Marketing

Marketing
Concepts and Strategy

Third Edition

Martin L. Bell
WASHINGTON UNIVERSITY

Houghton Mifflin Company   Boston
DALLAS   GENEVA, ILLINOIS   HOPEWELL,
NEW JERSEY   PALO ALTO   LONDON

Dedicated to Reavis Cox

Library of Congress Catalog Card Number: 78–69572

ISBN: 0–395–26503–7

Contents

Preface

The more things change, the more they remain the same.

Alphonse Karr, *Les Guepes* (January 1849)

The first edition of *Marketing: Concepts and Strategy* was written because of my conviction that significant changes had taken place in marketing and that a new approach was needed to convey the meaning of these changes. In some respects, the first edition was a revolutionary text and set the stage for a number of systems- and strategy-oriented books that followed. The second edition was prepared as the tide of interest in marketing crested. It extended and expanded the marketing concept while retaining the systematic approach introduced in the first edition.

This third edition is published at a time when marketing has achieved a degree of stability and recognition that it had not attained even six years ago. What was then revolutionary has become more commonplace today. Not only is marketing widely accepted as a natural and important function in commerce; it is seen as a viable process in not-for-profit organizations and in social and political entities as well.

However, because marketing has "come of age," it does not follow that the world of marketing today is the same as it was ten or even five years ago. Important changes continue to take place—as they always have and always will. But it seems apparent that marketing people are learning to cope with change. We accept it as a part of the marketing experience. If we look at marketing as a process to deal with change—external change to which the firm must respond and internal change initiated to achieve strategic objectives—we discover that in marketing, as in all of life, "the more things change, the more they remain the same."

In a fundamental way, marketing can be viewed as the function of managing change. The principal tool used in discharging this function is planning—the development of strategy. Thus, the major emphasis of the third edition of *Marketing: Concepts and Strategy* is on marketing planning in a changing environment.

This edition presents a blending of past, present, and future. Strong ties to the historical foundations of marketing are retained by direct utilization of the disciplines of economics, psychology, and sociology. Contemporary elements emerge naturally in discussions of systems concepts, consumer behavior, market segmentation, management science, and marketing information systems. The future is addressed in dealing with the new frontiers of marketing: services marketing, not-for-profit marketing; and international marketing. This future orientation emerges on an even more basic level in the text's focus on marketing planning—the development of future strategy under conditions of uncertainty.

Marketing: Concepts and Strategy has been revised to make it more appropriate for use in undergraduate courses whose instructors seek a little more demanding but entirely realistic approach. Teachers of introductory graduate level courses will find it equally appropriate.

The third edition retains the five major distinguishing characteristics of the earlier volumes. Briefly, these distinctive features are:

1. *The concept of "concepts"* My experience in teaching and consulting has convinced me that the planning of effective marketing strategy depends upon a thorough understanding of marketing concepts. A marketing concept is *not* a principle or law of marketing. Because marketing is a dynamic phenomenon, there are few if any genuine marketing

principles. The use of concepts rather than laws allows for both change and exception, for it involves essentially a realistic point of view rather than a set of static generalizations. In simple terms a concept can be thought of as "straight thinking about marketing based on sound marketing facts." This book encourages its readers to get the facts and then do their own straight thinking—or concept building.

2. *The concept of strategy* Marketing management is the strategic use of a firm's resources to take advantage of marketing opportunities. This view of management has been overshadowed in traditional textbooks by descriptions of marketing institutions and, more recently, by environmental treatments. Both are important, and this text does not ignore them. But its basic premise is that the crucial responsibilities facing today's marketing manager are the determination of objectives and the formulation of plans of action. This two-step management process is the essence of strategy.

3. *The systems concept* The first edition of *Marketing: Concepts and Strategy* contained one of the earliest textbook discussions of the systems approach in marketing. This revision retains the concept, but it has been given less prominence in the treatment. Although the systems approach has been applied successfully, for example, in engineering and information processing, it has not by any means been fully utilized in business administration. I was introduced to the intriguing possibilities of systems analysis by Professor Ralph Breyer at the University of Pennsylvania. More recently I have been increas-

ingly impressed with its general applicability to many phases of marketing, and I share the enthusiasm of a growing group who are convinced that it will become the basic approach to the teaching of marketing in the future.

4. *The ecological concept* The ecological concept is closely related to the systems concept. Relatively few authors have attempted to use human ecology as a basis for presenting the subject matter of the social sciences. In many ways, however, marketing readily lends itself to this approach, a fact which the late Wroe Alderson was among the first to recognize. Since ecology is the study of an organism (such as a consumer, a household, or a business establishment) in relation to its environment, an ecological theme permits the study of function, structure (organization), and adaptive behavior. The ecological theme pervades this book but does not dominate it. It is there for the interested instructor to apply, but it does not interfere with more conventional approaches to the subject of marketing.

5. *Integration* A major effort has been made to achieve integration in the treatment of marketing strategy. Indeed, a basic purpose of the text is to present a framework for preparing the *total marketing plan*—the complete marketing mix. A manager should not have separate plans for product development, distribution, promotion, and pricing. Rather, an overall, comprehensive plan that incorporates other plans involving all strategic areas is needed. To emphasize the integrated character of strategy formulation, I present a model of the marketing planning process in Chapter 3

and base the discussion of marketing planning on it. A comprehensive model of an integrated planning and control system is provided in Chapter 19.

The five distinctive features of this text make it particularly suitable for students with some background in economics or one of the behavioral fields, although previous work in these areas is not essential. For the instructor wishing to broaden the students' perspective, several excellent books of readings are available on such subjects as marketing management, consumerism, ecological impacts, and the like.

Cases are not included in the text. However, the *Instructor's Manual* does contain a guide to cases from the Intercollegiate Case Clearing House for teachers who would like to assign them. Case analysis is a logical and useful extension of the material presented in the text.

A number of questions and short problems have been placed at the close of each chapter. In general, these are intended to provoke class discussion, although a number of valuable *working* assignments have been suggested. Students are encouraged to associate with businesspeople in seeking answers to selected questions. In other assignments, the students are asked to observe and report on specific marketing activities. Obviously classroom requirements and local conditions may require some adaptation of these "field" problems.

Considerable attention is being devoted in the literature of marketing to the application of quantitative techniques. In response to this trend, I have included some contributions from the field of management science. For the convenience of those instructors who do not wish to expose beginning students to quantitative applications (even at a fairly elementary level), this material has been isolated from the rest of the text. Chapter 8, "Decision Tools for Marketing Management," is devoted entirely to the description of some of the more basic techniques of problem solving. The instructor can use or omit this material according to the objectives of the particular course.

I have borrowed from many sources over the years. Although a diligent effort has been made to credit specific individuals wherever possible, it has been virtually impossible to recall every specific source. For sins of omission or commission, I apologize in advance.

Inevitably every student of marketing is influenced by his or her teachers and contemporaries, and I am acutely aware of my inheritance. I continue to be grateful for the encouragement and suggestions of the late Wroe Alderson. The inspiration of his perception of marketing lives on in this book, as it does in the writings of his other friends and disciples. I owe a special tribute to my personal mentor and thesis advisor, Dr. Reavis Cox. Each year I am increasingly aware of how insightful and accurate his concepts of marketing were. It is my hope that some hint of his great contribution

endures in this book and will enrich yet another generation of marketing scholars.

The following reviewers have made suggestions for this edition: Professors William G. Browne, Oregon State University; Michael Houston of the University of Wisconsin at Madison; David Curry, University of Iowa; Gerald Linda of Tathan-Laird & Kunder; Richard J. Lutz of the University of California, Los Angeles; Noel Zabriskie, University of North Florida; Cecil V. Hynes, University of Maryland; Luis Dominguez of Case Western Reserve University; Richard A. Wald, New Mexico Highlands University; and Leland Beik, Pennsylvania State University. I thank them for their interest and help. Many secretaries and copy editors have worked on the manuscript. I am especially grateful to Mrs. Ruth Scheetz for her patience and skill in processing the book and teacher's manual.

With the hope that these pages will reveal some of the excitement and satisfaction that the study of marketing has brought to me, I offer this textbook to those who wish to accept the challenge of mastering a discipline which "the more it changes, the more it remains the same."

M.L.B.

Marketing

One

The Marketing Concept

1

Marketing: The Management Perspective

An interesting view of civilization is that progress is related not so much to the increased size of the human brain as it is to the greatness of the ideas that an expanding thought process has created. Many grand ideas have spelled progress for humanity. Of these, technological developments have received the most attention. The printing press, the steam engine, the radio, and nuclear energy are but four of the host of developments that have made it possible to produce an ever-expanding supply of goods and services. But without the idea of a market in which buyers and sellers could meet and exchange goods and services, the greatest inventions would have had little meaning. Goods had to be transferred from those who made them to those who used them in a manner that was satisfactory to all. And so trade emerged. What began as a simple barter of flints for food or hides for herbs developed through time into an elabo-

rate process by which the physical output of a society is distributed to its members for the satisfaction of their wants.

We can see elements of this elaborate system all around us. We visit a supermarket, and from among tens of thousands of items we select the few that we need and can afford. We observe the frenzied activity of a construction crew as it tops out a new high-rise office building to be occupied by a major marketing organization—perhaps IBM or Eastern Airlines. We enroll at a university. We spend a relaxing hour at the racquetball club or in front of the television. We attend a symphony or a rock concert. Each of these everyday incidents illustrates the delivery—directly or indirectly—of part of our standard of living. The process that brings these goods and services into being and to the marketplace, where we can exercise our role as buyers and consumers, is called *marketing*. And marketing is what this book is all about.

Two Views of Marketing

The term *marketing* has two important meanings, and both are vital to an understanding of the subject. Some observers advocate a broad view of marketing; they see it as cutting across the entire economic process. Others adopt a narrow concept, one drawn from the perspective of the individual business firm.

Macromarketing

The broad viewpoint considers marketing in relation to the national economy and other aspects of the total social and cultural complex. It sees marketing as a system of organizations and processes by which a nation's (or the world's) resources are distributed to people in order to satisfy their wants. We can liken this approach to the panoramic view an aviator has of a large geographical area. The pilot sees the big picture.

There is merit to this *macromarketing* approach. Viewed in the aggregate, marketing is a social institution and should be evaluated on how well it performs the role assigned to it. In the past this role has been considered to be primarily economic. Recently a broadened view has been suggested in which marketing is perceived not just in terms of market transactions but in terms of social exchanges generally.[1] Marketing is the process by which all needs of people are satisfied. We will return to this concept of marketing in Chapter 24.

[1]See P. Kotler and S. J. Levy, "Broadening the Concept of Marketing," *Journal of Marketing,* January 1969, pp. 10–15; P. Kotler, "A Generic Concept of Marketing," *Journal of Marketing,* April 1972, pp. 46–54; and R. P. Bagozzi, "Marketing as Exchange," *Journal of Marketing,* October 1975, pp. 32–39.

Micromarketing

The narrow view of marketing is called *micromarketing.*[2] It involves a close-up perspective, much like that of a scientist who inspects a small object through a microscope. Viewed in this narrow fashion, marketing is the process of managing an individual business firm in such a way as to satisfy its particular customers. As we will discover, marketing also involves many specialized tasks, such as product development, advertising, and pricing; but it is the relationship of these activities to the company's total effort that concerns us here. Marketing involves the management of every aspect of a business with the ultimate customer in mind. This is not easy to accomplish, particularly in businesses where finance, engineering, and manufacturing are important functions. But managing these activities as well as the traditional, customer-oriented marketing tasks is what marketing management is all about. It is from this microviewpoint that this book is largely written, and we will explore it thoroughly in this chapter and in those that follow. We will inspect in detail the specialized activities that go on every day in the marketing-oriented company, and we will see how these relate to the overall management of a firm. But we will look also at the big picture. We will consider issues that go beyond the boundaries of the business firm. Relations with other companies, with consumers, with the physical environment, and with the government will be discussed, notably as they influence business decisions.

[2]Some marketing authors maintain that this is the only valid perspective. See D. Luck, "Social Marketing: Confusion Compounded," *Journal of Marketing,* October 1974, pp. 70–72; and M. Bell, "The Floundering Marketing Concept," in H. W. Nash and D. P. Robin, eds., *Proceedings of the Southern Marketing Association* (1976), pp. 264–266.

We also will be concerned with the broad social implications of these relationships. And finally, we will look at nonbusiness applications of marketing and of marketing's broad social role.

The Marketing Revolution

Modern marketing emerged around 1900.[3] We can trace its origin to the Commercial and the Industrial Revolutions. The Commercial Revolution, which brought trade to the Western world, resulted from the breakdown of the feudal system and ushered in production for the purpose of exchange instead of self-sufficiency. The Industrial Revolution resulted from technological inventions and managerial innovations. Productivity increased so rapidly that manufacturing became known as *mass production.* In England the phenomenon progressed to such an extent that Adam Smith discussed it in his book *The Wealth of Nations,* which was published in 1775. But even Smith did not foresee the magnitude of the progress that was to follow.

It was almost 1850 before the Industrial Revolution made an impact on American manufacturing, and even then the problems of marketing did not emerge immediately. So long as goods were scarce relative to demand, there were no significant problems in disposing of them. Under conditions of scarcity consumers must approach sellers; manufacturers produce only when confronted with definite orders from middle-

men, and most goods are sold before they are made. This is a condition that prevailed throughout the nineteenth century and the first decade of the twentieth but then became quite uncommon until the energy crisis and similar shortages of other critical materials re-created, at least temporarily, these same circumstances in the 1970s.

The Stage of Mass Distribution

Between 1900 and 1920, the exact time varying somewhat from one industry to another, the deficit supply condition (sometimes called a *sellers' market*) disappeared. By 1920 most industries moved into a surplus supply situation (called a *buyers' market*); that is, immediate demand ran behind the industry's ability to produce. Thus a critical need arose to devise a system of *mass distribution.* A few individuals who were writing about business, especially businesspeople, were concerned with this situation. One such writer was Edward A. Filene. He wrote, "Mass production without mass distribution is unworkable."[4] Filene regarded department stores and the new, efficient types of wholesale operations as the natural outlets for the surplus created by mass production. It was a problem, he believed, of finding better methods of transferring merchandise from where it had been mass-produced to where it could be consumed.

The Stage of Aggressive Sales

The business system responded to this challenge. Organizations that were capable of

[3]For a classic discussion of how the marketing revolution has affected one firm, the Pillsbury Company, see Robert J. Keith, "The Marketing Revolution," *Journal of Marketing,* January 1960, p. 35.

[4]Edward A. Filene, *Speaking of Change* (New York: Former Associates of Edward A. Filene, 1939), p. 38.

mass distribution (such as chain stores, mail-order houses, and department stores) were created, but the problem of goods accumulating at factories and retail stores continued. Astute business executives realized that providing mass distribution could not solve the basic problem. Goods moved further from their production source but still did not sell.

Then came a second step in the marketing revolution; an awareness that selling was important emerged. The age of high-powered selling and aggressive advertising dawned. We discovered that, with enough expense and effort, almost anything could be sold. As the Great Depression of the 1930s set in, the pressure to keep selling increased. As a result marketing was subjected to a host of criticisms, including accusations of high-pressure tactics and misleading or false advertising.[5] The sales effort succeeded splendidly at first and then collapsed, and the failure of the sales approach was clearly evident by the end of the 1930s.

The Stage of the Marketing Concept

Something else was needed—something besides mass distribution and aggressive selling. Business had to avoid the disastrous effects first of producing the wrong goods and then of overselling them. Personal selling no longer could be used to correct the mistake of a buyer, a designer, or a production scheduler. Business managers learned to insist that products initially be designed to satisfy a particular customer need. Products would have to be made available at those stores where customers wanted to buy them. They would have to be promoted in a way that would win over consumers, not wear down their resistance through endless harassment. Goods must be priced reasonably. These new notions represented almost a complete turnabout in the approach to marketing. It was a dramatic shift from the producers' point of view to the consumers' point of view.[6] And it is this customer orientation that is the essential element in what we now call the *marketing concept.*

The Marketing Concept

The marketing concept emerged about 1940, but it was not generally recognized until the post–World War II period, when a number of large companies made major changes in their marketing organizations and procedures. Today the marketing concept is widely accepted in the business community. It has become the modus operandi of the modern firm. The concept has four essential elements.

Marketing Is Customer Oriented

We have noted that customer orientation is the principal element in the marketing concept. Its meaning is expressed aptly in the following excerpt from a large company's statement of corporate objectives:

Our primary objective is to increase profitability . . . to produce maximum long-term profit growth consistent with the balanced best interest of customers, shareholders, employees, suppliers, and society at large. . . . In achieving this

[5]For example, see S. Chase and F. J. Schlink, *Your Money's Worth* (New York: Macmillan, 1931); and A. Kallet and F. J. Schlink, *100,000,000 Guinea Pigs* (New York: Vanguard Press, 1932).

[6]The most widely known statement of this new orientation is found in T. Levitt, "Marketing Myopia," *Harvard Business Review,* reprinted September-October 1975, pp. 26–48.

goal we will . . . recognize that the primary purpose of our business is to perform a necessary economic service by creating, stimulating, and satisfying customers. We must be a marketing-oriented company, dedicated to the principle that in order to supply the right product or service at the right time and in the right way, we need first to establish what the customer wants, where, when, how, and at what price.[7]

The idea of customer orientation is clearly established in American business. In both consumer- and industrial-goods fields, managers equate the marketing concept with customer orientation. These people understand that marketing starts with the determination of customer wants and ends with the satisfaction of those wants. Marketing originates with the recognition that a need exists and terminates with the satisfaction of that need by the delivery of a usable product or service, at the right time, at the correct place, and at an acceptable price.

Marketing Is an Integrated Management Function

The marketing concept involves a recognition of the need to integrate and coordinate the diverse functions that historically have been classified as marketing. These functions include such activities as product development, physical distribution, control, forecasting, pricing, advertising, selling, and marketing research. To pull these activities together into a well-knit business operation, ideally under the supervision of a marketing manager, is to grasp this aspect of the marketing concept.

But it is not enough to integrate internal activities of the marketing division. These, in turn, must be coordinated closely with the

[7]From *Statement of Corporate Objectives,* Ralston Purina Company, St. Louis, Missouri, 1970.

other functional areas of a business. Marketing must be melded with finance; it must be dovetailed with personnel administration; it must utilize all the skills of accountancy and statistical control. For example, a business cannot have divergent personnel policies concerning hiring, compensation, and retirement for salespeople on the one hand and factory supervisors on the other and still expect the work force to perform harmoniously. Research and development cannot be allowed to work on one project while the marketing department is working on another. The advertising department cannot launch a campaign for a new product unless it is assured that the manufacturing department has produced adequate stock. Integration of effort is an absolute necessity, and it is usually the marketing manager's responsibility to see that this coordination takes place.

Marketing Is Results Directed

A third extremely important yet sometimes elusive element should be included in the marketing concept. Marketing effort must be related to results. We engage in marketing in order to achieve specific business objectives. The Ralston Purina statement of corporate objectives points out that the company's basic objective is "to produce maximum long-term profit growth." To this end the company's management has declared, "We must be a marketing-oriented company."

This view is in notable contrast to that which prevailed in most companies for many years—especially during the early years of marketing. The obsolete view is that the measure of marketing success is an increase in sales volume. The pursuit of this goal has led many firms to extravagant and costly endeavors to add new products, reach new markets, serve more customers.[8] In many instances sales increased but profits declined! The proper approach lies in seeking profitable sales volume, not sales volume per se. In some cases this actually is achieved by reducing sales—by dropping unprofitable products, territories, or customers. In other cases it is achieved by devising better methods of marketing, and closely matching these to the profit potential of a particular market.

Marketing is not restricted to profit-making organizations. Not-for-profit organizations, such as hospitals, universities, public transit systems, and governmental agencies, apply marketing techniques in ways that are very similar to those of profit-seeking businesses. Of course there also are important differences—notably in pricing—but the absence of a profit objective does not invalidate the marketing concept. A not-for-profit organization must be results oriented in its marketing. For example, the U.S. Postal Service is under as obvious pressure to deliver user satisfaction as is United Parcel Service, a private parcel delivery service. Both must plan their programs, ration their limited resources, and strive for efficiency in their marketing activities. Results are important, but profit is only one convenient way to state goals and to measure results.[9]

The Marketing Concept Requires Systematic Planning

The preceding discussion hinted at a fourth dimension of the marketing concept. This

[8]W. C. Fruhan, Jr., "Pyrrhic Victories in the Fight for Market Share," *Harvard Business Review,* September-October 1972, pp. 100–107.

[9]For an interesting book about the application of marketing in not-for-profit organizations see P. Kotler, *Marketing for Non-Profit Organizations* (New York: Prentice-Hall, 1975). We will return to the subject of not-for-profit marketing in Chapter 24.

element suggests that a particular type of management approach is necessary for a meaningful application of the concept. The approach demands the use of systematic planning and problem-solving techniques. Note these comments that business leaders have made to the author:

[The marketing concept] is the Marketing Plan—the plan of action, control, objectives, and follow-through.

[It means] developing a strategy to get it [the product] in front of customers so they have the opportunity to buy it . . . determining scientifically what products or services to make and how best to market them [distribution] to meet consumer needs.

Planning, developing strategy, systematically and scientifically selecting among available alternatives, and controlling the operation in order to provide customer satisfaction are relatively new implications in the marketing concept. Yet they are the principal concerns of the modern marketing manager.

Four elements, then, constitute the basic ingredients of the marketing concept—customer orientation, integrated effort, results direction, and the use of systematic and scientific methods of planning and problem solving. This is the contemporary concept of marketing as it has been accepted by many executives.

The Marketing Concept in the Future

We have seen that one reason for the shift from aggressive sales to marketing was the widespread criticism of business practices that arose in the late 1920s and early 1930s. This criticism was called the *consumer movement,* and it was the forerunner of the recent activism we call the *new consumerism.* We will look more thoroughly at these movements in Chapter 23, but it is important to point out here that serious questions have been raised about the extent to which the marketing concept really has been consumer oriented. It has been suggested that the concept is "bankrupt," or has at least "faltered."[10] The need for legislation to protect consumers from usurious interest, deceptive packaging, and fraudulent promotion is cited. The introduction of potentially hazardous products has come under attack. The pollution of our natural environment is scathingly criticized.

If respectable companies sometimes have done these things, what is the reason? The answer is relatively simple: Providing complete customer satisfaction and attaining maximum profits are incompatible goals. A trade-off must be made. Companies have been forced to resolve this incompatibility. Some have done so by concentrating their efforts on providing or promising only enough value to persuade the customer to buy, but not necessarily enough to render genuine satisafction. Others have become deeply concerned about the consumers' well-being and have responded to the challenge—even at the loss of some profitability.

What will be the ultimate impact of these developments? It seems fairly certain that consumers will continue to demand and to receive more satisfaction—better performance and fewer frills.[11] This will be at the expense of some profit for most companies. In short, the balance between profit attain-

ment and customer satisafaction will swing more toward serving the consumer. This will involve greater marketing costs, and high payoffs from questionable selling tactics will no longer exist. Marketing people will become much more selective in the projects they undertake, and they will manage every project with increased efficiency.

The marketing concept will go into a second formulation in which genuine consumer concern will replace customer orientation. Profit will no longer be the principal operational goal, nor will it be the sole criterion of effective marketing performance. Profit will be the reward for the skillful delivery of satisfaction. To be sure, the need for integrated effort and the use of scientific methods of planning and problem solving will be even greater. The marketing concept very likely will be the way of business life for many years to come.

The Marketing-Oriented Company

The adoption of the marketing concept has profoundly affected the organization and operation of many companies. The impact is visible at every level, from chief executive to marketing trainee. It is seen to some degree in every facet of a firm's activities. We see it in research and development, in manufacturing, in finance, and of course in sales.

Peter Drucker says that the purpose of a business is "to create a customer."[12] He also makes the remarkable statement that marketing is "a central dimension of the entire business. It is the whole business seen

[10]M. L. Bell and C. W. Emory, "The Faltering Marketing Concept," *Journal of Marketing,* October 1971, pp. 37–42.

[11]Another possible development is more intelligent decision making and behavior on the part of the consumer. See J. Rothe, "Intelligent Consumption: An Attractive Alternative to the Marketing Concept," *MSU Business Topics,* Winter 1974, pp. 29–34.

[12]P. F. Drucker, *Management: Tasks, Responsibilities, Practices* (New York: Harper & Row, 1974), p. 61.

from the point of view of its final result, that is, from the customer's point of view. Concern and responsibility for marketing must, therefore, permeate all areas of the enterprise."[13] Carrying out the marketing task is the responsibility of the entire company. Creating a customer is everybody's job. Let us look very briefly at the way the marketing-oriented company operates. Since the marketing task pervades the entire business, we will direct our attention to three organizational levels, starting at the top.[14]

Top Management's Marketing Role

The president and the executive staff decide on the basic direction a company should take. They determine the kind and size of company it should be. In the very broadest sense, the chief executive officer must answer the question, "Who is our customer—now and in the future?" By defining the customer it is possible to make plans to provide specific goods and services. It enables top management to determine which new ventures to investigate and which older ones to abandon. We refer to these kinds of marketing-oriented decisions as *corporate strategic planning*. The process also can be thought of as defining the company's mission—deciding on the kind of company it should be.

The company's top management also gives specific marketing-oriented direction to those at lower levels in the company, so

that these people can develop appropriate programs to carry out the company's mission. Top management establishes objectives for its various divisions. It also may set policies that will guide operating people in making lower-level decisions. Finally, of course, top management establishes an organization capable of carrying out the company's mission and creates a climate conducive to effective performance.

Divisional Management's Marketing Role

In decentralized companies the second tier of management often is called the *divisional level*. The divisional level may be an entire company, such as a subsidiary of a large parent corporation. Or, in smaller firms, the second level might be a group of similar products managed by a divisional vice president. Regardless of nomenclature, a hierarchy exists, and this next lower management level has its particular marketing role as well.

The division manager is responsible for developing a strategy consistent with the company's mission—one that will achieve the objectives assigned to the division. A strategy is a long-range plan, which usually involves programs lasting from three to five years. Marketing is a most important element in a division's overall plan. The marketing strategy is aimed at a particular group of potential customers (called a *market segment*). It includes decisions in the four critical areas of marketing management—products, distribution, promotion, and pricing. Decisions in these four areas are integrated carefully in a total program that we call the *marketing mix*. It goes without saying that this marketing strategy is not developed until exhaustive research concerning the

---

[13]Ibid., p. 63.

[14]An excellent description of the planning responsibilities of various organization levels is found in R. F. Vancil and P. Larange, "Strategic Planning in Diversified Companies," *Harvard Business Review,* January-February 1975, pp. 81–90.

consumer, the competition, and all the other external influences has been completed.

Obviously the division must have a total strategy involving more than marketing. Manufacturing plans, financial plans, and work force plans also are needed. But the principal thrust of a division's program almost always is marketing, because the basic purpose of a company—its very reason for existing—is to create customers and provide customer satisfaction. All of a division's plans are aimed at this goal.

Functional Management's Marketing Role

At the operational level almost every business is organized along functional lines. That is, a division normally is divided into at least three specialized areas—manufacturing, marketing, and finance. These functional departments are managed by persons who are responsible for developing the detailed programs necessary to carry out the divisional strategy. We call these action-oriented programs *tactics,* and we usually associate them with the short run (one year or less).

The marketing department is the key functional group in a company's effort to implement the marketing concept. It contributes in two very important ways. First, as a functional department specializing in marketing, it has the responsibility of working out the tactical details of a division's long-range marketing plan. Managers of specialized marketing activities, such as product planning, advertising, and personal selling, develop short-run programs for their areas. The manager of the marketing department makes sure that the various tactical plans are integrated.

The marketing department's second con-

tribution to the company's overall marketing effort is in its role as an intelligence-gathering arm of the firm. Corporate strategic planning and divisional long-range planning require information about customers, competition, and social, economic, and political developments. Similarly, information about the company's past sales and profits is required. It is often the responsibility of the marketing department to gather this information from external and internal sources. The subfunction of the marketing department that typically collects this data is called *marketing research.* Very large companies, with extensive and sophisticated marketing intelligence needs, expand the function into a complete marketing information and control system.

In carrying out these two important responsibilities, the marketing department becomes the key group in a company. But it does not run the company, nor do marketing managers intrude into the domains of other functional managers, dictating how their jobs should be done. Marketing gives purpose and direction, and a company operates best not when marketing people run it but when all those making business decisions do it from a marketing point of view.

Marketing Is Not a Panacea

The preceding description of how the marketing-oriented company operates may seem logical and basically simple. In practice it is difficult and only a relatively few companies seem to do it very well.

The obstacles are considerable. Regrettably not all managers accept the idea that the purpose of a company is to satisfy its customers. Some still cling to the outmoded notion that the purpose of a business is to manufacture and sell products. Production orientation is a fatal deterrent to effective marketing.

Even the marketing-oriented manager faces serious problems. There are other forces to be satisfied—employees, shareholders, and creditors. Resources always are limited. No company can do everything. Some customer wants must go unsatisfied because demand always exceeds supply. Moreover, there is an impressive list of things that can go wrong with the development and execution of a marketing program. The information that a company needs may not be available; data that it does collect may be obsolete or inaccurate. After all, the market is constantly changing. The wrong strategy may be selected and the tactics easily can be misconceived. There is always the uncertainty of what the competition is going to do. Add to all of these the increasing external pressure from government and consumer activists, and you can see that the marketing-oriented manager faces a most difficult task. But it is not an impossible assignment, and this book is intended to demonstrate just how a marketing-oriented business can be managed effectively.

Marketing Defined

This chapter began with the statement that there are two important views of marketing—one a broad macroview; the other a narrow microview. Definitions of marketing have been developed for each viewpoint.

From the macroview of marketing, the most widely accepted definition is that offered many years ago by the Committee on Definitions of the American Marketing As-

sociation. The committee has said that "marketing is the performance of business activities that direct the flow of goods and services from producer to consumer or user."[15] This is a broad definition because it embraces all goods and services, all consumers and users, and all business firms engaged in providing these goods and services.

The definition of micromarketing focuses on the activities of the business firm. Based on this chapter's discussion of the marketing concept, we define marketing as the *integrated activities of a business directed toward the satisfaction of customer needs at a profit.*

It is not necessary for you to understand the full import of these definitions after so brief an introduction. These concepts of marketing are not easy to grasp. They seldom dawn as a flash of inspiration; instead they evolve gradually. The subject of marketing must be worked at; it must be absorbed. A principal task of this entire book is to make these definitions of marketing clear and useful.

Summary

We have taken a first look at marketing. We have seen that it can be viewed from either a broad (macro) or a narrow (micro) perspective. For the present we have concentrated on the narrow view of marketing, which we define as the integrated activities of a business directed toward the satisfaction of customer needs at a profit.

This contemporary view of marketing has

[15]Reprinted from the Committee on Definitions, *Marketing Definitions: A Glossary of Marketing Terms* (Chicago: 1960), p. 15, published by the American Marketing Association.

evolved over time. The marketing revolution has brought us to the verge of seeing firms organized and operated from the basis of serving consumers, an orientation we call the marketing concept. It involves putting the customer first in making business decisions. It requires the integration of all business activities toward the goal of providing customer satisfaction. But this must be done efficiently. Planning and control, which involve the use of scientific tools of analysis and decision making, are required.

The focus of marketing management is on the development of strategy. In the marketing-oriented company, each level of management has its specific strategy-related responsibilities. Top management's marketing role is to define the company's mission, to establish its objectives, to designate its policies, and to provide an organization that can carry out the company's marketing programs. Divisional management has the responsibility to develop long-range strategic plans that incorporate the four elements of the marketing mix. Functional management translates the divisional strategy into short-run tactics that can be implemented. The marketing department has a second important responsibility—that of supplying the marketing intelligence needed by top and divisional managements to carry out their respective roles.

Questions and Problems

1. In this chapter we have looked at marketing primarily from the business point of view. What is the consumer's point of view? Discuss this question with a number of other people, such as a doctor or lawyer, a homemaker, and a liberal arts student. What are their views of marketing?

2. What is so revolutionary about the marketing revolution? Do you think that marketing may go through yet another stage? If so, what do you think it will be?

3. How can a company exhibit customer orientation? To answer this question, select a company with which you are familiar and explain the ways in which it responds to the needs and desires of consumers.

4. Three company presidents, each the head of a company in the computer industry, met at a trade convention. In the course of their conversation the following statements were made—one by each of these individuals:

   "We design and manufacture the most sophisticated computer equipment in the industry."

   "The day we stop responding to the wants of our customers will be the day we lose out to our competition."

   "The great forte of our company is its ability to sell effectively in the face of intense competition."

   What stage of the marketing revolution does each of these statements represent? What are the probable marketing implications of each president's view?

5. A small company that manufactured electronic components encountered difficulty because of its inability to develop really competitive new products. Its salespeople complained that nobody would listen to their suggestions. The marketing research manager said that the salespeople's opinions on new products were not reliable. The chief design engineer was a former production manager who had no contact with customers. What do you believe is the basic

problem in this company? What would you do about it?

6. The president of a large food company made these remarks to a group of marketing trainees: "This is a marketing company, and everybody in it makes decisions from this standpoint. It is true of the people you will work for—the product and sales managers. It is true of the people above them—the divisional and group vice presidents. And it is certainly true of me. Of course, we have different jobs to do; but we all do them from a marketing point of view." Explain how it is that people at all levels of management can be expected to operate in this way.

7. Why is it that two companies selling almost identical products can use very different methods and still succeed? For example, the Fuller Brush Company, Tupperware, and Avon sell exclusively on an in-home basis, whereas most of their competitors use retail stores. Can you think of other examples? Explain the marketing logic behind the different approaches.

8. Folklore provides the familiar mousetrap quotation, "If you . . . build a better mousetrap than your neighbor, the world will make a beaten path to your door." Someone did indeed build a better mousetrap. It was cleaner, safer, and more effective; it was also a miserable failure. Consumers preferred the old spring-type trap to the new plastic cage. Why do you think the better mousetrap failed?

2

Marketing Systems and Organization

The adoption of concepts that view marketing at different levels has made it necessary to apply a hierarchical perspective to understand the structure and organization of marketing establishments. We call this perspective the *systems approach*.[1]

What Is a System?

Since marketing is a system, we should know what the term implies. Kuhn aptly describes a system in terms that probably are familiar to most of us.

In its broadest sense a system is any set of interrelated components. Wires, tubes, capacitors, resistors, and speakers are components of a sound amplifier system. Locomotives, tracks, cars, switches, and signals are parts of a railroad system. Missiles, launching pads, tracking devices, computers, and control devices are components of a missile system. Parties, constitutions, elections, campaigns, nominations, and control of office are parts of a democratic political system—and so on.[2]

Briefly, then, a system is made up of components and their interrelationships. The first business applications of the systems approach were in production. The result was

---

[1] The systems approach has been used selectively by marketing scholars. Besides this text, other treatments can be found in E. Kelley and W. Lazer, *Managerial Marketing: Policies, Strategies, and Decisions* (Homewood, Ill.: Richard D. Irwin, 1973); L. Adler, "Systems Approach to Marketing," *Harvard Business Review,* May–June 1967, pp. 105–118; and G. Fisk, *Marketing Systems: An Introductory Analysis* (New York: Harper and Row, 1967).

[2] Reprinted with permission from A. Kuhn, *The Study of Society* (Homewood, Ill.: Richard D. Irwin, 1963, p.38.

rapid acceleration toward automation. The most notable example of systems application is found in the space program, especially in the outer space probes, such as the Mariner voyages to Mars. Closer to everyday life are examples of less complicated automated systems. A vending machine accepts or rejects coins, makes change if necessary, permits choice among alternative offerings, and delivers the desired item. A single reservation, ticketing, and seat assignment system has replaced the traditional method of handling each function separately at TWA. And there are numerous other instances of the trend toward automation and the application of the systems approach. These would include materials-handling systems, communications systems, electronic data-processing systems, and the like. Its extension into the behavioral and organizational aspects of management has been less pronounced. Progress in this field depends on an understanding of certain key concepts in the systems approach.

Key Concepts in the Systems Approach

There are a number of key concepts in the systems approach. In order to understand how the systems approach is applied to marketing, we should recognize the most important of these concepts. A complete discussion of the systems approach is beyond the scope of this text.[3]

[3]Several excellent treatments of the systems approach have been written. For example, see K. Boulding, "General Systems Theory: The Skeleton of Science," *Management Science,* April 1956, pp. 197–208; R. A. Johnson, F. E. Kast, and J. E. Rosenzweig, *The Theory and Management of Systems* (New York: McGraw-Hill, 1973); and S. L. Optner, *Systems Analysis for Business and Industrial Problem Solving* (Englewood Cliffs, N.J.: Prentice-Hall, 1965).

System Hierarchies

Most systems are composed of a hierarchy of subsystems. A telephone communications system provides a good example. At the lowest level is the individual telephone instrument.[4] The telephone is a system because it is composed of component parts linked together functionally for a specific purpose—the reception and transmission of audible messages. The instrument system is linked with other instruments, perhaps in an internal communications network within an office or hotel. This internal system may be joined, in turn, with an area communications network, possibly that of an independent telephone company. This company system then is connected with a national, and eventually an international, telephone system. Thus we see a hierarchy of systems in which the lesser systems are component parts of the larger systems.

In marketing terms, the largest system is the *macromarketing system* (the overall framework of all marketing and facilitating establishments). Next come the *industry system* (all those establishments involved in the marketing of a particular commodity), the *channel system* (all those components involved in the marketing of a particular brand, or product), and the *enterprise system* (the individual marketing firm). We also will be interested in some of the enterprise system's components. In particular we will look at the organization of the firm and of the marketing department.

Using the hardware industry as an example, we can see the various levels of marketing systems in Figure 2.1. The largest blocks

[4]Actually an instrument component such as the dialing mechanism or the bell circuit could be considered an even lower level system; but for the purpose of our analogy we can start with the instrument as the lowest-level system.

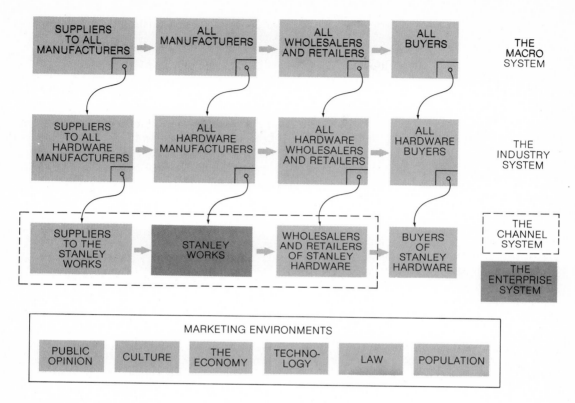

FIGURE 2.1   A hierarchy of marketing systems

in Figure 2.1 represent the macromarketing system. All manufacturers of goods (as well as providers of services) are linked with their suppliers, their various wholesalers and retailers, and, ultimately, their buyers and consumers. The smaller blocks within the macrocomponents represent the hardware industry. All makers of hardware and their suppliers, all hardware wholesalers, and all retail hardware dealers are included. They constitute an industry system. The small blocks within the industry represent a particular manufacturer of hardware, The Stanley Works, its suppliers, and the various wholesalers and retailers handling the Stanley line

of tools and builders' hardware. This arrangement is called the channel system. (It is enclosed within the broken line.) Finally, we can look at any one of the components in the channel system, in this case the Stanley Works. It too is a system comprised of component parts. We call it the enterprise system.

System Flows

The concept of a system involves the notion of linkage: a system's components are linked by flows. In probably the first major contribution of systems engineering to general

FIGURE 2.2   An elementary system (without control)

management, Forrester suggested several flows.

In other words, the company will come to be recognized not as a collection of separate functions but as a system in which the flows of information, materials, manpower, capital equipment, and money set up forces that determine the basic tendency toward growth, fluctuations, and decline.[5]

The flows mentioned in this statement, which is referred to often in systems literature, are representative of the activities that link components into systems. In Figure 2.1 we see only one flow—that of the physical product; but system components actually are linked by several flows, as Forrester's statement suggests.

System Boundaries

The boundaries of a system must be identified. By definition a system is a set of related components. Elements that are not involved in this relationship are outside the system, and we consider them to be part of the system's *environment*. The boundaries between a system and its environment depend on our perception of the system. They also depend on the level within the hierarchy about which we are concerned. For any particular system, the larger system to which

it belongs is part of its environment, while the smaller systems (subsystems) that it embraces are its components. In Figure 2.1 the broken line indicates the channel system. Everything outside the broken line is part of this system's environment.

System Management and Control

Systems that are meaningful in marketing management exist for a purpose. The system is designed to achieve a goal according to a plan that provides for the processing of inputs and the discharge of desired outputs. Figure 2.2 is a flow chart showing the relationships in a simple goal-oriented system. The components of this type of system are a plan, inputs that are applied according to the plan, a processor that converts the inputs, and outputs that are discharged according to the plan. In the absence of uncertainty, such a system, properly designed, might operate effectively. However, the typical marketing firm does not operate in this way—largely because it cannot be isolated completely from environmental influences and because the input-output relationships are not sufficiently stable.

A system operating under conditions of uncertainty requires *control*. Control is achieved by checking output against the plan. The flow of information required to check performance is known as feedback. This performance feedback is compared to standards stipulated in the plan. Significant deviations are identified and action to correct the problem is initiated. A diagram of a

[5]Jay W. Forrester, "Industrial Dynamics: A Major Breakthrough for Decision Makers," *Harvard Business Review,* July–August 1958, p. 52. Copyright © 1958 by the President and Fellows of Harvard College; all rights reserved.

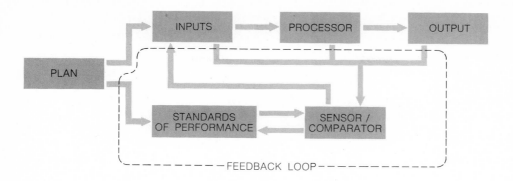

FIGURE 2.3   A system with feedback control

Source: Adapted from exhibits in R. A. Johnson, F. E. Kast, and J. E. Rosenzweig, *The Theory and Management of Systems* (New York: McGraw-Hill Book Co., 1973), pp. 75, 125.

system with this type of control is shown in Figure 2.3.

The Macromarketing System

The macromarketing system embraces all entities engaged directly or indirectly in the production and distribution of goods and services. Each establishment in the macromarketing system is linked formally or informally with many others. The system involves a complex arrangement of manufacturers, middlemen, retailers, and a host of specialized entities. These institutions and their relationships are referred to as the *structure of marketing.*

The attempt to present the macrosystem in its entirety involves an almost staggering amount of material. However, a few attempts to describe and measure the performance of the aggregate system have been made. Two of these, the first by Stewart and Dewhurst for the Twentieth Century Fund in 1939 and the second by Cox some twenty-five years later, resulted in thorough

studies of the entire marketing system, including attempts to portray graphically the flow of activity within it.[6]

Figure 2.4, an adaptation of a chart from the Cox book, shows the flow of ownership. Ownership flows back and forth within the system as a result of transactions among system components. The principal flow however is forward. It commences at the point where goods first emerge as tangible commodities. The sources of goods are shown in the upper left-hand corner of the chart as agriculture, imports, and extractive industry. The terminal points in the system are found in the lower right-hand corner. These are the consumers of the system's output—households, government, private capital formation, and exports. The rest of the macrosystem is involved in the creation of useful products and services, and their distribution. Roughly, the manufacturing, construction, public utilities, transportation, and service industries are responsible for the creation of goods and services. Intermediate

[6]P. W. Stewart, J. F. Dewhurst, and L. Field, *Does Distribution Cost Too Much?* (New York: The Twentieth Century Fund, 1939); and R. Cox, C. S. Goodman, and T. C. Fichandler, *Distribution in a High Level Economy* (Englewood Cliffs, N.J.: Prentice-Hall, 1965).

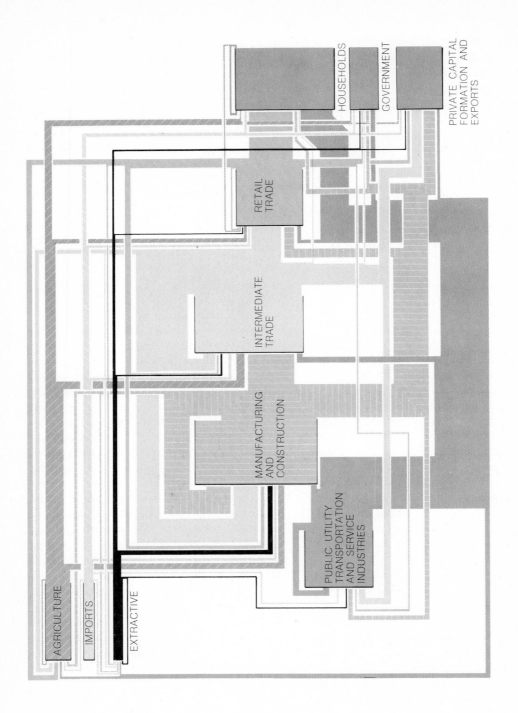

FIGURE 2.4   The macromarketing system

Source: Adapted from a chart of the flow of goods in Reavis Cox, C. S. Goodman, and T. C. Fichandler, *Distribution in a High-Level Economy,* © 1965. Reprinted by permission of Prentice-Hall, Inc., Englewood Cliffs, New Jersey.

trade establishments (wholesalers and retailers) are responsible for the distribution of goods. The linkage of these classes of components is indicated in the flow of ownership within the system. It is not a simple one-directional flow. Manufacturers sell to other manufacturers; wholesalers sell to manufacturers and to other wholesalers; and all types of components are seen to transfer ownership of goods to almost every other type. This flow of ownership creates an immensely complex arrangement, binding together the components of the macromarketing system.

The Industry System

The industry marketing system is a component of the macrosystem. It encompasses all those establishments involved in the manufacture and distribution of a general class of product. There are notable differences in the structure and operations of various industry systems. Compare, for example, the marketing of automobiles with that of packaged food products. In the automobile industry there are relatively few manufacturers—several of which have integrated backward into the production of some of the basic materials that go into automobile manufacturing. Cars usually are sold through a network of franchised dealers, without the use of other middlemen. Food products, in contrast, are produced by a large number of firms, some of which are very small. The farms that supply food manufacturers also tend to be quite small. There is relatively little vertical integration in the food industry. Farmers sell to middlemen (called *assemblers*), who in turn sell to food processors. The food processors convert the raw agricultural products into consumable foodstuffs

and sell them through an elaborate chain of dispersing middlemen, including brokers, wholesalers, and retailers.

It is interesting to look at marketing from an industry-wide point of view. It was from this perspective that some of the first marketing textbooks were written. However, very little practical marketing management is learned from this approach. Largely because of antitrust laws marketing seldom is managed on an industry-wide basis. Accordingly, we look to even smaller marketing systems to discover the structural units in which business decisions are made. One of these smaller systems is the channel system.

The Channel System

As early as 1948, Breyer proposed methods of marketing analysis and control that utilized channel systems concepts. He summarized his view of the channel as a marketing system as follows: "Embedded everywhere in the enormous complex of activities and agreements that characterize the marketing institution is an elemental piece of structure, the so-called marketing channel. . . . This channel is, of course, a system."[7] The components of a channel system are also members of the macro- and industry systems, although many fewer are involved in a channel system than are found in the larger complexes. The particular components that are included in a given channel are those establishments whose activities bring them together in connection with the flow of

[7]R. F. Breyer, "Some Observations on 'Structural' Formation and the Growth of Marketing Channels," in W. Alderson and S. Shapiro, eds., *Theory in Marketing* (Homewood, Ill.: Richard D. Irwin, 1964), p. 163.

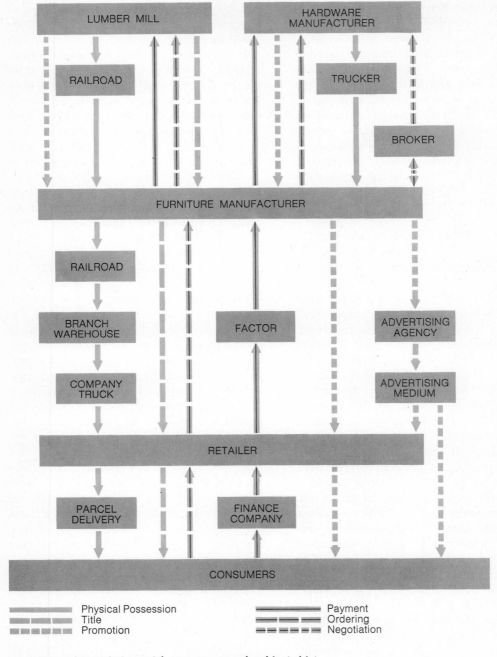

FIGURE 2.5 Partial channel for a consumer durable (table)

particular goods and services from resource to ultimate consumer.

A Consumer Durable-Goods Channel

It is possible to portray the channel of distribution for any product, but a complete portrayal of all flows and components is extremely unwieldy. For purposes of illustrating the channel system, it is more effective to treat a limited number of flows for a selected group of major components. Accordingly, a simplified channel with six flows—physical possession, title, promotion, payment, ordering, and negotiation—is shown in Figure 2.5. The figure models the channel for a consumer good of relatively high unit value, in this case a quality dining table made of expensive walnut with bronze hardware. The wood for the table is sold by the owner of a timber stand, who is also a sawmill operator. The lumber arrives by rail at the furniture factory. After manufacture, the table is shipped along with other items of furniture in a carload lot to the manufacturer's branch warehouse. After a period of storage at the warehouse, it is transported by a company-owned truck to a retail furniture store. This delivery takes place only after the retail buyer purchases the table, having seen it at the manufacturer's showroom (perhaps at the Merchandise Mart in Chicago). The retailer, buying four or five months ahead of the peak selling season, is not in a position to take advantage of offered cash discounts. The manufacturer, however, wants prompt payment in order to make a purchase of some especially fine lumber. Therefore the accounts receivable is sold at a discount to a factor, who in turn eventually collects from the retailer.

In the meantime promotion has begun.

Both of the primary producers promote the sale of their respective products to the furniture manufacturer. The furniture manufacturer selects an advertising agency to stimulate the sales of furniture not only to retail buyers but to the ultimate consumer as well. The agency plans appropriate campaigns and then places advertisements in various media, such as magazines, newspapers, and television. Advertising messages directed by the furniture retailer, using a local newspaper and radio station, also reach the ultimate consumer. The potential ultimate customer visits the store and purchases the table. The furniture eventually is delivered to the customer's home by an independent company's delivery truck. The consumer decides not to pay cash for the table and arranges for an installment loan from a finance company. The finance company makes its check payable to the retailer, and the customer agrees to make monthly or weekly payments to the finance company.

The Horizontal Dimension

We have considered so far only the vertical aspect of the channel system. Generally this is adequate, since an array of agencies related to each other by one or more marketing flows is the primary trait of the marketing channel. But the horizontal dimension also is important.

In the channel for the walnut dining table, only a single agency was depicted at each level. However, several—sometimes many—similar agencies operate at each channel stage. For instance, the furniture maker may negotiate with two, three, or a dozen lumber firms to obtain the right quality of wood at an acceptable price. Hardware may be purchased from two or more suppli-

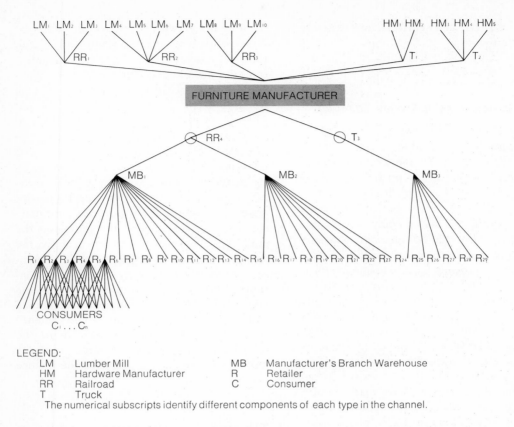

LEGEND:

LM	Lumber Mill	MB	Manufacturer's Branch Warehouse
HM	Hardware Manufacturer	R	Retailer
RR	Railroad	C	Consumer
T	Truck		

The numerical subscripts identify different components of each type in the channel.

FIGURE 2.6   Horizontal dimensions of physical flow in durable-goods channel (furniture)

ers. The manufacturer certainly must have several branch warehouses, each serving a considerable number of retail outlets. Figure 2.6 illustrates the changes and complexities involved when the horizontal dimension is introduced into only one flow in the channel. In this hypothetical example, there are no measurements on which to base the number of components operating at the various levels of the channel. The figure simply indicates the impact of horizontal relationships. The most important implication for management is, of course, the need to coordinate and supervise the marketing activities performed by the numerous agencies at each level of the distribution channel.

Collecting and Dispersing

Two important functions, called *collecting* and *dispersing,* are found in almost all channels. Suppose, for example, that a motorist finds it necessary to add oil to the crankcase of an automobile. This oil in its crude form probably comes from one of several possible sources in the United States or the Middle East. To deliver that oil directly to the motorist in the quantity and at the time that it is needed is the job of marketing. That marketing task is accomplished through the channel of distribution for oil. The vertical and horizontal dimensions of this channel are shown in Figure 2.7.

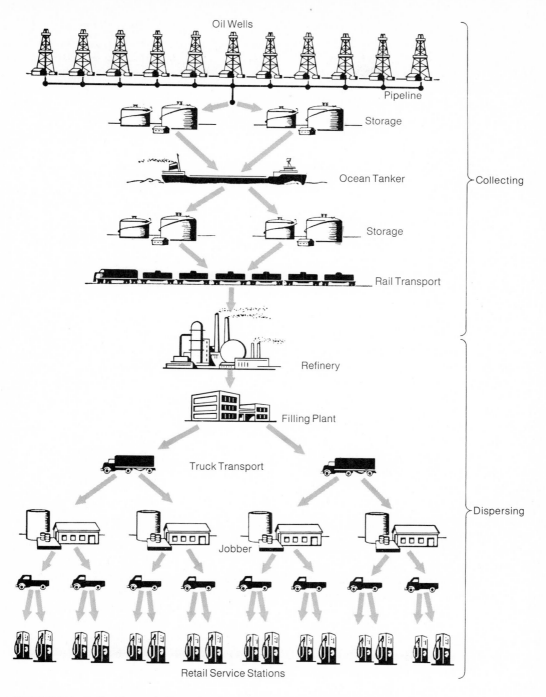

FIGURE 2.7   Collecting and dispersing in the channel system (motor oil)

Crude oil is extracted in large quantities; even a single well produces many barrels a day. No motorist, even if the crude product could be used, wants motor oil in wellhead quantities. Furthermore it is not economical to ship or store oil (crude or refined) in 1-quart cans. Shipping is done by pipeline, by ocean tanker, and by tank car. And it is necessary to change the scale of operation at successive levels of the channel in order to utilize agencies of the most economic size. A seagoing tanker or a river barge must have a larger capacity than a single well, and a refinery requires more than a tankerload. It becomes necessary then to collect and store quantities of oil at the well, at the shipping point, and at the refinery.

On the dispersion side, the filling plant is larger than the oil jobber, and the jobber is bigger than the service station. We can see the need to break down these accumulations of stock and distribute them in smaller quantities to jobbers and retailers. The petroleum company may ship in palletload quantities to the jobber by highway truck. The distributor in turn transports oil to the service station by the case. Finally the station attendant serves the motorist, dispensing a quart at a time. This process of dispersing permits each agency to operate at its optimum scale and still enables the motorist to buy a single quart of oil.

Collection and dispersion permit the utilization of components at their optimum size. As collection takes place the number of agencies at the next stage of the channel is reduced; in dispersion, the number is increased. In this way the horizontal dimensions of the channel change.

The Management System

Within the hierarchy of marketing systems, the smallest one that we will consider is the business firm. Systems engineers and management theorists have accepted the viewpoint that the firm is a system. Management, after all, is the force within an organization that coordinates the activities of its subsystems to achieve the organization's objectives. In Forrester's language, "Management is the task of designing and controlling an industrial system."[8]

Components of the Management System

The components of the management system are the various elements of its organization. Some of these are traditional functions or departments; others represent recent additions to corporate structure.

Traditional components Companies often use different terms to describe similar activities, but it still is apparent that most of the components of the microsystem have existed for many years. Included among these traditional components are:

Manufacturing
Engineering
Purchasing
Finance
Accounting
Sales
Advertising
Legal
Personnel

This list could be expanded, or several items could be combined. Some companies are organized very simply into three functional groups—manufacturing, sales, and finance. All other activities are subordinate to these

[8]J. W. Forrester, *Industrial Dynamics* (Boston: MIT Press, 1961), p. 8.

three. Other firms utilize very complex arrangements of these traditional components.

Newer components   Technological developments, the increased size and complexity of most businesses, and the closer contact between business and its environment have created many new activities or departments in the last decade and a half. Some of these activities represent organizational innovations. Others are modifications of traditional business activities. Nevertheless, each is important as a component in the modern microsystem. Some of these newcomers to systems structure are:

Corporate planning
Operations research
Data processing
Marketing research
Trade relations
Consumer relations
Government relations
Physical distribution
Materials management
New-venture management

To an even greater degree than with traditional components, the terminology used to describe the new activities is nonstandardized, and sometimes it is difficult to discover what actually is done in a particular department. However, it is probably not so important to have a complete and fixed list of system components as it is to recognize the dynamic character of the microsystem. It is certain that if the need for a new component activity arises, the adaptive processes within a microsystem will give expression to it.

Marketing Organization

There are two important ways in which the components of a micromarketing system are linked together. These are the flow of authority and the flow of information. We will look at each briefly.

The flow of authority   At the channel and macrolevel power is dispersed throughout the system. This is not true in the microsystem. Here power is concentrated in the hands of the owners or their hired managers. Operationally, power is centered in the office of the chief executive. To accomplish the system's objectives, this power is delegated to subordinates within the organization. The delegation of authority is not without restraints: It must take place within the framework of established policies, job descriptions, and job relationships.

One type of delegated authority is *line authority*. Line authority involves the power to issue instructions over other designated system components. A plant manager is authorized to operate a factory and may in turn delegate authority for performing specialized manufacturing activities to various foremen. Foremen in turn may delegate some authority to production group leaders. Sales authority is delegated to a general sales manager, who usually delegates authority to regional or district sales managers. The regional sales manager in turn delegates authority to the individual salesperson. Thus the components of a microsystem are linked by the flow of line authority.

Responsibility for performing staff (advisory) activities is often delegated to specialist components within the system. Staff executives have no power over other components. A staff executive, however, often requires the support and cooperation of these people. In place of line authority the power of persuasion and the influence of skill and knowledge must be exercised. In a way, the staff executive must rely on an authority of ideas instead of an authority of position.

The delegation of authority creates a one-on-one, vertical relationship between super-ior and subordinate. In multiperson organi-zations, such as the military and businesses, authority must be dispersed throughout the various levels within the system before dele-gation can take place. The dispersion is accomplished by decentralization.

Decentralization can be accomplished in several ways. First, the responsibility and authority to implement marketing plans may be assigned *geographically* to district or local managers. This method most commonly is used in organizing a sales department. It also is used in decentralized retail organizations, such as Sears, Roebuck and J. C. Penney.

Marketing positions also may be grouped *functionally*—the responsibility and authority for carrying out various functions are as-signed to separate managers. Advertising, selling, research, and physical distribution frequently are headed by individual func-tional managers.

A third way to decentralize the market-ing management authority is on the basis of *products*. Occasionally product decen-tralization is carried all the way through the organizational structure. The result is that a marketing department may have parallel organizational arrangements for different product lines. For instance, Procter & Gam-ble has separate marketing organizations servicing retail food stores. One group rep-resents such food products as cake mixes, another group sells P&G's soaps and deter-gents, and still another sells its health and beauty products. The product management system generally is used by firms that offer a wide line of products or brands to a relative-ly homogeneous group of customers.

A fourth method of decentralizing author-ity is through the use of *market managers*.[9] A

market manager is a person charged with the task of directing a company's efforts to serve a particular type of customer. For instance, an industrial products company that sells products both to manufacturers (called OEM—original equipment manufactu-rers—customers) and to distributors for use as replacement parts by the consumer might use a market manager organization. Fractional horsepower electric motors pro-vide a good example. GE sells motors to Maytag for installation in home laundry ma-chines. It also sells motors to electrical wholesalers who in turn sell them to appli-ance repair shops. GE very well might use two market managers—one for OEM cus-tomers and another for so-called aftermarket customers. The market manager system gen-erally is used when a firm has a relatively short and standardized line of products, which are used by customers in a number of rather different industries.

It is possible to combine two or more of these four methods of decentralization into a single complex method. Basic divisions may be made along product or market lines. Planning, marketing, research, and promo-tional tasks could be assigned to functional departments. And in the same organization, the sales force may be arranged on a geo-graphical basis. This method is used by operating divisions of AT&T.

Another way to combine methods of de-centralization is shown in Figure 2.8. The basic approach is functional. The marketing manager directs two product managers and also supervises a corporate staff of marketing specialists. These functional executives assist the marketing manager in developing overall plans and procedures. They also have func-tional responsibility for the activities of their counterparts who work for the product man-agers at the next lower level of the organiza-tion. For example, the Product A advertising manager would consult with the corporate

[9]M. Hanan, "Reorganize Your Company Around Its Markets," *Harvard Business Review,* November–December 1974, pp. 63–74.

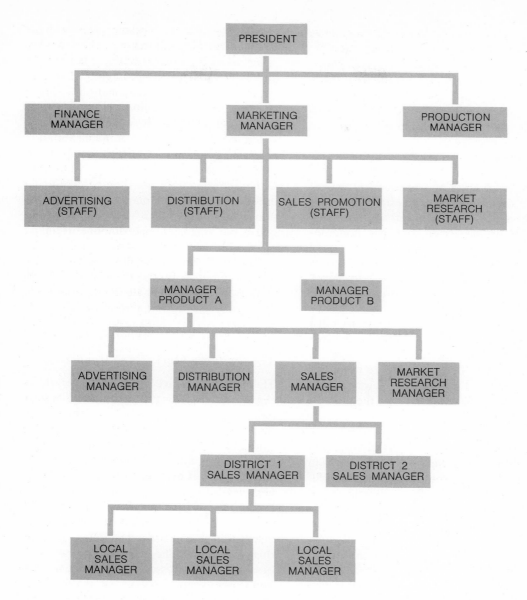

FIGURE 2.8   Combined method of decentralization of authority in a marketing organization (line product manager)

advertising manager on matters of company policy, such as the use of corporate identification marks, advertising agency selection, and the obtaining of frequency and space discounts in advertising media. The Product A advertising manager, however, reports to the product manager—not to the corporate advertising manager.

In Figure 2.8, the product manager is a line executive with direct responsibility for the total marketing of a product. However many product managers fill staff positions. They have no direct authority over anybody else in the organization, but they nonetheless have the responsibility for managing their assigned products at a profit. This is where "the authority of ideas" to which reference was made earlier comes into play. Any organizational conflict that might arise because of this lack of direct authority must ultimately be resolved by the line executives involved. But if the product manager is doing the job well, such crises are not likely to occur often. This remains, however, one of the most serious drawbacks of the product manager form of organization.

The flow of information   Probably the most important flow that links the components in the microsystem is the flow of information. Much of this flow is related directly to the flow of authority and to the staff's responsibility to prepare instructions and reports. However, the overall information flows move more frequently and in far more complex ways than do those required by the basic organization. As we noted staff executives have no line authority over other components within the system, but they do exchange information with them, carrying out assigned responsibilities through this exchange of ideas.

It is largely through this transfer of information that a business system becomes operative. Organizational relationships can be defined and communicated; but in the absence of dynamic information flows it is impossible for the system to be activated. Only by reacting to information about a change in its environment can a system adapt to external threats to its survival. Because of the functional importance of the information flow and the fact that serious management problems are encountered in connection with it, considerable attention has been paid in recent years to the management information system. This is a subsystem that involves the organizational components linked by the flow of information. Attempts to regulate and control this flow of information have resulted in formal management information systems. Chapter 20 describes the marketing information system in detail.

The Evolving Marketing Organization

The past twenty-five years have seen many changes in marketing organization. Contemporary forms bear slight resemblance to those that existed prior to World War II. In spite of the improvements, problems continue to exist. Since marketing is changing constantly, it is by no means certain that the best organizational form for the micromarketing system has been developed or that it ever can be developed. The discussion of marketing organization that follows reflects this viewpoint. The dynamic character of organization is stressed. Contemporary marketing organization as it has been affected by the adoption of the marketing concept is presented.

Marketing organization circa 1946   Figure 2.9 presents an organization chart of a typical firm engaged in marketing in the immediate post–World War II period. We see the three

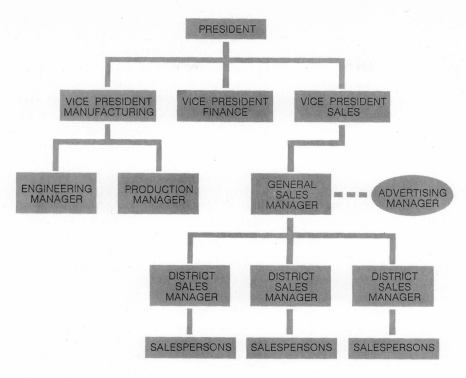

FIGURE 2.9   Marketing organization circa 1946

traditional organizational components—manufacturing, finance, and sales—dominating the organizational structure. Two important and distinct components exist within the manufacturing area: the engineering department, which is responsible for the design and development of products, and the production department, which is responsible for manufacturing the firm's products. Line authority within the sales division is delegated by the general sales manager to district sales managers. These individuals in turn assign sales authority to individual salespersons in the various territories. One staff marketing position is shown; an advertising manager reports to the general sales manager. This individual has no authority over others in the organization but is limited to

preparing advertising plans and serving as a point of contact with an advertising agency.

In the decade following the end of World War II, a number of important developments occurred. First, most companies experienced rapid and sometimes very disruptive growth. Doubling in size was quite normal, and tenfold increases in the level of company business were common. Many firms of this period diversified rapidly, partly driven by profit possibilities and partly to hedge against the uncertainty of single-line manufacture and marketing. Important technological developments occurred: changes in manufacturing methods, largely the result of automation; changes in the way in which customers used the products and raw materials they purchased; and dramatic changes in the level of sophistication in customers' purchasing practices. Another aspect of technological change was the research and development explosion. The pent-up technology that broke through in the postwar period made many prewar products obsolete. An increased level of research and development resulted in the rapid obsolescence of even some of the newest products, and the life expectancies of all products were cut substantially.

The generally favorable economic conditions that prevailed in the postwar period made it possible for many new businesses to get started. Their entry, together with diversification moves by established firms, resulted in increased competition of three distinct types. First, there were new firms selling products similar to those already on the market, and because of technological improvements the newcomers were able to sell at lower prices. Second, there was the competition of new products from established companies. Finally, there was the dramatic impact of new-product competition from entirely new businesses.

Changing technology, new products, and increased competition demanded tremendous capital outlay, and costs mushroomed. Growth, diversification, adaption of technological breakthroughs, massive research and development, and increased competitive pressure forced postwar firms into a period that might have been called *profitless prosperity*. Insistence on profit control, increased skill in selling, and greater attention to productivity became focal points of management's attention.

Marketing organization circa 1956 The economic and technological developments of the postwar period resulted in some important organizational changes between the years 1946 and 1956. Figure 2.10 presents a hypothetical organization that adapted to these developments, with the principal changes occurring in the manufacturing area. Growth and diversification forced the enlargement, and in some cases the decentralization, of manufacturing. The product blocks (A, B, and C) could represent either product or geographical separation in the manufacturing function, probably both. Some of the decentralization was also the result of companies' searching for lower-cost manufacturing locations. Within the engineering division, activities began to be specialized. Design engineering was required to support the manufacturing operation and a separate engineering activity was related to research and development. Although research and development groups and departments existed previously, they became more and more common in the early 1950s.

Some specialization also occurred in finance. Corporate financial planning, occasionally headed by a company economist, became a separate department within the financial division. Routine financial work, such as accounting or budget preparation, was handled in a second department.

Changes in the sales area were quite modest. In some firms another specialist arose— the marketing research manager. Marketing research was over fifty years old, but it had made relatively modest progress in attaining organizational status. Strangely enough, in some of the early organizational arrangements the marketing research manager reported to the company's financial officer.

The organizational changes that were made between 1946 and 1956 did not adequately solve the economic and technological problems that had developed. Indeed, some of the organizational developments actually aggravated the already-existing situations. Among the principal difficulties encountered in the mid-1950s was the strong product and manufacturing orientation in

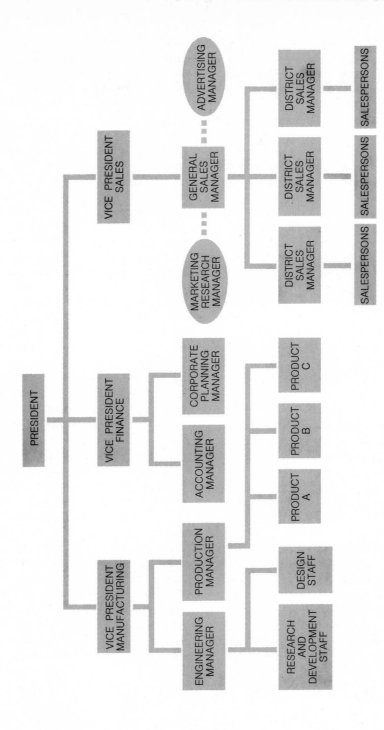

FIGURE 2.10   Marketing organization circa 1956

most managements. The changes that had taken place in manufacturing—decentralization, specialization of production, and the emergence of strong research and development groups—led naturally to a product-oriented company philosophy. The question was usually "Can we make it?" Seldom was it "Can it be sold?"

A second major problem that resulted from rapid growth and decentralization was a lack of coordination among sales, engineering, and manufacturing departments. Although engineering and production often reported to a common superior, there was little attempt to coordinate their activities more than was necessary to accommodate the manufacturing needs of the company. Coordination with sales seldom if ever occurred.

Following a brief post–Korean War slump in the economy, prosperity generally prevailed and most companies continued to grow. Unfortunately profit margins became tighter and tighter. In part this was the result of continuously rising costs. More important, however, was the decline in the number of profitable business opportunities. The cream apparently had been skimmed. Early on capital had been poured into those projects that offered the best return on investment. Only less profitable or marginal projects remained. It was in this condition that many companies entered the 1960s.

Marketing organization circa 1966 The economic and technological developments in the period between 1956 and 1966, and the problems created by them, led to some important changes in the philosophy and structure of business. The philosophical change involved the adoption of the marketing management concept. As we have seen, this concept involved the acceptance of cus-

tomer rather than product orientation. It demanded the integration of all marketing activities within the overall marketing effort, and the coordination of marketing with non-marketing activities within the firm. Finally, it emphasized the importance of profit goals rather than sales. The organizational impact of the marketing concept is shown in very simple form in Figure 2.11.

The organizational changes in the period were almost entirely within the old sales department. Even the name changed, and the term *sales* was replaced by *marketing.* But it was not simply a change in terminology, for a new top-level management post was created. It was a line management position, and its incumbent was charged with the responsibility of carrying out all of the marketing activities within the firm and of coordinating these with other company functions. This top marketing post carried different names in different companies. Whether called a vice president–marketing, director of marketing, or marketing manager, the position reflected the ascendancy of the marketing concept to a visible position in the organizational structure.

Important developments took place within the new marketing department. The older marketing activities—sales, advertising, and marketing research—now reported to a common supervisor, the top marketing executive. A new marketing staff position was developed to coordinate various aspects of marketing, to work out detailed marketing programs for particular products or markets, and to provide liaison with other parts of the company. As we already have noted, the market manager was charged with coordinating all company efforts on behalf of a selected group of customers. The person in the position of product manager, or *brand manager,* as the new marketing position com-

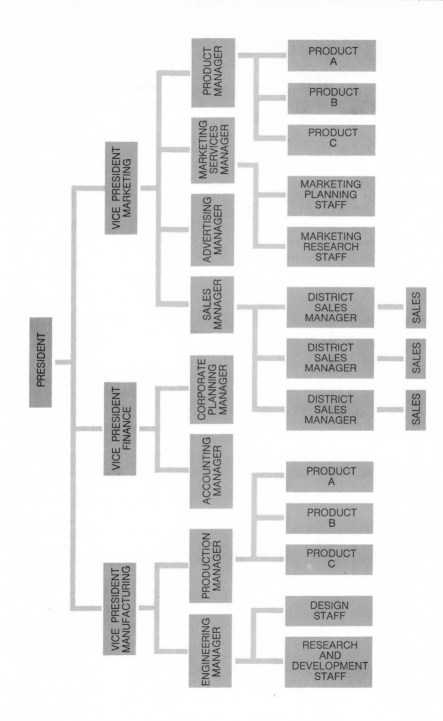

FIGURE 2.11   Marketing organization circa 1966

monly was called, was responsible for coordinating all company efforts on behalf of assigned products. We can use the terms *brand manager* and *product manager* synonymously, although distinctions are sometimes drawn. The most common is to use *brand manager* exclusively in connection with consumer packaged-goods marketing. *Product manager* seems to be used rather generally in both consumer and industrial marketing organizations. Often the product manager is charged with the responsibility of achieving programmed levels of profits.[10]

By 1970 many companies had adopted the product manager system. As might have been expected, companies in the consumer products field were the first to adopt it, and some industrial firms followed. Unfortunately, the product manager system failed to work satisfactorily in a number of companies. Uncertainty as to the type of person who should fill the position, failure to define the job carefully, and the inherent difficulties of achieving coordination in organizations long accustomed to operating independently hindered the development of a viable product manager system. Turnover rates were high, results were slow to materialize, disappointments grew, and some companies

returned to traditional organizational methods. Others attempted to find ways to make the product manager system work. Internal training, careful guidance and supervision by top management, and a great deal of patience have enabled many companies to make the system work satisfactorily. The shakedown seems to have occurred, and it appears that the general form of the organization shown in Figure 2.11 will be followed by most companies in the future.

Recent Developments in Marketing Organization

It is always difficult to recognize organizational trends in their early stages. Companies continually experiment, and it is only after the passage of time that clear indications of new developments can be seen. However, recent developments do suggest several new directions.

The considerable need for a constant flow of ideas for new products or other ventures has led some managements to separate the acquisition and expansion operations from the rest of the business. Often called a *new-venture department,* it usually is not a profit center. Operating divisions therefore are not burdened with the specific costs of searching for and developing new products. Also, the search for new products or other ventures is not hindered by vested interests in established products or by the failure to devote time, money, and attention to them.[11]

---

[10]The position of the product (brand) manager, its challenges, and its problems have received considerable attention in the recent literature. Selected references include G. H. Evans, *The Product Manager's Job,* Research Study No. 69 (New York: American Management Association, 1964); The Conference Board, *The Product Manager System* (New York: The Conference Board, 1965); V. P. Buell, "The Changing Role of the Product Manager in Consumer Goods Companies," *Journal of Marketing,* July 1975, pp. 3–11; G. R. Gemmill and D. L. Wileman, "The Product Manager as an Influence Agent," *Journal of Marketing,* January 1973, pp. 26–30; R. M. Clewett and S. F. Stasch, "Shifting Role for the Product Manager," *Harvard Business Review,* January–February 1975, pp. 65–73; and "The Brand Manager: No Longer King," *Business Week,* 9 June 1973, pp. 58–66.

[11]See Edgar A. Pessemier, *Managing Innovation and New-Product Development* (Cambridge, Mass.: Marketing Science Institute, 1975); R. M. Hill and J. D. Hlavacek, "The Venture Team: A New Concept in Marketing Organization," *Journal of Marketing,* July 1972, pp. 44–50; and J. D. Hlavacek, "Toward More Successful Venture Management," *Journal of Marketing,* October 1974, pp. 56–60.

The ultimate in marketing-oriented organization appears to have developed in a few very large industrial companies. This is sometimes called the *general manager* method of marketing organization. In organization chart form it looks very like the pre-World War II business organization, but it operates quite differently. The general manager is responsible for a strategic business unit, or profit center. Manufacturing, marketing, and finance executives report to the general manager. In one large firm, the Monsanto Company, product managers in one of the divisions are assigned the task of developing the total business plan for the unit. The plan, of course, is the general manager's plan; but the fact that it is prepared by a marketing person is significant. Since it is a general business plan, although heavily oriented toward marketing, it also embraces all of the other functions. Thus we see the marketing concept being put into practice: customer orientation, goal direction, integration of effort, and utilization of scientific planning and decision-making techniques.

Neither of these recent developments appears to herald a major change in marketing organization. What has evolved since 1956 seems appropriate for today's marketing task. Changes undoubtedly will take place in years to come. If the marketing task expands or contracts, there will be adaptations in marketing organization. It is difficult to predict what these changes may be; and it is equally difficult to anticipate the changes that will take place in the microsystem as a result. Of this, though, we can be sure—marketing organization will remain dynamic. It will continue to change as time goes on. The task of the alert manager is to make sure that the organization is suited to the times in which it must operate.

Summary

Marketing is a system. We can better understand marketing if we apply to it some of the key concepts in systems analysis. Among these are the ideas that there exists a hierarchy of systems in which small systems are components of the larger ones; that components are linked by flows; that the system can be distinguished from its environment; and that system performance can be regulated through various techniques of feedback and control.

We have looked at four levels of systems. The largest of these we call the macrosystem, or aggregate system. We have described the components of the macromarketing system and the ways in which they are linked by the flow of ownership of goods from their points of origin to their final consumption.

The industry system is a component of the macrosystem and includes all those establishments involved in making and distributing a general class of good. However, very little marketing (except industry-wide sales promotion) is managed on an industry system level. Accordingly we look to smaller system components to locate the structural units in which business decisions are made.

The marketing channel is a system. Channel components of many types are linked together by the various marketing flows. Collecting and dispersing are important channel functions, since they permit the utilization of components of the optimum size.

The business firm can be viewed as a micromarketing system. Its components, or subsystems, are the various functional departments and operating divisions. Today the business firm is composed of a combination of traditional and newer system components. Whether new or old, these components are linked by flows of authority and information. Marketing organization has been changing. The principal force behind these changes has been the adoption of the marketing concept. *Marketing* has replaced *sales* as the term used to identify the function and its place in the organization. The organization of the marketing department also has been modified substantially. Specialists in planning, research, product management, and market management have been added. Further changes in marketing organization can be expected to occur in the future as new technologies and environmental pressures are brought to bear on the micromarketing system.

Questions and Problems

1. Why is the systems approach particularly suited to the study of marketing?

2. Almost any company, church, or social organization can be viewed as a system. Select some firm or organization with which you are familiar (such as the organization of student government in your college) and show how it does or does not meet the characteristics of a system.

3. A number of mechanical systems were mentioned in this chapter as analogous to marketing, but none of these was actually a mechanical marketing system. Are you familiar with any? Can you find references in the business literature to marketing devices that might be considered mechanical marketing systems?

4. The macromarketing system can be viewed as an ecological system. This means that the components of the system must adapt to changes in the environment. Identify the important changes in the environment of the marketing system that you think have occurred in the last five to ten years. What kinds of marketing components have adapted best to these changes? What kinds have not adapted very well?

5. There are more retailers than there are any other type of marketing system component. This chapter suggests that this is because retailers have, generally speaking, smaller optimum size. Yet retailers seem to be getting bigger and bigger. What is happening?

6. Select a popular advertising theme, such as "When You've Said 'Budweiser,' You've Said It All" or Zenith's "The Quality Goes in Before the Name Goes On." Reconstruct the flow of this idea to you. What kinds of marketing components do you think were linked by the flow of this marketing idea?

7. Find out as much as you can about the channel of distribution for a particular product—either a consumer or an industrial good. In your investigation, find out if important changes have taken place in the channel arrangements in the past twenty-five years. If changes have occurred, discuss the reasons.

8. Select a consumer durable, such as an outboard motor or stereo equipment.

Draw as complete a flow diagram of its channel of distribution as you can. Explain why the various flows do not involve the same kinds and numbers of components.

9. What would the channel of distribution for a consumer service such as dental care be like?

10. Why is it appropriate to call a business firm a *system?*

11. If you were handed three undated or-ganization charts of a company, each from a different period of its history since 1945, what specific organizational clues would you look for in order to determine when each chart was proba-bly in effect?

12. Why do some firms decentralize mar-keting authority along product lines, others along market lines, and some along both?

3

Marketing Planning

Planning is the central activity in marketing management; and, as we observed in Chapter 1, planning is one of the essential elements of the marketing concept. We also learned that the principal method by which a marketing-oriented company directs its efforts to satisfy customer wants involves a systematic hierarchy of planning activities. Top management is responsible for the strategic planning. Divisional management develops long-range plans to carry out the company's mission. And functional management designs tactical short-range plans to execute the division's long-range program.

This arrangement is found in most large companies. For example, GE's chief executive officers are responsible for determining which businesses the company will pursue.[1]

In some cases this means entering new fields; and in other instances it means getting out of areas that will be unprofitable in the future. GE's entry into CB radios and its withdrawal from the computer field are good examples. The manager of each division, such as electronics, appliances, or wiring materials, develops three- to five-year plans to achieve the market positions that the company's strategic planners believe are desirable. Ultimately, functional managers in each division undertake the task of designing the tactical plans to be carried out in the marketplace.

Smaller companies often merge these re-

---

[1]An important outgrowth of GE's strategic planning has been the study of alternative strategies for attaining and maintaining high market share and profitability. See S. Schoeffler, R. D. Buzzell, and D. F. Heany, "Impact of Strategic Planning on Profit Performance," *Harvard Business Review,* March-April 1974, pp. 137–145; R. D. Buzzell, B. T. Gale, and R. G. Sultan, "Market Share—A Key to Probability," *Harvard Business Review,* January-February 1975, pp. 98–107; and P. N. Bloom and P. Kotler, "Strategies for High-Market Share Companies," *Harvard Business Review,* November-December 1975, pp. 63–72.

sponsibilities, but the fundamental elements still can be identified. The president of the Black Body Corporation, a modest-sized company manufacturing industrial equipment, makes very similar decisions. A few years ago he decided to concentrate his company's efforts in the area of manufacturing and marketing industrial ovens. His strategy to carry out this mission was to hire as sales manager a successful manufacturer's representative who was familiar with Black Body's products and with the market. This person in turn developed a new selling approach. Over the space of a few years, products were modified as a result of suggestions made by the sales department, and eventually a new and different long-range program was developed. Subsequently the company entered the fast-food industry, introducing a conveyorized oven for cooking pizzas and other foods. Now both parts of its business are prospering. While less elegant than GE's procedure, the Black Body planning approach is essentially the same and has achieved proportionally similar results.

Planning, then, is critical to the management of a marketing-oriented company, whether it is large or small. To see how marketing planning is done, let's look first at an example of a successful marketing company.

An Example of Marketing Planning

The Hooker Chemical Corporation prepares both a five-year general marketing plan and a one-year detailed marketing plan.[2] Although

[2]This description of the Hooker Chemical Company's planning process is adapted from a presentation in E. C. Miller, *Marketing Planning*, AMA Research Study

the director of marketing coordinates all planning, each division of Hooker prepares its own marketing plan, and the responsibility for preparing the plan is treated differently in the various divisions. In one, a product manager may work on the marketing plan; in another, perhaps an industry (market) manager.

After the divisional marketing plan has been prepared, it is reviewed by the general manager of the division and the corporate director of marketing, along with their respective marketing staffs. Following this review, it is submitted to the corporate marketing staff for inclusion in the company's consolidated marketing plan. The president of Hooker reviews and approves the divisional marketing plans as well as the consolidated corporate plan.

The basic document in the Hooker planning process is a long-range marketing plan for each product or market. The process by which this product or market plan is developed is illustrated in Figure 3.1. The company has described its process this way:[3]

Summarized in the six steps listed below [and shown in Figure 3.1] is the approach we have developed to achieve Hooker growth and profit objectives in all operations.

1. Selection of major market or product areas for growth and profit improvement.

No. 81 (New York: American Management Association, 1967), pp. 59–64. An interesting addendum to this description is found in an address by Hooker Chemical Company executive W. F. Christopher entitled "Three Basic Concepts of Long-Range Planning," in *The Marketing News*, 1 May 1970, pp. 4–7; and in W. F. Christopher, "Marketing Planning that Gets Things Done," *Harvard Business Review*, September-October 1970, pp. 56–64.

[3]The following excerpt is reprinted, by permission of the publisher, from *Marketing Planning*, AMA Research Study # 81, E. C. Miller, p. 62. © 1967 by American Management Association, Inc. All rights reserved.

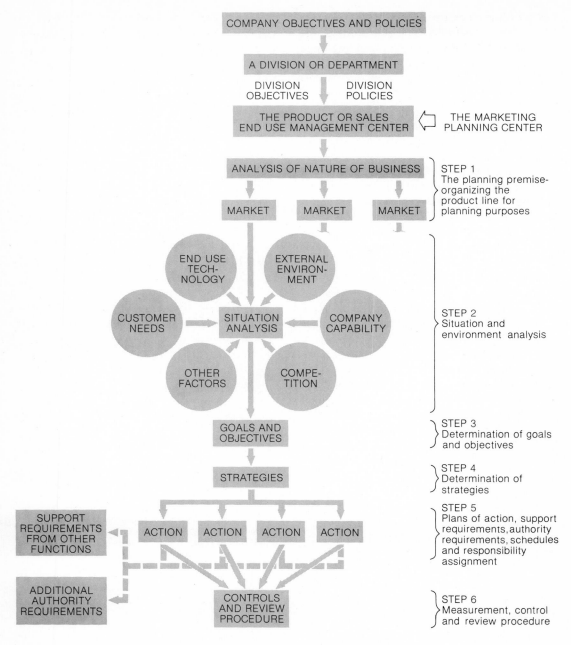

FIGURE 3.1   Hooker Chemical Corporation: Marketing planning process

Source: E. C. Miller, *Marketing Planning* (New York: American Management Association, 1967), p.60. Used with the permission of the American Management Association and James O. Rice Associates, Inc.

2. Evaluation of market and competitive situation in each selected area.
3. Establishment of goals for each area selected.
4. Determination of strategies to achieve goals.
5. Implementation of strategy through plans that include specific programs, completion dates, and responsibility assignments.
6. Aggressive, goal-centered leadership plus measurement and control of progress to achieve goals.

The planning process begins with an organized, objective evaluation of the business of each division. From this we identify the market or product areas for which we develop our forward plans. In general these areas will be defined in terms of markets or industries served, since we sell by markets. In our budget planning procedure each area selected becomes the subject for an LRP (Long-Range Plan). The LRP's, then, are summaries of Hooker's plans for growth and provide us the yardsticks we must live by to achieve our goals. The first step in budget planning is to define market or product areas for LRP's. Next we must be expert and highly professional in each of our LRP market or product areas. We must know customer needs and trends, competition and trends, and our own company capabilities. With this knowledge we can set goals that will give us the growth we seek, and we can determine the best Hooker strategy to achieve these goals. This strategy can then be implemented through specific plans which provide a basis for leadership and control.

If our plans are well thought out and specific, our daily, weekly, and monthly results can be measured against them to assure that we are on the track and on the way to achieving our goals. In this process nothing is static. The business situation changes, our capabilities change. So, in our leadership, measurement, and control we will constantly change our plans as we move to strengthen weaknesses or maximize newly discovered opportunities. In this sense our plans are not once a year—they are always. But the end result of each division's total performance for the year ahead must be the achievement of the division's profit objective, however much we may change the individual LRP plans.

The Complete Planning Process

As the Hooker Chemical Company example illustrates, the marketing planning process flows from the top of the organization to the bottom. In describing the detailed steps involved in marketing planning, it is helpful to elaborate on the particular responsibilities of each management level. It should not surprise you to discover that these planning chores closely parallel the marketing responsibilities at each tier of the organization. But we should not assume that these planning tasks are separate and distinct. On the contrary, they are part of a continuous and integrated activity. We cannot say that top management does its job, then divisional management takes over, and so on. There is only one planning process. In a very real sense, the president of the company is responsible for the outcome of the action plans that someone else much lower in the organization eventually develops. Marketing planning is a team effort, with each person's task contributing to or dependent on someone else's. The process is modeled in Figure 3.2.

The Planning Prerequisites

Top management sets the stage. It determines the framework within which others in the company develop specific marketing programs. This stage is extremely important, because it ultimately determines the kinds of

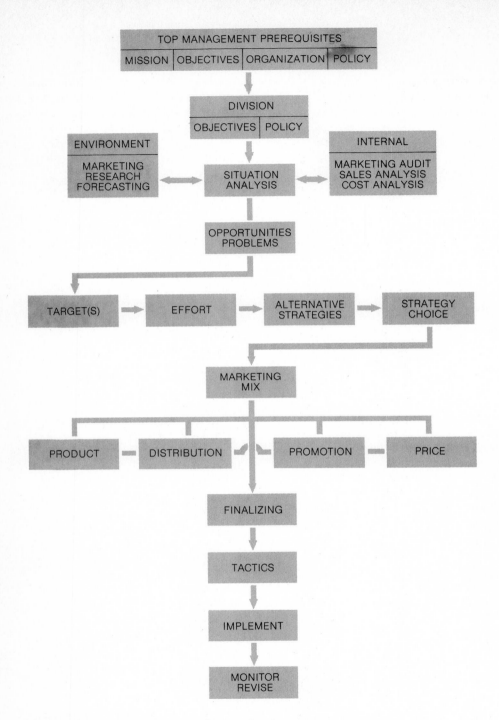

FIGURE 3.2 A model of the marketing planning process

marketing plans that are produced and the results that they achieve. Top management's contributions to the marketing planning process are so vital we call them *prerequisites.* This means that the people who are responsible for the actual development of the marketing plan cannot proceed until top management's responsibilities have been met. There are four basic prerequisites: defining the company's *mission,* stating its *objectives,* providing an adequate *organization,* and articulating *policies.*

Mission

The first top-management prerequisite for marketing planning is a statement of the company's mission. This statement defines the kind of company its leaders wish it to be. It identifies the customers and the markets the company intends to serve. The statement of company mission answers the question, "What business are we in?" That is, it focuses attention on the directions the company will pursue in the future. The importance to the marketing planner of understanding the company's mission should be evident: the mission defines the boundaries within which the planner looks for viable marketing opportunities. In some large companies the mission is refined further, and is assigned to divisions or subsidiaries through a statement called a *charter.*

Objectives

The second prerequisite is a statement of company objectives. The planner must understand the company's overall objectives in order to design a marketing strategy for attaining them. Company objectives may be stated in different ways. Some firms operate with the intention of attaining certain financial goals. Profit, expressed as a return on invested capital, constitutes the most common type of company objective. Some firms, however, may adopt a more general objective, such as a definition of the role they want to play in their industry. Other firms may state their marketing objectives in terms of attaining a certain market share. Still others may adopt company objectives that are related to innovation and technological advancement.

It normally is not the prerogative of the marketing manager to determine company objectives. These are matters of top-level administrative concern, in that boards of directors and chief executive officers are responsible for establishing them. The marketing manager, however, must understand these objectives, because it is possible to set specific marketing objectives only after the company's general objectives have been determined.[4] This relationship can be explained by a simple example. Suppose that an electronics company's top management has decided that its objective for the following year is to increase profits by $1 million. Furthermore, top management has determined that the best overall strategy to achieve this objective is to increase by $5 million the sales of the company's most profitable line of products, its integrated circuits. Increasing sales then becomes the objective of the company's marketing department. The marketing manager would consider various ways to increase sales by $5 million. One of these selling strategies might well be to do business in the booming digital watch industry by selling electronic move-

[4]See C. H. Granger, "The Hierarchy of Objectives," *Harvard Business Review,* May-June 1964, pp. 63ff.

ments to companies still making conventional mechanical watches. Selling these movements to such firms as Bulova and Timex becomes the objective for the sales department, which must develop an action plan. Thus a hierarchy of marketing objectives emerges. It begins at the top and extends down through the organization to the point where action programs can be designed and carried out.[5]

Organization

The third prerequisite that must be satisfied before operational plans can be made is the design and staffing of the marketing organization. Only after an operational organization and its necessary staff have been designed and incorporated into the overall organization is a company ready to undertake the preparation of strategic and tactical marketing plans. We looked at alternative organizational forms in Chapter 2.

Policies

The fourth prerequisite for operational planning is the establishment of necessary marketing policies. Policies establish a framework—a set of working rules—for administrative action. For instance, a company's decision regarding the type of competitive posture it wants to assume is a matter of policy. One company may decide to compete vigorously to increase market share; another firm may decide as a matter of policy

[5]A good discussion of setting objectives at the marketing department level is found in O. S. Sherwin, "Management of Objectives," *Harvard Business Review,* May-June 1976, pp. 149–160.

to engage in minimal competitive activities. A third company may decide as a matter of policy not to compete with its own customers; or alternatively it may instruct its people to seek business wherever they can find it. Policies create a framework within which strategy is formulated.

Developing the Long-Run Marketing Strategy

In a large decentralized firm, the next important level of planning responsibility is the divisional or business group. A division typically is responsible for a portion of a company's overall business. In some firms the division is an internal entity, such as the Grocery Products Division at Ralston Purina or the Pontiac Motor Division at GM or, a division may be a subsidiary operating company, such as one of the many autonomous operating companies within the ITT corporate structure.

The marketing planning responsibility at the division level is to develop a general strategy or long-range marketing plan. The specific responsibility for developing such a plan may be that of a top marketing executive—a vice president of marketing or a marketing manager. In a small division, the task of developing an overall business plan (including marketing) is often the responsibility of the division's manager.

There are no hard and fast rules regarding the exact steps to follow in developing a marketing strategy or the sequence in which the steps should be taken. Many useful books and articles have been written on the subject, and the author has distilled from them and from his own experience a general approach to marketing planning.[6] This approach is described in Figure 3.2 and explained in the discussion that follows.

Analyzing the Marketing Situation

The first step in planning is an organized analysis of the company and its marketing environment, which is frequently called a *situation analysis*. Four types of analyses are involved. First, a periodic and comprehensive review of the company's strengths and weaknesses is a necessary step in any planning activity. This periodic review of a company's marketing capacity is provided by a *marketing audit*. Much as the certified public accountant's scrutiny of a company's accounting procedures and financial reports acts as a guide to decisions in financial management, a marketing auditor's review of its marketing methods and capabilities serves as a guide to effective marketing management. A marketing audit includes a careful appraisal of a company's past performance as well as an evaluation of its existing marketing strengths. Particular attention is paid to the company's product line, its distribution channels, its promotional effectiveness, and its pricing. Thus, the results of a marketing audit bear directly on

the formulation of future marketing strategy. We will look more thoroughly at marketing auditing in Chapter 20.

The second phase of the situation analysis involves *researching the marketing environment.* This requires the use of marketing research techniques to answer questions that bear vitally on the management decisions to be made. The special environmental facts needed to develop strategy in each part of the marketing mix are collected at this point. Marketing research is discussed in Chapter 21.

The third step in analyzing the marketing situation is to conduct *thorough sales and marketing cost studies.* These may be special investigations conducted at irregular intervals. Preferably they should be part of the company's marketing information system. Chapters 20 and 22 explore these topics.

The fourth phase of the situation analysis involves *forecasting industry and company sales.* The sales forecast is the product of an analysis of the economic environment. Various types of sales forecasting methods are used, but the approach that is most appropriate at this early stage of the planning process commences with a forecast of general business conditions. On the well-established premise that general business conditions are major determinants of the direction and magnitude of industry and company sales, the forecast of the level of general business activity is a most important aspect of the situation survey. From this forecast the company can estimate both the sales of the industry and those of its own firm. On the basis of the sales forecast, a profit forecast can be made which in turn is based on the revenues and costs associated with the predicted level of sales. It is important to stress at this point that the forecast is an estimate of what the company can sell and the profit it will make

---

[6]A number of useful books and articles are devoted in whole or in part to the subject of marketing planning. For example, see L. Adler, "A New Orientation for Plotting Marketing Strategy," *Business Horizons,* Winter 1964, pp. 37–50; V. Buell, *Marketing Management in Action* (New York: McGraw-Hill, 1966); R. W. Ferrell, *Customer-Oriented Planning* (New York: American Management Association, 1964); W. I. Little, "The Integrated Management Approach to Marketing," *Journal of Marketing,* April 1967, pp. 32–36; E. C. Miller, *Marketing Planning* (New York: American Management Association, 1967); and M. E. Stern, *Marketing Planning: A Systems Approach* (New York: McGraw-Hill, 1966).

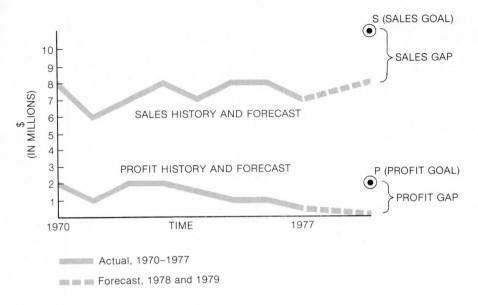

FIGURE 3.3   Gap analysis: The planning assignment

if it continues with its present strategy. It is relatively easy, then, to compare this forecast with the company's objectives to discover if a *planning gap* exists. Look at Figure 3.3. Company sales and profit have been plotted through 1977. Management has expressed dissatisfaction with the company's marketing performance and has set sales and profit goals, indicated by points *S* and *P*. Quite apparently this company cannot reach these goals without changing its strategy—or at least augmenting it. Closing the gap becomes the planning assignment. We will look further at demand measurement and forecasting in Chapter 7.

Assessing Opportunities and Problems

The second step in market planning is the identification of marketing problems and opportunities. It involves interpreting the findings of the situation analysis. Facts about the consumers, the economy, and the public environment are carefully considered in an appraisal of the alternative opportunities facing the enterprise. Opportunities always take the form of chances to provide consumer satisfaction. However, the specific marketing management opportunities that constitute guideposts to operational planning must be identified. These can be found in the form of opportunities to innovate, to improve efficiency, to create a competitive difference, or to carve out a market niche.

Marketing problems usually are easier to detect than are opportunities. They are situations calling for action to improve sales, profits, or market share. They almost always can be traced to competitive activity or to significant changes in the marketing environment. For a problem to exist, however, there must be alternative solutions available. If there is no solution or only one solution to a particular situation, that situation does not constitute a problem in the managerial sense. For example, if there are four service stations, one on each corner of a busy intersection, and one of the stations lowers its price by five cents a gallon, the other stations face a bad situation—but they don't have a problem. They have no choice: They must match the price cut to keep their business. Suppose however that one station begins to offer trading stamps. Now the other stations have a number of alternative promotional approaches that they might consider. Free merchandise or service, extended hours, contests or drawings, any of these might be just as successful as the trading stamps. A problem exists because a choice can be made.

Identifying Market Targets

The situation analysis and assessment of opportunities and problems usually enable the marketing manager to identify several possible market targets, or *segments*. The selection of a particular target, or of several targets, is influenced by a number of factors. The importance of the target as it relates to the company's objectives, the potential of the opportunity that the target represents, and the capacity of the organization to develop a program capable of reaching the target are the most important.

Chapter 6 is devoted to a complete discussion of segments and segmentation strategies. At this point in the text it is sufficient to point out that a segment is a part of an overall market. The consumers (or industrial customers) comprising a segment are unique in that their responses to a company's marketing efforts are different than those of others to whom the firm sells. For example,

a department store caters to different segments. Its teen-age customers look for certain kinds of wearing apparel; its older shoppers look for entirely different types of clothing. So, the department store does not mix the garments it offers to these two segments. Instead it uses different departments, managed by different people and stocking different kinds of goods. Recognizing the existence of segmented markets is a fundamental step in planning, because each major segment usually requires its own marketing strategy. At the very least, segmentation demands special consideration in any general marketing program directed at the market as a whole.

Determining the Scale of Effort

Management is concerned with the apportionment of limited resources among alternative targets. Since a basic objective always is company survival, the maintenance of reserves against unforeseen contingencies always is an intelligent allocation decision. Considering those targets that represent growth opportunities, the usual practice in determining the level of effort is to use an objective and task method. The manager identifies the activities, or tasks, that must be undertaken in order to reach the targets. The identification of the tasks leads naturally to an estimate of the effort required to fulfill them. Reaching some targets is more costly than reaching others, and a firm can muster only so much marketing effort at a particular time. Financial restrictions, limited production capacity, and work force shortages are the most important restraints on the amount of effort a company can generate.

After completing an objective and task approach to the estimate of the marketing

TABLE 3.1 "Menu" of marketing targets

Target	Priority	Probable cost
A	1	300,000
B*	3	200,000
C	6	200,000
D	2	500,000
E†	4	200,000
F*	5	500,000

*These targets may be postponed.

†This target is threatened by the probable introduction of a competitive product.

effort required to reach various targets, and after considering the level of effort in relation to existing capacity, the manager can make a final target selection. For purposes of illustration, assume that the market planner has identified six possible marketing targets (see Table 3.1). These have been assigned priorities that are based on overall company objectives. The amount of effort (expressed in dollars of cost) is estimated for each of these targets. It also has been determined that the maximum amount of effort (investment) the company can afford to commit to its marketing program is a sum in the neighborhood of $500,000. Table 3.1 presents a "menu" of marketing targets. The planner may select one expensive target or may spread the budget over several less costly projects.

In part the priority of the targets affects the decision. Obviously a low-priority target (F) that would require all of the company's marketing effort would be rejected, whereas a high-priority target (D) might well be selected in spite of the drain it will put on company resources. A program that cannot be postponed because of the threat of a potential competitor (E), should be selected immediately or not at all. On the other hand, plans for markets that would appear to be reasonably safe for some period of time (B

and F) may well be put off to a subsequent operating period.

The amount of risk involved in alternative projects may be a factor influencing the choice of a marketing target. The investment in a marketing program designed to produce future sales is much like a capital investment. Two targets of equal opportunity and comparable cost may be distinguished on the basis of the risk involved. In most cases a firm would choose the less risky venture, but we should not assume a general pattern. The choice among targets ultimately rests on a combination of factual and subjective evaluations. This much however is certain. Before the operational planning process can be continued a decision on targets must be made. In terms of the targets shown in Table 3.1, either targets A and E together or target D alone would probably be selected.

Considering Alternative Approaches and Choosing a Grand Strategy

It is the division manager's responsibility at this stage of the planning process to select an overall plan, or *grand strategy*. Experience in marketing, adeptness in strategic planning, and a high order of creative thinking contribute greatly at this juncture. The task is formidable, because the manager must visualize complete *alternative marketing plans*. Obviously, the manager need not anticipate the details involved in these alternatives; however, one must be able to conceive two or more alternative approaches. For example, consider the problem faced by the president of a medium-sized manufacturing company.

The ABC Manufacturing Company produces a line of closet accessories, such as clothes hangers, closet rods, shoetrees, and so forth. For many years these items have been sold in the notions departments of department stores. ABC's sales had increased steadily as it gradually expanded its product line. Subsequently sales leveled off, and further attempts to increase business through modest product improvements proved unsuccessful. The president of the firm decided to undertake a marketing program to boost the company's sales. Following a marketing audit and a survey of the market, two possible market targets were selected. One target was to increase sales through established department store channels. The other was to develop sales through an entirely new channel—discount department and variety stores. The president chose the first target, and an overall development budget was estimated.

Next, the president proceeded to visualize the alternative approaches that might be taken to increase sales. There appeared to be two diametrically opposed plans that might be followed. One involved the manufacture of a promotional line of closet accessories, designed to compete purely on a price basis with the company's established product line and with competitive low-priced merchandise. These products would be essentially the same as the existing line from a functional point of view, but less costly in design and packaging. It was hoped that segmentation on a quality basis would prevent serious damage to the sales of the existing line. Moreover with the multiple line some "trading up" might be possible, and sales of the existing line actually could benefit.

The other alternative involved the design of an entirely new product line distinguished by its quality and appearance—a prestige line. High-quality materials (walnut hardwood and 24-carat gold plating) would serve to distinguish dramatically between the new line and ABC's standard line. The core of the program would be its emphasis on high style and luxury, and the promotional and pricing strategies would be consistent with the product and its packaging.

The president estimated that either plan could be undertaken within the available budget. The choice of a particular approach to the department store market was clearly a matter of management choice. This choice was rendered in favor of the prestige line—a choice quite consistent with the marketing management opportunities to create a competitive difference, to innovate, and to carve out a market niche.

Again, we should stress that the planner does *not* develop the details of these alternative plans. These tactics are worked out by the next lower level of marketing management. The manager provides only a general statement of the approach to be followed. Still, the advantages, disadvantages, dangers, and possibilities of each alternative should be adequately visible at this point, so that the choice of a general type of plan can be made. The important point is that mapping a specific route to a marketing target cannot be carried out until a general direction is chosen.

Developing the Marketing Mix

At this point in the planning process the elements of the marketing program are developed. The integrated marketing plan is a complex and comprehensive statement of the total program of action designed to reach a specific target and to attain company objectives. It involves important strategy decisions relating to product, distribution, promotion, and price. We call this blend of elements the *marketing mix*. Professor Borden of Harvard first expanded on the concept, and it has become increasingly popular.[7] The precise way in which the marketing

[7]For Borden's description, see N. H. Borden, "The Concept of the Marketing Mix," *Journal of Advertising Research,* June 1964, p. 4. To illustrate how the concept has been applied to contemporary model building, see J. Lambin, "A Computer On-line Marketing Mix Model," *Journal of Marketing Research,* 19 May 1972, pp. 119–126.

mix is developed will be discussed at length in subsequent chapters. After the elements in the marketing mix have been determined, integrated, and coordinated, the marketing program is ready for presentation to management for approval.

Finalizing the Plan

Preparing the Written Document

All the steps that have been taken so far in the planning process have been leading to the adoption of a formal marketing plan. A most important part of the formalization of the plan is the preparation of a *written document.* It is vital that a marketing plan be written down and that the preparation of this document be included in the planning process. It is foolish to assume that the planning function has been completed before a vehicle for its approval, implementation, and control has been prepared.

Obtaining Approval

After final revision, the plan must be approved by top management. The marketing manager may find it necessary to sell the plan to his or her superiors. In this effort, the steps followed in preparing the plan provide the tools needed for this purpose.

1. A statement of company objectives
2. A list of possible marketing targets and the costs of reaching each
3. An integrated strategy designed to reach the target selected
4. A written document

If the planner has done the job well, final approval should be a logical step in the planning process. The marketing plan is then ready for implementation.

Designing Marketing Tactics

Once the various elements in the marketing mix have been determined, it is relatively simple to translate them into a short-run action plan. The specific elements in the tactical plan are:

1. A statement of the specific actions to be taken
2. Identification of the specific individual(s) responsible for each action
3. A schedule of when each action is to be initiated and completed
4. A comprehensive budget that specifies the expected cost of each action
5. A statement of the anticipated outcome of each action

In more familiar terms, the tactical details identify (1) *what* is to be done, (2) *who* is to do it, (3) *when* it is to be done, (4) *how much* it will cost, and (5) the *results* that are expected. It is easy to understand that until the strategy has been transformed into a marketing mix and the mix has been amplified in its tactical detail, marketing action is impossible. In fact, it can be justifiably maintained that it is only short-term tactical marketing planning that gets things done.

Communicate and Implement

The tactical marketing plan must be transmitted to the people in the organization who will carry it out. The written short-term plan is the basic medium of communication, but often a good deal of dramatics and persuasion are involved, especially when a sales organization or group of independent distributors are to be responsible for implementing the plan. The plan is presented at elaborate meetings, and high rewards for success are offered as incentives. But when the kick-off celebration is over and the organization settles down to the task of day-to-day marketing, the proof of the planner's skill should become clear. If the plan succeeds the planning was done well. If it does not succeed, the planner will have to discover the reasons and adjust the plan.

Monitor and Revise

This final step in the planning process involves the monitoring of the plan in action. Information feedback is provided to determine if the program is working. If the continuous audit suggests the need for adjustment or revision, the manager must initiate the changes necessary to keep the company's effort on target. This procedure of auditing and revision is called *marketing control* and will be discussed in Chapter 20.

The Cycle of Marketing Planning

As the Hooker Chemical Company planning process suggests, the completion of the marketing planning does not terminate the manager's responsibilities. Marketing involves

planning, directing, and controlling; and these functions are cyclical. Planning leads to the issuance of instructions, and directing leads to feedback monitoring and control. We can illustrate this cyclical process with a simple flow chart, Figure 3.4. The circular character of marketing planning is shown in the diagram. We see how the determination of strategy leads to the development of tactical plans. These, in turn, must be put into action by issuing the proper instructions to the operating organization. Performance is monitored and reviewed. The evaluation may lead to the issuing of amended instructions (corrective action), to a modification of tactics, or to a strategy change. Thus, the cycle of marketing planning goes on.

Two Cautionary Comments

The Impact of a Changing Environment

Although good marketing plans always are based on realistic facts, by the time a plan is unfolded reality may have changed. The marketplace is dynamic. Competitive reaction and interaction are impossible to anticipate precisely. But competition is not the only dynamic factor; any of the marketing environments may change and upset a carefully conceived plan. Even the best marketing plan is obsolete almost before it is initiated. Fortunately, not all environmental changes require alterations in the marketing plan. By modifying its tactics a firm can adjust its performance to compensate for minor changes in the environment, especially routine competitive reactions. Thus, the importance of having a flexible plan becomes clear. But it is true that major changes may completely upset a marketing plan at any

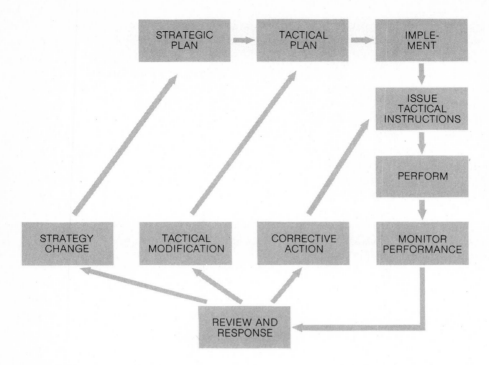

FIGURE 3.4   The cycle of planning and control

time. Unless these changing conditions are detected early, they may result in a marketing failure rather than an orderly retreat and subsequent counterattack. Good marketing control should permit the detection of flaws in performance early enough to enable the market planner to make critical changes in strategy. Having a standby or contingency strategy ready to replace one that is failing is a most practical reason for insisting on the development of several alternatives during the planning process.

The End-Means Confusion

In contemporary marketing the emphasis on planning may lead to *end-means confusion.* We should never lose sight of the fact that planning is only a means to a much more important end. Success is important, not strategy. Progress is needed, not a program for marketing action. In the last analysis, plans are not important; profits and social performance are. True, plans must be made before they can be implemented, but planning is not the purpose of marketing. Performance is critical, and the achievement of objectives is the ultimate goal.

Summary

We have looked at the way in which business firms, whether large or small, approach marketing planning. The process can be viewed in a generalized way as comprising four important elements. First, there are the planning prerequisites, which are the responsibility of top management. Mission, objectives, organization, and policy are the four areas of top-management concern.

The second aspect of the planning process is the development of a long-run marketing strategy, which is the responsibility of divisional management. Several steps are involved: analyzing the marketing situation, assessing marketing opportunities and problems, identifying market segments, determining the scale of effort, considering alternative approaches, and selecting an overall strategy.

Once a strategy has been selected, it is necessary to develop the marketing mix—the blending of the four key strategy areas, including product, distribution, promotion, and price.

Then the marketing plan must be finalized. To properly bring the planning process to its completion, the marketing manager must prepare a written document and obtain top-management approval. Next, working out the tactical details, the middle marketing manager specifies what is to be done, who is to do it, when it is to be done, how much it will cost, and the results that are expected. In the final steps, the planner must initiate implementation and monitor the plan's results, making tactical or strategic revisions as required.

Actually the planning process does not end. It is cyclical. Planning leads to direction, and direction leads to control. New strategies and tactics are evolved. The planning cycle rolls on.

Questions and Problems

1. What is the difference between a strategy and a tactic? Does the difference relate at all to whether the plan is long run or short run?

2. A drive-in restaurant was experiencing a substantial decline in business due to an involved and often-delayed highway construction project. Entrance to the restaurant was limited to traffic moving in one direction. Using the marketing-planning process in this chapter, suggest how the manager of the restaurant might increase its sales volume.

3. In what ways is marketing planning related to the marketing management concept?

4. Explain why some companies develop company-wide marketing plans while others rely exclusively on divisional plans.

5. Why are the prerequisites for marketing planning so important? Can a manager plan for marketing operations without them?

6. Planning can be thought of as a special aspect of decision making. Why?

7. Explain the concept of gap analysis.

8. A marketing manager who had just completed the finishing touches on a marketing plan was overheard to say, "Well, that job's done for another year." Point out the basic mistake(s) in this person's approach to planning.

Two Concepts of the Market

4 Understanding Consumer Behavior

Marketing's purpose is to create customers; to do this well the seller of goods and services must understand the consumer. The consumer's decisions to buy or not to buy, to consume or not to consume, and ultimately to repurchase or not to repurchase are the determinants of a company's marketing success. Consider how different people buy a product—a CB radio for example. One person shops, compares, and eventually decides on a selection. Another goes through much the same process but does not buy. A third appears to buy impulsively, without much thought or investigation. And of course a great many people show absolutely no interest in CB radios. Understanding such behaviors is the purpose of this chapter and the one that follows.

We must develop a theory of consumer behavior to serve as a foundation for marketing programs. This theory should form a central element in the manager's assembly of marketing concepts. Fortunately, each of us does not need to start from scratch; many helpful perspectives already have been developed. As early as the 1920s, marketing thinkers came remarkably close to many of the more advanced concepts now held. Time and effort have brought additional rewards. Today there is a considerably body of knowledge that we call the *theory of consumer behavior*.

The Interdisciplinary Approach

The contributions to our theory of consumer behavior have come from so many sources that we speak of the approach as *interdisciplinary*. Historically the field of psychology has provided the most substantial input, but the recent trend has been to look to several

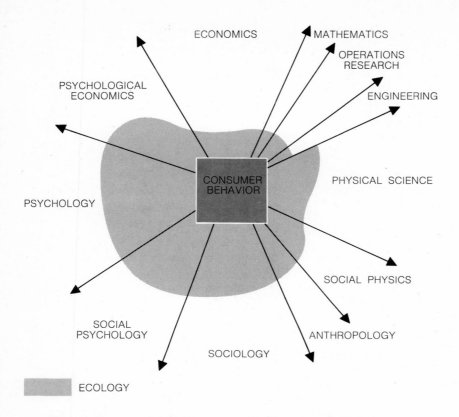

FIGURE 4.1   The interdisciplinary approach to consumer behavior

other areas of knowledge to gain further insights. Sociology, social psychology, anthropology, and even the physical sciences have made contributions. Although this interdisciplinary approach sometimes yields crazy-quilt results, its eclectic character does not lessen its value. Indeed it seems to help. One discipline explains what another cannot; or as is more often the case, the different perspectives complement and reinforce each other. Figure 4.1 presents a graphic concept of the interdisciplinary approach to consumer behavior.

Although it is both challenging and enlightening, the interdisciplinary approach has one great weakness—it lacks synthesis and structure. It is extremely difficult to develop an integrated general theory of consumer behavior based on so many different disciplinary foundations. Much that is extremely important to marketing is introduced, but a great deal of irrelevant material also is brought along. We need a comprehensive explanation of consumer behavior, and one such general theory can be found in the ecological concept.[1]

[1]The author credits Wroe Alderson for planting the first seeds of an ecological theory of marketing behavior. See W. Alderson, *Marketing Behavior and Executive Action* (Homewood, Ill.: Richard D. Irwin, 1957).

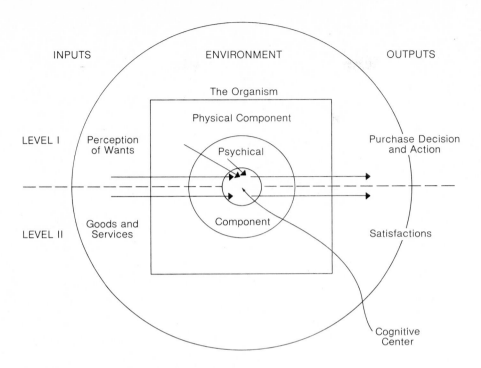

FIGURE 4.2   An ecological model of the consumer

An Ecological View of Consumer Behavior

Human ecology is the study of generic man in relation to the environment. It focuses attention on the human organism, its functions, and its adaptive processes. In a marketing context, ecological theory highlights the search for satisfaction of wants as a goal of consumer effort. The physical and psychological conditions of the organism are included as well as the physical and social phenomena in the environment. The ecological theory is interdisciplinary. Figure 4.1 shows it as a shaded area surrounding the consumer and includes some, but not all, of each of the other contributing disciplines.

Let us inspect a simple model of the consumer in relation to the environment. Figure 4.2 shows the consumer composed of two important and closely related elements—the physical and the psychical. At the very center is the cognitive center, which "manages" consumers' behaviors. Consumers, as ecological organisms, exist within an environment to which they must adapt in order to achieve satisfaction. Adaptation takes place in the following way. The cognitive center receives inputs from the environment, as well as stimuli originating within its own physical and psychical components. Processing those stimuli, it directs the consumer's output, or behavior. Figure 4.2 shows inputs and outputs at two levels. At the first level (above the broken line), the inputs involve the perception and disposition of various wants. The first-level outputs are buying decisions and actions (including nonactions, or decisions not to buy). At the second level, the inputs are goods and services that have been purchased as a result of the decisions reached at the first level. Goods and services are consumed, and the outcome is some degree of consumer satisfaction. In the balance of this chapter we will look in detail at the various parts of this model. We turn first to an inspection of the organism.

The Physical State of the Consumer

The consumer is a human being, a biological organism, and may be viewed from two perspectives—the physical and the psychical. Certain physical differences, such as sex, age, and physique, play an important role in consumer behavior. A male shopper's reaction to his marketing environment is usually different from that of a female. The shopping behavior of men in supermarkets varies considerably from that of women shopping under identical conditions. The age of consumers is also important in explaining their wants and the kinds of products or services that will satisfy them. The requirements to feed, clothe, shelter, and educate an eight-year-old boy are remarkably different from those required to sustain his ninety-year-old great-grandfather.

The relation of the physical state of the consumer to behavior is too obvious to require extensive discussion. In contrast, the psychical state of the consumer is complex and often changeable. Its impact on behavior is seldom direct or obvious. We must look at this aspect of the consumer organism in much greater depth.

The Psychical State of the Consumer

Human beings are distinguishable from other biological organisms primarily by their advanced mental ability. Except in some very primitive cultures, their physical state does not usually have as much influence as does their psychical state. Human beings are social creatures and are influenced greatly by others. Through the power of reason and as a result of contact with others, individuals perceive and learn. Attitudes are developed, and consumers evolve a unique set of self-perceptions as well as perceptions about the surrounding environment. In the following pages we will focus on those basic concepts that appear to be most important to an understanding of consumer behavior. These include motivation, perception, learning, and attitudes.

Motivation

A *motive* is any relatively stable inner condition of an organism that results in goal-directed behavior. A *buying motive* is an inner state that results in purchase behavior. Obviously, then, motivation lies at the crux of consumer behavior, and an understanding of it is essential. Because of vast differences among individuals, multiplicities of goals, and widely divergent environmental conditions, each individual tends to have a unique set of buying motives. But in the aggregate, patterns of motives appear to exist, and psychologists as well as marketing theorists have attempted to classify them. One of the first modern psychologists to do so was Abraham Maslow, and his classification commonly is accepted in marketing.[2] His arrangement, starting with the highest order of potency, is based on the relative importance of various motives as determined by behavioral research.

1. *The physiological needs* The human being who is deprived of everything in life strives first for the basic necessities of physical survival—food, drink, and protection from the elements.
2. *The safety needs* Once the physiological demands are met, the need for safety emerges. The desire of many individuals today for security and stability in their lives is evidence of this motive.
3. *The love needs* If the physiological and the safety needs of an individual are reasonably well satisfied, there exists the demand for love, affection, and belonging. The desire to be accepted as an integral part of a family or another close social group is of great importance to most people.
4. *The esteem needs* Almost all individuals strive for social acceptance. This begins with a need for self-respect, which is carried over to a motive for esteem by others.
5. *The need for self-actualization* In contemporary terms, people want "to do their own thing." We must express ourselves by doing what is important to us. Maslow calls this the need for self-actualization.

Maslow's classification has several important features. First, it distinguishes among needs that are physical, social, and personal.

Second, it suggests the relative importance of the various needs. Third, since it appears that the first three types of needs are relatively well satisfied for the majority of American consumers, Maslow's classification suggests that marketers should direct their efforts to satisfy the other needs—esteem and self-actualization.

Perception

A second important aspect of the psychical state of consumers is their capacity to perceive. A motive merely creates a disposition to act. It needs to be triggered by a sensory cue in order to cause behavior. Perception is the process by which people detect, interpret, and classify sensory cues.

The importance of perception People receive many more sensory cues than they are able to process. A prominent marketing executive, echoing a commonly held belief, once remarked that members of an average family are exposed to about fifteen hundred advertisements during a normal day. Subsequently Bauer and Greyser took exception to this statement, pointing out that it is absurd to believe that an average person could possibly be aware of so many commercial stimuli. They write "that only a fraction of these ads could make any meaningful impact on the individual family members seems certain . . . the 1,500 figure represents opportunities for exposure, not exposures themselves."[3]

---

[2]A. H. Maslow, "A Theory of Human Motivation," *Psychological Review*, July 1943, pp. 370–396.

[3]R. A. Bauer and S. A. Greyser, *Advertising in America: The Consumer View* (Boston: Division of Research, Graduate School of Business Administration, Harvard University, 1968), p. 174. Britt and others subsequently concluded that the number is much closer to one hundred; see S. H. Britt, S. C. Adams, and A. S. Miller, "How Many Advertising Exposures per Day?" *Journal of Advertising Research*, December 1972, pp. 3–10.

For several reasons the typical consumer is simply not able to handle all of the sensory cues to which he or she is exposed. In the first place, although individuals vary widely in their capacity to consider a number of different things at the same time, the average span of attention is remarkably small. It is estimated that a typical person can extend thought to cover only about eight different things at the same time. The ability to handle the vast amount of advertising stimuli to which we are exposed is further complicated by the fact that consumers usually do not have much time to devote to the consideration of buying problems. Other activities of living demand attention. Making buying decisions is often difficult, and consumers ration their energies to conserve them for other purposes. Finally, most consumers cannot indulge every whim or want that they may have. Limited purchasing power and the desire to avoid a spendthrift label deny the satisfaction of many wants. The sensory cues and motivations that produce these wants must be pushed aside. Perception is the process by which consumers limit the number of stimuli to which they respond.

We should consider briefly how consumers achieve some balance between the inflow of information and their capacity to process it. There are three ways in which an information cue can fail to trigger consumer response. It will not affect behavior (1) if it does not attract attention—that is, if it is not perceived at all; (2) if it is filtered out by a process of selective perception; or (3) if it is classified as unimportant and rejected. If a sensory input avoids these three roadblocks, it can be expected to affect consumer action. Let us look at these roadblocks more carefully.

Attention   Attention focuses perception. It involves recognition of a stimulus and a decision to interpret and classify it. A stimulus that does not attract attention is not perceived. Marketers understand this and use various devices to attract attention to their products and advertising. By dramatic use of color, size, shape, display, position, and motion, and a novelty of approach sellers attempt to thrust their products into the consumers' awareness. We see examples of this in unique advertising forms. Who doesn't remember the great ads for Volkswagen, Alka Seltzer, and Hathaway shirts?

Selective perception   Even if a stimulus succeeds in passing a threshold of attention, there is no assurance that it automatically will affect behavior. It still must pass a perceptual screening. Selective perception is the result of the screening of stimuli. The two most important factors performing the screening role are motives and attitudes. Their filtration can produce several consequences. Figure 4.3 illustrates three of them. First, if the stimulus has passed the attention threshold, it may be accepted and passed undistorted through the filtering mechanism. Second, filtration may result in a distorted interpretation of the cue. Third, the cue may be rejected completely by a process known as *perceptual defense.*

It is not hard to find evidence that distortion of stimuli takes place. For example, many readers of advertisements subsequently associate the message with the wrong company. Remember Goodrich's humorous attempt to remind tire buyers that "we're the other guys—the ones without the blimp"? Avis worked very hard to convince car rental prospects that being "Number Two" was an advantage. Without this type of effort, companies often find that their identities are lost in the confusion of the marketplace.

Sensory cues can be rejected. Individuals

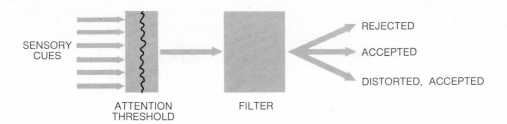

FIGURE 4.3   Perceptual filtration

have a tendency to refuse to accept ideas with which they disagree or that threaten their value systems. Psychological studies suggest that most people set higher thresholds of perception for sensory cues that challenge their existing norms. In marketing terms, nondrinkers seldom read beer advertisements, and loyal Chevrolet owners refuse to consider a visit to a Ford showroom.

Subliminal perception   Our discussion of perception would be incomplete without mentioning subliminal perception. This term refers to the possibility that stimuli below the awareness threshold actually are perceived and therefore do affect behavior. The use of subliminal (we might think of it as *subconscious*) influence in advertising caused considerable controversy a number of years ago.[4] As a result of some research findings, it was concluded that consumers respond to stimuli below the attentive threshold. In a now classic experiment, movie audiences were exposed to the words "Drink Coke" and "Eat Popcorn" on the movie screen at speeds so fast that the impressions were well below conscious visual perception.[5] Accord-

ing to the researcher's results, cola sales increased almost 60 per cent, and popcorn sales almost 20 per cent, at the refreshment counter in the theater. Although subsequent research has not confirmed the effectiveness of subliminal suggestion, considerable criticism was raised of the advertisers' presumed attempts to manipulate consumers by its use.[6] There is no evidence, however, that large numbers of advertisers ever attempted to make use of the technique.

Totality of perception   The preceding discussion may have given the false impression that the process of perception involves the receipt in rapid succession of stimuli by the consumer—much like a telegraph receiver accepting messages in code, one signal after the other. In fact, many sensations reach the individual at the same time—like meteorites striking the earth's atmosphere from all directions. These sensations are received, interpreted, and classified more or less simultaneously, according to the individual's capacity to handle them. What the person perceives is a total picture, and what is accepted depends on how well it fits into this overall perception.

[4]For an early criticism, see Vance Packard, *The Hidden Persuaders* (New York: Pocket Books, 1957), chap. 23.

[5]J. Brooks, "The Little Ad that Isn't There," *Consumer Reports,* January 1958, pp. 5–11.

[6]See W. B. Key, *Subliminal Seduction: Ad Media's Manipulation of a Not-so-Innocent America* (Englewood Cliffs, N.J.: Prentice-Hall, 1973).

Learning

We learn from experience, and what we learn affects our behavior. Buying is no exception; it is critically affected by learning experiences. Learning is defined as any change in response resulting from experience. We already have seen that the consumer receives stimuli and filters them through a framework of motives and attitudes. These sensory cues, perceived, identified, and classified, cause some type of response behavior. The process goes on continuously, and the cumulative effect of behavioral experiences causes changes in subsequent patterns of perception and response. In other words consumers behave because they learn, and they learn as a result of behavioral experiences. What they learn, how they learn it, and the way in which this learning affects subsequent action are important to understanding their psychical state.

What is learned   What is learned depends on the kinds of experiences consumers have—with whom and with what they come in contact. People, products, advertising messages, and marketing events (for example, warehouse sales, exclusive fashion exhibits, and grand openings) become the subject matter of consumer learning. Wants also can be learned. The smoker acquires a desire for tobacco, just as the family kitten develops a demand for fresh dairy cream. In both cases experience is the teacher, and learning of wants is the result. In addition, other subjective behavioral elements, such as attitudes and brand preferences, are changed through learning experiences. Recall, "Try it. You'll like it." In short, almost any behavior-related factor is subject to learning to some degree. Whether it becomes an important influence of behavior depends partly on how it is learned and how well it is retained.

How consumers learn   The literature on the subject of learning is immense. We will limit our consideration to two of the most important influences on learning as it affects consumer behavior: learning by acquiring information and learning by building associations.

The least complicated way in which consumers learn is to *acquire information.* The exposure to marketing information may be through advertising, informal communications with others, or shopping experiences. It is important to recognize that exposure to information is not in itself a learning experience unless it has some effect on subsequent behavior. Only when the acquired information has been absorbed and translated into some change in the influential factors, a change in motives or attitudes for example, or when it has directly affected some aspect of consumer action, can it be said to have had a learning effect. This point is important because, while it is relatively easy to expose consumers to marketing information, it is exceptionally difficult to create communications that will result in behavioral change.

Learning also occurs through the *building of associations.* Two types of association building, sometimes referred to as *conditioning,* are recognized. The first is *classical conditioning.* Through repetition, consumers learn to associate a particular stimulus (even a quite meaningless one) with a particular type of response. For example, a shopper conditioned to cents-off sales may purchase a food item that nobody in the household really likes simply because of a "10¢ Off" panel on the package. To the extent that classical conditioning takes place, consumers learn to react to all sorts of strong and subtle stimuli.

A more meaningful type of conditioning or association building occurs when consumers achieve some goal or objective. A young homemaker may struggle for several months with various types of shortening and still produce consistently poor pie crusts. When finally a brand of shortening "works," that brand usually will be purchased regularly. It wouldn't really matter that the homemaker's baking skill had improved over the period. If the improved result was associated with the particular brand of shortening, a conditioned learning situation would have been created. Once conditioned in this way, consumers become accustomed to turning to the same company for products that meet particular needs. In marketing we refer to this type of conditional behavior as *brand loyalty*. Thousands of examples could be cited. Shavers turn to Gillette for smoother shaves, car owners look to Goodyear for longer mileage, and so on down the list of products that have achieved a measure of brand loyalty. We will look at this phenomenon more fully in connection with memory.

Memory Another critically important aspect of learning is memory, or the ability to retain and recall experience consequences. There are two areas of marketing in which memory building is an important element of strategy. First, memory determines how well consumers recall a brand name and how regularly they purchase it. Second, memory affects how well a company's advertising is retained.

The tendency of some consumers to stick with a particular brand is well established. Haven't you heard someone refer to "my brand" of coffee, of beer, or of chewing gum? You may ask, "What makes some customers so loyal to a brand that they never buy competing products? Is brand loyalty the result of an effective marketing strategy, or does the customer feel a personal need to be brand-loyal?" Surprising as it may seem, there is experimental evidence that suggests that consumers' own needs as well as the corporate marketing strategy jointly deter-

mine brand loyalty.[7] Study subjects actually established brand preferences among products that were in all respects identical except for their names. And even the names were meaningless, for example Product X and Product Y. Another instance is seen in the amazing fact that consumers who profess a preference for a brand of beer or soft drink frequently are unable to select it from among a group of competitive products when the brand names and identifications have been disguised or removed. In view of this, it is reasonable to believe that brand loyalty is not merely the result of particularly effective marketing by the seller of the brand. It is also a phenomenon of the consumers' psychical state.

Two explanations are possible. First, a product is more than a physical commodity to consumers. It possesses a character or personality that consumers perceive as an image. Consumers feel more comfortable with the image of one brand than with the image of another and accordingly are loyal to the brand whose image is most acceptable. Another explanation is that consumers seek ways in which to become efficient in buying. One way to do this is to routinize the buying process, making purchase decisions quickly by identifying a favorite brand and buying it regularly. Regardless of the reason for brand loyalty, however, it is a reality of the market and the marketing manager must understand its importance and something about the ways to build customer allegiance for a brand.

A second area of memory that is important to marketers involves communications—especially advertising—remembrance. One method of evaluating advertising involves the measurement of the number of people who recall specific ads. If the message is remembered clearly, it is avail-

[7]W. T. Tucker, "The Development of Brand Loyalty," *Journal of Marketing Research*, August 1964, pp. 32–35.

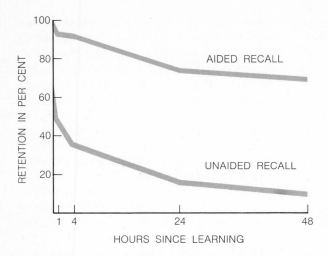

These curves show percentage of learned material remembered within a 48-hour period, according to the type of recall aid provided.

FIGURE 4.4   Remembrance curves

Source: Adapted from J. H. Myers and W. H. Reynolds, *Consumer Behavior and Marketing Management* (Boston: Houghton Mifflin Co., 1967).

able for the consumer to use whenever a solution to a buying problem is sought. If however the message is lost or forgotten before the decision situation arises, the advertising can have no influence on the buying outcome.

It is important, then, to know something about how much the consumer remembers and for how long it is remembered. One clue to this problem is found in the traditional forgetting curve, a version of which is presented in Figure 4.4. The figure actually shows two retention curves, illustrating the percentage of learned material retained over a forty-eight-hour period. The higher of the two curves represents the proportion of material that was recognized when individuals subsequently were re-exposed to it. We call this type of memory *aided recall.* The lower curve indicates the proportion retained in memory when no subsequent aid to remem-

brance was present. We can see from the figure why repetition is so important in the learning process and why the attempt to build strong consumer awareness over time is so difficult.

Cognition and cognitive dissonance Cognition refers to learning that is retained and becomes part of the consumer's behavioral capability. Retention, therefore, is the key factor in affecting behavior; and as we have seen most consumers do not remember very much or for very long. Moreover, that which is retained is simplified and modified to fit the individual consumer's cognitive capacity.

However, not every retained perception fits easily into the consumer's existing set of attitudes and beliefs. When new information is learned that conflicts with existing cognitive elements, tension, or *cognitive dissonance* as Festinger calls it, arises.[8] The consumer is strongly motivated to reduce the tension. This can be done in three ways. First, the consumer can change the balance of the cognitive material by accepting the new information, rejecting some older learned material that disagrees with it, and assimilating all of the elements into a new and more comfortable cognitive state. On the other hand, the person can reject or discredit the new information in order to restore the original cognitive stability and thus remove the dissonance. A third approach is for the individual to seek additional information, generally that which will support and strengthen the previous cognitive position. For example, a buyer of a new automobile frequently spends more time reading advertisements about the car *after* the purchase than before. Real estate salespersons call on recent home buyers for the specific purpose of reassuring them that they have made a good buying decision. However, these measures are sometimes only temporary, because if dissonance persists, the consumer ultimately faces the challenge of adapting to it. This is the real effect of learning, and without it all consumers would sooner or later follow purely stereotyped behavior patterns.

Attitudes

In considering the psychical state of the consumer, we turn next to attitudes. Attitudes are pervasive—there is no one place or function at which they can be isolated. They weave in and out of the behavioral process as both cause and consequence of behavior. Attitudes are complicated, but an understanding of the nature of attitudes, how they are formed, and how they affect behavior is

[8]L. Festinger, *A Theory of Cognitive Dissonance* (New York: Harper & Row, 1957).

vital to an understanding of consumer behavior.

What is an attitude? An attitude is a state of mind or feeling that establishes a basic orientation for or against particular objects or individuals. It induces a predisposition to behave in some way.

Marketers must be aware of several important considerations concerning the nature of attitudes. First, it should be clear that consumers do possess attitudes about buying. Some of these may be at the cognitive level; others may not. Second, all attitudes are related in what we call an *attitude system.* Maintaining consistency within this system is as important as it is in connection with perceptions and cognitive material generally. Third, attitudes are related closely to other elements in the consumer's psychical state. We already have seen how motives, perceptions, and learning affect behavior. They do so directly and also indirectly, in that they affect the formation of attitudes. These attitudes in turn affect behavior. Fourth, there is a relationship between attitudes. Attitudes are acquired, and those related to physical needs actually are formed as a person attempts to find ways to satisfy such needs. A person tends to develop favorable attitudes toward individuals and things that contribute to the satisfaction of physiological needs, and unfavorable attitudes toward those that do not. However, most consumer attitudes relate not to physical but to social needs, the result of the learning involved when the individual comes into contact with others. This probably explains why consumer attitudes appear to differ considerably among different ethnic groups, among members of different social classes, and among consumers in different geographical locations. These people are in natural, frequent contact with each other and much less so with other groups. Hence the similarity of attitudes within groups and the distinctions between different groups.

The attitude system   Attitudes do not exist in isolation. In an informal way they are programmed into the consumer's entire psychical state. We have seen that the individual strives to achieve balance and congruity both within and among the elements. Attitudes must exist in a reasonably stable balance that resists change. Internal consistency among attitudes is probably the most important feature of this balance. The individual attitudes support each other and also surround and protect the person's self-concept. This system can be thought of as a latticework of interlocking attitudinal components. Like any latticework, its strength depends on its structure. A modest break here or there in the structure may effect no permanent change in the attitudinal system, since the individual tends to repair the damage promptly. If kept in good repair, the lattice of attitudes tends to resist major threats and to provide the stability that the individual's psychical state requires.

The functions of attitudes   There are two critical functions that the attitude system performs. One is *perceptual screening;* the other has to do with the development of habitual or *routinized behavior.*

We have seen that attitudes provide a perceptual filter through which stimuli are screened before being evaluated and classified. This filtration function is an attitude's most important role. There is ample evidence to indicate that individuals perceive and interpret stimuli in ways that are consistent with their established dispositions. Attitudes affect perception in other ways as well. First, they tend to influence the manner in which people are exposed to stimuli. The phrase *selective exposure* refers to individuals' tendency not to expose themselves to those aspects of the environment that would result in unpleasant experiences. For example, we all know people who tune down or turn off the television set during commercials. Electronic devices for this purpose have been sold for a number of years. Other viewers leave the room when commercials come on. The water department of a large midwestern city reported a noticeable drop in water pressure during commercial time in the evening hours. Finally, some individuals mentally tune out the commercial, focusing attention on other thoughts to such an extent that they subsequently are unable to recall even having been exposed to the message.

Another function of attitudes is to produce habitual or routinized behavior. Through experience, consumers discover that a particular product or brand satisfactorily meets a particular need. Rather than struggle periodically with the same question of what product or brand to buy, consumers make a routine or habitual purchase. Studies of consumers on shopping expeditions indicate that a considerable amount of purchasing is done this way. A homemaker may spend as little as twenty minutes in a supermarket selecting the week's groceries, because he or she knows exactly which items to choose from the many that are available.

The nature of habitual purchasing is worth considering. Older explanations of habit suggest that it is the result of subconscious evaluations. The more recent view is that habit should be considered a routinized problem-solving process. A repetitive want, regardless of its importance, does not require a new search of the environment or a complete reappraisal of alternatives each time it arises. Once consumers have a satisfactory solution for a recurring want, they develop a routine procedure for purchasing it. What seems to be unconscious habit is in fact a rational method of problem solving.

Attitude change   It must be obvious that it would be of extreme importance to a company marketing goods and services to be able to modify consumers' attitudes, making them more inclined to buy its offerings than those of its competitors. People in advertising are generally convinced that attitudes can be changed and that a principal function of mass communications is to effect changes in behavior by causing changes in beliefs or attitudes. But can attitudes be modified? And, if so, how is this accomplished?

The most effective method of attitude change is first to affect behavior by some other means and then allow the consequent behavior to produce the desired attitude shift. Most adults, for example, possess the belief that they could not possibly learn to become rapid readers. They think they have been away from school too long, that they are too old to learn, or perhaps that speed reading is just a gimmick and to take a course in it would be a foolish waste of time and money. To counter these strong negative attitudes, Evelyn Woods' Reading Dynamics Institute offers free sample lessons in which the participants actually see results. The people discover that it is possible to read faster and comprehend more with relatively little effort. The company converts a high proportion of those attending the free lessons into paying customers. This example demonstrates the importance of participation in learning. It also shows how attitudes can be circumvented, in this case by appealing to a strong motive—the desire to get something of value without cost. The resulting behavior then builds more favorable attitudes.

But what if there is no way to circumvent an attitude? In such a case the attitude must be directly changed to affect behavior. Can this be done? In general the answer is "Yes," but it must be qualified. Some attitudes are much more difficult to change than

are others, and some cannot be changed at all. Whether an attitude can be changed depends on its strength and the degree of commitment the individual has to it. The strength of an attitude (either its absolute or relative importance) can be measured, and naturally the stronger the attitude the less the chance of changing it. By commitment we mean the extent to which the individual intends to stick with an attitude. As might be suspected, the degree of commitment is somewhat harder to measure, but still the greater the commitment to an attitude the less likely it is to be changed.

Attitudes, then, have two dimensions. We might measure their strength on a vertical scale and their degree of commitment on a horizontal one (Figure 4.5). Any attitude falling close to the diagonal broken line represents approximately equal measures for importance and commitment. The further along the curve in quadrant I, the more difficult is the task of changing an attitude. A life-loyal owner of Oldsmobiles is an example. This person might be positioned at point *A*. In contrast, an individual buying a staple, undifferentiated product, such as construction lumber, might be found at position *B*. Consumers at positions *C* and *D* represent more interesting (and more complex) marketing situations. An individual at point *C* has a strong commitment to a relatively unimportant attitude. Possibly it is an attitude about a brand of cigarette. Remember the ads showing a smoker with a black eye proclaiming "I'd rather fight than switch"? In contrast, consider an independent voter's attitude toward a candidate for public office. The voter may feel strongly that experience in government is very important in a public candidate. At the same time the voter easily may be persuaded to change this view when confronted with information about another equally strong criterion.

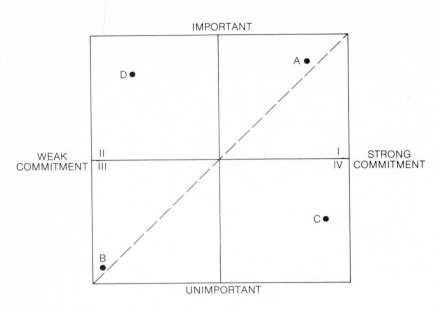

FIGURE 4.5   Hypothetical map of consumer perceptions

A generally accepted model for explaining how attitude modification occurs is found in *information-processing theory*. This theory assumes that the consumer is a rational decisionmaker who deals with information logically and is willing to accept a change in belief if conclusive arguments lead to this result. The theory suggests that attitude modification occurs as the result of the completion of a series of behavioral steps, each one of which has a probability of occurring. Since all of the steps must be completed before a behavioral change takes place, the probability of a modification occurring is the product of the probabilities associated with each step in the process. This step-by-step process is illustrated in Figure 4.6.

The first step is the presentation of new information—information that the marketer hopes will eventually result in an attitude change. In the next step, the consumer's attention must be drawn to the informa-tion—a particularly difficult task if the existing attitude is well established and acts as a filter, screening out the new information. The consumer must accept the new information and yield to the conclusion it presents. This occurs in the third and fourth steps. The third step involves the comprehension of the arguments that the new information presents and the conclusion that they impel. In the fourth step, the consumer yields to the conclusion—at least temporarily—and adopts the new belief. The fifth step assures that the belief becomes part of the consumer's permanent attitude set. And in the final step, the consumer acts on the basis of the new belief.

Modification of attitudes is generally attempted through marketing communications. A change will most likely take place if the message fits the consumer's overall framework of attitudes, even though it conflicts with the particular element it is intend-

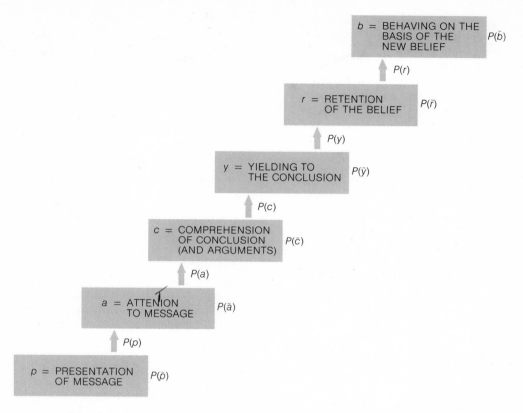

PROBABILITY OF DESIRED BEHAVIOR $= P(p) \cdot P(a) \cdot P(c) \cdot P(y) \cdot P(r) \cdot P(b)$

FIGURE 4.6 Steps in the attitude modification process

Source: Scott Ward, Thomas S. Robertson, *Consumer Behavior: Theoretical Sources,* copyright ©1973, p. 326. Reprinted by permission of Prentice-Hall, Inc., Englewood Cliffs, New Jersey.

ed to displace. Suppose a consumer likes to go to the movies but is not particularly interested in documentary-type films. This attitude easily might prevent the consumer from going to see *All the President's Men,* a 1976 semidocumentary film dealing with the Watergate episode. What might have been needed was a message that would upset this person's bias against documentaries. Several appeals could work. One approach might emphasize the dramatic character of the film, which starred two top box-office personalities. Another might capitalize on the sensational events depicted in the movie, giving it the image of a mystery film. Both of these approaches conform to a generally favorable attitude toward movies and could help offset a negative feeling about documentaries. The spectacular success of the movie suggests that a great many people who do not ordinarily go to the theater turned out to see this particular film.

Not all programs of marketing communication are so successful. The information-processing model in Figure 4.6 suggests why this is so. Take the example of a cereal manufacturer attempting to persuade consumers to try a particular brand. Network television is selected to present the message, and a particularly popular program is picked on which to run the commercial. Assume that over a period of time, the following rather typical results occur:

Step 1	*Presentation* The cumulative unduplicated reach of the message is	.50
Step 2	*Attention* The average recall of the commercial is	.30
Step 3	*Comprehension* The proportion of those reached who understand the message is	.50
Step 4	*Yielding* The percentage accepting the conclusion is	.40
Step 5	*Retention* The percentage retaining the new belief is	.50
Step 6	*Behavior change* The proportion behaving on the basis of the new belief is	.50
	Total probability	.0075

If this total probability of producing a behavioral change were applied against a potential population of 200 million persons, approximately 1.5 million might be expected to try the cereal. Some of these might like and repurchase it; others would not. Ultimately, somewhat fewer than half of 1 per cent of the population might become consumers of the brand as a result of this marketing effort. For some companies this response might be acceptable; for others it probably would not.

Attitude measurement Our discussion of attitudes has been based on the assumption that they can be measured. Psychologists and marketing researchers are still only at the threshold of effective attitude measurement. The subject is technical, and the amount of material on it is considerable. In this book, we can present only one example of a basic method of attitude measurement. It is the now widely used technique of attitude scaling.

Attitude scaling involves the assignment of numerical values to verbalized expressions of consumer attitudes. The scaling device is the starting point. One of the most commonly used is the semantic differential scale developed by Osgood and others.[9] In this technique, the respondent to an attitude survey is asked to position a feeling between two statements of polar extremes. A five- or seven-position scale is then presented, making it possible for a person to profess a neutral or indifferent attitude on any point between the extremes. For example, a shopper at a department store might be asked, "Do you think that a revolving charge account is 'very helpful' or 'very dangerous' to the shopper on a limited budget, or is your feeling some place between these two points of view?" The respondent might be asked to convert the answer into a quantitative one by assigning values to the various positions on the scale. The assignment of numbers has no particular meaning except that it permits the use of statistical tools and the tabulation of the study results. Involved and interesting methods for processing attitudinal data have been developed, including multidimensional scaling and cluster analysis.[10] We expect to see much progress in attitude research and

[9]C. E. Osgood, G. J. Suci, and P. H. Tannenbaum, *The Measurement of Meaning* (Urbana, Ill.: University of Illinois Press, 1937).

[10]See P. E. Green and Y. Wind, *Multivariate Decisions in Marketing: A Measurement Approach* (Hinsdale, Ill.: Dryden Press, 1973).

measurement in the future. Attitude scaling appears to be only the first step. It is, however, a useful research tool that has considerable application in marketing.

The Goals of the Consumer

The goals or objectives of the consumer are the same as those of any organism in relation to its environment. The consumer desires, most of all, want satisfaction. At the very least, but at the most basic level, is the desire to survive.

Satisfaction depends on the degree to which a want is met. While it might be tempting for a consumer to contemplate the complete satisfaction of all wants, this is unrealistic for most people because of limited income. Only the most demanding wants can be satisfied completely. Lesser wants may be partially satisfied and the buyer may be reasonably content with this outcome. For instance, a consumer might like to purchase a new automobile to replace a six-year-old model that has become more and more troublesome. Complete satisfaction probably would occur if a new car of the same make and model as the old one could be obtained. However, because of income limitations and other pressing wants (perhaps a child in college), the consumer may be forced to purchase a new but less expensive automobile. Or, adequate satisfaction may be achieved by replacing the old car with a more recent model used car. Finally, the consumer may have to be content to repair and continue to use the old junker.

Only wants of an extremely high order demand complete satisfaction. A basic physical want such as the need for food or water may fall into this category. But in a crisis, such as drought, war, or depression, an individual may be forced to accept partial satisfaction even for basic physical wants and probably no satisfaction for all other wants. Under ideal conditions, an affluent consumer may require that all wants be satisfied at the maximum level attainable. However, few persons are wealthy enough to command complete satisfaction of all wants. Most of us achieve satisfaction for a few wants and partial satisfaction for the rest.

A marketer is most successful when satisfactions are delivered that fit the wants of the particular consumers being served. Theoretically, it is as possible to oversatisfy as to undersatisfy these wants. For example, a customer may resent a restaurant that serves too much just as much as one whose portions are too small. Customer satisfaction is always relative to the ranking of the need and the degree of satisfaction desired. This is a key concept in the development of an effective marketing strategy.

The Nature of Consumer Wants

Marketing creates customers by providing satisfactions for consumer wants. What are these wants? From what sources do they spring? The answers to these questions are important if we are to understand the ways in which consumers behave. We will begin by looking at the basic nature of consumer wants.

Wants Versus Needs

Needs are those conditions—whether physical, psychological, or social in origin—that require satisfaction. The need for companionship, the need for peace of mind, and the need for physical comfort are equally compelling. Needs create wants for goods and services. A want, therefore, is a drive state that exists toward a specific object. A marketer, accordingly, does not create needs; rather the marketer creates wants by making consumers aware of their needs and by informing consumers of goods and services that can satisfy those needs. A want, therefore, can be thought of as a perceived need that motivates the consumer to act.

Some needs may exist but not be recognized. A person may need dental work, for example, without realizing it. Until this need is recognized, it does not become a want. An executive, pressed for time, may work through the normal lunch hour. But not until the clock or a complaining stomach reminds the executive that noon has long since passed does a desire for food arise. Yet, the physiological need for food existed hours earlier.

Demands

A *demand* is a want supported by purchasing power. Unperceived needs are not direct determinants of demand, even though they offer latent opportunities for demand creation. Furthermore, wants that cannot be backed up by purchasing power do not provide valid marketing opportunities. You might like the idea of owning an expensive Italian sports car, but unless you are unusually well off you probably cannot afford one. You may have a want, possibly even a need, but you certainly do not have a demand. All three elements must exist to establish an effective demand. There must be a need; the need must be perceived as a want; and the want must be backed up by purchasing power. Thus, the logical analysis of consumer

demand rests on the study of needs, their perception by the individual as wants, and the distribution of disposable income.

The Sources of Wants

Wants may arise either within the individual or from environmental contact, but wants ultimately must be centered within the individual because they are the result of perception. This is obviously true of physiological wants; and so we turn first to this important source of consumer wants.

Wants Originating Within the Individual

Wants originating within the organism are the result of both physical and psychical drives. The physical needs are well known. The human body, in order to survive, requires food for energy and growth. For proper functioning, the body must be maintained at temperatures within a rather narrow range. The body also requires adequate amounts of air, water, and minerals. Attempts to measure the relative importance of physical wants in relation to all other wants have not been especially productive. However, it is generally agreed that from one fourth to one third of all consumer expenditures are made to satisfy basic physical wants.

The psychical characteristics of a human being give rise to relatively few wants in their own right. Intellect, attitudes, and perception are more important for their bearing on the observation, interpretation, and activation of wants perceived in the physical self and in the environment. However, a person as a psychological entity does appear to have certain wants that arise simply because of this high level of intelligence. Curiosity, humor, and fear of the unknown are typically human, although lower organisms sometimes express these characteristics to a lesser degree. The urge to satisfy one's curiosity, for example, leads some people to explore the unknown and to consume goods and services simply for this purpose. Likewise, the human mind is amused or entertained by what it observes as comical. It also is diverted, absorbed, or challenged by more serious intellectual activity and by cultural experiences. The rising popularity of municipal orchestras and local theatrical productions are examples of the importance of this type of psychical want.

Although emulation of others and social respectability are closely related to the efforts of consumers to improve themselves through education and cultural activity, much of the recent increase in consumer outlays in these areas can be attributed to the fact that psychical wants of this type are being assigned more and more importance by consumers generally.

Wants Originating in the Environment

There are a number of external, or environmental, factors that give rise to consumer wants. We will explore several of the more important ones, including membership in small groups, social class, culture, and elements of physical, economic, and marketing systems to which the consumer belongs.

Small-group influence   Most consumers are influenced by others because of personal contacts arising from membership in small groups, both formal and informal. The personal influence of these associations is a

well-established sociological fact. The family or household is the most important formally structured small group to which almost everybody belongs. Others are work groups, professional societies, social clubs, and so forth. Membership in or reference to a number of *informal* small groups is characteristic of most individuals. Typically, the informal groups include an individual's neighborhood and various groupings of social acquaintances. Membership in informal groups of this type creates specific wants. For instance, it is quite common for people in the same neighborhood or in the same entertainment circle to live in approximately the same kind of house, to drive the same make of car, and to consume goods and services in roughly the same manner. Conformity to group standards is typical of consumer behavior.

It is not, however, simply the process of copying a neighbor's behavior that explains the importance of small-group influence. Even more to the point is the fact that informal groups have established communication patterns. The interaction of the members of a small informal group is the essential bond that unites the group. Some individuals are more communicative than others and are known as *opinion leaders*. Their ideas, attitudes, and behavior spread quickly and are adopted by other members of the group. Several interesting studies have been made of the characteristics of opinion leaders.[11] These studies suggest that directing marketing efforts toward opinion leaders is a sound marketing practice. The expectation is, of course, that their influence on other group

[11]E. Katz and P. F. Lazarsfeld, *Personal Influence* (Glencoe, Ill.: Free Press, 1955); E. M. Rogers, *Diffusion of Innovation* (New York: Free Press of Glencoe, 1962); and E. Katz, "The Two-Step Flow of Communication: An Up-to-Date Report on Hypothesis," *Public Opinion Quarterly* 21 (Spring 1957): 61–78.

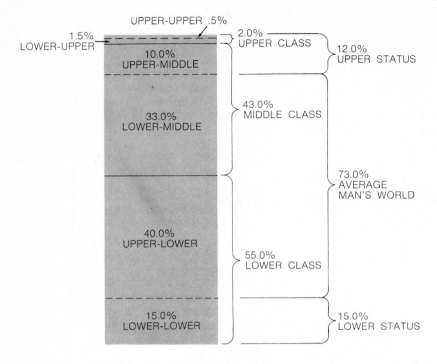

FIGURE 4.7   Social class in the United States

members will result in broader consumer acceptance.

An individual is influenced more by some groups than by others. A person may be an important member, perhaps even a leader, in one group and may exist only at the edge of another. A corporation executive may be a very inactive church member. A production line worker may be the captain of a company bowling team. A homemaker may be an active officer of a parent-teacher association, a willing volunteer worker at a local hospital, and an indifferent attendant at garden club meetings. Despite varying degrees of participation, membership in all three groups will influence not only the individual's behavior but also the actions of other people with whom he or she comes in contact. This overlapping of group member-

ship is important to the marketing manager, because it explains how ideas and modes of behavior sweep through a market. The phenomenon was once called *the web of word of mouth*—a phrase that cleverly describes the way in which small-group and interpersonal influence affect consumer behavior.

Social class   A second important way that social contact in the environment gives rise to wants is through social stratification. Sociologists have long recognized that a social hierarchy, usually referred to as *social class,* exists in American society. W. Lloyd Warner and his associates developed a theory of social class based on studies of New England communities over thirty years ago. Many different approaches can now be found in the literature. One of these is seen in Figure

4.7, which presents six levels of social class. They can be described as follows:[12]

1. The upper-upper or "Social Register" class is composed of prominent families, usually with at least second-generation wealth. This is the smallest of the six classes, with no more than 0.5 per cent of the population able to claim membership. The basic values of upper-upper class people are summarized in these phrases: living graciously, upholding the family reputation, and displaying community responsibility.

2. The lower-upper class is made up of the recently arrived but never quite accepted wealthy families. Included in this class are members of each city's "executive elite," as well as founders of large businesses and newly well-to-do doctors and lawyers. Only 1.5 per cent of Americans fit into the lower-upper level. The goals of these people are a blend of the upper-upper pursuit of gracious living and the upper-middle class drive for success.

3. In the upper-middle class are moderately successful professionals, owners of medium-sized businesses, and "organization" people at the managerial level. Also included are younger persons who are expected to arrive at this occupational status—and possibly higher—by their middle or late thirties. About 10 per cent of all Americans are part of this social class, and the great majority of them are college educated. The motivating concerns of upper-middle class persons are success in a career and a tasteful lifestyle.

4. At the top of the "average man's world" is the lower-middle class. Approximately one third of all citizens are members. For the most part, they are drawn from the ranks of nonmanagerial office workers, small business owners, and those highly paid blue-collar families who are concerned with being accepted in white collar–dominated clubs, churches, and neighborhoods. The key words in understanding the motivations and goals of the lower-middle class are *respectability* and *striving*. This means living in a well maintained, neatly furnished home, buying suits and dresses from "nice stores," and saving for a college education for the kids.

5. At the lower half of the "average man's world" is the upper-lower class, sometimes called the "working man's" class. Nearly 40 per cent of all consumers belong in this stratum, making it the single biggest group. Many of these people have very good incomes, but they do not bother to become respectable in middle-class ways. They are oriented more toward enjoying life from day to day than toward saving for the future or caring what the middle class thinks of them.

6. The lower-lower class consists of unskilled workers, unassimilated ethnics, and the sporadically employed. It comprises about 15 per cent of the population but has less than 10 per cent of its purchasing power. Many of the households in this class are afflicted with real poverty. Apathy and fatalism seem to be the natural outcomes of this condition, and these psychical characteristics influence buying behavior.

The marketing significance of social stratification is indicated in the description of the

[12]Adapted from R. P. Coleman, "The Significance of Social Stratification in Selling," in M. L. Bell, *Marketing: A Maturing Discipline* (Chicago: American Marketing Association, 1961), pp. 171–192.

six social classes. The assumption is that there is a tendency, although it is by no means without exception, for people in a given social class to behave in more or less the same ways. They have the same kinds of backgrounds, the same tastes, and they encounter more or less the same kinds of experiences. Their physical and psychological needs tend to be quite similar. Their environments are virtually identical.

These factors combine, then, to create segments of society with relatively homogeneous attitude sets. Members of a given social class adopt similar lifestyles and tend to respond in more or less similar ways to external influences. The marketing manager needs, then, to become familiar with the patterns of behavior within each social class in order to identify those wants that represent marketing opportunities for the firm.

In looking at Figure 4.7 it seems apparent that the greatest marketing opportunities lie in serving the all-important middle majority, consisting of the lower-middle and upper-lower classes. We must make two qualifications, however, about the overriding importance of this broad middle segment of the market. First, the wants of consumers usually are influenced not only by the social class to which they belong but also by the social class to which they aspire. This is especially true of middle-majority persons who are said to be socially "upward mobile." They are greatly influenced by the higher social environment to which they hope someday to belong. Their aspiration level is particularly useful in explaining expenditures on discretionary items—the kind of home one occupies, the model car one drives, and the school to which one sends son or daughter.

A second qualification involves the implied relationship between income and social class. A close general relationship does exist; but there are important exceptions. There are always individuals or households within a given social class receiving incomes greater or less than the average for the group as a whole. Consider the case of new arrivals in the upper-middle class, such as young doctors or lawyers who have only recently started public practice. These people find it a strain to spread relatively meager incomes over those expenditures required to maintain class status. They accordingly compromise on some purchases in order to conform on others. They may drive Fords or Chevrolets, but they maintain homes in prestigious suburban communities. People in this situation are said to be *underprivileged*. They are not in want in any real sense, but they find it difficult to meet the basic demands of upper-middle-class life.

Overprivilege also occurs. For example, blue-collar workers in the upper-lower class may enjoy incomes well above the average for that class. Perhaps they are production foremen or members of a craft union that enjoys especially high wages. Frequently, spouses in upper-lower class families also work, possibly as sales people in department stores. Thus, family incomes may range as high as $30,000, and family members may enjoy what amounts to over $5,000 of discretionary purchasing power. This type of family tends to spend its money rather than save it. The products it buys are those with status appeal. Their home may be modest, but it will boast a color television set in the living room. A late-model car, perhaps more than one, will be parked prominently in the driveway.

However important income level and social class may be in explaining the origins of consumer wants, they are not the only relevant factors. A complete understanding of the origins of consumer wants must include the linking of social class with all these other individual and environmental considerations. Often cultural influences provide such a link.

The influence of culture   Culture is a pervasive environmental determinant of behavior. Certainly, the contrasts that can be drawn between oriental and occidental consumers can best be understood in terms of culture and only secondarily in terms of individual psychical and physical differences. Differences in behavior among various western nations, for instance, France and the United Kingdom, also can be explained adequately by cultural distinction. Even contrasts in American consumer behavior can be explained culturally. Consider, for example, lifestyles in Boston and in Los Angeles.

Culture is the study of the accumulated effects of people in relation to people, and of societies in relation to their environments. More specifically, we use the term *culture* both to refer to the complex of values, attitudes, and other meaningful symbols created by a society to govern its behavior and to refer to the instruments or artifacts of that behavior. We shall look briefly at the elements of culture that influence consumer behavior at any given time.

Mores are standards of behavior that have strong moral sanction. They are deeply ingrained and generally accepted as norms of behavior. For example, tasting food in a supermarket is not an accepted practice in America, whereas in other cultures a shopper would not think of purchasing produce without first sampling it.

Many mores are so important, or their violation so critical, that they are codified in the form of *law*. On the other hand, some progressive legislation may run counter to mores—for example, open housing, school busing, and other civil rights laws. In general, however, the legal framework of marketing, most of which affects competitive behavior, reflects the mores of American capitalism.

Folkways are conventional behavior patterns that are accepted as appropriate by society but that are not strictly enforced. Styles in men's fashions, for example, provide an interesting case. Appropriate business dress in New York City until a few years ago was the traditional gray flannel suit. Today, even off Madison Avenue, sometimes bizarre and often colorful clothing is accepted.

Customs are standards of behavior that are gradually accepted and that become norms of conduct. Although originally rooted in behavior standards appropriate for their time, many customs appear to outlast their usefulness. Sometimes, custom is reflected in law. For example, so-called Blue Laws prevent the operation of many commercial establishments on Sunday. Violation of the law by some merchants and the overwhelming popularity of the violating establishments indicate that the custom of Sunday closing and the laws requiring it are no longer in tune with the times.

On the other hand, many customs that benefit marketing persist, either with or without the sanction of law. Holidays such as Christmas and Easter provide seasonal surges in sales for many companies. The family vacation supports the tourism industries and has given rise to fantastic parks such as Six Flags and Disneyland. The church wedding, the retirement banquet, the public funeral, and scores of other custom-related behavior patterns also influence aspects of marketing. Industrial behavior is not exempt. Codes of conduct for industrial salespeople exist. Custom prevents the hiring of competitors' employees. Likewise, it is customary to inform distributors of price changes before announcing them to the public. At a different level, consider the business lunch—a custom that takes many businesspeople away from their desks two or three hours a day.

Influences of the marketing system   Each individual comes in daily contact with many businesses anxious to sell goods and services. Sometimes this contact is passive or accidental. An office worker, for example, passes a display in a store window. Often, however, the contact is neither passive nor accidental. An insurance salesperson calling on a new customer may intrude into the prospect's environment. A viewer of "Monday Night Football" is exposed to fifty or more commercials in a two-and-one-half-hour period. A customer may initiate the contact. For example, some people without particular wants in mind frequently shop as a matter of routine or simply for enjoyment.

Thus, in one way or another, individual consumers come in almost ceaseless contact with sellers of goods and services. Such contact frequently leads to the perception of wants. The office worker, passing the department store windows, is reminded of the need for a new topcoat. The insurance salesperson's prospect may realize a need for protection. The homemaker, on a shopping excursion from store to store, may remember a dozen items that are needed at home.

Influence of the physical environment   Wants are influenced by both geography and climate. There are broad differences in the kinds of products and services consumed in various climates and locations. Wants for food, clothing, and shelter are the most commonly affected. Central heating systems, for example, are used widely in northern states, where central air conditioning is still somewhat exceptional. The opposite is true in the South. A person in San Francisco owns a topcoat; another, in Los Angeles, does not; and a third, in New York City, needs both topcoat and overcoat. Geographical differences also are found in tastes for food. New Orleans coffee, heavy with chicory, is almost unpalatable to a northerner. Midwesterners prefer black coffee; New Englanders usually use sugar and cream. Bostonians like brown eggs; New Yorkers demand white. Such differences, although not always logical, exist. They are partially explained by cultural and historical influences, but differences in climate and location are important determinants.

Influence of the economic environment   An individual's wealth, income, and stock of material goods also influence wants. Wealth and income, as we have seen, are associated with social class; however, the relationship is not always clear-cut. Not only do wealth and income give rise to certain wants, but their absence severely limits the ability of the average consumer to satisfy all wants. In this sense, the limitations or restrictions that the environment places on wants are as important as the wants themselves.

A consumer's stock of goods and services (or recent purchases of them) can vitally affect wants in either of two ways. A person emerging from a barber shop does not want another haircut. A homemaker whose kitchen cupboards are well stocked has little incentive to shop for food. A recently satisfied want, or an anticipated want that can be satisfied with goods already on hand, is not a marketing opportunity. Usually, however, a consumer's stock of goods and services affects only the relative importance of wants in the short run. Within a few days the store of groceries will diminish, and the consumer must shop once again to satisfy the family's needs for food.

A consumer's inventory of durable goods tends to affect wants over a longer period of time. Few families trade cars more often than once a year. Many purchase a new car infrequently. Certainly a new car in the garage affects a family's want for transportation (or status) for many months. In like manner, all durable assets influence to some degree the pattern of wants that an individual seeks to satisfy.

So far, we have implied that the existence of a stock of goods diminishes an individual's wants. However, the opposite effect also can prevail if the stock contains *complementary* goods or goods with related demands. For instance, an individual without a car has no need for tires, oil, and gasoline; but a car owner cannot operate a vehicle without them. A hunter with a rifle but without ammunition isn't a hunter at all. A high-fidelity stereophonic system gives rise to wants for tapes or records. Such wants would not exist were it not for the ownership of the set itself.

America is a land of abundance—a land of marketing opportunity. American consumer wants and purchasing power support the greatest marketing mechanism in the world. At least two of every three American families have some discretionary purchasing power, and in 1975, 15 per cent had family incomes of $15,000 or more. But in the midst of this relative prosperity is considerable poverty. Poverty has a special impact on marketing. The poor, in fact, constitute a special market segment whose needs are no less urgent (and frequently are more so) than those of the prosperous. Ideally, marketing should deliver a rising standard of living to *all*—probably not an identical standard, but certainly an ever-improving one, especially at the lower end of the economic scale.

Summary

Marketing is concerned with people and their behavior, especially their behavior as consumers. Our understanding of consumer behavior rests on contributions from many fields. The behavioral sciences have been the most helpful source of concepts relating to consumer behavior, but other disciplines have made contributions. We call the study of these contributions the interdisciplinary approach.

An ecological view of the consumer as an organism with a physical and psychical state is a helpful perspective from which to view consumer behavior. The influence of the physical state is clear. Basic needs for food, clothing, and physical comfort stem from the physical state of the individual. The psychical state is more complicated, since more than basic motives are affected.

Motivation, perception, learning, and attitudes are the most important factors affecting the consumer's psychical state. A motive is a stable inner condition that results in goal-directed behavior. Maslow's hierarchy of motives is a useful classification. Perception is the behavioral process that involves the detection, interpretation, and classification of sensory cues. Not all sensory cues affect behavior. Attention may not be attracted to them; or, by a process called selective perception, the cue may be distorted or rejected. Learning is more than exposure to information. For learning to have occurred, a change in response must result from an experience. In general, consumers learn by acquiring information or by building associations. Cognitive dissonance is a critical aspect of learning that involves a disruption of the consumers set of cognitive materials. Attitudes are predispositions to behave in particular ways. They are very important in explaining consumer behavior.

They provide a perceptual filter for screening new stimuli and arranging existing behaviors into predictable patterns. Attitudes can be measured. Attitudes can be changed or circumvented if they present a roadblock to effective marketing.

We discovered that the goal of the consumer is to achieve satisfaction. How much satisfaction the consumer seeks in connection with a particular want depends on the importance of the want and the sacrifice required to satisfy it.

Needs are defined as those conditions, whether physical, psychological, or social in origin, that require satisfaction. Wants are perceived needs. Demand is a want backed up with purchasing power. We saw that wants arising within the individual can be either physical or psychical in nature. Most consumer wants arise by reason of the consumer's contacts with the environment. These may be personal contacts involving the individual's membership in a small group or alignment with a particular social class. Cultural contacts also exert an influence, since many wants arise simply because of the mores and folkways of the society to which the consumer belongs. The marketing system, including the goods and services that are available and the marketing information about them, likewise influences consumer wants. Geography and climate exert an additional force. And, the economic environment is of great importance as well.

Questions and Problems

1. Why do you think it is that psychologists and sociologists have contributed more to the understanding of consumer behavior than have scientists in other disciplines?

2. Select an introductory textbook in economics and review its explanation of consumer behavior. Summarize the economist's explanation of consumer behavior. Contrast it with the approach taken in this chapter.

3. Using the Maslow classification, explain how the various motives might be involved in the purchase of the following:
   a. A color television set
   b. Lunch at a cafeteria
   c. A diamond engagement ring
   d. A dusk-to-dawn automatic lighting system
   e. A set of encyclopedias
   f. A life insurance policy
   g. An automobile liability policy

4. It has been obvious for a number of years that most automobile buyers have not been willing to pay for extra safety features. How might one explain this reluctance in terms of the consumer's psychical state?

5. Loan a friend a recent copy of a magazine and later on interview your friend about it. Make sure that the magazine has actually been read. Ask for a description of the specific advertisements he or she remembers seeing. Then ask that he or she thumb through the magazine and mark all of the ads that were looked at. Report your findings to the class. Comment on what your experiment contributes to your understanding of perception and memory.

6. Discover some examples of marketing situations where cognitive dissonance is likely to occur. What can the marketer do in these instances?

7. It appears that people's attitudes are gradually changing toward selected phenomena, for example, energy,

environmental protection, minority rights, and so on. Select one of these examples (or another of your own choice), and explain how people's behaviors have been changed by the process of attitude change.

8. In Chapter 1 we learned that customer orientation is one of the important aspects of the marketing concept. Now that we have looked at the nature of consumer wants, what complications do you see in connection with the businessperson's effort to satisfy these wants?

9. Consumers' wants change over time. Find out something about the wants of Americans fifty years ago and compare them with the wants of today. (One approach would be to compare the products available in the early mail-order catalogs with those sold in recent years. Early editions of Sears, Roebuck and Montgomery Ward catalogs have been republished lately.)

10. List the twenty most important wants you have at the moment. Arrange them in a hierarchy of importance and put the list aside. In approximately six hours, draw up another list without referring to the first. Compare them. Are the items on the second list the same as those on the first? Has the hierarchy changed? In what ways? How do you explain the differences between the two lists? How do you explain the similarities?

11. Identify the various small groups to which you belong. What is your role in each? In what ways did your belonging to these groups affect some important decision, such as your selection of a college to attend?

12. Which is more important as a want-provoking source: social class or small-group membership? Can a clear-cut line be drawn between the two? Explain.

5

The Buying Decision Process

In the preceding chapter we explored the nature of consumers. We saw consumers as ecological organisms whose needs and wants emerge from within themselves or as a result of contact with their environment. We are now ready to look at the ways in which consumers process wants and arrive at buying decisions.

In looking at the buying decision process, we will begin by constructing a model of how consumers perceive and dispose of various wants. We will then explore how consumers go about finding satisfactions for these wants in the marketplace. We also will review the ways in which business buying decisions are reached, for business buying behavior is just as important to many marketers as the behavior of ultimate consumers.

An Ecological Model of Consumer Behavior

It has become popular and helpful to present many aspects of marketing in the form of models. We have seen how diagrammatic models can be used in the portrayal of marketing systems. Attempts also have been made to describe consumer behavior in more or less the same way. It is quite natural to use a flow diagram for this purpose, since it enables us to view consumer behavior as a system within which various behavior-affecting elements are linked by flows of direct and indirect influence.

Several important flow diagrams of consumer behavior have been developed.[1] However, we will use a model designed specifically for this book. Not surprisingly, we call it an *ecological model*. Figure 5.1 is a diagram of the perception and disposition of consumer wants. It is an elaboration of Figure 4.2 and deals with the specific ways in

[1]Among these are: A. R. Andreasan, "Attitudes and Consumer Behavior: A Decision Model," in L. E. Preston, ed., *New Research in Marketing* (Berkeley, Calif.: Institute of Business and Economic Research, University of California, 1965), pp. 1–16; J. F. Engel, D. T. Kollat, and R. D. Blackwell, *Consumer Behavior* (New York: Holt, Rinehart and Winston, 1968); J. A. Howard and J. N. Sheth, *The Theory of Buyer Behavior* (New York: Wiley, 1969); and F. M. Nicosia, *Consumer Decision Process* (Englewood Cliffs, N.J.: Prentice-Hall, 1966).

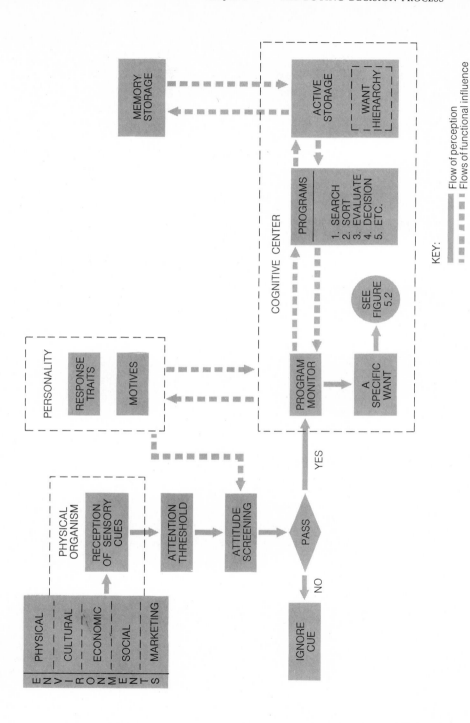

FIGURE 5.1   The perception of consumer wants

which consumers perceive and process need-related stimuli. It depicts consumers as organisms coming into contact with various environments. These contacts result in the detection of sensory cues. Whether these stimuli eventually affect behavior depends on the consumers' perceptive processes. It is therefore with the perception of wants that we begin a detailed discussion of the model.

The Perception of Stimuli

Needs arise within the individual or through contact with the environment. For marketing purposes, needs become effective only when recognized. This process of perception is therefore extremely important. An unrecognized need has no influence on a consumer's buying behavior.

The wants emanating from the individual are recognized through the physical senses. Often the needs that give rise to these wants are so imperative or so persistent that the incidence of the need and its perception are practically simultaneous. In fact, the want that results from the perception of a physical need is so strong that we sometimes refer to it as a *drive*. A drive is characterized by high priority and, often, extreme urgency. The drives to satisfy hunger, thirst, and the like are important factors in explaining consumer behavior under emergency conditions. However, as we learned in Chapter 4, most American consumers are directed by less urgent influences than physical drives. Their wants for food, clothing, and shelter are reasonably well satisfied. Thus, it is the perception of other wants that explains much of their marketing behavior.

The physical senses also enable the individual to perceive these other wants, most of which arise in the environment. The pace of the typical American consumer is rapid, and

attention constantly is being diverted from one environmental element to another. Therefore the life span of some wants is exceedingly short. A fleeting glance at an outdoor poster showing an appetizing soft drink may remind a motorist of being hot and thirsty. Within seconds, however, the driver's attention may be diverted to something else, perhaps something giving rise to an entirely different want.

Before such perception can occur, however, a sensory cue must pass the individual's attention threshold. Many stimuli do not attract sufficient attention to penetrate this barrier, but some do pass it for reasons we already have discussed. Those cues of which the consumer does become aware pass next through an attitude screening. Attitudes may reject a cue as incongruent or irrelevant, or they may pass the stimulus along to the cognitive center. Of course, as we have seen, attitudinal screening may actually distort the stimulus, so that it arrives in conscious thought in a disguise that may eventually cause considerable confusion. We can assume, however, that for the most part sensory cues that pass through the attitudinal screening avoid serious distortion and become the focal point of subsequent consumer action.

The Disposition of Perceived Stimuli

New information, coming in the form of perceived cues, usually demands additional screening in conscious thought for a determination of its disposition. For purposes of explaining consumer behavior, the most important disposition concerns whether the new information adds to the consumer's existing bundle of wants. If not, the information is irrelevant to immediate consumer activity, and it is filed in the memory along with other thought experiences. If the information reinforces some existing want or creates an entirely new one, it is filed in a somewhat more tightly controlled category of stored wants.

In our model, we assume the consumer possesses a program for this process of sorting and evaluating perceived stimuli. The program monitor selects the appropriate routine, and the sensory cue is properly classified and sorted. When such a program or routine is applied to the perception of wants, it results in a hierarchy, or ranking, which enables the consumer to select certain ones for immediate attention.

The Hierarchy of Wants

After an individual perceives a set of wants, it is arranged in a hierarchy of potency or urgency. This hierarchy is fairly stable in the long run, being dictated by a reasonably permanent set of values. Only when a dramatic change takes place in the individual or in the environment is the long-run stability of the hierarchy of wants disturbed. A job promotion, a move, or a change in family composition may cause a permanent readjustment in a consumer's scale of wants. But such changes occur infrequently, and we can reasonably anticipate their impact.

In the short run, the relative importance of various wants in the hierarchy changes drastically. For example, a consumer who has just finished a dinner of clams on the half shell, onion soup, tossed salad with Roquefort dressing, charcoal-broiled steak, baked potato, and French pastry hardly places the want for food very high in the hierarchy. In contrast, a hiker who has just completed a long trek in the country without refreshment ranks the want for food, even for a lowly hot dog, very high. This short-run instability in

the hierarchy of consumer wants makes predicting individual behavior at any particular place and time especially difficult.

In the aggregate, however, the differences between various individuals' sets of wants tend to disappear. Conventional modes of behavior influence many consumers to want approximately the same sorts of things at the same place and time. The eight-hour working day, the practice of eating three meals a day, and other traditional behavior patterns force some uniformity even on short-run hierarchies. For example, there always are individuals seeking meals at restaurants, morning, noon, and evening; seeking transportation to and from work; and searching for goods and services during conventional shopping hours. Behavior that is difficult to predict on an individual basis becomes somewhat easier to estimate in the aggregate.

The Consumer Decision Process

The process of perceiving sensory cues goes on continuously. But not all cues are stored away. Some information remains in conscious thought and bestirs the individual to act. What triggers this action? Some wants are so urgent, so strong, that they impel the consumer to take immediate steps to solve them. Physiological drives are of this type. But less urgent demands, even rather unimportant ones, eventually are considered. Routines exist for this purpose. The flow diagram in Figure 5.1 shows us that such a routine involves sorting and evaluating the wants that have been stored. Much as a cook checks the pantry for needed items, or as a retailer checks inventory, the consumer periodically sorts out various wants and selects one or more for immediate attention. The manner in which the consumer then seeks a satisfaction for this want is called the *consumer decision process.*

Rational Problem Solving

An underlying assumption in the ecological model of consumer behavior is that the organism seeks satisfaction in a rational manner. The essence of this rationality is problem solving. A problem may involve a physical want or a psychical desire. The recognition of the want and the orderly evaluation of alternative ways of satisfying it constitute a rational procedure. It is true that many purchases appear to be either *habitual* (without conscious evaluation of alternatives) or *impulsive* (without benefit of any evaluation). But these apparent exceptions to the general rule of rational buying can be explained. And it still is true that most consumer buying behavior is rational, as long as we recognize that it is just as reasonable to make a purchase for psychological or social reasons as it is to do so for the satisfaction of a physiological drive.

We have seen that the consumer assembles a collection of wants. These are arranged in a hierarchy that possesses long-run stability, but that in the short run is highly dynamic. At any given time, some wants in the hierarchy are more active than others. Presumably these are the wants at the top of the priority list; however, the continuous input of information into the cognitive center results in an almost constant reordering of priorities. Thus, the short-run wants about which the consumer must make immediate buying decisions are forever changing.

Of course, the consumer does not simply select one want at a time, solve it, and then proceed to the next. For example, a family may go on a shopping expedition to look for a new car; but this does not mean that the search for solutions to other problems stops while the car buying goes on. Family members continue to think about other needs and perhaps to advance the decision process concerning them even while shopping for the automobile. In many cases, consumers economize on time and effort by consciously solving more than one buying problem at a time. A trip to the supermarket or to the shopping center usually is undertaken in a search for products and services to meet several needs.

However, for purposes of studying consumer behavior, it is convenient to consider the way in which a single want is satisfied. This is a much less complicated process than when decisions about several different wants are made concurrently. But the basic problem-solving approach is the same, and the consumer decision process is not distorted, only simplified. You, however, should recognize the simplification and bear in mind that the decision process for a single want is actually only one of many similar and related processes going on simultaneously.

An Ecological Model of the Consumer Decision Process

Figure 5.2 illustrates the consumer decision process. It begins with the identification of a specific want. Either because of the tension that a particular want exerts or as the result of following a sorting and evaluating routine, a specific want is identified for possible satisfaction. (This process was shown in Figure 5.1.)

Consumer inventory as a source of satisfaction The first decision about the want concerns

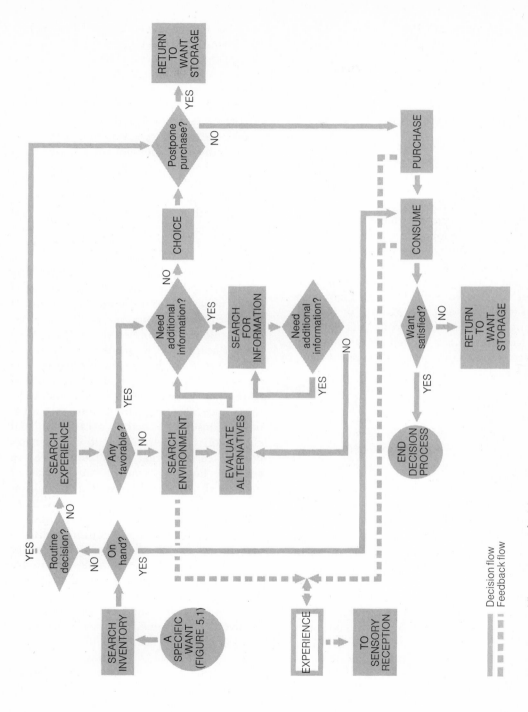

FIGURE 5.2   The consumer decision process

the possibility of satisfying it with a product already on hand. If the consumer has an appropriate product (or claim on a service) in inventory, it will be used. For most wants, however, the consumer is not likely to have a want-satisfying product or service claim in stock. A purchase must be made.

Routine buying decisions The consumer must decide whether to follow a routine buying procedure in acquiring the needed product. We have already considered this question in connection with consumer learning and the development of brand loyalty. The consumer utilizes habitual purchases, or routinized buying processes, to conserve time and energy. It is clearly not worth the effort to re-solve every want problem each time it arises. Rather, programs for routine buying are stored in the consumer's cognitive center and can be called on whenever the consumer considers them appropriate. Standardized, routinized, or habitual purchases then are made quickly in accordance with the program adopted. In Figure 5.2 a decision to follow an established buying program leads the consumer immediately to determine if more information is needed and if not to consider whether to buy immediately or to postpone the purchase.

The Search for want-satisfying goods and services Want-satisfying goods and services exist in the consumer's environment, in the marketing system. A search is necessary to locate them. Search programs are stored in the consumer's cognitive center, including a program of market search. For instance, a person may visit department stores and specialty shops in a definite sequence. This order may be based on prior experience in finding satisfactory goods and services, or it may be the result of experiments to deter-

mine the most convenient way to shop all of the stores in a given period of time. The point is that the consumer tends to follow set patterns of shopping, which we call *search programs,* that are retained in the cognitive center for use when needed. There are two important search methods: to search prior experience and to search the environment.

An individual does not institute an environmental search every time a want is perceived. Wants recur and, as we have seen, patterns of problem solving develop. When dealing with a repetitive type of want, but one for which a buying routine has not been adopted, the consumer searches memory rather than the actual environment. A couple, having decided to dine out, may rely entirely on information already gathered concerning various restaurants. If satisfied that the recalled solutions present an adequate selection from which to choose, no further search will be made. But the possibility that some important alternative may have been forgotten or that new restaurants recently may have been opened complicates the choice. To safeguard against this situation, consumers make occasional spot checks of the environment to discover important changes that are taking place. In general, however, the inconvenience of making a complete search of the environment is not justified by the improvement that the additional information brings. In Figure 5.2 we see that the consumer discovers from a search of memory that either there has been some favorable experience on which to base a buying decision or there has not. Even if there has been some satisfactory experience, the buyer should ask the question, "Do I need more information?" If the answer is "No," the buying process proceeds. If "Yes," the consumer gathers more information before making a choice.

New wants usually require a search of the

environment for appropriate products and services. Even old wants that arise when the consumer encounters a new or strange environment necessitate a search for means for their satisfaction. Consider the situation of a traveler arriving for the first time in San Francisco. Routine wants, such as those for food and shelter, arise. Unusual wants, perhaps for a new raincoat and umbrella to replace those left on the airplane, also may arise. In this situation, the individual cannot benefit from local shopping experience. A search of the environment for goods and services is required. The traveler will first arrange for lodging. To save time and also to use local advice, another person might be consulted—perhaps a taxicab driver. The driver may mention several hotels. If the traveler remembers something favorable about one of them, it will be selected. If not, an arbitrary choice may be made. On the other hand, the visitor might ask to be driven past various hotels, making a selection on the basis of observation. Each of these approaches illustrates an alternative method of searching the environment for solutions to a lodging need. The traveler's routine need for food involves a similar search and solution. The nonroutine want for a raincoat and umbrella is approached in the same general way. The environment is searched. The same two methods of *inquiring* and *observing* are available. Either path leads to a list of various stores at which to shop. Would it be surprising to learn that the visitor stays at the Mark Hopkins, dines on Fisherman's Wharf, and buys a coat and umbrella at the Emporium?

Evaluation of alternatives The search of experience or the search of environment produces alternative ways of satisfying a want. These alternatives must be evaluated and a choice made. Four factors are in-

volved. First, there is the want itself. Second, there is the degree of satisfaction that the consumer seeks. Third, there is the sacrifice required to obtain the satisfaction. And fourth, there is the fact that each want is positioned within a hierarchy of wants.

The shopping behavior of homemakers in a supermarket provides an example. As is quite typical, they may enter the store without a shopping list. Nevertheless, they have a fairly definite idea of the hierarchy of wants that must be satisfied. They also are aware of their budget limitations. However, some wants, regardless of cost, must be satisfied completely. If there is a new baby in the household, the pediatrician's feeding recommendations will be followed explicitly. Other wants may be satisfied partially. If planning to entertain a spouse's employer at dinner, that homemaker may consider first the purchase of a standing rib roast. If the meat costs twenty dollars, the homemaker may decide to adjust downward the degree of satisfaction sought in entertaining. It is possible, of course, that the standing rib will be bought with a corresponding scaling down of the degree of satisfaction sought on other needs. If the homemaker buys the expensive cut of meat, the family may dine on hamburgers, hot dogs, and eggs for the rest of the week. So each shopping decision relates to all others. In Figure 5.2, we can see feedback lines going from various stages in the decision process back to the consumer's cognitive center. This feedback, in the form of direct experience, is evaluated, classified, and placed in active or inactive storage by the various programs retained in the cognitive center. The simultaneous search of the environment for want-satisfying goods and services and the evaluation of alternatives necessitate a constant reappraisal of wants, goods, and sacrifices. The result is a composite solution, involving decisions relating to those wants that will be satisfied, the degree of satisfaction that will be sought, and the sacrifice of time, effort, and money required.

Purchase Evaluation of alternatives might proceed endlessly. Indeed, some consumers never seem to make up their minds. But if a want is genuine, the shopper eventually must select among alternatives and make a purchase. As this event approaches, the question arises, "Am I ready to decide, or do I need additional information?" If more information is required, the environmental search continues until it is apparent that further search will not contribute enough to make it worthwhile. When this point in the evaluation process is reached, the consumer makes a choice. One of the various alternatives must be selected, and this decision determines which product or service will be purchased and which seller's marketing program will succeed.

Postponement We should not assume, however, that the process of evaluation always drives the consumer relentlessly toward a logical and imperative action. A decision is seldom mandatory. The consumer must ask the question, "Should I postpone the purchase?" The consumer knows what to buy and where to purchase it, but can be uncertain about when to do so. It is a question of timing.

Several factors influence this decision. The importance of a major want and the considerable sacrifice involved mean that large and important expenditures are not made hastily. Lesser outlays to satisfy relatively unimportant wants are made quickly and with minimal attention to the problem-solving process.

Another way of explaining the uneasiness of making some purchase decisions is in terms of *perceived risk.*[2] Every purchase involves some risk, because it is never certain that the product will deliver the desired satisfaction or that its price is worth the sacrifice involved. The more information the consumer has and the more reliable it is judged to be, the less the perceived risk. In fact, we can explain the entire process of information search as an attempt to reduce risk. Obviously the safest decision in the face of great uncertainty is not to buy, or at least to postpone the decision.

Risk in buying is lessened and the need to postpone less critical when the purchase is *reversible.* For example, a consumer may have the privilege of returning a product that fails to live up to expectations. It is sometimes said that consumers do their shopping after their buying. Returns and allowances are substantial deductions from gross sales in many retail establishments. On the other hand, some products cannot be returned because the terms of sale do not permit it. A sign on a merchant's wall proclaiming "All Sales Final" announces that the purchase decisions made in the store are not reversible. Naturally, irreversible decisions tend to be made more deliberately and postponed more frequently than are reversible ones.

Eventually, however, consumers do buy. Some purchases are postponed and others are reversed, but wants must be satisfied and purchases are made—to a staggering degree. In 1975 alone, consumers spent $973 billion on goods and services. When we add to that sum the value of commercial and industrial transactions, the total volume of purchasing is almost beyond belief.

Consumption and satisfaction For the most part, buying is done well in advance of

[2]J. W. Taylor, "The Role of Risk in Consumer Behavior," *Journal of Marketing,* April 1974, pp. 54–60.

consumption. Services, of course, must be consumed immediately, although the satisfaction may endure for some time. Not only are the majority of purchase decisions made before consumption takes place, but also they are often made in anticipation of future wants. However, satisfaction usually is achieved only through consumption, not through purchasing. One retailing expert remarked that "shopping is a bore," meaning that the buying process itself brings little or no satisfaction. The want is only satisfied while the product is used.

Although marketing managers have long recognized that postsale dissatisfaction can arise, only in recent years has much attention been directed to the consumer after the purchase. Returns of merchandise, especially following Christmas and Easter, have always plagued retail store managers. It is not unusual for returns of seasonal merchandise to run as high as 20 per cent of sales.

The phenomenon of postsale customer behavior has been explored by a number of psychologists and marketing theorists. Their observations generally are classified as studies of consumer dissonance, a concept which we discussed in Chapter 4. In the present context, we can use this term to refer to the postpurchase anxiety that consumers often feel after making a buying decision. Consumer dissonance arises in two ways:

1. Postdecision dissonance occurs because of product disfeatures that actually were known prior to the purchase but that were outweighed by positive features when the buying decision was reached.

2. Cognitive intrusion creates dissonance after the purchase by injecting disturbing new information.

This concept of consumer dissonance identifies the dissatisfaction that may gener-

ate a new appraisal of wants and may eventually trigger a whole new decision cycle. Even the end is a beginning. As one product is consumed, the individual's hierarchy of wants is at least temporarily changed. Other wants assume higher priority. Moreover, the satisfying of a want through the purchase and consumption of a product, or the failure of a product to provide satisfaction, are new factors in the individual's experience that inevitably affect subsequent attitudes and behavior. Buying behavior, then, is a continuous process, as the feedback lines in our ecological model suggest.

The Business Buying Decision Process

It is also important for the marketing manager to understand business buying behavior. Many firms sell not to ultimate consumers but to other businesses. True, the demands of business establishments are almost always derived from ultimate-consumer demands; but intermediate customers must also be "sold," and marketing efforts must be directed toward them. Industrial, institutional, and resale buying practices are extremely important to the marketing programs of firms selling to these customers. Although the purchasing behavior of such business customers is less complex than that of ultimate consumers, there are complicating factors in the nonconsumer markets.

The Characteristics of Business Buying Behavior

All buyer behavior is related to want detection, search for products, and purchase. In this sense business buying behavior is basically the same as its consumer counterpart. However, business buying does possess several characteristics that make it sufficiently different to require explanation.

The rational (problem-solving) approach Most business buyers view their function as a problem-solving activity. Moreover, rationality has been assumed to characterize the business buying process. The objective nature of most business wants encourages the problem-solving or want-search-solution approach. In contrast to consumer buying, there are no important exceptions to this characteristic in business buying.

Use of formal procedures The development of formal procedures, or routines, typifies most business buying. Routinization of buying, as we have noted, saves time and effort. It also encourages uniformity of action if more than one person is involved in performing the same function. Moreover, it permits orderly recordkeeping and facilitates the control of purchasing. Most purchasing executives occupy organizational positions that are thoroughly described and for which clear-cut tested procedures have been established. Notwithstanding, truly habitual purchases seldom occur in industry, and the impulsive purchase probably never happens. Routinization in business buying, therefore, does not lead to these two "soft spots" in consumer behavior.

Multiple purchase influences The presence of a purchasing executive in a company tends to obscure the fact that other individuals also are involved in the buying process. It has been estimated that, on the average, three to four executives take part in every industrial purchase, and many more can be involved. The number and executive level of individuals influencing purchasing depends on the kind and the importance of the decision to be made.[3] For instance, the purchase of paint may involve only the maintenance supervisor and a purchasing agent, while the decision to purchase expensive manufacturing equipment might involve engineers, production managers, plant managers, and financial officers. A labor relations person also might be included and of course a purchasing executive. Regrettably, it is not always easy for a seller to identify or approach the specific individuals involved when they are not part of the purchasing department.

Importance of inventories Consumers for the most part live on a hand-to-mouth basis and do not have to manage large inventories of goods. Such is not the case in business. In fact, we can view industrial purchasing as an effort to maintain the correct assortment of goods in inventory. The purchase of steel by automobile manufacturers, for example, is influenced not only by current demands for steel in new-car production but also by inventory policy related to steel. Having on hand enough steel, plastic, glass, engine parts, and the thousands of other items to keep production lines running is mandatory. But the purchasing or materials-management people must be concerned that they not tie up working capital unnecessarily or risk a loss from obsolescence by overstocking such items.

Disposition of waste and scrap It is often the responsibility of the purchasing executive to dispose of waste and scrap. This problem is not important to most consumers, although trash removal has become a distressing problem in some cities. It is,

[3]For an excellent treatment of the organizational impacts on industrial buying, see F. E. Webster and Y. Wind, "A General Model for Understanding Organizational Buying Behavior," *Journal of Marketing,* April 1972, pp. 12–19.

however, an almost universal problem influencing purchasing at the industrial and resale levels. Waste material is created in almost all manufacturing and must be disposed of economically and in an ecologically acceptable manner. Surplus or excess stock is accumulated occasionally in manufacturing and, with unfortunate frequency, in wholesaling and retailing. This excess also must be disposed of as profitably (or at as little loss) as possible.

Industrial Procurement

Before World War II, purchasing was a poor cousin of manufacturing. The purchasing department performed its chores without much assistance or recognition. World War II brought a dramatic change. It was during the war years, when there was a drastic shortage of most goods required in business, that purchasing agents became known as *procurement executives.* The wartime success of these executives was measured mainly in terms of their ability to "deliver the goods." After the war, rising prices, the increased quantities involved in most purchases, the growing importance of inventory management, the increasing complexity of industrial goods, and the critical shortages of some metals and petrochemicals required the continuation of a high level of purchasing skills. The procurement function has continued to gain in importance, and it is now one of the most vital factors in the smooth operation of a modern business or institution. In the period of extreme shortage in the years 1973 and 1974, the purchasing function became so critical that marketing managers—long accustomed to ignoring the purchasing function—had to turn much of their energy to helping procure needed materials.

The scope of the procurement function appears to be constantly widening. In recent years, the phrase *materials management* has been used to describe its expanded range. The most important difference between the materials manager and the procurement executive is that the former is responsible for the management of inventories as well as purchasing.

A Model of Industrial Buying

The Marketing Science Institute made an exhaustive study of industrial buying.[4] The investigation included not only an inspection of the various elements of the procurement process but also a study of its environmental influences and the interpersonal relations among its participants. Several interesting case studies were contained within the report. One of them, concerning the purchase of a machine tool, is illustrated by the decision network diagram in Figure 5.3. This PERT-type diagram shows the various decision elements in a procurement process, the departments or functions that are responsible for them, and the order in which the steps of the process are carried out. We see that there are eight fundamental procurement activities involved in the purchase of a machine tool, and these steps are typical of all industrial procurement. They are:

1. *Anticipation or recognition of a problem (need)* Needs are recognized when engineering analyses suggest that a new tool is economically justifiable or is required for the manufacture of a new product.

[4]P. J. Robinson, C. W. Faris, and Y. Wind, *Industrial Buying and Creative Marketing* (Boston: Allyn and Bacon, 1967). Other models have been developed. See Webster and Wind, "Understanding Organizational Buying Behavior," and J. N. Sheth, "A Model of Industrial Buyer Behavior," *Journal of Marketing,* October 1973, pp. 30–36.

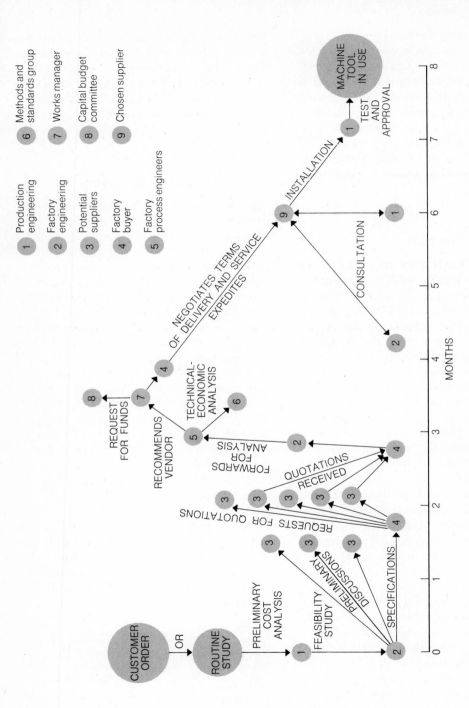

FIGURE 5.3 Decision network diagram of the procurement process (standard machine tool)

Source: P. J. Robinson, C. W. Faris, and Y. Wind, *Industrial Buying and Creative Marketing* (Boston: Allyn and Bacon, Inc., 1967), p. 50. Reprinted with permission.

2. *Determination of the characteristics and quantity of the needed item* Production engineering determines the type and quantity of equipment that is needed.

3. *Description of the characteristics and quantity of the needed item* Factory engineering, having identified the requirement, formulates specifications and furnishes them to the factory buyer in the form of a request for quotation. In formulating the specifications the factory-engineering group may hold preliminary discussions with prospective suppliers.

4. *Search for and qualification of potential sources* The initial selection is made by the factory engineers in their selection of vendors with whom to discuss their problems. Factory purchasing personnel suggest additional suppliers to bring the total number within the company policy of considering three to five sources. The policy of considering at least three suppliers is not followed when machine tools are needed for special applications. This suggests that on such applications the choices made by the engineering group become final unless the purchase itself is disapproved at a higher level.

5. *Acquisition and analysis of proposals* The buyer invites quotations from potential sources. Quotations are analyzed by a factory process engineer, who evaluates each proposal on technical and economic grounds.

6. *Selection of suppliers* The factory process engineer selects the supplier. This recommendation is forwarded to top management for approval on capital planning and financial grounds. If the recommendation is approved, the factory then sends a requisition to the buyer, directing that person to place the order with the designated supplier and to negotiate terms of delivery and service.

7. *Selection of an order routine* The factory buyer prepares and forwards the purchase order, and undertakes expediting and other follow-up activities.

8. *Performance feedback and evaluation* The system of performance feedback is informal, confined to the production and production-engineering groups within the plant.

Figure 5.3 also shows that seven separate departments or company functions, as well as an unspecified number of potential suppliers of the needed machine tool, are involved in the decision process. Add to these the unnamed purchasing influences and the complex character of industrial buying becomes very clear.

This example of industrial buying demonstrates that the process is essentially one of identifying a want to be satisfied, searching for a solution, and negotiating the purchase. The process is orderly and systematic, although complicated by a multitude of influences. In spite of its unique characteristics, this model is still remarkably similar to our model of consumer behavior and no great distortion is created by viewing them similarly in our study of marketing.

Buying for Resale

Resellers are business establishments that buy and sell goods in essentially the same form. They may break bulk, or subdivide large orders; they may combine goods from various sources into new assortments; but they seldom change the material structure of the product. Wholesalers and retailers are important types of resellers. In spite of persistent efforts of manufacturers to find ways of marketing directly to the ultimate consumer, strong independent merchants continue to operate at the wholesale and retail levels. The persistence of such firms is explained partly by their strong roots in history. However, most resellers have changed considerably in the last fifty years. They have altered both form and function in order to adapt to changes in their economic and social environments. Resellers exist today because they continue to provide important marketing services.

The characteristics of industrial procurement also apply to buying for resale. Because of institutional differences and the distinction between manufacturing and selling, these characteristics are seen in somewhat different form. But their influences are nonetheless felt. The rational or problem-solving approach is followed, as are formal buying procedures. Multiple-purchase influences are found, although they tend to be less important than in industry. Inventory considerations are of vital importance however.

Among resellers, the buying function is closely connected with the overall merchandise-management activity. We use the term *merchandising* to describe the sum of merchandise-oriented activities, including buying, pricing, controlling inventory, and selling. All four activities are necessarily coordinated, and it is impossible to discuss buying without reference to the other three.

Central to the whole idea of merchandising is the fact that resellers perform a purchasing function for their customers. Customer orientation was accepted in retailing long before the marketing management concept became popular. Retailers always have been proud to consider themselves purchasing agents for their customers. In many respects, this is the role they perform best. Retailers must recognize and understand their customers' wants in order to satisfy them. Beyond this, they must anticipate customer wants.

A second way of viewing reselling is to see its basic responsibility as that of maintaining adequate assortments for which consumers can select want-satisfying goods and services. For most shoppers, searching the environment is tedious, time consuming, and costly. Retailers, through effective buying, lighten this task. Since their maintenance of an assortment is closely related to inventory control, we see the intricate relationships among buying, pricing, inventory management, and sales. Certainly, the ultimate success of an overall retail merchandising strategy depends on the skill used to conceive and purchase the merchandise assortments.

Retail Buying Procedures

Retail buying involves three important steps: (1) the determination of what and how much to buy, (2) the selection of resources, and (3) the selection of specific items. Of course, as defined above, the total merchandising function extends beyond buying. However, we will discuss only those aspects of merchandising that affect resale buying behavior.

Determination of what and how much to buy is based on knowledge about the consumer. Some stores conduct research to discover the wants of retail store customers. However, to a considerable degree, retailers rely on experience and intuition in determining what to buy. Mistakes are made, but for the most part buyers exhibit remarkable ability to develop acceptable assortments of merchandise. Many consumer wants are repetitive, and buyers rely to a large degree on past sales experience to guide current buying. An important part of determining what and how much to buy, therefore, involves analyses of past sales and careful examinations of inventories. Some buying is done more or less mechanically, to fill in the existing stock. Of course complicating factors develop, such as changes in consumer tastes and the actions of competitors. Their ability to anticipate changes in consumer wants and quickly to adjust to expected competition marks good buyers.

In spite of the freedom that retail buyers generally enjoy, most of them operate under formal merchandising policies imposed by top management. In some stores, buying is regulated by an overall *merchandising plan.* The plan sets forth in detail the kinds of goods that are to be handled, inventory levels, and the prices at which merchandise will be resold. Deviations from the established plan require top merchandise-management approval. This is especially true in the case of buying for units of corporate chains. Basic inventory policies are established by the headquarters organization. Store managers have some freedom to cater to local wants and to buy locally to fill gaps in inventory. However, for the most part, they select the kinds and amounts of merchandise indicated by the overall plan.

The selection of suppliers, called *vendors* or *resources,* is an important aspect in resale buying. The vendors' reliability and ability to deliver merchandise according to the terms of purchase are key considerations. Retail buyers establish continuing relationships with proven resources. Changes are made from time to time, and most retailers continually shop the market before making final resource decisions.

Retail buying takes place in the store or in the market. Buying *in the store* may result from a salesperson's visit or on the basis of samples, catalogs, and advertising material. Traveling sales representatives frequently visit retail stores in order to display merchandise and personally present a sales message. Often the salesperson brings samples into the buyer's office. On occasion, a display is set up in a nearby hotel and buyers are invited to inspect the line. This practice has become less important in recent years as regional and national merchandise marts and shows have become popular. A *mart* is a building in which manufacturers display merchandise, especially new or seasonal lines. A *show* is a periodic event held in a public exposition hall, such as McCormick Place in Chicago, at which vendors display their lines for inspection by retail buyers. Buyers visit marts and shows regularly in order to compare competitive lines directly.

Some individual stores and most store groups maintain buying offices in major markets. Buyers visit these offices two or three times a year, depending on the type of merchandise in which they are interested. Imported merchandise has become more and more popular in America, and retail buyers frequently travel abroad. Foreign marketers also exhibit their lines in major American markets.

Item selection and the selection of source are closely connected in the buying process. However, most resources present wide lines of merchandise from which buyers can choose. Buyers must carefully select specific items—such as color, style, price, and the like. Experience, a thorough understanding of the store's customers, imagination, and a flair for the sales possibilities of the merchandise guide successful buyers. This is the art of retail buying.

A Model of Resale Buying

We can use flow models to portray the retail buying process. In some respects, it is much easier to diagram the decisions made by a marketing establishment than it is to depict the consumer buying process. Massy and Savvas, for example, illustrate the buying activity of a major appliance department in a logical flow diagram presented in Figure

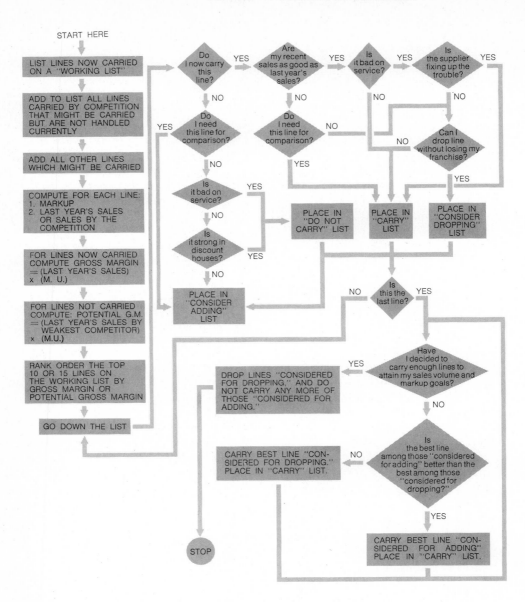

FIGURE 5.4   How a major appliance department decides which suppliers' lines to carry

Source: Reprinted from "Logical Flow Models for Marketing Analysis" by V. F. Massy and J. D. Savvas, *Journal of Marketing,* January 1964, p. 35, published by the American Marketing Association.

5.4.[5] While the general process is apparent from the diagram, several points are important enough to consider in detail.

1. Gross margin (last year's sales multiplied by the markup percent) is used as the buyer's primary criterion for ranking lines. For lines not carried now, the sales of the weakest major competitor are utilized. Thus, the method for forecasting gross ✓ margin is biased in favor of products now carried.

2. Lines now carried enjoy a second advantage. Provided that (a) they are among the top 10 or 15 lines on the working list (this cutoff rarely eliminates currently carried items), (b) their sales have not declined during the last year, and (c) service has been satisfactory; these products are automatically placed in the "carry" list, regardless of alternatives that might be available.

3. Satisfactory lines that are not currently carried are placed in the "consider buying" list. They are considered further only if the buyer has not been able to meet sales and markup goals exclusively from the "carry list." If additional lines are needed, the best potential new line is compared with the best of the old lines on the "consider dropping" list; and the one with highest gross margin is chosen.

4. Potential new lines must have satisfactory service and must not be strong in discount houses. The discount house question does come up in evaluating currently carried products, although service considerations remain important. Exceptions are made when the lines are needed for comparison purposes (trading the customer up or down).[6]

So far we have stressed the buying practices of general merchandise establishments, such as department stores. Most retailing literature is similarly directed, because, in many respects, all retail buying conforms to the same pattern.[7] The same general buying decisions must be made. However, the majority of small independent stores exercise relatively little buying initiative. Small independent merchants—and there are a great many of them—rely on wholesale suppliers for guidance in selecting goods. Units of chain-store organizations likewise have little buying responsibility. Exceptions exist, but in general these stores stock an assortment determined by the chain headquarters, and their requirements are filled by requisitions to a chain-store warehouse. Limited-price variety stores are stocked in the same manner.

Wholesale Buying Procedures

Wholesale buying, like retail buying, involves purchasing goods for resale. The parallels are pronounced. The approach is rational and formal buying procedures are followed. The buying decisions are the same: (1) what and how much to buy, (2) which suppliers to purchase from, and (3) what particular lines of items to buy.

Determining *what* to buy is a matter of discovering those products that the wholesaler's customers want. If these are retail stores, the wholesaler either attempts to carry what the stores want or, as mentioned earlier, attempts to anticipate the store's needs and to supply them. Many wholesalers sell industrial goods, such as component parts and maintenance and supply items. These wholesalers buy to meet their industrial customers' needs.

[5]W. F. Massy and J. D. Savvas, "Logical Flow Models for Marketing Analysis," *Journal of Marketing,* January 1964, p. 35.

[6]Ibid.

[7]For a model of selecting new products for a supermarket, see D. B. Montgomery, "New Product Distribution: An Analysis of Supermarket Buyer Decisions," *Journal of Marketing Research,* August 1975, pp. 225–264.

TABLE 5.1   Effect of stock turn on item profitability

	Item A	Item B
Value of inventory		
at cost	4,250.00	4,250.00
Turnover	5	10
Sales	25,000.00	50,000.00
Margin	3,750.00	7,500.00
Costs		
Investment	340.00	340.00
Physical handling	750.00	1,500.00
Space (rent, light, etc.)	1,000.00	1,000.00
Total	2,090.00	2,840.00
Profit contribution	1,660.00	4,660.00

To some extent wholesalers (as well as retailers) buy what they are sold. They are selected by their various suppliers as part of a marketing channel. But most channel systems are flexible and wholesalers not only have considerable freedom of choice, they sometimes carry the products of competing manufacturers. They do this, of course, to increase sales and to provide broad assortments to their customers. Even in well-managed systems, resellers have considerable freedom of choice in buying.

The expense of carrying inventory has a profound impact on the wholesaler's costs and profits. Many buying decisions, therefore, are made on the basis of inventory considerations. This can be demonstrated by a simple example shown in Table 5.1. Suppose a wholesaler carries an average inventory of 5,000 units of each of two items of the same unit value ($1). Both items produce a margin of 15 per cent. Item A has a turn of 5; Item B has a turn of 10. Compare the effect of the difference in turnover. The profit contribution is greater for Item B for two reasons. First, it produces twice the margin.

Second, and this is the point being illustrated, some costs (investment and space) vary with the size of inventory and are therefore unchanged as turnover increases. Thus Item B's profit contribution is higher than that of the slower moving Item A. Prompt turnover of stock is an important profit factor. Because most wholesalers handle tens of thousands of products, many of low unit value, it is imperative that they maintain a rapid rate of turnover in order to generate adequate profit.

Resale considerations are important. Wholesalers must persuade retailers to buy. However, since the sales effort is spread over many thousands of items and since selling time is at a premium, it is very costly to devote special attention to selected items in a line. Wholesale buyers, therefore, prefer to carry higher-profit items with built-in sales appeal that will sell rapidly without intensive sales effort. Wholesale drug firms, for instance, make important buying decisions on the basis of product movement and unit price. The *average line extension* is a measure used to estimate an item's relative profitability. The number of units ordered by a wholesaler's customer times the unit price is the *line extension*. Since it costs about the same to sell and process a large order for an item as it does a small order, it always is more profitable to sell as many units of an item as possible each time an order is written. The buying decision, accordingly, is very much affected by the product's impact on sales, sales expense, turnover, and inventory cost. The author once visited a wholesale hardware company shortly before it went into bankruptcy. Besides an obsolete warehouse and archaic order-filling procedures, the company had actually lost control of its inventory. Items were still on the shelves that had been bought twenty years earlier! No wonder the company failed.

Modern hardware wholesalers operate quite differently and compete efficiently. The changes in buying and merchandising practices have been almost revolutionary. It is a good example of why and how wholesalers continue to flourish in the marketing system.

Summary

This chapter has been concerned with the perception and disposition of wants. A logical flow model was used to demonstrate the way in which people perceive sensory cues and process information about wants. This model representing the perception and disposition of wants suggests that wants arising within individuals or the environment are detected by sensory cues that are screened by the individuals' attitude sets. The cues may be ignored or passed into the cognitive center. Here a monitor selects one or more programs to dispose of the want. It may be sent immediately into a decision routine, or it may be stored to be acted on at a later time.

The consumer decision routine involves a search for want-satisfying goods and services, and a choice among alternative solutions. Important related decisions involve the questions of information search and purchase postponement. If eventually a decision is reached, consumption occurs and the consumer evaluates this experience in terms of the degree of satisfaction attained. Thus, the process ends either with the satisfaction of the want or its return to the beginning of the cycle, where it rests in a memory cell of the consumer's cognitive center.

Business wants are not unlike consumer wants. They arise either within the business or by reason of its relations with the environment. Business people tend to follow rational, orderly routines in seeking satisfactions for wants. These were presented in flow diagrams. Two types of business buying were considered, resale buying and industrial procurement. They are similar except that the wants in resale buying arise almost exclusively as a result of a firm's relations with its customers.

Questions and Problems

1. The want-perception model in this chapter utilizes the concept that the consumer's cognitive center receives and processes sensory want cues. This processing utilizes various routines for classifying, storing, and retrieving wants. This sounds much like a system. Do you think the connection is accidental or meaningful? Explain.

2. Recall the most recent relatively expensive purchase you have made, such as a suit or a camera. Analyze your search and decision process, using the consumer decision model in this chapter.

3. Compare the ways in which purchasing decisions are made for a major purchase (like carpeting) and a minor one (like toothpaste).

4. List five products that you buy out of habit. How did these habitual purchase patterns get started? Have you ever switched brands? What do you think it would take to get you to switch brands now?

5. A well-known natural scientist recently remarked, "We don't consume things;

we just *use* them." How does this statement modify your ideas about consumption? Focus your analysis on specific aspects of consumption—for example, consider the difference between the returnable soda bottle and the aluminum can. What about a car? Do we really "consume" it?

6. How do you know when a want has been satisfied?

7. Locate several people who have recently bought a durable good, such as a car or a washing machine. Find out how satisfied they are with the product purchased. See if you can detect the existence of any consumer dissonance. If you do, what conclusions can you draw as to (a) what the manufacturer might have done before the sale and (b) what the manufacturer or retailer might do now to improve the customer's post-purchase satisfaction?

8. When computers first came on the market many companies ordered them. Some had well-defined needs; others appeared to buy computers simply because "it's the thing to do" or "it makes us look good to have our own computer." These last two reasons sound very irrational. How might you explain this type of purchase behavior?

9. During a recent period of extreme shortage of certain petrochemicals, the salespeople and product managers of one large chemical manufacturer spent most of their time trying to find other sources of products for their company's customers. Why do you think they did this rather than just allocate their limited supply among the various customers?

10. Interview a purchasing executive of a medium- or large-sized company. Have the executive describe the purchasing procedures followed by the firm. Draw a flow chart of the process and compare it with the model presented in this chapter. Explain any differences.

11. Why is it that most demands for business goods are derived? Can you think of any business demands that are not derived? List and explain.

12. Are business decisions postponed? What reasons might a company have for postponing a decision to replace office equipment? Are these kinds of decisions more important in marketing than decisions by consumers to put off buying? Similarly, are business purchase decisions reversible? What are the consequences of business decisions to postpone or to reverse a purchase?

6

Market
Segmentation

In preceding chapters we looked at the ways in which marketing companies are organized and make plans. We explored the nature of consumer behavior and explained why and how consumer purchase decisions are made. It is now possible to describe the way in which these topics are related. The linkage occurs as a marketing manager develops marketing plans that direct a company's resources to the satisfying of consumer wants. A marketing plan by definition must focus on a market, and the precise way in which this is done involves the application of the concept of market segmentation.

The Concept of a Segment

In 1977 there were about 217 million people in the United States, most of them consum-

ers. If we looked at any large group of consumers from some distance away—say we were to watch a crowd of people from the twentieth floor of an office building—they would appear remarkably similar. However, if we went lower, certain obvious differences would become clear—men and women, short and tall. If we descended to the street and joined the people there, we would naturally discover that each person was in some respects unique. But we also would discover similarities that we had not seen before. Some smile, others don't. Some walk fast and purposefully, others loiter and gaze at shop windows. We discover an amazing fact: People are at the same time similar and different. We have discovered the concept of a population segment.

Just so we look at consumers. First we look at them in the aggregate. Then we study them from a closer vantage point and discover the basic ways in which consumers can be differentiated. Finally, we look at those groups of consumers that are alike in their marketing characteristics but different from consumers as a whole. We call these groups *market segments,* and this chapter is concerned with them. Let us turn first, however, to the concept of the market and the ways in which it can be described.

The Nature of Markets

The Market as a Place

Historically, markets have been considered geographical places. The term *marketplace* suggests this heritage. In today's view of marketing there is a hierarchy of places that constitute markets. There is a world market; there are international, European, and American markets. The domestic American market can be subdivided into regions, states, and localities. Urbanization has created a new kind of marketplace—the metropolitan area. Larger than a city, larger than a county, and sometimes embracing parts of two or more states, the metropolitan area is the major geographical place of marketing for many companies. However, markets as places can be even smaller than a city. A shopping center, a block, a portion of a block, and even the site of a single retail store can be called a market. Since goods must be delivered to and customers attracted toward particular places where transactions are made, the geographical identification of markets is important for marketing management purposes. Such issues as location of facilities, routing of salespeople, and direction of promotional efforts are affected by the concept of geographical marketplaces.

The Market as People

Markets also can be fruitfully viewed as collections of people. People with overt or latent wants constitute markets. People with wants create marketing opportunities. People with wants and purchasing power make these markets effective. A market as people implies the existence of people with purchasing power—people with money to spend. A market, then, is composed of people, people with money, people with money wanting goods and services; and the basic opportunity in marketing is to provide these people with want-satisfying goods and services.

When speaking of markets as people we are not concerned exclusively with ultimate consumers, although individuals and members of households do constitute the most important and largest category of market. Still, business establishments and other organizations must be viewed as capable of supporting marketing effort as well. People, individually or in groups, create markets.

The Consumer Market

By the consumer market we mean those individuals and households that buy and consume goods and services for the satisfaction of personal wants. They are ultimate consumers in that they do not purchase for resale or for industrial use.

This market is tremendous. Millions of people, hundreds of millions of differing wants and desires, and billions of dollars of purchasing power are found in it. How shall we look at this huge multidimensional market? One approach is to inspect each signifi-

TABLE 6.1 Population of the United States for selected years, 1800–1970, and projections, 1980 and 2000

Year	Population (millions)
1800	5.3
1820	9.6
1840	17.1
1860	31.4
1880	50.2
1900	76.0
1920	106.5
1940	132.6
1960	179.3
1965	194.3
1970	204.9
1975	213.5
1980	220.2
2000	249.1

Source: U.S. Department of Commerce, "Population Estimates," *Current Population Reports,* series P–25, no. 310 (30 June 1965), no. 311 (2 July 1965), no. 519 (April 1974), and no. 601 (October 1975) (Washington, D.C.: U.S. Government Printing Office).

cant aspect of the consumer market separately—that is, its demographic, geographic, economic, and social dimensions. Even though this tends to oversimplify the complex nature of the consumer market, we have little choice. If we remember that a consumer is a complex creature, embracing all of these elements to some degree, we will not be misled by the oversimplification.

Demographic Factors

Population In order to survive and enjoy life, people need the goods and services that marketing provides. By 1977 the U.S. population was slightly over 217 million persons. Even if we eliminate a fraction of this total

because certain individuals do not directly affect the market (such as infants and incompetents), the remaining figure is almost staggering, and the population continues to increase. Table 6.1 shows the growth of the population of the United States since 1800, projecting the data to 2000. By 2000 there will be approximately 250 million persons constituting the American market.[1]

Age distribution of the population The age distribution of a population at any given time helps us to understand the kinds of goods and services that are demanded by consumers as well as the different types of consumer behavior exhibited. For example, not only does a young, recently married couple demand different products and services than do an older couple, but the young people tend to approach the problem of seeking satisfactions for their wants in quite different ways from those of their older counterparts. Table 6.2 shows the distribution of the population by age groups for four selected years. Of a total population of approximately 181 million persons in 1960, 53 million (about 30 per cent) were under 14 years of age. Marketers were well aware of the importance of this youth market segment.[2] Not only manufacturers of toys, infants' clothing, bicycles, and juvenile furniture, but makers of products less directly affected

[1] It is important to realize that population projections can be subject to considerable error. Also, forecasters disagree on the basic assumptions that must be made before attempting to project demographic data. For example, the Department of Commerce in 1967 estimated the U.S. population in 2000 A.D. would be approximately 320 million. A drastic decline in the birthrate and changed assumptions about the future caused a major reduction in the population projections published eight years later.

[2] G. W. Schule, "How to Reach the Young Consumer," *Harvard Business Review,* March-April 1974, pp. 77–86.

DeBow's categories

TABLE 6.2 United States population by age, 1960 and 1970, and projected to 1980 and 1990

U.S. population	In millions				Per cent change		
	1960	1970	1980	1990	1960–1970	1970–1980	1980–1990
Total	180.7	204.9	222.8	245.1	+13.4	+8.7	+10.0
Under 5 years	20.3	17.2	17.3	20.1	−15.3	+0.6	+16.2
5–13	33.0	36.6	30.2	34.6	+10.9	−17.5	+14.6
14–17	11.2	15.9	15.8	12.9	+42.0	−0.6	−18.4
18–21	9.6	14.7	17.1	14.5	+53.1	+16.3	−15.2
22–24	6.6	10.0	12.3	10.6	+51.5	+23.0	−13.8
25–34	22.9	25.3	36.2	41.1	+10.5	+43.1	+13.5
35–44	24.2	23.1	25.7	36.5	−4.5	+11.3	+42.0
45–54	20.6	23.3	22.6	25.2	+13.1	−3.0	+11.5
55–64	15.6	18.7	21.0	20.5	+19.9	+12.3	−2.3
65 and over	16.7	20.1	24.5	28.9	+20.4	+21.9	+18.0
Median age	29.4	27.9	29.9	32.2	−5.1	+7.2	+8.0

Source: U.S. Department of Commerce, "Population Estimates," *Current Population Reports,* series P–25, no. 310 (30 June 1965), no. 311 (2 July 1965), no. 519 (April 1974), and no. 601 (October 1975) (Washington, D.C.: U.S. Government Printing Office).

by the demands of children found it profitable to adapt their products and promotional strategies to make them appealing to younger consumers. For example, at least a few manufacturers of furniture had items in their lines designed for use by children. A marketer of adult water skis actually made a pair less than 3 feet long for use by toddlers. By 1970, the percentage of children under 14 had fallen from 30 to 26, but the actual number had remained almost constant. The subteens of the sixties became the teen-agers and young adults of the seventies. (The percentage of persons 18 to 24 increased 52 per cent between 1960 and 1970.) Blue jeans and track shoes, motorbikes and colas, eight-tracks and hard-rock tapes were the products of this generation.

At the other end of the population is a growing number of older citizens. The specialized needs of older consumers have created what is known as the *senior market.*

Special foods, health aids, recreational and entertainment services, and the like have been developed and promoted to satisfy the needs of the older segment in the population. Heavy concentrations of older persons are found in the well-known retirement centers in Florida, Arizona, and California. In these markets, the whole tempo of marketing is keyed to the leisurely pace of retired persons.

Educational background of the population The American population is well educated. Illiteracy rates, except in some localized markets and for certain population groups, are exceedingly low. In 1975, the total population 25 years and older had completed an average of 12.3 years of formal schooling. Table 6.3 shows the number of years of school completed by persons 25 and over. Except for the young (who are excluded from the table) and those over 55, educa-

TABLE 6.3   Years of school completed—Total population, by age, 1975
(Persons 25 years old and over as of March 1975)

Item	Population (1,000)	Years of school completed (per cent distribution)							Median school years completed
		Elementary school			High school		College		
		Less than 5 years	5–7 Years	8 Years	1–3 Years	4 Years	1–3 Years	4 years or more	
Total, 25 and over	116,897	4.2	7.4	10.3	15.6	36.2	12.4	13.9	12.3
25–29 years	16,393	1.0	2.2	2.5	11.2	41.5	19.7	21.9	12.8
30–34 years	13,699	1.1	2.8	3.5	14.0	41.9	15.8	20.8	12.7
35–44 years	22,607	2.3	4.6	5.4	16.2	42.2	13.2	16.1	12.5
45–54 years	23,586	3.3	6.4	9.2	17.3	40.2	11.4	12.1	12.3
55 years and over	40,613	8.1	13.0	19.1	16.6	26.6	8.5	8.1	10.6

Source: U.S. Bureau of the Census, ''Population Characteristics,'' *Current Population Reports,* Series P–20 (Washington, D.C.: U.S. Government Printing Office, 1976).

tional attainment is one of the factors that explain the maturity and sophistication of the American consumer. Of the adult population, 74 per cent has finished high school. These consumers are intelligent and articulate buyers. For the most part they understand their needs and are capable of making rational selections of goods and services. There persists an unfortunate temptation to underestimate the intelligence and educational attainments of the American consumer. This concept of the consumer usually comes back to haunt the misinformed seller. Most consumers refuse to be insulted or duped by marketing efforts based on an assumption of consumer ignorance. At the same time, however, it is well for the marketing manager to reflect that the typical consumer is not a college graduate. The design of products and instructions for the use of products should be developed with the customers' educational attainments in mind. Too often, for example, owners' manuals or assembly instructions appear to have

been written for use by graduate engineers and not for use by average owners. Sales presentations and advertising copy used by some firms appear to be similarly inappropriate. A firm that is customer oriented must adapt its marketing program to the educational attainment of the market segment it seeks to serve.

Race and national origin   The importance of the civil rights movement in the United States highlights that the American population is not nearly so homogeneous as is popularly assumed. We are tempted to think that the American melting pot of the turn of the century has long since been removed from the sociological stove. We assume, for the most part, that the varied racial and national groups that immigrated here in the last hundred years have been assimilated into the American population. To a considerable extent this is true, but differences continue to exist. Although 90 per cent of the population in the United States in 1975

TABLE 6.4 Nativity and parentage of the population, 1900, 1930, 1960, and 1970
In millions and percent of total

| Year | Total population | Native born | | | Foreign born |
		Total	Native parentage	Foreign or mixed parentage	
1970	203.2	193.6	169.6	24.0	9.6
1960	179.3	169.6	145.3	24.3	9.7
1930	110.3	96.3	70.4	25.9	14.0
1900	66.8	56.6	40.9	15.6	10.2
		Per cent of total population			
1970	100.0	95.3	83.5	11.8	4.7
1960	100.0	94.1	79.1	15.0	5.9
1930	100.0	87.3	63.8	23.5	12.7
1900	100.0	84.7	61.3	23.4	15.3

Source: 1970 Census of Population, Characteristics of the Population, United States Summary (Part 1, Section 1) (Washington, D.C.: U.S. Government Printing Office, 1973), p. 361.

was classified as white, there are large numbers of nonwhite consumers who constitute important market segments. For example, the approximately 25 million black persons in the United States are one of the most important single market segments.[3] Special products, unique distribution methods, and specially designed media have emerged to serve this market. For instance, *Ebony* magazine has a circulation penetration in its own market segment equal to that of the most popular national consumer magazines.

Of course, the nonwhite population is not spread evenly across the nation. Certain geographical areas have much higher proportions of nonwhite consumers than do others. Migration from the deep South to northern industrial centers in the last thirty years has moderated the extreme differences in the geographical distribution of the non-

[3]D. E. Sexton, "Black Buyer Behavior," *Journal of Marketing,* October 1972, pp. 36–39.

white population. However, considerable geographical differences continue to exist. A typical large metropolitan market in Pennsylvania, Michigan, or Illinois may have 50 per cent of its population in the nonwhite category. Suburban areas of metropolitan centers and intermountain rural communities have far less than the national average.

Table 6.4 presents the nativity and parentage of the population in 1900, 1930, 1960, and 1970. At the beginning of this century, 61 per cent of the population was of native parentage. This proportion has increased steadily in succeeding generations. According to the 1970 census, 84 per cent of all Americans were native born of American parents. Foreign born in 1900 accounted for 15 per cent of the population, and this percentage has declined in seventy years to less than 5 per cent. The slowing of immigration into the United States is a principal cause. Of course, almost 400,000 foreign persons enter the United States each year.

DeBow's categories

TABLE 6.5   Population of the United States, excluding armed forces overseas, by geographic division

	Population (in thousands)			
	1950	1960	1970	1975
New England	9,314	10,509	11,883	12,198
Middle Atlantic	30,164	34,168	37,274	37,263
East North Central	30,399	36,225	40,313	40,979
West North Central	14,062	15,394	16,360	16,690
South Atlantic	21,182	25,971	30,805	33,715
East South Central	11,477	12,050	12,839	13,544
West South Central	14,538	16,951	19,388	20,855
Mountain	5,075	6,855	8,348	9,644
Pacific	15,115	21,198	26,600	28,234

Sources: *1960 Census of the Population, Characteristics of the Population, United States Summary* (Part 1—Section 1) (Washington, D.C.: U.S. Government Printing Office, 1964), pp. 1–16. *Current Population Reports*, series P-25, no. 430 (29 August 1969), no. 460 (7 June 1971), no. 520 (July 1974), no. 533 (October 1974), and no. 615 (November 1975) (Washington, D.C.: U.S. Government Printing Office).

However, the total American population swallows up this modest influx with no appreciable change in its overall character.

Whereas national origin had considerable bearing on markets at the turn of the century, these differences tend to be less important today. However, as with racial differences, pockets of individuals of common national descent are found here and there in the United States. Frequently these are second- or third-generation citizens who retain many of the attitudes and tastes of their forebears on other continents. Some groups are recent arrivals. Puerto Ricans have entered the United States in sizable numbers only since 1950, and many have settled in New York's Harlem area. Cuban refugees have established their own communities in several Florida cities. Some 600,000 Asians from the Philippines, Korea, and Vietnam entered the United States between 1971 and 1975. Of less recent but of considerable market importance are the Scandinavians in Wisconsin and Minnesota. Communities of German, Italian, and Polish consumers are found in almost every city. These consumers have specialized wants and often exhibit buying behavior that differs from the rest of the population. These differences are most obvious in food buying; but national differences also account for particular demands in books, phonograph records, motion pictures, clothing, home furnishings, and the like.

Spatial Factors

Geographical distribution   The population of the United States is not distributed evenly over the nation. Historical, geographic, and climatic factors influence spatial distribution. Two types of locational distributions are of particular importance. First, the distribution of the population among the important regions of the country is important in locating the consumer market.

Table 6.5 shows the population of the United States according to major census regions for four selected years. Although the two most heavily populated regions of the United States are the Middle Atlantic and the East North Central areas, these are not the regions experiencing the greatest rates of population increase. Since the 1930s, the Pacific area, in particular California, has experienced a constant influx of people from other states seeking the benefits of employment or climate. The Mountain region, stretching from the Rockies to the Sierras, is the least populous area of the country and primarily for this reason has shown the largest rate of increase, even though the absolute population gains since 1950 have been relatively modest. The South Atlantic region also has grown. Florida in particular has undergone the second big population and economic explosion in its recent history.

Those regions in which rapid population changes have taken place are important to firms seeking opportunities in marketing. New families in an area mean new homes, new shopping centers, new schools, new highways, and the host of goods and services required to establish these consumers in the manner of living they seek. In general, population increases generate marketing activity.

The second important aspect of the spatial distribution of the population involves the concentration of persons in urban communities. Table 6.6 shows the distribution of the population in 1960 and 1970 in large cities, suburbia, and rural communities. As we see, three fourths of all twentieth-century Americans live in urban markets, and well over half dwell in or close to the largest cities in the nation. However, a sizable proportion still make their homes in typically rural areas. We should not conclude that these rural residents are necessarily living on farms or dependent on farming for their support. In 1970 there were approximately 3 million

TABLE 6.6   Urbanization of the population

	Number (in thousands)	
	1960	1970
Central cities	57,975	63,922
Urban fringe	37,873	54,525
Suburban	29,420	30,878
Total urban population	125,268	149,325
Rural population	54,054	53,887

Sources: 1970 Census of the Population, Characteristics of the Population, United States Summary (Part 1—Section 1) (Washington, D.C.: U.S. Government Printing Office, 1973), pp. 46–47.

farms. Assuming the national average of three to four persons per family, it is clear that almost four nonfarm families reside in rural areas for every farm household. These nonfarm families are supported either by decentralized industry or by service establishments required to maintain the local economy.

Mobility of the population The data we have looked at so far might leave the impression that the population is relatively fixed geographically, since absolute gains are shown for every region of the nation. The regional changes in population shown in Table 6.5 were spread, of course, over a period of twenty-five years. Actually a remarkable number of people are always on the move. About half of the 1970 population had moved by 1975.

A great deal of the movement, of course, is local (within the same Standard Metropolitan Statistical Area). But approximately one fifth of all households actually made nonlocal moves. The moving of a household and its relocation in a new market always gives rise to new and expanded demands for goods and services.

Another aspect of mobility that is important in marketing is the day-to-day movement of people within a market. Modern life requires an individual to leave a residence frequently and to cover a considerable amount of ground. Certain elements in the marketing world are especially interested in this type of local mobility. The outdoor advertising industry, for example, is extremely concerned with the numbers and types of persons who are on the move in any market. Automobile dealers, bus firms, taxicab companies, and the like find their basic marketing opportunities in consumer mobility.

Household Characteristics

Obviously, many items are neither purchased for nor consumed by individuals alone. For marketing purposes, therefore, certain groups have more meaning than do individual consumers. The most significant group for consumer-goods marketing is the family or household.[4] In 1975, there were 71 million households, which together are the target of a vast consumer marketing effort. Household formations tend to follow population patterns by approximately a twenty-year lag. For instance, the baby boom of the

---

[4]"A family consists of two or more persons living in the same household who are related to each other by blood, marriage, or adoption; all persons living in one household who are related to each other are regarded as one family. . . . A household consists of all the persons who occupy a housing unit. A house, an apartment, or other group of rooms, or a single room is regarded as a housing unit when it is occupied or intended as occupancy as separate living quarters." *1960, Census of Population Characteristics of the Population, United States Summary* (Washington, D.C.: U.S. Government Printing Office, 1964), pp. xxii–xxiii. A household, therefore, might be made up of more than one family; or a family might be broken up into two or more households. The distinction is important in statistical analysis of the population; it tends to be less important in describing group behavior in marketing.

TABLE 6.7   Households in the United States for selected years, 1960 to 1975, and projections, 1980 and 1990

Year	Number of households (thousands)
1960	52,799
1965	57,436
1970	63,041
1975	71,120
1980	79,356
1990	94,270

Source: U.S. Bureau of the Census, "Population Estimates," *Current Population Reports,* Series P–25, no. 607 (Washington, D.C.: U.S. Government Printing Office, August 1975).

postwar period had an important effect on the formation of households in the mid-1960s. Table 6.7 shows the trend of the number of households as well as projections for 1980 and 1990.

The household is a key factor in consumer analysis. Characteristics of households are important in explaining wants and purchases. The same types of general population statistics used to describe individuals are usually available for households. For instance, Table 6.8 presents selected characteristics of households—color, age of head of the family, and size of the family. Just as these types of population data help explain the wants and behavior of individuals, the data in Table 6.8 can help us to understand the nature of wants and the patterns of household behavior.

Economic Factors

Income A distribution of household income for the year 1974 is shown in Table 6.9. Almost half of all American households received income between $5,000 and $15,000. About 20 per cent had less, and

TABLE 6.8   Characteristics of families in 1975

	Number (in thousands)	Per cent of total
All households	71,120	100.0
Color		
White	62,945	88.5
Nonwhite	8,175	11.5
Age of head		
14–24 years	5,832	8.2
25–34 years	14,935	21.0
35–44 years	11,877	16.7
45–54 years	12,944	18.2
55–64 years	11,308	15.9
65 years and over	14,295	20.1
		100.0
Size of household		
1 person	13.9	19.6
2 persons	21.8	30.6
3 persons	12.4	17.4
4 persons	11.1	15.6
5 persons	6.4	9.0
6 persons	3.1	4.3
7 persons or more	2.5	3.5
		100.0

Source: U.S. Bureau of the Census, "Population Characteristics," Current Population Reports, series P–20, no. 291 (Washington, D.C.: U.S. Government Printing Office, 1976).

about 35 per cent received more. Currently, almost 80 per cent of all American households have an income over $5,000. But what of the poor? Twenty-six million persons (12.3 per cent of the population) are members of households living below the poverty level. These persons experience genuine hardship and often are unable to purchase even the necessities of life. But, for many families much purchasing power remains to be spent on discretionary goods and services. It is this ability and willingness to spend discretionary cash that supports a tremendous marketing opportunity.[5]

[5]Discretionary income is that amount that remains from gross income after taxes and the cost of food, clothing, and shelter have been deducted.

TABLE 6.9   Per cent of 1974 income of households

Family income	Number (in thousands)	Per cent
Under $5,000	15,025	21.1
$5,000 to 9,999	16,799	23.6
$10,000 to 14,999	15,695	22.1
$15,000 to 24,999	16,843	23.7
$25,000 and over	6,758	9.5

Source: U.S. Bureau of the Census, "Consumer Income," Current Population Reports, series P–60, no. 100 (Washington, D.C.: U.S. Government Printing Office, 1975).

Credit Not all purchasing power arises from current income. Another important source is savings. And credit is still another. In many marketing situations, credit has proven to be a means not only of selling additional goods but of materially increasing the standard of living of lower-income and middle-income segments of the population.

It has been estimated that as much as one third of all retail sales are made on credit. The percentage, of course, is much higher on the purchases of certain consumer durables, such as automobiles, furniture, and boats. In 1976, for example, $193.3 billion of installment credit were extended to consumers for the following purposes:[6]

Purchase of automobiles	$63.0 billion
Purchase of mobile homes	4.8 billion
Home improvement	6.7 billion
Revolving credit	29.7 billion
All other, including personal loans	88.1 billion

At any given moment there are substantial amounts of consumer credit outstanding or owed. The amount outstanding on December 31, 1976, was $185.5 billion.[7] This consumer indebtedness breaks down as follows:

[6]*Federal Reserve Bulletin,* December 1977, p. A43.

Automobiles	$66.1 billion
Mobile homes	14.6 billion
Home improvement	11.0 billion
Revolving credit	14.4 billion
All other, including personal loans	79.4 billion

Some economists view this amount of consumer indebtedness with concern. The experience of the Great Depression tells us that a period of protracted economic recession results in many individual bankruptcies. Much of the outstanding consumer debt is secured by mortgages on real or personal property. Repossessions could result and, as in the 1930s, the market value of the collateral might not cover the debt. Some people believe that we will never again face such a depression because the federal government now has the power and the instruments to protect the economy from drastic swings in the business cycle. However, the deep recession of 1974 to 1975 raised again a basic concern over the amount of consumer debt outstanding. We find some optimism in the fact that most households seem able to weather short-term downturns reasonably well. A study of one postwar period of unemployment showed that fewer than 7 per cent of a sample of households owning or buying automobiles lost them by sale or repossession during a period of extended unemployment for the household head. These households made many adjustments in their spending patterns, but they did not become insolvent.

Family expenditure patterns For many years economists and sociologists have been interested in differences in spending patterns in different market segments. Probably the first observations of differences in

[7]Ibid., p. A42.

spending patterns according to income level were made by a German statistician, Ernest Engel, over a century ago. Engel studied the spending patterns of low-income working-class families. His observations, which were reinforced later by studies in England and in the United States, gave rise to a number of generalizations we know as Engel's laws.

1. As a family's income increases, a smaller percentage is spent on food.
2. As a family's income increases, approximately the same percentage is spent on clothing.
3. As a family's income increases, approximately the same percentage is spent on rent, fuel, and household operations.
4. As a family's income increases, an increasing percentage is spent on all other items.

The generalizations are based on data showing the relationship between percentages of income spent on various categories by families in different income groups. Contemporary consumer income-expenditure relationships are shown in Figure 6.1. Such information is useful in explaining the differences in wants among families of different incomes *at a given point in time.* It does not really imply what would happen over time as income changed. The concept of market segmentation suggests a more appropriate statement of these relationships. Income-segment laws might be stated as follows:

1. A low-income family spends a higher proportion of its income on food than does a high-income family.
2. Regardless of the level of income, families tend to spend about the same proportion of income on clothing, rent, fuel, and household operations.
3. A low-income family spends relatively less on discretionary items than does a high-income family.

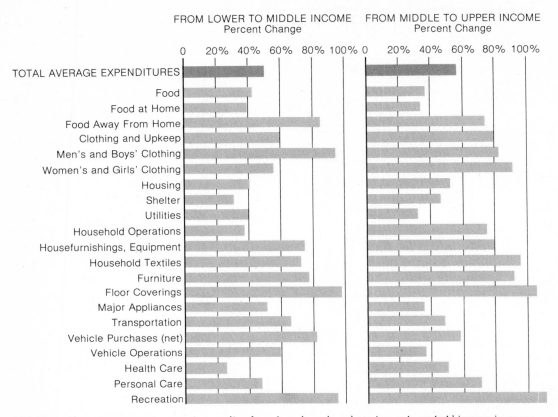

This chart shows the percent increase in spending for selected goods and services as household income increases. For example, as we move from the middle to the upper income brackets, total household expenditures for consumption rise by somewhat over 55%. Total spending for food, however, grows by about 35%, while outlays for recreation more than double. As defined in this presentation, "lower income" includes households in the $5,000–$10,000 earning bracket; "middle income," the $10,000–$20,000 bracket; and "upper income," the $20,000-and-over bracket. All data are based on a survey by the Bureau of Labor Statistics on consumer expenditures in the year 1973.

FIGURE 6.1   Relation of changes in income to expenditure patterns

Source: F. Linden, "Downstairs, Upstairs," *Across the Board* 14, no. 10. Copyright © 1977, The Conference Bureau.

On the basis of Figure 6.1, it is not altogether accurate to say that as a family's income increases it will necessarily or immediately alter its spending pattern to conform to its new income. As a matter of fact, experience indicates that this does not happen and that individuals whose income changes radically tend either to change their spending patterns slowly or to overadjust them beyond the patterns of the group they have joined.

Closely related to the analysis of expenditures by income is the study of the apparent effect of changes in the composition of the family over time. The changes that come about as children join the household, mature, and eventually leave to start families of their own are referred to as the *family life cycle.* The results of an investigation of the effect of family life cycle on the purchase of recreational products and services is shown in Table 6.10. Logically, a high proportion (43.0 per cent) of toys and play equipment is bought by families with small children. Spectator- and participant-sports expenditures are high for families with teen-agers. Families without children patronize clubs, raise pets, and travel.

Consumer Expectations

Besides the many obvious demographic and economic factors that describe consumers in their marketing environments, a psychological element also is important. It is not simply what consumers are able to spend on consumer goods and services that influences their purchase decisions. The marketing manager also must anticipate what these consumers *plan* to buy. Periodic studies are made of consumers' buying intentions. The results of one such study, published by the Conference Board, are shown in Table 6.11. This table compares consumer intentions to purchase automobiles, houses, selected household durables, and travel from January 1973 through February 1976. This kind of information is useful to marketing managers in planning new product introductions, scheduling inventories, and designing promotional strategies. Consumer intentions reflect not only present economic conditions but future expectations. Thus, a marketer can utilize information on consumer intentions to gauge the optimism or pessimism of consumers and guide the marketing program accordingly.

Nonconsumer markets

Business Establishments

Other groups besides ultimate consumers or households are important in the marketing system. A group may be *formal,* such as a church or a corporation, or *informal,* such as a social club or a neighborhood. At this point, it is useful to mention one type of formal group in the marketing environment—the business establishment. Every business buys goods and services in the open market, as a study of the expense section of any profit and loss statement will indicate. How large is the business market? Table 6.12 presents a breakdown of the approximately 13 million business establishments. Most of the businesses clearly are marketing firms—retailers and wholesalers—but all are important in creating demand.

Institutions

Another important segment of demand is made up of various types of nonprofit institutions, such as schools, hospitals, prisons, and so on.[8] The institutional population of the United States (excluding schoolchildren) in 1970 was 2,119,066. The enrollment in schools of persons five to thirty-four years of age for the same year was 51,913,000, more than half of the population in that age group. Institutions are important customers. In 1974, there were 7,174 hospitals, of which 2,698 were operated by the government. Almost $42 billion (exclusive of new construction) was spent by hospitals in the same

---

[8]Data in this paragraph are from the *Statistical Abstract of the United States, 1976* (Washington, D.C.: U.S. Government Printing Office).

TABLE 6.10   Estimated consumer expenditures for recreation according to family life cycle, 1966

Item	Total	Families with children				Families without children	
		Child under 6		6 or over only			
		Some under 6	All under 6	All 6 to 11	Any 12 or over	Husband wife	Other
Distribution of all families	100%	13.5%	11.5%	4.0%	26.5%	24.5%	20.0%
Recreation	100	17.0	12.5	6.0	36.5	19.0	9.0
TV, radios, musical instruments	100	16.0	12.0	6.0	36.0	20.5	9.5
Television, portable or table	100	16.0	12.5	4.5	27.0	25.0	15.0
Other television sets	100	15.5	14.0	4.0	33.5	24.5	8.5
Radios, portable or table	100	17.5	9.0	5.5	39.0	19.0	10.0
Other radios	100	17.0	21.5	5.0	34.5	13.0	9.0
TV and radio repairs	100	15.5	10.0	5.0	31.5	26.5	11.5
Phonographs, tape recorders	100	16.5	10.5	6.5	42.5	14.0	10.0
Hi fi components, kits, parts	100	16.0	15.0	3.0	37.0	13.0	16.0
Records, magnetic tapes, reels	100	14.0	12.5	6.0	43.5	14.5	9.5
Pianos and organs	100	14.5	10.0	12.5	38.5	17.0	7.5
Other items	100	22.0	4.5	14.0	49.5	6.5	3.5
Spectator admissions	100	14.0	10.5	4.0	45.0	16.0	10.5
Movies, indoor	100	14.0	8.5	4.0	50.0	14.0	9.5
Movies, drive-in	100	20.0	21.0	4.0	39.0	11.5	4.5
Sports events	100	14.0	9.5	5.0	44.0	18.5	9.0
Concerts, plays, other admissions	100	10.0	9.5	3.5	36.0	22.5	18.5
Participant sports	100	16.5	12.5	6.0	40.0	19.0	6.0
Hunting and fishing equipment	100	18.0	13.0	6.0	36.0	22.0	5.0
Other sports equipment	100	18.0	11.0	6.5	42.0	15.5	7.0
Dues and fees for sports	100	16.0	13.0	5.5	41.5	18.0	6.0
Club dues and memberships	100	13.5	8.0	6.0	37.0	27.0	8.5
Hobbies	100	13.5	12.0	5.5	36.5	23.5	9.0
Cameras	100	12.5	19.0	6.0	34.5	20.0	8.0
Other photographic items	100	15.0	17.0	5.0	33.0	20.0	10.0
Crafts and other hobbies	100	11.5	8.5	5.5	41.0	22.0	11.5
Pets (purchase, supplies, equipment)	100	16.5	10.5	7.0	36.5	23.0	6.5
Pet food	100	13.5	9.0	5.5	36.5	27.0	8.5

TABLE 6.10   Estimated consumer expenditures for recreation according to family life cycle, 1966 (*cont.*)

| | | Families with children | | | | Families without children | |
| | | Child under 6 | | 6 or over only | | | |
Item	Total	Some under 6	All under 6	All 6 to 11	Any 12 or over	Husband wife	Other
Toys and play equipment	100	43.0	26.0	8.5	20.0	2.0	.5
Dolls and accessories	100	43.0	22.0	11.5	19.5	2.5	1.5
Stuffed toys and infant toys	100	30.5	44.5	3.5	17.5	3.0	1.0
Tricycles	100	42.5	41.5	3.5	10.5	1.0	1.0
Wagons, skates, sleds	100	37.5	17.5	9.5	32.5	2.0	1.0
Games, puzzles, mechanical toys	100	38.5	18.0	11.5	28.5	2.5	1.0
Other toys and equipment	100	38.0	29.5	9.0	21.5	1.5	.5
Lump-sum expenditures	100	48.5	26.0	7.0	16.0	1.5	1.0
Recreation out of home city	100	12.0	9.5	5.0	39.5	23.5	10.5
Other recreation	100	12.5	7.0	5.0	35.0	20.5	20.0

Source: F. Linden, ed., *Market Profiles of Consumer Products* (New York: National Industrial Conference Board, 1967), pp. 132–133.

TABLE 6.11   Consumer expectations and intentions

| | 1976 | 1975 | | 1974 | | 1973 | |
	Jan-Feb	July-Aug	Jan-Feb	July-Aug	Jan-Feb	July-Aug	Jan-Feb
Consumer confidence index*	93.3	77.3	50.9	69.1	56.0	83.3	99.4
Buying plans index	126.3	104.6	80.0	81.1	89.2	111.6	102.7
Percentage planning to buy within 6 months							
New car	5.4	3.4	2.9	3.7	2.7	4.1	5.0
Used car	4.6	3.8	2.2	3.1	2.1	3.4	2.9
Home	4.0	2.9	2.0	2.9	2.7	3.8	3.1
Refrigerator	4.7	4.6	4.1	5.5	5.2	5.3	4.1
Color TV	6.5	7.1	5.3	5.4	5.8	5.8	5.8
Percentage planning to vacation within 6 months							
Within state	6.1	10.8	10.6	12.9	11.3	12.3	10.3
Other states	35.5	30.7	25.6	28.4	23.4	30.5	30.9
Abroad	3.9	3.6	3.4	3.6	3.6	4.3	5.3
Means of travel							
Automobile	34.5	36.1	30.4	33.8	27.1	36.7	34.1
Airplane	11.1	9.1	7.3	9.7	8.7	8.9	10.2
Other	2.1	2.6	2.3	2.6	3.1	2.4	1.8

*The confidence index measures overall consumer optimism.

Source: "Consumer Attitudes and Buying Plans," *Conference Board Record,* March 1974, March 1975, and March 1976.

TABLE 6.12   Numbers of business establishments

(in thousands), 1966 and 1973

	1966	1973
Agriculture, forestry, fishing	3,357	3,586
Mining	73	86
Construction	856	1,099
Manufacturing	402	449
Transportation, public utilities	359	434
Wholesaling	434	548
Retailing	2,047	2,329
Finance, insurance, real estate	1,223	1,576
Services	2,714	3,367
	11,465	13,474

Source: U.S. Internal Revenue Service *Statistics of Income, Business Income Tax Returns,* preliminary reports (annual).

TABLE 6.13   Selected years, governmental units in the United States

Type of government	1962	1967	1972
U.S. federal	1	1	1
States	50	50	50
Local	91,185	81,248	78,218
Counties	3,043	3,049	3,044
Municipalities	17,997	18,048	18,517
Townships	17,144	17,105	16,991
School districts	34,678	21,782	15,781
Special districts	18,323	21,264	23,885
Total	91,236	81,299	78,269

Sources: U.S. Department of Commerce, *Government Units in 1962* (Washington, D.C.: U.S. Government Printing Office, 1962); and U.S. Department of Commerce, "Governmental Organization," *U.S. Census of Governments, 1967 and 1972* (Washington, D.C.: U.S. Government Printing Office).

year. Much of this was payroll expense, but a substantial part of it represented demands for goods and services purchased in the marketplace. In 1974 there were 109,517 schools. Expenditures in public and private schools for plant operation and maintenance in the same year were $9.5 billion.

Clearly, the institutional market is an important source of demand. Opportunities to provide goods and services for the various types of institutions are expanding somewhat faster than the population is increasing, since each year more attention is being paid to the expansion of institutional services.

Government

Table 6.13 presents a classification of government units during selected years. In addition to the local governments, there are, of course, the federal and state governmental bodies. Governments of all types are extremely important customers. In 1974 government expenditures amounted to $408.1 billion. Of this, $297.2 billion was spent by

federal departments and agencies; the balance was spent by state and local units. Much of this outlay (41.6 per cent) was in the form of payments for personal services. However, estimates of government purchases of goods and services from business suggest that they amounted to about half of the total outlay.

Segments and Segmentation Strategy

The concept of the market has been presented, and various markets of importance have been described. These markets, whether consumer or industrial, were presented as aggregates embracing many different kinds of individual customers. Variables, such as age and income, were used to describe *all* customers. Special insight into the consumer market was gained as these variables were inspected; however, the overall impression should have remained that the consumer market is an aggregate composed of individuals who are not identical but similar enough to present the appearance of homogeneity. The concept of the market segment is based on the opposing point of view, that the differences are more important than the similarities. The balance of this chapter is concerned with this opposite perspective.

What Is a Market Segment

The idea of market homogeneity originated in economics. The theory of perfect competition did not explicitly stipulate buyer homogeneity (except in terms of rational behavior), but until the theory of imperfect competition was presented, the notion of buyer similarity appeared implicitly in economic reasoning. This is because the explicit requirement of product homogeneity is logical only if buyers also are identical. Both assumptions are relaxed in the theory of imperfect competition, and special applications of it, such as the theory of price discrimination, are based on the explicit requirement of different demands for the same product. The illusion of market homogeneity in contemporary marketing theory was dashed by Alderson.[9] His theory of marketing was based on the concept of the heterogeneous market. In the extreme case, this means that each consumer is unique in at least one important respect, and in this respect is like no other person. In other respects, consumers may be more or less similar. In view of all of the variables that affect consumer behavior and the varying degrees to which these variables may influence specific individuals, it must be obvious that the blending of these variables creates

[9]For example, see W. Alderson, *Dynamic Marketing Behavior* (Homewood, Ill.: Richard D. Irwin, 1965), chaps. 1 and 2.

an almost infinite number of combinations. The result of these different combinations is market heterogeneity.

Complete market heterogeneity overstates reality. Pockets of similarity, known as *segments,* do exist. Thus, in spite of the fact that each consumer differs from every other, it is still true that each consumer tends to be more like some consumers than like others. For example, although each teen-ager has unique physical and psychological characteristics, he or she tends also to be more like other teen-agers than like any person in a different age bracket. Such a group of consumers, similar to each other in some respects but not in all, is said to be a *market segment.* Obviously, the basis of similarity among consumers in a segment must hold marketing significance.

All markets are composed of segments. So-called mass markets are actually made up of segments, and these segments in turn usually are composed of subsegments. For example, the teen-age segment might be further divided on the basis of age, sex, or some interest. Ultimately, because of the heterogeneity of demand, the process of seeking subsegments within segments drives the analyst to the identification of individual consumers.

What Is Market Segmentation?

Market segmentation involves the development of separate marketing programs designed to meet the needs of one or more particular segments of the market. The process is twofold: (1) identifying viable segments and (2) targeting programs toward them. It is the opposite of a general program designed to appeal to an overall market. In the extreme, a strategy of segmentation would involve the development of a different marketing program for each consumer, and we can cite examples of companies that market on this basis. Custom yacht building, some home construction, and the making of such personal products as hair pieces provide instances of marketing situations in which extreme cases of customer heterogeneity are matched by corresponding product heterogeneity.

For the most part, however, marketers √ attempt to serve market segments rather than individual consumers. It always has been true that some brands of products sell well to some consumers but not in the market as a whole. Regional differences in the preferences for various nationally advertised brands are well known. Marketing managers do not attribute these differences to chance. They know that there are basic differences among market segments. Sound marketing practice requires that a manager know how market segments differ in their attitudes toward and susceptibilities to marketing effort. From this knowledge separate segmentation strategies can be developed—assuming of course that a segmentation approach is worth the additional cost and effort involved. In many cases manufacturers do introduce multiple brands or other differences in strategy in order to meet the needs of particular segments.

In summary, a market segment is a meaningful buyer group. Segmentation is a customer-oriented approach designed to identify and serve that group. These are two highly important, related concepts. But not all segments present marketing opportunities. To be meaningful they must satisfy each of five requirements.

Requirements for Segmentation

A segment must be specifically identified and measured   The segment must be clearly defined. Who is in the segment? Who is out-side the segment? After these questions have been answered, it is then important that demographic, social, and cultural data about segment members be obtained. These data should permit the measurements of the size and importance of the segment as a potential object of marketing strategy. Unfortunately, obtaining segment data is seldom easy, especially when the segment is defined in terms of behavioral characteristics.

A segment must evidence adequate potential   Either an actual or a potential need must exist in order for a segment to present an opportunity. *Actual needs* are recognized needs—overt demands for existing goods and services. *Potential needs* can be transformed into perceived wants through education or persuasion. Potential needs are more difficult to ascertain than are actual needs, but there are usually many more of them.

Marketers should develop strategies only for substantial segments, whether actual or potential. If the segment is too small to justify a separate marketing program, it should not be used to develop a segmentation strategy. This requirement demands the ability to measure both the intensity of need and the strength of the purchasing power to support it. Needs plus purchasing power create effective demand. The ability to buy stems from income, savings, and credit. Purchasing power stemming from one or more of these three sources must belong to the members of a market segment in order for it to represent a meaningful marketing opportunity.

A segment must be economically accessible   Segmentation involves a search for enough similarity among buyers to permit the seller to reach these potential customers economically. For example, segment members could be concentrated geographically, shop at the same stores, or read the same kinds of magazines. Regrettably, many important segments, for instance those based on motivational characteristics, cannot be reached economically. Consider the problem of Beecham, Inc., marketers of MacLean's toothpaste, in attempting to reach a segment of the dentifrice market identified by the user's desire to enhance sex appeal. This company is forced to advertise to the general market, purchasing prime-time television spots in major markets. Without doubt this advertiser does reach the desired segment by the use of television, but it also reaches many other consumers as well. The cost per segment member reached is accordingly much higher than the cost per television viewer. Sometimes specific market segments can be reached economically with mass media. Gillette has been able to reach its market segment by placing radio and television commercials on major sporting-event programs. The characteristics of viewers of these programs match the characteristics of major users of Gillette products. Other advertisers, such as Ford, have used the same programs without the same closeness of fit between audience and market segment. In the case of Ford, its relevant segment is probably larger than the audience reached by sporting-event programs. Accordingly, it also places advertisements in prime-time evening hours. Similar coverage for Gillette would be extremely wasteful.

A segment must react uniquely to marketing efforts A fourth criterion for determining the advisability of segmenting a market in some particular way is differential response by segment consumers to marketing effort. There must be a reason for using different marketing approaches in the various segments. Different segments, unless they re-spond in unique ways to particular marketing inputs, hardly justify the use of separate marketing programs.

Another way of describing this requirement is to point out that what the marketer wants is equal marginal response from the last unit of marketing input applied in each market.[10] If different segments responded in the same way to additional increments of marketing input, the manager would simply allocate effort to the various segments using essentially the same marketing approach but varying the level of activity in each segment to correspond to its potential. However, when the shapes of the response functions differ among segments, the only way to optimize the marketing operations is to vary the type of input and the amount. This calls for differences in program as well as spending levels. Thus, for segmentation to be meaningful, segments should differ in their responsiveness to marketing effort.

A segment must be reasonably stable over time Marketing strategies are long-range plans that project three to five years into the future. Moreover, lead times of up to a year often are needed to analyze a market and to prepare a plan. Segments that emerge rapidly and disappear just as quickly do not offer very good marketing opportunities for a firm that follows the generally accepted approach. Highly innovative entrepreneurs can, however, and at considerable risk, attempt to serve these segments. The marketer of Pet Rocks fared well. In contrast the firms that produced souvenirs for the Bicentennial were sadly disappointed. Some big companies have been similarly misled. Consider the Edsel and E. J. Korvette's huge discount stores. Both attempted to serve segments that were shrinking at the time.

[10]H. Assael, "Segmenting Markets by Response Elasticity," *Journal of Advertising Research,* April 1976, pp. 27–36.

Bases of Segmentation

In discussing the requirements for a meaningful market segment, various ways of identifying segments were mentioned.[11] It is important to inspect these bases thoroughly and to describe those that are used commonly.

How are market segments identified?[12] We identify a segment by searching for those factors that make some consumers more like one another than they are like the market as a whole. The descriptions of various aspects of the consumer market in the first part of this chapter provide a good starting place. In all, we will discuss seven different bases used to identify market segments.

Geographic bases Historically the first, and probably the most obvious, basis for segmenting markets has been geography. Regional differences in consumer tastes for products as a whole are well known. Markets identified according to location are readily pinpointed, and considerable data about them can be obtained. Practical limitations, such as a lack of production capacity and financial restrictions, confine many compa-

nies to marketing on a local or regional basis. Geographical segmentation is thrust on them. Some national concerns also have been able to benefit by the use of segmentation strategies rooted in geographical differences. The advantages of this approach are obvious. Marketing effort can be concentrated in exactly the places where potential customers reside. Local or regional advertising media can be used efficiently. The sales organization and physical distribution facilities can be optimally assigned.

The obvious disadvantage to a geographical basis of segmentation is that consumer preferences often bear no clear-cut relationship to location. Also, geographic market segments tend to be rather large. It would be unusual and uneconomical for a national company to develop separate segmentation strategies for more than two or three geographical segments. A geographical segment, for instance the southeastern part of the United States, obviously contains many meaningful subsegments, and the geographical coincidence of the people residing in that area may be more than offset by other influences on behavior. Members of a geographic segment tend, therefore, to be far too heterogeneous to qualify as a meaningful target for marketing action.

Demographic bases By far the most common approach to segmentation has been the identification of buyer groups according to selected demographic characteristics. Although demographic segmentation has been challenged, it offers the obvious advantage that segments can be easily identified. For example, the marketing manager of a carpet manufacturing company might decide that three factors, family income, size of family, and home ownership, are the basic segmentation variables. Ideally, the manager would like a cross-tabulation of these varia-

[11]Discussions of segmentation usually are devoted to consumer-goods marketing. Industrial market segmentation also is practiced. The same principles apply. Commonly used bases of industrial market segmentation are geography, type of industry, channel of distribution, type of technology, usage of particular raw materials, and common buying practices.

[12]The analysis of segments has become one of the most popular areas of marketing research. New concepts and techniques have been developed. For the most part they involve sophisticated quantitative methods that go beyond the scope of this text. For readers interested in exploring this topic, the following articles are suggested: H. Assael and A. M. Roscoe, Jr., "Approaches to Market Segmentation Analysis," *Journal of Marketing,* October 1976, pp. 67–76; N. K. Dhalla and W. H. Mahatoo, "Expanding the Scope of Segmentation Research," *Journal of Marketing,* April 1976, pp. 34–41; and L. Percy, "How Market Segmentation Guides Advertising Strategy," *Journal of Advertising Research,* October 1976, pp. 11–26.

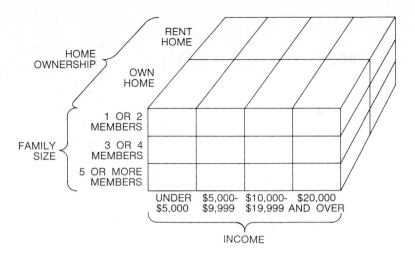

FIGURE 6.2   Three-dimensional market segment matrix for a carpet manufacturer

bles to pinpoint targets precisely. Figure 6.2 shows how the carpet market might be segmented into a three-dimensional matrix using these three demographic breakdowns. Since household income contains four breakdowns, family size contains three, and home ownership, two, there are twenty-four possible cells in this three-dimensional matrix.

The analyst next must determine the exact number of households in each segment or cell of the matrix. Approximate annual usage rates can be applied to the population data to determine the absolute potential of each segment. In an extremely sophisticated approach the profitability of the higher-potential segments might be estimated by considering such other data as brand share, competitive activity, and the probable expense of attaining a target level of sales. Segments with the highest sales level or profit potential can thus be identified. Of these, only those that are accessible are selected. One determination of accessibility would be the availability of advertising

media capable of being directed to the particular segment. Finally, when all requirements for segmentation have been satisfied, strategies can be developed for each selected segment and used as a basis for marketing activity.

Vast amounts of demographic information are available, and differences in population characteristics appear to explain general differences in usage rates for product classes fairly well. The relationships seem almost too obvious to require statistical verification. Baby foods are bought primarily by families with very young children, and nationality foods are most popular with ethnic groups in the population. Young people drive motorcycles and sports cars; families with small children purchase station wagons; and successful businesspeople drive large comfortable sedans. These are obvious and expected. However, other less obvious relations also exist. Baby foods also are consumed by invalids and senior citizens; and nationality foods are particularly popular with young mobiles. Carpenters and painters usually drive station wagons, and high-powered sports cars are not exclusively preferred by young drivers.

Notwithstanding its apparent advantages, there is considerable uncertainty about demographic segmentation. The method frequently is misused. Too often, detailed cross-tabulations are ignored, and oversimplified demographic analyses are used. A typical misuse of the approach has been to construct profiles of product users. For example, it might be said that the typical consumer of Mexican food is under thirty-five years of age, has a college education, earns over $15,000 a year, lives in a suburban fringe of a moderate-sized community, and resides in the West. True, these characteristics do describe many consumers of Mexican food, but they also describe a lot of other people as well. The crude process of averaging that produces this profile hides the extreme differences that exist among consumers of Mexican food as well as the principal motivational forces influencing its consumption. A most important influence on a preference for Mexican food is a consumer's exposure to it through travel or residence in

Mexico or the southwestern United States. The existence of this influence is seldom ascertainable from even refined demographic analysis. Recent attempts to explain consumer usage of products or brands of products have tended to concentrate on qualitative aspects of consumer segmentation. It is argued by some that such qualitative factors as opinion, attitude, and motivation are more important determinants of product usage than are demographic characteristics.

Research was undertaken in the early 1960s to test how well demographic variables explain differences in consumption. Since the problem is particularly critical to marketers of packaged consumer goods and since data on household consumption of food and proprietary drug products were available, most of the research involved these kinds of products. In general, studies that have been undertaken have failed to confirm the intuitive notion that demographic variables affect consumption. In one of these studies it was determined through multiple-regression analysis that, in forty-six of fifty-seven product categories, less than 20 per cent of the variation in consumption could be explained

TABLE 6.14   Distribution of users and nonusers of selected personal-care products

	All users	Heavy users	Moderate users	Light users	Nonusers
Females					
Home permanents	16.5	3.1	5.1	8.4	83.5
Hair sprays	53.5	4.9	19.6	29.0	46.5
Hair coloring	28.3	3.5	8.9	15.9	71.7
Lipstick	70.7	20.2	20.2	30.3	29.3
Nail polish	54.5	12.5	17.3	24.7	45.5
Males					
Talcum powder	37.3	3.7	14.1	19.4	62.7
Electric shavers	35.4	2.7	20.0	12.7	64.6
Shave cream	64.3	38.6	15.8	9.9	35.7
Hair coloring	5.8	.9	1.3	3.7	94.2
Cologne	49.1	4.2	17.9	27.0	50.9

Source: *Target Group Index*® *1977* (New York: Axiom Market Research Bureau, 1977).

by a total of fourteen socioeconomic characteristics. The highest proportion of explained variation was 29 per cent for one product, and for twenty-five product categories the proportion of explained variation in consumption was less than 10 per cent!

The conclusion that a demographic basis of segmentation is not helpful in predicting consumer purchasing has not gone unchallenged. Bass suggests that, while no significant relationship between purchasing by households and their socioeconomic characteristics has been found, it is entirely possible that *groups* of households with similar characteristics may still evidence distinct consumption patterns. Bass, Tigert, and Lonsdale studied selected demographic data for light buyers and heavy buyers of ten different packaged consumer products. They concluded that "it is clear from the range of variation of mean purchase rates between the segments that socioeconomic measurements provide a meaningful basis for segmentation."[13] Obviously, more research will be necessary before these two somewhat conflicting views are resolved. Meanwhile, the most recent segmentation studies follow the approach of identifying a segment on some nondemographic basis and then of using demographic data to profile the members of the segment.

Usage as a basis for segmentation Historically, the first departure from pure demographic segmentation was an approach suggested by Twedt, in which he stressed the importance of the *heavy user* as a basis for developing marketing strategy. Twedt's analysis of household consumption data from a panel of *Chicago Tribune* subscribers indicated that purchase concentration "is *not*

a simple function of such obvious demographic variables as income or size of household."[14] His solution is to measure consumption directly, isolate the heavy users, and then aim promotion input directly at them. Twedt's heavy user (sometimes called *heavy half*) theory has been widely accepted. Table 6.14 shows the usage data for selected product categories.

One of the charms of the usage approach is that particular companies are often in a good position to identify their own high-volume customers.[15] Internal or industry-wide sales analyses are generally feasible through normal data processing. For example, banks can determine heavy users of banking services because the customers' names are recorded in connection with each service used. Insurance companies can study policy holders in depth because of the vast amounts of information obtained from insurance applications. Department stores can analyze their charge account and other credit customers. Marketers of durable goods frequently make use of information obtained from warranty registration cards. Public information, such as boat and automobile registrations, often can isolate heavy users. Finally, all marketers of consumer packaged products can make use of several nationwide panels of households that are maintained by marketing research companies.

Psychographic segmentation Psychographics, a recent approach to market segmentation, has emerged as a major alternative to the older methods. In a fundamental sense, it is not a different approach. Researchers in the 1950s and 1960s explored the possibility

[13]F. M. Bass, D. J. Tigert, and R. T. Lonsdale, "Market Segmentation: Group Versus Individual Behavior," *Journal of Marketing Research* 5 (August 1968): 266.

[14]D. W. Twedt, "How Important to Marketing Strategy Is the 'Heavy User'?" *Journal of Marketing,* January 1964, p. 71.

[15]S. M. Barker and J. F. Trost, "Cultivate the High-Volume Consumer," *Harvard Business Review,* March-April 1973, pp. 118–122.

of segmenting on such bases as personality and attitudes but were generally unable to produce definitive results. In retrospect, it is easy to understand the failure of the first attempts. The studies generally embraced only one behavioral independent variable—for example, personality. We now know that consumer behavior is multidimensional and that numerous independent variables must be considered. Not until large computers were designed and sophisticated statistical techniques were developed could marketing analysts cope with multiple variable psychological segmentation. But this is now possible, and we refer to the approach as *psychographics.*[16]

Emanuel Denby is said to have coined the term. He defines it as follows: "Psychographics seeks to describe the human characteristics of consumers that bear on their responses to products, packaging, advertising, and public relations efforts."[17] What differentiates psychographics is not its purpose, or even its content; it is its methodology. Its method has two principal elements: the use of large probability samples and the use of sophisticated statistical techniques.

The use of large probability samples ensures that a data base adequate for obtaining statistically significant results that can be extrapolated to the national market will be obtained. By using such powerful statistical techniques as multiple-regression analysis, factor analysis, cluster analysis, multiple-dimensional scaling, perceptual mapping, and multiple-discriminant analysis it is possi-

ble to analyze a market for segmentation purposes with far greater precision than was possible even ten years ago.

Psychographic studies can employ any or all of several consumer descriptors. Among these are the traditional bases of usage and demographics, which we have already described. In addition, three other variables are usually employed. They are (1) product attributes, (2) life-style variables, and (3) psychological variables, such as self-image, personality, and attitudes.[18]

Product attributes The painfully slow progress in establishing operational validity to the theory of market segmentation has stimulated the development of an approach that has been called *product segmentation.*[19] Its basis is found in the differences that people perceive in the various products that are available to them. The approach is based on the fact that consumers can differentiate between products and, on the basis of their respective needs, identify those that satisfy their needs best. Thus product preferences emerge. Presumably, product segments can then be classified according to the kind and extent of product characteristics exhibited. A segment, then, is composed of those consumers who prefer a particular product.

A key concept in using product attributes is the idea of *product space.* All products can be thought of as occupying a position in a universe of products. Start with the simplest example, a two-dimensional map. Figure 6.3 shows the positioning of various personal sporting activities along two dimensions—cost and safety. If other variables, such as social prestige and a degree of physical exertion, are important, a concept of multidi-

[16]For an excellent review of the development of psychographics and its present status, see W. D. Wells, "Psychographics: A Critical Review," *Journal of Marketing Research,* May 1975, pp. 196–213. The 148-item bibliography accompanying this article is as comprehensive as most readers will need to become thoroughly familiar with the development of psychographics.

[17]E. Denby, "Psychographics and from Whence It Came," in W. D. Wells, ed., *Life Style and Psychographics* (Chicago: American Marketing Association, 1974), p. 13.

[18]Ibid., p. 18.

[19]N. L. Barnett, "Beyond Market Segmentation," *Harvard Business Review,* January-February 1969, pp. 152–266.

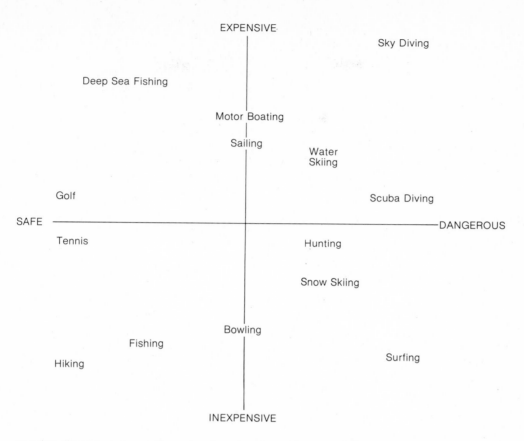

FIGURE 6.3   Map of two-dimensional product space for personal recreation

mensional product space would be appropriate. Statistical techniques for performing the more complex mapping function are available, but the basis is in the consumers' perceptions of various products' (or services') attributes.

A logical extension of this concept is the search for new or potential product segments. Segmentation becomes a search for areas of opportunity, defined in terms of product characteristics that are not provided by existing products. Significant unsatisfied consumer demands create opportunities for marketers to design products whose characteristics match these needs. The entire pro-

cess of marketing, including distribution, promotion, and pricing, can be tuned to this opportunity.

The contrast between this approach and traditional methods of market segmentation should be obvious. The segment is identified in terms of perceived product characteristics rather than in terms of user characteristics. True, a segment is still composed of people (not products), but these individuals are completely homogeneous with respect to their perceptions of a particular product or brand. Market segments defined exclusively in terms of user characteristics often include many individuals who do not have any inter-

TABLE 6.15   Benefit segmentation of the toothpaste market

	Segment name			
	The sensory segment	The sociables	The worriers	The independent segment
Principal benefit sought	Flavor, product appearance	Brightness of teeth	Decay prevention	Price
Demographic strengths	Children	Teens, young people	Large families	Men
Special behavioral characteristics	Users of spear-mint-flavored toothpaste	Smokers	Heavy users	Heavy users
Brands disproportionately favored	Colgate, Stripe	MacLean's, Plus White, Ultra Brite	Crest	Brands on sale
Personality characteristics	High self-involvement	High sociability	High hypo-chondriasis	High autonomy
Life-style characteristics	Hedonistic	Active	Conservative	Value oriented

Source: Reprinted from R. I. Haley, "Benefit Segmentation: A Decision-Oriented Research Tool," *Journal of Marketing,* July 1968, p. 33, published by the American Marketing Association.

est in the product that the marketer wants to provide.

In product segmentation we assume that consumers perceive products as bundles of characteristics that may satisfy needs. This is particularly true of new products introduced to match specific unmet consumer demands. It is reasonable to inquire whether segments might not be identified directly on the basis of satisfactions desired as opposed to product characteristics. This is precisely the concept behind Russel Haley's approach, which he calls *benefit segmentation.*[20] Consumers, he argues, can be classified on the basis of the kind of product benefits demanded. To be significant, these benefits must differ considerably from one group to another. For example, the benefits sought by buyers of Chevrolets differ considerably from the benefits sought by purchasers of Oldsmobiles.

Table 6.15 presents a hypothetical seg-

[20]R. I. Haley, "Benefit Segmentation: A Decision-Oriented Research Tool," *Journal of Marketing,* July 1968, pp. 30–35.

mentation analysis for the toothpaste market. It assumes that a benefit segmentation study has been conducted and that four major segments have been identified. One of these segments is health oriented, concerned primarily with preventing decay. Another segment, presumably socially oriented, is most concerned with the appearance or brightness of the teeth. A third segment seeks personal gratification in the use of the product, being concerned principally with flavor and appearance. The final segment is economically motivated, looking primarily for a price benefit. In order to profile the segments shown in Table 6.15, a good deal of demographic and behavioral information about toothpaste consumers has been gathered. This is a good example of a psychographic study involving a number of variables.

Life-style variables   *Life style* refers to the mode of living of a whole society or any of its segments. It is often the principal focus in

TABLE 6.16   Variables in life-style segmentation

Activities	Interests	Opinions	Demographics
Work	Family	Themselves	Age
Hobbies	Home	Social issues	Education
Social events	Job	Politics	Income
Vacation	Community	Business	Occupation
Entertainment	Recreation	Economics	Family size
Club membership	Fashion	Education	Dwelling
Community	Food	Products	Geography
Shopping	Media	Future	City size
Sports	Achievements	Culture	Stage in life cycle

Source: Reprinted from J. T. Plummer, "The Concept and Application of Life-Style Segmentation," *Journal of Marketing,* January 1974, p. 34, published by the American Marketing Association.

psychographic research. Life style is composed of a number of elements. A team of researchers at the University of Chicago developed sets of three widely applicable elements: activity, interest, and opinion (AIO).[21] Plummer used the same general AIO classification, but added demographics to complete a segmentation analysis.[22] Plummer's list of life-style variables are found in Table 6.16. While this is not the only scheme for classifying life-style variables, it is illustrative of the life-style approach.

For marketing purposes, a segment defined in terms of its style of living must respond uniquely to marketing efforts—as well as satisfy the other criteria of importance, economic accessibility, and stability. Psychographic studies have indicated that life style does provide a useful basis for segmentation, especially when segments also

are profiled on demographic, attitudinal, and media-preference dimensions.

The marketing implications of psychographic segmentation appear obvious. Product development can be based on a clear impression of the benefits consumers seek. Competitive action can be framed on the basis of consumers' perceptions of how well alternative brands provide the benefits sought. Advertising and sales promotion strategies can be cued directly to particular market segments. Copy strategy and media selection can be geared to appeal to particular audiences. Finally, pricing decisions can be reached more intelligently when the needs of consumers, balanced against the benefits sought, can be appraised in terms of willingness and ability to buy.

Psychological variables We already have learned how important the psychical factors are in explaining consumer behavior. In fact the first attempts to go beyond demographics explored the basic psychological dimensions: personality, self-concept, and attitude. But attempts to segment on these bases alone almost always were unsuccessful. It was not until two important methodologi-

[21]T. P. Hustad and E. A. Pessemier, "The Development and Application of Psychographic Life Style and Associated Activity and Attitude Measures," in W. D. Wells, ed., *Life Style and Psychographics* (Chicago: American Marketing Association, 1974), pp. 31–70.

[22]J. T. Plummer, "The Concept and Application of Life-Style Segmentation," *Journal of Marketing,* January 1974, pp. 33–37.

cal changes were made in segmentation analysis that psychological variables became fruitful descriptors of consumer behavior. The first involved the development of special scales (measuring devices) to identify market-relevant psychological variables. The second methodological change was to blend psychological and life-style variables in the forerunners of contemporary psychographic studies. Today, a whole battery of psychological variables can be incorporated in psychographic segmentation studies.

Application of Segmentation Concepts

Although the present-day theory of market segmentation seems clear, its application is not simple. A number of steps are involved. The first step is to define precisely the basis for segmentation that will be used. A great deal of knowledge about the market and considerable experience with it are highly desirable. Research into consumer motivation is almost mandatory.

On the basis of the general rule that from four to seven segments usually are found, the next step in the application of segmentation theory is the collection and analysis of data concerning each market segment. At this stage, it is particularly important that the number of consumers in each segment and the extent of their effective demand be estimated. Clearly, only important market segments are meaningful for marketing action.

The third step in segmentation strategy is to apply the criteria of a good segment. These are, as we recall, that (1) a segment must be identified and measured, (2) a segment must be important, (3) a segment must be economically accessible, (4) each segment

must differ in its response to a marketing effort, and (5) a segment must be reasonably stable over time. It is apparent that more than one segment might qualify for consideration as the basis for marketing action, and it also ought to be clear that none might do so. It may be as important at this stage to learn that a segment is not an area of potential opportunity as to discover that it is.

The last step in segmentation strategy is the development of action programs to deliver the benefits consumers want. This involves the development of marketing programs for both the short- and the long-run. A thorough discussion of this step would take us far beyond the scope of this chapter. At this stage it is enough to contemplate three alternative types of strategies based on the concept of market segmentation.

Alternative Segmentation Strategies

Undifferentiated marketing The first approach is really not a segmentation strategy. It is based on the assumption that the marketer finds no basis for segmenting and attempts to reach the market as a whole. Not everyone will buy; but a general appeal should attract sufficient volume without the necessity of tailoring the company's products and methods of marketing to particular segments. For certain types of widely consumed convenience items, the unsegmented marketing approach may be reasonable. Gasoline marketing is an example. Although brands of gasoline are sold in at least three types—regular, premium, and unleaded— the general promotion of the brand does not appear to reflect this distinction. Shell promotes its "extra mileage ingredients"; car owners are told that Gulf is "good"; Conoco is "the hottest brand going." Simple general appeals in mass advertising media and constant reminders at the point of sale characterize this kind of undifferentiated marketing. Many packaged food products are also sold across the board. Campbell's soups, Pillsbury cake mixes, C&H sugar, and Jeno's pizza rolls are offered to all consumers.

Undifferentiated, or unsegmented, marketing makes sense for products that have more or less universal appeal. It offers certain advantages over segmented marketing. It makes possible the use of economies of scale in manufacturing and marketing by avoiding multiple products, competing brands, and duplicated inventories. Generally, the cost of marketing per unit of product sold is minimized under an undifferentiated approach.

It is apparent, however, that relatively few companies today base their approach on this notion. Exceptions can be found even in the examples cited above. The advantages of even a crude segmentation approach appear to be too obvious. The undifferentiated approach, when followed by two or more sellers attempting to capture the same general market, results in very intense competition—especially in advertising. Though there is cost efficiency in using mass media, profitability actually may decline as the spending among competitors increases. Individual products and services become victims of unpredictable brand switching. In this way the company marketing fails to take advantage of a basic opportunity to create a differential advantage and to establish for itself an unassailable market niche.

Differentiated marketing A company using the second approach attempts to modify its product and methods of marketing to more or less match the demands of two or more market segments. Examples of differentiated marketing surround us. The soft drink companies clearly have moved away from the generalized, undifferentiated approach that

they used a few years ago. Almost all major soda companies market to at least two segments—the regular and the diet markets. Since young people consume more than 40 per cent of all cola beverages, both Coca Cola and Pepsi Cola have made particular efforts to appeal to the youth market. Sometimes they do so with a special product, such as Pepsi's Mountain Dew. More often, they employ selected advertising appeals. The same company urged young consumers to join the "Pepsi Generation."

There is almost no end to the list of consumer-product marketers who use the differentiated approach. Radio and television manufacturers, automobile firms, sporting-goods firms, clothing manufacturers, and the like, all develop unique products and promotions designed to appeal to two or more segments in the overall market.

The advantages are rooted in the concept of segmentation. A customer-oriented firm must adapt to the needs of particular customers. By so doing it places itself in a unique competitive position where it stands to serve these customers best. This is a true competitive advantage. In many respects it is easier to develop marketing programs for segments than for the market as a whole. Of necessity, consumers within a single segment are more homogeneous. Their needs are uniform and more easily detected. To these considerations should be added the prospect of greater sales by serving more than one market segment. Theoretically, there is greater potential in developing marketing programs for two or more segments than in trying to persuade all customers to buy a single product not quite suited to their particular needs.

But there is a price to be paid for the advantages. Generally, the costs of manufacturing and marketing increase when a strategy of differentiated marketing is followed. Economies of scale are sacrificed. Administrative problems arise. Larger and more complicated organizational structures are usually involved. Planning becomes more difficult, and control, less effective. On balance, the advantages of differentiated marketing outweigh the drawbacks. The prospects of greater sales, a stronger competitive position, and hoped-for greater profit in the aggregate entice most American firms toward differentiated marketing.

Concentrated marketing A third approach to market segmentation involves the selection of one, or at the very least a few, market segments, as the precise and only targets on the company's marketing action. We call this *concentrated marketing.* Examples are easy to find. The Rolls-Royce appeals to only the wealthiest and highest socially positioned automobile buyers. Volkswagen, in contrast, has not attempted to trade outside of the lower price range. Timex carved itself a niche in the "disposable" watch market. Similar examples can be found in almost every category of consumer-goods marketing. It is even more obvious in industrial marketing where firms elect to concentrate their technical and manufacturing talents in providing goods and services for narrowly defined market segments. Some manufacturers of automotive parts, for example, sell only to one or two manufacturers.

Concentrated marketing has special appeal. It permits the seller to direct the full force of the company's effort in a narrow area of opportunity. If successful in adapting to the needs of that single market, the company can virtually dominate it. The strategy is economical and particularly attractive to a company without extensive resources. While it suffers from the disadvantage of limiting the potential to a single segment, this strategy is the major means by which a company creates for itself an impregnable market niche.

A good example of concentrated marketing is found in the strategy followed by Zenith Radio Corporation. It defined its target segment as that part of the buying public primarily motivated by a desire for product reliability. (This is a good example of the benefit segmentation described earlier in the chapter.) In selecting this segment, Zenith probably was influenced by the strong position it had attained in the television receiver market by becoming established in the minds of consumers as the leading exemplar of product reliability. Zenith had long produced products of good workmanship. This became particularly important to consumers facing the mounting threat of poor service, delays in service, expensive service, or no service at all on sets that broke down in the home. Zenith set out to convince the public of its products' reliability, emphasizing the use of hand-wired rather than printed circuits. Servicepeople and retail stores in the Zenith channel system lent strong support. Advertising drove home the message to every potential buyer. Zenith's market share soared to the point where one out of five sets sold carried its name. True, some people bought Zeniths for another reason, price for example. And many bought competitors' brands for other reasons, probably styling and prestige. But the Zenith strategy of concentrated marketing carved out a permanent position for Zenith in the television industry. The example would not be complete without mention of the approach of its major competitor. RCA vigorously pursued its development of color and maintained its claim to leadership by this action. Other manufacturers elected to concentrate their efforts on segments seeking convenience, portability, or the prestige of beautiful cabinetry. Each of these was in some degree a reflection of a concentrated marketing strategy, based on the benefits sought by different consumers. These companies survived and prospered at least in part because of their segmented approaches. They did not attempt to market some theoretically optimum receiver. Rather they directed their attention to a definitive segment of the market that they were uniquely fitted to serve. The firms that did not make the grade, the ones that were shaken out, were those that were not able to distinguish themselves as peculiarly capable of serving the needs of some particular market segment.

The dangers of concentrated marketing are rather obvious. Putting all of one's eggs in a single basket restricts growth opportunities and makes one particularly vulnerable to a successful competitive attack. Many firms, while using a concentrated strategy at the core of their marketing effort, do not leave themselves unprotected. Some seek a hedge in other corporate activities. Others flank out from the core segment and seek additional business in other markets. In the last analysis, the difference between differentiated and concentrated marketing is one of degree and emphasis. Probably most firms prefer the advantages derived from concentrated marketing but seek the insurance brought by an appeal to additional segments of the market.

Dynamic Segmentation

A final word of caution: We should not conclude that once a company finds its segment its problems will be solved forever. The market is changing constantly. Segments are loose aggregations that are subject to considerable modification over time. Developments in the television industry provide a good example. Competition from foreign companies forced a number of firms, including Zenith, to change their strategies and even to abandon the market altogether.

Change is particularly critical in segments based on psychographic variables. Perceptions and attitudes are volatile; benefits are subject to dramatic alteration. Consider the so-called status symbols of the new rich or affluent blue-collar workers. These markets were once important for black and white television, then for color, and recently for neither as other products have replaced them as symbols of status. Because of such changes, marketers must monitor the market constantly to detect changes in it, adapting their strategy accordingly. We call this process *dynamic segmentation.*

Summary

Marketing takes place to serve markets, to deliver a standard of living. We can define a market as a geographical place or as a group of persons. Usually both elements are involved.

There are various types of markets. The most important, from many viewpoints, is the consumer market. The consumer market, composed of individuals and households, can be analyzed according to various characteristics. These include demographic factors, spatial considerations, family aspects, and economic factors. Some awareness of each of these areas and of the changes taking place in them is important in understanding the consumer market.

There are nonconsumer markets, including businesses, institutions, and various branches and levels of government. Numerically these markets are far smaller than the consumer market, but they represent a disproportionately greater demand for goods and services.

Market segments are parts of the overall market. Members of a segment are more like each other than they are like the market as a whole. Segments can be identified on geographic, demographic, usage, psychological, product, and benefit bases. Geographic and demographic bases are the easiest to apply, but there is some doubt among marketing practitioners as to their usefulness in isolating unique pockets of demand. Psychographic segmentation is an attempt to incorporate life style and other variables in ways that provide statistically significant results.

To be useful as a basis for developing marketing strategy, a market segment must meet five tests or requirements. It must be specifically identified and measured; it must evidence adequate potential; it must be economically accessible; it must react uniquely to marketing efforts; and it should be reasonably stable through time. Once a marketer has identified the existence of one or more market segments, there are three general approaches that can be followed. There is undifferentiated marketing, which does not involve any effort to match the program to a particular segment. Differentiated marketing is an attempt to develop separate programs for each of several market segments. Finally, concentrated marketing, in which the marketing strategy is aimed at a single important market segment, can be considered.

Questions and Problems

1. What is a market segment? Why is the concept said to be the single most powerful tool of modern marketing?

2. Find examples of specific products, distribution methods, and advertising campaigns for a particular market segment.

3. On what bases could your class be divided into market segments? Identify some product or services that one segment might purchase but another segment would not.

4. What is psychographic segmentation? How does it differ from traditional approaches?

5. Identify at least three products not mentioned in this chapter that are marketed by an undifferentiated approach. Why do you think these products are sold in this way?

6. Select a product and thoroughly analyze the ways in which its overall market might be segmented. Explain the logic of your segmentation scheme. Test each segment against the requirements mentioned in this chapter. Which segment(s) would you recommend using to plan marketing strategy?

7. What kinds of segmentation might you expect to find for the following products:
   a. A ten-speed bicycle
   b. A portable hair dryer
   c. An inexpensive sports car
   d. A dishwasher
   e. A high-energy cereal
   f. A vitamin candy

8. What significance do you see in the absolute and relative increases in population to the marketing of the following:
   a. Automobiles
   b. Chemicals
   c. Building materials
   d. Personal services
   e. Metal-working equipment

9. It has been said that the American population is becoming older and younger at the same time. Is this possi-

ble? What are the facts about the changing age structure? What might these changes mean to such marketing activities as new-product development, pricing, and advertising?

10. A great deal of interest has been generated in recent years in the black market. Find out as much as you can about this market segment. In what specific ways, if any, does it differ from other market segments? Since only about 10 per cent of the population is black, do you think the interest in this market is justified from a marketing point of view?

11. Assume that you have to make some recommendations regarding the location of shoe stores that a vertically integrated shoe company plans to operate. In 1975 the company had 250 stores distributed geographically as follows:

New England	25
Middle Atlantic	80
East North Central	60
West North Central	15
South Atlantic	20
East South Central	10
West South Central	15
Mountain	5
Pacific	20

The company plans to have 300 stores by 1980. Where should these stores be located? Explain.

12. According to the heavy-half, or usage, approach to segmentation, 87 per cent of all hair tonics is used by 24 per cent of the consumers. What are the implications of this fact to the marketing of such products as Vitalis or Brylcreme?

7

Market Measurement and Forecasting

Market measurement and forecasting are critical tasks in marketing management. They contribute data that help answer these three vital questions:

1. *What is the potential of a given market segment?* As we learned in Chapter 6, only segments with adequate potential represent good marketing opportunities. Measurement of the potential of a market segment is an important step in the development of a strategy of market segmentation.
2. *What is the planning gap?* As we recall from Chapter 3, the planning gap is the difference between an objective and the forecast of sales given no change in the existing marketing strategy.[1] A forecast is needed to identify the planning gap.
3. *What kind and amount of marketing effort will be required to close the planning gap?* This question involves the prediction of an outcome of a possible strategy. We

call this kind of prediction *conditional forecasting.*

The answers to all three questions are based, at least to a degree, on the theory of demand. We will look briefly at some of the elements of demand theory before considering the practical aspects of its application.

The Determinants of Demand

To the economist, demand is the willingness and the ability to buy. Behind it lie a host of influences we know as *demand determinants.*[2] Until recently, economics has been concerned almost exclusively with the determinants of demand that are measurable. Thus,

___

[1]You will find it useful to reexamine Figure 3.2. The flow chart shows the relation between the topics covered in this chapter and the overall marketing planning process.

[2]Readers with a background in economics will recognize that the treatment in this chapter is an abbreviated version of selected topics in managerial economics. If an expanded discussion is desired, there are intermediate economic theory texts that can provide appropriate background reading. For example, see E. Mansfield, *Economics: Principles, Problems, Decisions* (New York: W. W. Norton, 1974).

demand analysis originally considered only such objective phenomena as population, price, and income. Contemporary analyses, however, also incorporate the findings of opinion research, thereby including in demand analysis information on attitudes and expectations.

Demand is a complex subtle economic phenomenon; but even in highly sophisticated mathematical treatments, three fundamental determinants play a very important part.

Consumer Tastes and Preferences

Demand is rooted in consumer wants—in buyers' basic tastes and preferences. In the aggregate these tend to be fairly stable in the short run, but they are subject to change over a longer period. Shifts in demand may result from changes in cultural, economic, attitudinal, or demographic factors, or from sellers' promotional efforts. We explored these phenomena in Chapters 4 and 5.

Income

Disposable personal income—the income people have left after paying taxes—is a second important factor influencing consumer demand. Consumption of almost all types of products, except the humblest necessities, increases as disposable income rises. This is shown in Figure 7.1. In the aggregate, consumption rises as income increases but by less than the amount of the income increase.

Although this declining propensity to consume appears characteristic of consumption generally, the demand for most goods does increase absolutely as consumer incomes rise. However, the demand for some goods and services rises much more noticeably

Table 7.1   Income sensitivity coefficients, selected commodity groups

Commodity group	Coefficient
Total personal expenditures	1.0
Durable goods	1.1
Nondurable goods	1.0
Services	.9
Automobiles and parts	1.0
New cars and net value of used cars	1.2
Tires, accessories, and parts	.7
Clothing and shoes	.5
Food and beverages	.8
Household operation	1.4
Personal services	.6

Source: U.S. Department of Commerce, Office of Business Economics.

than do others. We use the phrase *income sensitivity of demand* to identify the relationship between an increase in disposable income and the corresponding change in the consumption of particular types of goods and services.[3] Table 7.1 presents a tabulation of sensitivity measurements for selected products and services. In analyzing consumer demand for any particular product, it is helpful to know the precise relationship between changes in income and changes in consumption. It is possible, by using such sensitivity measures, to predict with fair accuracy the level of demand for any forecasted level of disposable personal income. For example, if 6.7 million new cars were sold in a recession year such as 1975, and economic forecasters predicted a 3 per cent increase in real disposable income for 1976, the anticipated level of automobile sales would be around 6.9 million (6.7 + 6.7 (.03 × 1.2) = 6.94). Of course sales might be

[3]The sensitivity coefficient indicates the average per cent by which consumption increases over a base period, corresponding to a 1 per cent increase in disposable income.

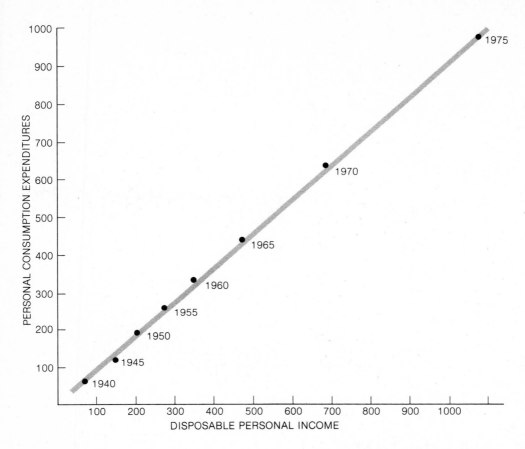

FIGURE 7.1 Personal expenditures related to personal disposable income, 1940–1975

Source: U.S. Department of Commerce, *Business Statistics,* 1969; *Statistical Supplement to Survey of Current Business,* 1975; and *Survey of Current Business,* August 1976.

forecast at more or less than 6.9 million, depending on other demand determinants—such as the availability of gasoline, expected price increases, and the like.

Substitute Products

The availability of substitutes is another factor that affects the pattern of consumer demand. Built into a consumer's desire for a particular product is the awareness of alternative ways of satisfying a need. For instance, consumer demand for automobiles is affected by the availability of public transportation. The degree of substitutability of one product for another is difficult to measure, however. One approach is to analyze the effect of a price change for one product against the corresponding change in sales of

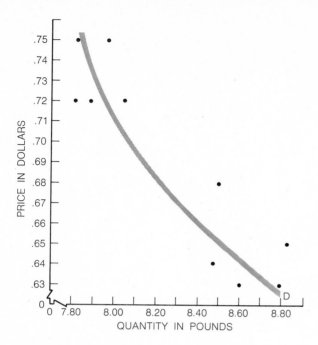

FIGURE 7.2   The demand curve (poultry, meat, and fish)

Source: Data adapted from J. S. Duesenberry and L. C. Preston, *Cases and Problems in Economics* (Englewood Cliffs, N. J.: Prentice Hall, © 1960), p. 45.

a substitute product. If there is a measurable influence, the products are said to be *close substitutes*.[4]

For most products, the relationship between the availability of substitutes and the amount of demand is inverse. However, the opposite situation also can occur when the relationship between two products is complementary. For example, the demand for automobile accessories, such as tires and

batteries, is influenced by automobile ownership and usage. The demand for TBA (tires, batteries, and accessories) items in service stations is said to be *derived from* and *complementary to* the demand for automobiles.

Price

Price has always been considered the principal determinant of demand. Other potential demand determinants are assumed to be relatively constant, particularly in the short run. Regardless if the market prices that prevail are competitive or are administered, the relationship between price and demand

[4]The phrase *cross-elasticity of demand* identifies this type of measurement. Specifically, the relative change in the sales of one product is divided by the relative price change of its substitute. The higher the ratio, the greater the substitutability of the two products.

is fundamental.[5] Ordinarily this relationship is inverse; that is, a regression line showing the relationship between price and quantity has a negative slope. For example, Figure 7.2 shows a scatter diagram and a freehand regression line depicting the price-quantity relationship in the demand for poultry, meat, and fish. The regression line in the figure is frequently called a *demand curve.* Demand curves may take any shape, depending on the situation being described. Often, for convenience, they are drawn as straight lines. However, it is generally believed that most demand curves are nonlinear and assume shapes quite similar to that shown in Figure 7.2.

Price-quantity relationships also are expressed mathematically. If the scatter diagram permits the fitting of a curve with known mathematical properties, the appropriate equation can be constructed. Even for an erratic regression, mathematical measurements can be applied to specific price and quantity data. The most commonly used measurement is that of *price elasticity of demand.* This is the ratio between a relative change in quantity demanded divided by the relative change in price. The price elasticity of demand is expressed in the form of an equation:

$$E = \frac{Q_1 - Q_2}{Q_1 + Q_2} \bigg/ \frac{P_1 - P_2}{P_1 + P_2}$$

in which Q_1 is the quantity demanded prior to the price change, Q_2 is the quantity demanded following the price change, P_1 is the price prior to the price change, and P_2 is the price following the price change.

We use this formula for calculating price elasticity to infinity. A price elasticity of

precisely -1 is said to be *unitary.*[6] Any value less than -1 (for example, -0.7) is said to be *inelastic;* and any value greater than -1 (for example, -1.7) represents an *elastic* demand. Marketing executives often generalize concerning the elasticity of a product's demand. A manufacturer and marketer of table salt, for example, might logically say that the demand for the company's product is inelastic. This means that a price change would be accompanied by a less than proportionate change in quantity demanded. Such a relationship is important, because a company's total revenue from the sales of a product always is affected by the price that it charges and the quantity that it sells. For instance, in the case of an inelastic demand, we can assume that a price increase will result in a substantial increase in total revenue, while a price decrease might have a devastating result. Figure 7.3 shows such a case as well as two other hypothetical demand curves. Part A represents a demand that is inelastic; part B, a unitary demand curve; and part C, an elastic demand situation.[7]

Demand Functions

We might assume that one determinant of demand, such as price or income, can be studied at a time and its effects isolated from those of all other determinants. This as-

---

[5]A *competitive price* is one set by the interaction of buyers and sellers. An *administered price* is one set by a seller or by a group of sellers—for example, the price for oil set by OPEC.

[6]Elasticity measures typically carry a negative sign since the slope of the demand curve is normally negative—that is, most sales (Q) increases come from lower not from higher prices.

[7]Actually the price elasticity is different at all points along the straight-line demand curves shown in parts A and C of Figure 7.3. However, application of the elasticity formula to any pair of data on each curve would yield a result consistent with its designation as generally inelastic (part A) or elastic (part C).

A.
AN INELASTIC DEMAND CURVE

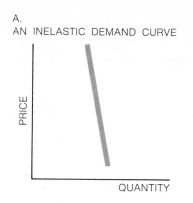

B.
A UNITARY DEMAND CURVE

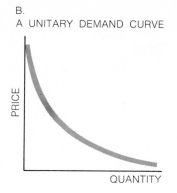

C.
AN ELASTIC DEMAND CURVE

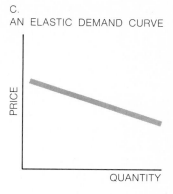

FIGURE 7.3   Three hypothetical demand curves

sumption, although convenient, is misleading. Actually, all determinants are variable, and all of them affect demand simultaneously. It is necessary, therefore, to express demand in terms of multivariable determinants. Hopefully adequate data can be generated and converted into a set of equations by fitting regression lines with known mathematical properties to the data. These equations can then be combined to predict the value of demand under any given combination of variables. Thus, the demand function is a composite mathematical statement of the relationship of the various determinants of demand. We can express it as

$$D = f(N, I, S, P)$$

in which N represents customer needs, I represents income, S represents sales of substitute products, and P represents price.

The demand for a particular product, such as gasoline, could be stated more specifically in terms of the determinants that analyses have shown to be related to changes in the level of gasoline sales. Logically, the sales of gasoline might be expected to vary with the number of vehicles in use (trucks, cars, and buses), income, and price. If G represents gasoline consumption, the demand function

for gasoline might be expressed generally as

$$G = f[(T + C + B), I, P]$$

where $T, C,$ and B represent trucks, cars, and buses in use; $I,$ discretionary income; and $P,$ price.

To be most useful for predicting demand and allocating marketing effort to specific sectors of the market and to the various elements of the marketing mix, it is desirable that such a general demand function be stated in precise quantitative terms. Of course, extensive study of the variables that affect gasoline sales would be necessary for a precise indication of the demand function. Colburn developed this demand function for gasoline:

$$G = \{[1.66T + C + 5.5B]$$
$$\times [.458 (3.151)^{1.65}] 4.74P^{-.52}\} 17TT$$

in which $TT,$ the trend factor, has been added to the symbols used in the general equation.[8]

Demand functions have been constructed

[8]L. D. Colburn, "Forecasting Sales of Demi-Durable and Perishable Goods," reported in M. Spencer and L. Siegelman, *Managerial Economics* (Homewood, Ill.: Richard D. Irwin, 1959), pp. 162–165.

for almost every type of product. A favorite object of econometric analysis has been the passenger automobile. The Department of Commerce devised the following demand equation for automobiles:

$$Y = 0.0003 X_1{}^{2.5} \; X_2{}^{2.3} \; X_3{}^{-1.4} \; (0.032) X_4$$

in which Y represents new private-passenger car registrations per 1,000 households; X_1 is real disposable income per household in base year dollars; X_2 is current annual real disposable income per household as a percentage of the preceding year in base year dollars; X_3 is the percentage of average retail price of cars to all consumers' prices, the latter measured by the consumer price index; and X_4 is the average scrappage age.[9]

Unfortunately, the extreme segmentation that has developed in recent years for various types and makes of automobiles has made this general demand function less meaningful. Demand functions for particular kinds or makes of cars are difficult to construct. Notwithstanding, demand functions such as these can be developed for any product for which the major demand determinants can be isolated and data collected. Thus, the demand equation continues to be an important tool for understanding and predicting market demand.

Market Potential

The Concept of Market Potential

The first application of the theory of demand is the measurement of potential. This measure is needed to answer the question, "What is the potential of a given market segment?" The *industry sales function* is the volume of sales that all firms in the industry enjoy at various levels of industry marketing effort. *Market potential* measures the ability of a market segment to absorb the products of an industry in a specified period of time in which the industry's collective marketing effort has been extended to the maximum (see Figure 7.4a). Market potential is the industry sales level attained when industry effort is at *I,* its theoretical maximum. Potential can be expressed in units, such as units of automobiles sold, or in dollars. Obviously, the use of the measurement of market potential depends on our definitions of the terms *market, product,* and *industry.* Sometimes these definitions present problems, particularly when attempting to identify relevant product categories or industries. For example, when estimating the market potential for trucks, should the demand for all trucks, even pick-ups and panel vehicles, be included? To do so might give a very misleading picture to a firm interested in over-the-highway, diesel-powered, tractor-trailer rigs. On the other hand, a fabricator of campers would only be interested in the potential for the pick-up variety. A food manufacturer discovered that overall estimates of market potential for Mexican foods were quite meaningless, since in various parts of the country extreme differences existed in the relative popularity of the canned versus the frozen forms. There is almost no demand for canned Mexican foods in the Northeast, where frozen Mexican entrees sell reasonably well. In contrast, there is a substantial potential for many types of canned Mexican foods in the Southwest.

The *company sales function* is the share of business that a given company can expect as it increases effort relative to the competition. *Sales potential* is the share it can expect at its maximum level of marketing effort (see

[9]"Consumer Markets for Durable Goods," *Survey of Current Business,* April 1958, p. 19.

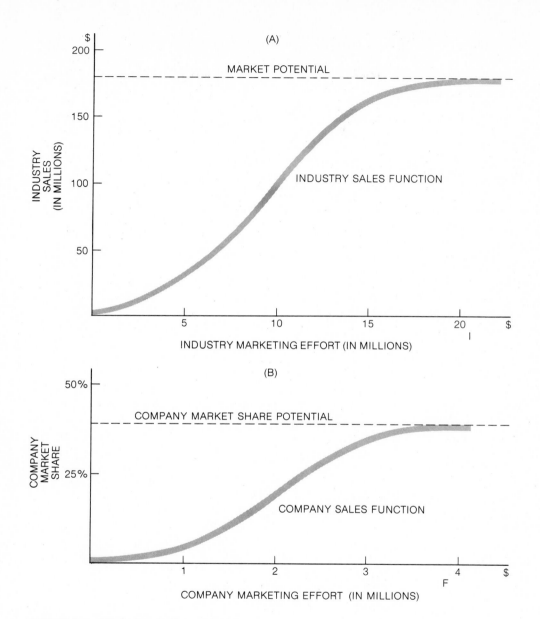

FIGURE 7.4   Market and sales potential

Figure 7.4b). As in the case of market potential, the term refers to the sales of a particular product to a specific segment. Not surprisingly, most companies' sales potentials vary considerably from one market area to the next. Sales potentials, therefore, are significantly harder to estimate than are market potentials. Also they tend to fluctuate considerably from year to year as competitors vie to strengthen their positions. Thus, it is difficult to project sales potential measurements into the future. Consider what happened over a four-year period in the share positions of two leading makers of packaged pizza mix in one southern California market. At one time, the leading pizza mix had a 34.2 per cent market share, but its principal competitor was close behind with a 33.3 per cent share. Three years later the former leader had fallen to a poor second place with a 23.9 per cent share, whereas the new leader had increased its share by almost a third to a substantial 41.0 per cent of the market. This improvement in market position was attributed to an aggressive advertising program. But most marketers would not have been willing to project such a level of change in sales potential because of the uncertainties surrounding competitive marketing.

Methods of Measuring Potential

Direct-data measurement of potential is seldom possible. There are some exceptions however. Sales of some products, such as motor vehicles and liquor, which are reported by government agencies, are relatively easy to determine. Potential for these kinds of goods does not seem to change a great deal from year to year. Thus, direct measurement of past sales often provides an adequate approximation of potential. Moreover, for some items like automobiles, both competitors' sales as well as total sales can be obtained from public records. For most other products, however, indirect measurements of market and sales potential must be made.

Regional demand functions The type of demand function described earlier in this chapter can be used to estimate market and sales potential. These equations can take one of two general forms. We can use an aggregate demand function for the nation as a whole by utilizing regional data instead of national figures. Using such a procedure assumes that the same functional relationship exists between the independent and dependent variables in a particular area as exists for the market as a whole. This is not always a sound assumption, particularly where consumer tastes differ considerably in various parts of the country. For example, per capita consumption of selected food products differs substantially in New York and California, even though income and other demand variables are fairly similar. When such a situation prevails, it is necessary to develop separate regional demand functions for the purpose of measuring potential and forecasting sales for each market area.

The great difficulty in producing regional demand functions is the lack of adequate regional economic data. Advances have been made in recent years in the collection and publication of localized economic data, but much progress remains to be made before useful regional demand functions will be available to aid in measuring potential.

Survey methods It is always possible to conduct a research study to estimate market or sales potential. This appears to be most practical when a company sells to a limited number of customers in a particular area. The smaller the market for which the measurement is sought, the easier it is to conduct a survey of buyers' intentions. For example, it is not uncommon for companies to have their regional sales offices obtain information from customers as a basis for estimating market potential. The reliability of the sales force in providing these data is, of course, somewhat questionable. For this

TABLE 7.2   Single-factor market index

Region	1975 retail sales (estimated in $1,000,000)	Index
New England	35,024	5.87
Mideast	115,592	19.37
Great Lakes	115,725	19.39
Plains	44,989	7.54
Southeast.	127,583	21.38
Southwest	54,339	9.11
Rocky Mountain	16,453	2.76
Far West	87,007	14.58
Total	596,712	100.0

Source: From "1976 Survey of Buying Power," *Sales Management,* July 26, 1976, p. A–8. Used with permission of Sales Management, Inc. Copyright 1976 by Sales Management, Inc. Further reproduction is forbidden.

reason, some firms prefer to use commercial survey services. One prominent service of this type is provided by the F. W. Dodge division of McGraw-Hill. Dodge offers a subscription service that reports new construction of various types in most of the major construction markets of the country. Using this survey, a client may make special studies that permit the preparation of reasonably accurate estimates of potential for various products used in building construction.

Market indexes   A *market index* is a number that indicates the proportion of total demand that can be expected in a particular market area. The index can be based on a single demand factor or on several. Retail sales might be used as a basis for constructing a simple index. Table 7.2 shows the distribution of retail sales in eight geographic regions and the single-factor market index that results from this distribution. According to the index, a company selling a consumer good of general appeal in the national market should expect to sell approximately 5.87 per cent of total volume in New England. It

should be pointed out, however, that most indexes are not this simple; rather they are based on several factors that regression analysis has shown to be closely correlated to sales.

A number of already-prepared market indexes are available to assist managers in estimating market potential. In the past, magazines (both industrial and consumer) have been a principal source of these indexes. For a number of years, the Curtis Publishing Company issued an index of consumer demand that utilized circulation of its magazines in addition to economic data. The Chilton Company has prepared an index and map for use by industrial companies selling to automobile parts distributors. By far the best known and most widely used of the commercial market indexes is *Sales Management* magazine's "Annual Survey of Buying Power."

The "Survey of Buying Power" includes three special indexes in addition to the single-factor indexes of population, retail sales, and effective buying (disposable) income. These three special indexes are

1. *Buying Power Index (BPI)*   The Buying Power Index is a weighted index in which a weight of .5 is given to an area's percentage of total U.S. effective buying income, a weight of .3 to its percentage of U.S. retail sales, and a weight of .2 to its percentage of the total population of the United States. Index values for two standard metropolitan areas are shown in Table 7.3.

2. *Sales Activity Index (SAI)*   This index is a measure of the per capita retail sales of an area compared with that of the nation. It is computed by dividing an area's percentage of retail sales by its percentage of U.S. population. The SAI's for the Boston and St. Louis standard metropolitan areas are shown

TABLE 7.3   Buying Power Index (BPI)

Area	Per cent effective buying income ($w = .5$)	Per cent retail sales ($w = .3$)	Per cent population ($w = .2$)	Index ($w = 1.0$)
Boston, Mass.	2.0145	1.9008	1.8321	
× weight	1.0072	.5702	.3664	1.9438
St. Louis, Mo.	1.1212	1.0990	1.0996	
× weight	.5606	.3297	.2199	1.1102

Source: Calculated from data in "1976 Survey of Buying Power," *Sales Management,* July 26, 1976.

in Table 7.4. From a comparison of these two SAI's, it is apparent that Boston has modestly greater sales activity than does St. Louis, but St. Louis is almost exactly at the national average (1.0). Presumably, Boston attracts more retail business from people who reside outside of the area—possibly tourists or commuters from outlying areas.

3. *Quality Index (QI)* This index compares the buying power per capita of an area to the corresponding figure for the country as a whole. It is computed by dividing an area's Buying Power Index (BPI) by its percentage of the U.S. population. The calculations for Boston and St. Louis in Table 7.5 show that Boston's Quality Index is 106 and St. Louis's is 105. Thus both are above par for the nation as a whole, but Boston enjoys a slightly higher overall rating.

A great deal of useful information is found in market indexes such as these. As we probe deeper into the development of marketing strategy, we shall see that these measurements of market potential have many applications, including the selection of test markets, the allocation of salespeople, the appointment of distributors, and the selection of advertising media.

Store audits The drug and grocery-product industries are particularly interested in obtaining knowledge of market and sales potential. Partly because of the explosive growth in the food industry and partly because of intense competition, marketers of packaged food products have been at the forefront of the search for this knowledge. They had discovered that statistics of manufacturers' sales and shipments provided very misleading pictures of actual demand. The

TABLE 7.4   Sales Activity Index (SAI) of two markets

	Per cent retail sales (A)	Per cent U.S. population (B)	Index 100 (A ÷ B)
Boston, Mass.	1.9008	1.8321	104
St. Louis, Mo.	1.0990	1.0996	100

Source: Calculated from data in "1976 Survey of Buying Power," *Sales Management,* July 26, 1976.

TABLE 7.5   Quality Index (QI) for two markets

	Buying Power Index (A)	Per cent U.S. population (B)	Index 100 (A ÷ B)
Boston, Mass.	1.9438	1.8321	106
St. Louis, Mo.	1.1556	1.0996	105

Source: Calculated from data in "1976 Survey of Buying Power," *Sales Management,* July 26, 1976.

principal reason is the lag between the time a manufacturer sells products and the time that they are purchased by consumers. The lag for a hypothetical new product is shown in Figure 7.5. The manufacturer's sales in six successive periods are shown by the height of the lighter bars. Retail sales of the product in the same periods are shown by the darker bars. Considerable distortion of reality occurs when we simply look at the manufacturer's sales record. From this point of view, the product apparently received immediate and substantial acceptance. Orders almost doubled in periods 2 and 3. Then disaster appeared to strike. Orders in period 4 fell to less than half of those in period 3, and they continued to decline in periods 5 and 6. However, consumer purchases actually were increasing throughout the six periods, although at a more gradual pace than that shown in the manufacturer's early order record. The reason is simple: The sales enjoyed by the producer in the first three periods were "pipeline" sales. Wholesalers and retailers were building up inventories from which consumers eventually purchased. When these stocks were complete, wholesalers cut back on their purchase rates even though consumer sales continued to improve. A hasty decision by the manufacturer to withdraw the product or to engage in a costly program of promotion could be avoided if a current measurement of retail sales such as the one shown here were available.

Except in a vertically integrated firm like Sears, Roebuck, such consumer data are not normally available from retailers. But they can be obtained in the drug and packaged food-product industries from several marketing research firms that specialize in conducting store audits. The most famous of these firms is the A. C. Nielsen Company, which maintains a panel of representative groceries and drugstores in which it conducts periodic counts of stock movement.[10].

Store-audit data are useful not only in estimating market and sales potential but also in monitoring competitors' activities and in evaluating advertising and sales promotion programs. Exhibit 7.1 lists various kinds of data available from a store-audit organization. With proper controls, it is possible to use the audit to compare movement in several market areas in which different marketing strategies have been utilized.

Warehouse withdrawal data   Store audits are expensive, but for many years they provided the only data available. However, with the computerization of chain-store warehouse operations, it became possible to obtain data on the movement of products from

[10]A relatively new service makes use of computer-generated retail sales stock movement by the use of the universal product code (UPC). Electronic scanning equipment reads the UPC identification as the customer is checked out. Proportionately few retail stores have installed the scanning equipment; therefore, the data base for the service remains rather modest.

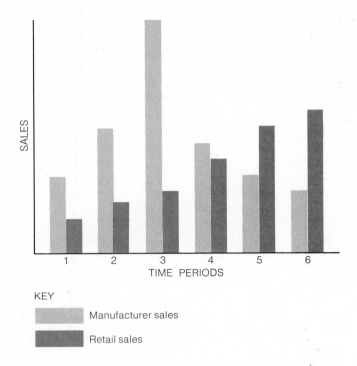

FIGURE 7.5   Comparison of manufacturer and retail sales of a
new product

EXHIBIT 7.1   Intelligence provided by store
audits

Sales to consumers
Purchases by retailers
Inventories
Facings
Average day's supply on hand
Number of stores carrying product
Distribution of all commodities
Out of stock
Retail and wholesale prices
Retail margins
Special factory packs
Dealer support, including displays, local
   advertising, coupon redemption, sampling
Special price deals
New competitive products
Competitors' test-marketing results

---

the warehouse to the retail store. This information is known as *warehouse withdrawal data.* Time, Inc., was one of the first to provide such data through a subsidiary known as Selling Areas Marketing, Inc. Its withdrawal data, often called *SAMI,* are purchased from cooperating chains and wholesalers, are consolidated, and are sold on a subscription basis to grocery manufacturers.

The warehouse withdrawal report is also fairly expensive, but it covers many more products and includes a much greater proportion of total sales than do store-audit figures. It lacks the pinpoint precision of audit information in that it reports movement *to* retail stores, not movement out of them. However, since the turnover of prod-

TABLE 7.6   Determination of market potential for frozen pie shells by the use of the chain-ratio method for the Marvelous Pie Shell Company

Population, age six and over	200 million
× Per capita consumption of pies of all types	3.3
= Number of pies consumed	667 million
× Per cent of pies consumed at home	75%
= Number of pies consumed at home	500 million
× Per cent of pies prepared at home	72%
= Number of pies prepared at home	360 million
× Per cent of pies prepared at home with prepared pie shell	28%
= Number of pies prepared at home with prepared pie shell	100.8 million
× Per cent of prepared pie shells which are frozen	88%
= Number of pies prepared at home with frozen pie shells	88.7 million
= Market potential for frozen pie shells	88.7 million
× Marvelous Pie Shell Company's share of market	.20
= Sales potential for Marvelous Pie Shell Company	17.7 million

ucts at the retail store is much faster than at the warehouse level, it is felt by many manufacturers that warehouse withdrawal information provides a relatively satisfactory indication of consumer purchases. Certainly annual or accumulated warehouse data provide quite a satisfactory measure of regional sales and market shares.

Chain ratio Market and sales potentials can be estimated by applying a series of usage ratios to an estimate of total demand. Suppose that the Marvelous Pie Shell Company is interested in estimating the number of frozen pie shells it might sell. The starting point might well be the entire population, aged six and over. This number would be multiplied by the per capita consumption of pies to determine the total number of pies consumed in a year. Since some desserts are not eaten at home or are bought already baked from retail stores, the total number of pies must be multiplied by the percentage of

all pies consumed that are prepared at home. Of those cooks that prepare pies at home, some (a given percentage) work from scratch, preparing the dough and baking the crust; some use a prepared crust; and some use a frozen pie shell. Table 7.6 illustrates how this chain of ratios might be applied to produce an estimate of sales potential for this fictitious company.

SIC data Market potential, but not sales potential, can be estimated for industrial products by use of Standard Industrial Classification (SIC) data. The U.S. Department of Commerce classifies all manufacturing establishments according to a series of code numbers. There are twenty-one two-digit-code industrial classifications, each representing a major industry group. Three- and four-digit codes break out even finer degrees of classification.

In order to use SIC data to estimate market potential for a product it is first

TABLE 7.7   Estimates of potential for containers in three markets

	Containers		
	Cost of materials purchased (million $)	Purchases per $ total materials	Potential (thousand $)
Duluth-Superior, Minn. SMSA			
SIC 20 Food and kindred products	92.5	.021	1943.5
23 Apparel and other textiles	11.6	.011	127.6
27 Printing and publishing	4.7	.011	51.7
			2122.8
Columbus, Ohio SMSA			
SIC 20 Food and kindred products	362.6	.021	1614.6
23 Apparel and other textiles	13.9	.011	152.9
27 Printing and publishing	50.8	.011	558.8
			8326.3
Albuquerque, N.M. SMSA			
SIC 20 Food and kindred products	44.1	.021	926.1
27 Printing and publishing	5.6	.011	61.6
			987.7

Sources: Materials purchased from *1972 Census of Manufacturers,* vol. 3, Area Statistics, parts 1 and 2. (Washington, D.C.: U.S. Government Printing Office, 1976). Container purchases from *Survey of Current Business* (Washington, D.C.: U.S. Government Printing Office, 1969).

necessary to discover the SIC classification of manufacturers that use it. This is not as easy as it might seem, since an establishment is classified by what it makes, not by what it buys. The most practical approach for a company is (1) to analyze the SIC classifications of its past customers and (2) to estimate the relationship between sales to a given SIC category and one or more of the data series published in the *Census of Manufacturers.* Table 7.7 shows how a paper box manufacturer might estimate the market potential in three markets. The first step in such an analysis is to determine the types of companies (by SIC code) that are heavy users of paper boxes. A company's sales might provide this data; or perhaps a trade association might publish shipment figures. It also is

necessary to ascertain how much each type of customer spends on containers. This information is available from the same sources. Next, the manager must find out where these prospective buyers are located. The 1972 *Census of Manufacturers* reports, along with a great deal of other data, the purchase of materials by SIC code for each state and standard metropolitan statistical area (SMSA). To determine the potential in any area, such as Columbus, Ohio, we multiply the container purchase rate by the value of materials purchased for each SIC code. These products are totaled to obtain an estimate of area potential. In this example the box manufacturer might expect to obtain some share of a market potential of $8.3 million.

Sales Forecasting

Another aspect of marketing to which demand theory can be applied is sales forecasting. The forecast is critical to the identification of the planning gap. It leads directly to the definition of the strategy assignment. A sales forecast, in contrast to measures of potential, is concerned not with historical data but with *estimates* of future sales. Uncertainty limits the accuracy of these estimates, but the effort must be made.

Uses of the Sales Forecast

Forecasting plays an extremely important role in almost all aspects of business management. For example, sales forecasting can be used as a basis for decision making in the following areas:

Scheduling production

Planning inventory, both raw material and finished goods

Making procurement decisions

Establishing sales goals and standards

Determining advertising budgets

Establishing financial needs, including those for worker capital and capital spending

Price setting

Expansion or contraction of manufacturing facilities or distribution

Determining organization and personnel requirements

Planning and scheduling research and development activities

Some of these are short-run decisions. They require immediate decisions that affect current operations. Scheduling production,

planning inventory levels, setting sales targets, estimating working-capital needs, and establishing advertising budgets are short-run considerations. Ordinarily, a projection of sales for a period of between three and twelve months is adequate for these kinds of operational decisions. Accordingly, sales forecasts for these purposes are often called *short-run forecasts.* Projection of sales covering periods longer than one year, although seldom more than five years, are classified as *long-run forecasts.* A few companies attempt to forecast ten, twenty-five, or even fifty years in advance. These very long run projections are used to define a company's mission, in contrast to the more limited long-run forecasts that affect decisions on such things as plant expansion, research and development expenditures, and organizational changes.

Steps in Sales Forecasting

The Conference Board in a study of business policies presented the steps involved in sales forecasting.[11] They may be summarized as follows:

1. *Determine purposes for which forecasts are to be used*   In common with all information gathering, forecasting should always be undertaken to help solve specific problems. The general purposes of forecasting have already been mentioned. These purposes relate to short-term decision making and to the formulation of marketing strategy.

[11]The Conference Board has periodically published reports on sales forecasting. For the most recent, see D. L. Hurwood, E. S. Grossman, and E. L. Bailey, *Sales Forecasting* (New York: The Conference Board, 1978).

2. *Divide company products into homogeneous groups* If a company offers a diversified line of products, it usually is impractical to make a single forecast for the entire line. This is especially true if a company's program is based on market segmentation, because the planning gap may differ among the several segments that the company serves.

3. *Determine factors affecting sales of each product and their relative importance* This information results from an understanding of the theory of demand and from a study of the market. A program of demand analysis, including studies of economic factors, motivational considerations, and competition, is usually necessary in order to isolate and measure the impact of the various factors influencing sales.

4. *Choose a forecasting method* There are numerous forecasting techniques available, some of which are described briefly in this chapter. Usually a choice must be made among these techniques, because it is uneconomical to try to use all of them. The choice of the technique is generally determined by the purposes of the forecast and the kinds of information that can be obtained.

5. *Gather available data* The choice of the forecasting method in the previous step paves the way for gathering all available information relevant to the factors influencing sales and to the methods being used.

6. *Analyze the data* The analysis of forecasting data is often difficult. For example, even when statistical techniques are used to project past sales, some judgment usually is involved. When opinion methods of forecasting are utilized, a great deal of subjectivity enters into the analysis.

7. *Check and cross-check deductions* The future is always uncertain, and conclusions drawn from forecast data always involve some margin of error. In order to reduce this error, it is wise for the analyst to check and recheck the work. Ideally, two or more analysts should inspect and interpret the same data. Differences in their deductions should be carefully studied and the best possible final forecast adopted.

8. *Make assumptions regarding other factors* The ability to forecast accurately depends on either (1) the ability of the forecaster to make good assumptions regarding factors that cannot be measured or (2) the relative unimportance of such factors in influencing sales. Most sales forecasts involve a certain amount of error because one or more influencing factors cannot be included. These factors may be exceedingly important. For instance, the character and intensity of competitors' future programs may be the single most important element affecting a company's sales. Obviously, some assumption must be made regarding competitors' actions and reactions in order to forecast future sales performance with any degree of realism.

9. *Convert deductions and assumptions into specific forecasts* The deductions and assumptions made in the preceding steps must be translated into specific sales projections. These estimates are most useful for planning purposes when they are broken down into product, territorial, or customer categories. If a grassroots forecasting method is used, this distribution is not difficult. If, on the other hand, an aggregate forecast is made, the allocation of the total forecast to specific products or

territories usually is based on past experience weighted by reasonable assumptions regarding changes expected in the future.

10. *Apply the forecast to company operations* This step really takes the forecaster into decision making. Together with other types of information, such as various marketing research findings, the forecast must be transformed into a marketing strategy.

Forecasting Methods

If every minor variation that can be introduced into forecasting were classified as a separate forecasting method, the number of such methods would be astronomical. Yet, for important reasons, every forecast is different. Each forecast is made from a slightly different vantage point in time. The factors that influence sales are changing constantly. The forecaster grows in experience and confidence. The amount of time available for forecasting frequently changes. For reasons such as these no two forecasting procedures are likely to be identical. However, there are four general categories of forecasting methods: (1) naive (unscientific) methods, (2) correlation methods, (3) survey methods, and (4) input-output methods. Within each of these methods several specific forecasting techniques can be mentioned.

Naive (Unscientific) Methods

Naive methods are unsophisticated and unscientific projections based on guesses or on mechanical extrapolations of historical data.

Two naive methods that frequently are used are factor listing and extrapolation.

Factor listing Factor listing as a forecasting method takes one no further than the third step in the forecasting process. The forecaster only identifies those factors expected to influence sales and attempts subjectively to estimate the extent of their influence. The factor-listing method is quick and easy. It can easily be used on an interim basis, allowing a detailed forecast to be postponed until some indication of an important economic change is detected. The great danger, however, is that the simplicity of the method may cause the forecaster to miss a subtle sign of an important change.

Extrapolation A second naive method is the extrapolation of historical data. One of two types of extrapolation is usually adopted. Spencer and Siegelman refer to these two types as the *no change model* and the *proportional change model.*[12] Using the no change model, the forecaster assumes that the level of predicted sales will be the same as the level of current sales. In the proportional change model, the assumption is made that predicted sales will reflect an increase over the current period proportional to the increase in the current period over the one preceding it.

In considering extrapolation methods, we should draw a distinction between the intelligent use of trend and cycle analysis for forecasting purposes and the arbitrary projection of prior years' sales. Sophisticated applications of business cycle and trend analyses are made in many company forecasts. But we always should remember that, regardless of how careful the analysis of time-

[12]Spencer and Siegelman, *Managerial Economics,* pp. 45–46.

series data may have been with respect to trend, seasonal variations, and cyclical fluctuations, the projection of future sales is based on the assumption that the directions and rates of change experienced in the past will continue in the future. It is this assumption that is naive, not the technique itself.

Correlation Methods

We already have seen how correlation (regression) analysis is applied in the development of a demand function. Regression analysis can involve a single demand determinant or it can involve multiple determinants. The correlative relationships may be either linear or nonlinear. As the analysis moves from single to multiple factors and from linear to nonlinear relationships, correlation studies become increasingly complex. However, standardized computer programs have been developed so that a multiple regression, whether linear or nonlinear, can be prepared with relative ease.

Regression analysis is not in itself a forecast. When applied to a marketing problem it isolates and measures the influence of so-called independent variables (demand determinants) on a dependent variable (sales). In order to use the technique as a forecasting device, the demand determinants must be projected. Usually, these determinants can be predicted more readily than can sales.

The use of such a multiple regression analysis is illustrated by the National Industrial Conference Board in its description of the Chesapeake and Ohio Railway Company. This company experimented for several years with correlation studies relating economic indicators to various classes of the company's traffic. The experimentation culminated in the development of a linear multiple regression program. Using a com-

puter, the company fed in various formulations of a predicting equation for each of the company's traffic groups. The best formula in each case was the one that would have provided the most accurate forecast when past period car loadings were studied. After the predicting formulas were tested in this way, a final set of forecasting equations was adopted for use by the financial planning office in its preparation of preliminary traffic projections for the company.[13]

Another example is the American Can Company, which has found it necessary to forecast the sales of each of its customer groups in order to predict, in turn, its own container sales. One of American Can's important customer groups is made up of breweries that package beer for consumption in the home. For the prediction of this consumption, a regression analysis including number of families, per cent of families owning homes, and family income established an accurate basis for predicting the demand for cans by the brewing industry. Similarly, a prediction of the demand for cans for motor oil was based on a multiple regression of motor oil sales in terms of car ownership, the declining frequency of oil changes, and declining crankcase capacities. The resulting equation enabled the company to predict consumption of motor oil and the associated demand for cans to package this product.[14]

✓ Survey Methods

With the exception of the factor-listing method, the forecasting techniques described to this point are based principally on statistical analysis. In many forecasting situa-

[13]National Industrial Conference Board, *Forecasting Sales*, p. 90.

[14]Ibid., pp. 46–48.

tions, however, lack of data, lack of time, and the inability of the average forecaster to utilize sophisticated statistical techniques combine to make such techniques unworkable. But the need for forecasting is no less critical. In these cases, survey methods of forecasting often are utilized. They are superior to naive methods because they employ controlled techniques of information gathering. There are three important survey techniques used in forecasting.

The jury of executive opinion   It is common practice in some companies to consider the opinions of key executives in establishing the forecast. These executives, of course, do not venture opinions of future sales without adequate study. In some cases they back up their opinions with sophisticated techniques of sales analysis. Such a jury of executive opinion produces a forecast quickly and often minimizes the amount of effort required. One of its greatest advantages is that it brings a diversity of viewpoints and experience to the forecasting problem. The result, however, is usually extremely subjective and tends to be based on the barest minimum of facts even in situations where data are available. But when opinion and data can be combined, a good forecast often results. The Conference Board reports that "for a number of years the Lockheed Aircraft Corporation, a manufacturer of airplanes and missiles, has used a forecasting technique dubbed 'prudent manager forecasting' as part of its long-range forecasting procedure."[15] This "prudent manager forecasting" is supported by a considerable amount of background information provided by the marketing research department. The jury of executives in this case is well fortified by market studies and statistical analysis.

Sales force composite method   In contrast to the jury of executive opinion, this technique makes use of the judgments of salespeople, who after all should know the market well. The forecast is built up from grassroots estimates of future sales. The Pensalt Chemical Corporation has utilized such an approach for a number of years.[16] Specific estimates are made of the expected volume of products to be sold to each major customer—including current customers, old customers, and customers expected to be added in the forecast period. This type of forecasting is quite common in large industrial marketing companies. Corporations, such as Otis Elevator and Westinghouse, build up sales forecasts by using this general technique.

Customer intentions   Closely related to the sales-force composite method is the technique of obtaining estimates of future business directly from customers. It is used principally by direct-selling industrial firms, and it is especially valuable when a lack of data concerning the demand determinants precludes the preparation of forecasts in any other way. User-expectation surveys are of critical importance in cases where a firm relies on a limited number of large customers. Marketers of electrical generating equipment, such as GE and Westinghouse, rely on the expansion and modernization plans of public utilities as a basis for estimating future sales. Some research sources, such as the McGraw-Hill publishing company's department of research, periodically publish summaries of user expectations. Similarly, capital-spending plans are reported quarterly for most industrial sectors. Process machinery manufacturers, construction firms, machine tool builders, and the like

[15]Ibid., p. 48.

[16]Ibid., p. 25.

TABLE 7.8   Input-output table for use in industry forecasting

	Input (buying) industry							
	Motor vehicles				Office, computing, accounting machines			
	Input coefficients*		Dollar flow (000)		Input Coefficients*		Dollar flow (000)	
Output (selling) industry	1958	1970	1958	1970	1958	1970	1958	1970
Iron and steel	.08774	.08407	$205,917	$502,125	.01887	.01036	$4,265	$8,913
Plastics	.00470	.02270	11,030	135,580	.00132	.00216	298	1,858
Aluminum	.00547	.01053	12,838	62,893	.00543	.00569	1,227	4,895
Rubber	.02376	.02293	55,762	136,954	.01021	.00983	2,307	8,457
Copper	.00510	.00280	11,969	16,724	.00812	.00755	1,835	6,495
Other nonferrous	.00082	.00074	1,924	4,420	.00528	.00726	1,193	6,246
	Aircraft				Household appliances			
Iron and steel	.03193	.02666	$40,714	$54,080	.07616	.05962	$27,380	$44,924
Plastics	.00325	.00520	4,144	10,548	.01952	.03355	7,017	25,280
Aluminum	.02003	.02445	25,540	49,597	.01600	.01733	5,752	13,058
Rubber	.00366	.00395	4,667	8,013	.01573	.01452	5,655	10,941
Copper	.00517	.00553	6,592	11,218	.01238	.01565	9,328	11,792
Other nonferrous	.00166	.00736	2,117	14,930	.01371	.01025	4,929	7,723

*Coefficients are for direct sales only; that is, for example, for products sold directly by the aluminum industry to the motor vehicles industry.
Source: "Input-Output Searches the Seventies." Reprinted by permission from Sales Management, The Marketing Magazine, 1 August 1968. Copyright 1968, Sales Management, Inc., pp. 27–29.

make use of this kind of customer-intention analysis.

Input-Output Analysis

Of interest in marketing is the use of input-output (I-O) analysis to forecast demand within an industry.[17] The starting point is an input-output table of the entire economy.

[17]For a selection of articles on the use of input-output analysis in forecasting, see "After Many Years Comes a Matrix," Sales Management, 15 January 1970, pp. 54–55; N. C. Mohn, "Input-Output Modeling— New Sales Forecasting Tool," Michigan Business Review, July 1976, pp. 7–15; and E. D. Ranard, "Use of Input-Output Concepts in Sales Forecasting," Journal of Marketing Research, February 1972, pp. 53–58.

From this, the industry forecaster culls those selling and buying industries that are not relevant. The table is then reconstructed including only the remaining segments. This reconstructed I-O table shows exactly what the past sales of a vendor industry were to each buying industry. These past sales can be expressed in two ways. The actual dollar sales to each buying industry can be shown; or the sales can be expressed as percentages of total output, known as *coefficients*. The coefficient is calculated by dividing the total output of an industry into each of its customer industries' inputs. As one might expect, the coefficients demonstrate more long-run stability than do the dollar sales; but both are subject to change, and input-output matrixes must be continually updated to reflect economic growth and changing patterns of industry demand.

To use an input-output matrix for forecasting, the analyst has two choices. One is to project future sales of an industry, using a prior year's coefficients and a projected estimate of sales in the entire economy. The other is to modify the coefficients. Such modification would be based on assumptions about the changing structure of the industry, technological developments, competitive activity, and the like. The final result, using either approach, is an input-output table of dollar sales for the forecast period. An example of the calculations of projected sales for six selling industries to four buying industries is shown in Table 7.8. The table vividly illustrates how both the level of overall economic activity and the technical coefficients affect the sales of the plastic industry to automobile companies between 1958 and 1970.

The use of input-output as a forecasting method is still in its infancy. Lack of familiarity with the approach and the paucity of data on many smaller industries are the principal restraining factors. As more detailed information becomes available and as marketing forecasters become more adept at using this approach, we can expect to see this type of analysis become an important tool in sales forecasting.

Using More than One Method

A company seldom restricts its forecasting to a single technique. Generally, several techniques are used, depending on the sophistication, the importance, and the complexity of the forecasting situation. One approach is to ask the marketing research department to prepare an overall economic forecast using correlation techniques and the study of economic indicators. At the same time, either the jury of executive opinion or the salesforce composite method is used to build up a forecast from the other direction. The final result is a compromise or combination of the two forecasts.

Pitfalls in Forecasting

No one seriously expects a forecast to be absolutely accurate. But in some cases forecasts fail even to approximate actual performance. There are a number of reasons for this.

Faulty Concepts of Demand First, in no area of marketing management are clear concepts of demand more important than in forecasting sales. One must measure the right determinants in order to predict sales. Faulty assumptions regarding the influences on demand result in the design of forecasting methods quite inappropriate to the real nature of the market.

Failure to detect market trends Naive methods of forecasting are most likely to involve this type of pitfall. However, correlation techniques and internally generated survey methods also may fail to detect subtle or incipient market changes. Theoretically, the customer-intentions survey should reveal important changes in market requirements. However, even this technique may not produce a satisfactory warning if the inquiry is made only in terms of customers' intentions to buy "old" products. The market analyst must be constantly on the alert to detect changes in customer needs and base predictions on company opportunities to supply the appropriate satisfactions.

Difficulty of anticipating competitors' plans This point has been mentioned previously, but it must be stressed that it is the most important factor limiting accurate forecasting of company sales. To ignore competitive action is to omit a major element in marketing. Attempts constantly must be made to anticipate competitors' plans. A continuous review of sales performance in relation to forecasted sales provides an opportunity to change assumptions and conclusions in the light of competitive actions.

Attempting to forecast with pinpoint accuracy Forecasting, although it utilizes highly precise methods of measurement, produces only estimates. A certain amount of error always is involved. For this reason, the appropriate way in which to state a forecast is by the use of a *range*. This becomes especially important when attempting to forecast sales for a period in the very distant future—say, four or five years ahead.

Failure to use more than one method A few firms succumb to the temptation to limit their forecasting to a single technique. The analyst is thus deprived of an immediate check on forecasting accuracy. Sales forecasts are like the proverbial rubber ruler. Only if several measurements are made with different measuring sticks can some certainty be established as to the reliability of the estimate.

Long-Range Forecasting

It has become more and more common for companies to look well into the future in order to make decisions about capital spending, research and development, and marketing strategy. Although most sales forecasts are still limited in their time horizon to one or two years, a few firms attempt to predict sales for five years in advance, or even longer.

Economic Forecasting

Long-range forecasting for the whole economy is somewhat more prevalent than is long-range sales forecasting. It is not uncommon for governmental and private research agencies to project gross national product into the distant future, perhaps twenty-five or more years away. These forecasts are generally based on extrapolations of historical rates of economic growth. Those who make them are always careful to point out the inherent limitations of a long-term economic forecast, indicating that important demographic, political, and technological changes can easily upset the prediction.

Although a company can make some use of these long-range economic forecasts in developing its own long-range marketing plans, it is obvious that as one moves from the economy as a whole to a particular industry, and eventually to an individual firm, the long-range economic forecast becomes less and less relevant. The principal reason for this is technological change. While advancing technology may be expected to exert a rather gradual and steady influence on the overall economy, it can cause dramatic changes in specific industries and have even more impact on an individual company. For example, computers and high-speed office copying machines have revolutionized traditional methods and systems of bookkeeping and communications. Powerful new companies like IBM and Xerox have come into existence. Established firms like National Cash Register and A. B. Dick have had to make drastic changes in their products and methods of operation to compete with the newcomers. Very clearly, the long-range planning in these firms would have been immensely improved if some method of forecasting technological change had been available. Today such a method exists and is expected to become of increasing importance in forecasting and in the development of very long range marketing plans.

Technological Forecasting

While some companies, especially those with extreme technical orientation, always have attempted to study the course of technological change, the formal attempt to produce a forecast of such change is a relatively recent development.[18] Two companies that seem to be in the forefront of this development have published considerable information about their approaches. One of them TRW, Inc., has defined its method of technological forecasting as "the prediction of likely inventions, specific scientific refinements, or discoveries in technology, including applications or products which may become possible."[19] The other is the Rand Corporation, whose Delphi technique has been widely adopted.[20]

In many ways, the technological forecast is similar to an economic or sales forecast. The

---

[18]The literature of technological forecasting goes back to the early 1960s. Three books of readings and contributed papers that provide a good survey of the discipline are G. Willis, D. Ashton and B. Taylor, eds., *Technological Forecasting and Corporate Strategy* (New York: American Elsevier Publishing, 1969); J. R. Bright and M. E. F. Schoeman, eds., *Guide to Practical Technological Forecasting* (Englewood Cliffs, N.J.: Prentice-Hall, 1973); and J. Martino, *Introduction to Technological Forecasting* (New York: Gordon and Breach, 1973).

[19]H. Q. North and D. L. Pyke, " 'Probes' of the Technological Future," *Harvard Business Review*, May-June 1969, p. 69.

[20]See R. J. Tersine and W. E. Riggs, "The Delphi Technique—A Long-Range Planning Tool," *Business Horizons*, April 1967, pp. 51–56; and R. F. Scott and D. B. Inmans, "Programmer Productivity and the Delphi Technique," *Datamation*, May 1974, pp. 71–73.

---

techniques vary somewhat, but the purposes and limitations are comparable. This is particularly true of the precision that should be expected. No sophisticated manager expects the forecaster to come up with a pinpoint estimate. What is wanted is a reasonable estimate of the expected level of technology and an indication of the probability that other levels of technology may occur instead.

Conditional Forecasting

In terms of marketing planning, the main purpose of sales forecasting is to determine if a planning gap exists. Any disparity between an objective and the forecast means that the manager must make a strategy change in an effort to fill the gap.

What if there is no gap? This is not likely, because most companies are under constant pressure to achieve ever higher levels of sales, profit, and market share. But if it does occur, it has two implications for the marketing manager. First, the overall strategy should not be altered even though there may be considerable pressure to do so from those who are bored or who for some reason do not accept the goal. (Recall, however, that the marketing strategist cannot change the goal, which emanates higher in the organization, because to do so would upset the end-means hierarchy.) So the manager in this case would stick with the existing strategy. The second implication of a zero gap is the opportunity it provides to fine tune the strategy—that is, to make minor adjustments in the tactics. The motivation is the desire to improve efficiency and to become more knowledgeable about the cause and effect relationships in the marketing mix. However, as already mentioned, the zero

TABLE 7.9 Conditional forecasting and the payoff matrix

(Sales in millions of dollars)

| Alternative strategies | States of nature: Competitors' advertising level | |
	Heavy	Light
A	3.1	5.2
B	4.9	6.4

gap condition seldom occurs, and we should turn our attention to the more agonizing reality "that we can't get there from here."

How to Fill the Gap

We fill the gap with a new or improved marketing strategy—a long-range marketing plan designed to produce the needed increase. We learned in Chapter 3 that once a marketing problem or opportunity has been identified, a number of alternative approaches should be considered and a choice of the best overall plan, or grand strategy should be made. Because the choice of the best strategy is fraught with doubts about the outcomes of the various alternatives, the most applicable decision model is the payoff matrix.[21]

The payoff matrix is simply a way of structuring the decision. As illustrated in Table 7.9, the matrix identifies alternative strategies and the various states of nature (environment) assumed to have impact on the outcomes of the various strategies. For example, suppose a supermarket chain, Big Boy Markets, has identified a planning gap of $5.5 million. Specifically, the company's president wants to achieve sales of $25 million, but the forecast indicates that only $19.5 million will be possible unless some strategy change is made. The president believes that the best way to fill the gap is to advertise, although it is recognized that the degree to which competitors also advertise will drastically affect the success of the approach. Alternative strategies (A and B) are developed. Strategy B involves a large budget, using television; strategy A is less expensive, relying on radio and newspapers.

The Conditional Forecast

Before the choice among alternatives can be made, the cells of the matrix must be filled in. Where do these numbers come from? Not from the sales forecast because the strategy on which it was based is not among the alternatives. A different kind of forecast is required—a forecast that is essentially an estimate of the outcome of a strategy. H. Claycamp calls this a *conditional forecast*.[22]

An estimate of the outcome of a strategy is conditional in two respects. First, it is conditional on the strategy; and second, it is conditional on the state of nature. A good way to understand the nature of the conditional forecast is to think of it as an "If . . . then . . ." statement: "If we adopt strategy A, sales will be $5.2 million." Actually, a single statement will not suffice, since strategy A sales would be different under each state of nature. Thus, our "If . . . then . . ." statement should take this form: "If we adopt strategy A *and* if our competitor advertises heavily, then sales will be $3.1 million." The payoffs for strategy B are similarly stated.

---

[21]The payoff matrix and other methods of structuring a decision are described more completely in the next chapter.

[22]It has been suggested that the concept may have been first formulated by H. Claycamp in an unpublished manuscript (Palo Alto, Calif.: Stanford University, 1966).

Illustrating the conditional forecast is, as one might suspect, a great deal easier than doing it. Fortunately, there are two conceptual tools that assist the marketing executive in making the conditional forecast. One is the concept of the marketing mix; the other is the concept of the marketing response function—both of which have been mentioned previously.

Conditional forecasting and the marketing mix   To produce a conditional forecast for a strategy, it is first necessary to determine the marketing mix that will be employed. Only by determining the kinds and amounts of marketing inputs that will be utilized is it possible to estimate the sales and cost outcomes. In Chapters 9 through 19 we will be looking very carefully at the elements of the marketing mix and how they are combined to create the complete marketing plan. At this point it is necessary to describe only the general approach.

Each element of the marketing mix—that is, product or service offering, distribution, promotion, and price—can be thought of as a marketing effort that contributes individually and in concert with the other elements of the mix to the attainment of sales or another goal. In the context of this discussion it would be a sales goal; but any output of a marketing mix, such as customer awareness, market share, or profit, can be the object of a conditional forecast. The analytical tool we use to make a conditional forecast for a mix element is the response function.

The response function   A response function is a model (either graphic or mathematical) that shows the relationship between a dependent variable (sales for example) and a single independent variable (such as advertising expenditures). We already have

looked at a response function in this chapter (see Figure 7.4). Let's assume that the principal element in a company's marketing mix is advertising. We might depict this response as in Figure 7.6. We can use the figure to illustrate conditional forecasting. Two states of nature are possible. The company's major competitor might advertise heavily, or it might not. The firm has many levels of advertising from which to choose, only two of which are specifically identified (level *A* and level *B*). The shape of the response function determines the outcome of each level. Thus the conditional forecast would be expressed by the following four statements:

1. If we spend at the *A* level of advertising expenditures and if our major competitor does not advertise heavily, then sales will amount to $5.2 million.
2. If we spend at the *A* level of advertising expenditures and if our major competitor does advertise heavily, then sales will amount to $3.1 million.
3. If we spend at the *B* level of advertising expenditures and if our major competitor does not advertise heavily, then sales will amount to $6.4 million.
4. If we advertise at the *B* level of advertising expenditures and if our major competitor does advertise heavily, then sales will amount to $4.9 million.

These conditional forecasts might be placed in the cells of a decision matrix as shown in Table 7.9.

Actually, the process is not nearly so simple because most marketing strategies involve all four elements of the mix, each with a different response function. The conditional forecasts of each mix element must be related and combined. Tools for doing this will be introduced in Chapter 8.

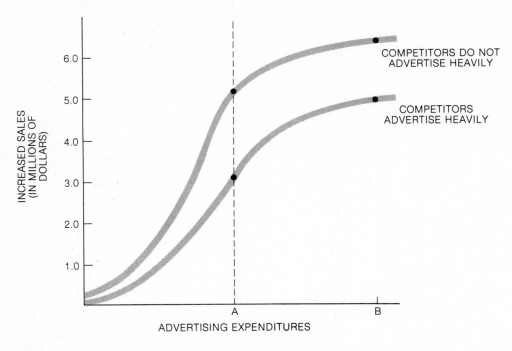

FIGURE 7.6   Advertising response functions

Conditional Forecasting of Other Marketing Outcomes

The output of marketing effort can be forecast in other ways besides sales volume. In fact, sales volume per se may not be the best measure, because company objectives might be better expressed in terms of market share or profit.

To forecast market share it is necessary to predict both industry and company sales. In some forecasting approaches, forecasting industry sales is an integral part of the company's forecasting process and the prediction of market share is relatively simple. However, it is not always easy to forecast industry sales because the total amount and effectiveness of competitors' marketing efforts may be hard to predict. Philip Kotler suggests

that each company's share of market depends on the following:

1. The total amount of its marketing expenditure
2. Its marketing mix
3. The effectiveness of its marketing effort
4. The elasticity of its marketing effort[23]

Total industry sales, therefore, are dependent on a number of factors that are hard enough to identify, let alone predict. Yet these kinds of estimates are essential for

[23]P. Kotler, *Marketing Decision Making: A Model Building Approach* (New York: Holt, Rinehart and Winston, 1971), pp. 92–97.

conditional forecasting when the outcome to be forecast is market share.

A conditional forecast can be stated in terms of profit contribution. This further complicates the forecasting problem. Changes in the cost structure and the prices of input factors affect future costs, and these must be incorporated in the conditional forecast. The measurement of marketing profitability involves complicated accounting procedures. This is a subject that we will explore in Chapter 22.

Summary

Market measurement and forecasting are important analytical assignments in marketing management because they produce data needed to answer three important questions: (1) What is the potential of a given market segment? (2) What is the planning gap? (3) What kind and amount of marketing effort will be required to close the planning gap?

Measurement and forecasting properly begin with an understanding of demand theory. This theory helps to isolate the various determinants of demand, including consumer tastes and preferences, income, availability of substitutes, and price. Demand theory also suggests how these various determinants are related in their aggregate effect on demand. It does this through the use of the demand function, which is a mathematical statement of the relationship between the demand influences and sales.

Once these aspects of demand theory are understood, it is possible to explore the three uses of sales data. The first use of sales data is in the measurement of market potential, which is defined as the amount that is purchased as industry marketing effort approaches infinity. Closely related is the measurement of sales potential, the amount that is sold as the sales effort of a particular company reaches its maximum. There are several methods of measuring potential, and most companies rely on one or more outside information services to supply the needed data.

The second use of demand theory, the forecasting of future sales, is one of the most important aspects of marketing management. Its influence goes far beyond the planning of sales activities. Production, finance, and almost every other facet of the business are affected by the sales forecast. There are several methods of forecasting that can be fitted into an overall forecasting procedure. Although there are pitfalls that must be avoided in forecasting, there is no substitute for the forecast as a basis on which to plan future marketing operations.

Most forecasts for marketing purposes are made on a short-term basis, but long-range forecasting is beginning to be more widely utilized. It takes two forms. There is long-range economic forecasting, in which an attempt is made to estimate industry and company sales five or more years into the future. There is also technological forecasting, which has an even longer time horizon. In this relatively new approach to long-range prediction, an attempt is made to foresee the impact that technical developments will have on business opportunities.

Conditional forecasting is the process of estimating the outcome of a strategy. It takes the form of an "If . . . then . . ." statement. Conditional forecast data are inserted in the decision matrix and become the basis of making a strategic choice. Conditional forecasting is dependent on the development of response functions, which permit the manager to estimate the outcome of a given strategy.

Questions and Problems

1. *Econometrics* is a term applied to the measurement and analysis of economic data. Would it make sense to use the term *marketmetrics* to describe the subject matter of this chapter?

2. A businessperson once said, "What's all this fuss about *demand?* My customers don't demand anything. They have to be sold!" What is the difference between this person's concept of demand and the concept presented in this chapter?

3. Why is it that the sales of some kinds of products respond much more dramatically to price reductions than do others? What do you think are the marketing implications of this?

4. What is a demand function? Identify several different applications that might be made of a demand function in marketing management.

5. Using hypothetical figures, illustrate how the chain-ratio method of estimating market potential might be used by a battery manufacturer attempting to measure the market for replacement car batteries.

6. Forecasting is difficult and seldom very accurate. Some companies give this as a reason for not attempting to make forecasts. Does such an explanation make sense to you?

7. Distinguish among the following:
   a. A sales forecast
   b. Market potential
   c. Sales potential

8. If you were going to select a forecasting method, which would you choose for use by a company in each of the following industries:
   a. Electronic computers
   b. Outboard motors
   c. Metal doors and frames used in nonresidential construction
   d. Frozen foods
   e. Jet-powered private aircraft

9. Investigate the long-range forecasting method(s) used by a medium- to large-sized company. What are its methods? Why do you believe it is using them? Would you recommend the use of different methods?

10. Using a readily available marketing index, such as *Sales Management Survey of Buying Power,* determine the potential in three different market areas for one of the following product categories:
    a. Grocery products
    b. Gasoline additives
    c. Children's clothing
    d. Color televisions

11. The construction industry appears to be undergoing a great deal of technological change as modular construction and industrialization enter into a situation once dominated by on-site fabrication by the building trades. Write a 500-word technological forecast for the construction industry based on your own knowledge of what is happening in this field. If you were going to make a genuine technological forecast, what method(s) would you use?

12. What is a conditional forecast? On what is the forecast conditional? How is the conditional forecast used in making marketing decisions?

Three
Marketing Strategy

8

Decision Tools for Marketing Strategy

Until a few years ago most marketing decisions were made "by guess and by gosh." Nobody was particularly proud of the fact, nor was anybody especially concerned. "Marketing," it was said, "is an art—not a science." However, a few short years have changed this situation. Today, more and more attention is being devoted to the application of scientific approaches to marketing decision making.

The application of management science, or the use of a new set of quantitative techniques to help make marketing decisions, is probably the most important development in marketing management in the last ten years. Every student of marketing should be familiar with the most basic applications and should understand how they help the manager perform more effectively. This does not mean that every manager of the future will have to be an accomplished mathematician. It is most likely, however, that marketing executives of tomorrow will need to communicate intelligently with specialists

in quantitative techniques. Like all sophisticated tools, management science techniques will be applied by persons trained to use them; but the manager must recognize when a problem is susceptible to quantitative analysis and have a general understanding of tools that the specialist may recommend. The purpose of this chapter is to survey the most popular techniques and to equip you to deal with them from a managerial point of view.[1]

Decision Criteria for Marketing

The most distinctive contribution of management science to marketing has been its emphasis on finding the best possible strate-

[1] For a summary of other analytical tools, see D. A. Heenan and R. B. Addleman, "Quantitative Techniques for Today's Decision Makers," *Harvard Business Review,* May-June 1976, pp. 32–62.

TABLE 8.1   Linear revenue and cost data for break-even analysis

| Unit price | Quantity (1,000) | Total revenue (1,000) | Fixed cost (1,000) | Variable cost | | Total cost (1,000) | Profit (1,000) |
				Unit (1,000)	Total (1,000)		
0	0	0	5,000	0	0	5,000	(5,000)*
50	100	5,000	5,000	30	3,000	8,000	(3,000)*
50	200	10,000	5,000	30	6,000	11,000	(1,000)*
50	300	15,000	5,000	30	9,000	14,000	1,000
50	400	20,000	5,000	30	12,000	17,000	3,000
50	500	25,000	5,000	30	15,000	20,000	5,000

*Figures in parentheses are losses.

gy or solution to a marketing problem. Of course there are model-building techniques that merely describe what is observed and do not provide alternative approaches to problem solving. The consumer behavior models that we looked at in Chapter 5 are of this type. At this point, we primarily are interested in those techniques that do supply criteria for managers seeking to select the best possible strategy. There are numerous such decision criteria that can be built into marketing models. We will concern ourselves only with the two most notable: profit maximization under conditions of certainty and maximization of expected payoff under conditions of uncertainty.

Profit Maximization Under Conditions of Certainty

The concept of profit maximization is well known to students of economics. The practical difficulties of actually maximizing profits are equally well recognized by business managers. The essential difference between theory and practice is that in traditional economic models the outcomes of decisions concerning output and price (for example) are presumed to be known in advance. That is, certainty prevails—which, of course, it

really does not. However, let us set aside for the moment the fact that uncertainty usually exists in business decision situations and let us look at the classical economic model. In doing so, we can observe some useful things about profit maximization.

Linear break-even analysis The simplest model of profit maximization under conditions of certainty is the well-known break-even chart. An example is shown in Figure 8.1. Dollars of total revenue, profit, and cost are measured on the vertical axis. The data base for this exhibit is found in Table 8.1. In mathematical terms, the cost and revenue functions are linear—that is, they appear as straight lines with constant slopes in the break-even chart. At any given level of output (or sales), the profit (or loss) is determined by the following equation:

$$\text{Profit} = \text{total revenue} - \text{total cost}$$

The equation can be expanded to reflect in more detail the relationships shown in Figure 8.1.

$$P = p \times Q - FC + (VC \times Q)$$
where P = profit
$\quad\quad p$ = the unit price

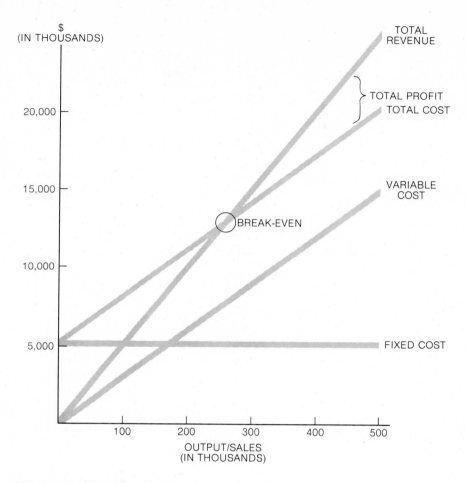

FIGURE 8.1   Linear break-even chart

Q = the quantity produced (or sold)
FC = the total fixed cost
VC = the variable cost per unit

An examination of Figure 8.1 confirms the importance of this equation. Revenue results from selling goods and services. The greater the volume of output and sales, the higher total revenue rises. Marketing, in its broadest sense, is responsible for producing sales. But the marketing manager is interest-ed in more than sales income. Profit is the goal; and costs also are important. Fixed costs do not vary with sales volume. They occur, in the short run, even if no goods are produced or sold. Rent, depreciation, and executive salaries are all fixed costs. Other costs are variable with output or sales. Some manufacturing expenses, such as material and labor, and some marketing costs, such as salespersons' commissions, are variable. Thus, the higher the level of output or sales, the greater is the total of variable costs.

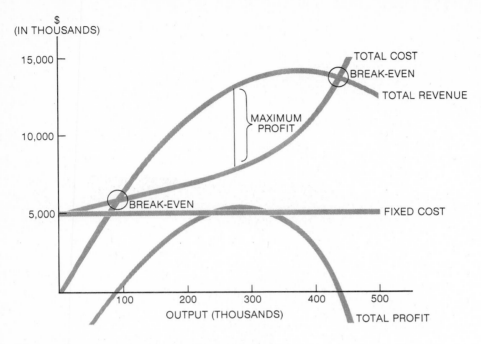

FIGURE   8.2   Nonlinear profits maximization chart

The preceeding equation is often restated in the form of a break-even equation:

$$BE = \frac{FC}{p - VC}$$

The break-even point is shown in Figure 8.1 at that sales volume where total revenue equals total cost. Applying this formula to the data in Table 8.1, we note that

$$\frac{5,000,000}{50 - 30} = 250,000$$

Break-even is an interesting concept, and reaching it is an important step in attaining profit; but it is not per se a useful profit-maximization model. *Any* output beyond break-even is profitable; and the greater the level of sales, the greater the profit. "Beautiful," you say; but regrettably every econo-

mist and all businesspeople know that it is simply not a valid model of the great majority of real-world situations.

Nonlinear break-even analysis The reason the classical break-even analysis is a poor model is that usually neither the total-revenue function nor the total-cost function is linear. We can see a truer picture of these curves in Figure 8.2. Note that the total-revenue curve (after a brief period of increasing returns) increases at a constantly decreasing rate until it reaches a maximum, and then it actually turns down. This phenomenon is fully explored in economics. We can explain it briefly here by recalling that in order to persuade consumers to buy increased amounts of a particular product, the product will have to be sold at a lower price. The greater the sales volume desired, the lower the price will have to be. Columns 1,

TABLE 8.2   Nonlinear revenue and cost data for profits maximization

(1) Price	(2) Quantity (1,000)	(3) Total revenue (1,000)	(4) Fixed cost (1,000)	Variable cost		(7) Total cost (1,000)	(8) Total profit (1,000)
				(5) Unit	(6) Total (1,000)		
70.00	50	3,500	5,000	6.00	300	5,300	(1,800)*
65.00	100	6,500	5,000	10.00	1,000	6,000	500
60.00	150	9,000	5,000	9.33	1,400	6,400	2,600
55.00	200	11,000	5,000	9.25	1,850	6,850	4,150
50.00	250	12,500	5,000	9.60	2,400	7,400	5,100
45.00	300	13,500	5,000	10.50	3,150	8,150	5,350
40.00	350	14,000	5,000	12.28	4,300	9,300	4,700
35.00	400	14,000	5,000	15.63	6,250	11,250	2,750
30.00	450	13,500	5,000	21.78	9,800	1,480	(1,300)*
25.00	500	12,500	5,000	33.10	16,500	21,550	(9,050)*

*Figures in parentheses are losses.

2, and 3 of Table 8.2 present hypothetical data reflecting this assumption.

Nor is the total cost function linear, although the fixed-cost function must remain so. But variable costs behave quite differently. As output and sales increase, total costs increase, initially quite slowly. Then suddenly as maximum efficiency is attained, total costs increase at an ever-accelerating pace. Economists call this the *stage of diminishing returns.* Table 8.2 presents the relevant cost data in columns 4, 5, 6, and 7.

In Figure 8.2 we find two break-even points, and we also observe that total profit (total revenue minus total cost) reaches a maximum at an output between these two zero-profit points. Now we have a model that permits us to maximize profits. We can identify the most profitable output (sales volume) in any of three ways. First, we can use Figure 8.2 and visually identify from the graph the most profitable level of operations. (See the total-profit line in the exhibit.) Second, we might use calculus to determine the precise mathematical solution.

Third, we could apply the marginality principle, using a mixture of trial and error and some simple algebra to find the correct management decision to maximize profits.

The Marginality Principle

There is no more powerful tool in marketing decision making than the marginality principle. It permits the manager to compute precisely or to approximate practically the maximum profit strategy. Let us apply it first to a simple illustration in sales management and then return to the general discussion of profits maximization.

Bob Essen owns a chain of five suburban hardware stores in a large midwestern city. One of the key factors that influences the sales, costs, and profit of this chain is the number of salespersons employed. When Essen hires new salespeople he does not promise them that they will work permanently at any particular store. In fact, he frequently transfers salespeople among the five stores in an attempt to utilize his sales force most effectively. Essen has discovered that it is not easy to find competent salespeople—those with hardware experience and the right personality characteristics. For this reason, he often is forced to operate his chain of stores with fewer (and occasionally more) salespeople than optimal. Faced with these operating circumstances, Essen has these marketing management decisions to make:

1. How many salespeople in total should be employed in order to maximize profits?
2. How should the sales force be allocated among the five stores?

Essen can answer these questions by applying the marginality principle. The principle of marginality states that any variable resource should be employed as long as the incremental revenue resulting from its use exceeds (or is equal to) the incremental cost of adding it. For example, if hiring an additional salesperson will cost Bob Essen $10,000 in salary and commissions, it is necessary that the additional salesperson produce at least $10,000 in extra gross profit.

Let's see how this principle works in relation to the two questions Essen has to answer. Fortunately he has kept careful records and knows what has happened in the past in each of the stores as the number of salespersons has been altered. These data are summarized in Table 8.3. For example, at store 1, when 4 salespeople have been used, annual gross profit amounted to $277,500. When 5 were employed, the gross profit rose to $295,500. The incremental contribution of the addition of the fifth salesperson to the staff at store 1 was $295,500 less $277,500, or $18,000. Clearly, adding the fifth salesperson was worthwhile

because the incremental (marginal) cost of hiring the person was only $10,000. Should a sixth person be hired? Yes, because the increase in gross profit (now $13,500) is still greater than the incremental (marginal) cost. How about a seventh? Yes, because the seventh salesperson brings in exactly the amount of additional gross profit ($10,000) that is necessary to offset the cost. Eight? Definitely not! The eighth salesperson will actually cost more than the amount he or she contributes to gross profit ($9,000).

It should now be apparent that profits maximization is approached as the number of salespeople is increased. Adding salespersons continues to improve total profits because each new salesperson contributes more gross profit than is required to pay for his or her services. But eventually a salesperson is hired whose contribution to gross profit is exactly offset by the cost. This is the point of profits maximization. Hiring fewer, or more, salespeople actually would reduce total profits.

Now Essen has a way to answer his two questions. From Table 8.3 it is apparent that the best (the most profitable) number of salespeople is as follows:

Store 1	7
Store 2	5
Store 3	9
Store 4	5
Store 5	6
	32

Bob should employ 32 salespeople and assign them so that each store has the number that maximizes profits at that store and thereby maximizes overall profits for the entire chain.

We can summarize the marginality principle that has just been illustrated. In order to

TABLE 8.3 Essen Hardware Company stores average annual gross profit related to the number of salespersons employed

(All figures in thousands of dollars)

Number of salespersons	Cost Total	Cost Marginal	Store 1 Total	Store 1 Marginal	Store 2 Total	Store 2 Marginal	Store 3 Total	Store 3 Marginal	Store 4 Total	Store 4 Marginal	Store 5 Total	Store 5 Marginal
1	10.0		125.5		130.5		149.0		89.0		81.0	
		10.0		80.0		15.0		300.0		17.5		40.0
2	20.0		205.5		145.5		449.0		106.5		121.0	
		10.0		40.0		12.5		150.0		12.5		25.0
3	30.0		245.5		158.0		599.0		119.0		146.0	
		10.00		32.0		11.0		35.5		10.5		16.0
4	40.0		277.5		169.0		634.5		129.5		162.0	
		10.00		18.0		10.0		17.5		10.0		12.0
5	50.0		295.5		179.0		652.0		139.5		184.0	
		10.00		13.5		9.5		14.0		9.5		10.0
6	60.0		309.0		188.5		666.0		149.0		194.0	
		10.00		10.0		9.0		12.0		9.0		9.0
7	70.0		319.0		197.5		678.0		158.0		203.0	
		10.00		9.0		8.5		11.0		9.0		8.0
8	80.0		328.0		206.0		689.0		167.0		211.0	
		10.00		7.5		7.5		10.0		8.5		7.0
9	90.0		335.5		213.5		699.0		175.5		218.0	
		10.00		6.0		6.0		9.5		7.0		6.0
10	100.0		341.5		219.5		708.5		182.5		224.0	

maximize profits, the variable resource should be used at that level at which incremental revenue equals incremental cost. This can be expressed in equation form as

$$MR = MC$$

or alternatively

$$MR - MC = 0$$

Applying the marginality principle with a fixed resource Up to this point we have assumed that Bob Essen easily might increase or decrease the size of his company's sales force. We call such a situation *unconstrained.* However, as you recall, Essen actu-

ally has considerable difficulty in finding competent salespeople, and at any given time his sales force is fixed in number. We call this a *constrained* situation. It usually is not possible to maximize profits when a resource is constrained. Instead, the manager must suboptimize—that is, achieve the highest level of profits possible given the fact that a variable resource is constrained.

For example, suppose that one of Essen's senior salespeople decides to go into business and hires nine other Essen employees to work in the new venture. Essen now has 22 salespeople. How should he assign them to the five stores? To begin, he probably will inspect the profitability of each store with two less salespeople:

	Number of salespersons	Marginal-profit contribution
Store 1	5	8.0
Store 2	3	2.5
Store 3	7	2.0
Store 4	3	2.5
Store 5	4	6.0
	22	

The marginal-profit contributions (gross profit less salesperson expense) of these salespeople are shown on line 1 of Table 8.4 (iteration 1). Essen immediately notes that the seventh salesperson at store 3 produces a $2,000 contribution and that the fifth salesperson at store 1 generates $8,000. Why not move a salesperson from store 3 to store 1? Logic suggests that this person would produce more than $2,000 at store 1, although probably less than the $8,000 generated by the fifth salesperson. We look at the result of this reallocation on line 2 (iteration 2). Obviously the move was desirable. The sixth salesperson at store 1 produces $3,500 compared to the $2,000 when at store 3. Can the allocation be further improved? Essen thinks so. He shifts a salesperson from store 2 to store 5 (see iteration 3). This move does not appear to help very much. In fact, it now appears that the best thing to do is to reverse the decision that has just been made. (A decision to move a salesperson from store 4 to store 5 would have resulted in the same situation. You may want to check this out.)

Nothing is to be gained by further attempts at reallocation. Essen has come as close as he can to the application of the marginality principle in the constrained situation.

It is not possible in the strictest sense to maximize profits when a constraint exists; although from a practical viewpoint, the optimizing solution is the best attainable under the circumstances. The highest attainable profit will be realized when a variable resource is constrained if the marginal profit (contribution) in each market (such as a store, area, product, or·so on) is equal. This can be expressed as

$$MP_1 = MP_2 = MP_3 = MP_n = k$$

Note that the constant k will be greater than zero, due to the constraint. Over the long run the astute manager endeavors to remove the constraint and thereby approach the ideal profit attainment. But this usually is very difficult to do because of the many circumstances over which the manager has no control.

Marginality principle and profits maximization under certainty We can now return to the discussion of profits maximization under certainty and show how the marginality principle relates to the model in Figure 8.2. The easiest way to do this is to compute two additional sets of numbers from the data in Table 8.2. These are marginal revenue and

TABLE 8.4   Essen Hardware Company stores' marginal contribution of sales force
(Profit figures in thousands of dollars)

Iteration	Store 1		Store 2		Store 3		Store 4		Store 5	
	Number of sales force	Marginal profit	Number of sales force	Marginal profit	Number of sales force	Marginal profit	Number of sales force	Marginal profit	Number of sales force	Marginal profit
1	5	8.0	3	2.5	7	2.0	3	2.5	4	6.0
2	6	3.5	3	2.5	6	4.0	3	2.5	4	6.0
3	6	3.5	2	5.0	6	4.0	3	2.5	5	2.0

TABLE 8.5   Nonlinear revenue and cost data for profits maximization*

Price	Quantity (1,000)	Total revenue (1,000)	Fixed cost (1,000)	Variable cost Unit	Variable cost Total (1,000)	Total cost (1,000)	Total profit (1,000)	Marginal cost	Marginal revenue
65.00	100	6,500	5,000	10.00	1,000	6,000	500		
60.00	150	9,000	5,000	9.33	1,400	6,400	2,600	8.00	50.00
55.00	200	11,000	5,000	9.25	1,850	6,850	4,150	9.00	40.00
50.00	250	12,500	5,000	9.60	2,400	7,400	5,100	11.00	30.00
45.00	300	13,500	5,000	10.50	3,150	8,150	5,350	15.00	20.00
40.00	350	14,000	5,000	12.28	4,300	9,300	4,700	23.00	10.00
35.00	400	14,000	5,000	15.63	6,250	11,250	2,750	39.00	0
30.00	450	13,500	5,000	21.78	9.800	14,800	(1,300)*	71.00	(10.00)*
25.00	500	12,500	5,000	33.10	16,550	21,550	(9,050)*	135.00	(20.00)*

Figures in parentheses are losses.

marginal cost. They are calculated as follows:

$$MR = \frac{dTR}{dQ}$$

where MR is marginal revenue, dTR denotes the change in total revenue, and dQ indicates the change in output or sales that caused the change in total revenue. And,

$$MC = \frac{dTC}{dQ}$$

where MC is marginal cost, dTC is the change in total cost, and dQ is the change in output or sales that caused the change in total cost. Marginal revenue and marginal cost have been calculated for the data in Table 8.2. They are found in Table 8.5, which also includes the total-revenue and total-cost figures. By inspecting Table 8.5 and applying the marginality rules learned in the Essen Hardware Company example, we find that marginal revenue equals marginal-cost output between 250 and 300 units, or at approximately 280 units. Not

surprisingly, this is the same output at which the difference between total revenue and total cost is the greatest.

If the mathematical relationship is not evident, one more chart will suffice to demonstrate the connection between the marginality principle and profits maximization. Figure 8.3 has two parts. The upper part (part A) is a replication of Figure 8.2. The other part (part B) portrays the marginal-revenue and marginal-cost data found in Table 8.5. The output scales on the horizontal axes of the two charts are identical. The vertical axis in the upper chart indicates total dollars of revenue, cost, and profit. The vertical axis in the lower chart is scaled in dollars per unit of output—in this case marginal cost and marginal revenue for unit changes in output. Note that marginal revenue declines continuously, reflecting the fact that total revenue increases at a decreasing rate, which we learned earlier was due to the lower prices charged to encourage increased sales. Marginal cost increases consistently at an increasing rate. This behavior of marginal cost is traceable to the decreasing productivity of

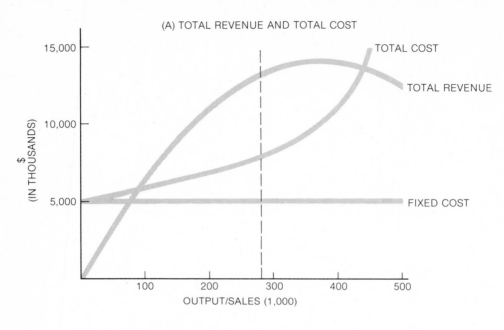

(A) TOTAL REVENUE AND TOTAL COST

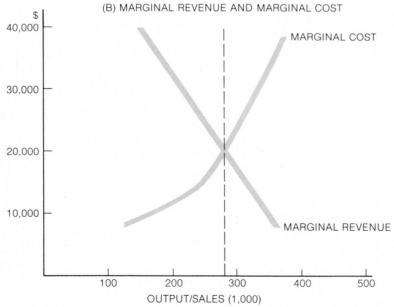

(B) MARGINAL REVENUE AND MARGINAL COST

FIGURE 8.3   Total and marginal profits maximization models

TABLE 8.6   Expected payoffs for two product strategies

(Figures in millions of dollars)

Alternative strategies	State of the economy			
	Excellent p=.10	Good p=.20	Fair p=.50	Poor p=.20
Introduce Grow!	2.00	1.80	.20	(.20)*
Introduce Clobber!	4.00	2.00	(.40)*	(1.00)*

*Figures in parentheses are losses.

the variable factor. (We saw how additional hardware salespeople were progressively less productive.)

Maximization of Expected Payoff Under Uncertainty

Expected payoff is quite similar to profit maximization. Both concepts emphasize finding the best possible return from some choice of action, such as the number of salespeople to assign to a territory or the output to schedule for a product. The concepts, however, do differ somewhat in their particulars. As we already have seen, profit maximization generally assumes that only one kind of result, or outcome, will occur in response to a firm's actions. We called this *decision making under certainty*, because there is no doubt as to the effect of a selection of a particular strategy.

In contrast, one of the most important features found in the payoff model is the provision for several possible profit outcomes for each of the strategies under consideration (see Table 8.6). The table shows four possible outcomes or payoffs for each of two alternative product-introduction strategies. The reason for showing four possible outcomes is that the manager is uncertain about the future state of the economy.

Grow! is a lawn fertilizer with more or less the same features as other products on the market. Its principal advantage to the consumer is its low price. Because of its low price and the almost "necessity" character of the demand for a basic lawn fertilizer, the manager expects that, although Grow! will suffer somewhat if business conditions are poor, it will be relatively less affected than the other product offering. Clobber! is a fertilizer with a remarkable pest-control feature. It will sell at a premium price. This innovative product clearly will be the most profitable if economic conditions are good or excellent; but it might be a potential disaster if the economy should turn down.

The payoff matrix in Table 8.6 highlights the usefulness of this type of model in making decisions. The company is not interested simply in the expected profit contribution of one product, say, Grow!, given a number of possible profit outcomes. Rather, it is interested in comparing the expected profit from Grow! with the expected profit from a different type of lawn fertilizer—Clobber! Used in this way, the payoff model not only provides a better estimate of expected profit, but permits the comparison of payoffs from two (or more) different marketing strategies. However, before we can discuss the decision rule by which the maximum expected payoff can be determined, we need to understand the concept of subjective probability.

Subjective probability   In everyday life we often guess at the chance that something will happen. Usually, the event is familiar to us—such as the possibility of rain tomorrow or of seeing a home run hit by a well-known baseball player. These events, when expressed in terms of their relative chances of occurrence, illustrate an essential element of subjective probability—namely that it is possible to state an opinion about the probability of occurrence of a one-time event. For example, how often do we hear someone say, "The chances are fifty-fifty that it will rain tomorrow," or "The chances are one in a hundred that that bum will hit a home run."

Similar kinds of educated guesses are possible in many business situations. For instance, a wholesaler may guess at the chances that a retailer will order two cases of canned peaches; an advertising agency executive may guess at the chances of a client switching to another shop; and a pricing analyst may guess at the chances of earning a desired return on investment from a particular product. Until the 1950s, however, such subjective judgments about the future were rarely discussed in business texts and probably seldom admitted to in business practice.

However, statisticians have come to realize that personalistic probability estimates have a place in business decision making when they are used appropriately. Such subjective probabilities regarding the future state of the economy are shown in Table 8.6. They indicate that the manager's best thinking about economic conditions in the next selling season ranges from a fairly modest belief that the economy will be strong to a rather firm belief that it will be depressed. In this example, the decisionmaker thinks that the probability of various economic conditions prevailing in the next selling season are as follows:

The chances that economic conditions will be excellent are	.10
The chances that economic conditions will be good are	.20
The chances that economic conditions will be fair are	.50
The chances that economic conditions will be poor are	.20
Total	1.00

Note that these probabilities must add up to 1.0, because it is absolutely certain that one of the four possible states will occur.

Expected value We can now illustrate how the payoff model and the concept of subjective probability can be combined to provide a decision model. A strategy choice criterion known as *expected value* is utilized. The expected value of a strategy is the weighted average of its various payoffs, using as weights the subjective probabilities of the states of nature. To illustrate, the expected value of introducing Grow! in Table 8.6 is:

$$\$2.00(.10) + \$1.80(.20) + \$.20(.50)$$
$$- \$.20(.20) = \$.420$$

The expected value of introducing Clobber! is:

$$\$4.00(.10) + \$2.00(.20) - \$.40(.50)$$
$$- \$1.00(.20) = \$.400$$

The manager probably will elect to introduce Grow!, because its expected value of $420,000 exceeds the expected value of Clobber! by $20,000. However, the difference is not very great, and the manager might be inclined for other reasons to go ahead with the more innovative product. Looking beyond a single year, the expected value of the two products over the next five to ten years might be projected. Or, the manager might believe that the image of the company with the public and in the trade would be enhanced by introducing Clobber!, and that this improvement in image would more than offset the $20,000. These two alternative lines of reasoning simply illustrate the fact that the final decision is up to the manager. Expected value is simply a decision criterion. It is a good criterion, but there are others to be considered. And in the last analysis it is the manager, not the

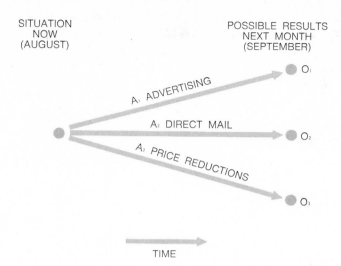

SITUATION
NOW
(AUGUST)

POSSIBLE RESULTS
NEXT MONTH
(SEPTEMBER)

A_1 ADVERTISING

A_2 DIRECT MAIL

A_3 PRICE REDUCTIONS

O_1

O_2

O_3

TIME

FIGURE 8.4   Rapp's Supermarket: A one-stage decision tree

model, who makes the choice among alternatives.

Decision-Tree Models

Another type of model that can illustrate the use of subjective probability as well as payoff maximization is called the *decision-tree model.* The name comes from the branching out of possible alternatives from a starting point, as can be seen in Figure 8.4. Decision trees are properly regarded as decision models because they summarize all of the possible strategies from which a manager can choose. The following examples show how decision trees can help to clarify and predict the best course of action for a business.[2]

[2]Two useful references that provide further details are John F. Magee, "Decision Trees for Decision Making," *Harvard Business Review,* July-August 1964, pp. 126–138; and Paul E. Green and Donald S. Tull, *Research for Marketing Decisions,* 2nd ed. (Englewood Cliffs, N.J.: Prentice-Hall, 1970).

A Basic Example of a Decision Tree

Suppose that in August the manager of Rapp's Supermarket decides to increase the store's sales in September by spending $2,000 on a special promotion. Given this budget, there are only three possible promotional strategies: (a) using local newspaper and radio advertising, (b) sending a direct-mail circular to every residence in the neighborhood, and (c) offering special low prices on some competitive items to the extent of a $2,000 reduction in their gross margin contribution. For the sake of simplicity, we will assume that the manager cannot choose a combination of these strategies. Each method is therefore a self-contained alternative, and only one of them can be selected. Diagramatically, the manager can portray the situation as a decision tree. As drawn, Figure 8.4 shows the three alternative courses of action, A_1, A_2, and A_3, as pathways extending from a *node,* or decision point, to three outcomes, O_1, O_2, and O_3, which are not yet known.

Presumably, the manager of Rapp's Su-

TABLE 8.7   Rapp's Supermarket: Payoff distributions for alternative strategies

Advertising (A_1)		Direct mail (A_2)		Price reductions (A_3)	
Chances	Sales increase	Chances	Sales increase	Chances	Sales increase
.10	$1,000	.20	$1,000	.10	$1,000
.50	1,500	.20	1,500	.20	1,500
.20	2,500	.20	2,500	.40	2,500
.10	3,500	.20	3,500	.20	3,500
.10	4,000	.20	4,000	.10	4,000
1.00		1.00		1.00	

permarket has had the business experience to permit the prediction of possible outcomes of each strategy. Table 8.7 summarizes the results. For each alternative the left-hand column shows the probability that the sales increase listed in the column to its right will occur.[3] Notice again that the probabilities of the various outcomes add up to 1.0, which implies that all possible outcomes have been accounted for.

The manager's problem now becomes solvable. By simple calculations, A_1 (advertising) is found to have an expected payoff of $2,100.

Chances (probability)		Sales increase		Payoff
.10	×	$1,000	=	$100
.50	×	1,500	=	750
.20	×	2,500	=	500
.10	×	3,500	=	350
.10	×	4,000	=	400
				$2,100

Using the same method, A_2 (direct mail) has an expected payoff of $2,500, and A_3 (price reductions) also has an expected payoff of

$2,500. The manager then determines the resulting expected profit contributions by subtracting the costs of each promotional strategy from its expected payoff:

	A_1 (advertising)	A_2 (direct mail)
Expected payoff	$2,100	$2,500
Minus expenditures	2,000	2,000
Expected profit contribution	$100	$500

	A_3 (price reductions)
Expected payoff	$2,500
Minus expenditures	2,000
Expected profit contribution	$500

These results show that A_2 and A_3 apparently are equally desirable and that both are superior to A_1. Either A_2 or A_3 should add $500 to September's profits.

Tie breaking   At least two methods can be used to choose between A_2 and A_3. One method, which emphasizes risk considerations, is to examine the probability distribution for the outcomes of A_2 and A_3. Which distribution appears more likely to yield a payoff of at least a certain amount, say

[3]Each alternative in this example has an identical set of possible sales increases. This has been done to simplify the problem and to bring out a related issue: choosing among alternatives with identical payoffs.

$2,500? A_3 is the better choice according to this method, because Table 8.7 shows that the manager thinks there is only a 60 per cent chance that direct mail will produce $2,500 or more, whereas he believes there is a 70 per cent chance that price reductions will produce at least $2,500.

Another procedure is to ask how the expected profits for A_1, A_2, and A_3 might change if the proposed expenditure of $2,000 were increased, for example, to $2,500. Note that A_1 should be examined in this approach even though it currently appears to be an unwise choice, because it might become a better choice than A_2 or A_3 if the budget were increased. This is because increasing the promotion budget will affect the sales increase. It may even alter the distribution of the probabilities. In a sense, it is a whole new ballgame, and an entirely different strategy might be best. For example, if the budget went as high as $5,000, television advertising might become feasible and possibly could be the best strategy. This emphasizes the importance of constraints, such as the amount of the budget and the size of the sales force, in identifying alternative courses of action.

Two-Stage Decision Trees

Not all problems are as easily solved as the Rapp's Supermarket example might imply. Consider this example. Suppose that Sheila Worth must decide whether to stock a new novelty item, Pet Rocks, in her chain of ten gift shops. The only aids that Worth has to help her make this decision are a fact sheet from a sales representative, the knowledge that Pet Rocks will not be advertised nationally, and her own intuitive judgment.

From an analytical point of view, Worth's problem is to choose between maintaining her present assortment of gifts or making the

new product available to her customers. Since these two alternatives are controllable, we shall call them *strategies* and think of them as the possible solutions to the problem. How well Pet Rocks would be accepted by customers is not nearly so controllable as are the alternative actions, however. It is possible that the item will be popular; but then again it may not be popular. For this reason, the customers' responses are to be regarded as *states of nature* or events not under the manager's control. (Recall how economic conditions were treated in the example of the fertilizers Grow! and Clobber!) For simplicity's sake, we shall assume that customers can exhibit only two responses: either they like Pet Rocks and are satisfied, or they dislike the product and are not satisifed. We also shall assume that the actions and states of nature are independent of each other.

Four possible results can occur, since there are two strategies and two possible states of nature. We can use the following notation to identify these results:

Strategies A_1 Worth does not stock Pet Rocks

                        A_2 Worth stocks Pet Rocks

States of nature S_1 Customers do not like Pet Rocks

                        S_2 Customers like Pet Rocks

We can describe the four possible results as follows:

1. $(A_1 S_1)$ Worth does not stock Pet Rocks and its sales in other stores strongly suggest that the item was not popular with consumers. This result can be regarded as producing no loss or gain for Worth inasmuch as she never stocked the product.

2. $(A_1 S_2)$ Worth does not stock Pet Rocks

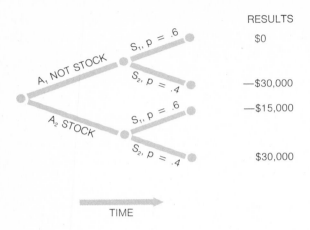

RESULTS

$0

$S_1, p = .6$

A, NOT STOCK

$S_2, p = .4$ —$30,000

$S_1, p = .6$ —$15,000

A₂ STOCK

$S_2, p = .4$ $30,000

TIME

FIGURE 8.5   Worth's Gift Shops: A two-stage decision tree

and its sales in other stores suggest that the item would have contributed $30,000 to annual profits. In effect, Worth loses $30,000 because she did not stock Pet Rocks.

3. (A_2S_1) Worth decides to stock Pet Rocks and then discovers that very few of her customers buy it. The result is a net loss of $15,000 because of her inventory carrying costs, merchandise handling costs, and price markdowns.

4. (A_2S_2) Worth stocks Pet Rocks and finds that her customers like the item. The result is a $30,000 increase in annual profits.

These combinations can be diagrammed in the form of a two-stage decision tree such as that shown in Figure 8.5. The same notation scheme has been used to label the tree's branches. The two-stage tree is much like the single-stage tree, except for the branching that takes place at the second set of nodes—called, in this instance, *chance nodes* because they lead to outcomes based on the different states of nature that might prevail.

This decision tree helps to reduce and

simplify the problem, and should make the issue clearer to the manager. But we should recognize its limitations as well. One of the major limitations is that Worth cannot select a course of action and then manipulate her customers to achieve a desired state of nature. She cannot attempt to control an event that is basically uncontrollable. That is, she cannot put Pet Rocks in her gift shops (A_2) and then make her customers like the item (S_2) in order to achieve the best expected payoff. In fact, if Worth did have any further action options after deciding to stock the product (such as advertising or reducing price), a three-stage decision tree with two action stages would be the appropriate model. Decision trees can be as elaborate as is the decision process that they are intended to represent.

Another limitation of the decision-tree model is that, although it may help the manager to understand the problem, it cannot by itself solve the problem. The manager also must know the expected value of each possible result before a final choice can be made on the most appropriate course of action. As we have seen in other examples,

Worth must determine the chances that each state of nature will occur. To do this she will employ the concept of subjective probability. We will assume that she believes that there is a .40 chance that her customers will go for Pet Rocks (S_2) and a .60 chance that they will not (S_1). Sheila's expected profit from choosing A_1 (not to stock Pet Rocks) is then found by multiplying the results of each strategy by the probabilities that each will occur. Thus, for strategy A_1 the expected value is

$$\$0.0(.60) - \$30,000(.40) = -\$12,000$$

Similarly, the expected value of strategy A_2 (to stock Pet Rocks) is

$$-\$15,000(.60) + \$30,000(.40) = \$3,000$$

Thus, A_2, the stocking of Pet Rocks, which results in an expected gain of $3,000, should be selected. (Fortunately, Pet Rocks turned out to be a very big thing in 1975, the year in which Worth was faced with this particular merchandising decision. She actually had trouble keeping them in stock!)

The Expected Value of Perfect Information

A manager can attempt to reduce the uncertainty that clouds the selection of the most profitable strategy. By conducting research to discover the true state of the market, a manager can avoid those strategies that would lead to losses. We call this foreknowledge that completely dispels uncertainty *perfect information*.[4]

---

[4]It should be readily apparent that perfect information is usually impossible or extremely expensive to collect. Nevertheless, the example illustrates an important concept.

By continuing the example of Worth's gift shops, it is possible to calculate an expected value of perfect information for the problem. This value is the amount that Worth would be willing to pay for perfect knowledge of her customers' reactions to Pet Rocks, so that she could always choose the best strategy. Such a value, it should be emphasized, assumes no changes in the probabilities and payoffs already estimated—it merely shows the gain from always choosing correctly.

Suppose that Worth used research to obtain foreknowledge of her customers' responses to Pet Rocks. If this research showed that her customers dislike Pet Rocks, her proper choice of action of course would be not to stock the product (A_1). Her payoff, as we have seen, would then be zero ($0). Conversely, if she knew that her customers would like Pet Rocks, her best choice of action would be to go ahead and stock the item (A_2). The result would be a payoff of $30,000.

We can use a slightly different version of the two-stage decision tree to model this situation (see Figure 8.6). The decision and chance nodes are reversed. It is possible to compute the expected value with perfect information by multiplying the payoffs for the best strategy by its probability of occurring. Thus

$$\$0(.60) + \$30,000(.40) = \$12,000$$

This value is compared with the expected value of the best choice under uncertainty, which as we recall was $3,000. The expected value with perfect information ($12,000) minus the expected value under uncertainty ($3,000) equals $9,000; and this is the maximum amount that Sheila Worth should be willing to spend on research. Therefore we also call it the *value of perfect information*.

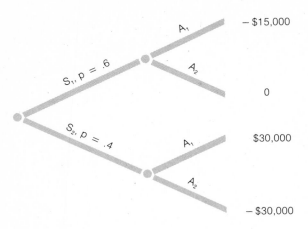

FIGURE 8.6   The inverted decision tree

PERT and Critical-Path Models

PERT-CPM[5] models are close relatives to the decision-tree models just described. However, they are primarily useful for project planning and scheduling purposes. Their applications include determining the least time necessary to plan a marketing program or an advertising campaign, or to launch a new product.[6] Alternatively, PERT-CPM models can be used to find the obstacles that prevent any of the foregoing from more rapid completion. Dramatic reductions in the lead times required to complete such projects have been reported by firms that

have made PERT-CPM project analysis a standard operating procedure.

Like the decision-tree models, applications of PERT-CPM are exceedingly simple, even though many elaborations and extensions of them have been developed over the years. The new-product example that will be discussed below illustrates only the fundamentals.

Introducing new products to the buying public has been one of the most successful marketing applications of PERT and CPM. Whenever a company is putting a new product on the market, it should do so promptly and efficiently. This is even more urgent if a competitor is following close behind with another version of the same type of product.

The first step in using a PERT-CPM model for product introduction or any other purpose is to define its so-called events. *Events* include such things as completion of a media schedule, completion of a test-marketing program, and receipt of all raw materials needed to make a product. The distinctive characteristic of an event is that it is always a fully completed task.

---

[5]The abbreviations stand for two phrases originally used by the military: *Program Evaluation and Review Technique* and *Critical-Path Method*. Originally the terms referred to two somewhat different techniques, but they have since come to be used almost interchangeably. Further details of both techniques are available in Richard I. Levin and C. A. Kirkpatrick, *Planning and Control with PERT/CPM* (New York: McGraw-Hill, 1966).

[6]See, for example, Warren Dusenbury, "CPM for New Product Introductions," *Harvard Business Review,* July-August 1967, pp. 124–139.

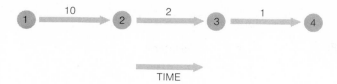

TIME

Lines denote activities; the number above a line shows the maximum number of days needed to complete an activity.
Circles denote completed events. The number within a circle is arbitrarily assigned. It denotes the character of the event according to the following code:

Event Number	*Event*
1	Start
2	Engineering drawings prepared
3	Engineering drawings released to factory
4	And so on

FIGURE 8.7   An example of sequential activities for the manufacture of a new product

Linking one event to another are *activities*. The activities leading up to the events just mentioned could consist of developing a media schedule, selecting a test market, and taking delivery of the raw materials. In summary, activities describe the actions needed to bring about results, and events describe the results that are achieved.

By way of illustration, Figure 8.7 shows a PERT sequence of events and activities for the introduction of a new manufactured product. Notice that the events are listed in the order in which they must be performed, with arrows marked on the connecting lines to show the direction of activity. Examining this figure, we can see that a total of 13 days are required to complete the events shown and that each event must be completed before the next activity is begun. Accordingly, Figure 8.7 illustrates what we call *sequential activities*.

Sometimes, however, several activities can be performed at the same time. Such activities are termed *concurrent*. Usually activities that can be performed concurrently have no direct relationship to each other as, for example, when some production and marketing tasks can be completed simultaneously but independently of one another. Events 2, 3, and 4 in Figure 8.8 are concurrent activities since they can be completed in any order.

The activity requiring the longest time in Figure 8.8 is warehouse stocking—event 3. It is expected to take 10 days. After this and the other concurrent activities have been completed, the product is available for sale. It is the completion of event 3, however, that is the most critical task, since any delay in its completion will delay the product's availability on the market. This is true because we have assumed that no additional activities are required after the completion of events 2, 3, and 4. Accordingly, we have joined those events to event 5 by means of three fictitious activities that require no time for their completion. The fictitious activities are merely a way to link all the concurrent activities to their common terminating point. Fictitious activities can be used as

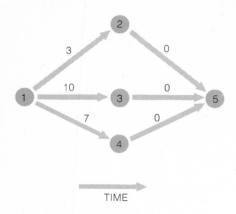

TIME

Event Number	Event
1	Start
2	Salespeople informed about product
3	Warehouse stocked with product
4	Advertising budgeted for product
5	Product available for sale

FIGURE 8.8   Concurrent activities in the marketing of a new product

necessary in PERT-CPM diagrams to specify interrelationships among events and to create pathways through the network.

All of the foregoing ideas can now be brought together in a more complex diagram, such as that shown in Figure 8.9. This figure illustrates a network for a new-product introduction. In it are sequential activities, concurrent activities, and fictitious activities. The arrangement of the activities suggests that the company is eager to get the jump on its competitors, because it has scheduled the manufacture of the product concurrently with the planning for its marketing. (Note especially events 3, 5, and 6.)

We can now ask two questions that will illustrate the usefulness of this network dia-

gram. "What is the shortest possible time in which the product can be made available for sale?" "Which events might delay the product's introduction?"[7] Both of these questions can be answered by finding the *critical path*—the most time-consuming path in the network. In Figure 8.9 the critical path includes events 1, 2, 4, 5, 8, and 9. It is shown by the heavy line. The total time along this path is 122 days from start to finish. Any other path from event 1 to event 9 will take less time and, therefore, will fail to recognize all of the potential impediments to the project's completion. In other words, there is no event in any other path that could impede the product's progress toward introduction more seriously than could the events in the critical path. Accordingly, the shortest feasible time to be allowed for the introduction of the product is the time required by the events in the critical path. Any delay in completing activities along this path necessarily increases the total time that will be required. Hence we refer to the path as *critical*.

We can glean other useful information from the further analysis of Figure 8.9. The long lead time between the product's availability (9) and the approval of its advertising budget (8) implies that stocking the warehouse (6) can be delayed for as long as 70 days, since pathway 1–2–3–6–9 requires only 52 days. Similarly, there is an excess of time available between the time the company's salespeople are informed (7) and the time the product becomes available (9). In both instances, delays can be tolerated without

[7]Alternatively, the company might want to know if the product could be marketed by a certain date. This question can be answered by working backward from the desired completion date to the origin of the network in order to determine if the necessary activities can be completed on time.

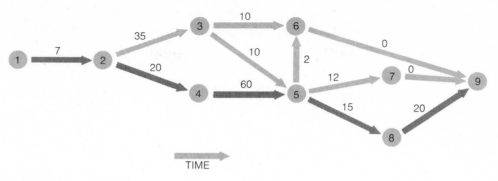

Event Number	Event
1	Research and development completed
2	Budget for manufacturing and marketing activities approved
3	Initial production completed
4	Overall marketing plan approved
5	Test marketing completed
6	Warehouse stocked with product
7	Salespeople informed
8	Advertising budgeted
9	Product available for sale

FIGURE 8.9   A new-product introduction network

postponement of the product's intended introductory date. And so the major contributions of the PERT-CPM analysis is that it shows which activities are crucial to keeping on schedule and which other activities safely can be allowed to run behind.

Programming Models

Resource-Allocation Models

Another class of model that has been useful to marketers is the resource-allocation model. This model focuses on finding the best possible uses for a given set of resources (sales force, warehouse capacities, supermarket check-out stands, capital funds, and so on) during a certain period of time, such as a month or a year.

Without a doubt the technique most commonly used in connection with resource-allocation models is *linear programming*.[8] This type of programming has gained wide acceptance because of its conceptual simplicity, its ease of use on a computer, and its wide range of applications. Formally, linear programming provides a means for finding an optimum result, or payoff, given that a business has various alternatives, or activities, open to it. These activities are best regarded as possible ways to accomplish the

[8]For further information on linear programming, see William A. Clark and Donald E. Sexton, *Marketing and Management Service* (Homewood, Ill.: Richard D. Irwin, 1970), pp. 293–315 and 438. Many other texts also contain expositions of programming.

TABLE 8.8   Data for product-mix allocation problem

Row number	Input information	Sweeties	Roasties
1	Profit contribution per case sold, net of all traceable costs	$0.30	$0.10
2	Hours of time required, on the average, to sell one case	0.26	0.13
3	Profit contribution, expressed in dollars per hour of selling time (row 1 divided by row 2)	$1.27	$0.77
4	Maximum number of cases that wholesalers will accept	8,000	15,000
5	Maximum number of cases the sales force can sell if its entire time is devoted to one product (row 6 divided by row 2)	10,000	20,000
6	Total hours of time available for selling in fourth quarter of 1972 (10 persons × 20 hours per person per week × 13 weeks)	2,600	

results that a firm desires, such as making and selling products.

Linear programming often is explained in economics and quantitative-method textbooks through an example of a manufacturing company concerned with allocating its resources to the production of several possible products. The problem of resource allocation, however, is not unique to manufacturing, and linear programming techniques also can be applied to decisions involving resource allocation in marketing. For example, allocating an advertising budget to determine an optimum media schedule, allocating salespeople to regional offices, and determining an optimum product-line mix are all marketing problems that can be subjected to linear programming. The example given below is relatively brief and simple. Of course, much more sophisticated program-

ming models are needed to solve real-world problems, but the widespread acceptance of linear programming in American industry today is ample proof that realistic models can be devised and that they can provide useful results.

A Product-Mix Example of a Linear-Programming Model

Suppose that a sales manager in charge of 10 salespeople is interested in finding out what quantities of two dry cereals, *Sweeties* and *Roasties,* her staff should sell to wholesalers in order to maximize the district's contribution to company profits in the fourth quarter. We shall assume that the manager has decided to analyze the problem by means of linear programming and that she has obtained the information listed in Table 8.8, all of which is based on the best available estimates for the calendar quarter. For the sake of simplicity, we shall further assume that wholesalers who buy Sweeties refuse to buy Roasties and vice versa, because the two cereals look and taste remarkably like each other.

A quick glance at Table 8.8 shows that Sweeties is the more profitable product. Each case of Sweeties should yield a profit contribution of $.30 net of all traceable costs, such as sales time, shipping costs, and manufacturing costs. In view of the total amount of selling time available (2,600 hours), it would be possible to sell as many as 10,000 cases of Sweeties.

However, the manager knows that wholesalers will not buy more than 8,000 cases in the quarter because of their unwillingness to purchase more than they believe they can reasonably sell. It becomes obvious, then, that some selling time must be devoted to Roasties, since it is better to sell this product than to do nothing after having sold as many cases of Sweeties as possible.

By now the optimum solution to the problem may be evident, but we shall nonetheless work out the solution in a systematic manner to illustrate the basic mechanics of linear programming. The solution procedure will utilize the graphical analysis shown in Figure 8.10. In addition, an algebraic statement of the problem will be presented for those of you who already are familiar with programming.

As we have said, the sales manager can have the sales force sell either or both products. Figure 8.10 illustrates the possible amounts of each product, with cases of Sweeties on the vertical axis and cases of Roasties on the horizontal axis. Each axis, in other words, shows the possible outputs of

the selling work in physical terms. More precisely, each axis is a possible activity, and the amounts of output shown on the axis are known as *activity levels.*

On the vertical axis a dot has been marked at the 10,000-case level to show the maximum number of cases of Sweeties that could be sold (1) if the wholesalers were willing to buy that many, and (2) if no Roasties were sold. Similarly, the horizontal axis shows a dot at the 20,000-case level to mark the maximum number of cases of Roasties that could be sold if there were no customer demand problems and no need to sell Sweeties.

Joining the two dots on the axes is a downward-sloping line. The darker segment of this line is called a *production frontier;* any point along that segment describes the maximum number of cases of Sweeties and Roasties that could be sold in combination without spending more than 2,600 hours of selling time. This can be illustrated by calculating the hours of work needed to sell two or three arbitrarily chosen combinations lying on the production frontier. Table 8.8 gives the necessary hours-per-case data.

Also shown on the graph is a darker line segment extending horizontally at 8,000 cases of Sweeties and a similar vertical segment at 15,000 cases of Roasties. These two segments represent the wholesalers' unwillingness to buy more than the quantities specified. Technically, the segments are called constraints—they limit the brands' sales.

In addition to these constraints, Figure 8.10 includes a number of equal-profit lines, which show the various combinations of Sweeties and Roasties that can be sold to yield a specific dollar profit. For any given profit line, for example, $2,000, there exists an almost infinite number of possible

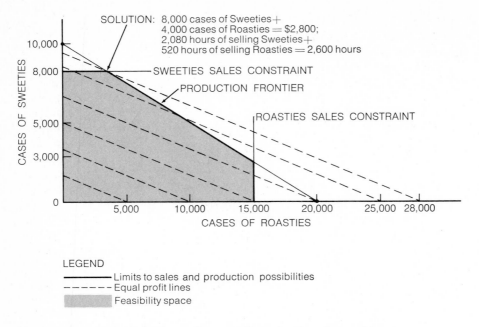

FIGURE 8.10   Graphical solution for a product-mix allocation problem

product-mix combinations. Six equal-profit lines are shown in the diagram. Actually, there could be many more, covering all possible levels of profit. For simplicity, the profit lines drawn in Figure 8.10 have been positioned at equal increments of $500. As long as the profit-contribution ratio of the two products remains constant, as it does in this example, the equal-profit lines will be parallel.

Now that the production frontier, the two constraints, and the equal-profit lines have been drawn in, we can see that all the limitations on the ability to sell create a polygon enclosing what is called the *feasibility space*. This space includes every possible combination of Sweeties and Roasties that can be sold by the sales force. Also we can see that any point below or to the left of the darker-line segments will not be as

profitable as a point lying along those segments. This implies that we need to consider only the points along the outside of the polygon in trying to arrive at an optimum solution.

The last step before reaching such a solution is to examine the profit implications for any combination of case sales of the two cereals. As can be seen from the graph, the most profitable combination turns out to be 8,000 cases of Sweeties and 4,000 cases of Roasties. This is the point on the production frontier that is just tangent to the highest equal-profit line included in the company's feasibility space. Another, but lower, profit line (about $2,200) also is tangent to the production frontier at a combination of 15,000 cases of Roasties and 2,000 cases of Sweeties. However, the first solution is preferred since it involves greater total profit.

Moreover, a verification that this solution does, in fact, represent the maximum possible profit can be made by checking the resources that the solution needs. In terms of selling time, the first solution requires that 2,080 hours should be devoted to selling Sweeties and that 520 hours should be allocated to Roasties, for a total of the requisite 2,600 hours.[9]

Advantages of Programming Models

Three advantages of programming models are suggested by the foregoing example. Of these, the most important is that such models can provide the manager with a systematic way of thinking about problems involving the optimum allocation of scarce resources (selling time for instance) to multiple uses (sales of Sweeties and sales of Roasties). Stating any problem about the optimum use of resources as a programming problem—regardless of whether linear programming can be appropriately used—always is helpful

[9]Readers who are familiar with the mathematics of linear programming will see that the linear algebraic formulation of this problem (before introducing slack variables) is as follows:

The objective function

$$\$0.30\,x_1 + \$0.10\,x_2 = Max\ f(x)$$

is subject to operating constraints

$$.26\,x_1 + .13\,x_2 \leq 2{,}600 \text{ hours}$$
$$x_1 \leq 8{,}000 \text{ cases}$$
$$x_2 \leq 15{,}000 \text{ cases}$$

and the nonnegativity constraints

$$x_1,\ x_2 \geq 0 \text{ cases}$$

where   activity x_1 = cases of Sweeties

and   activity x_2 = cases of Roasties

in clarifying optimum-seeking behavior and in identifying the trade-offs between the activities involved (for example, what is the profit-consequence of selling one additional case of Roasties instead of one additional case of Sweeties?).

The second important advantage of programming is that it encourages a manager to think of an allocation problem in terms of its basic components: the activities themselves, the activities' payoff functions, the resources used by the activities, and the situational constraints applying to the problem. The manager then can consider whether to have a specialist in management science analyze the problem in greater detail. Without an understanding of the basic concepts of programming, however, the manager is not likely to be aware of the potentialities of a thorough scientific analysis.

Finally, once the allocation problem has been defined in programming terms, the manager can consider whether the analysis has dealt with the fundamental problem. Is it truly reasonable, for example, to limit oneself to selling only two products, Sweeties and Roasties? Why not broaden the product line? Is it reasonable that only 10 salespeople should be used to sell the products? Why not more? Also, is it reasonable that the customers should refuse to buy more than 8,000 cases of Sweeties? All of these questions illustrate that new insights and alternatives nearly always appear after programming concepts are applied to problems in resource allocation.

Implementing Marketing Models

This chapter suggests that systematic techniques for making decisions are desirable and that they are valuable in marketing management. But have these techniques been widely accepted by managers? Have they made a substantial contribution to marketing management? Can their costs be justified in relation to the information they provide?

The honest answer to all these questions is "Yes and no." One survey indicated that model-building techniques have made some headway but that there is by no means a universal acceptance of them.[10] A more recent informal investigation by the author indicated that about one in five of the firms contacted had made use of one or more of the models described in this chapter. Such evidence suggests that corporate managers have acted with discretion—perhaps too much discretion—in implementing the techniques. At least two possible reasons for this caution can be identified. First, many managers are probably not yet sufficiently aware of these techniques to be able to use them. And second, the techniques are costly relative to the value of their results. But this situation is bound to change as persons with more quantitative skills enter marketing management and as managers and management scientists learn to work together more effectively.

On balance, and particularly in view of the generalized nature of the decision tools presented in this chapter, you should recognize that models are more important for the approach they represent than as instruments to be directly applied. A set of frameworks for decision making has been presented. Each model presents a systematic way of viewing a marketing problem and each contains these critical elements:

1. A set of objectives stated in quantitative terms
2. A set of relevant variables, including inputs, outputs, and constraints—all in measurable terms
3. A decision structure that permits the manager to make a choice among alternative courses of action

A systematic framework aids the manager in making strategic decisions; but as has been emphasized several times, the model does not make the choice. A management consultant once said, "The choice of a strategy may sometimes be more spiritual than statistical." Decision tools are only as useful as the skill of the user, and that skill includes the ability to judge when to use the tool at all.

As we plunge into the following chapters on marketing strategy, many instances in which the new decision tools can be used will be encountered. But they will not be the only tools to be employed. We will explore the artistry of marketing management and will discover that decision making in marketing is in fact a blend of science and art. This is one of the things that makes marketing one of the most fascinating (and sometimes frustrating) elements of modern business.

Summary

Until recently marketing was not thought to be very scientific. Most decisions were made by intuition or on the basis of past experience. But management science, defined as the use of quantitative techniques to help make marketing decisions, has significantly changed the approach to marketing management—at least in some companies. True, the marketing manager has not become a mathematical whiz kid, nor is it likely that the

---

[10]John J. Caldwell, "Marketing and Management Science—A Marriage on the Rocks?" *California Management Review* 10 (Summer 1968): 3–12.

future manager will have to be an accomplished management scientist. But the manager needs to understand how quantitative techniques can be used to help solve marketing problems and how to communicate effectively with the management scientists who are asked to help solve them.

We have looked at several quantitative techniques, beginning with the decision rules that the management scientist applies. The rules discussed were (1) profits maximization under certainty and (2) maximization of expected payoff under uncertainty. Both criteria have a place in marketing management. The classical break-even chart and the more refined nonlinear profits maximization models have been illustrated and explained. Both involve the condition of certainty, since the models assume that only one outcome will occur for any given strategy.

The marginality principle is the keystone of profits maximization analysis. This principle states that a variable resource should be employed as long as the incremental revenue resulting from its use equals or exceeds the incremental cost of adding it. We have seen how the marginality principle can be applied when the resource is unconstrained (unlimited) and when it is constrained (limited).

Maximization of expected payoff under uncertainty is a more realistic decision model. It is based on the assumption that several possible outcomes may result from a particular strategy, depending on the particular state of nature that prevails. However, since the state of nature is unknown (or at least uncertain), the manager uses subjective probabilities to weight the various payoffs and to compute an expected value. This gives an average payoff under all possible states of nature. By comparing the expected value of two or more strategies, the manager can make an intelligent choice—in spite of the uncertainty that exists. If the manager

would like to reduce the uncertainty, marketing research can be undertaken. If the marketing research produces perfect information, the manager will know which is the best strategy to adopt. The expected value of always making the right choice can be compared with the expected value without conducting the research. We call the difference the value of perfect information; the manager is justified in spending up to that amount for research to eliminate uncertainty.

Decision-tree models are very similar to payoff models, except that they portray the decision choices and states of nature as branches stemming from nodes in the model. The decision tree is a helpful method of visualizing a marketing problem because it emphasizes the alternatives among which the manager must choose. In extremely complex situations that require the use of two- or three-stage decision-tree models, this approach is an excellent way to systematize the complicated decision variables with which the manager must contend.

PERT-CPM models are close relatives to decision-tree models. They are used primarily for planning and scheduling marketing projects—such as the introduction of new products or the development of advertising campaigns. The critical-path model is especially useful. It identifies the most time-consuming path of events in the network of activities. If the schedule of events any place on the critical path is not met, the project as a whole is certain to be delayed.

We also looked at a programming model. The principal use of such a technique is to allocate resources when one or more constraining elements exist. The model most frequently used is called linear programming. An example of allocating the sales force to two products was presented.

There is no doubt that quantitative techniques are here to stay. They make an important contribution to marketing management. At present, however, they are still not extensively used. We expect this to change, especially as marketing managers and management scientists learn to work effectively together.

Questions and Problems

1. Benjamin Franklin wrote in 1789 the frequently quoted remark, "In this world nothing is certain but death and taxes." Assuming the universal validity of the statement, how is it that marketing decisionmakers can benefit from understanding the concept of profits maximization under conditions of certainty?

2. The manager of the Valley Car Wash in San Jose wants to use break-even analysis to operate the company more profitably. A business-school class collected the following information for the manager:

Production function		Demand schedule	
Variable input (number of salespeople)	Total product (cars per hour)	Price per car	Quantity demanded per hour
1	3.4	3.50	0.0
2	7.0	3.25	1.5
3	10.0	3.00	3.0
4	12.4	2.75	4.5
5	14.2	2.50	6.0
6	15.4	2.25	7.5
7	16.0	2.00	9.0
8	16.0	1.75	10.5
9	15.4	1.50	12.0
10	14.2	1.25	13.5
		1.00	15.0
		.75	16.5
		.50	18.0
		.25	19.5

In addition, the class determined that the labor cost is $2.00 per hour; the fixed cost is $5.00 per hour; and water, soap, and other supplies cost $0.20 per car.

a. Draw break-even charts for Valley Car Wash (1) if a car wash sells for $2.00 and (2) if the demand schedule in question 2 applies.

b. Identify the break-even points.

c. What is the most profitable volume?

3. What is the marginality principle?

4. Using the data provided in question 2, construct the marginal-cost and marginal-revenue schedules.

a. Plot the two curves.

b. Determine the most profitable volume at which to operate the firm.

c. Is this the same answer you obtain for question 2, part c? Why?

5. The sales promotion manager of a chain of supermarkets in Atlanta is considering three possible strategies to increase her stores' share of the area's grocery business. Strategy 1 involves an increase in the company's advertising budget from $200,000 to $300,000. Strategy 2 calls for selective price decreases on popular products amounting to a $100,000 reduction in sales income. Strategy 3 involves a consumer contest in which the value of the prizes and the expense of administration would total $100,000. The manager believes that the state of the economy in Atlanta will have considerable bearing on the outcomes of these three alternatives. For example, if consumer income is high, the advertising strategy should work best; if consumer income is down, the price reductions should be most effective. If the economy is neither strong nor weak, the excitement of the contest should make it the most successful.

TABLE 8.9

Event number	Event	Must follow after event(s)	Days required to complete event
1	Start	—	—
2	Problem defined	1	3
3	Search of secondary sources completed	2	10
4	Sample survey design completed	2	15
5	Questionnaire completed	3, 4	5 days after event 3; 0 days after event 4
6	Field survey completed	5	20
7	Data edited, tabulated, and analyzed	6	15
8	Final report completed	7	10

a. Set up a payoff matrix for this situation.

b. Establish some hypothetical subjective probabilities for each alternative.

c. Fill in the cells of the payoff matrix with data that represent possible payoffs in gross profit contribution.

d. Calculate the expected value for each strategy and indicate the one that is superior.

e. Under what circumstances might the manager elect not to select the strategy with the highest expected value?

6. Draw a decision tree for the following situation (probabilities and payoffs have been omitted in order to simplify the problem): The advertising manager for Smith's, a large discount department store, is preparing a promotional plan intended to combat a loss of customers to Brown's a newly opened promotional discount store in the same city. The advertising manager is concerned that the owner of Smith's may not approve his plan. If his plan is approved, there is a considerable chance that Brown's will retaliate with a similar promotion to counteract Smith's campaign. Construct a tree showing all the possibilities that the advertising manager should consider. Label each branch to identify it.

7. Find the critical path and minimum possible completion time for the market research project described in Table 8.9. (Such a table is customary in applications of PERT-CPM.)

8. Describe, in words, how a linear-programming model could be used to allocate funds from an advertising budget to various publications, all of which are newspapers or magazines. Answers to the following questions should help you to think through the problem:

a. What should be the payoff function (objective function)? Two possible answers are maximum number of advertising exposures and minimum total cost.

b. What limitations (constraints) should be considered? The amount of money budgeted for the campaign? A minimum (or maximum) number of insertions in any given publication? A minimum size for any ad?

c. How many publications should be considered?

9

Product Strategy

We commence our discussion of the specifics of marketing management with the topic of product strategy. Why do we begin here? Mainly because the product is the principal means by which a company provides consumer satisfactions. For example, the package in which a product is contained may satisfy a need for convenience or safety. The brand name or identity of a product adds meaning—perhaps assurance or status. The seller of a product may extend a service, such as delivery or financing. All of these things enhance the consumer's satisfaction and are, by definition, part of the company's product offering. It is the engine that pulls the rest of the marketing program. Without a product, there is nothing to distribute, nothing to promote, nothing to price.

What Is a Product?

The term *product* refers not only to a physical commodity but also to anything used by a firm to provide customer satisfaction. A product can be a single commodity or a service, a group of commodities or a group of services, a product-service combination, or even a combination of several products and services.

Theodore Levitt suggests a useful term to describe this concept of a product.[1] He refers to the *augmented product,* or the aggregate of the satisfactions that a user obtains. When an industrial marketer sells a major item of machinery, it may augment the product in several ways. A diesel engine manufacturer might (1) provide long-term financing, (2) assure a constant supply of maintenance and replacement parts, (3) guarantee the performance of the engine for a specified period of time, (4) make technicians available to advise the customer on the installation and use of the product, and (5) train the customer's people who actually will operate the engine. The customer doesn't just buy a diesel engine; the customer pur-

[1]T. Levitt, *Marketing for Business Growth* (New York: McGraw-Hill, 1975), p. 9.

200

chases an augmented product—a product augmented by financial, warranty, service, and training benefits.

Classifications of Goods

Consumer Goods

Consumer Goods and services are those used by ultimate consumers (or households) for the satisfaction of personal wants. There are various ways to classify consumer goods, each method of classification contributing some useful perspectives on product strategy.

Durables and nondurables   One of the most common means of classification is the durability of products. *Durable goods* are those that are expected to deliver a stream of satisfactions over a period of time. The length of the period is not as critical as the fact that a product's utility is not consumed immediately. A watch that may last twenty-five years or a fountain pen that may last ten are both durable goods. An orange, a sport shirt, and dry cleaning (like all services) are *nondurables*. Durable goods often are more expensive than nondurables, but not always. (A Super Bowl ticket may cost more than a transistor radio.)

Luxuries and necessities   Another way to classify consumer goods is the rather nebulous distinction between *luxuries* and *necessities*. There is no doubt that consumers do distinguish between things that are musts and those that are not. However, disparities in family income and living standards have been disappearing, at least in the technologically advanced countries. In the United States, considerable poverty remains, but the majority of Americans are relatively well off. Thus, rather than to speak of necessities and luxuries in the modern American market, it makes more sense to distinguish between necessities and nonnecessities. Nonnecessities broadly include those items and services competing for the discretionary purchasing dollar. The marketing significance of such a classification is clear. A so-called necessity has first claim on the consumer dollar. Competitive marketing of necessities is largely restricted to brand competition among various sellers. On the other hand, the marketer of a nonnecessity first must compete with all other sellers of discretionary products and then compete with other sellers of comparable items.

Convenience, shopping, and specialty goods Another classification that has long been used in marketing separates manufactured goods into three groups: convenience, shopping, and specialty.[2] A *convenience good* is one that a shopper wishes to buy with a minimum of effort. It should be readily available. Vending machines typically dispense convenience goods. These products are usually of low unit value, they are highly standardized, and frequently they are nationally advertised. Such characteristics, together with the necessity for widespread distribution, make the marketing of convenience goods extremely involved, although not especially difficult.

---

[2]This is the classification accepted by the definitions committee of the American Marketing Association. Its origin can be traced to M. T. Copeland, "Relation of Consumers' Buying Habits to Marketing Methods," *Harvard Business Review,* April 1923, pp. 282–289. Modifications have been proposed over the years. For example, see L. Aspinwall, *Four Marketing Theories* (Boulder, Colorado: 1961); L. P. Bucklin, "Retail Strategy and the Classification of Consumer Goods," *Journal of Marketing,* January 1963, pp. 50–55; and J. M. Rathmell, "What Is Meant by Services?" *Journal of Marketing,* October 1966, p. 27.

Shopping goods are goods that consumers wish to compare with other available offerings before making a selection. Household furnishings, clothing, and recreation equipment are in this group. Shoppers are willing to go to some lengths to compare values, and therefore these goods need not be distributed widely. Many shopping goods are nationally advertised, but often it is retail differentiation that attracts shoppers. The market for shopping goods tends to be more segmented than is the market for convenience goods. Discounting, or promotional price cutting, is characteristic of many shopping goods because retailers want to provide attractive shopping values.

Specialty goods are goods that buyers are willing to go to considerable lengths to seek out and purchase. Price is seldom a principal factor affecting the sale of specialty goods. Such goods may be custom-made, or they simply may be very successfully differentiated products. Regardless of the reason, the specialty product is considered so unique by its buyers that they rarely accept substitutes and usually are willing to wait, if necessary, for delivery. It is generally desirable for a marketer to lift a product from the shopping to the specialty class and keep it there. Hence, most of the marketing activities associated with shopping goods, except price cutting, also apply to the sale of specialty goods.

Business Goods

Consumer goods are not the only concern of marketing strategists. There are also important wants for industrial goods, and industrial and business demands present marketing opportunities as important as those for consumer goods. The methods of industrial marketing are somewhat specialized, but in general the concepts presented in this text are valid for the industrial market as well as for the consumer-goods market. There are several important types of industrial goods.

Agricultural and other extractive products Farms, forests, mines, and quarries provide raw materials. Although certain farm products are ready for consumption on leaving the farm, most agricultural products and all extractive products undergo some processing before consumption. Demands for extractive products are derived from the demands for the goods into which they are transformed. Since many firms that require these raw materials do not own their own sources, they must seek them in the market. Thus, a market demand arises and a marketing opportunity is born.

Manufactured industrial products Manufactured products are those that have undergone some processing. The demands for manufactured industrial goods usually are derived from the demands for ultimate consumer goods. There are a number of specific types of manufactured industrial goods.

Semimanufactured goods are raw materials that have gone through some stages of manufacturing but require further processing before they can be used. Products such as copper billets, lumber, and crude oil are examples. *Parts* are manufactured items that are ready to be incorporated into other products. *Process machinery* (sometimes called *installations*) refers to major pieces of equipment used in the manufacture of other goods. These are manufacturing plant or capital items that often require top-management approval before they are acquired. Boilers, lathes, blast furnaces, elevators, and conveyor systems are examples of process machinery. *Equipment* involves lesser items of a productive nature. Bench tools, lift trucks, typewriters, and store fixtures are examples of equipment. *Supplies* are materials used in the course of business that are destroyed or consumed in the process.

Classification of industrial products by buying attributes The classification of industrial goods according to buying behavior (remember, this is the basis for identifying convenience, shopping, and specialty goods) was attempted by Lehmann and O'Shaughnessy.[3] They suggest that industrial products can be classified into four categories according to the problems that purchasing agents contend with in purchasing them.

Routine-order products are products that are used regularly and ordered frequently. Few if any problems arise. Examples are office supplies, component parts of very well established products, and standardized packaging materials.

Procedural-problem products are those that may reasonably be expected to perform well, but will require changes in operations to integrate them properly. A decision in a small advertising agency to buy a small offset-printing press to do work internally that had previously been sent outside caused considerable turmoil and delay until office personnel could be trained to use the press efficiently.

Performance-problem products are products that may not perform up to expectations. Is the technology correct for a specific application? A typesetting company considering the purchase of a computer-assisted system would be concerned whether this equipment was actually well suited to the type of work its customers required.

Political-problem products pose problems because of disagreements among those involved in the decision to buy or use the items. If more than one department will

[3]D. R. Lehmann and J. O'Shaughnessy, "Difference in Attribute Importance for Different Industrial Products," *Journal of Marketing,* April 1974, pp. 36–42, published by the American Marketing Association.

have to use a given piece of equipment or if completely unconnected departments are competing for scarce funds, political problems arise. *Reciprocity* (the practice of buying from one's customer) raises issues between the purchasing department and sales.

These are commonly encountered problems in industrial purchasing. The classification of goods to reflect these conditions makes good sense. The implications to the marketing manager in an industrial-products company are apparent. Strategies and tactics to minimize these buyer problems are important parts of the industrial company's marketing mix.

Product Strategy and the Product Life Cycle

A *product strategy* is a company's plan for marketing its products. It is one part of the total marketing mix. As such, it has the same elements as the overall marketing plan. It starts with a statement of product objectives. These objectives may be goals that the company wishes to achieve, or they may take the form of product-line problems that the company needs to solve. In either event, a statement of product objectives is the first step in developing a product strategy. The second step in developing a product strategy is the design of a product line to achieve the stated objectives or to solve troublesome problems that have arisen. Whereas the overall marketing strategy takes the form of an integrated marketing mix involving product, distribution, promotion, and pricing strategies, the product strategy takes the form of answers to a series of problems or issues faced in the course of product planning. To a considerable extent these problems and issues vary according to the prod-

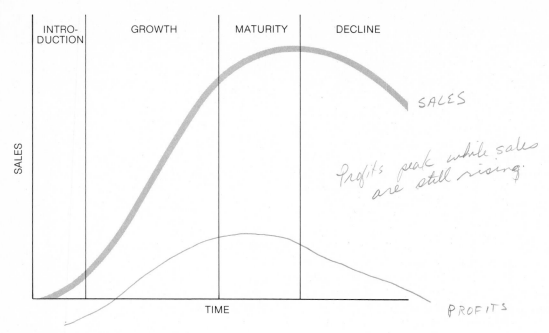

| INTRO-DUCTION | GROWTH | MATURITY | DECLINE |

SALES

Profits peak while sales are still rising.

PROFITS

SALES

TIME

FIGURE 9.1   The product life cycle

uct's position in the life cycle. We will now look at each of these elements in more detail.

The Product Life Cycle

The product life-cycle model is one of the most frequently encountered concepts in marketing management. Its earliest applications were in fashion merchandising, but it has gained acceptance in almost all areas of marketing. Levitt popularized the concept; others have extended and elaborated on it.[4]

⁴See T. Levitt, "Exploit the Product Life Cycle," *Harvard Business Review,* November-December 1965, pp. 81–94, and *Marketing for Business Growth;* C. R. Wassen, *Product Management: Product Life Cycles and Competitive Marketing Strategy* (St. Charles, Ill.: Challenge Books, 1971); B. Catry and M. Chevalier, "Market Share Strategy and the Product Life Cycle," *Journal of Marketing,* October 1974, pp. 28–34; and D. J. Luck, *Product Policy and Strategy* (Englewood Cliffs, N.J.: Prentice-Hall, 1972).

The life cycle is simply a graphic portrayal of the sales history of a product from the time it is introduced to the point when it is withdrawn. See Figure 9.1. There are four major stages to the product life cycle. They are

1. *Introduction*—the period during which a new product is introduced. Initial distribution is obtained and promotion is initiated.
2. *Growth*—the period during which the product is accepted by consumers and the trade. Initial distribution is expanded, promotion is increased, repeat orders from initial buyers are obtained, and word-of-mouth advertising leads to more and more sales.
3. *Maturity*—the period during which competition becomes serious. Toward the end of this period, competitors' products cut deeply into the company's market growth.

4. *Decline*—the product becomes obsolete, and its loss of competitive advantages results in sales declines.

The different competitive conditions that prevail in each of these periods dictate different marketing approaches. In no area is this more apparent than in the area of product strategy. The product is the firm's chief competitive weapon, and contending with the product life cycle is best accomplished by changes in the product itself. Of course, we will see in this and subsequent chapters that changes in other elements of the marketing mix also can contribute to a strengthened competitive position. For example, a vigorous promotional program or a dramatic lowering of price may improve the sales picture in the decline period, at least temporarily. But the improvements brought about by nonproduct tactics tend to be relatively short lived. Basic alterations in product offerings plus changes in the rest of the marketing mix usually are required for longer-run benefits. Thus, we return to product strategy as the chief instrument of adapting to the competitive changes inherent in the product life cycle.

Of the four stages in a product's life cycle, product strategy is most critical in the first and last. Obviously a new product is necessary for a life cycle even to begin. The competitive distinctiveness or technological superiority of a new product determines its success in the introductory stage. It must survive infancy in order to move on in the life cycle. New products are also the ultimate solution to the problems of maturity and decline. In these periods, decisions eventually must be reached on the abandonment of a declining product. But the strategies of marketing mature products are not restricted to the elimination of them. This is a relatively unexplored topic in marketing management, but it is one of growing impor-

tance. We will look at it more closely in Chapter 11.

The Adoption Process

A more sophisticated exploration of the product life cycle is found in the behavioral concept known as the *consumer adoption process*. This process is concerned with the way in which consumers become aware of and eventually adopt a new product. As more and different people move through the adoption process, sales increase until the market is saturated. This process usually takes time. People become aware of new items only after they have been on the market for some time, and they accept such innovations gradually. Rogers has identified the steps in this innovation adoption process as

1. *Awareness* The individual becomes aware of the innovation but lacks information about it.
2. *Interest* The individual is stimulated to search for information about the innovation.
3. *Evaluation* The individual considers whether to try the innovation.
4. *Trial* The individual tries the innovation on a small scale to test its usefulness.
5. *Adoption* The individual decides to make use of the innovation on a regular basis.[5]

Rogers drew his original conclusions from research on the adoption of new agricultural

[5]The most complete discussion of the adoption and diffusion processes is found in E. M. Rogers, *Diffusion of Innovations* (New York: Free Press of Glencoe, 1962), pp. 81ff. A relatively recent study of adoption is found in J. H. Donnelly, Jr., and M. T. Etzel, "Degrees of Product Newness and Early Trial," *Journal of Marketing Research*, August 1972, pp. 295–300.

methods and products by farmers. Isolated research in the acceptance of innovations by physicians and industrial buyers tends to confirm Rogers' findings. Evidence of the adoption process among ultimate consumers also exists.

Adoption theory provides further insight into the product life cycle by its extension into what is known as the *diffusion process.* This refers to the spread of a new idea from its introduction to its final general acceptance. Such a spread might follow a normal pattern of communications were it not for the fact that some people are more prone than others to accept new products or ideas.[6] Rogers classifies the adopters of innovations using five categories.[7]

1. *Innovators* are the first people to accept a new product. There are relatively few of them. Rogers estimates that only about 2.5 per cent of all adopters falls into this category. These people are venturesome and willing to assume risk. They also tend to be socially aggressive and communicative.

2. *Early adopters* comprise about 13.5 percent of innovation acceptors. They are less venturesome than innovators, but they enjoy the leadership and prestige that early adoption brings. They tend to be the opinion leaders and tastemakers in the community. Others respect their judgments and follow their examples.

3. The *early majority* of adopters are those who precede the other half of the majority of innovation acceptors. What

they are like and why they buy at this relatively early stage are hard questions to answer. The best correlate of early adoption seems to be upper-class social status. It also would seem logical to suppose that these people are gregarious, communicative, and attentive to the information cues to which they are exposed. About 34 per cent of adopters falls into this class.

4. *Late majority* adopters also account for about 34 per cent of all innovation acceptors. We have practically identified these buyers by exclusion. They are less cosmopolitan and tend to be less responsive to change. Consumers with ethnic backgrounds, people of lower economic and social status, and those past middle age tend to fall into this group.

5. The last 16 per cent of the adopting public, which we classify as *laggards,* constitutes a more extreme segment. These people are often price conscious and wait until an innovation has passed well into its mature stage before making a move to adopt it. They also tend to be extremely suspicious of novelty and change. Caution, conservatism, and cost consciousness characterize the laggards in the diffusion process.

Rogers' distribution of adopter types provides further insights into the product life cycle when it is retabulated on a cumulative basis. Such a retabulation suggests that by the time innovators have purchased the new product only 2.5 per cent of its eventual total market has been realized. When we add the early adopters, the percentage of saturation rises to 16.0. Not until the laggards have stepped into line is 100 per cent of the market achieved. These data are shown in Figure 9.2. The bars are smoothed by averaging the adoption percentages over the

[6]A growing chain of personal influence and communication might well explain the growth in the first stages of the product life cycle. If each person who hears about an innovation tells only two others about it each week, within ten weeks more than a thousand people will have learned about it. Of course, like the broken chain letter, the process breaks down when noncommunicators slip into the network.

[7]Rogers, *Diffusion of Innovations,* pp. 156ff.

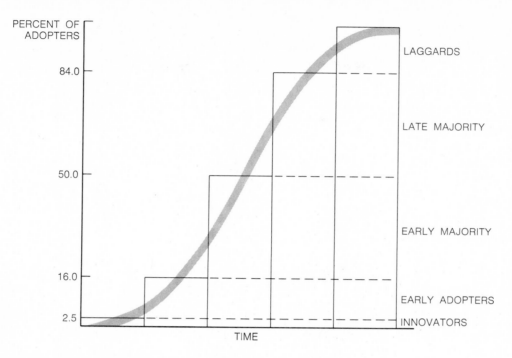

FIGURE 9.2   A cumulative distribution of innovation adopters

Source: Adapted from E. M. Rogers, *Diffusion of Innovations* (New York: Free Press of Glencoe, 1962), pp. 81 ff.

range, which gives a curve that remarkably resembles the product life-cycle curve.

The implications of adoption theory for product strategy seem clear. The secret of getting a new product underway is to get a small but important innovative group to use it. This group must be quickly followed by a larger set of early adopters. Since these people tend to be highly influential and communicative opinion leaders, the importance of getting the product and marketing information about it into their hands is readily apparent. The appeal in promotion to opinion leaders and, through them, to the larger market is sometimes referred to as the *two-step process.* Beyond this stage, the marketing task is largely one of making the product readily available to the early and late majority. The laggards generally come along by themselves. It is interesting to note that

this diffusion process also explains some of the difficulties a company encounters in the period of decline. What happens is that many original customers begin experimenting with competitors' products. The mix of a company's customers therefore changes over the product life cycle.

"Forget the Product Life Cycle Concept!"

This is the irreverent title of an article by Dhalla and Yuspeh. [8] The authors attack the product life cycle on several counts. They

[8]Nariman K. Dhalla and Sonia Yuspeh, "Forget the Product Life Cycle Concept!" *Harvard Business Review,* January-February 1976, pp. 102–110. Copyright © 1975 by the President and Fellows of Harvard College; all rights reserved.

TABLE 9.1   How PLC advocates view the implications of the cycle for marketing action

| Effects and responses | Stages of the PLC | | | |
	Introduction	Growth	Maturity	Decline
Competition	None of importance	Some emulators	Many rivals competing for a small piece of the pie	Few in number with a rapid shakeout of weak members
Overall strategy	Market establishment; persuade early adopters to try the product	Market penetration; persuade mass market to prefer the brand	Defense of brand position; check the inroads of competition	Preparations for removal; milk the brand dry of all possible benefits
Profits	Negligible because of high production and marketing costs	Reach peak levels as a result of high prices and growing demand	Increasing competition cuts into profit margins and ultimately into total profits	Declining volume pushes costs up to levels that eliminate profits entirely
Retail prices	High, to recover some of the excessive costs of launching	High, to take advantage of heavy consumer demand	What the traffic will bear; need to avoid price wars	Low enough to permit quick liquidation of inventory
Distribution	Selective, as distribution is slowly built up	Intensive; employ small trade discounts since dealers are eager to store	Intensive; heavy trade allowances to retain shelf space	Selective; unprofitable outlets slowly phased out
Advertising strategy	Aim at the needs of early adopters	Make the mass market aware of brand benefits	Use advertising as a vehicle for differentiation among otherwise similar brands	Emphasize low price to reduce stock
Advertising emphasis	High, to generate awareness and interest among early adopters and persuade dealers to stock the brand	Moderate, to let sales rise on the sheer momentum of word-of-mouth recommendations	Moderate, since most buyers are aware of brand characteristics	Minimum expenditures required to phase out the product
Consumer sales and promotion expenditures	Heavy, to entice target groups with samples, coupons, and other inducements to try the brand	Moderate, to create brand preference (advertising is better suited to do this job)	Heavy, to encourage brand switching, hoping to convert some buyers into loyal users	Minimal, to let the brand coast by itself

* *Source:* Nariman K. Dhalla and Sonia Yuspeh, ''Forgot The Product Life Cycle Concept!'' *Harvard Business Review,* January-February 1976, p. 104. Copyright © 1975 by the President and Fellows of Harvard College; all rights reserved.

remind us that there is very little empirical evidence to support the notion that products do go through the classical stages depicted in Figure 9.1.[9] There are explanations for this lack of data. Long-term statistics (some life cycles, for example automobiles and cigarettes, last many decades) are hard to obtain. The definition of the term *product* is hard to establish. For example, the product might be all products in a class (say automobiles), a type of product in a class (convertibles), or a brand of product (Packard). There would be different life-cycle curves for each. Lastly,

[9] R. Polli and V. J. Cook, *A Test of the Product Life Cycle as a Model of Sales Behavior* (Cambridge, Mass.: Marketing Science Institute, 1967).

we must recognize that the product's sales curve through time is a dependent variable—dependent on many forces, both internal and external. The external forces are largely uncontrollable, but the internal ones are manageable. Such actions as product improvement, advertising, and lowering price are designed to alter the typical product life-cycle curve—to accelerate its growth, to extend its period of maturity, to reverse or at least to postpone its decline.

Notwithstanding its title, "Forget the Product Life Cycle Concept!" provides some useful insights into the idea. Its authors present a very useful summary of the traditional applications of the concept (see Table 9.1). This exhibit suggests ways in which product life-cycle advocates view the implications of the cycle for marketing action. Dhalla and Yuspeh use this table in part to criticize the disregard of mature and declining products in favor of products in the introductory stage. To the extent that this occurs, it reflects a regrettable aspect of marketing management. As we will see in Chapter 11, mature products offer important challenges and opportunities—not just problems.

Determining Product Objectives

Sources of Product Objectives

Product objectives should be derived from marketing objectives, which in turn emanate from corporate objectives. They constitute subobjectives in the hierarchy. This is an important point, because it means that a given marketing objective (say, increased sales) will create subobjectives in all four areas of the marketing mix. We learned in Chapter 3 how this hierarchy of objectives

functions in a general way. It is well here to review it briefly as it relates to the identification of specific product objectives (refer to Figure 9.3). The company goal is growth, presumably measured by sales income. Top management is exploring two strategies to achieve this growth: the acquisition of another firm, which is primarily the responsibility of the legal and financial departments, and an increase in sales of the present firm—a direct responsibility of the marketing department. Thus, increased sales (again, quantitatively expressed) becomes the marketing department's objective. Four marketing strategies materialize, one in each area of the mix. (Actually there could be many more, involving combinations of the four.) The company can (1) actively promote its existing line of products through advertising and personal selling; (2) expand its distribution system; (3) adjust its prices to increase volume; or (4) introduce one or more new products. The fourth marketing strategy is the direct responsibility of the product management function and therefore becomes its objective. How this product subobjective is carried out is a matter of marketing tactics, and as we shall see in Chapter 10 involves such activities as generating new-product ideas, screening them, designing and developing the new product, and finally bringing it to market.

Seldom, if ever, should a marketing company pursue product objectives arising solely within the product management area. For example, the perpetuation, for its own sake, of an obsolete product that is declining in customer popularity would be ill advised unless the need to utilize manufacturing capacity, to maintain a sales organization, or to service an existing trade channel makes such a decision temporarily correct. Ordinarily, product objectives relate to such higher goals as growth and increased market share.

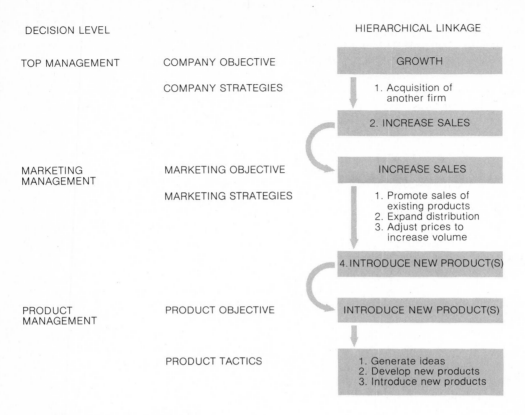

DECISION LEVEL

TOP MANAGEMENT   COMPANY OBJECTIVE

COMPANY STRATEGIES

MARKETING
MANAGEMENT   MARKETING OBJECTIVE

MARKETING STRATEGIES

PRODUCT
MANAGEMENT   PRODUCT OBJECTIVE

PRODUCT TACTICS

HIERARCHICAL LINKAGE

GROWTH

1. Acquisition of
   another firm

2. INCREASE SALES

INCREASE SALES

1. Promote sales of
   existing products
2. Expand distribution
3. Adjust prices to
   increase volume

4. INTRODUCE NEW PRODUCT(S)

INTRODUCE NEW PRODUCT(S)

1. Generate ideas
2. Develop new products
3. Introduce new products

FIGURE 9.3   A hierarchy of objectives

Typical Product Objectives

It would be impossible to list all of the objectives that bear on the development of product strategy. We can, however, point out a number of typical objectives that a manager might establish as a result of a study of the company, its marketing targets, and the position of its products in their respective life cycles.

Growth The first such objective is growth in sales by the introduction of new products or the improvement of existing products. This is an almost universal objective that guides the product strategy of most firms.

Closely related is the objective to achieve growth in sales by finding new uses for established products. Generally easier than developing new products, the search for new uses of older products goes on endlessly. For example, literally hundreds of industrial and consumer uses have been found for silicone sprays; GE has adapted its hair dryer to enable women to dry lingerie; IBM has expanded its basic computers into multipurpose data-processing systems. New uses have been found for some established products even where no physical change in the products has been made. For example, baking soda is used more widely as a household antacid or deodorant than as a baking ingredient; an industrial hand soap, Goop, doubles as a home laundry product; a drain cleanser is used by marinas in the Midwest to clean algae from boat hulls. The explosion of such new uses creates a prime objective for product strategy.

Utilizing excess capacity   A common product objective is to utilize excess capacity. Because of the rapid turnover of products and resulting changes in market shares, the utilization of excess capacity (whether in manufacturing or distribution) may give direction to a company's product effort. Of course such utilization is always a short-run consideration. Over a longer period of time, only those products that can be justified by continuing marketing opportunities should be retained, regardless of the problem of excess capacity.

Maintaining or improving market share   Many firms direct their marketing efforts toward the objective of maintaining or improving market share. In effect, these companies are more interested in sustaining or bettering their competitive positions than they are in attaining a target level of profits.[10] Although there are many ways in which a firm competes, the most basic methods build on product differentiation. Several aspects of product strategy can be involved here. Design, packaging, and identification are three important ways to differentiate products, and without such differentiation the maintenance or improvement of market share is extremely difficult.

Offering a complete line   A fourth typical objective is to develop a full line of prod-

ucts. A company with a partial line may well consider the objective of rounding out its product offerings. Such a goal relates directly to product strategy, as does a final typical objective of satisfying distributor requirements. Wholesalers and retailers have different product-assortment requirements from manufacturers. In order to satisfy these channel members it may be necessary for a firm to expand or alter its product offerings.

The list of typical product objectives could be expanded greatly. The examples are only illustrative. In each marketing situation, corporate and marketing objectives that bear on product strategy usually can be identified without much difficulty. The important point is that there must be a reason for all marketing activity. These reasons are best expressed in the form of specific product objectives.

An interesting approach to such objectives is shown in Table 9.2.[11] The matrix condenses product objectives into two possible areas: (1) an improvement in the product's technological newness and (2) an increase in the product's market newness. Combinations are possible. For example, a company such as Toastmaster might decide that there is to be no change in the product's market position, but that there are two possible degrees of technological change. One is to replace its existing product with a completely new item; the other is to modify the product to achieve some advantage in cost or quality. On the other hand, Toastmaster might determine that no technological improvement is immediately possible and thus look for ways to improve market position instead. According to Table 9.2, the

---

[10]The PIMS (profit impact of marketing strategy) studies have highlighted the finding that in many companies profitability is a function of market share. See S. Schoeffler, R. D. Buzzell, and F. F. Heeny, "Impact of Strategic Planning on Profit Performance," *Harvard Business Review*, March-April 1974, pp. 137–145.

[11]The following discussion is based on E. A. Pessemier, *New Product Decisions: An Analytical Approach* (New York: McGraw-Hill, 1966), p. 8. Pessemier credits S. C. Johnson and C. Jones, "How to Organize for New Products," *Harvard Business Review*, May-June 1957, p. 52, as the source of the matrix idea.

TABLE 9.2   New products classified by product objective

| Product objectives | | *Increasing technological newness* ⟶ | | |
		No technological change	Improved technology	New technology
Increasing marketing newness ↓	No market change		*Reformulation* Make minor modifications in product to reduce cost and/or improve quality	*Replacement* Make major modifications in product to reduce cost and/or improve quality.
	Strengthen market	*Remerchandising* Make present products more attractive to the type of customers presently served	*Improved product* Make present product more useful to present customers by improving present technology.	*Product-line extension* Widen the line of products offered to present customers by adopting a new technology.
	New market	*New use* Extend sale of present products to types of customers not presently served.	*Market extension* Extend sales to types of customers not presently served by offering a modified present product.	*Diversification* Extend sales to types of customers not presently served by offering products of a new technology.

Source: E.A. Pessemier, *New Product Decisions: An Analytical Approach* (New York: McGraw-Hill, 1966), p. 9. Copyright © 1966 by McGraw-Hill, Inc., New York. Used with permission of McGraw-Hill Book Company.

company might utilize remerchandising programs to established customers such as department stores, or it might design programs to present the product to entirely new customers, for example discount houses. The cell in the lower right-hand corner of the matrix represents the ultimate in product and market diversification: the development of new products for new customers.

Issues in Product Strategy

There is no easy path to the development of product strategy. A considerable number of elements are involved, and many of them appear, at least superficially, to be hopelessly entangled with each other. By a systematic approach to strategy design, however, these entanglements can be straightened out.

First, the various issues involved in developing product strategy must be isolated. The planner can do so by breaking down the general problem into its component decisions, which permits concentrating separately on each of several important considerations. It usually is discovered that each issue is indeed related to or dependent on some other issue, but that the lines of this dependence are logical and clear. We will see that the elements of product strategy are not terribly complicated. Once the orderliness of the relationships is recognized, the process of developing strategy becomes a system of decisions in which the components are the individual issues that need to be resolved.

Determining the Product Line

What product, or products, should we sell? This is the basic question in product strategy. Recalling that the fundamental marketing opportunity is not to sell things but rather to provide satisfaction, the question should probably be rephrased: "What satisfactions should we provide?" However, in most firms the form in which satisfactions are delivered is that of products, services, or product-service combinations. For this reason, even in a customer-oriented firm, the question "What products shall we sell?" is of paramount importance.

The first step in deciding what to sell is the identification of a potential product's ultimate consumers or users. This step should have already been accomplished through the analysis of the marketing situation. The marketing strategist should have all the market information needed to identify potential users of the product. The key to undertaking this step is in the word *identify*. Much more than a casual description of the potential users is required. Their precise demographic, economic, and behavioral characteristics must be known.

Having identified the consumer, the product planner next determines the use (satisfaction) specifications that the potential product will have to provide. Unfortunately, this important step often is omitted in product planning. The product planner may be tempted to jump immediately from the identification of the customer to the design of product characteristics. The omission can be a critical mistake however. The product designer needs to know exactly what the product is supposed to do; how the product will be used; how often it will be used; and with what efficiency it is supposed to operate. From a marketing viewpoint, it is not as important to know what a product is *capable* of doing as it is to understand what consumers *expect* it to do. To be well designed, a product should provide exactly the satisfactions desired—neither more nor less. To build in more than the desired satisfaction is

wasteful; to create less than the desired satisfaction is a costly mistake. Being on target with a product means designing one that exactly matches the consumption specifications of potential users.

This process of matching the product to the specific needs of customers is referred to as *targeting* or *positioning*. It becomes of critical importance when a segementation strategy is pursued. Segmenting as a strategy is successful only when a company is able to tailor its offerings precisely. To miss a segment completely is disastrous; to overlap a segment is wasteful and confusing to customers.

It is not sufficient to satisfy ultimate consumers. A product must provide satisfactions for wholesalers and retailers as well. These are not consumption satisfactions but resale satisfactions. For a product to fit into a retail assortment, it must match the resellers' expectations in terms of inventory requirements, stock turnover, margin, packaging, and so forth. If it fails to meet these needs, the product will not be stocked. The expectations of resellers are therefore important considerations in the design of the product, its package, and its brand identification.

The final step in answering the question "What products should we sell?" involves matching both the customers' specifications and the resellers' specifications with appropriate product characteristics. Generally, product design involves developing three important characteristics: (1) appearance, (2) performance, and (3) cost. These characteristics affect both the product and its package. The form of a product (that is, its specifications) should match its function, and its function is to satisfy consumers and resellers. True it must do so profitably, and this is the product's principal function insofar as the manufacturer is concerned. In addition, other objectives may dictate product functions. For example, it may have to be made in existing facilities or it may have to be designed in such a way as to fit into a line of products.

Introducing New Products

The question is not really whether a company *should* introduce new products but rather *when* new products should be developed and introduced. A few decades ago a company might well have considered whether even to undertake such a task, but today there is little choice. The rapid technological obsolescence of most products forces every seller to consider the necessity of introducing new products in order to survive and grow.

Even without technological obsolescence, however, declining competitive distinctiveness demands a planned program of new products in order to maintain market share. The concept of the product life cycle provides a useful basis for determining the appropriate strategy of product introduction as well as of product competition in subsequent stages. The development and marketing of new products have become vitally important parts of product strategy. The next chapter is devoted exclusively to these subjects.

Determining the Width and Depth of a Product Line

The appropriate breadth for a product line resembles the proverbial question, "How long is a piece of string?" Obviously, the product line should be complete enough to do the job. Most companies handle multiple products. Thus, they must make important decisions concerning the number of different items in each product line and the number of different lines to be handled.

The composite of products a company offers is sometimes called its *product mix.* Those items in the mix that are closely related are referred to as a *product line.* Ralston Purina Company has an extensive mix, ranging from animal feeds to human foods to ski resorts (see Exhibit 9.1). It has a line of formula feeds—horse feed, poultry feed, and so on. Its line of grocery products is extensive and illustrates well the concepts of width and depth of product line. *Width* refers to how many different products are offered. *Depth* defines how many items of each type are sold. Ralston Purina's grocery-products line is of typical width, with three major categories of offering. Depth varies considerably from one entry to another. Seafood has three items, cereals and snacks has six, and pet foods has twelve.

Why should a company offer so many products? Is such diversity necessary? A consumer generally buys only one product at a time, unless the products are complementary in nature. However, since different customers have different requirements, it may be necessary to offer a number of products in order to satisfy several different market segments. Retailers, in particular, usually like to have some depth of assortment in a given product category. In addition to greater selection, the retailer has the opportunity of trading up a shopper from a lower- to a higher-priced item. To satisfy these customer and reseller requirements, as well as to build volume and utilize manufacturing and marketing capacity, most firms opt to offer several products.

However, the addition of new products cannot go on endlessly. Ultimately the manufacturer must decide on an optimum width and depth of line. This optimum is the one that is most profitable in the long run. Theoretically, a company should continue to add products so long as incremental revenues generated by a new product are greater

EXHIBIT 9.1   Ralston Purina Company's product mix

FORMULA FEEDS
Purina Hog Chow
Purina Dairy Chow
Purina Cattle Chow
Purina Poultry Laying Chow
Purina Broiler Chow
Purina Horse Chow
Purina Turkey Chow
Purina Laboratory Chows
Purina Specialty Chows

POULTRY PRODUCTS
Ralston Purina Rock Cornish Game Hens
Ralston Purina Basted Young Turkeys
Ralston Purina Turkey Roasts
Ralston Purina Fried Chicken
Ralston Purina Gravy and Sliced Turkey

PROTEIN PRODUCTS
Soybean Oil
Soybean Meal
Industrial protein
Pro-Cote
Food protein
Supro
Edi-Pro
Dairy Pro
Purina Protein

GROCERY PRODUCTS
Sea foods
Chicken of the Sea Tuna
Van Camp's Tuna
Chicken of the Sea Canned Oyster Stew
Pet foods
Purina Dog Chow

Purina Puppy Chow
Purina High Protein Dog Meal
Purina Chuck Wagon
Purina Fit & Trim
Purina Cat Chow
Purina Variety Menu
Purina Tender Vittles
Purina Lovin Spoonfuls
Purina Special Dinners
Purina Kitten Chow
Purina Meow Mix
Cereals and snacks
Rice, Wheat, and Corn Chex
Freakies
Grins & Smiles & Giggles & Laughs
Hot Ralston
Moonstones
Ry Krisp

RESTAURANTS
Jack in the Box
Boar's Head
Hungry Hunter
Stag and Hound

OTHER PRODUCTS AND SERVICES
Grain Merchandising
Animal Health Products
Mushrooms
All-Season Resort
Sales of Breeding Hogs
Institutional
Foodservice
Candy
Chemical Specialties
Contract Research

Source: From *Ralston Purina Company 1976 Annual Report* (St. Louis: Ralston Purina Annual Report, 1976), p. 51.

than the incremental costs of adding it. Occasionally, a product may be added even though its contribution to profit is negligible. Offering a full line to serve retailers or providing special products for the handicapped are examples.

A critical factor in determining the proper product mix is the element of *consistency*. The very term *line* means that the products must be related in some meaningful way. The Ralston Purina product mix provides a good example. Products may be related by utilizing common manufacturing processes. Some of Ralston's pet food products are manufactured by essentially the same methods. The products in a line may move through the same distribution channel. This is true of all of the company's grocery products. Finally, the items in a line are consistent if they emerge in similar end use, or consumption, circumstances. Ralston's animal feeds meet this test. Many companies have product lines that are not nearly so consistent as is Ralston Purina's. The attempt to market a diverse line of products can be confusing and wasteful if not handled carefully. It usually is accomplished best by decentralizing marketing responsibility and not attempting to market such disparate items as smoke alarms and razors as part of a single line. Such decentralization is practiced by Gillette with apparent success.

Deleting Products

The general issue of dropping unprofitable products has already been mentioned several times. This question becomes specifically relevant when it is applied to particular products. Candidates for product deletion should be identified well in advance of the time they are to be dropped from the product line. The detection of "sick" products, the timing of their abandonment, and the method of their withdrawal from the company's line are all important aspects of this particular problem. Abandonment is not the only strategy available for the mature product. Generally it is a last resort. Alternative approaches to the management of older products include product improvement, re-

packaging, private branding, and so on. We will explore these topics in Chapter 11.

Timing Product-Line Changes

The timing of changes in the product line is always a troublesome issue. New products seldom are available at the exact moment a company would like to introduce them. The process of development is usually longer than anticipated, and on occasion a competitor may actually beat a company "to the punch." The timing of product deletions is also a thorny problem. Sales departments usually are reluctant to abandon products that are producing any sales. Theoretically, a product should be dropped when it ceases to contribute to overhead. In practice, this point may be hard to detect. Moreover if no replacement is available, it may be better to continue to sell the unprofitable item than to leave a gap in the product line. Ideally there should be an unbroken continuity of product offerings. New products should be nurtured and developed while the older ones are in their declining stages, and the introduction of the replacement product should be timed to coincide with or slightly lead the removal of the old.

Packaging

Packaging is almost always an important consideration in the development of product strategy. In contrast to a generation ago, the vast majority of today's consumer goods are packaged in some way or another. Many industrial products also are packaged—especially shelf items that are sold through warehouse distributors and jobbers. As is true of so many aspects of marketing strategy, the creation of a good package is itself a complicated task. There are many vital considerations to be attended to, only the most important of which can be touched on here.

Product packaging has come under considerable attack from environmentalists. Beverage containers have been a prime target. So called one-way containers—cans and nonreturnable bottles—have actually been outlawed in some areas. Product development engineers have come up with remarkable package improvements in response to the environmentalists' criticisms. Reusable and recyclable containers, self-disposing closures, and biodegradable package materials have been developed, often at considerable expense.[12]

The first thing to note is that the product and its package may be inseparable. Certain commodities, such as fluids, cannot be marketed unpackaged. Others can be marketed most efficiently only when attention has been given to packaging—from both functional and aesthetic points of view. Certain features of the packaging are of particular importance. The type of packaging *material* usually is dictated by the need to preserve or protect the commodity until it reaches the consumer. However, this is not an unalterable choice. The development of new packaging materials and changes in consumer requirements foster frequent alterations in the type of packaging. For instance, Maxwell House coffee has been sold in several different kinds of containers, including plain paper bags, cans, glass jars, and foil-lined bags. The closure (the cap, flap, or cover) is an important feature of these and many other packages. A reusable package or a package with a secondary use also may be an important feature of a product program. The *size* of the package is another consideration

that may be dictated by either consumer or distributor requirements or by both. For years, cereal manufacturers persisted in packaging breakfast foods in jumbo-sized boxes that were taller than the average pantry shelf. Recently, however, breakfast cereals have been marketed in compact packages. The size and appearance of these packages are important promotional considerations.

Obviously, package design is closely related to product identification. Such relationships must be carefully considered before a product package is chosen. Whenever self-service and mass merchandising of consumer products is involved, packaging and identification assume considerable significance. For example, impulse buying is the direct result of the delivery of a sensory cue at the point of sale. Thus, it is an important function of consumer packaging. In fact unique packaging may be, for some companies, the only technique available for attracting consumers to their products. Various brands of detergents, dehydrated milk, salt, sugar, and other staples, which are almost identical in content, can be differentiated effectively on the basis of differences in consumer packaging.

Resellers' needs The manufacturer should never ignore the requirements of resellers in connection with packaging. From the retailers' point of view, a good consumer package is one that has *display impact*. It moves merchandise off the shelves. In addition, resellers' mechanical requirements must be met. Packages must be of appropriate size. They should shelve or stack conveniently. They should be easy to pricemark. Moreover, packages should be strong enough to withstand routine handling by store personnel and by shoppers. Packages that fail to come up to these reseller requirements seldom enjoy repeat dealer business.

[12]W. N. Gunn, "Packages and the Environmental Challenge," *Harvard Business Review,* July-August 1972, pp. 103–111.

The universal product code In the early 1970s an interesting packaging development occurred, which it was thought for a short time would revolutionize the check-out process in self-service retail stores. A universal product code (UPC) was developed and manufacturers modified their packages to display the code. Electronic scanning devices at the check-out counter identified the code and recorded the transaction. The computer processed the customer's order, priced and extended each category purchased, and printed an itemized listing and receipt at a point-of-sale terminal. The advantages of the system were (1) a faster and more accurate check-out, (2) the elimination of the necessity of pricemarking each item, (3) the immediate implementation of price changes without remarking goods, and (4) the on-line feedback of product movement enabled a store to have current data on sales and inventory. However, UPC systems did not take over. Early models did not work perfectly. The entire process was mysterious and threatening to the consumer. Some local ordinances were enacted to prohibit the use of the system or to require individual price marking (which eliminated a major cost saving). Some version of it eventually will be in rather widespread use, especially as electronic funds-transfer systems are adopted. The timing of these developments is difficult to anticipate at the present time, however.

Cost A final important consideration in connection with packaging concerns its cost. The more elaborate and attractive a package becomes, the costlier it is likely to be. For some types of products, such as aerosol insecticides and shave cream, the cost of the container may be greater than that of the contents. Careful attention always must be paid to the cost of the package in relation to its contribution to marketing strategy. Occasionally, a package comes under the ax of a drive to cut costs despite the negative effect on sales that the package change may have.

Branding

In addition to uniqueness of appearance and performance, products can be identified by *branding* and the use of a *trademark*. A *brand name* is a copyrighted word that labels a company's product or product group. A *trademark* is a registered symbol that distinguishes the products of one company from those of another. Frequently, unique brand names are given special artistic treatment and registered as corporate trademarks. For example, Coca-Cola is not only a brand of carbonated beverage, but its printed name in the familiar script (as well as the abbreviated word *Coke*) are legally registered trademarks.

The process of product identification by branding may take several forms. Consumer products usually are branded by the manufacturer, the manufacturer's brand often being called a *national brand*. A manufacturer may, of course, use more than one brand. For example, there may be a family brand composed of a number of subsidiary brands, which allows the manufacturer to take advantage of favorable customer acceptance of an established product name. The various pet food products in Figure 9.4 have their own names as well as the family brand name Purina. On the other hand, if the general marketing approach calls for an aggressive promotion of a low-priced product, the manufacturer may wish to disassociate such a promotion from its regular marketing activities. This can be accomplished by the use of a *fighting,* or secondary, *brand.* Or a manufacturer may choose to differentiate between two or more product lines by the use of separate national brand designations. OMC (Outboard Marine Corporation) markets both Johnson and Evinrude outboard motors.

In contrast, a product may be identified with a distributor's brand or *private brand.* Private brands, sometimes called *private labels,* can be used by wholesalers or retailers. Topmost (General Grocer) and IGA (Independent Grocer's Alliance) are wholesalers' private brands. Kenmore (Sears, Roebuck) and Fieldcrest (Marshall Field) are examples of retailers' private labels.

The creation of such brand names, whether private, secondary, or national, and the design of trademarks often are assigned to a company's advertising department or to an outside advertising agency. [13] Various techniques are used in developing them. A functional approach would attempt to set forth the product identification requirements that could then be followed by a creative effort that seeks to incorporate these requirements.

The design of a trademark is equally important and somewhat more difficult, since it involves the use of graphic arts. Both the trademark and the brand name must be researched carefully from a legal standpoint to make sure that they do not violate existing copyright or trademark registrations. After being tested for marketing effectiveness, the trademark and brand should then be legally protected by their own copyright or trademark registration.

Brand names and trademarks are extremely important in the identification of products. Brand names, in fact, are mandatory if the manufacturer or distributor intends to promote the product through mass-communications media. Brand names also make word-of-mouth advertising effective. Without them, repeat purchases of a particular product would be virtually impossible. Almost every product that is purchased by ultimate customers and many products that are consumed industrially are branded in some way. A product strategy that does not give due consideration to this problem of product identification omits a most important element in the marketing mix.

Providing Customer Service

Since a firm is in business to provide satisfactions, its marketing effort is not complete until the satisfaction has been delivered. When products are not consumed and satisfactions thus not completely delivered at the time of purchase, the need for postsales servicing often arises. The longer the period over which a product is intended to provide satisfaction, the more likely that some type of warranty and service must be included in the marketing mix. Sears has found it an effective marketing device to remind its customers, "We Service What We Sell"; GM emphasizes its Mr. Goodwrench program; and all car manufacturers promote warranties of their products. [14]

As with consumer durables, the marketing of almost all industrial products also involves postsales servicing. For example, the marketing of installations and equipment often requires that the vendor supply technical service for setup, maintenance, and repair. This type of activity is important in keeping

---

[13]Automobile companies are constantly looking for names for new models. The ironic naming of the ill-fated Edsel is chronicled in John Brooks, *The Fate of the Edsel and Other Business Adventures* (New York: Harper & Row, 1963). The manner in which GM named its Chevrolet Camaro is described in "What's in a Name? Soul-Searching Agony and Woe, says Detroit," *Wall Street Journal,* 30 June 1966, p. 1. For a more sophisticated approach, see R. A. Peterson and I. Ross, "How to Name New Brands," *Journal of Advertising Research,* December 1972, pp. 29–34.

[14]J. G. Udell and E. E. Anderson, "The Product Warranty as an Element of Competitive Strategy," *Journal of Marketing,* October 1968, pp. 1–8.

the customer "sold" and encourages repeat purchases. Thus, its effect on longer-run marketing success makes postsales servicing a vital part of the continuing marketing program.

From time to time a consumer actually is harmed by the use or misuse of a product. The courts have long held that a manufacturer (and more recently the wholesalers and retailers) of a product are liable for injury or damage inflicted on a consumer. Claims for heavy damages and extremely liberal awards by the courts have caused the premiums of product liability insurance to increase drastically.[15] Companies have made strenuous efforts to make products safer. The Consumer Product Safety Commission has hastened the trend by establishing standards to which hazardous products must conform. The addition of mandatory or voluntary safety features almost always increases the cost and eventually the price of a product. This is an important reason why automobile companies have been reluctant to install air bags on a voluntary basis.

Organizing for Product Management

How should a company be organized to implement product strategy effectively? The basic marketing organization should be created before the planning of any product strategy is undertaken. But in the development of a new operational plan, certain special organizational needs arise. This is especially true when so-called nonmarketing activities must be coordinated with marketing. How this coordination can be achieved is partially a question of organization. Should a committee be used to bring together sales, advertising, manufacturing, engi-

neering, and finance? Or should a separate department be organized for new-product development? If such a department is organized, how should it function and to whom should it report? These are critical questions that must be answered as a part of the development of marketing strategy.

There are two major directions in which the organizing for product planning and development has moved in recent years. As we saw in Chapter 2, one has been the creation of the position of product or brand manager. Usually a staff executive, the product manager is responsible for product planning and for coordination of the various departments and individuals assigned to implement the plan.

The second approach has been the creation of a special new-product or new-venture department. This department is responsible for generating new-product ideas, screening them, and moving the best candidates through the stages of design, development, and market testing. In the Monsanto Chemical Company, the new-venture group also is responsible for the actual introduction of the new product. The product is turned over to the regular sales organization only after it has been successfully launched. Other firms that are well known for use of this type of organization are General Foods, IBM, and the Burroughs Corporation.[16]

Summary

We have now started to consider the detailed development of marketing strategy.

---

[15]L. A. Dennison and A. I. Benningson, "Product Liability: Manufacturers Beware," *Harvard Business Review,* May-June 1974, pp. 122–131.

[16]J. D. Hlavacek, "Toward More Successful Venture Management," *Harvard Business Review,* September-October 1974, pp. 56–60; and R. M. Hill and J. D. Hlavacek, "The Venture Team: A New Concept in Marketing Organization," *Journal of Marketing,* July 1972, pp. 44–50.

The process rightly begins with the product, for that is the foundation on which the rest of the marketing program is built. As long as we remember that a product also can be a service or a product-service combination, we can see that without a product there would be no marketing program. There would be nothing to promote, nothing to distribute, nothing to price.

Products have been classified in several ways. The major distinction is between consumer goods and business goods. Some of the more detailed classifications are based on the physical characteristics of the goods. Even more useful is a breakdown based on their marketing characteristics. The well-known classification of consumer products as convenience, shopping, or specialty goods is an example.

The development of an appropriate product srategy for any type of goods begins with consideration of the key concept of product life cycle. New products must be introduced before the life cycle even begins. Others must be developed to replace older products in the declining stage of the life cycle. Modifications and improvements are important elements of the marketing program in the growth and maturity stages of the cycle.

The adoption and diffusion processes provide a useful explanation of this product life-cycle concept. They suggest that certain segments of the population are more inclined to try and adopt new products than are others. These early adopters are the prime targets when new products are introduced. But eventually the innovation is diffused throughout the population. More and more people buy it until the market is saturated. After a period of time the market actually begins to decline, as some users drift away to newer products offered by competitors.

Understanding the product life cycle provides a useful framework in which to consider the major issues that must be resolved in the course of developing a product strategy. Of critical importance is the determination of the product line. The manager must decide what products to sell. This is done by looking at consumer needs and the opportunity to satisfy them. As we have seen, the manager uses such information to make decisions on the introduction of new products and, from time to time, the dropping of old ones. Of course, these decisions must be considered in light of other product issues. For example, how broad a line of products should the company sell, and when should needed product-line changes be made? Two remaining issues involving products somewhat less directly are the matters of packaging and branding.

No other aspect of marketing planning has had such a profound impact on company organization as has product management. Entirely new forms of organization emerged as the marketing concept took hold. At the center of these was the creation of a new position in marketing—the product or brand manager. It is this manager's job to make marketing plans for assigned products and to coordinate the activities of those who must carry out the product programs. Another aspect of company organization that is rooted in product management is the new-product development department or the new-venture group that has been formed in some companies.

Questions and Problems

1. Select a product that you would like to own, such as a typewriter or a stereo set. Draw up a list of your personal use specifications for this product—that is, write down explicitly what you expect

the product to do. Match these use specifications with the product characteristics of two or three alternative products that you find for sale. What conclusions do you draw from this comparison?

2. An automobile can be considered an augmented product. Why? What are the various services that augment the satisfaction that a car buyer obtains?

3. Name at least five products that you believe are in (a) the introductory stage, (b) the growth stage, (c) the maturity stage, and (d) the decline stage of the product life cycle. Defend your classifications.

4. Critics of the various classifications of consumer goods argue that any particular product usually can be placed in more than one category. Do you see this as a serious problem? Explain.

5. Explain the adoption process and how it relates to product strategy.

6. Why is it that some products diffuse more rapidly than do others? For example, new clothing styles are quickly adopted by a large portion of the population, whereas products such as Teflon-coated kitchenware take several years to be widely accepted.

7. What is meant by *positioning* a new product? What might the term *repositioning* mean?

8. Many companies describe their product offering in their annual reports. Obtain an annual report and analyze the company's product mix. In your analysis, apply the concepts of width, depth, and consistency presented in this chapter.

9. Using the matrix in Table 9.2 select a new product, such as one of the new American subcompact cars, and suggest the kind of product objectives that the manufacturer might have had in introducing the product.

10. Assume that you are the marketing manager of a medium-sized chemical company. The product development department has recently come up with a liquid household detergent. The product has some unique cleaning features, but top management feels that in order to succeed the product must have a truly distinctive package. What factors should be considered in planning the package for this liquid detergent?

11. It is thought by some that private brands are taking over in the battle of the brands. Draw up three lists: (a) products that are predominantly sold under national brands, (b) products that are predominantly sold under private labels, and (c) products that are about evenly divided between the two. What do you conclude from your lists?

12. Within the past year or so there have been experiments at marketing no-brand grocery products. The packages simply identified the contents (for example, peaches) together with basic ingredient information. The no-brand products sold at prices that were lower than comparable branded products. Suppose the practice of nonbranding becomes common. What would be its effects on (a) marketing management and (b) consumer behavior?

10

New
Product
Strategy

This chapter is concerned with the development and introduction of new products. The scope of new-product management is broad and varied. It involves making decisions on practically all of the issues raised in Chapter 9. It generally demands the efforts of a number of different individuals and job functions over a considerable period of time. Substantial sums of money often are required, both in the development period and in the market introduction stage. Pressures to develop new products, the uncertainties that are inherent in the activity, and the risk of failure make it an aspect of marketing management that requires orderly procedures, careful consideration of data, and intelligent decision making.

The Development Process

The appropriate way to begin the discussion of new-product strategy is to describe the general process by which new products are conceived, developed, and brought to the marketplace.[1] Figure 10.1 presents a model of this process. Our discussion will be based on the steps shown. The process commences with the generation of new-product ideas. These ideas immediately must be screened to eliminate those that are inappropriate. Any new product idea that survives the screening process is then subjected to a careful business analysis. At this stage, the demand for the new product is studied, the costs of making and marketing it are estimated, and an attempt is made to determine its potential contribution to the firm. If the product idea stands up under this scrutiny, it is sent to research and development for technical work and to marketing for exploratory consumer testing. The activities of the

[1] The consulting firm of Booz-Allen-Hamilton, Inc., was among the first to formalize a systematic approach to the development of new products. The discussion in this chapter parallels the Booz-Allen-Hamilton approach; see *Management of New Products,* 4th ed. (New York: Booz-Allen-Hamilton, 1968).

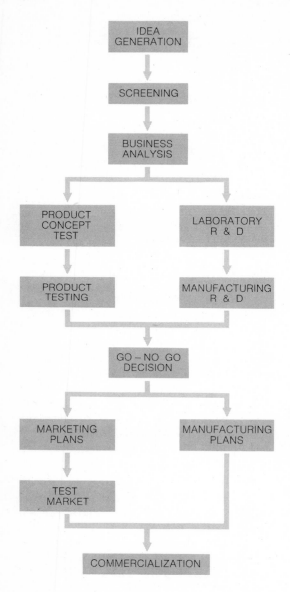

FIGURE 10.1 The new-product development process

tunity to complete their preliminary work, a decision is reached on whether or not to go into full-scale commercialization. The new product can be abandoned or shelved or approved for manufacture and marketing. If it receives approval, it is sent to manufacturing for a plan of final production methods. Meanwhile, the marketing department develops an overall plan for market introduction and, if desirable, initiates test marketing to ensure that the product and its marketing program are ready for a major-market introduction.

Idea Generation

The basic inputs for the development of new products are ideas.[2] The real difficulty is not in gathering ideas but in identifying good ones. The mortality rate of ideas for new products is exceptionally high—even higher than the failure rate for products that are actually introduced. Figure 10.2 shows the decay curve of new-product ideas, indicating that, in fifty-one companies studied, an average of only three products out of almost sixty reached the market-testing stage, two of these went into commercialization, and only one was successful.[3] As the diagram shows, more than half of the new-product ideas were wiped out at the screening stage,

engineering and marketing departments should, of course, be carefully coordinated during this stage of development. After these two departments have had an oppor-

[2]C. L. Alford and J. B. Mason, "Generating New Product Ideas," *Journal of Advertising Research,* December 1975, pp. 19–26.

[3]New products or brands fail for many reasons, and there is a considerable body of literature on the topic. Some interesting examples include R. Hartley, *Marketing Mistakes* (Columbus, Ohio: Grid, 1976); W. T. Moran, "Why New Products Fail," *Journal of Advertising Research,* April 1973, pp. 5–13; and J. H. Davidson, "Why Most New Consumer Brands Fail," *Harvard Business Review,* March-April 1976, pp. 117–132.

Totally a business system. Never mind the public.

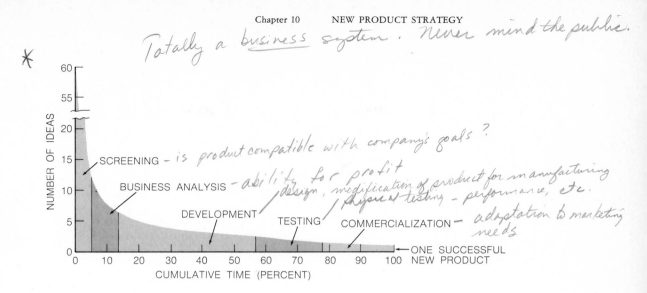

is product compatible with company's goals?

ability for profit

design, modification of product for manufacturing

physical testing — performance, etc.

adaptation to marketing needs

FIGURE 10.2   A mortality curve of new-product ideas

Source: Adapted from *Management of New Products* (New York: Booz, Allen & Hamilton, 1968), p. 9.

and all but six were eliminated after the business analysis had been completed. The demand for new-product ideas is obvious; the need for good ideas that can pass the screening and analysis stages in the development process is even greater. Since a company has little control over the idea generation phase, however, it is very important that a constant stream of ideas, good or marginal, be channeled into the system.

Internal Sources of New-Product Ideas

Where do new-product ideas come from? Actually they can come from many internal and external sources. Internal sources of new-product ideas include basic research, manufacturing, salespersons, and top management.

Basic research   Almost all large companies engage in some basic research. Research and development often is divided between the development of product ideas that already

have passed the initial screening stages and research into areas of technology that give promise of producing totally new product concepts. Some of the most important new products have come from this latter source. Nylon was discovered in the laboratory; Teflon was the result of applying basic research done for the space program. IBM, GE, AT&T, and many of the other largest corporations in the country devote substantial sums to basic research.

Manufacturing   People who manufacture products often have ideas about modifications and improvements. They also come up with ideas for completely new products. Sometimes, however, there are problems with their ideas. For example, they often tend to suggest products that the company is capable of making but that are not well conceived from a consumer point of view.

Salespeople   Company sales representatives can be a helpful source of new-product ideas. These people are on the competitive firing line. They know what customers want and what they are not getting. They are often the first to learn about competitors' new products.

Top management Top executives can play an important part in the generation of new-product ideas. Their ideas ought to be good ones—ones that the company is capable of developing. They know the company's needs and resources. They usually are keen observers of technological trends and of competitive activity. If nothing else, the top company managers should set an example. If they expect the rest of the organization to be generating new-product ideas, they should be doing so as well. Moreover, management must encourage all new ideas and provide an organizational means by which they can be speedily and effectively screened.

External Sources of New-Product Ideas

Secondary sources of information There are published lists of new products.[4] Lists of available licenses also provide clues for new-product ventures. Most magazines have a new-products section, and some business publications are devoted almost entirely to the subject of new-product news.

Competitors By the time a competitor has a new product it is pretty late to be trying to do anything about it. New-product developments are usually closely guarded secrets, and it often is difficult to discover what actually is being developed. But most development activities are at least partially exposed, and information about them inevita-

bly finds its way to competitors.[5] Good inferences about competitive product development can be made on the basis of indirect evidence gained from salespeople and from other external sources, including suppliers, resellers, and customers.

Customers. Customers frequently generate new-product ideas, or at least they relay information regarding problems that new and improved products would help to solve. Household consumers often write directly to manufacturers with suggestions for product changes. Retail buyers visit the factories and showrooms of manufacturers. Specification-buying retailers, such as Sears, actually design the new products they want to have developed. Industrial purchasing and engineering personnel often visit the plants and laboratories of their suppliers to discuss product needs.

Resellers Resellers can be considered customers, so the points made in the previous section also apply here. However, contacts with resellers often go beyond customer-supplier relationships. Resellers are component parts of a firm's marketing system. They too have a stake in the manufacturer's new-product development activity. Their needs in building a profitable line naturally are reflected in the products that their suppliers develop. A number of firms use councils or committees made up of representative resellers to assist in solving various problems, including product development. For example, McQuay-Norris, an automotive-parts manufacturer, and Hussman Refrigeration Division of Pet, Inc., a leading maker of

---

[4]See E. P. McGuire, *Generating New Product Ideas* (New York: The Conference Board, 1972).

[5]For an interesting account of how one company's new-product activities are monitored, see L. Edwards, "P and G Watcher Sees Lots of New Products Ahead," *Advertising Age,* 24 January 1977, p. 1.

store display equipment, have distributor councils that meet periodically. These groups are useful in maintaining healthy channel relationships, in assessing market developments, and in tackling a number of issues that affect dealers and distributors. They also can contribute ideas for new products.

Foreign markets   The United States has no monopoly on new-product development. In some fields, the post–World War II period has seen the most active new-product leadership come from Western Europe. The countries there had to look for new and unique products to build a favorable trade balance after the war. They also had the advantage of starting almost from scratch; they had little fixed investment in equipment and facilities. The classic example of European product innovation is the Bug—the Volkswagen automobile that revolutionized American car buying. Scandinavian furniture, Italian shoes, and French wines and perfumes are categories in which Europeans traditionally maintain new-product leadership.

Organizing and Managing the Generation of New-Product Ideas

Who is responsible for managing the generation of new-product ideas? In some companies there is a single individual, often with several assistants, responsible for this task. This person may be called a *new-product manager.* In other companies a committee of manufacturing, marketing, and financial executives is charged with the organizational responsibility of new-product idea control. This committee usually has one or more staff assistants to handle routine tasks and clerical duties. In extremely large firms, each product division may have its own new-product manager or department. New-product ideas are assigned to the appropriate operating division. If the suggestion is for an entirely new venture, it generally is processed by a corporate development department.

Screening New-Product Ideas

The second step in the new-product development process is screening. It is a critical part of the development activity. If a poor product idea is allowed to pass the screening stage, it wastes effort and money in subsequent stages until it is later abandoned. Perhaps even more frightening is the prospect of screening out a worthwhile idea. The practical manager knows that on occasion both events can occur. The ideal approach is minimize the possibility that either will happen, and this is best done by using orderly and effective screening procedures.

There are three reasons why the number of ideas must be cut down. First, poor suggestions should not be allowed to go any farther in the development process. Second, a company simply cannot handle more than a few new development projects simultaneously. Business analysis and technical and market development are time consuming and expensive. The cost of product development would be outrageously high if all new ideas were given the full treatment. Third, the cost of performing the development function rises as the process continues.

The Techniques of Screening

There are two techniques for screening new products. Both involve the comparison of a

TABLE 10.1   A comprehensive rating chart

		Very good	Good
A	**Marketing characteristics**		
1	Distribution	Can be distributed to prime markets via present channels	Can use present channels for majority of prime markets, but some new ones needed
2	Relationship to present product lines	Reinforces present product line, which is not complete	A suitable fit with current line, but not really necessary. Easily handled, however
3	Price-quality comparison with competitive products	Of equal quality but priced below competitors	Priced below majority of competitors
4	Merchandising potential	Product characteristics superior to competition. Lends itself to type of promotion and advertising that company knows best	Has demonstrable features that compare favorably with competing products
5	Effect on present products	Should complement sales of present products	May aid sales of present products
B	**Demand**		
1	Durability	Basic demand for product expected to be constant	Product demand expected to last long enough to return investment plus years of additional profits
2	Market dimensions	Wide range of customers spread throughout entire nation plus excellent overseas potential	Wide range of customers nationally, but little foreign potential
3	Dependence on economic climate	Easily sold regardless of general economic conditions	Strongly resistant to economic changes
4	Seasonal stability	Demand unchanged throughout entire year	Very minor seasonal variations
C	**Potential**		
1	Originality	Patents will afford complete protection against imitators	Resistant to patent infringement but not considered foolproof
2	Market position	Product that will supply a need not currently filled	Product that is a definite improvement over existing products
3	Future customers	Customers should increase substantially in number	Customers should increase moderately

Source: A. C. Nielsen Co. Adapted from a chart originally published in *The Nielsen Researcher* 4 (1962): 10–11.

Fair	Poor
Will have to distribute equally between new and present channels	Will require many or all new channels of distribution
Can be introduced to current product line	A rather poor fit
Equal in price, same quality	Higher priced than most competitive brands and of no better quality
Has features that are equal to competitors'	Has a few promotable features, but generally does not measure up to competition
No effect	May hinder
Product demand expected to return investments and at least several years of profits	Product should return investment but profit returns highly speculative
Nationwide appeal but narrow range of customers	Limited customer and area appeal
Sales will reflect average sensitivity to economic changes	Highly sensitive to economic change and may precede general decline
Definite but predictable seasonal fluctuations. Adverse effects can be modified by careful planning	Strong seasonal fluctuations of varying intensities, which will cause severe manufacturing, personnel, and storage problems
Not possible to patent but product features would defy easy imitation	No patent possibilities and product features reasonably easy to copy
A product possessing certain characteristics that should have reasonably wide consumer appeal	A product with barely distinguishable characteristics
Number of customers should increase slightly	Customers will remain the same or decrease in number

potential product idea against criteria of acceptable new products. The first technique makes use of a simple check list. For example, H. R. Hamilton calls for rating new business opportunities in a multistage approach each with its own set of criteria.[6] Criteria that typically are employed in screening new product ideas include

Sales volume and future growth
Type and number of competitors
Technical opportunity
Patent protection
Raw-material requirements
Available manufacturing capacity
Potential profitability
Similarity to existing business
Effect on present products

Check lists of this type present two problems. The first is the difficulty of defining what is "good" or "poor." The analyst's opinion is not enough. More definitive criteria are necessary to rate a new-product idea. These are at least partially provided in a more elaborate type of rating that supplies verbal descriptions of the various ratings. An example of such a chart is shown in Table 10.1. This type of rating scheme should produce more consistent and understandable results than the simple categorizing of new-product ideas as "good" or "poor."

However, another difficulty arises. How does a manager determine with any precision exactly how good a new-product idea actually is? Even if it is good, the question remains, "Is it good enough to justify the time and expense of a thorough business analysis?" Or suppose a manager has two or more good new-product ideas and can only

commit one of them to further study. How does one choose between them? Clearly an even more precise rating measurement is needed.

We have seen how rating scales are used in measuring consumer attitudes. The same technique can be applied to product screening. How this is done is illustrated in the example that follows.

An Example of Rating a New Product

The Superior Candy Company is a manufacturer of specialty candy items such as wafers, lollipops, and jawbreakers. These are marketed through candy jobbers to various types of retail outlets in which children's candy is sold, such as confectioneries, five- and ten-cent stores, and neighborhood drugstores. The candy is priced from 5 cents to 10 cents at retail.

The company has isolated five factors of its marketing program that it would like to use to evaluate new-product ideas. It has assigned weights to each of these factors, indicating their relative importance in the new-product screening process. The factors and the weights are shown in Table 10.2.

The marketing research manager presented a suggestion that the company should introduce a line of 20-cent candy bars. She pointed out that only 10 per cent of total candy consumption was accounted for by the type of candy Superior currently produced. In comparison, candy bars of all types accounted for over 50 per cent of total candy consumption. The research manager also noted some consumer dissatisfaction with competitors' bars, particularly in hot weather. Thus, an opportunity presented itself for Superior to introduce a new line of bars that could withstand high summer temperatures without discoloring and becoming stale.

[6]H. R. Hamilton, "Screening Business Development Opportunities," *Business Horizons,* August 1974, pp. 20–21.

TABLE 10.2   A rating chart for new products—Superior Candy Company

Factor	Weight	Score				
		5	4	3	2	1
1 Relationship to present product line	.20	Complements product line that needs to be filled	Complements product line that does not need but can handle product	Fits into product line	Does not fit entirely into present product line	Does not fit into any existing product line
2 Exclusiveness of design	.30	Can be patented by a copyproof patent	Can be patented, but patent can be circumvented	Cannot be patented, but copying is difficult	Cannot be patented, but can be copied only by large companies	Can be copied easily
3 Effect on sales of present products	.10	Will increase sales of present line	May increase sales of present line	Will have no effect on present sales	May hinder sales of present line	Will reduce sales of present line
4 Relationship to present channels of distribution	.30	Fits well into present channel of distribution	Slight change in current channels must be made	Major change in current channel must be made	New channels must be sought, but channels are available	No channel exists for distribution of this product
5 Availability of production knowledge	.10	Present knowledge available	Present knowledge needs minor adaptations	Present knowledge needs major adaptations	A ratio of 50–50 will prevail between new and old knowledge	Mostly new knowledge is needed

TABLE 10.3   New-product rating—Superior Candy Company (candy bar)

	Score	Weight	Weighted score
Relationship to present product line: The line of proposed candy bars does not fit entirely into the present line, which is composed of flavored candy specialty items.	3	.20	.6
Exclusiveness of design: The candy bar is somewhat unique. It can probably not be patented, but copying it would be difficult.	3	.30	.9
Effect on sales of present products: May increase sales of present line as candy bar users become familiar with the brand.	4	.10	.4
Relationship to present channels of distribution: Slight change in current channels must be made, since company is not now strong in vending machines or supermarkets.	4	.30	1.2
Availability of production knowledge: Present knowledge is available. The assistant plant manager formerly worked as a manufacturing methods supervisor for a major candy bar manufacturer.	5	.10	$\underline{.5}$ 3.6

A study by the marketing research manager enabled her to appraise the proposal and to assign an appropriate score. The assigned values are shown in Table 10.3. The table also shows the weighted rating score for the proposed new product. The equation for this computation can be expressed as

$$I_i = \sum_{j=1}^{n} w_j S_{ji}$$

where

I_i = the overall index of product i
w_j = the weight of the factor, which reflects its relative importance

S_{ji} = the score of new product i in area j
n = the number of factors considered

In line with Superior's previous use of this rating system, the product suggestion was passed on to a thorough business analysis, since the overall rating of 3.6 was slightly higher than the score of 3.5 that was considered necessary to pass the screening stage.

Eventually, the company decided to enter the 20-cent candy bar market, electing to start this move with the most unique candy bar it had developed. This was a white candy bar, which proved to be superior to those already on the market. Appropriate brand identification, attractive packaging, and consumer promotion made the new product successful.

Business Analysis

The third major step in the development of new products involves thorough demand, cost, and profit studies of the proposal. The purpose of this business analysis is to determine the long-run contribution of the proposed new product. The focus of the analysis is primarily on expected profit performance but other considerations, such as social responsibilities, also may be involved.

Demand Analysis

The first step in the detailed business analysis of the new product is a study of demand. Several types of analysis that we have discussed in preceding chapters are involved. Initially an estimate of total demand must be made. Ideally a demand function is formulated on which projections of future sales can be based. Estimates of market and sales potential also may be necessary, especially if segmented marketing appears to be a useful approach. Another important aspect of this analysis may be a technological forecast of likely subsequent developments in fields related to the proposed product. It will be particularly helpful to anticipate the probable date on which competitive products can be expected and the time at which the product will become obsolete. All of these considerations will affect the appraisal of the product idea from a demand point of view.

Cost Analysis

A complete cost appraisal is necessary as a part of the business analysis. It is difficult to anticipate all of the costs that will be involved in a new product, since the product idea has not yet entered the development stage. However, it generally is possible to project a range of costs that will be incurred. Both manufacturing and marketing costs must be included. An estimate of the capital investment required usually can be made, as well as a projection of the direct and indirect costs of manufacture. Marketing costs, however, will depend on the type of marketing program anticipated. Will a great deal of advertising be involved? What physical-distribution costs and reseller margins will have to be covered? Since these strategic considerations also enter into the estimate of demand, it generally is possible to interpret the answers in terms of expected marketing costs.

Profitability Analysis

Two methods of profitability analysis are often used in evaluating new-product ideas. One is break-even analysis and the other is rate-of-return analysis. An example should prove helpful.[7]

At the Trolex Sales Company a group of young people developed and patented a device to measure the speed of a boat so that a fisherman could select and maintain a proper trolling speed. Original cost estimates indicated that about $3,500.00 would be required for dies, materials, and other start-up costs. The dies would have a useful life of three years. The product itself was simple and easy to assemble. Purchased parts cost about $.30 per unit. The five required castings, made from the dies included in the start-up costs, could be purchased from a metal-working fabricator for $.64 each if bought in lots of 500 or more. A time study indicated that a person could

[7]This example is adapted from a case written by Gordon E. Miracle, Michigan State University, "Trolex Sales Company" (Intercollegiate Case Clearing House, n.d.). Case materials, as adapted, are used by permission of the author.

TABLE 10.4 Analysis of Costs and Calculation
of Break-Even Volume—Trolex Sales Company

Fixed costs

1. Dies and patterns $\dfrac{3,000}{3} = \$1,000$
   (assume three-year life)
2. Rent   300
3. Administrative time, 80 hours   400
                                              $1,700

Variable costs

1. Purchased piece parts $0.30
2. Five castings   0.64
3. Labor @ $2.50 per hour   0.125
4. Shipping   .06
                                              $1.125

assemble the device and pack it for shipment
in 3 minutes. Suitable labor was available
from college students at $2.50 per hour.
Shipping costs were estimated at $.06 per
unit in lots of 100; this was considered the
maximum-sized order that would be obtained. A suitable place for the storage of
materials and assembly could be rented for
$300.00 per year. The developers of the
project agreed to perform such managerial
supervision as was required (about 80 hours
during the first year) at a rate of $5.00 per
hour.

The owners of the device wanted to know
what volume of sales they would have to
obtain in order to cover the fixed costs,
including the managerial time of the developers. To make this determination some
information on pricing was necessary. They
learned that mechanical fishing devices, such
as lures, gadgets, and accessories, usually
sold for under $10.00. In order to fit into this
pattern, a retail price of $7.95 was consid-
ered appropriate for their product. Retail
sporting-goods stores require approximately
a 40 per cent markup on their selling price.

Therefore, a wholesale price of $4.75 was
selected.

The calculation of the break-even point at
this price is shown in Table 10.4 and Figure
10.3. The steps involved are as follows:
First, the fixed costs of producing and selling
the new products are determined. These
costs were $1,700.00. Second, the variable
costs of manufacturing and shipping are
computed. As we can see from Table 10.4,
these totaled $1.125 per unit. The data are
then plotted as shown in Figure 10.3. The
fixed costs appear as a straight line at $1,
700.00, since they do not vary with volume.
Variable costs appear as a straight line, beginning at zero output. The total cost line is
obtained by a vertical summation of the
fixed and variable costs.

The third step in this break-even analysis
is the plotting of total revenue. This is also a
straight line, indicating the various total
revenues associated with different levels of
sales at a price of $4.75 to retailers. The
break-even point is determined by the intersection of the total-cost and total-revenue
lines. In this case break-even volume is 469
units.[8]

Break-even analysis does not depend on
an estimate of actual sales. Accordingly it
does not permit the analyst to estimate what
profits will be. All that is known is that if the
break-even volume is surpassed profits will
result, and that the greater the volume, the
higher the profits. Thus, break-even analysis
does provide some help in reaching an eventual go–no go decision, but it does not

[8]The equation for the calculation of the break-even
point is

$$BE = \frac{F}{P - V}$$

where *BE* is the break-even volumne, *F* is the total fixed
cost, *P* is the selling price, and *V* is the variable unit
cost.

$$BE = \frac{1.700}{4.75 - 1.125} = 469 \text{ units}$$

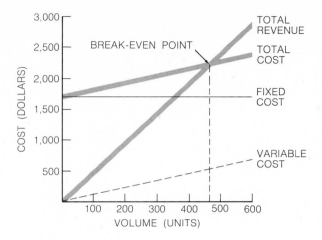

FIGURE 10.3   A break-even chart—Trolex Sales Company

possess the precision necessary to choose among alternative projects.

Rate-of-return or return-on-investment (ROI) analysis does make strategic comparisons possible.[9] The rate of return can be determined for a single year, for several years, or for the expected life of the project. We will demonstrate its use for one-year and six-year projections, taking the same data presented in the break-even analysis. Before we can proceed, however, one additional estimate is necessary. This is a projection of sales at the planned wholesale price. A market survey of sporting-goods stores in the Midwest indicated that approximately 800 units would be sold during the first year at a price of $4.75 and that a 10 per cent increase in sales could be expected each year thereafter. This sales volume could be achieved, however, only if $400.00 were spent on direct-mail advertising the first year and if

this budget were increased by $100.00 each year thereafter.

The rate of return for the first year is computed from a projected earnings statement as seen in Table 10.5. The statement shows that based on the given cost and sales

TABLE 10.5   Projected earnings statement—Trolex Sales Company

Net sales		$3,800
Cost of goods sold		
Ammortization of dies	$1,000	
Rent	300	
Parts	240	
Castings	512	
Labor	90	
Shipping	48	
Total		2,190
Gross profit		$1,610
Administrative and selling Expense		
Administration	$400	
Advertising	400	
Total		$800
Net profit		$810

[9]Return-on-investment analysis is receiving more attention in marketing. For example, see F. H. Mossman, P. M. Fischer, and W. J. E. Crissy, "New Approaches to Analyzing Marketing Profitability," *Journal of Marketing*, April 1974, pp. 43–48.

TABLE 10.6   Six-year earnings projection—Trolex Sales Company

	Years					
	1	2	3	4	5	6
Sales ($)	3,800	4,180	4,598	5,058	5,564	6,120
(Units)	(800)	(880)	(968)	(1,065)	(1,172)	(1,289)
Cost of goods sold						
Ammortization of dies	1,000	1,000	1,000	1,666	1,667	1,667
Rent	300	300	300	300	300	300
Parts	240	264	290	320	352	387
Castings	512	563	619	681	749	824
Labor	90	99	109	120	132	145
Shipping	48	53	58	64	70	77
Total	2,190	2,279	2,376	3,151	3,270	3,400
Gross profit	1,610	1,901	2,222	1,907	2,294	2,720
Administrative and selling expense						
Administration	400	400	400	400	400	400
Advertising	400	500	600	700	800	900
Total	800	900	1,000	1,100	1,200	1,300
Net profit	810	1,001	1,222	807	1,094	1,420

estimated, Trolex should earn a net profit of $810, representing a 27 per cent pretax return on the $3,000 investment. This rate appears sufficiently high to encourage the investors to put their money into this project rather than into some other alternative (such as common stocks or certificates of deposit paying about 7 per cent).

But what about the longer run? Is this level of profit likely to continue? Here is where the concept of return on investment becomes more complicated and meaningful. Revenues and costs for the venture must be projected over the period for which the analysis is to be made, in this case six years. What new capital costs will be involved? Will increases in advertising, management, and so forth be encountered? What will happen to sales volume? Will prices hold, or will competition force a downward revision? These questions must be answered before a long-term ROI can be computed.

In our case, the developers of Trolex

assumed that price would remain at $4.75 and that sales volume would increase each year by 10 per cent. Advertising costs would increase yearly by $100.00. New dies would be purchased in three years and would have a cost of $5,000 and a useful life of another three years. Material and shipping costs would not change. In computing the average rate of return for a longer period, then, we must add these future investments to the original investment and relate the stream of future profits to the total investment.

The projections through year 6 are shown in Table 10.6. The average annual rate of return for the six-year period is derived from the formula[10]

[10]This is actually a very simple formulation of a rate-of-return analysis. Capital-budgeting theory requires that future streams of income and investment be discounted to their present value to permit the computation of the rate of return. An explanation of present value goes beyond the scope of this text. The student interested in it should consult a finance text or a book on managerial economics.

$$R = \frac{\sum\limits_{i=1}^{n} P_i}{\sum\limits_{i=1}^{n} I_i}$$

where

R = the average annual rate of return
P = the expected net profit in each of 6 years
I = the owner's investment
n = the number of years

Inserting the data from the Trolex case, we find that the average annual rate of return for the six-year period is 26.5 per cent. This is approximately the same as the first year's return, notwithstanding that the new dies were expected to be more expensive and increased levels of advertising also were planned. The return continues to be more attractive than conventional alternatives. The risk however is also greater. The final decision of the developers, then, must be based on a balancing of this risk against the prospect of a long-run return of 26.5 per cent on investment.

Product Development

A product that has passed the screening and business analysis stages is ready for technical and marketing development. We will look briefly at these two aspects of product development and at the importance of coordinating them properly.

Technical Development

Technical development involves two steps. The first is the applied-engineering research required to develop exact product specifications. The goal of this research is to construct a prototype model of the product that can be subjected to further study. Once the prototype has been created, manufacturing-methods research can be undertaken to plan the best way of making the product in commercial quantities under normal manufacturing conditions. This is an extremely important step, because there is significant distinction between what an engineer can assemble in a laboratory and what a factory worker can produce. An electronics manufacturer discovered that of fifty tape recorders produced in the factory after successful laboratory assembly only two or three passed inspection. Realistic testing of manufacturing methods is therefore an essential part of product development.

Marketing Development

While the laboratory technicians are working on the prototype, the marketing department should be testing the new product with its intended consumers and developing the other elements of the marketing mix. The testing generally is done in two stages. First, a product concept test may be conducted early in the process. The product concept was defined by D. K. Hardin:[11]

Basically the product concept is a synthesis or a description of the product idea embodied in the proposed new product. It may be a very simple, straightforward, objective statement; it may be a highly subjective simulation of an advertisement.

For example, here is how an evaporated milk

[11]D. K. Hardin, "Successful New Products Without Test Marketing," an address to The New Product Marketing Conference, Detroit, Michigan, 17 March 1966.

company might have stated its product concept for a proposed cat cream:

The objective statement	*The subjective statement*
Kitty Kreme—an evaporated milk with cream-like consistency and flavor for use as a supplemental cat food.	Treat your cat to Kitty Kreme. A wholesome and delicious treat for your favorite pet. She'll love the flavor and love you. And at less than half the price of dairy cream.

Motivation research methods often are used in product concept tests. Focused group interviews or depth interviews may be conducted. Respondents are asked to express their views about existing products and possible new products. "How about something that would do . . .?" is a question that might be asked. For example, a farm publication was interested in knowing if a market existed for a special type of market news service. Group interviews were held with farmers and other agribusinesspeople in several midwestern states. Respondents talked about the ways in which they obtained and used this type of farm news. The conclusion reached was that potential subscribers already had adequate information and that the only additional thing they might be willing to pay for was an extremely fast news service. As a result of concept testing, the original idea of a weekly newsletter was abandoned, and a study was initiated of the feasibility of a hot-line service using Wide Area Telephone Service (WATS).

The second aspect of market development involves consumer testing of the product itself. This activity usually must await the construction of the prototype, or preferably limited-run production models. Various kinds of consumer preference tests can be conducted. The product can be exposed to consumer taste or use tests. Packaging, labeling, and other elements in the mix similarly can be studied. Straight-use tests are frequently administered. The consumer is asked to use a new product and give an opinion of it. Comparison tests are even more common, since the degree of consumer acceptance of existing products usually is known. The new product then can be compared to products of known acceptability. Consumers are asked to rank a number of products, including the new item; or the products are exposed in pairs to consumers, and by proper research design the relative rankings of the various items are determined. Even durable goods can be consumer tested, although the time period involved is usually quite long. It is not uncommon for makers of household appliances, for example, to provide prototypes of new equipment to selected households in order to determine how they work under actual use conditions and to obtain consumer opinions about their competitive merits and disadvantages.

Coordinating Marketing and Technical Research and Development

Nothing is more disastrous to effective product development than for marketing and technical research to be pulling in different directions or for marketing research to be ignored until the technical R&D has been completed. An example drawn from an actual experience in the chemical field illustrates this.

The research department of a large organic chemicals manufacturer had discovered a compound which appeared to have exciting possibilities as a rocket propellant. With the objective of gaining access to the expanding military and space markets, the company approved a large R&D effort to both develop this product and at the same time carry out research for additional propellants. After several years, many thousands of man-hours, and many millions of dollars, the entire project was cancelled. Failure of the project was not due to faulty R&D—the product was a good propellant, and production difficulties were not an obstacle. The project was dropped because little or no research had been conducted on the nature of the market, profits to be expected, and competitive conditions. Only after much R&D effort had been expended did the company discover that profit margins were much lower than the company's average, competition was intense, and prime contractors were very wary of dealing with organizations who had no prior experience in the field. Though the company was able to license or sell some of its technology, it did not cover costs, and there was no way to replace the lost effort which could have been expended on more commercially feasible projects.[12]

How is coordination to be achieved so that mistakes like this can be avoided? One way is for the R&D projects to be initiated in marketing—not in technical departments. In fact, this is one of the principal advantages of the product management system of organization. The product manager is the person who initiates all activity on behalf of the product and coordinates the various marketing and nonmarketing activities that must be undertaken. In companies with new-product departments, the coordination is achieved through a person in the department who is assigned responsibility for the entire development process.

[12]N. W. Jones, "Coordinating Industrial R&D with Marketing," an unpublished research report, Graduate School of Business, Washington University.

The Go–No Go Decision

Once initiated, the product development process is expected to produce a commercially successful product. A "go" decision is expected, particularly once the business analysis step has been passed. But a "no go" decision also can be made at almost any point if the development process breaks down. For example, engineering may not be able to develop an economically feasible prototype. Or marketing may encounter unexpected consumer indifference. Thus, the product development manager must stand ready at any time to reevaluate the implied decision to go with the new product.

This reevaluation is essential because as expensive and time consuming as the development stages are, they cannot compare with the financial drain that an actual market entry involves. For that entry, plant facilities must be obtained or diverted from other uses. Enough production must be scheduled to supply manufacturer and reseller inventories even before orders are received. Some marketing costs also are required, such as for packaging, point-of-purchase materials, and the like. It pays, then, to give one last thorough look at the project to make sure that it possesses the promise of success that justifies sinking further and substantial resources into it.

There are no special techniques to be used at this stage. It consists mainly of a careful review by top management of all of the facts gathered in the preceding steps, including the original screening, the business analysis, the compromises made in the product during its technical development, and the results of concept and consumer testing. If the project still looks like a successful venture, a go decision is made. If, however, there is some question about the project, a decision may be made to shelve it temporarily and to schedule a later review. The project may, of course, be abandoned. We have looked at the possible consequences of these three alternatives in Figure 10.2.

Manufacturing Planning

The go–no go decision sets the stage for final precommercialization activities. The product is approved, and the manufacturing department is asked to prepare plans for producing it. We cannot be concerned here with the details of manufacturing planning. Broadly, however, the manufacturing plan provides for facilities—including manufacturing space, equipment, dies, and other accessory tools. Personnel needs also must be estimated and the employment department instructed to assign or hire the work force. The procurement (materials management) department makes plans for the purchase of raw materials and for other manufacturing-logistics activities that fall within its sphere of responsibility. All of these manufacturing plans generally are coordinated by a production-planning department.

Close communication with the marketing group is still desirable at this stage, even though the final "go" decision already has been reached. Communications are particularly important in connection with scheduling. It is essential that the product be available when the marketing plan is ready to roll. Often, however, it is difficult to obtain sufficient quantities of the product. Occasionally, the whole market entry plan must be postponed because of a failure to coordinate with the manufacturing department. Emergencies can always occur; but the errors that close coordination would eliminate should

not be allowed to affect the success of the new-product development process.

Marketing Planning

It is at this point that the marketing department, especially a product manager, moves into high gear. We have reached the apex of the development process so far as marketing is concerned. It is here that the product planner's grasp of marketing concepts and an understanding of the planning process merge in the development of a strategy for the introduction of the new product. The product planner must prepare a complete marketing plan—one that starts with a statement of objectives and ends with the fusion of product, distribution, promotion, and pricing decisions into an integrated program of marketing action.

The Life-Cycle Plan

In formulating the plan, the alert marketing planner looks beyond the introduction of the new product. The product's entire life span is important. Although all of the events that will transpire in the history of the young product cannot be foreseen, plans can be laid based on the assumption that it will move through the stages of introduction, growth, maturity, and eventual decline. As we shall see in subsequent chapters on distribution, promotion, and pricing, it is very important for the planner to anticipate the complete marketing program that eventually will evolve for the embryonic product. One can then work toward the program's goal and avoid making introductory decisions that may make it more difficult to achieve the right program at a subsequent date. For example, extremely low introductory pricing should not be used if one expects to sell at somewhat higher prices later on. In terms of selecting market segments, an introductory program that is aimed at teen-agers will make an appeal to an older group in future advertising quite difficult. The older consumers most likely will react unfavorably to a kids' product. In some respects, this is the obstacle that Pepsi faced in its long struggle with Coke. Pepsi started its life span in a 12-ounce bottle selling for 5 cents—"Twice as much for a nickel." Sophisticated cola drinkers were not impressed by the appeal. Young people were, and their acceptance of Pepsi-Cola created a product image of lower quality and lower price—an image that took many years and millions of dollars to change.

Test Marketing

The final step in the product development process is test marketing. Formerly, test marketing was used principally as a screening device. The products that could not make it in the test did not get a chance at national marketing. In effect, the marketing planner extrapolated the results of the test to the national market and made a final go–no go decision on the basis of the test results. A decade ago this was probably the basic reason for test marketing.[13]

A new view of test marketing A newer view, however, is that test marketing should test those variables in the marketing plan other

than the product. Of course, product modifications might be recommended as a result of a test-marketing effort, but this is not the principal reason why it is undertaken. As a prominent marketing research company puts it:

It is well to remember that a good test market operation is (or by all means should be) a marketing plan carried out in miniature and scaled in every detail as to its relationship to the total intended market. It should involve two kinds of predictions:

1. A prediction of how a marketing plan will work at full scale.
2. A prediction of the eventual effect of the plan.[14]

The same company goes on to emphasize that test marketing is not a screening device. "It should be undertaken with the prior knowledge that all the important odds for success are high."[15]

What specific questions can be answered by this newer type of test-marketing operation?[16] First, the overall workability of the marketing plan can be assessed. In some respects, the test is like a shakedown cruise. Indeed, it is reported that many grocery manufacturers actually use the test-marketing activity as the first step in a planned program of market entry. Minor adjustments in subsequent markets may be made, but the *roll-out* (market-by-market introduction) is planned from the day the product is first introduced in the test market.

A second type of question that test marketing can answer involves the evaluation of

[13]See, for example, "Product Tryouts: Sales Tests in Selected Cities Help Trim Risks of National Marketing," *Wall Street Journal,* 10 August 1961, p. 1; and L. A. Fourt and J. W. Woodcock, "Early Prediction of Market Success for New Grocery Products," *Journal of Marketing,* October 1960, pp. 31–38.

[14]*Test Marketing* (Toledo, Ohio: National Family Opinion, undated), p. 4.

[15]Ibid.

[16]An interesting account of how Cadbury Limited, a well known British producer of confectionery and grocery products uses test marketing is found in N. D. Cadbury, "When, Where and How to Test Market," *Harvard Business Review,* May-June 1975, pp. 96–105.

alternative allocations of the budget. The level of spending can be varied in each of several test markets and changes in consumer response measured. Similarly, apportionment of the budget among various elements of the mix may be tested. In one market, the principal effort may be put behind in-store promotion and merchandising deals. In another area, the main thrust of the introduction may be through consumer sampling and mass-media advertising. Different advertising media may be tested in the different markets. Radio and newspapers might be used in one area, television in the other. These experiments always are carried on under conditions that are controlled as closely as possible. Store-audit data and warehouse withdrawal information, brand-awareness studies, coupon redemptions, and the like are used to measure the relative effectiveness of various approaches to market entry.

Objections to test marketing   Test marketing by no means meets with universal approval, even from sellers in those industries where it is used a great deal. There are several reasons for this. First, test marketing is expensive. This is undoubtedly why many companies now use test marketing as the first phase of national distribution. Second, it takes considerable time to complete a market test—the average duration appears to be about six months. This is more than enough time for dangerous developments to occur. For example, the distinctiveness of the innovation can decay drastically. It will no longer be a new product when it goes into the national market.

Third, test marketing is criticized because it prematurely tips one's hand to competitors. A test-marketing effort is very visible, and any good marketing-intelligence system will report its existence to a competitor's management almost immediately. The least that can happen is that the competitor will be ready to meet the threat of the new product when it enters national marketing. Other competitive tactics, however, may be more disastrous. Some competitors "jam" a test-marketing experimentation by purposely altering their programs in areas where another firm is known to be testing a new product. And competitive counteraction is not limited to jamming test-market results. A small competitor sometimes actually can beat a national marketer to full-scale distribution even while the larger seller is still involved in test marketing.

In addition to these major complaints about test marketing, which urge caution on those who intend to use it, there are a number of technical pitfalls that should be avoided. Briefly, these are the don'ts of test marketing, which if violated give rise to the types of complaints we've already discussed.

1. Don't confuse test marketing with concept testing. Test marketing is supposed to test the complete plan, not simply the product concept.
2. Don't test too early in the development program. Wait until the complete entry plan has been prepared.
3. Don't select test markets without careful study. Test markets should be representative of the national market, but they also should be different from each other in important respects that may affect the outcome of the marketing plan. (For example, one market may not have television.)
4. Move quickly, but not in haste. Allow enough time to get good results, but don't expect decimal-point accuracy. Certainly allow enough time for repeat sales, if any, to materialize.

5. Don't forget to have a control market, which is important for estimating the impact of competitive effort, seasonality, and the like.

Commercialization

The product is finally ready to go. It has survived the development process and is poised on the brink of market introduction. How can it now be guided to eventual marketing success? It is the purpose of the life-cycle marketing plan to answer this question. Such a complete marketing program will, of course, involve decisions about distribution, promotion, and pricing. Since it is very difficult to discuss the launching of a new product without getting into these other areas, we will have to do so briefly in order to show how the development process culminates in a market entry plan and to lay the groundwork for the discussion of marketing mature products in Chapter 11.

Launching the New Product

There are several dimensions of choice open to the market planner. Two of these are of primary importance. First, a decision must be made on whether to market to a selected segment or to approach the entire market. The second is between a roll-out (market-by-market) introduction and an attempt to obtain immediate national distribution.

We discussed the first matter of market segmentation in some detail in Chapter 6. The decision must be made on the basis of potential in the various segments and on the relative profitability of developing separate strategies for them. Test marketing might be used to resolve this issue. Careful analysis of all available data should indicate the approach to take. We must remember the criteria for segmentation that were presented. The market must be different, important, measurable, and accessible. If true segments exist and if the cost of preparing individualized programs can be justified, a segmented approach usually is desirable, since the appeal of the product and its promotion can be keyed more closely to specific consumer needs than they can in an undifferentiated marketing program.

The choice between a roll-out program and one of national marketing rests on a number of other factors. If new distribution must be established, national marketing cannot be achieved quickly. On the other hand, market potential may dictate a national effort. If the total amount of business to be had is spread very thinly, it may not be worth the effort to try to cultivate any particular market area intensively. Another factor that sometimes influences the decision to go national is the threat of potential competition. A market-by-market introduction may take as long as eighteen months to complete—plenty of time for energetic competitors to enter the picture. Finally, if a marketing program is to rely heavily on national advertising media, the waste of going through a series of local markets may be substantial.

Figure 10.4 is a two-by-two matrix showing this choice between segmented versus nonsegmented and national versus roll-out marketing. Within each of the four matrix cells there are almost countless mixes of distribution, promotion, and pricing that are possible. It is difficult even to suggest the many combinations that could exist. An example may be helpful.

DISTRIBUTION / SEGMENTATION	ROLL-OUT	NATIONAL
SEGMENTED	SEGMENTED – ROLL-OUT	SEGMENTED – NATIONAL
UNDIFFERENTIATED	UNDIFFERENTIATED ROLL-OUT	UNDIFFERENTIATED – NATIONAL

FIGURE 10.4   Alternative market entry strategies

An Example of New-Product Introduction

Admiral Chemical Company's new household detergent was ready for market introduction at the beginning of the fall season. Early in the summer, advance publicity releases were issued announcing that Admiral would introduce a revolutionary new product on October 1. This teaser campaign was followed in mid-July by a series of meetings with the company's brokers, introducing the new product to them. Sales promotion materials were provided for the brokers' initial presentations to chain headquarters, wholesalers, and voluntary buying groups. As soon as the broker sales organizations were fully informed of the new product and ready to start making calls, meetings of store buyers were held in each major market. At these breakfast meetings, the broker introduced a sales promotion manager from Admiral, who made a product presentation to those attending. Samples were distributed, a door prize (a new automatic clothes washer) was given away, and tickets for a family outing at the first professional football game in the area were handed out to each trade buyer attending.

Following this trade introduction, broker salespeople and company sales promotion representatives called on chain and buying-group headquarters and local stores. Advance orders were booked. On the Thurs-

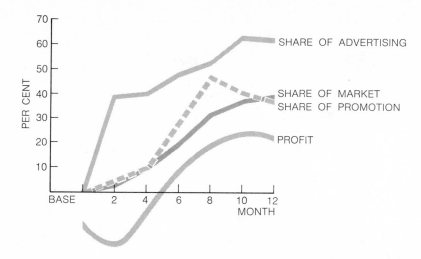

FIGURE 10.5   Results of an introductory marketing program—The Admiral Chemical Company (hypothetical)

day, Friday, and Saturday before the introduction, every major store in each market was visited. Point-of-purchase displays were erected and stock availability confirmed. On the weekend, television commercials were aired. Large-space newspaper ads were inserted in the Sunday papers. A cents-off coupon was included in the newspaper ad. Outdoor posters were erected the following week.

The program was under way. A somewhat diminished level of promotion was maintained for the next eight weeks, and then a sustained effort involving gradually increasing levels of spending continued for the rest of the year. Figure 10.5 plots the product's progress in national marketing for this first 12-month period. At the end of the introductory period (January 31), the product had earned and maintained 10 per cent of the market. Its share of advertising for that product category was a sizable 40 per cent. However, introductory marketing expenses were within budget, and sales results slightly

exceeded expectations. The new product was judged a successful market entry.

Marketing in the Growth Stage

We will not have much to say about marketing in the growth stage except to point out that the momentum of a successful entry must be maintained. Distribution gaps must be filled. Promotion is cut back somewhat as a percentage of sales dollars, but overall spending increases drastically. Minor product modifications may be made—perhaps in packaging. Flanker items may be introduced, such as larger or smaller sizes. But in general marketing in the growth stage is an extension of the introductory period. In the introduction stage, direct and specific product expenses exceed sales revenue by a considerable amount. The venture is temporarily unprofitable. In the growth period, however, the profit curve rises sharply, and the maximum point of profit usually is encountered sometime during this period. Toward the end of the period, competitive products begin to appear, and the company's own marketing effort encounters diminishing returns. Costs start to rise and profits to decline somewhat. Targeted rate of return, however, should continue to be more than satisfactory.

Summary

In contemporary marketing, introducing new products is the name of the game. We find that in many industries new-product development absorbs all of the attention of marketing managers. Although, as we saw in the preceding chapter, there is a great deal more to formulating a sound product strategy than just the introduction of new products, this is undoubtedly one of the most important and exciting topics in all of marketing.

The process of new-product development naturally begins with the generation of new-product ideas. Ideas for product innovations can come from internal sources, including basic research, the manufacturing department, the sales force, and top management. Good ideas also can come from outside the company. Among external sources are secondary-information data, competitors, customers, resellers, and foreign markets. A constant flow of new-product ideas is important, and it must be properly organized, managed, and nurtured.

Usually, however, a company gets far more unworkable ideas than good ones. A procedure to screen out the undesirable ideas is needed. There are several techniques of screening, including check lists,

rating charts, and indexes. Products that pass the initial screening generally are subjected to a more thorough business analysis. This investigation embraces three critical considerations—demand, cost, and profit. The profitability analysis may employ conventional accounting methodology, break-even studies, or rate-of-return calculations.

While a new-product idea is being scrutinized from the standpoint of its business prospects, it also must be studied from the standpoint of its technical and marketing feasibility. The technical research and development department constructs product designs and produces a prototype for testing. The marketing department evaluates customers' reactions—both to the product concept and to the prototype when it becomes available. The proper coordination of these two product development activities is extremely important.

If all goes well in the business analysis and in the technical and marketing phases of product development, the new-product idea comes back to management for a final go–no go decision. There are no special techniques to help the manager at this stage. The recommendations of all the people who have screened and developed the idea must be considered and then the decision whether to swallow the cost sunk in the project or to incur even greater sums in sending it on to commercialization must be made.

The go-no go decision sets the stage for the final precommercialization activities. These involve the formulation of manufacturing and marketing plans. A complete marketing program is developed at this point, and, if deemed desirable, the new product is committed to test marketing. There are sound reasons to test market and also good reasons not to do so. Testing prohibits the company from moving quickly to capture a marketing opportunity. It reveals company plans to competitors, one or more of whom may attempt to jam the test. Moreover, test marketing is expensive. But it does provide the manager with much information needed to select the right market segments, to determine the proper strategy to employ, and to decide how to allocate the budget among the various elements of the marketing mix. Some firms compromise between testing and not testing by using market tests as the first stage in the roll-out of a national marketing program. The results of the test cannot stop the program, but they may suggest important modifications.

The new product is thus launched into a market fraught with uncertainty and pitfalls. The product may fail, or it may succeed. If it finds consumer acceptance, it moves from the introductory to the growth stage of the product life cycle. Profits result, and the fortunate company chalks up a success in an area of marketing where failure is the rule rather than the exception.

Questions and Problems

1. An executive once likened the new-product development process to a beauty pageant in which scores of likely candidates are screened out until only one winner remains. What do you think of the analogy?

2. A company in the field of industrial maintenance products produced and marketed a rather wide line of floor cleaners, waxes, and the like. This firm generated a large number of new-product ideas, but almost none of them passed the screening investigation conducted by a new-product committee. What might have been wrong with this company's new-product development procedure?

3. After seeing the company's latest new product fail, the president bitterly remarked, "What this company needs is one good idea—just *one good idea*. You would think with all the people we have around here that somebody could come up with just one single good idea for a new product." What are the implications of this remark?

4. What kinds of analyses are conducted during the business analysis stage of the new-product development process?

5. Using the Trolex Sales Company illustration in this chapter, recalculate the break-even point and the average rate of return on the basis of the following information:

   Original dies and patterns cost $8,000.00 and will last five years.
   Administrative time is computed at $10.00 per hour.
   Purchased piece parts cost $.25 each.
   Labor will cost $3.50 per hour.
   A retail sales price of $9.95 has been selected.
   An annual growth rate of 25 per cent is expected.
   All other data in the case remain the same.

6. Suggest several specific areas in which it is particularly important for marketing and technical product development to be coordinated.

7. What is meant by a life-cycle plan? Using either Ford's Mustang II or Chevrolet's Camaro outline what you think might have been a reasonable overall life-cycle plan for the car at the time of its introduction. Indicate the time period covered by your plan, critical decision stages in it, and the general strategy that you think should have been used.

8. Chevrolet dropped its Vega models in 1978, presumably because of problems with the aluminum engine as well as the excellent market reception of its subcompact Chevette. Does this mean that the introduction of Vega had been a mistake?

9. The years 1977 and 1978 saw a rash of new products in the small electric-appliance industry. The public seemed to like the appliances very much. How do you square both the companys' decision to introduce such products and consumers' willingness to buy them with the apparent energy crisis?

10. A product manager recommended to her marketing manager that a new product should be test marketed before being marketed nationally. The marketing manager disagreed. He said, "In the toiletries field, getting a jump on the competition is more important than doing research." What arguments do you think these two people might pose to defend their points of view?

11. Do you believe that salespeople should be consulted before a product is added to the line? How else can the sales organization be used in connection with new-product development?

12. Identify several products that appear to be in the growth stage of the life cycle. Select one of these and find out as much as you can about the way it is being marketed. Why are such marketing methods appropriate for the growth stage?

11

Mature Product Strategy

In this chapter we will look at the unique challenge of marketing mature products. The nature of the mature product and the importance of planning a marketing program especially suited to it provide the point of departure for a more detailed discussion of the developments that usually occur in the maturity and decline stages of the product life cycle. We will look at some examples of products that have moved into the mature stage and at alternative strategies for marketing them. The chapter concludes with a discussion of the strategy of product deletion. While this is actually one of several strategies available for mature products, it is all too often neglected and deserves the special attention that life-cycle planning focuses on it.

What Is a Mature Product?

A *mature product* is one that has entered the maturity stage of the life cycle or has passed

beyond it into the stage of decline. As we shall soon see, so-called extension strategies can be applied to mature products with the result that a second take-off may materialize. Ordinarily, these life-cycle extensions do not assume the proportions of the original growth stage. Occasionally, however, such major changes are made in the mature product that its extension really becomes a new-product introduction. The dividing line between a major product improvement and a completely new product can be extremely hard to detect. In general, we will assume that if major changes are made in a product, a new life cycle has been started; but if relatively minor modifications have been incorporated, the product is still in its maturity stage.

An Example of a Product in Maturity

We traced the Admiral Chemical Company's new consumer product through its successful introductory and growth stages in Chapter 10. The subsequent history of this prod-

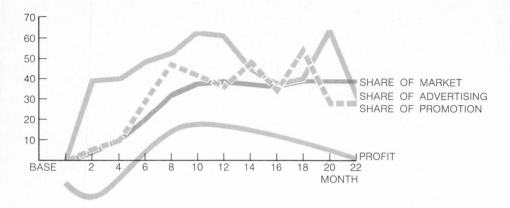

FIGURE 11.1   The product in maturity—The Admiral Chemical Company (hypothetical)

uct is shown in Figure 11.1. It achieved its maximum share of market in the twelfth month after introduction. From that point on, it was able to maintain approximately the 40 per cent share of market that it enjoyed at the height of its growth period. This was attributed to the relatively high levels of promotion and advertising maintained in the maturity stage. Clearly, it is now a mature product but has not yet entered the decline stage. We can assume that its product manager worked vigorously to forestall such a development. The profit curve, however, declined steadily as competitive pressures pushed prices lower while marketing expenses remained fairly high. Without question, the time is approaching—perhaps in two months, perhaps in twenty—when the sales of this product will decline and other strategies will have to be considered for it.

The Importance of Special Strategies for Mature Products

In spite of the glamour of new products and the considerable amount of money and attention that is devoted to their support,

mature products account for a far greater proportion of most companies' product offerings and sales volume. The importance of mature products is borne out by studies like the Nielsen report of nonseasonal sales trends of 275 brands from 37 grocery-product categories.[1] This report indicated that only 72, or 26 per cent, of the brands were in their introductory or growth stages. However, approximately 44 brands, or 16 per cent, either were already failing or were such recent entries that their success in the introductory stage could not be determined. Thus, the study showed that at least 60 per cent of the products of the typical grocery company are mature. Considering the uncertain status of the above 16 per cent, we may assume that the true proportion of mature products is closer to 75 per cent.

A second reason for stressing special strategies in the marketing of mature products is

[1] "The 'Life Cycle' of Grocery Brands," *The Nielsen Researcher*, no. 1 (1968): 8. Regrettably this unique study has not been updated. Plans to do so were abandoned when the inflationary pressures and then the recession disrupted the data base for the period 1974–1976. The earlier report (1968) is used here because of the lack of more recent published data.

that sooner or later product maturity is inevitable. All new products pass out of the growth stage at some point and the evidence indicates that products are becoming mature at an ever-quickening pace. This is partly the result of the rapid rate of new-product introduction, which means simply that older items are driven faster to maturity and eventual obsolescence.

A third important reason for emphasizing the marketing of mature products is that changes can and must be made to prolong their life expectancies. The reason for the *must* should be quite clear. In Chapter 10 we saw how difficult, time consuming, and uncertain it is to develop new products. We also saw in Figure 11.1 that old products do produce considerable profit and that a product's overall long-run profit record depends on a company's ability to sustain the product's sales and profit contribution through a healthy stage of market maturity.

That successful changes *can* be made in the marketing of mature products is well documented by reports of mature-product successes. Arm and Hammer baking soda has found many new uses and the original product has been flanked by a number of new personal-care items. A prominent electrical products manufacturer enjoys a resurging demand for ceiling fans. Sears continues to feature such old-time favorites as Franklin stoves, ice-cream makers, and push-type, nonmotorized lawn mowers. Faced with rising prices of motors and fuel, recreational boaters are buying sailboats in greater and greater numbers.

The popularity of these mature products can be explained in various ways. Sometimes their sales are the result of fashion throwbacks, such as the demand for home ice-cream freezers and granny spectacles. The nostalgia kick of the mid-1970s stimulated demand for many long-neglected products.

Economic considerations and a quest for security in products of the past are other reasons for buying older products. Probably the most important factor, however, is the streamlined marketing effort applied to mature products. Consider this example:

A soft-drink manufacturer noted that one product had been declining steadily in sales for several years despite advertising and marketing efforts that were equivalent to those maintained at the peak of its sales. Since marketing costs had been increasing steadily as a percentage of sales, even sizable manufacturing economies had not changed a sharply declining profit pattern. Faced with a loss operation in the coming year on this product (and a general tightening of profits in other products), the company studied the probable sales effects of cutting back the marketing effort. As a result of this analysis, the soft-drink company eliminated all advertising, shortened the product line, and tightened marketing backup support in the form of sales and product management. Now, five years later, sales are still 50 per cent more than those at the time of the cutback on frills, and the product has become one of the most profitable in the company's line.

The soft-drink manufacturer had considered a number of alternative actions before selecting the course that seemed to hold the greatest possibility of optimizing profits. He found that a different marketing strategy was required for the product in decline than was appropriate during the product's growth and maturity.[2]

Fortunately, marketing managers are now able to spot weakening products much sooner than they could in the past. Store audits, warehouse withdrawal information, and consumer brand-preference studies make it possible for a manager to detect at a relatively early date that a product in the growth stage is moving toward maturity and will therefore

[2]W. J. Talley, Jr., "Profiting from the Declining Product," *Business Horizons*, Spring 1964, pp. 77–78.

require the special and different attention that a mature product demands.

Marketing Developments in Maturity

In describing the product life cycle in Chapter 9, some of the characteristic developments of the mature and declining stages were introduced. It is important to review and expand on these developments for two reasons. First, it is imperative that a marketing manager be able to recognize when a product is in the mature stage, especially if adequate product sales data are not available. As we already have seen, we can tell when a product is in maturity by the kinds of competitive conditions that it faces. Second, the strategies that are most appropriate for any particular mature product depend on the specific developments encountered in its mature and declining stages.

Market Saturation

Market saturation appears to be an important reason why packaged consumer goods go into maturity. The following specific developments occur:

1. A brand reaches maximum distribution. A high percentage of package placement, commensurate with outlet potential, is achieved. We sometimes refer to this as *100 per cent distribution.*
2. Sales of a brand reach a maximum share of the market. Most marketers assume that there is a peak share that they can expect to attain. In Figure 11.1 we saw that Admiral's product achieved a 40 per cent market share and maintained this

over a considerable period of time. For most firms, this would be an exceptionally good performance.
3. At the same time that peak share and distribution are attained, relatively high levels of consumer awareness and recognition are enjoyed. Further efforts in advertising probably would result in very few additional purchases, since all of the potential buyers already have been informed about it.

Decline in Product Distinctiveness

A decline in product distinctiveness is a fundamental fact of product maturity. As long as a product possesses some degree of uniqueness, it maintains a competitive advantage. As its distinctiveness wanes, however, the product experiences a weakening in the market, which in turn leads to wavering consumer loyalty. Buyers are less likely to insist on the brand, substitution becomes common, and formerly loyal customers experiment with new products. Moreover, as customers begin to shop among competitive brands and are exposed to new-product advertising from other firms, product disfeatures in the mature product begin to be important deterrents. An inconvenient or undesirable attribute that might have been excused or overlooked previously now becomes a reason not to buy. All of these developments are related to the decline in the mature product's distinctiveness.

Dealer Apathy and Disenchantment

Wholesalers and retailers tend to be more loyal than ultimate consumers; but in the last analysis their allegiance is to their own customers, not to their suppliers. As a product becomes mature, the factors that deter the manufacturer's sales also affect the dealer's sales. Mature products help to sustain the dealer's business, but they do not contribute to its growth. When an older product actually begins to decline in sales, the dealer usually is more interested in replacing it than in finding ways to build it back to its previous volume.

Dealer apathy is reflected in the lack of attention given to the mature item. The product seldom receives promotional support, except as a loss leader. Reorders often are slow and usually in minimum amounts. Careful inventory control lapses and stockouts are tolerated. Disenchantment eventually leads the dealer to look for new products. To find room for these new items, mature products are pushed into smaller and less desirable shelf positions. The dealer knows that the easiest way to maintain the sales of mature products is through price cutting; thus, they are often used as price "footballs." In these cases, the dealer seldom is willing to bear the full weight of the reduced margin and puts pressure on the manufacturer to provide price relief. Eventually purchases are limited to special deals and promotions, which allow the dealer to stock mature products at the low prices needed for price reductions to the final buyers.

Intensified Competition

Competition in the mature stage comes from several sources. One major source is new and improved products. Once their introductory phase has been passed, these exciting and different substitutes drive deeply into the sales of established products. Competition—often on a price basis—comes also from other established products in the same category. Morevoer, wholesalers and manufacturers provide private-label merchandise to retailers. Such private-label merchandise usually sells at prices somewhat below manufacturers' brands.

Direct competition from other products is not the only competitive disadvantage that the mature product suffers. Other elements in the marketing mix become less effective in maturity. The competitive edge of the company's advertising and sales promotion program becomes dull in the mature stage. Several factors are involved. First, the absolute level of spending on mature products often declines. This means that the brand's share of industry advertising and promotion falls. It is already at a competitive disadvantage in terms of product distinctiveness; the absolute and relative decline in promotional impact worsens the product's competitive position. Also, those dollars that are committed to the promotion of mature products tend to be less effective than similar amounts spent to support new products. Market saturation, declining product distinctiveness, and increased competitive promotion combine to push the promotion response curve well into the stage of diminishing returns.

Changing Market Composition

Another development that often affects products in maturity is the changing composition of the market. In this connection, it is well to recall the adoption process, which we outlined in our discussion of new products. By the time a product reaches its peak in the life cycle, the loyalty of innovators and early adopters already may be wavering. A hypothetical projection of the life cycle using this "disadoption" concept is shown in Figure 11.2. The figure indicates that the first customers to leave the mature product are the innovators—those who made its entry successful in the first place. The decline in sales from this point on is due to the movement

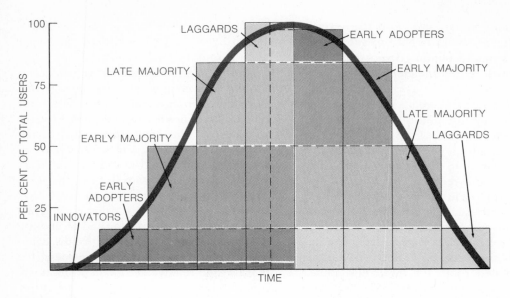

FIGURE 11.2   The disadoption process and the product life cycle

of early-adopter and early-majority buyers to substitute products. If the product were allowed to continue almost to the zero sales point (which of course is seldom practical), the last customers to abandon it would be laggards, who, as we recall, were also the last to adopt the product. According to the disadoption concept, customers in the mature and declining stages should have characteristics different from those in the introductory and growth stages. These differences may be economic, social, or behavioral.[3]

Not all of the changes in maturity are negative in their impact. Mature products tend to find new uses and new users. If these are substantial enough, the downward trend in sales may be suspended for a period of time. We shall see in the next section how

the decline can be postponed by the use of extension strategies to locate new uses and new users.

A final and generally favorable aspect of changing market composition for mature products is the solidification or stabilization of market segments. The discussion of disadoption suggests one reason why this may occur: Only the late adopters and laggards continue to buy in the mature stage. Another reason is that brand loyalties tend to be built up over time, and the core of the heavy-user segment seldom is identified until the product has been marketed for a considerable period. It also should be apparent that successful marketing itself tends to create segmentation. By product modification, packaging improvement, and promotion the seller adopts marketing programs to appeal to particular segments. If the programs are successful, usage segmentation materializes. Thus, it is not surprising to find

[3]These differences are about the same as we described in Chapter 9 for the innovators, early adopters, early majority, late majority, and laggards.

TABLE 11.1   Factors influencing the close of the product life cycle
(Per cent of cycles studied)

	Primary cycle	Recycle
Manufacturer's own action	12	16
Competitive action	72	55
New brand introduced	46	27
Matching action	11	16
Increased or resumed spending	11	7
Price advantage gained	4	5
Market saturation	10	23
Miscellaneous	6	6
	100	100

Source: Adapted from "The 'Life Cycle' of Grocery Brands," *The Nielsen Researcher*, no. 1 (1968): p. 11.

that in the mature stage the characteristics of users and nonusers tend to be well established.

The Life Cycle Comes to a Close

We may summarize the developments in the mature stage by highlighting the factors that influence the close of the product life cycle. Table 11.1 presents the findings of the previously mentioned study of grocery products throughout their life cycles. The most important factor causing closure of the life cycle is competitive actions—this factor accounting in total for almost three out of four cycle terminations. Almost half of these cycles ended as a result of a competitor introducing a new brand. Matching actions on the part of competitors, increased or resumed spending on advertising and promotion, and price competition accounted for the rest of the decline in competitive advantage.

It also is interesting to note that the manufacturer's own action caused termination of the life cycle in one out of eight

cases. What does a manufacturer do to destroy a mature product? Why is it done? One reason is that spending in support of the product may have to be cut back for financial reasons. Product problems sometimes are encountered, either in the field or in production, and the cost or difficulty of resolving them may be unwarranted. Of course, the manufacturer may simply be dissatisfied with the results obtained from a given product and decide to channel resources into support of other products or into the development of new ones. Finally, many companies render their own products obsolete by the introduction of new ones in order to beat the competitors to the punch. This type of preemptive strategy is competitively sound, but it has numerous hidden costs. The most important of these is the profit that the mature product would have earned had it been allowed to remain on the market. Another is the significant waste that is involved.

If nothing else does, then market saturation usually brings a product's life cycle to a close. If the product is a novelty item or one of temporary consumer appeal, there is little

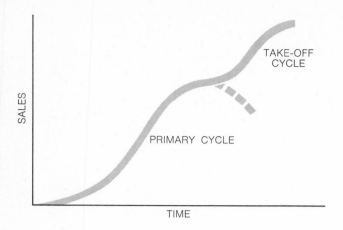

FIGURE 11.3   The take-off cycle

reason to expect the manufacturer to support it indefinitely. Similarly, if the market itself is limited or if the product appeals only to a small segment, further support of the product may not be justified.

Strategies for Marketing Mature Products

Take-Off Strategies

A *take-off strategy* for a mature product is one that is designed to send it into a new phase of consumer acceptance. In effect, the plateau of success in the mature stage becomes the launching platform from which the product is sent into a period of renewed growth. The take-off cycle, shown in Figure 11.3, begins when the primary cycle starts to decline.

A vivid illustration of this type of rebirth is presented by Theodore Levitt, who suggests that four extensions of the life cycle of nylon were made possible by four distinct strategies for the mature product.[4] These strategies were

1. Promoting more frequent usage of the product among current users
2. Developing more varied usage of nylon among current users
3. Attracting new users by expanding the market
4. Finding new uses for the basic material

Specific examples of product applications of nylon in new uses over a twenty-year period are shown in Figure 11.4. If its manufacturers had not found new uses and users, nylon would likely have been replaced in the market by substitute products in the early 1950s.

Another example of how a consumer-products company revitalized a mature product and moved it into a new stage of consumer acceptance is the take-off strategy used by Quaker Oats for its Aunt Jemima pancake mix. This product was plagued with

[4]T. Levitt, *Marketing for Business Growth* (New York: McGraw-Hill, 1965), p. 163.

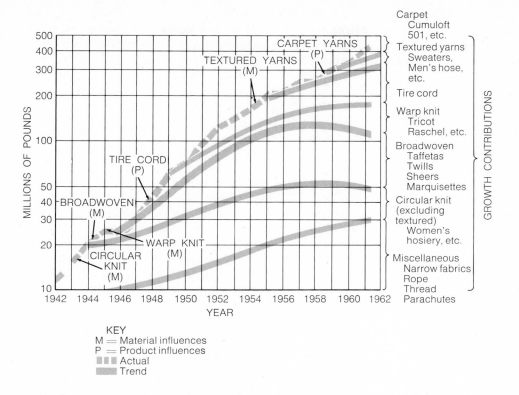

FIGURE 11.4   The product life cycle of nylon

Source: Jordan P. Yale, "The Strategy of Nylon's Growth: Create New Markets," *Modern Textiles Magazine* (February 1964), p. 33. Copyright © 1962 by Jordan P. Yale. Reproduced by permission.

an image of appealing to hearty eaters and being extremely rich and filling. With the advent of slenderizing foods, the image was particularly damaging. To counteract it, Quaker Oats developed a new method of preparing pancake batter. This method, which eliminated the old mixing-bowl approach, was called the *shaker method.* Quaker Oats also developed new ways of using the pancake mix—a tuna waffle casserole, waffle-burgers, and waffle rarebit. To help present these new ideas, Quaker Oats designed a new package for the mix. Originally the box was covered with a picture of Aunt Jemima. The new package, however, emphasized the new-use ideas with recipes. By doing these things and also by beginning an appeal to the younger generation, the company changed the Aunt Jemima image.

In producing this revitalized Aunt Jemima, Quaker Oats capitalized on two important ideas that are essential to marketing a mature product. First, the company was able to identify the market segments they were going to enter; namely, the youth market and the summer market. Second, Quaker Oats knew what these two segments wanted. The new method of preparing the batter saved time and was easy, so that even a youngster could mix pancakes without making a mess in the kitchen. Also, the new recipes were introduced in the summertime, when pancakes usually are not advertised. Finally, in appealing to the diet-conscious market segment, Quaker Oats got away from the idea of the high caloric content of pancakes. Sometimes this type of strategy is referred to as *repositioning*.

Take-off strategies provide a natural route for expanding the sales of mature products. Of course, the ability to use this approach depends on technological breakthroughs that permit the adaptation of the product to new uses or on changes in consumer demand that the mature product can, with some modification, satisfy. In this sense, the take-off approach depends on the emergence of a new opportunity. Development of an appropriate strategy to grasp this opportunity for an established, mature product is the key to the take-off approach.

Dynamic Adaptation

In contrast to seizing an opportunity for a second take-off, dynamic adaptation implies making changes in the existing marketing program for the mature product. Such adaptation is defensive rather than offensive. Its objective is not so much to increase sales or market share as to hold on to what already has been earned. The success of this approach to the marketing of a mature product depends on two things. First, good marketing intelligence must be received promptly enough to permit the product manager to take immediate and effective measures to meet competitive challenges. Second, the mature marketer must be ready and willing to make important changes in approach, perhaps even concessions in traditional ways of marketing. While it is impossible to gen-

eralize about the best adaptation strategy, observation of mature-marketing methods indicates that the following kinds of actions are most frequently used.

Package changes One of the easiest ways to adapt quickly is to change the package rather than the product. The Frozen Foods Division of Pet, Inc., has frequently used package changes to sustain the position of its Downyflake brand of frozen waffles. Curiously, there is no discernible pattern to these moves, but it is this very fact that classifies package changes under such circumstances as dynamic adaptation. For example, when Downyflake was faced with severe price competition from private-label waffles in some markets, the product was repackaged in extremely large polyethylene bags and priced as an economy package. Subsequently, in other markets the Frozen Foods Division moved away from plastic bags to colorful boxes, part of a family of packages that also included those for French toast, honey buns, and other breakfast specialties. The company's food brokers then concentrated on getting retailers to reserve a separate section in the display freezer for Downyflake breakfast products.

Steady imaginative advertising In the mature stage a product is usually well known, and massive splashy advertising is no longer necessary. Instead, many companies prefer to promote mature products by steady, but reduced, advertising expenditures. Often small amounts of newspaper space and short radio and television spots are used, tying in with retailers' local promotions.

Trade deals Probably the most effective weapon of marketing in maturity is a special inducement offered to the trade. This is because a periodic exciting deal to wholesalers and retailers is often the best device to

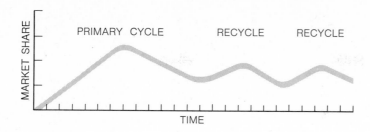

FIGURE 11.5   The primary growth cycle and two recycles

Source: "The Life Cycle of Grocery Brands," *The Nielsen Researcher,* no. 1 (1968), p. 6

keep dealer interest and activity at a high level. It is not uncommon for marketers of mature products to plan from two to six major promotions for a single product each year.

Anticipation of competition The mature marketer also must attempt to anticipate competitors' actions. If it is possible to anticipate when and where competitors will move against a product, the manager can commit reserves to its protection.

Recycle Strategies

The third major marketing approach for mature products is the recycle strategy. Recycling differs from take-off strategy in that it involves a total life-cycle plan, intended to project the sales of a mature product over a planned period of time. Take-off strategies are based on new opportunities to raise product sales by developing new uses and finding new users. Recycling, on the other hand, is designed primarily to preserve a product's share of its original market by protecting it against the effects of declining competitive distinctiveness. According to the A. C. Nielsen Company, a recycle is "any significant, non-seasonal improvement or revitalization in share trend after a pri-

mary cycle has run its course."[5] The primary cycle is the period that we have previously referred to as the *product life cycle,* involving the stages of introduction, growth, maturity, and decline. Such a product life cycle with the two recycle stages is shown in Figure 11.5. *The Nielsen Researcher* suggests that recycles can be identified by three kinds of sales developments.

1. An acceleration of an upward trend (similar to the effect of a take-off strategy).
2. A reversal of a previously declining share trend.
3. The arresting of a declining trend in share of sales.[6]

How long do recycles last? We can partially answer this question by comparing the average length of primary cycles in selected categories of grocery products with the average length of recycles for the same products. Such a comparison is shown in Figure 11.6. The average length of the primary cycle for all product types is 26 months. As might be expected, recycles tend to be of shorter duration—averaging only 15 months. In general, slightly more than one third of all grocery products go into one or more recycle periods. This means that for the average

[5] "'Life Cycle' of Grocery Brands," p. 6.
[6] Ibid.

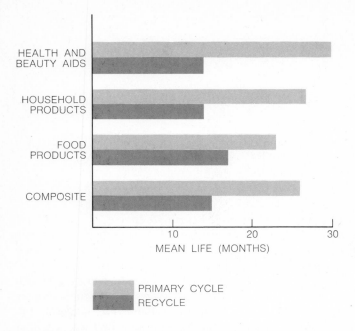

FIGURE 11.6   Length of primary cycles and recycles of grocery products

Source: "The Life Cycle of Grocery Brands," *The Nielsen Researcher,* no. 1
(1968), pp. 10 and 12.

grocery product with a primary life expectancy of 26 months, we can anticipate extending the life span by about 75 per cent.
Although each successive recycle tends to be
somewhat shorter than the preceding one,
we can assume that a typical grocery product
going through two recycles before being
withdrawn from the market will have a life
span more than twice as long as its primary
life expectancy. Marketing for grocery products might even entail three recycle efforts,
the decision on the third depending on the
success of the two that preceded it. A timetable for such a four-phase life-cycle plan is
shown in Figure 11.7.

Recycling has pronounced effects. It extends the period of time in which a company
can be developing a new generation of products. It also extends sales and profits beyond

those of the primary cycle. Nielsen data
compare share trends of established products that went through recycle stages with
those that did not. Increases in market share
were experienced by 42 per cent of the
recycled brands, compared with 13 per cent
of the brands that went through only pro-
longed primary cycles.

Marketing mix for recycle strategies   Recycling efforts tend to be most successful if
more than one element of the marketing mix
is involved. Figure 11.8 reports on the proportion of recycles using various mix elements. Advertising, as expected, is a major
weapon. In total, about 20 per cent of
recycling efforts involve either increased
advertising expenditures or changes in creative approach. Forty-one per cent of recy-

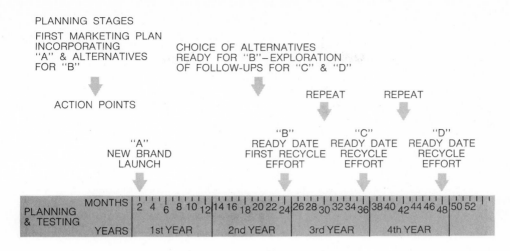

FIGURE 11.7   A timetable for planning over the product life cycle

Source: "The Life Cycle of Grocery Brands," *The Nielsen Researcher,* no. 1 (1968), p. 18.

cling strategies also involve some product improvement, which may range from a product change to the introduction of additional sizes, flavors, colors, and the like. Pricing advantages also are sought in recycle programs. These include direct price reductions or consumer and trade deals. The "Other" category in Figure 11.8 covers the indirect benefits of decay in competitors' effectiveness. That is, the easing of competitive pressure, such as product withdrawal or advertising cutbacks by competitors, may benefit an aggressive recycle program.

Thus far we have discussed recycling only in terms of grocery products. The concept also is applicable to consumer durables and industrial goods. The Lincoln Continental's successful designer series is credited with extending that automobile's life cycle by two to three years. Black and white television sales have been temporarily rejuvenated by product-line pricing changes. Industrial products, such as electrical motors and controls, water treatment chemicals, and data-processing equipment, have been successfully guided through recycles.

Why recycles come to a close Even good recycling efforts, however, will not perpetuate a mature product indefinitely. Eventually new products will dominate, and old ones must give way. Recycles close for much the same reasons that primary cycles are terminated; although as was shown in Table 11.1, distinct differences can be noted in the relative importance of the various factors. For example, new-brand introduction by competitors accounts for 46 per cent of primary-cycle closings, while this factor influences only 27 per cent of recycle terminations. Obviously, recycle programs are undertaken after competitors have made their new-product moves. Market saturation, on the other hand, is more important in ending recycles than in ending primary cycles. Almost one fourth of all recycles close because saturation in some form is reached. Recycles are closed slightly more frequently on the manufacturer's own action than are primary cycles, and a competitor's matching action (presumably promotion) also tends to influence their end more often than the primary-cycle closings.

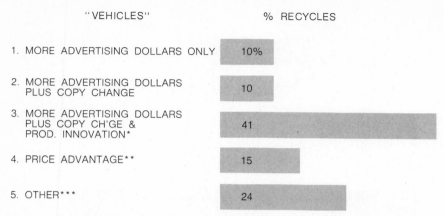

"VEHICLES"   % RECYCLES

1. MORE ADVERTISING DOLLARS ONLY   10%

2. MORE ADVERTISING DOLLARS
   PLUS COPY CHANGE   10

3. MORE ADVERTISING DOLLARS
   PLUS COPY CH'GE &
   PROD. INNOVATION*   41

4. PRICE ADVANTAGE**   15

5. OTHER***   24

  * Basic product change, new type, addit. sizes, flavors, colors, etc.
 ** Price increase, price reduction, more "deal" (Trade or Consumer), commodity price change, etc.
*** Easement of competitive pressure such as adv. and prom. cutbacks, copy diversions,
     maturity of new brands or recycling efforts, etc.

FIGURE 11.8   Vehicles used in recycles

Source: "The Life Cycle of Grocery Brands," *The Nielsen Researcher,* no. 1 (1968), p. 14.

Stretch and Harvest

Mature products are sometimes referred to as *cash cows,,* and the strategy of sustaining their flow of cash to support other ventures is called *milking.* The phrase *stretch and harvest* seems more appropriate and better describes what the strategy actually involves. *Stretching* is the effort to protract the product's life cycle without making major financial investments. A product lending itself to this approach usually has attained a high share of market and requires relatively little support to maintain it. Competitive threat is minimal, and the company is able to keep its prices at profitable levels. Since all tooling and introductory investments have long since been written off, the product is exceptionally profitable and generates an excellent cash flow. And, the scheme is to maintain that flow as long as possible.

Not all mature products become cash cows. The competitive situation may be very keen; prices, and profits, may be depressed. It may require massive sums of money to maintain market share. A stretch-and-harvest strategy is not appropriate in such a case. More likely, this mature product should be a candidate for early deletion.

An Example of Mature-Product Strategy

Figure 11.9 traces the primary cycle and two recycle stages of a typical grocery brand. The new Brand X was introduced and moved rapidly into its growth stage, supported by the distribution of free samples and a strong advertising program. At the end of twelve months of domination by Brand X, competitive Brand A entered the market. The distinctiveness of Brand X waned, competitive pressure was felt, and sales declined. During

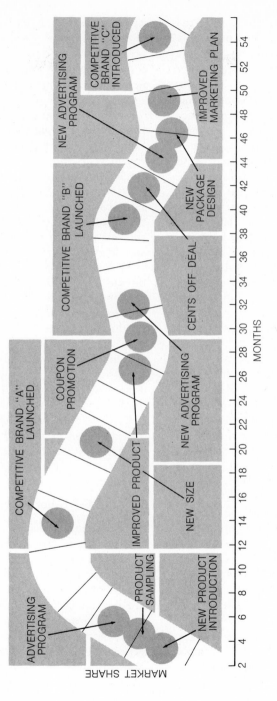

FIGURE 11.9 The product life cycle, showing strategies in the primary and recycle stages

Source: "The Life Cycle of Grocery Brands," *The Nielsen Researcher,* no. 1 (1968), pp. 4–5.

the second year, Brand X's company introduced a new package size. Although this failed to change the downward sales trend, it may have somewhat slowed the accelerating rate of decline.

Meanwhile, work on an improved Brand X was advancing. It was ready for introduction in the third year. This new product, Brand X^1 was supported by a coupon promotion and a completely new advertising approach. The first recycle was underway. Sales improved, and market share climbed again to approximately 25 per cent. At this point, competitive Brand B was launched, and the sales of X^1 again began to fall. The company retaliated immediately with a cents-off deal, and when this failed to stem the decline it introduced a new advertising program, followed shortly thereafter by a new package design.

The new package became the basis for an improved marketing plan, and sales and share of market in the second recycle stage again improved. With the introduction of a third competitive brand, the sales of X^1 once more began to fall, approaching levels at which serious thought was given either to deleting the product or making substantial improvements in it. After careful consideration of these two alternatives and review of new-product ideas already in the development stage, the decision was reached to withdraw Product X^1 as soon as test marketing on a replacement item was completed.

The Strategy of Product Deletion

A decision on product deletion, such as the one in the previous example, is not simply an ultimate strategy that eventually must be considered. Rather it is an alternative that is open at all times to product managers. As we already have seen, products probably should go into at least one or two recycle stages. However, under some circumstances product deletion at the end of the primary cycle may be the best alternative.

Product deletion as a strategy for mature products is a neglected topic in marketing. Some attention has been devoted to it in recent years, but interest in the subject lags far behind interest in the development of new products. In view of all that has been said about the importance of managing mature products effectively, it is surprising that this last phase of mature product marketing should be so disregarded.

To help correct this deficiency, we will devote the remainder of this chapter to the most important aspects of product deletion. We look first at the reasons for deleting products, and then at the factors that cause managers to ignore or to delay deletion decisions. Next, examples of product deletions from both consumer- and industrial-goods marketing will be presented to demonstrate the importance of developing definite deletion procedures. A discussion of a continuous system of review of mature products concludes the chapter.

Reasons for Deleting Mature Products

At first glance the reasons for deleting mature products may not seem worth considering. Such products are deleted when they are simply too old to go on. However, not all old products are ready for deletion, nor are deletion candidates necessarily those that have been around for a long time. Moreover, the various factors that should result in product abandonment are not always easy to detect. Certainly, as we have seen, age of product is not a sound basis for deletion.

There are, however, a number of other, more reliable criteria that can serve as signals for deletion consideration.

Negative profit contribution When a product is losing money it is a prime deletion candidate. It is important, however, to be sure that the product is not simply sustaining paper losses. Conventional accounting analysis may load a particular product with overhead and other expenses for which it is not responsible. For product-abandonment purposes, only direct or escapable costs should be considered.[7]

Moreover, projected rather than past profit contribution should be used in evaluating a product. Thus, a forecast of profit contribution must be made for each mature product and a judgment rendered on the basis of such a forecast as to whether the product should be retained. Obviously a product with a projected negative profit contribution is, at least by this standard, a prospect for removal.

Proliferation of product line Companies with long product lines encounter problems that can, to a degree, be lessened if the weakest of these products are dropped. This thinning of the line is referred to as *product-line simplification*. The advantages of simplifying a line should be clear. As the number of products offered by a firm increases numerically, the range of management problems seems to grow geometrically. Product overpopulation spreads a company's productive, financial, and marketing resources very thin. Further problems are the result. Forecasting becomes more difficult, and even the mechanics of product pricing become complex and time consuming. Moreover, an excess of products in the line, some of which serve overlapping markets, not only creates internal competition among the company's own products but also creates confusion in the minds of consumers. Planning and controlling a large number of products likewise present serious problems. As product managers attempt to spread their efforts over a product mix of hundreds of items, their ability to coordinate and control them is weakened. Some products with underdeveloped potential undoubtedly are ignored. Incipient problems with mature products go undetected. Even new products fail to receive the close attention that they require.

Problem products absorb too much management attention A weak mature product, of course, demands far more care than its contribution to company profits justifies. Unfortunately, this drain of attention also can go unrecognized; or, if detected, it is excused on the basis that "something has to be done." Philip Kotler points out that the costs incurred by weak products usually are indirect and seldom are reflected in expenses actually assigned.[8] This is because

1. Weak products tend to consume a disproportionate amount of a manager's time.
2. A declining product often requires frequent price and inventory adjustment.
3. Mature products, with declining sales shares, ordinarily involve short production runs. The problem is compounded when setup times are extensive.
4. The mature product, notably one in a recycling stage, requires both advertis-

---

[7]*Direct costs* are those that vary with the manufacture and sale of the product; *escapable costs* are those that would be eliminated if the product were dropped. Escapable costs include direct costs and some elements of overhead that could be eliminated if the product were abandoned.

[8]P. Kotler, "Phasing Out Weak Products," *Harvard Business Review*, March-April 1965, p. 109.

ing and sales attention that might be better used for new and healthy products.

5. The sagging product may damage a company's image and reputation.
6. The floundering attempt to preserve an old product may divert the agressive search for replacement times and weaken a firm's foothold for the future.

Opportunity cost   Even if a mature product is making a profit contribution and its indirect cost consequences are recognized and considered justifiable, a company still might be better off without the product because of its opportunity cost. The *opportunity cost* of a mature product is the profit contribution that a new and healthy product could produce if the effort and resources being devoted to the mature item were redirected. For example, if a business analysis indicates that a new product would produce 25 per cent return on investment but that this investment is presently committed to a mature product producing only a 5 per cent return, the opportunity cost that should be charged against the older product is the 25 per cent that could be earned on the alternative investment. Only if excess capacity exists or if no new-product opportunities are available should a mature product escape the burden that opportunity-cost analysis imposes.

Reasons Why Product Deletion Often Is Ignored

In many cases, products that should be deleted are allowed to remain in the product line. This is a fairly well accepted fact of marketing life. Should this be? There are a number of reasons, most of which are rooted in a lack of information, in personal considerations, or in the absence of procedures for reviewing mature products.

Lack of information   If cost studies, whether profitability analysis or opportunity costing, are not undertaken, it is quite likely that unprofitable products will remain undetected. Not until sales or share-of-market data indicate a dangerous condition is product deletion considered. We know from the product life-cycle curve, however, that profits on mature products tend to fall sooner and faster than do sales. With characteristic optimism, costly efforts to maintain or regain market share are made without a measurement of the effect of these efforts on product profitability.

Personal considerations   Product deletion is a drab business and often precipitates "much of the sadness of a final parting with old and tried friends."[9] Personal circumstances affect product deletion in several ways. Deleting products is an unsavory task, and it tends to be put off as long as possible. Since it is seldom something that "must be done today," it is relatively easy to postpone.

Moreover, vested interests tend to perpetuate mature products. Various people in the comapny—top management, manufacturing personnel, and salespeople—are inclined to have very subjective, personal biases toward older products. The individual who brought a product into being in the first place or the one who was responsible for its first big order seldom is willing to pull the switch on its final execution. Salespeople are particularly reluctant to see old products withdrawn. As long as a product generates any sales, the sales force is not willing to allow it to disappear. Older products often are easier to sell—at least to some customers; and they certainly require less study and effort.

[9]R. S. Alexander, "The Death and Burial of Sick Products," *Journal of Marketing*, April 1964, p. 1.

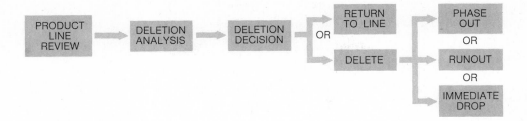

FIGURE 11.10   The deletion process

Finally, a sense of guilt often surrounds the discussion of abandoning a particular product. The question always arises, "Did we give it a decent chance to succeed?" This carries us back to the problem of product-line proliferation. No product can ever receive a fair chance under circumstances in which products that should be deleted are retained in order to be given another opportunity.

Product Deletion Procedures

As we already noted, one of the major reasons for the failure to delete products at the appropriate time is the absence in many companies of a definite procedure for the review of old products and the elimination of those that do not justify further support. Ad hoc deletion studies generally are inadequate and usually are too late. A procedure should be built into the management of mature products that guarantees that each is inspected carefully on a periodic basis. If this is not done, the problems of product-line proliferation and diffused management effort inevitably set in.

What is needed, in other words, is the counterpart of the product development procedure—a step-by-step process in which each mature product is isolated for study and carefully analyzed. Then decisions are made about its future status. It is not exactly the

reverse of the product development process; we do not "undevelop" products. But we do go through a parallel type of management review. We call this the *deletion process*. A sample deletion process is shown in Figure 11.10. The sections below briefly describe the deletion steps.

Product-line review   A review of the entire product line should be undertaken periodically, perhaps semiannually or possibly even monthly, by companies with long lines and high product turnover.[10] All products are given an initial screening. Such factors as the following provide convenient bases for the initial screening:

Actual sales volume
Sales volume compared to forecast
Share of market
Profit contribution

If a mature product shows signs of weakness in one or more of these areas, it is designated for a thorough deletion analysis.

Deletion analysis   The deletion analysis is similar to the business analysis step in the development process. The crux of the inves-

[10]J. T. Rothe, "The Product Elimination Decision," *MSU Business Topics,* Autumn 1970, pp. 45–51; and P. W. Hamelman and E. M. Mazze, "Improving Product Abandonment Decisions," *Journal of Marketing,* April 1972, pp. 20–26.

TABLE 15.2   A rating scale for product deletion

Components	(A) Relative Weight	(B) Product value (Low to High)											A × B
		.0	.1	.2	.3	.4	.5	.6	.7	.8	.9	1.0	
1. Is the value as seen by the customer (what is received for the money) high or low?													
2. Does it meet consumer buying habits, motives, and satisfaction?													
3. How strong is brand loyalty?													
4. What would be the consumer reaction if the product were dropped (little, rate low; great, rate high)?													
Total weight	1.00											Total score	

tigation is to determine whether a product should be allowed to remain in the line. This question is not unlike the problem of whether a new product should be introduced. It is not surprising, then, to find that the procedures used in deletion analysis are quite similar to those used in the development process.

Let us think back for a moment. It is reasonable to expect that a mature product should pass the same fitness test as does a new-product idea. Except for its degree of distinctiveness, a mature product should have a better chance of passing such a test, since it already has survived the test of the market and probably has been improved substantially since its original entry. Thus, the starting point in any deletion analysis is to go back to the original development

screening procedures and run the mature product through the same rating instruments.

A rating chart for use in evaluating a deletion candidate is shown in Table 11.2. It is only one of several such charts that should be used, since it is concerned solely with the effect of the proposed deletion on the product's consumers. As in the case of new-product ratings, weights must be assigned for each factor, scores given to each factor (in this case, on a 10-point scale), and an overall weighted factor score determined. This score for consumer impact would be combined with scores obtained from rating other deletion considerations, and a final total product value would be determined. Presumably, some standard of acceptance or rejection can be set. Generally, however, this standard can be used only as one of several considerations in the final decision on whether to delete the product.

Deletion decisions are forward decisions, involving predictions of a mature product's future. A product sales forecast therefore is necessary. A product may meet all of the criteria of acceptability, but the prediction of its future volume and share of market may not justify further commitment to it. A convenient starting point in making such a forecast is the product's past sales history. If this history conforms generally to the company's typical primary and recycle patterns, an extrapolation may be possible. Often, however, unique problems affect individual products. These must be carefully noted, and their probable consequences on the product's future must be taken into consideration.

Another important part of the deletion analysis is the study of the mature product's profit contribution, if any. From this a projection of future profits can be made. If the item appears to be declining in profitability and if there are no feasible ways by which to reverse this trend, it is probably time for the product to be removed from the line. Often, however, changing a manufacturing method, dropping parts of the line, or eliminating the expensive frills in marketing can make a mature product a profit contributor. A hasty decision by the manufacturer to delete a product before a search for cost-saving steps has been made is not wise.

Deletion decision   After the deletion analysis has been completed, a choice must be made regarding the product's future. Should it be retained in the line, or should it be dropped? If it has passed the various tests imposed in the analysis stage, it can reasonably be expected to perform satisfactorily—at least until the next scheduled deletion review. If it has failed to stand up to the

deletion scrutiny, the product should be scheduled for abandonment.

Deletion timing   There are three basic courses to follow once a product has been scheduled for removal. These have to do mainly with the speed with which the product is removed and the amount of support that is given it during its removal stage.

A normal way to abandon a product is to let it run its present course in the downward stage of its last recycle. This is called a product *phase-out*. It still produces some volume, even a slight profit contribution. Modest advertising and dealer support may be rendered. In other words, this approach involves an attempt to buy a little extra time. If the next generation of product in the same category is not yet ready for introduction, it may be important to try to hold shelf space and consumer loyalty by continuing to support the older product in its last recycle period.

A modification of the phase-out program is called the product *run-out*. It differs in that specific strategies are imposed that capitalize on the remaining strength of the mature product. These strategies are based on one of two alternatives.

1. Concentrate selling and advertising efforts in the stronger markets, geographical or vertical, for the product
2. Completely eliminate or substantially tighten total market effort

An example of how a company benefited from this second approach is as follows:

A manufacturer of a number of general product lines for supermarkets found itself with a line of farmer (kitchen) matches which had been steadily declining in sales for several years. To arrest the decline, a revitalized marketing program was launched which included redesigning the match box, instituting a sizable national advertising campaign, and lowering prices. The results were catastrophic—the decline in dollar sales continued, and the only figures that mounted were the red ones on the profit and loss statement.[11]

A subsequent detailed evaluation of the unique market demands for the product was made. The basic courses of action that we have discussed thus far were weighed by the study team and by management to determine their probable effects on the rate of decline.

The following assumptions were felt to be realistic: The current rate of decline would continue under a phase-out program; the current rate of decline would continue in metropolitan markets, but would double in other markets under the first type of run-out program; and the current rate of decline would double under the second type of run-out program.

After working out detailed models for each alternative course of action, the third—run-out program eliminating all advertising and promotion—clearly was shown to provide the optimum profit contribution. In actual practice, however, the rate of decline, rather than doubling, showed no significant change; thus profits proved much better than estimates had indicated.[12]

The last and most drastic tactic of deletion is the *immediate drop.* It is appropriate under either of two circumstances: when the product is unprofitable on the basis of direct or escapable costs, or when a substitute product is ready for market introduction. The second situation is the more desirable, but it seldom prevails.

The choice between phase-out, run-out, and immediate drop really depends on just how unprofitable the product is. Several examples of companies that benefited from

product-line simplifcation have already been cited. Simplification, of course, is not as drastic as the dropping of a complete product line, but judicious pruning often results in remarkable profit improvement and even some sales improvement as marketing effort is directed toward more healthy products.

Unfortunately, however, the heartrending decision to abandon at once an important product or a complete line occasionally must be made. A number of automobile companies have faced this decision, as have many manufacturers of grocery products. The products involved often are marketing failures that have not even gone into the maturity stage; but sometimes they are old favorites. When strong sentiment surrounds the abandonment of such products, an immediate drop may be easier to administer than a slower withdrawal from the market.

Summary

Borrowing General MacArthur's statement, we might say, "Old products never die; they just fade away." In this chapter, we have seen that mature products do not have to fade away—indeed they should not be permitted to do so. There are appropriate strategies for marketing mature products. These include programs for revitalizing them or, when necessary, for carefully deleting them from the product line.

The number of mature products on the market is far greater than the number of new ones. These products require considerable attention, because they are the backbone of their companies' marketing programs. Unfortunately, this attention often is lacking, possibly because mature products lack the glamour and excitement of new ones.

The developments in the mature stage of

[11]Talley, "Profiting from the Declining Product," p. 80.

[12]Ibid., p. 83.

the product life cycle, however, do pose interesting and important challenges. The successful marketing executive learns to recognize and cope with them. Among the most important challenges are saturation of the market and a decline in the product's competitive distinctiveness. This combination of circumstances can be a deadly threat. In addition, dealers tend to be uninterested in mature products and fail to give them the display space and merchandising support required to meet the intensified competition that arises. The market composition for a mature product also tends to change. A hard core of loyal buyers remains, but most previous customers switch to new brands. Unless some management action is taken to adapt to these changes, the product's life cycle comes to a close.

Fortunately, there are workable strategies for adapting to mature-product marketing conditions. The take-off strategy is employed when entirely new opportunities open up. In other words, new uses and new users may create a new life cycle for an established product. Most firms, however, do not find take-off opportunities. They must be content with other approaches. One is called dynamic adaptation and involves tactical changes in the marketing program to adjust it to the changing market and competitive conditions. Another approach is known as recycling and involves the development of new marketing plans for the mature product. As many as two or three recycle stages are possible for an effectively marketed mature product. A final strategy for the mature product is to stretch its life cycle and harvest as much return from it as possible. Sometimes referred to as milking, the strategy concentrates on having the mature product generate a positive flow of cash to support other ventures—presumably products at earlier stages of their life cycles.

All product life cycles, including recycles

and stretched cycles, come to a close, and eventually the issue of dropping an older product must be faced. Understandably, most managers do not like to think about product abandonment, but there are important reasons why they must do so. Declining products can be real losers. Having too many products in a line is costly and spreads management too thin. In addition, problem products tend to absorb a disproportionate amount of executive time. And when the opportunity costs of more profitable new products are considered, most old products are seen to be very unattractive.

Thus, it is necessary for a company to have systematic product deletion procedures. An orderly review of products for the purpose of screening out those to be considered for deletion is the important first step. Deletion analysis may involve forecasts of future sales, detailed profit contribution studies, and the rating of the product on the basis of various criteria. Once a deletion decision has been reached, the question of the timing of the product's abandonment must be considered. A product can be phased out according to a definite timetable; it can be allowed to run its course without further marketing support; or it can be dropped immediately. The ideal approach to product deletion involves a continuous review of all mature products, not only for the purpose of isolating those that should be considered for deletion but also to spot others for which the life cycle can be extended by new marketing plans.

Questions and Problems

1. What is a mature product? Name at least five products that you think are

mature. What are your reasons for classifying them as mature?

2. Name at least three products that are less than two years old but are, nevertheless, mature. Why is it that age has no bearing on the mature character of these products?

3. Select one of the products that you identified in question 1 or 2, and find out as much as you can about the way it is marketed. What do you think of this program as a strategy for a mature product?

4. Why do the various elements of the marketing mix differ in their relative effectiveness over the product life cycle?

5. In 1950, the radio was a mature product rapidly being displaced by television. Suddenly the radio business took off. How do you explain this phenomenon?

6. What is a recycle? Why is the recycle concept so important in the marketing of mature products?

7. How can dynamic adaptation help the marketer of a mature product?

8. You are the product manager of a mature product, a popular 20-cent candy bar. Sales of the product have peaked out, and your company has been experiencing a gradual loss of market share for several years. Select one of the several candy bars on the market as your product, and develop an adaptive strategy that you think might improve its market position.

9. A marketing consultant recommended to a client company that it should abandon one of its products. As a matter of fact, it was the company's first product and had been invented by the father of the current company president. The consultant presented the suggestion to the company's president, the director of marketing, the sales manager, and the treasurer. Only one of these people agreed to the recommendation, and that person agreed for the wrong reasons. What do you think were the positions of the four executives on this issue?

10. Would you rather be a product manager of a new product or a mature one? Why?

11. Why can we say that product deletion is like product development?

12. What are the advantages and disadvantages of a system of continuous review of mature products?

12

Channel Strategy

In this chapter we shall look at the second element in the marketing mix—the channel of distribution. We will see that channel selection is not a static once-and-for-all choice, but that it is a dynamic part of marketing planning. The chapter opens with a brief discussion of where channel decisions fit in the sequence of steps used to develop an integrated marketing plan. We are then ready to review the nature of the channel as an intermediate marketing system and to suggest how two prevailing misconceptions about channel selection often result in grave mistakes. Since channel selection is strategic, we also shall have to look at objectives for channel selection and at the various problems and issues that must be solved as one develops a channel plan. The chapter closes with a reminder that dynamic channel management is a vital part of short- and long-run marketing planning.

Defining the Role of Channel Strategy

In the sequence of steps involved in designing a complete marketing plan, channel decisions follow the development of product strategy. Channel decisions can be reached more efficiently if prior consideration has been given to product planning. If a firm decides to develop a product-service combination to meet a particular customer need, this same customer need may suggest channel problems that also must be resolved. A market for a highly engineered product, for example, may require an extensive and technically oriented sales and service organization.

Equally important is the idea that channel decisions should precede consideration of promotion and pricing. For example, if a program of advertising to resellers is consid-

273

ered an integral part of the promotion mix, the prior determination of the type, number, and location of wholesale and retail channel components must be made before such a campaign can be designed. Similarly, pricing decisions require that the channel system first be determined. To illustrate, whether provision for a wholesale markup must be made in the final price of a product depends on whether wholesalers will be used in the distribution channel.

The Channel Is a System

In Chapter 2, we were introduced to the concept of the channel of distribution, which, as we recall, includes not only channel components but also their interrelationships. All kinds of middlemen and many kinds of facilitating agencies (such as common carriers, financial institutions, and advertising agencies) are potential channel components. These components are linked in the channel system by one or more of the marketing flows, which include transfers of ownership, physical movement of merchandise, transmission of information, and payment and repayment of funds.

Channel Choice Is Strategic

Although channel arrangements are often long lived and channel decisions tend to become fixed features of a company's marketing activity, this situation is not especially desirable. It is always prudent to identify the channel requirements of each new marketing plan. True, a company does not upset its existing setup every time it considers a new marketing program. However, the best channel arrangements are those that are developed in accordance with the rest of the marketing mix and as part of an integrated marketing plan. If an overall strategy dictates a modification of existing channel arrangements or perhaps even calls for a sweeping reorganization, the need to do so should be recognized. In other words, existing trade channels are not a constraint in the design of marketing strategy. For this reason, channel decisions are included as a part of strategy rather than as a part of the marketing organization.

Two serious channel misconceptions The theory and practice of channel design have long been disrupted by two pernicious misconceptions. To dramatize these, let us call them the *shipping-platform approach* and the *product-feature approach.* Both are fundamentally incorrect and potentially dangerous because they tend to produce bad channel decisions.

The shipping-platform approach is a practical error. It is the mistake of concentrating only on the first link in the distribution channel. The error often arises from the production of goods without an advance knowledge of the consumers who will use them. The merchandise is assembled in the warehouse, and management's attention is directed to the shipping platform over which the goods must pass to make room for another production run. The cry to the sales department is "Move these out of here!" An immediate buyer must be found. Where to ship the material becomes the problem to be resolved—and it is often resolved without regard to the ultimate destination of the merchandise. Thus, the channel is created by a series of sales, not by the logical structuring of a distribution system through which the goods can be moved most efficiently from manufacturer to ultimate user.

The product-feature approach is a theoretical mistake. It has long been held that the type of distribution channel required is determined by such product features as physi-

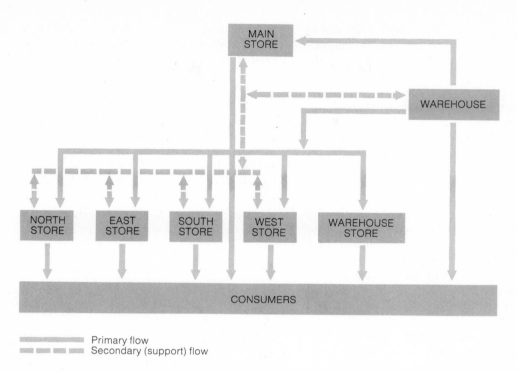

Primary flow
Secondary (support) flow

FIGURE 12.1   Flows of merchandise within a local department store organization

cal size, unit value, perishability, technical nature, and length of product line. The admittedly frequent association of these features with certain channels does not logically substantiate a cause-and-effect relationship between the two.

It is true that customer requirements determine product features, and it also is true that customer requirements dictate channel features. But these two facts do not mean that product features actually determine the kind of channel to be used. As we shall see later in this chapter, the only factors that directly determine channel characteristics are the requirements of the customers and resellers. One should not inspect the product to discover how it should be sold. Rather, one must look to its ultimate users and to those from whom consumers buy.

Reseller channel strategy   Does the middle-man need a channel strategy? Or is the reseller part of the manufacturer's channel system? The closer we get to the ultimate consumer, the less likelihood there is that a particular marketing establishment needs to develop a distribution channel. In most cases, sales are made directly to ultimate consumers or industrial buyers. Retailers, in this sense, do not develop channel strategies, although large integrated retailers do have locational and logistical problems that parallel those that manufacturers solve by making appropriate channel decisions. Figure 12.1 shows an organization chart of a large center-city department store with four branch stores, a warehouse store, and a warehouse. Merchandise moves from warehouse to the stores, from the center-city store to consumers and to branch stores, from the warehouse to consumers, and between stores. The primary flow of merchandise represents major inventory allocations. The secondary flow, shown by the broken line, is a support flow to provide merchandise from some units to meet unusual demands at other units.

A wholesaler faces a more conventional channel problem. A pharmaceutical wholesaler or a hardware distributor, for instance, must decide on the types and numbers of retail outlets through which to sell. The wholesaler's options are fewer and the considerations somewhat less complicated than those faced by manufacturers, but the same basic channel decisions must be made.

In Chapter 2 we saw that a channel system has a power structure. A locus of power usually emerges within this structure, perhaps at the reseller level. Extremely large retailers are often the most instrumental components in the channels to which they belong. Corporate food chains, such as A&P, Kroger, and Safeway, exert great pressure on other members of the food marketing system. Similarly, large general-merchandise retailers, including department store giants and the newer mass merchandisers, profoundly influence the marketing decisions that are made concerning the consumer soft and hard goods that they sell.

We call a dominant component in a channel system the *channel leader* or *channel captain*. This position usually is occupied by the manufacturer, but the leadership can be held by a retailer or a wholesaler. If the real authority in the system exists at the reseller level, the channel is more affected by buying decisions than by selling decisions. Suppliers, not resellers, are selected. The difference is of considerable importance, but the final effect is similar. A channel system is formed, and its components are joined together by flows of products, funds, and communications. These components cooperate in the marketing of the products that bind them together in order to achieve their own organizational goals and objectives.

For the most part, however, channels are created by the selling and distribution decisions of manufacturers. Thus, resellers ordinarily are chosen; they do not choose. They are selected as members of another's channel, but they are not less important for this reason. It is just that the basic channel issues are resolved within another company, and the power center usually rests where the decisions actually are made.

Objectives of Channel Strategy

Sources of Channel Objectives

Channel objectives, whether dramatic or routine, usually can be found in a review of corporate and marketing objectives. As with product objectives, a firm seldom has channel objectives that are distinct and separate from those of the rest of the marketing program.

Channel objectives can be dominant, as in the case of a company that is just getting under way or in an older firm attempting to carve out a new and different market niche. In these instances, getting to the market may be the most important problem; and channel development, rather than product development, may be the greatest obstacle to penetration of a new market. For example, small manufacturers often encounter great difficulty in expanding distribution outside their local market. One reason is that shelf space, especially in supermarkets, is jealously guarded. Only so many "facings" of a particular product category are permitted. The addition of a new product to the shelves generally means that space previously assigned to competitive products must be obtained. Competitors resist such inroads vigorously. Distribution in these cases often must be forced by superior selling efforts. In cases such as these, the distribution objective is the principal marketing objective of such a firm.

Similar problems are encountered by industrial firms seeking to develop new markets, since it often is difficult to obtain distribution through established industrial resellers. These distributors are no more anxious to proliferate their product offerings than are retail merchants. If manufacturers' representatives are to be used, obtaining representation by competent individuals in all important markets is often a serious problem. A manufacturer of automotive-repair equipment, for example, had to postpone introducing a new product for over a year while waiting to develop a minimum distribution system. The delay was costly in terms of lost sales, but it was inevitable in view of the necessity of obtaining twenty or twenty-five experienced manufacturers' representatives who were not already handling competitive items.

Typical Channel Objectives

There are an almost unlimited number of marketing or corporate objectives that can be related to channel strategy. To illustrate the diversity of form that channel objectives can take, a few examples are mentioned below.

Growth in sales by obtaining distribution in new markets The new markets may be in areas of the country or of the world that have not yet been served. On the other hand, this goal may imply distribution to new customers—to market segments not previously covered.

Maintenance or improvement of market share through existing channels The pressure to maintain a company's competitive position often can be translated into pressure to increase the flow of goods through existing channels. Increasing the flow to maintain or to expand market share is difficult. Some channel components operate very close to capacity; they cannot handle an increased load. Other channel components may lack the incentive to increase their efforts on behalf of the manufacturer. Such components must be educated or assisted so that they will cooperate to achieve the desired increase in sales.

Achievement of a predetermined pattern of distribution Aside from its effect on sales or market share, a specific pattern of distribution may be useful. As noted earlier, this may be a critical objective for a new company or a company introducing a new product. Similarly, an established firm may desire to streamline or otherwise change its basic channel arrangement. To effect such changes may constitute an important channel objective.

Creation of an efficient channel system A channel system is a complex arrangement of marketing components. Money, work force, materials, and information flow back and forth through system components. The efficiency of the channel is determined by the amount of effort required to keep such flows in motion and on the marketing results achieved. Channel objectives may relate to any or all of the flows. In particular, channel efficiency usually is sought by improving the flows of goods and information. Bottlenecks of materials and the loss or distortion of information are critical handicaps. A principal objective may be to improve channel performance by eliminating these bottlenecks and information traps.

Channel Issues and Problems

At first glance, channel issues would appear to be less complicated than those involved in product planning. The shipping-platform misconception suggests that the only channel issue is "How do we sell the goods that we have manufactured?" This is, of course, a basic question, but it is not the only one, nor is its answer as simple as the shipping-platform approach seems to imply. The hundreds of potential channel components and the almost infinite number of ways in which they can be combined intimate that channel planning is a complicated process. There are eight basic issues that usually arise in channel planning.

Direct versus Indirect Marketing

The question "Should we sell direct?" comes up sooner or later in almost every marketing program. Often it arises after some type of indirect marketing system has been utilized. For example, it is common practice for headquarters sales organizations to take over large customers from representatives, distributors, and even company salespersons, and handle them as house accounts. Dissension and occasional conflict result from such takeovers, however. Other firms, having developed a market through manufacturers' representatives, may decide in subsequent years to take over and sell direct through their own salespeople. There

has been a growing tendency for both manufacturers and large retailers to bypass the wholesaler. Developments such as these suggest that the question of direct selling is an important channel issue. If the manager expects this issue to arise at a later date, the problems should be considered at the outset because the answers will directly influence the rest of the channel planning. If, for example, a firm does decide to sell direct to its user-customers, all the other channel questions tend to merge with those of company organization. On the other hand, if direct marketing is not desirable (or will not be for several years), the other channel issues relating to the use of independent channel components still must be solved.

Selecting Channel System Components

Selecting channel components is almost as important as selecting a product to sell. It also is almost as difficult to do. Consider, for example, the many types of retail establishments in which a camera might be purchased. A list would include camera stores, department stores, sporting-goods stores, discount houses, drugstores, mail-order establishments, some grocery stores, hardware stores, variety stores, automotive-supply stores, art supply stores, and audiovisual equipment stores. Which of these types of retailers should a company introducing a new camera use? Answering this question is a major step in developing a distribution system.

The question is repeated at the wholesale level. There are several types of wholesalers who handle similar kinds of merchandise. For example, cameras might be handled by photographic-supply distributors, jewelry wholesalers, drug wholesalers, hardware wholesalers, and general-merchandise distributors. Although the list is not as long as that of possible types of retail outlets, the problem of choice among wholesalers is still serious. It must be answered before the vertical arrangements in the channel can be established.

Start with the ultimate user   "Who are our ultimate users and buyers?" is the most significant question to be answered in resolving the channel issues. Instead of "To whom shall we sell this merchandise immediately?" as is implied in the shipping-platform approach, the question is "To whom is this merchandise finally to be sold?" The identification of ultimate users must be precise. One must know the exact market segment for which a product is intended. Who are these customers? Where do they live? How many may we expect to find in each market? The answers to such questions provide important data required in the identification of ultimate users.

While planners of both product strategy and channel strategy are interested in the ultimate users of the product, the channel strategist also is very much concerned with its buyers or purchasers. If users and buyers are the same, there is no problem. However, in many marketing situations the buyer and user are not the same individual. This is especially true in industrial marketing. The purchasing agent or the materials manager for an industrial plant generally buys on behalf of those who ultimately will use the product. Thus, both the user and the buyer are important targets in an industrial marketer's program. Even in the consumer market a great deal of buying is done on behalf of users. We can view the homemaker as the purchasing agent for the family. Whereas the users of a particular product, for example, breakfast cereal, may be the entire family, the actual purchase frequently is made by

one member of the household. The attitudes and habits of this designated purchaser are of critical importance to the design of channel strategy for consumer products.

Consumer buying specifications   Whether one considers users who are also purchasers or purchasers buying on behalf of users, the buying requirements or specifications of these consumers provide important information that is necessary for the development of the channel plan. What are buying specifications? These specifications identify the way in which a purchaser buys, the place where a purchase is made, the frequency with which purchasing is done, and the time when it is performed. For example, the typical buying specifications for the purchase of a grocery item such as bread by a suburban shopper might be as follows:

1. Purchased once a week, or more often if necessary, to replenish stock
2. Purchased on a Friday or Saturday following the publication of food section advertising in the local newspapers on Thursday
3. Purchased in a large supermarket in conjunction with other grocery staples
4. Purchased generally on impulse without reference to a shopping list
5. Purchased on a convenience basis at any hour, day or night, at a nearby store
6. Purchased according to an established brand preference but easily switched, if necessary, to another label

In contrast, the buying specifications for the purchase of a color television set might be as follows:

1. Purchased only from a well-established reputable television dealer
2. Purchased only after considerable shop-

ping to compare prices and features of competitive products

3. Purchaser willing to go to some inconvenience (time and distance) to locate the most acceptable product
4. Purchased only after extended conversations (and negotiations) involving all interested parties, including dealer, users, and purchaser
5. Purchase may be postponed
6. Purchased only from a dealer equipped to render prompt and reasonable product service
7. Purchased on the basis of definite brand preference that is difficult to shift to another brand

These buying specifications illustrate the kinds of information that the manufacturer must discover. In most cases, purchase specifications are fairly obvious and can be discovered without great difficulty. On the other hand, some are difficult to determine. For example, certain consumers will not dine at restaurants that serve liquor; others refuse to patronize restaurants that do not. Some grocery buyers only patronize grocery stores that exhibit definite ethnic characteristics in their merchandising.

Knowing the buying specifications of the consumers, the planner can decide on the type, or types, of retailer through which a product should be sold. As we recall, the question is not "To whom can we sell?" but "From whom will our ultimate purchasers buy?" The product must be where the action is. Matching consumer buying specifications with particular types of retail establishments is relatively easy. The final decision depends on the degree to which the characteristics of the various retailers meet the buying requirements of purchasers. Referring to the buying specifications suggested for purchasers of bread and of color televi-

sions, we can easily see what types of retail outlets would be most appropriate for these products. The issue becomes somewhat more involved when less obvious retail outlets are considered. For instance, should bread be sold not only in grocery stores and confectioneries, but also in drugstores and service stations? Should color televisions be distributed not only through department stores and franchised electronics dealers, but also through furniture stores, appliance dealers, discount houses, and auto parts suppliers? It always is difficult to decide whether to use such outlets because buyer specifications seldom fit reseller performance exactly. How well they must match in order to justify the use of a particular type of retailer is a matter to be decided in each channel strategy. In part, the answer depends on the availability of the type of dealer desired. It might be extremely difficult for a manufacturer just entering the color television market to obtain distribution through major department stores and leading electronics retailers. This manufacturer might be forced to use secondary types of outlets in order to obtain any distribution at all.

Reseller buying (purchase) specifications In much the same way that buying specifications of users and purchasers are determined, the manufacturer also must discover buying specifications of resellers. Of particular importance is the question "From whom do retail outlets prefer to buy?" The answer to this question determines the types of wholesalers, if any, that the manufacturer should use. One might assume that all retailers prefer to buy directly from the manufacturer. This is not true however. The way most manufacturers must sell in order to make a profit makes them less than ideal suppliers for many small retailers. Infrequent visits, large order requirements, and stringent credit terms are typical conditions for dealing with manufacturers. Many retailers prefer to buy in small quantities and at frequent intervals. Local distributors tend to be somewhat more lenient in extending credit terms and in enforcing payment than are credit departments of remote manufacturing concerns. Retailers also are inclined to buy from vendors who offer a wider assortment of merchandise than most manufacturers do. A retail buyer cannot afford to tie up time in visiting with manufacturers' sales representatives. Buying time is economized by concentrating purchases with a single supplier. Ordinarily, a jobbing or distributing organization best meets the smaller retailer's buying specifications.

Of course, as just intimated, some retailers, especially large outlets, such as department stores and regional headquarters of grocery chains, find it economical and desirable to buy direct from the manufacturer. In these cases, the use of a distributor or wholesaler is neither necessary nor desirable. The important point to stress is that from a marketing point of view (in contrast to the shipping-platform approach), the determination of intermediate resellers in the channel is based on the buying preferences of retail customers rather than on the convenience and preferences of the manufacturer. In such an approach, the market planner works backward (or upstream) from the marketplace, determining in each case the supplier preferences of each successive link in the distribution channel. Ultimately, the process uncovers those types of middlemen who generally expect to buy direct from the manufacturer. At this point, and only at this point, does the manufacturer know who the immediate customers should be.

The buying specifications of these wholesalers are not identical but are similar to those of retailers. Most wholesalers, except local jobbers, tend to buy direct from manufacturers or their representatives. Their average order size, annual volume of business, service expectations, and the like, all suggest that the manufacturer alone is in a position to serve the wholesaler effectively. The identification of wholesale buying specifications is, therefore, not especially critical in determining from whom these channel components will buy. However, these same specifications are tremendously important in outlining to the manufacturer the selling policies that should be adopted in order to serve wholesale customers effectively. Thus, although they will not be pursued in this discussion of channel strategy, wholesalers' buying specifications (or those of retailers who buy direct) must be considered in the development of product-line, promotion, and pricing strategies.

Selecting facilitating channel components The channel issues discussed thus far have all concentrated on the development of the channel created by the flow of ownership. However, as we know, the complete channel involves other flows and many different types of channel components. The roles, if any, of an advertising agency, an independent marketing-research organization, a public warehouse, or a lending institution can all be anticipated from the nature of the overall plan. Frequently, the use of particular types of retail and wholesale outlets in the plan suggests the need for related types of channel components. For instance, manufacturers' representatives seldom take physical possession of merchandise. Either the manufacturer provides regional warehouses or hires the services of public warehouses. The decision to utilize certain types of retail outlets likewise may suggest the need for related marketing-research services. For example, when a manufacturer uses a wholesaler-retailer distribution system in the grocery business, direct access to data about sales to or through retail outlets seldom is possible. To compensate for this lack of information, the manufacturer purchases store-audit or warehouse withdrawal information from a marketing-research company.

Another example of how the need for special channel components may develop is found in the promotional area. When using a large number of retail outlets in an extensive distribution system, the manufacturer cannot rely on a great deal of aggressive sales effort at wholesale or retail levels to push the merchandise. Instead, a manufacturer must generate market pull. Merchandise is said to be *pulled through the channel* when consumer brand insistence is generated principally by sales promotion activities. An extensive sales promotion program usually is planned and coordinated by an advertising agency. There also are companies that specialize in providing incentive programs for sales promotion purposes. Maritz, Inc., prepares complete programs of channel promotion. Trading-stamp firms provide similar services, often using stamps as a device for rewarding participants. All such facilitating channel components serve to complete the channel system, making it capable of implementing the overall marketing plan.

Determining the Number of Channel System Components

Determining the actual number of channel components involves specifying the horizontal dimensions of the channel. This channel issue originates at the retail level. How many retailers in a particular market should be included in the distribution network? The answer is never simple and must always suit the general marketing plan being developed. There are limitless possibilities ranging from distribution through a single outlet to distribution through every store of a given type in the market.

Exclusive distribution   The use of a single retail outlet is referred to as *exclusive distribution*. Exclusiveness in marketing carries with it significant marketing advantages, although it is not without commensurate limitations. Strong dealer loyalty and active sales support usually are obtained when exclusive distribution privileges are granted. In addition, control over retail marketing generally is greater when there is a single outlet. Better forecasting, more efficient inventory allocation, and greater merchandising efficiency also are possible with exclusive distribution. The principal sacrifice is the lost sales volume that might have been obtained through wider distribution. Exclusive marketing usually suggests high-price and high-margin operations. If there is a high price elasticity of demand, exclusive marketing tends to reduce revenues and profits. Moreover, a manufacturer who sells through only one retail outlet is at the mercy of that single distributor. Success or failure in the market depends on the effectiveness of this exclusive retailer in developing sales.

Extensive distribution   At the other extreme is *broadcast* or *extensive distribution*. With this type of distribution, a manufacturer attempts to get as many retailers of a particular type as possible to carry the product. The advantages of extensive distribution are increased sales volume, wide consumer recognition, and considerable impulse purchasing. Problems associated with it relate to inventory and turnover. Low price, low margin, and small order sizes often result, tend-

TABLE 12.1   Number of accounts and sales by number of units purchased

Customer volume groups, number of units of product purchased	Number of accounts (per cent of total)	Sales in physical units (per cent of total)
Under 1,000	75	2
1,000–5,000	15	4
5,000–15,000	6	5
Over 15,000	4	89
Total	100	100

ing to generate unprofitable sales. In addition, it is extremely difficult to stimulate or control a large number of customers.

Limited distribution Between the two extremes of exclusive and extensive distribution is found a compromise that meets the requirements of both manufacturers and resellers. We call it *limited distribution.* Most shopping goods are distributed in each market through a number of retail outlets that falls far short of extensive distribution. The exact number of outlets that should be maintained in any given market area varies according to market potential, density of population, dispersion or concentration of retail sales in shipping centers, and competitors' distribution policies. The actual number of retail components is likely to be fewer than the manufacturer ordinarily would desire but somewhat more than the retailers would like to have. This is illustrated by a simple mathematical example. If the share of a market going to a particular manufacturer is $100,000 when distributing through 10 retail outlets, the share of each retailer is $10,000. If this volume can be increased by 50 per cent with 10 additional retail outlets, the manufacturer would undoubtedly be anxious to do so. However, doubling the number of retail outlets would mean that each retailer

would, on the average, obtain only $7,500 of sales volume. Under these circumstances, retailers tend to resist an increase in the number of retail outlets, while manufacturers ordinarily consider some increase in distribution desirable.

Selective distribution A special aspect of limited distribution is the selection of those particular resellers through whom the manufacturer can sell most profitably. The manufacturer elects to distribute only through those outlets whose sales volume, rate of inventory turnover, order size, and so forth create profitable business. This is known as *selective distribution.* For example, a local ice-cream company adopted a policy that prohibits its driver-salespeople from soliciting business from retail stores that do not buy a minimum number of gallons per week. Industrial-marketing companies have adopted similar policies of selective distribution. The reason is illustrated in the hypothetical data in Table 12.1.

According to Table 12.1, three fourths of the number of accounts of this industrial firm were responsible for only 2 per cent of sales in physical units. In contrast, the largest customers (those buying over 15,000 units annually) purchased almost 90 per cent of the company's output. To remedy this situation, the firm applied a policy of selection distribution. The smallest of the direct customers were transferred to a dealer organization. Ultimately about two thirds of the firm's customers were no longer called on directly by company representatives. The firm thus realized a substantial reduction in total marketing expenses with very little reduction in total sales.

Examples of channel decisions involving the number of retailers The manufacturer's preference regarding the extent of distribution must frequently be modified by the requirements of consumers and distributors. Such compromises are described in the following examples—one for bread, the other for television. It is important to bear in mind that the planner must make the decision on a local basis, working up to the total market, rather than determining the overall number of retail outlets to be used, allocating these among the various local markets.

Bread, by virtue of its consumers' buying specifications, is a convenience good and normally must be marketed in as many retail outlets as possible. Thus, a strategy of extensive distribution ordinarily prevails. Starting with this premise, the marketing manager for a bread company would locate on a map all the retail outlets through which the company expects to sell. These retail outlets are then assigned to delivery routes. The limiting factors that determine the number of stores to be covered on a particular route include such considerations as the expected volume at each store, the physical capacity of the vehicle, the distance between stores, the time required to service each store, the travel time involved in covering the route, and the number of hours the driver can devote to route servicing. When routes are constructed in this manner, it is unlikely that any two routes will be identical. Differences in driving conditions, in the location and size of stores, and in other variable market conditions also contribute to the likelihood of very different routes. One route may involve as few as ten large supermarkets in an urban area; another route may include as many as forty smaller stores spread over a wide suburban and semirural territory.

Occasionally a bread company may decide to eliminate certain retail shops on a delivery route. Credit problems, slow turnover, spoilage of product, and insufficient business may be factors influencing a decision to turn to selective distribution. In some instances routes are adjusted because of the driver. A trainee may be assigned half a normal route while learning the job. The route of an older driver, perhaps nearing retirement, also might be reduced. Sometimes, in order to retain or reward especially productive personnel, a company may assign them routes with particularly good profit potential. Competitive conditions also may affect the design of market coverage. Ultimately, after all such considerations have been disposed of, a pattern of distribution is set up. This pattern incorporates the route decisions that determine the specific number of retail establishments to be covered in the market.

The marketing manager of an electronic company works from two directions in determining the number of dealers who will carry the product line. Starting from the market, the locations of potential customers and competing dealers are determined. On the basis of the buying specifications mentioned previously, the manager determines the optimum number of retail outlets required to provide the coverage needed to be competitive for shopping goods. This means in the case of color televisions that distribution in all major department stores would be mandatory. In addition, an outlet in each of the major shopping centers would be necessary. How many other outlets would be required to serve customers and to be competitive would depend on the geographic characteristics of the market area and the location of competing dealers. For black-and-white television sets, dealers in every neighborhood shopping district would probably have to be appointed. For color televisions, at least until about 1965, relatively few neighborhood-type outlets were necessary to satisfy customer requirements. Since color television was still almost in a specialty category, consumers were willing to go to considerable inconvenience to purchase the product. Recently, however, more and more households have been buying color television sets. The need for more dealers to handle them has risen accordingly. Today, it is almost impossible to find a television dealer who does not handle both black-and-white and color sets.

Starting from the other direction, the marketing manager would also estimate the total market potential for color sets in a given area. The company's probable share of that market must be estimated and the number of sets to be sold in a given period of time calculated. More specifically, on the basis of previous experience with retail outlets, the manager would estimate the average number of color receivers a dealer should sell in order to (1) make a profit and (2) justify the required service facilities. If, for example, the manager estimated that the company should sell five thousand color sets in a metropolitan market in a year's time and that the average dealer should sell at least fifty sets, the number of outlets to be used in the market would be estimated at about one hundred. This number, however, is probably too large. Some dealers will sell far more

than one color set a week, while others would be expected to sell fewer. In order to satisfy the needs of these smaller dealers (by reducing the amount of retail competition), the manager might decide to franchise considerably fewer than one hundred stores.[1]

Ultimately, the number of outlets to be used in a particular market is a compromise between the manufacturer's distribution objectives and the dealers' desires for exclusiveness. Of course the number of outlets is seldom static. As a market grows, competition becomes more intense; or as a company's market share increases, there is an inevitable tendency for the number of dealers in a particular market also to increase.

Determining the number of wholesalers to use Having determined the type and number of retailers, it is relatively easy to determine the number of wholesalers to be used in a particular channel design. Two important factors influence this decision. First, most wholesalers operate in a limited geographical area, often referred to as a *wholesale trading area*. The manufacturer is aided in planning by U.S. Department of Commerce and trade publications, which provide maps that divide the United States into a number of wholesale trading areas. Generally speaking, a single wholesale establishment would be appointed for each of the trading areas. Of course, these trading areas differ considerably for different kinds of wholesaling opera-

---

[1] The writer talked at one time with the manager of a successful automobile agency. This executive estimated that if more than five dealerships were franchised in his market, one or more of them could not operate profitably. In contrast, the automobile manufacturer apparently believed that more extensive distribution was necessary in order to maintain market position. No fewer than twenty-three dealers have since been franchised in that metropolitan market.

tions. The areas for industrial goods tend to be much larger than do those for consumer products. Wholesale trading areas for firms selling to convenience-type outlets are much smaller than those of wholesalers selling to customers in the shopping- and specialty-goods categories. Obviously, the size of the market area is determined not only by the geographical space to be covered but also by the number of retail accounts to be served. Where a heavy concentration of retail outlets exists in a given market, the size of the wholesale trading area is correspondingly reduced. Where there is a low density of retail outlets, the wholesale trading area tends to be larger.

The second factor influencing the number of wholesalers to be used relates to the number of retail accounts that can be efficiently and profitably handled. The manufacturer often is in a position to estimate the average number of retail outlets a typical wholesaler should be able to service efficiently. The total number of wholesalers to be included in the channel system can then be determined by dividing the number of retail outlets by this average value. If, for instance, the typical wholesaler should service approximately 100 retail accounts and the manufacturer already has identified 2,500 key retail outlets in the national market, then 25 wholesale establishments would be required to serve these retail customers. However, as was the case in determining the number of retailers, the number of wholesalers likewise must be adjusted to meet the needs of those who can attract a sufficient volume of business only through exclusive-distribution privileges. It is necessary, therefore, to adjust the total number of wholesalers to ensure that those used will be able to operate profitably. Thus, the determination of the number of these components in the channel is again a compromise between the ideal distribution system from the manufacturer's point of view and the needs of resellers.

Using Multiple Channels

For many companies, the question of using multiple channels never arises. Companies that sell direct, either to users or to resellers, and firms that sell through a well-established pattern of wholesale and retail outlets are not likely to encounter the problem of more than one type of channel. However, a manufacturer who finds it necessary to distribute through a wide variety of retail outlets or whose retail trade structure is undergoing considerable change may be faced with the thorny problem of multiple-distribution networks. Companies selling diversified product lines to two or more distinct market segments often develop multiple-channel structures. The decision depends almost entirely on the markets that the company serves.

Multiple channels can be either *complementary* (noncompetitive) or *competitive*. Complementary channels are created when a company sells multiple products to two or more unrelated market segments. The most obvious example is a company marketing both industrial and consumer products. Consider, for instance, a typewriter manufacturer selling direct to large industrial and commercial customers (see Figure 12.2). Consumer products, on the other hand, are marketed either directly to large retail accounts or indirectly through office equipment distributors to small retailers and ultimately to final users. Similarly, a manufacturer of hydraulic brake fluid sells through three different marketing channels. A considerable proportion of total production is marketed direct to the OEM (original

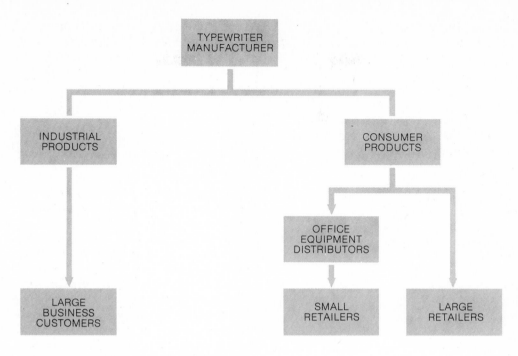

FIGURE 12.2   Using multiple channels

equipment manufacturer) market—in this case to automobile manufacturers. Another sizable portion is marked for distribution under private brands by major oil companies. The last and largest part of the output is marketed in large containers through warehouse distributors to automotive jobbers and ultimately to service stations, repair garages, and automotive dealerships.

In the typewriter example, the industrial- and consumer-product channels are noncompetitive. An ultimate consumer cannot under most circumstances buy direct from the manufacturer. Similarly, a commercial firm would seldom buy a typewriter from a retail store. However, the two consumer-product channels are competitive. The small retailer who buys from the office equipment distributor is in direct competition with the larger retailer who buys direct from the manufacturer. The brake fluid channels also are basically noncompetitive. OEM customers generally buy direct from the manufacturer. The brake fluid marketed through the oil companies appears as private-label merchandise, usually shelf goods in small containers, and is not used by mechanics in the repair of automotive brake systems. Brake fluid marketed through automotive distributors and jobbers, however, definitely is intended for use by mechanics.

Companies develop, willingly or unwillingly, competitive marketing channels. For years, automobile manufacturers have used separate franchised retail outlets for major divisions of their product line. Cadillac, Oldsmobile, Buick, Pontiac, and Chevrolet cars are more or less competitive, and the dealer organizations that handle them are in competition as well. A classic example of the dangers involved in using such multiple competitive channels is seen in the marketing mix for the ill-fated Edsel. A principal element in this marketing mix was the development of an entirely new distribution system. As it turned out, one of the probable reasons for the failure of the project was the great difficulty encountered in acquiring a dealer organization. The considerable overlap of the Edsel with the Mercury made their two distribution systems extremely competitive—probably more competitive than the new product could stand in its early market period.

An example of the development of an involuntary competitive channel is seen in the experience of Mead Johnson and Company. Primarily an ethical drug manufacturer, Mead Johnson traditionally relied on distribution through drugstores. It also marketed for many years a line of proprietary foods, of which Pablum is best known. In the early history of baby food marketing, customers expected to purchase Pablum in drugstores, so no distribution problem was encountered. However, with the revolution in postwar retailing, mothers soon expected to find Pablum in grocery stores. Mead Johnson then had an important decision to make, Should it distribute Pablum through grocery stores and drugstores? Actually, the company had little choice, and in spite of its reluctance to create a channel competitive to the traditional drug channel, it was forced to go into the grocery business.

Few resellers are happy with a manufacturer's decision to use multiple channels. Just as most retailers would like exclusive-distribution privileges, so they look with disfavor on competitive channel arrangements. However, resellers' attitudes are not the only factors to be considered. The manufacturer also must weigh, as in all distribution questions, the advantages to be gained in increased sales, increased market share, and increased profits by the use of multiple competitive channels.

Supervising and Controlling Channel Components

To those unfamiliar with marketing, the fact that supervising and controlling channel components sometimes presents problems usually comes as a surprise. Why should there be any problem in working with resellers? Aren't the mutual interests of manufacturer, wholesaler, and retailer sufficiently strong to impel effective cooperation and coordination? On further thought, however, perhaps we should be surprised that a manufacturer has any reason to expect more than minimum cooperation from wholesalers and retailers. Wholesalers and retailers are, after all, in business for themselves, not for the manufacturer. We should not expect them to serve the interests of the manufacturer exclusively. Even though the systems concept suggests that manufacturer, wholesaler, and retailer—as well as many other types of channel components—are functionally linked together in a vital distribution system, this is seldom appreciated by the managers of independent channel components. It is, therefore, up to the manufacturer, as the principal decision center in the trade channel, to motivate, stimulate, and direct channel components in such a way as to create an effective channel system.

Internal conflict   As we just intimated, the need for channel supervision and control arises because most channel components are independent. Their independence can in some instances lead to a real conflict of interest among channel components.[2] Such conflict is not likely to arise if each component is performing its own designated role in the marketing system. Nevertheless, the tendency of manufacturers to bypass wholesalers, absorb distributors' customers as house accounts, and terminate arrangements with manufacturers' representatives have not created the friendliest climate in which to develop an integrated channel effort. But the fault does not lie all on one side. Retailers and wholesalers have been just as guilty of invading each other's and the manufacturer's domain. Wholesalers get into retailing, and retailers get into the jobbing business. Both types of resellers have been known to establish manufacturing activities. Where such competitive overlapping exists, a genuine conflict of interest may occur, and such a conflict usually is attended by serious problems.

Lack of interest Lack of interest on the part of wholesalers and retailers in the manufacturer's product and related marketing problems is a more common cause of poor relationships. The lack of interest may reflect genuine resistance or inertia. There is a tendency among resellers not to compete aggressively or change traditional ways of doing business. However, most lack of concern with the manufacturer's problems may only reflect the nature of the reseller's business. Wholesalers and retailers handle the products of hundreds, sometimes thousands, of manufacturers. The reseller's concern with suppliers' problems is spread over so many manufacturers that very little attention can be devoted to any single one. This is probably as it should be, for any special

attention a manufacturer gets should be earned. Therefore, when developing a channel strategy, it is important that the manufacturer recognize the need for reseller cooperation and set up a program to achieve it.

Why not pay for channel cooperation? It is logical at this point to ask why such cooperation cannot be encouraged by direct monetary compensation. A larger trade discount, tied to the performance of certain specific manufacturer-sponsored activities, presumably would develop the kind and amount of cooperation desired. In practice, however, it seldom works out that way. First, there is a general tendency among resellers to pass extra discounts along to customers in the form of lower prices or else to absorb the additional discount as an increased operating margin. Because of the intensity of retail price competition, the pressure to pass the discount on always is strong. Another problem in granting special discounts for reseller cooperation is that competitors easily can match them and require the same or even less cooperation. Finally, there is no way of making sure that the added financial incentive will produce the desired result. Unless the reseller's efforts on behalf of the manufacturer are carefully supervised and controlled, it is more than likely that the funds provided will be used ineffectively or even wasted.

Channel assistance and control programs Now that we have seen why it is necessary, we may ask what specific kinds of assistance or control can be used by a manufacturer to keep the channel system operating efficiently.[3] An almost endless detailed list of activi-

---

[2]For an interesting discussion of channel conflict, see M. Edgar, "Channel Domination and Countervailing Power," *Journal of Marketing Research,* August 1976, pp. 254–262.

[3]P. Bucklin, "A Theory of Channel Control," *Journal of Marketing,* January 1973, pp. 39–47; and A. E. El-Ansery and R. A. Robicheaux, "A Theory of Channel Control: Revisited," *Journal of Marketing,* January 1974, pp. 2–7.

ties has been developed by manufacturers working with their resellers. However, there are three major directions toward which this assistance or control usually heads: (1) direct personal supervision, (2) management service, and (3) stimulation.

The most effective way for a manufacturer to stimulate, assist, or control the activities of its resellers is by sending a personal representative into the field to work with the channel members. The most frequently used type of personal representative is the *missionary salesperson*, whose job is to help the reseller develop a market for the manufacturer's product. This may be done by assisting in making sales to ultimate customers, by working with dealer salespeople, or by engaging in any type of promotional activity designed to help the dealer move the manufacturer's goods. In some industries, these personal representatives have slightly different responsibilities and are known by different names. In the industrial market, for instance, they usually are called *factory representatives*. Often trained engineers, the factory representatives call on customers to render special technical services in connection with products that already have been sold or new items that are being considered. In the pharmaceutical industry, factory representatives also call on hospital administrators, doctors, and nurses in order to render technical assistance and promote the sale of company products. The work of these people is known as *detailing*.

Another way to maintain an effective channel system is to equip channel components with the management skill that will enable them to operate efficiently. Many types of management services are provided by manufacturers to their dealers. These range from a complete array of management counsel to very specific assistance in rather narrow areas of dealer operation. The services most frequently rendered, however, are in the areas of training, merchandising, and inventory control.

Training may be provided for sales or service personnel. It is not uncommon for a manufacturer's representative to address a group of department store clerks at one of their periodic sales meetings to demonstrate new products or to suggest especially effective ways of presenting older ones. If the maintenance and repair of the manufacturer's products are important parts of the marketing task, service training may be provided at the reseller's facility or at the manufacturer's location. For example, service is a very important part of GM's marketing programs. This company maintains training centers throughout the country that offer specialized training services to dealers' mechanics.

Another type of management service that may be offered to channel components is *merchandising assistance*. Such considerations as store layout, merchandise display, advertising, and sales promotion fall within the scope of many manufacturers' merchandising assistance to distributors and dealers. For example, an independent service station may be guided in almost every detail of its operations by suggestions from the major oil company whose products it sells. Similarly, a diversified retailer such as a hardware store may rely on a manufacturer's merchandising services for an entire department. If the hardware store handles one major line of house paints, for instance, the manufacturer of this line may be called on for assistance in all aspects of paint merchandising.

A third important service a manufacturer can render to its resellers involves *inventory management*. Some manufacturers have developed model inventory plans for use by their dealers. On the basis of such factors as regional characteristics of demand and size of store, manufacturers can come remarkably close in their estimation of the appropriate level of inventory for a dealer to handle. In addition to helping in the determination of inventory requirements, the manufacturer often assists the dealer in maintaining inventory control. Printed forms to be used either in taking inventory or in keeping perpetual inventory records are supplied. The systematic use of good inventory records can assist in proper scheduling of purchases and in determining optimum order sizes.

In order to overcome inertia and encourage dealers to cooperate and support their programs, manufacturers have conceived various methods of dealer stimulation. The various techniques of stimulation include dealer contests, cooperative advertising programs, special incentives for dealer participation, sales aids, and sales quotas.

Dealer contests, which are frequently used in connection with an overall sales promotion program, can take many forms. If the object is to stimulate the reseller's sales force, a contest designed specifically to reward sales performance can be used. If the object is to generate overall dealer activity, a contest that rewards the dealer's key management personnel would be more appropriate. Prizes for such dealer contests range from modest awards of merchandise to all-expenses-paid vacation trips.

Cooperative advertising involves sharing by the manufacturer of some of the expense (usually 50 per cent) incurred by the dealer for advertising the manufacturer's products. A common procedure is for the manufacturer to put aside a small percentage of the revenue from each dealer into a cooperative advertising fund. Whenever a participating dealer reports having advertised the manufacturer's product, the manufacturer reimburses the customer from the advertising fund.

Another method of securing dealer cooperation through stimulation is the use of *special-merchandise* or *financial deals.* Particularly in getting initial distribution for a new product, a manufacturer may entice a distributor into stocking an item by offering attractive price discounts or free-merchandise bonuses. For example, if merchandise is packed twelve to the carton, a special deal might involve an offer of two free with ten.

The importance of such assistance to dealers should now be clear. The channel of distribution is the system through which the manufacturer must work in order to achieve marketing objectives. Unless this system is tuned up to the manufacturer's level of activity and the marketing task is approached with the same enthusiasm and drive by resellers as by the manufacturer's own sales personnel, the dealer organization becomes the weakest link in the system. In the development of an integrated marketing program, strengthening this potentially flimsy link in the channel system is of tremendous importance. Unfortunately, activities to assist or stimulate the channel components often are neglected or left to the last minute in the planning process. Nevertheless, the design of a successful channel strategy must include attention to the problem of working with the entire channel system.

Vertical Marketing Systems

The assistance and control activities of the manufacturer (or other channel leader) create one form of what we call a *vertical marketing system.* According to B. C. McCammon, vertical marketing systems are "professionally managed and centrally programmed networks, preengineered to achieve operating economies and maximum market impact."[4] Unfortunately, the administered vertical marketing system that we have described in the preceding pages is relatively ineffective because the channel leader (captain or administrator) lacks the power to enforce channelwide allegiance. Persuasion, assistance, and incentives play a role; but they are poor substitutes for absolute authority.

Absolute authority is obtained only through ownership. The *corporate vertical marketing system* involves the outright ownership of channel components. The integration may be forward, as when a manufacturer operates its own distribution centers or retail stores. Edison Stores, the Singer Company, and GE are among the many manufacturers that actually own some if not all of their channel components. The integration may be backward, where wholesaler or retailer owns a component upstream in the channel system. For instance, Sears owns substantial interest in a number of its suppliers. The hardware industry provides a very unusual example. The Cotter Company is a wholesale cooperative owned by the retail hardware stores it serves. Cotter, in turn, owns a subsidiary manufacturing company that produces such items as paint and lawnmowers.

Outright ownership is not always feasible or desirable. However, the channel still can be vertically coordinated by a *contractual arrangement* under which the parties agree to operate. The most common form of contractual arrangement is the distributor or dealer *franchise.* The awarder of the franchise may be a manufacturer, such as an automobile company, or a corporate organization whose principal business is franchising. Dunkin Donuts and Holiday Inns of America are two well-known firms that operate in this manner. Industrial firms, such as Cummins Engine Company, Moog, American Standard, and Emerson Electric, franchise wholesale distributors. These are all examples of forward contractual arrangements. It is possible for the arrangement to work backward. It is quite common for a large retailer to contract with a supplier for a specified volume of goods. Sears does this in a number of staple product lines where it wants to assure itself of a regular supply at a predetermined cost. According to W. R. Davidson, the development of the vertical marketing system is one of the most important events in contemporary marketing.[5] There is reason to expect that the trends in this direction will continue, because the necessity of instituting channel controls should become even greater as the demand for overall marketing efficiency increases and competitive pressures become stronger.

Managing Channel Costs

Seldom are the costs of developing and controlling a channel considered part of the budget of a marketing program. Except in companies with a trade relations department, these costs are submerged in other categories of marketing expense. The costs of maintaining day-to-day channel relationships are especially difficult to isolate. Much

[4]B. C. McCammon, "Perspectives for Distribution Programming," in L. D. Bucklin, ed., *Vertical Marketing Systems* (Glenview, Ill.: Scott, Foresman, 1970), p. 43.

[5]W. R. Davidson, "Changes in Distributive Institutions," *Journal of Marketing,* January 1970, pp. 7–10.

of the responsibility for channel supervision is delegated to the sales organization. A considerable part of channel expense, therefore, is generated as a result of the company's personal-selling effort. Outlays for special deals, discounts, premiums, advertising allowances, and contests usually appear in the advertising and sales promotion budget.

Ideally, if the need for channel development is critical, a formal allocation of funds to this activity should be considered. Dollars spent for channel development, especially for personal supervision of channel components, represent a long-run investment. These expenditures may not bear fruit for some years, but their benefits usually are expected to endure for a considerable period of time. The budgeting of such expenditures, therefore, is somewhat akin to the allocation of funds for institutional advertising and product development. Since so few companies have formally allocated marketing costs to channel-related activities, however, there are no general standards or bench marks available on how much to spend. Nevertheless, such allocations are entirely practicable, and it is probable that increased attention will be paid to this type of cost analysis in the future and that cost standards for channel expenditures will be developed.

Organizing for Channel Management

Traditionally, the sales organization has been responsible for developing and maintaining relations with channel components. It has been common practice for many years to require salespeople to perform some nonselling activities in connection with dealer training, supervision, and control.

For the most part, such methods of obtaining dealer cooperation have worked fairly well. To supplement them, however, some companies require sales managers, sales promotion managers, and advertising managers to spend a certain amount of time in the field working with resellers. In part, this activity is intended to keep the management group in touch with the trade. Moreover, these contacts by the management group with the dealer organizations also make a contribution to the program of channel supervision and control. With the development of market-planning groups and the rise in the importance of marketing managers, the advantages of dealer contact and control have been more fully appreciated. Thus, today, staff personnel often work directly with the dealer organization.

A recent development along these lines, which we already have mentioned, is the emergence of the so-called trade relations department. This is a separate staff department charged with the responsibility of maintaining good working relations with resellers, customers, and suppliers. Such a department is seldom large and ordinarily is not responsible for maintaining direct and continuing contact with the trade. However, the trade relations director is responsible for identifying problems arising in the distribution channel and for working out plans for their correction. The trade relations director also logically could be expected to contribute to future planning for new marketing strategies.

Dynamic Channel Strategy

We noted earlier the tendency for a channel arrangement, once established, to take on a quasi permanent status. In the minds of marketing planners, it may become one of the givens in the strategy-making process. Even though it is obvious that there are weak spots in an existing channel system, executives are inclined not to tinker with it. Their greatest fear is the disruption of long-standing relationships with resellers that may adversely affect sales. Since channel modifications are very difficult to pretest, the uncertainty that surrounds a change in channels encourages caution in introducing improvements.

Distribution channels can be managed; they are not once-and-for-all structures within which a firm must operate. Certainly it is difficult to make changes. The channel leader does not have direct control over other channel components. There also may be conflict and disagreement among channel members. But such differences in opinion and difficulties are not really so different from other problems encountered within a large corporation. Diplomacy, persuasion, development, and incentive often can be put to work to achieve what direct authority cannot. Appropriate use of such tools means that a company is not wedded to its existing distribution system. In fact, the decision to change that system may be one of the most important a company ever has to make.

There are many reasons for making channel alterations. Marketing conditions may change. There can be dramatic and momentous shifts in demand, as when a company changes from defense products to civilian marketing. Market segments also may shift, creating new pockets of demand and diminishing the importance of others. Changes in public policy—perhaps a new law or a critical court decision—likewise may force a modification in channel arrangements.

The problems faced by Arnold, Schwinn & Company illustrate how environmental (external) developments caused this firm to reconsider its distribution policies.[6] Schwinn was long a leader in the quality bicycle market. Competition from inexpensive but glamorous bikes from Japan began to cut into Schwinn sales. This competition was particularly tough in discount houses, where the products often were displayed side by side. Schwinn decided to cut back the number of its dealers from 15,000 general-merchandise stores to about 3,000 fully franchised dealers. The Justice Department regarded this move as a restraint of trade. The Supreme Court upheld the Justice Department and ruled that Schwinn could adopt the dealer franchising policy only if it retained ownership of bicycles in the dealers' hands.[7] Substantial changes in Schwinn's historic methods of distribution were thus called for by this series of legal developments.

Another important reason why a channel arrangement must sometimes be changed is that the existing structure originally may have been an expedient channel, not necessarily the right one. For example, a shoe manufacturer might instruct its sales representatives to get its line placed in the "best store in town." If this is impossible, then try for "the next best." The chances are that most initial distribution will be in the "next best" stores. Eventually, as the product line becomes well known, the company may be in a position to move over to the "best" store in each market. This explains why

[6]B. Bock, *Antitrust Issues in Restricting Sales Territories and Outlets* (New York: National Industrial Conference Board, 1967); and *United States* v. *Arnold, Schwinn & Co., et al.,* 388 U.S. 365 (1967).

[7]A 1977 Supreme Court decision (*Continental TV* v. *Sylvania*) tempered the Schwinn ruling to apply the traditional "rule of reason." It is not proper, therefore, to conclude that vertical restraints per se are a violation of the Sherman Act. They are illegal only if the restraint of trade is "unreasonable."

channel changes may appear to reverse decisions made at an earlier date. Alternatives are open later that did not exist when the channel was first formed.

In summary, we may say that channels constantly are evolving. The entry of new firms and the departure of old ones; the development of entirely new distribution technologies that make older methods obsolete; and the changing size and composition of markets all demand a constantly changing distribution system. Such changes may be drastic, as when a sudden environmental disturbance occurs. More often they are gradual, and the alterations in the channel system are correspondingly slow. But there is no question that channels change, and it is part of marketing planning—especially for the long run—to consider what these changes should be.

Summary

The channel is a distribution system, composed of various components linked together by one or more of the marketing flows. Decisions about these system components comprise channel strategy. The channel provides the structure within which the rest of the marketing plan is carried out. However, the channel plan differs from an organizational plan in that it is essentially strategic. A particular channel is selected because it adds to the achievement of certain marketing objectives.

Unfortunately, not all channels are strategically designed. Two widely held misconceptions appear to explain this. The first misconception, called the shipping-platform approach, suggests that the channel is formed by selling products to a customer. A succession of sales creates a channel. However, as we have seen, the proper way to identify a channel is to start with the customer and work backward to the origin of the goods. The other misconception is called the product-feature approach and implies that the nature of the product determines the type of channel to be used. Again, this is incorrect because we must look to the customer—not to the product—to find out how the system should be arranged.

For the most part, channel arrangements are made by manufacturers, who select various kinds of resellers and facilitating components to comprise the system. Sometimes, when the reseller is stonger than the manufacturer, the channel is created by the decisions of the reseller. In either case, one component in the system usually emerges as the channel captain or channel leader. Generally speaking, however, retailers do not wield much power in the channel. Since they are chosen by the manufacturer, they do not have a channel strategy of their own but are instead part of the manufacturer's distribution system.

Strategic channel objectives stem from company and marketing objectives. Frequently, a company will have to identify specific channel objectives. This is particularly true when new or expanded distribution is being sought.

As is the case with the other elements of the marketing mix, there are a number of important channel issues and problems that must be considered and resolved before a channel strategy can emerge. The very first channel issue that usually must be faced is whether to market directly to the user. If a firm decides to sell direct, its channel problems become problems in company operations, since most of the system's components are part of the company organization. If, on the other hand, a firm chooses the indirect route, it must consider such issues as the type and number of middlemen to include and the methods to be used in stimulating and controlling them.

Once a channel system has been designed, it is up to the marketing manager to make sure that it operates effectively. This is achieved through supervision and control. The job is difficult, however, because most channel components are independent, and conflict often arises among them. In addition, apathy and inertia retard the marketing performance of some channel members. Assistance and control programs to overcome such channel deficiencies involve direct personal supervision, management services, and various kinds of rewards and incentives.

Unfortunately, there is a tendency for a channel arrangement, once established, to take on a rather permanent status. But distribution strategy should be dynamic. Channels can be managed to achieve company objectives, and they can be changed if they are not working out properly.

Questions and Problems

1. Strange as it may seem, manufacturers of food products in Korea often operate their own retail stores there. This is largely a remnant of a distribution system that existed before the influence of American marketing methods was felt. Under what circumstances in an underdeveloped country do you think direct marketing of staple food products might be feasible? Could it occur in the United States? Under what conditions?

2. Explain why a shipping-platform ap-
proach might result in very wrong channel decisions for each of the following types of companies:
   a. An automobile manufacturer
   b. A drug manufacturer
   c. An electronic-computers manufacturer
   d. A manufacturer of quality reproductions of Early American antiques
   e. A manufacturer of frozen portioned meat servings.

3. What kind of information about the ultimate customer would a marketing manager use in selecting a channel of distribution for
   a. A consumer durable, such as a refrigerator or power saw
   b. A consumer nondurable, such as a carbonated beverage
   c. An industrial item, such as a machine tool
   d. A consumer service, such as income tax preparation

4. Certain types of retail outlets are fast disappearing—for example, neighborhood drugstores and five- and ten-cent stores. Why do you think this is happening? What does it do to a manufacturer that has traditionally made use of this type of retail store to reach consumers?

5. Prepare a list of consumer products that historically have been purchased direct from the manufacturer. Are all of these items being sold direct today? Explain any changes that may have taken place in direct selling to ultimate consumers in recent years.

6. Draw up a list of all the various types of establishments at which you would expect to be able to buy
   a. Adhesive tape

b. A wrist watch

c. A transistor radio

d. Automobile antifreeze

7. The manufacturer of a line of power-driven lawn and garden equipment is considering the number of middlemen to use and where they should be located. What arguments can be raised for and against the use of exclusive distribution for this product line at the retail level? Would you allocate your outlets in suburban areas according to population, or would you use some other approach? Explain.

8. The owner of a large and prosperous salvage company in New Jersey attributes the success of the company to a policy that was instituted early in the firm's history. The company only accepted salvage material in truckload quantities and sold only in railroad-carload quantities. Explain how this two-directional policy of selectivity compared with the policies of typical scrap dealers might have been a factor in the company's success.

9. Find at least three examples of manufacturers' using multiple channels. Are these channels competitive or comple-mentary? Explain the channel arrangements.

10. A manufacturer of metal-working equipment sells through a network of manufacturers' representatives who also handle complementary products of other manufacturers. The manager of this firm feels that the "reps" are not pushing the company's products. What might the manager do about the situation?

11. A food-products manufacturer sells a line of canned Mexican food through food brokers who call on retail stores. Company salespeople work with the brokers, who are judged to be doing a reasonably good job. Retailers, particularly in the eastern part of the country, however, have not been featuring or promoting the company's products. Outline a program of dealer assistance, stimulation, and control that will improve sales of the Mexican food line in eastern markets.

12. Find an example of a company that has abandoned its former distribution method in favor of a completely new approach. Why do you think the change was made?

13 Physical Distribution Strategy

Most marketing involves the movement of goods and the occasional holding of them to increase their value. The specific relation of physical distribution to marketing has long been recognized. Transportation and storage were among the functions of marketing discussed in the earliest textbooks. But until recently only in certain kinds of firms was physical distribution a critical aspect of marketing management. For example, when transportation costs were a large proportion of total costs, as in the case of steel, lumber, and fuel oil, considerable attention was paid to the location of facilities, the quotation of delivered prices, and the management of traffic and transportation services. Also, companies that marketed perishable or fragile products paid careful heed to the problems of physical distribution, since the preservation of their products depended as much on the conditions of moving and storing them as on producing them.

Developments in recent years, however, have made almost all firms responsive to the need to manage physical distribution wisely. Rising transportation rates and increasing costs of maintaining inventories have caused managers to become aware of the dent that physical distribution makes in profits. In some companies the need to improve efficiency also has focused attention for the first time on the costs of holding and moving goods. At the same time, customers have demanded better distribution services and have become less tolerant of stock-outs, back orders, and substitutions. Meeting the customer's delivery needs has thus become part of the bundle of satisfactions that the seller must offer. In the effort to provide these services better than can the competition, the management of physical distribution has become *strategic*. It is no longer simply a facilitating service, rather it is a full-fledged partner in the marketing mix. Moreover, it is closely related to channel strategy, since many channel members perform physical-distribution functions. But there are some aspects of physical distribution that deserve special attention. We will look at these aspects in this chapter.

What Is Physical Distribution?

Physical distribution and *logistics* are terms frequently used interchangeably to refer to activities associated with the handling of goods. The National Council of Physical Distribution Management (NCPDM) has defined physical distribution as

a term employed in manufacturing and commerce to describe the broad range of activities concerned with efficient movement of finished products from the end of the production line to the consumer, and in some cases included the movement of raw materials from the source of supply to the beginning of the production line. These activities include freight transportation, warehousing, material handling, protective packaging, inventory control, plant and warehouse site selection, order processing, market forecasting, and customer service.[1]

The term *logistics,* although borrowed from the military, likewise can refer to all of these activities and more. It is defined as "the procurement, distribution, maintenance, and replacement of material and personnel."[2]

From these definitions we can infer certain characteristics of logistical or distributional activities. First, while some of the activities are quite dissimilar, they are all related by the common bond of an efficient flow of goods. Second, a decision involving one of the logistics activities automatically may force a decision affecting another activity. If management decides, for instance, to reduce transportation costs by ordering or shipping in carload or truckload lots, one effect of that decision is to change warehousing requirements. A third characteristic of logistics activities is that a decision concerning them may be felt in another division or function of the firm. If the number of distribution points is increased, additional working capital for inventory is required.

A fourth characteristic is that logistics activities may be used as elements of marketing strategy. The redesign of a distribution system, for example, may make it possible for the marketing department to improve its service to customers and thus protect or increase sales. Another characteristic of logistics activities is that a small reduction in their costs may add substantially to profit. This is because such a large proportion of costs is incurred in the physical-distribution sector of the firm. For example, in the case of food products, physical-distribution costs take about 35 per cent of the sales dollar. A moderate reduction of about 6 per cent would save approximately $.02 of each sales dollar—as much as some firms earn in profit.

A sixth and final characteristic that emerges from these definitions is that logistics is best viewed as a system. There are components performing different functions but linked together by the flow of goods. The integration and management of the various activities is enhanced considerably when the process is viewed as a subsystem of the overall marketing channel.[3]

---

[1]D. J. Bowersox, *Logistical Management* (New York: Macmillan, 1974), p. 1. Copyright © 1974, Macmillan Publishing Co., Inc.

[2]William Morris, ed, *The American Heritage Dictionary of the English Language* (Boston: Houghton Mifflin and American Heritage, 1976), p. 767. Copyright © 1969, 1970, 1971, 1973, 1975, 1976, 1978, Houghton Mifflin Company. Reprinted by permission from *The American Heritage Dictionary of the English Language.*

[3]D. W. Bowersox and others, *Dynamic Simulation of Physical Distribution Systems* (East Lansing, Mich.: Michigan State University, 1972), pp. 15–34.

The Environment of Logistics Decisions

Like other systems, logistics takes place in a external environment. In this section, we will concentrate on five of the important external forces that influence logistics decisions: transportation companies, transportation rates, transportation services, warehouses, and the phenomena of physical, economic, and temporal proximity to the market.

Transportation Companies

Many firms perform some of their own transportation. These firms are known as *private carriers*. While practically all forms of transportation are used by private carriers, truck transport is the most prevalent. The firms engaged in this type of private carriage may range from a small appliance store operating a single panel truck to a giant corporation with a fleet of hundreds of highway rigs.

Of course, firms that are not private carriers must use other forms of transportation, such as common carriers, contract carriers, and exempt carriers. *Common Carriers* are companies that serve the public in the movement of people and certain categories of goods. Ordinarily, common carriers do not agree to carry everything; for example, a rail common carrier usually will not handle such items as money, jewelry, and other valuables, while a truck carrier may be a common carrier only of frozen foods, automobiles, or liquid petroleum (LP) gas.

Contract Carriers are those that provide one or a few shippers with a transportation service as defined by contract. Generally, contract carriers offer some particular service, often requiring specialized equipment. *Exempt carriers* are for-hire carriers that are exempt by law from economic regulation by the federal government. Some commodities moved by water and most agricultural commodities are exempt from such regulation.[4]

In addition to these familiar types of transportation companies, there are other transport services that are important facets of the distribution system. Government parcel post is one example. Other examples are private parcel services, typified by United Parcel Service, and express companies. Not so well known, however, are the services offered by freight forwarders and shippers' associations. Both organizations perform essentially the same type of transportation function. The major distinction is that the freight forwarder holds itself out to the public for hire, while the shippers' association is a cooperative venture designed to save transport costs for its members. More specifically, the freight forwarder collects shipments from a number of companies and consolidates them into one larger shipment to be transported by common rail, motor, or air carrier. This type of organization makes its profit by the spread between less-than-truckload (ltl) or less-than-carload (lcl) rates that the shipper would otherwise have to pay and the volume rates for carload (cl) or truckload (tl) movements that the forwarder pays. Speed in service is the primary advantage to the shipper of using a freight forwarder. This advantage also can be gained through the services of *shippers' associations*. These associations usually are local in nature—a group of companies that receives or ships significant amounts of freight forms a cooperative venture and employs a paid staff to arrange for the consolidation of the members' shipments at the point of origin.

---

[4]The legal aspects of exempt transportation are very complicated. Since the value received by the reader of this book would be very small compared with the effort required to gain a good understanding, no attempt is made to unravel this subject.

Transportation Rates

The price structure of transportation has no equal in its degree of complexity. Business in general has a comparatively simple pricing problem, for any given firm handles only a relatively limited number of products. The transportation companies, however, have to provide a price for transportation not only on every item shipped, but also on every possible combination of origins and destinations.

Class rates and commodity rates are the two basic types of freight rates. Since class rates often are modified by exceptions, however, it frequently is said that there are three types of rates: class, commodity, and exceptions.

Class rates   Every commodity subject to a classification rate is listed in a book called *classification manual,* where it is placed in one of a limited number of groups called *classes.* The basic group is Class 100, and all other groups are expressed as percentages of it. Thus, if a particular commodity is placed in Class 85, it will carry a transportation rate that is 85 per cent of the basic rate for Class 100 commodities. There are a dozen or so criteria used to determine the class into which a given commodity fits. Theoretically, these criteria have to do with the nature of the demand for service and the cost of providing that service.

Exceptions to the classification   The basic classification applies to all parts of the country and to all carriers. For a number of reasons, however, certain carriers may feel that they cannot operate under the classification. Perhaps competition from other carriers in one region, or from one destination, or to one market, causes a serious problem. Perhaps competition faced by the shipper in certain markets is so severe that a reduced

charge for transportation is considered essential. Such a reduction can be granted only if the shippers or the carriers take exception to the classification. There are four items in a classification to which they may object: description of articles, minimum weights, lcl ratings, and cl ratings. An exception may be taken to any one or a combination of these four items. To effect such a change, the carrier files an exception to the classification in the appropriate tariff, and barring any legal difficulty, the ICC ultimately approves it.

Commodity rates   This type of rate is published directly for a commodity or group of commodities rather than indirectly through classification. The rate usually is applicable to a limited geographical area. For example, a hypothetical but completely realistic schedule of rail rates for the shipment of packaged television antennas from St. Louis to selected cities in the Midwest is shown in Table 13.1. Note the variation in cost (rate) of transport per 100 miles between these points in the same general area.

This illustration is designed to show the complex and confusing relationships that exist within a single rate schedule for a given type of product. Of course, in the real world

TABLE 13.1   Hypothetical rail rates from St. Louis to selected cities

From St. Louis to	Distance (miles)	CWT rate (cents per 100 miles)
Indianapolis, Ind.	241	35
Columbus, Ohio (via Indianapolis)	371	30
Springfield, Mo.	239	45
Ft. Smith, Ark. (via Springfield)	417	46
Kansas City, Mo.	283	48

the confusion is multiplied thousands of times by the infinite combinations of products and distances. Moreover, with class, commodity, and exception rates in effect at the same time, how does one ever know which to use? A good general rule is that the lowest published rate applies. Unless a very unusual situation exists, exception rates take precedence over class rates; and commodity rates, over both.

Transporation Services

Transportation companies offer a wide variety of services that are helpful not only to the logistics manager but also to the marketing manager. Also, a few of the rail and motor services are especially vital to marketing strategy.

Piggyback   Piggyback refers to the transporting of loaded highway trailers on a railroad flatcar. There are half a dozen piggyback plans that railroads offer. They range from moving trailers of common motor carriers to providing the power to pull a shipper's flatcar loaded with the shipper's trailers.

Transit privileges   The idea behind the transit privilege is to allow a through rate to apply even though goods are stopped at some intermediate point. Why would anyone want to stop and unload a shipment short of the final destination? Possibly the production manager wants to have something done to the goods before they get to market. Perhaps a shipment of pipe needs to be stopped en route to be threaded. Or, steel in certain shapes may be stopped at a fabricating firm en route from the mill supplier to the market. A logistics manager may find it desirable to stop goods in transit for storage. Sometimes charges are made for

this service, but the through transportation rate usually applies.

Diversion and reconsignment   These services enable goods to be shipped in the general direction of the market even before the owner knows who the buyer will be or where the goods must be delivered. This is a valuable service to shippers of perishables, such as bananas and citrus fruits, because they can be placed in transit without first being sold. For example, to save time, the owner of a shipment of bananas in Galveston may consign them to his or her own company in Chicago but, after they are sold, reconsign them to the buyer and divert them to the buyer's destination, perhaps in Boston.

Transloading   This rail service enables the seller to ship a carload to a point where parts of the load are transferred to other cars going to different destinations.

Of course, piggyback, transit privileges, diversion and reconsignment, and transloading are not the only transportation services available. Transportation companies, particularly airlines, railroads, and some motor carriers, are becoming more and more committed to improving both the marketing and logistics functions. The effects of this commitment are that the carriers actively seek out opportunities to meet the unusual needs of shippers and to bring them greater satisfactions.

Warehouses

Moving goods is but part of the physical-distribution process. Holding them is equally important, as are the functions of assembling and breaking bulk. These activities of assembling, holding (storing), and breaking bulk typically are performed by warehouses, of which there are several types.

Public versus private warehouses   A *public warehouse* is one that offers its services to the public. A *private warehouse*, like a private carrier, is for the exclusive use of its owner. There are a number of reasons why companies employ public warehouses, their own private ones, or do both. The decision on which to use turns on a combination of economic and service factors.

For large companies, the economic advantages of private warehousing exceed those of using public facilities. However there are exceptions. Some services can be obtained only from bonded public warehouses. In some cases, the investment in private warehouse facilities cannot be justified because of a relatively low return on investment. Once established, a network of private distribution centers is costly and difficult to modify. Using public warehouses provides much more flexibility.

General-merchandise versus special warehouses   Of the several types of warehousing facilities classified by the U.S. Bureau of the Census, general-merchandise warehouses are the most important to marketing people. This type handles almost all kinds of goods, ranging from appliances to zippers. Some general warehouses also have controlled-temperature facilities. Other more specialized types of warehouses include those for refrigerated items, household goods, farm products, and so on.

Financial services of warehouses   One of the important services of warehouses is financing. The *warehouse receipt* is evidence that goods actually exist and are in the hands of a responsible third party, the warehouseman. The receipt can be used as collateral for loans. Through the practice of *field warehous-*

ing, receipts can be issued by a public warehouse on goods stored in a private warehouse or on the premises of the owner. The public operator merely takes legal, rather than physical, possession of the goods and becomes responsible for them even though they are on the owner's premises. The field warehouser may fence in items, lock them in a special room, or segregate them in some other way, and thus accept responsibility for them physically.

Some warehouses are bonded and under government regulations can store goods on which taxes ultimately will be due. The owner, however, does not have to pay those taxes until the goods are withdrawn. For example, imported goods may be put in a bonded warehouse and duties paid only when the goods leave the custody of the warehouse.

Physical, Economic, and Temporal Proximity to Markets

Physical distribution is concerned with moving goods to the marketplace. The closer a seller is to the market, the less burdensome and costly is the logistics task. Conversely, the further away a seller is from the market, the greater is the cost and difficulty of serving it. Proximity to the market is a decided competitive advantage, and it has three important dimensions—physical, economic, and temporal.

Physical proximity   The physical space separating buyer and seller represents a barrier to marketing, and the difficulty of overcoming this space limits the geographical area in which a company can compete. This limitation is particularly severe for companies whose logistics costs in general and transportation costs in particular are significant elements of total cost. Aside from the cost, about which we will say more in a moment, there are some products that simply are difficult to move very far. Consider large yachts or electric turbines. Some are dangerous, such as liquid petroleum gas. Others are perishable and easily damaged in transit. For companies that manufacture this type of product, physical proximity to a market is almost mandatory; and, typically, they are not able to serve customers situated very far away.

Economic proximity   Economic proximity is closeness to a market measured in terms of the cost of reaching it, rather than in terms of geographical distance. Aren't they the same? Not necessarily. Generally speaking, it costs more to move goods a long distance than it does to move them a short distance. But there are exceptions, some of which we already have discussed.

1. *Mode of transport*   It generally costs less to ship by barge than by rail, by rail than by truck, and by truck than by air.
2. *Transit privileges*   As we have seen, it may cost less to ship to an intermediate point if an in-transit privilege is utilized than if two short-haul rates are charged.
3. *Zones rates*   Rates are seldom quoted per mile. A flat rate per CWT (hundred weight) may be charged for delivery any place in a zone. It costs less per mile, therefore, to ship to buyers at the far edge of a zone than to those located closer to the seller.
4. *Rate equalization*   Regulatory authorities have arbitrarily set rates to equalize the cost of shipping to a market from two different locations. For example, it costs about the same for a seller in Florida to ship oranges to Chicago as it does a seller in Southern California. Presumably, this is done to preserve competition.

Notwithstanding the exceptions, the general principle applies that rate times distance equals cost of transit. Like all other costs, transportation costs must be covered by the final price of the product if a profit is to be realized. But this does not mean that the seller always pays for the cost of moving goods, although this often is the case. Sometimes the buyers pay, and therefore they try to purchase from the closest seller. Sometimes the seller pays the cost of transport if the amount is not great, or even when it is if the size of the order is large and the seller needs the business. When done to match the price of a competitor situated closer to the buyer's location, the practice is called *freight absorption*. Systematic methods of quoting delivered prices, such as the basing-point pricing system, have been generally considered illegal, because of the price discrimination involved.[5]

Regardless of which party, seller or buyer, pays the transportation bill, the economic impact is important. It determines in large part where companies buy and sell, therefore affecting the degree of competition that prevails. Economic proximity turns out, then, to be of considerably more importance than is physical proximity.

Temporal proximity   Time is a third critical concept in logistics, and its impact is very similar to that of space. In this section, we will analyze some of the time options available to the planner when marketing strategy places a temporal constraint on logistics decisions. This can best be done by posing a logistics problem subject to the constraint that the only practical means of delivery is by truck. The customer is located in St. Louis, where one of several supplying firms also is located. Other suppliers are located in

[5]See Chapter 18 for a description of basing-point pricing.

Springfield, Missouri, Chicago, and Tulsa. In round numbers, these out-of-town suppliers are 150, 300, and 400 miles away, respectively; in terms of time, they are approximately three, seven, and nine hours away. Although the physical relationship of customer and suppliers is obvious, in most cases neither the number of miles nor the number of hours is relevant. The important fact is that all four suppliers can deliver goods the next morning. As long as overnight delivery meets the needs of the St. Louis customer, the sellers in all four markets are of equal temporal proximity. Their equality would disappear, however, if the customer were to demand next-hour service. Only the St. Louis firm could supply such prompt delivery.

It is possible for other suppliers, even those thousands of miles away, to overcome a temporal disadvantage of this type. Suppose this distant firm is located in Los Angeles. It has several options. First, if the midwest market as a whole could support it, a branch plant might be established. Second, it could open a company-owned distribution facility. Third, it could utilize a public warehouse. Finally, it could utilize a faster mode of transport, probably air freight. All four solutions would be costly, some more so than others; but each would permit the Los Angeles firm to achieve temporal proximity. It could compete effectively with firms located much closer to the market.

other aspect of the business. Objectives must be established, plans must be made to achieve them, and decisions must be reached on the basis of the plans and objectives. The objectives also serve as standards against which the effectiveness of the logistics strategy can later be tested. For example, if management sets as an objective the reduction of total cost in getting goods to the right place at the right time, this would constitute both a criterion for the design of the logistics system and a standard by which its performance could later be measured.

As we shift our thinking from cost reduction to the increase of profits, our horizon is broadened, and our management options are increased. The integration of the distribution system with the marketing system is the essence of our approach to logistics management. In order to demonstrate this systems approach, we will examine logistics decisions at successively higher levels of the hierarchy, beginning with the transportaiton system and moving through the logistics system, the logistics-marketing system, and finally the system of the entire firm. More specifically, we will demonstrate that only through the management of logistics costs to reflect marketing and other systems requirements can we give concrete meaning to the organizational goal of good service at low cost. And only if we analyze such logistics costs in terms of economic and temporal proximity to the market can we actually implement this goal.

A General Approach to Logistics Management

We now turn to the process of logistics management. Managing the physical-distribution activities of a firm involves the same general approach as managing any

A Transportation System Decision

Place yourself in the position of a distribution manager who is asked to identify the best means of getting a product to the customer. Before reading on, pause and think for a moment about the nature of your answer. You will probably answer the question with another question: What do you mean by "best"? Is it the fastest means? Or is it the cheapest means? If you are told that either of these goals is satisfactory, you can proceed to solve the transport problem because you now have a criterion on which to base your decision. But it is still only a transportation decision. It does not provide answers to the many other related questions that are involved. For example, to how many distribution points should the product be transported? How much will this cost? Will the customers get adequate service? To answer these questions, we must look at the overall logistics system rather than at just the transportation system.

A Logistics System Decision

We now move up a level in the systems hierarchy. As distribution manager, you are now asked to determine the best number of locations to use as distribution points. Again, what is meant by "best?" Suppose you interpret it to mean lowest total cost. After some analysis, you estimate that the total cost (transportation, warehousing, inventory, and so on) of physical distribution from several points would be as follows:

```
  5 points: $4,475,000
 17 points: $4,693,000
 25 points: $4,840,000
 50 points: $5,400,000
100 points: $6,310,000
```

Applying the criterion of lowest total cost, you settle on 5 distribution points. In this instance you have applied a broader systems concept, but you have reached your decision without taking into account its implications on marketing or on other divisions of the firm.

A Logistics-Marketing System Decision

It is necessary again to move up a notch in the systems hierarchy and to include the marketing requirements. Table 13.2 presents a hypothetical marketing-logistics situation. Column 1, in the upper part, lists several cost components.[6] Columns 2, 4, 6, 8, and 10 show the costs of each of the components when varying numbers of distribution points are used. The fifth line in the table shows the total cost for 5, 17, 25, 50, and 100 distribution points. As in the previous example, the lowest-cost system (column 2) calls for 5 distribution points.

But what happens when we include marketing considerations? The bottom part of Table 13.2 shows that only 33 per cent of the customers would receive an order one day after it is placed if as few as 5 distributoin points were used. Another 53 percent would get second-day service. On the other hand, if 100 distribution points were used, 99 per cent of the customers would get one-day service. (To keep this illustration simple, we have not considered the reliability of this level of service. Obviously it will make a difference in both the cost and the quality of service if the plan is to ensure a certain speed of service 100 per cent of the time or only, for example, 80 per cent of the time.) If marketing people were looking only at the marketing aspects of the problem on a non-system basis, they would certainly want 100 distribution points and 99 per cent of the customers getting one-day service all of the time.

[6]Assume that all cost components are included in one or another of the categories shown. Nothing would be gained (other than complicating an otherwise simple illustration) by showing a separate set of data for materials handling or order processing; so assume that those and other costs are included in warehousing, data processing, and so on.

TABLE 13.2   Cost of physical-distribution components from various numbers of distribution points (Index: total cost from 5 points = 100)

Component of cost (1)	5 points		17 points		25 points		50 points		100 points	
	$000 (2)	Index (3)	$000 (4)	Index (5)	$000 (6)	Index (7)	$000 (8)	Index (9)	$000 (10)	Index (11)
Transportation	2,632	58.8	2,211	49.4	2,082	46.5	1,939	43.2	1,847	41.3
Warehousing	190	4.2	235	5.3	265	5.9	368	8.2	514	11.5
Inventory (22 per cent of investment)	1,205	26.9	1,761	39.4	1,997	44.6	2,513	56.2	3,172	70.9
Data processing	448	10.0	486	10.9	496	11.1	585	13.1	777	17.4
Total cost*	4,475	100.0	4,693	104.9	4,840	108.2	5,400	120.7	6,310	141.0

Service levels	Per cent	Index	Per cent	Index	Per cent	Index	Per cent	Index	Per cent	Index
Customers receiving										
First-day service	33	100	81	245	90	273	96	291	99	300
Second-day service	53	—	16	—	10	—	4	—	1	—

*Some totals may not add to figures shown because of rounding.

Source: Clayton W. Hill, "Reorganizing Distribution for Higher Profits," *Industrial Marketing* 48, no. 2 (February 1963): 77–84. Reprinted from *Industrial Marketing.* Copyright 1963 by Crain Communications, Inc., Chicago, Illinois. (Basic data are from the reference cited; calculations are by this author.)

However, this view might be changed if they were to look at the index found in columns 3, 5, 7, 9, and 11. This index shows the relationship of each of the cost components at various numbers of distribution points to the total cost of distribution from 5 points. For example, transportation cost from 5 points (column 3) is nearly 59 per cent of the total cost, whereas from 100 points (column 11) it is only 41 per cent of the total cost from 5 points.

Using this index and at the same time bringing marketing service into the picture, we can note what happens to both cost and service levels as the number of distribution points increases. Moving from 5 distribution points to 25 results in the cost index rising from 100 to 108.2, or about 8 per cent. However, this 8 per cent increase in cost results in nearly two and three quarters times as many customers being given one-

day service. This does not appear to be a very high price to pay for the increased level of customer service.

Moving on from 25 to 50 points, total distribution cost rises from $4.8 million to $5.4 million, or nearly 12 per cent, but the proportion of customers receiving one-day service rises less than 7 per cent. From these figures, the marketing department must determine whether it places such a high value on providing one-day service to 96 per cent of its customers rather than to 90 per cent that it is willing to increase logistics costs by 12 per cent. If its goal is to render good service at reasonable cost, the marketing department may conclude that serving 90 per cent of its customers at the cost shown meets this standard but that serving 96 or 99 per cent at the accompanying higher costs is unreasonably expensive. Thus, a trade-off is made; the marketing department sacrifices a

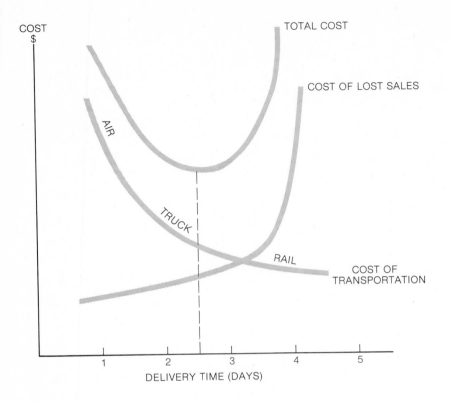

FIGURE 13.1   Combined marketing-logistics costs

small increase in service in order to permit a substantial cost savings.

Another critical aspect of the management of the logistics-marketing system involves the selection of a mode of transport that satisfies both the standard of economical transportation cost and the criterion of customer service. Figure 13.1 illustrates how these two sometimes conflicting requirements can be met. It usually is less costly to use rail than truck and truck than air, and one reason shippers are willing to pay the premium is the speed of delivery. But it is not simply the desire to serve the customer that leads to the choice of a more costly mode of transport—important as that may be as a marketing consideration. There is also a cost of not serving the customer through late delivery. The principal element of this cost is the revenue that is lost when the customer turns to another supplier. The cost can be even greater if the customer makes a permanent shift in resources in order to ensure better service.[7] The cost of lost sales mounts rapidly as the delivery time (especially delay) increases. The transportation cost and the cost of lost sales are shown in Figure 13.1. The manager cannot utilize the lowest cost mode of transport because the cost of lost sales is too high. Nor can the cost of lost sales be held low without using the most expensive method of transporta-

[7]H. N. Shycon and C. R. Sprague, "Put a Price Tag on Your Customer Servicing Levels," *Harvard Business Review*, July-August 1975, pp. 71–78.

tion, air freight. The solution is to minimize total cost; which in Figure 13.1 is at the delivery time of 2.5 days. Note that this decision probably doesn't really please either marketing or logistics, but is acceptable to both.

Total System Considerations

Although the marketing and logistics people have bilaterally reached a decision that meets their respective requirements and goals, other affected segments of the firm have been ignored. The decision reached may or may not mesh with such functions as finance and production. For example, working-capital requirements rise dramatically as the number of distribution points increases. We see in Table 13.2 that inventory costs of $1.205 million for 5 distribution points increase to $1.997 million for 25 points. It has been estimated that on the average 30 per cent of the working capital of a firm is tied up in inventory. In our hypothetical illustration, inventory costs were set at 22 per cent of investment. Using these percentages, the following calculations show the changes in working capital and investment in inventory as the number of distribution points increase:

	5 Points ($000)	25 Points ($000)	Per cent increase
Inventory cost (22% of investment)	1,205	1,997	65.7
Investment (30% of working capital)	5,478	9,077	65.7
Working capital	18,260	30,258	41.1

Of course these are representative values in a hypothetical situation, but they serve to illustrate the point that the effects of a revision of marketing-logistics policy to improve customer service by shifting the number of distribution points will definitely be felt in other segments of the firm. Similarly, some production policies involving scheduling and length of runs may require adaptation as inventory adjustments are made.

The Design and Operation of a Logistics System

The achievement of logistics objectives, the efficient operation of the system, and the melding of the logistics function with other functional areas into an overall marketing program do not just happen; they must be carefully planned and administered.

Planning the System

There is a wide latitude for strategic logistics planning because of the many variables that can affect logistics decisions and the many types of system components that are available. For our discussion, let us assume that one of the goals that affects logistics is that the firm must ensure delivery to customers within three days after an order has been received and that this quality of service will be provided at least 90 per cent of the time.[8] As we have done before, we will further assume that the logistics decisions reached must be consonant with the other goals of the organization.

In planning the system to meet this basic

[8]While guidelines also would be established for inbound materials ordering, transporting, warehousing, and so on, we will ignore the supply side of logistics because the same principles apply.

service goal, the many components of logistics can be combined in a variety of ways. To simplify our illustration, we will consider the transportation and warehousing components as the only controlling variables in the strategic logistics decision. For those customers located three days away or less there is no great challenge in developing a logistics plan. The principal choice involves the type of carrier to use, whether private or public, common or contract. For customers located more than three days away, however, the problem is not quite so simple. There are two broad options available: direct service or indirect service. These options require strategic choice and commitment of resources. They may even necessitate the acquisition of additional resources.

Direct service Direct service involves shipping from the supplier to the customer without the use of intermediate warehouse facilities or other holdover procedures. The customer's order may be shipped by air freight, or arrangements may be made for the customer to receive periodic surface deliveries of specified amounts, with unanticipated needs being filled by emergency air shipments. This method might require some adjustments of the customer's procurement practices, but it would permit goods to flow in a more or less steady stream via surface carrier rather than air carrier. In either case the service is direct to the customer.

Indirect service An alternative is to use surface transportation in combination with warehouses. This indirect alternative has five decision elements:

1. The type and ownership of transport to the warehouse

2. The size and timing of shipments to the warehouse
3. The use of public or private warehouses
4. The type and ownership of transport from the warehouse
5. The size and timing of shipments from the warehouse

It is not difficult to see that the logistics system would be defined by the decisions reached on these five points. The components of the system are identified when the type and ownership of transportation and warehousing facilities are determined. The flow of product linking these components is established by decisions regarding the size and timing of shipments to and from warehouse points. The system is goal oriented, since it would be planned to achieve the objective of maintaining three-day delivery to all customers at least 90 per cent of the time.

Administering the System

Let us assume that, in the planning process, management has decided that indirect service provides the best method for implementing the goal of three-day delivery. It is now necessary for the logistics manager to select the warehouse locations and inventory order points that will make the most efficient use of the company's resources.

Warehouse location The principal task in choosing a warehouse location is to select the site from among several alternatives that best satisfies the profit and customer service goals of the firm. We can approach this kind of question by using an example. We will assume that public warehousing will be used, that only one warehouse location is needed to serve a given market, and that there is only one point of origin, the factory. We will further assume that the major market is three days away by truck and that the average truck speed is 35 miles per hour over the road. Given our goal of three-day delivery service, we know that if the warehouse receives an order on Monday morning it must be delivered sometime Wednesday. Allowing the working day for processing the order and getting it to the carrier by 3:30 P.M. for over-the-road departure at 8:00 P.M. leaves 4 hours on Monday, 24 hours on Tuesday, and 6 hours on Wednesday for arrival at the terminal by 6:00 A.M. and all that day for delivery to the customer. The territory that could be served by the warehouse under these conditions would have a radius of about 1,200 miles (34 hours times 35 miles per hour).[9]

Our problem is to select an appropriate warehouse site to serve this territory. The first consideration is, of course, time. Accordingly, several potential sites can be isolated by drawing circles around locations within radii that are equivalent to three days' time from the factory—in our illustration about 1,200 miles. Since several places will probably meet the three-day requirement, however, the logistics manager must turn to the expected cost of serving the market from each of these places. The cost factors would be inbound transport cost plus warehouse cost plus outbound transport cost.

If the company information system is adequate, these costs should not be too difficult to obtain. First, the amount of demand in

each town in the territory should be determined so that total tonnage can be estimated. On the basis of this estimate, the logistics manager can obtain from carriers (rail, truck, or water) or from the files of the company's traffic department the volume rate for transporting goods from the factory to each of the several possible sites, say points A, B, and C. We will assume that rail transport is found to be most economical.

Next, warehouse charges on the expected volume of goods to be handled can be determined. These charges, which constitute the second element of cost, probably will vary at points A, B, and C. So also will the third element of cost, outbound transportation charges. Less-than-optimum-volume outbound shipments from the warehouse could be made by common carrier truck, the warehouseman's trucks, or freight forwarders. The actual rates are obtained from Sites A, B, and C to all of the final destination points. A weighted average charge to each destination from each of the potential warehouse sites easily can be calculated. The transportation charge (weight times the rate) to each town is determined, and the sum of all charges to all towns is divided by total weight to yield the average rate per hundred weight (CWT). For illustration purposes, assume there are 100 towns or cities to be served in an area. The weight of shipments to each town has been estimated. The costs of moving these weights from each possible warehouse site also have been determined. A work sheet might be constructed to facilitate the computation of the weighted average cost of shipment from each site to the 100 towns and cities in the area (see Table 13.3).

If private carriage is used for the outbound movement, outbound charges would have to be estimated rather than based on

[9]As a practical matter, the territory probably will not be that large, because if shipments have to move by two or more carriers, much time is lost in unloading and reloading. Furthermore, direct service to some towns in the area may not be available, and special deliveries may have to be scheduled to them.

TABLE 13.3   Worksheet showing calculations of weighted average outbound transportation costs from three possible warehouse sites to 100 customer locations

Customer Location (1)	Weight of Shipment (CWT) (2)	Site A		Site B		Site C	
		Rate (CWT) (3)	Cost (4)	Rate (CWT) (5)	Cost (6)	Rate (CWT (7)	Cost (8)
1. Des Moines	5,000	.50	2,500	.60	3,000	.75	3,750
2. Omaha	8,000	2.00	16,000	2.25	18,000	2.50	20,000
3. Ft. Dodge	3,000	1.50	4,500	1.70	5,100	1.00	3,000
100. Fargo	6,000	2.50	15,000	2.50	15,000	3.00	18,000
Total	700,000		725,900		733,600		841,400
Weighted Cost (CWT)		1.037*		1.048†		1.202‡	

*Column 4 divided by column 2.
†Column 6 divided by column 2.
‡Column 8 divided by column 2.

published rate schedules. In either case, the cost elements of serving the market from Sites A, B, and C are summed, and the end results may be as follows:

	Cost per CWT		
	Site A	Site B	Site C
Rail rate to warehouse	$ .550	$ .590	$ .468
Warehouse charges	.050	.050	.040
Weighted average outbound cost from warehouse	1.037	1.048	1.202
	$1.637	$1.688	$1.710

Although all three points meet the time requirement of three-day service, it is clear from these figures that site A is the preferred location because it entails the lowest cost.

We must recall that this example represents a simple situation in which only one warehouse was needed to serve each market. If more than one warehouse were necessary in a given market area, it also would be fairly simple to divide the area into two or more

territories by approximately the same process that we used to find the lowest-cost warehouse locations. First, the tonnage to each location would be estimated, the rates determined, and the transport charge calculated. Warehouse charges at each location then would be added to show the cost of goods before outbound movement starts. According to the above data, these costs would be $.600 for site A and $.640 for site B. Assuming that the company plan calls for private carriage, we will use a per-mile charge instead of a 100-pound charge to show distance costs. A reasonable estimate would be $.40 per vehicle mile. For shipments of 40,000 pounds, the $.40-per-mile cost converts to $.20 per 100 pounds for each 200 miles covered.

Figure 13.2 shows how the territory would be divided between warehouses at A and B when the cost of delivery is the deciding factor. The boundary between the two territories is drawn through the locations where the cost of delivery is identical from the two warehouses. Since the inbound transporta-

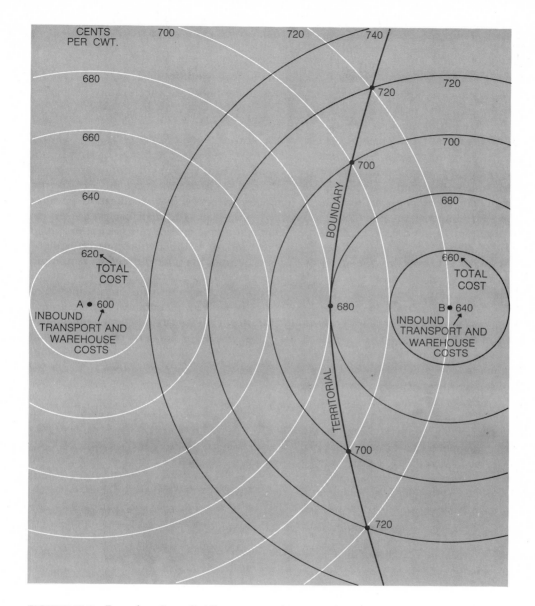

FIGURE 13.2   Boundary lines dividing two warehouse territories

tion and warehousing costs at location A are less than at location B, the warehouse at A is able to penetrate farther than the warehouse at B for the same costs of delivery.

The method of determining warehouse location that we have just described is useful when only a few points are involved. It is not able to cope with very complex systems involving dozens of warehouse locations, multiple plant origins, and thousands of delivery points. There are other methods available, however, to deal with such highly complex situations.[10]

Inventory management   Administering a logistics system involves a number of problems in inventory management, the most obvious of which is running out of stock. Other problems center on the investment tied up in inventory and the difficulty in deciding on the objectives of the inventory function. Moreover, there are problems associated with forecasting not only the amount of a product that will be needed and the time it will be required, but also such product specifications as style, color, and size. Every new product means an increase in the complexity of the inventory problem, not to mention a considerable increase in the cost of carrying inventory. A further cause of difficulty in inventory management is that the lag between production and use often is long, and the channels of distribution often are complex. With inadequate flows of information among channel members concerning the amount of product on hand, there is relatively little control over inventory throughout the system.

In order to explore some of the ways in which a logistics manager might attack such problems, we will return to the same basic illustration that we used in discussing warehouse location. The company's specification of three-day delivery 90 per cent of the time affected not only transportation and warehousing policies but also the amount of stock required to implement the delivery goal.

[10]For an excellent treatment of a comprehensive logistics model, including warehouse location, see Bowersox and others, *Dynamic Simulation.* Another interesting and less technical approach is found in A. M. Geoffrian, "Better Distribution Planning with Computer Models," *Harvard Business Review,* July-August 1976, pp. 92–99.

The manager of inventory thus became concerned both with having goods available for the customer within a given time after receiving an order and with the proportion of time that this availability requirement must be met. In other words, administering the logistics system involves determining economic order quantities (EOQ) and deciding when to place orders to replenish stock.

The economic order quantity   It is commonly accepted that the cost of maintaining inventory is 20 to 25 per cent of the investment in that inventory. Because of the magnitude of the expense, the decision of how much inventory to keep on hand is an important one in managing and controlling logistics costs. To help make the decision correctly, a basic formula for determining the economic order quantity (EOQ) has been devised.

$$\text{EOQ} = \sqrt{\frac{2RS}{CK}}$$

where EOQ = the economic order quantity
R = the annual rate of usage
S = the cost of placing the order
C = the cost per unit
K = the inventory carrying-cost percentage

In this formula, R is estimated from the forecast of demand for the product. S is derived from company records but can be only as accurate as the underlying cost analysis will allow it to be since many cost analysis procedures involve arbitrary methods of allocating overhead expenses. If the product is bought outside the firm, the same problems are present as in determining the cost of placing an order, and C is likely to be an estimate. K is also an estimate, and it is an aggregate of various items. Included are such costs as storage, insurance, taxes, handling, interest, depreciation, and the like.

If we assign values to each variable, we can determine the number of units to order at one time, other things remaining constant. Assume, for example, that

$$R = 15{,}271 \text{ units}$$
$$S = \$5.62$$
$$C = \$13.11$$
$$K = 22.5 \text{ per cent}$$

Thus

$$\text{EOQ} = \sqrt{\frac{(2)\,(15{,}271)\,(5.62)}{(13.11)\,(.225)}}$$

$$= 241.226$$

We can see that the application of the estimated values results in an economic order quantity of about 241 units, if other things remain constant. But do they? If the product is bought outside, suppose the seller sells in multiples of 100 units only. If it is manufactured, suppose the economic production run is 350 units. Suppose truckloads or carloads consist of 300 units. What if palletloads are 275 units? If any of these conditions prevail, the manager may not be able to order exactly 241 units. Thus, the size of the order will be an even 350 units if manufactured or 300 units if bought outside.

Timing orders The next problem for the inventory manager is to establish a decision base for when to place an order. If withdrawals from an inventory of 300 units were at the rate of one seventy-second per day and the lead time were twelve days, the order could be placed every sixty days with assurance that, as the last unit went out one door, the new order would appear on the shelves. Although this state of affairs is not likely, we now have some idea of the type of information required to set a reorder point.

More specifically, the *reorder point* can be determined by the interaction of three separate forces. First, the lead time required for delivery of the order after it is placed; second, the estimated mean demand during the lead time; and third, the allowable number of stock-outs or the per cent of time stock will be available when customers ask for it. In addition, we need to know the standard deviation from the mean demand. In mathematical terms, these components of the reorder point (ROP) can be expressed as follows:

$$\text{ROP} = (L)\,(\overline{D}) + (L)\,(X)\,\sigma$$

where $L =$ the lead time in weeks
$\overline{D} =$ the average (mean) amount demanded during the lead time
$X =$ the number of standard deviations
$\sigma =$ the standard deviation

The mean demand may be calculated from historical data. If the arithmetic mean of weekly demand were 200 units, it could be assumed that with a normal distribution demand would be met 50 per cent of the time. However, since the distribution of demand may vary, the probability of the mean being 200 may be either more or less than 50 per cent. We can compute this standard deviation from the mean using company records. For purposes of our decision, let us assume that we have calculated the standard deviation and found it to be 104 units.[11] Since the mean plus 1 standard deviation would cover only 84 per cent of the area under the curve in a normal distribution, more than 1 stan-

[11]The $\overline{D}$ of 200 and σ of 104 are merely assumed numbers to fill out the illustration. To have derived the mean and standard deviation would have meant building a historical record for the company.

dard deviation is necessary to reach the 90 per cent level. From standard statistical tables we know that 1.28 standard deviations plus the mean will provide the desired service level. If we further assume a 2-week lead time, we now have values for all the components of the ROP formula:

$$ROP = (L)\,(\overline{D}) + (L)\,(X)\,\sigma$$

where $\overline{D}$ = 200 units per week during lead time
X = 1.28 standard deviations
σ = 104
L = 2-week lead time

Substituting, we find that

ROP = (2) (200) + (2) (1.28) (104)
    = 666

With a reorder point of 666 units, a cushion against stock-outs has been built into the system. Putting it differently, we can say that a safety stock of 666 units is required to cover demand during the lead time and to ensure that demand will be met 90 per cent of the time. This number of units provides excessive protection during the first days of the lead time, but since the use rate is not known, such a level of protection is necessary.

Note that no allowance is made for late delivery or any other delays that would extend the lead time beyond 2 weeks. Furthermore, these neat calculations would be upset if inventory were at 888 units and unexpectedly three orders for 330 units each came in on the same day. Statistically these situations should not arise over 10 per cent of the time, for our analysis was based on 90 per cent service.

Organizing for Logistics Management

Where Should Logistics Be Managed?

Throughout our discussion of planning and administering the logistics system, we have assumed that these activities take place within the framework of a corporate structure. But exactly where in that structure should the logistics function be housed? We can begin to answer this question by looking at a fairly typical situation. Assume that in the Reliable Engine Company there are four executives who report directly to the president, all of whom have responsibility for some facet of logistics along with their other duties. The controller is responsible for traffic, order processing, and finished-goods inventory control. The production planning manager is responsible for the planning of warehouse space. The sales manager is in charge of order status inquiry. The factory manager, through industrial engineering, is charged with the supervision of the factory warehouse and a branch warehouse, as well as with some responsibility for finished-goods inventory control.

All of the elements of a distribution system are present in this firm. However, the elements do not operate as an integrated system, so a genuine logistics function does not arise. It is likely that the persons responsible for the various distribution tasks perform them well as independent tasks, but it is very unlikely that these tasks are coordinated in any meaningful way. In fact, the situation is almost chaotic. Inventory requirements are not revised when sales differ from forecasts; the sales department cannot respond intelligently to customer inquiries, because the traffic department has the orders and traffic policy prohibits partial shipments; moreover, there is little coordination between information concerning demand and information concerning inventory levels, the result being that the plant occasionally works overtime on some products while inventories of others are excessive. Unfortunately this type of situation is not unusual. It is found both in small firms and in very large firms serving national markets.

Let us consider how such a situation might be remedied. First, logistics responsibility needs to be vested in a single executive, the distribution manager, with full responsibility for all of the elements of logistics. Since the distribution manager would have no other functions to manage, the logistics would not be subordinated to any other area. Since the manager would be placed on the same level as other functional managers, logistics would not be dominated by other functions. This does not necessarily mean that the logistics manager should always be a top-level executive. In some organizations, the logistics manager reports to the person in charge of marketing or production, or to the controller. The only caveat about such organizational subordination is that the manager in charge of logistics must not subordinate the function. As conflicting goals arise, the systems viewpoint and the overall objectives of the firm must prevail.

Organizational Alternatives

The top-level logistics executive   Ideally, the logistics manager should be a vice president and should be on the same level as other vice presidents. However, this is not always realistic for several reasons. First, the company may be so large and other priorities so great that this structure would not be administratively feasible. Controlling the function would be beyond the ability of one person or department. Second, the company may be

so small that it cannot afford an executive whose time is devoted exclusively to logistics matters. In fact, logistics matters in a small company may not be complex enough to justify a full-time top manager even if the company could afford one. Third, logistics may be so much a part of the functioning of another division, such as marketing, that separating the two functions would accomplish nothing except to foster confusion and duplication of effort. Finally, neither the cost nor contribution of logistics may warrant the arrangement.

Logistics with another function   A second organizational scheme is to put the logistics function under another functional manager. There are several logical places for the function to be housed in a large firm: with the controller or financial vice president; with the marketing vice president; or with the production vice president. In small firms with executives who wear several functional hats, logistics can be placed under the most likely one, probably the executive who is not already overburdened or the one who has the most understanding of the activities involved.

The logistics planning staff   A third organizational scheme can be used by large companies with planning staffs that include management science specialists. The responsibility for logistics planning may be given to this group because of its importance in overall strategic planning for the firm. A logistics specialist should be a member of the group. Its potential for solving difficult logistics problems would thus be very great. That is, a logistics planning staff would not be limited to the simple service goals that we have used in our illustrations. Large amounts of data and sophisticated logistics models could be developed. Simulation models might be of particular value.

But planning staffs do not implement programs. Other people within the firm would have to be charged with the responsibility of carrying out the logistics plans developed by the staff. There may be a physical-distribution manager or a materials management executive. Or, the administration may be assigned to one of the functional divisions of the firm. In extremely large, diversified firms there may be several such individuals—perhaps assigned to particular plants or product lines.

Summary

It has long been recognized that physical distribution is an important part of marketing. However, until recently, the only companies that devoted very much attention to managing the logistical aspects of their operations were those whose physical-distribution costs were a substantial proportion of their total costs. This situation is now changing. The rising costs of moving goods and of warehousing them have made managers more alert to the possibilities of improving profits by controlling physical-distribution outlays. At the same time, customers have become more insistent on prompt reliable delivery service. Offering such service thus constitutes a significant part of a company's strategic marketing plan.

It is clear, however, that providing good distribution services to customers at a reasonable cost to the firm does not merely happen. This function must be managed. Physical-distribution (logistics) management is defined as the planning and operation of a system of internal and external flows of goods and of related information. In this chapter we saw that logistics management involves four specific areas of knowledge: (1) the environment in which logistics decisions must be made; (2) the relation of logistics decisions to the total systems approach; (3) the design of a logistics system suited to the specific needs of the company; and (4) the organization of a logistics system.

The environment of logistics decisions is both structural and conceptual. The structure of the environment involves those system components that provide transportation and warehousing services. Of equal importance are the rates or prices that these establishments charge for their services. The transportation system in the United States is complex, and the rate structure borders on chaos; but an understanding of this aspect of the logistics environment is essential if correct physical-distribution decisions are to be made. The warehousing structure is less complicated, but both public and private warehousing present special problems and opportunities for the logistics manager.

The conceptual aspects of the logistics environment involve the correct understanding of a number of important relationships. These can be expressed in terms of three proximity concepts. Physical proximity refers to geographical distance; economic proximity involves the cost of moving goods from seller to buyer; and temporal proximity refers to the time that it takes to move goods from origin to destination.

Logistics decisions can be made at any of several levels in the systems hierarchy. Simple decisions, such as the type of carrier to use, can be made at the transportation system level. Decisions that involve maintaining a certain limit on physical-distribution expenses can be made at the logistics system level. Decisions relating to the physical movement of goods and the maintenance of some level of customer service would have to be resolved at the logistics-marketing system level. Finally, the total firm may be the appropriate system level for making logistics decisions if several functional areas are involved, such as manufacturing, finance, marketing, and the like.

The sophistication of the system's organization and its position within the firm must be determined by the cost and the relative importance of the logistics function to the company. These considerations also indicate whether the logistics function is located high in the company with a top-level executive in charge or whether it is assigned to another functional area.

Questions and Problems

1. Some people think that providing a high level of customer service inevitably results in much higher physical-distribution costs. Do you agree? Explain your position.

2. One of the great obstacles to the mass production of housing has been the prohibitive cost of transporting prefabricated houses. With the rise of on-site construction costs, however, this disadvantage gradually is being reduced. For a manufacturer of prefabricated building components, design a physical-distribution plan that might accelerate the trend toward industrialized housing.

3. Does it not follow that the optimum logistics arrangement from the seller's viewpoint automatically must produce a satisfactory level of customer service? Explain your position.

4. What is the difference between storage and warehousing? How do both relate to wholesaling?

5. Of the three kinds of proximity (physical, economic, and temporal), which do you think is most important in developing a logistics system? Why?

6. Construct a chart similar to Figure 13.2, but demonstrate how it might be adapted to include a warehouse at point C, which is located to the south of points A and B and is equally distant from them.

7. Show how the calculation of the economic order quantity would be changed in the example on page 315 if
   a. The cost per unit is $6.75 instead of $5.62
   b. The cost per unit remains the same, but the per cent of inventory carrying cost is 27.5 instead of 22.5

8. What would be the effect on the reorder point in the example on page 315 if the company wanted to provide 95 per cent service to its customers?

9. A company decided to create a logistics function and to locate it in one of the established departments of the firm. Heated debate arose as to whether it should be located in the marketing or the manufacturing department. What arguments were probably raised to support each possibility? How would you lean in such a debate?

10. Identify the various departments or functions in a large manufacturing company that might be concerned with some aspect of logistics. Indicate briefly what the interest of each department would be. Given these respective interests, how do you think the logistics function should be organized in the firm?

14

Promotion Strategy: General Considerations

In this chapter we will look at some general aspects of promotion. The role of promotion strategy will be defined and its place in the marketing program will be explored, as will the objectives of promotion and the general issues and problems that arise in developing a promotional plan. Such general considerations apply to all types of demand creation—advertising, publicity, personal selling, and specialized sales promotions. However, there are other special and very important issues that arise in connection with the advertising and selling aspects of the promotion program. We will look at some of these special issues in Chapters 15 and 16.

Defining the Role of Promotion Strategy

The marketing planner often turns to the design of promotion strategy with mixed emotions. The development of promotion pushes us to the very frontiers of marketing knowledge. We must feel some trepidation as we tread the uncertain path through a maze of conflicting conceptions of consumer behavior. Simultaneously, we must sense an exhilaration when we realize that our personal creativity can make the difference between a merely acceptable marketing program and one that is truly distinctive.

The term *promotion* describes all types of marketing activities designed to stimulate demand. Promotion can be divided into four basic categories: advertising, publicity, personal selling, and specialized sales promotion activities. Unfortunately these categories are not clear-cut. However, an understanding of the term *advertising* is a helpful starting point for distinguishing among them. Advertising involves the communication by nonpersonal means of messages to selected large audiences for the purpose of informing and influencing them. As contrasted with publicity, advertising messages are identified with the advertiser and involve payment to the media employed. The definition gives us a key to the scope of advertising in the phrase "addressed to selected audiences." Advertising is sometimes referred to as *mass selling*. Although some advertising is directed to specific individuals (as, for example, in the use of direct mail), most advertising messages are directed at large numbers of people.

Publicity refers to the communication of information, by either personal or nonpersonal means, that is not directly paid for and that does not clearly identify the source of the message. Publicity can be used for many nonmarketing communications purposes; for example, in connection with a company's dealings with the financial community or in connection with a collective-bargaining situation. To isolate the part of publicity that is properly part of the promotion mix, we use the phrase *marketing public relations*. Marketing public relations can be an important part of a company's promotion strategy. For instance, when a marketer introduces a new product, it is highly desirable to have articles about it appear in magazines and newspapers. It is helpful to have the product featured on television programs, perhaps as a prize on a give-away show. The principal problem with publicity as a marketing tool is that it is very difficult to control. There is no assurance that the information will be published, and even if it is published the marketer has very little to say about the way it is presented. A good example of the impact of publicity is the benefit that Walt Disney World receives from the hundreds of references that are made to the amusement complex in the public media and in other companies' advertising. A spokesperson for the organization once reported that it received in publicity the equivalent of over $20 million in promotion—all without cost to Walt Disney World.

In contrast to advertising and publicity, *personal selling* is tailored to a specific individual or very small group. The emphasis is on the presentation of sales messages and the negotiation of transactions by personal contact with the customer. The essential difference, therefore, between advertising and personal selling is that the former is an impersonal method of communicating with large groups of consumers, while the latter is a personalized method of getting a message to individual consumers.

Sales promotion is a catch-all phrase that includes all methods of stimulating demand not specifically identified as advertising or selling. The American Marketing Association defines sales promotion in the specific sense as

those marketing activities, other than personal selling, advertising and publicity, that stimulate consumer purchasing and dealer effectiveness, such as displays, shows, and exhibitions, demonstrations and various non-recurrent selling efforts not in the ordinary routine.[1]

In addition to the ones mentioned in the AMA definition, sales promotion includes such activities and devices as

Motion picture and videotape films

Contests

Premiums

Coupons

Trading stamps

Display or dispensing equipment

Sampling

[1]Reprinted from R. S. Alexander, Chairman, Committee on Definitions of the American Marketing Association, *Marketing Definitions: A Glossary of Marketing Terms* (Chicago: 1960), published by the American Marketing Association.

Visual aids for salespeople

Catalogs and price sheets

Demonstrations

Special deals (including temporary price reductions)

Tie-in promotions

Most of these can be used in stimulating sales either to consumers or to the trade; although such items as training films, dealer contests, and display and dispensing equipment generally are restricted to trade promotion. Often, trade promotions are coordinated with consumer promotion. A consumer contest, for example, might be held simultaneously with a contest for dealer salespeople. A premium offered to consumers (such as a piggyback offer in which two items are joined and sold for a low price) might be coupled with a *dealer loader* (special-purchase discount) offered to the reseller.

The Promotion Mix

In exactly the same way that the overall elements of a marketing plan are blended together to create the marketing mix, so the various elements of the sales promotion plan are combined in what we call the *promotion mix*. The term *mix* implies that there are many ways of blending the ingredients to obtain different total effects. It suggests a synergism, in which the total promotional effort is greater than the sum of the elements going into it. In other words, the promotional mix is an overall creative plan as well as a thoughtfully designed combination of selected ingredients. There is a great deal of artistry involved. Of particular importance is the proper integration of the various ingredients. These elements, of course, must

work together toward the same promotional objectives. The proper coordination of advertising, selling, publicity, and sales promotion produces a far more efficient program than an attempt to carry out these activities without regard to their effects on each other. For example, it is easier to complete a sales transaction if the customer has been preconditioned or even presold by advertising. Advertising, in turn, is made more effective when it is coordinated with the use of sales promotion devices. And sales promotion, for its part, seldom can operate independently of either selling or advertising.

The Role of Promotion in the Marketing Mix

The definitions of promotion that we have cited suggest the extent of its role in the marketing mix. However, for reasons that are never altogether clear to marketing people, some business executives are extremely naive about promotion. They tend to think either that it is all there is to marketing or that it has, on the whole, very little importance. A sizable number of executives who think of promotion as the only significant element of marketing also believe, as we mentioned in Chapter 1, that marketing and sales amount to about the same thing. This misconception is dispelled by the marketing management concept.

At the other extreme is the mistaken view that promotion is an unimportant part of the marketing mix. Product, channels, and pricing are generally accepted to be the mandatory elements of every marketing strategy. About promotion, however, there is less conviction that it is really necessary. Skeptics are quick to suggest examples of companies that have succeeded exceptionally well without advertising. Many industrial concerns and a few engaged in marketing consumer products have indeed dispensed with all but token advertising programs. One case in point is the Hershey Chocolate Company, which for many years never aggressively advertised its products to consumers. However, this does not mean that the company did not promote its products. Promotional considerations in product design and packaging, in channel merchandising, and in pricing always have been present. Intensive distribution and prominent display of Hershey chocolate bars also provided this company with considerable promotional impact. Sixty-six years of success without advertising might cloud the certainty that advertising would have enhanced the success of the marketing program were it not for the fact that in 1969 Hershey named the Ogilvy and Mather advertising agency to handle a substantial advertising program. The disinclination of many industrial firms to make use of advertising is aptly expressed in this comment by the president of an electrical products company. "In good times," he said, "we don't need to advertise. In bad times, we can't afford to."

The Purposes of Promotion

There are three specific purposes of promotion: (1) to communicate, (2) to convince, and (3) to compete. Harion Harper, a prominent marketing executive, maintains that communication is the basis of all marketing effort and that it involves much besides the stimulation of sales. However, in practice most marketing communications are promotional, and it is in this context that communicating is included as a purpose of promotion. The dissemination of ideas, whether by advertising, by publicity, or by personal selling, is the principal activity of promotion.

The second purpose of promotion, to convince, follows from the first. It is not enough merely to communicate. Ideas must be convincing enough to impel the consumer to take action. In Chapters 4 and 5 the process of consumer behavior was explained and illustrated. Promotion enters into this process by providing the information or stimulation needed to convince the consumer to reach a decision favorable to the seller. It is one thing to distribute information; it is quite another to do so in a manner that will produce marketing results.

The third important purpose of promotion is to compete. A company's promotional program is the cutting edge of its competitive effort. Carving out a market niche and creating a differential advantage often can be accomplished by effective promotion. A good product, an efficient channel, and an appropriate price seldom are enough. Without a strong promotional element in its marketing strategy, a company's overall marketing program would be dull and unconvincing in contrast to the efforts of its competition. Since the struggle for market share is the principal characteristic of American marketing, it is apparent that whatever contributes to an improved competitive position is an integral part of marketing. Thus, it is the competitive characteristic of promotion that defines its vital role in marketing strategy.

An interesting way of looking at the three purposes of promotion is to inspect the many points at which they can affect consumer behavior. Figure 14.1 (A and B) presents two models that were introduced in Chapter 5: the perception of consumer wants and the consumer decision process. The models are the same as those in the earlier chapter, except that here they identify the various points where promotion might be expected to influence consumer behavior. Brief explanations of how promotion

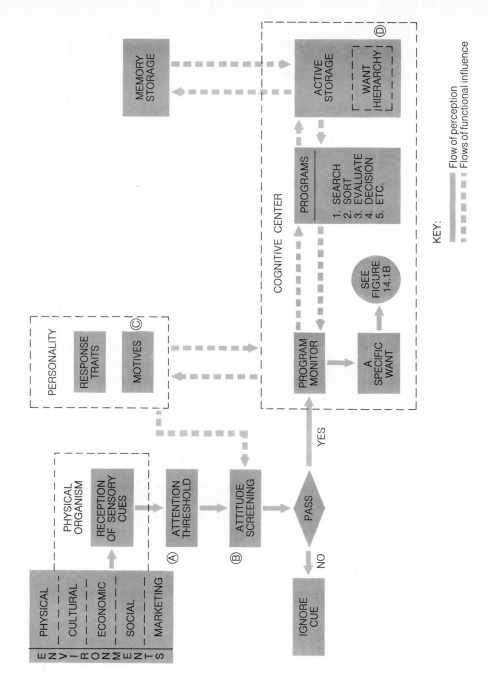

FIGURE 14.1 A. The perception of consumer wants and points where it may be affected by promotion

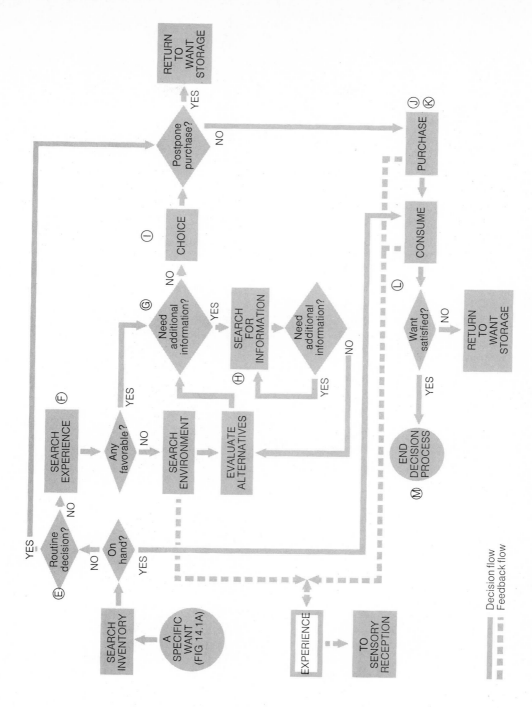

FIGURE 14.1 B. The consumer decision process and points where it may be affected by promotion

Decision flow
Feedback flow

FIGURE 14.1   *(continued)*

A. Promotion (as a want sensory cue) may arouse an awareness of a latent need and transform it ultimately into a perceived want.

B. Promotional messages (as want sensory cues) must pass through an attitude screening in order to establish a perceived want. Promotion also may be directed at altering specific attitudes.

C. Promotional messages (sensory cues) ultimately must affect motives in order to establish a perceived want.

D. Promotional messages may be designed to readjust the hierarchy of wants—for example, to assign a higher priority to a new car than to a new carpet.

E. Promotion often is used to establish routinized buying decisions. Brand insistence is the result of a routine buying decision.

F. So-called reminder promotion is intended to keep the results of favorable past experience fresh in the consumer's thought so that further searching of the environment will not be necessary.

G. Reminder promotion also should convince the buyer that further information is not necessary. At this point, the advantage goes to the seller who has previously done business with the consumer. A seed of doubt, sown by a competitor's promotion, may cause the buyer to seek additional information, however.

H. Promotional messages are part of the buyer's environment. The search of the environment inevitably involves a more or less careful comparison of competitive promotional messages. This information is then used to delineate and evaluate alternative ways to satisfy the perceived want.

I. Information, including what is gleaned from promotional messages, is usually the consumer's basis for evaluating alternative choices.

J. Promotion, especially sales promotion activities, may be designed to produce an *immediate* purchase. On the other hand, a competitor has the last chance to delay the process by urging postponement—for example, "Don't buy any new car until you have seen the new _____."

K. Consummating the purchase agreement is a selling function. Promotional effort usually is required to get the consumer to agree to buy *now*. Personal selling and point-of-purchase advertising are used to close the sale.

L. Sensory cues of satisfactions may be physical or psychological. They do not necessarily rise to a conscious level in the consumer's thought. Satisfaction is usually assumed; dissatisfaction is more likely to be recognized consciously. It is the function of promotion to make consumers *aware of satisfactions*. Promotion also may neutralize any tendency toward postpurchase dissonance.

M. The buying process stops with the establishment of a satisfaction for the perceived want. Promotion does not stop, however. It continues to reinforce the satisfaction in an effort to establish brand insistence. Promotion also begins the decision cycle again by arousing the consumer to a new or recurring need.

affects the perception of wants and the consumer decision process at each lettered point follow the diagrams.

Promotion as a Communications Flow

Communications theory has important applications in promotion.[2] After all, promotion involves the transmission of ideas, and, as we have seen, one of its purposes is to communicate. We will look at this purpose more carefully, since it really incorporates the other two functions of promotion. That is, promotion could neither convince nor compete except through communications.

The flow of promotion communications   Promotion generally involves a *forward* communication flow. Manufacturers promote to wholesalers, retailers, and ultimate consumers. Resellers promote to their customers. Promotion flows also can be horizontal. A firm might direct promotional messages to other companies in its own industry. Per-

[2]For a text devoted to the topic of communications in marketing, see E. Crane, *Marketing Communications* (New York: John Wiley, 1965).

X   FIGURE 14.2   The elements of communication in promotion

haps it wants them to support a particular position regarding a social or political question. Since information tends to flow rather easily among channel components at any given level, it is not unusual to find such information spreading out horizontally. A satisfied or dissatisfied purchasing executive often tells friends in other companies about experiences with particular vendors. The same thing happens on the customer level. Consumers are notoriously inclined to spread marketing information horizontally. In fact, we even talk about word-of-mouth advertising as if it were a type of promotion. However, important as these horizontal flows may be, the kinds of promotion that generally are found in a marketing plan involve vertical forward flows among trading and nontrading components in the marketing channel.

Elements of communication   There are four important elements of communication that help us understand its relation to promotion.

1. The *source* is the originator of the promotion. In terms of promotional strategy, the source is a marketing company that wants to transmit some idea to its customers or resellers.
2. The *message* is the commercial idea being communicated. In selling terms, it is the sales story; in advertising terminology, it is the copy theme. The message is what flows from sender to receiver.
3. The *medium* carries the message. It may be a salesperson, a television commer-

cial, or a piece of literature sent through the mail.
4. The *receiver* is the person, or one of many persons, to whom the message is directed. In most cases the receiver is a potential customer. However, he or she may be a purchase influencer or a reseller, who then becomes a medium to transmit the message to others.

The role of these four communications elements is illustrated in Figure 14.2. The source is an advertiser, for example, Ford Motor Company. The medium, or vehicle, is a national network television show—perhaps, "Monday Night Football." The message is a commercial promoting the company's Mustang II. The receiver is a potential customer in New York City who views the advertisement over WNBC-TV.

Types of promotional communications   The example in Figure 14.2 is an oversimplification of a highly complex mass-communications system. Such a system can be further explained by another figure using three diagrams, which permit the classification of two additional types of promotion flows. Looking at Figure 14.3, we will start with the simplest and work down to the more complicated mass-communications flow.

Specific communications   Specific communications are simplest. They involve the direct transmission of a message from a single source to a single, specific receiver. Sup-

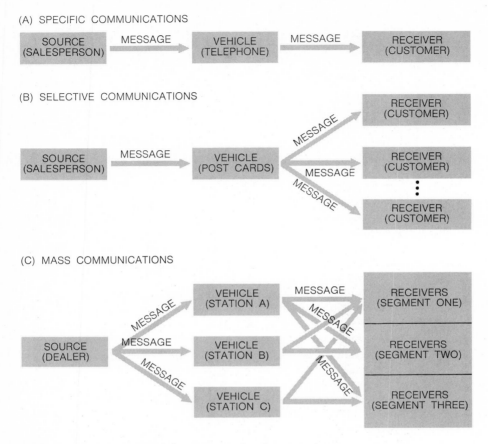

FIGURE 14.3   Three types of communication in promotion

pose, for example, that Joe Malachek, a salesperson working for a Ford dealer in Stamford, Connecticut, telephones a customer who owns a Maverick that had been purchased from Malachek several years before. Malachek thinks that the customer might be ready to trade for a new car, possibly a Fairmont. This specific communication from the source, Joe Malacheck, to his customer is shown in part A.

Selective communications   Selective communications involve the direction of messages through a single vehicle to a limited number of receivers. For example, after Malachek finishes talking on the telephone, he might decide to send a colorful postcard showing the new Fairmont to everybody who purchased intermediate-sized cars from him three years earlier. There might be several dozen such people. Part B of Figure 14.3 illustrates this communications flow.

Mass communications   Mass communications involve the use of one or more vehicles to reach an extremely large number of unknown receivers. Part C of the figure shows such a program. Instead of Malachek being the source, his dealer-employer fills this communications role. Three radio stations are selected as the vehicles to carry a commercial message to the entire market. Each radio station reaches some but not all of the potential customers. However, every potential buyer is exposed to at least one radio station. This is mass communication.

The message form Communication involves the transmission of ideas, not simply words. Of course, words are often used in promotion—usually overused—and the correct use of language is very important to effective promotion. But let us look at other ways in which ideas can be transmitted.

A picture communicates a message very effectively. The abundant use of illustrations in magazine and newspaper advertisements suggests the power of a picture to communicate. Notice how many magazine ads use illustrations that almost fill the entire page.

The spoken word also is an effective communications tool. More than the words themselves, the speaker's voice and interpretation enrich the message and improve its credibility. Likewise, music contributes to effective communication. A hit tune is remembered longer than its lyrics. One justification for the singing commercial is its memorability.

We can understand, then, why television is thought of as the perfect advertising medium. It combines all of the elements of communication—written words, illustrations, spoken words, and music. These are the message forms of a comprehensive promotion program.

Distortion and noise in the promotion channel Not every communication reaches its intended receiver, and some that do are hopelessly distorted. *Distortion* is most likely to occur in long communications flows, where several successive vehicles participate. The use of persons to transmit messages often creates distortion. A manufacturer whose product is purchased and resold first by a wholesaler and then by a retailer really has little control over the sales message that eventually is delivered to the ultimate consumer.

Noise is an even more serious problem. It can arise because of faulty transmission, faulty reception, or interference. A small newspaper advertisement that is crowded in among many others on a cluttered page will certainly be lost because of intereference. Bad reception and interference are even more likely in electronic communications. Consumers are not especially interested in advertising, and as a rule they do not pay close attention to it. They frequently will tune down or turn off the radio or television whenever a commercial starts. The noise level in the communications flow at the receiving end is usually very high.

The loudest and most serious noise results from competitive interference. The typical consumer is simultaneously exposed to many communications flows. Often these are directly competitive. Look at a newspaper and note how many directly competitive advertising messages it contains. In the same way, how many beer commercials do you see in one evening of television watching?

How can a marketer overcome this type of interference? In part, our discussion of promotion strategy will answer that question. For now we can say that one must communicate meaningfully to the right people, at the right time, with the right message. But there is more to effective promotion. It demands conspicuous creativity. It also requires a consistent and persistent effort. The effect of promotion is largely cumulative. The noise at any one time is too great for one to expect immediate results. Over the period of an entire campaign, however, and certainly in the long run, the impact of a well conceived, continuous, and creative promotion program will bear fruit for the marketing manager.

Objectives of Promotion Strategy

Sources of Promotion Objectives

The design of promotion strategy begins with a statement of its objectives. As we shall see, these objectives also become the basis for a subsequent evaluation of the program's success.

Most promotion objectives can be traced directly to broader marketing objectives. However, other forces, both internal and external to a firm, may dictate promotional objectives. It is not uncommon, for example, for such objectives to arise in connection with trade association and public-relations activities. Frequently, a company will participate in a joint promotional effort with other members of the industry's trade association. It also is possible for public- and employee-relations objectives to be translated into promotional objectives. For example, when the Great Atlantic and Pacific Tea Company (A&P) was defending itself in an antitrust action, the company made extensive use of advertising to present its case to the public. In another situation during World War II, when many companies were unable to supply the consumer market, public-relations messages were transmitted through media normally used for product advertising. One of the most famous promo-

tional programs of this sort was developed by Nash-Kelvinator. It encouraged patriotism, especially the purchase of war bonds. Occasionally, when a firm is engaged in negotiations with a labor organization, the company or union may use conventional promotional methods to inform employees and the general public of the company's or union's position in the negotiations. These examples suggest only a few of the many ways in which nonmarketing objectives may be converted into promotional objectives.

Typical Promotion Objectives

The numerous promotional objectives that could be cited might easily fill an entire chapter. The versatility of promotion and the many aspects of corporate activity to which it can be applied create not only a large number but also a wide range of promotional objectives. Here are a few examples.

To increase sales Sales can be increased in different ways. One way is to promote particular products. The objective may be to expand one part of the company's line while holding other parts reasonably firm. Or the objective may require the expansion of sales of all products. Growth in sales also can be achieved by increasing the amount of business done with particular customers. Almost all companies attract more business from some customers than from others. The proportions can be almost staggering. For example, one metal fabricator discovered that 90 per cent of all sales came from only 10 per cent of its customers. In this case, growth in sales obviously could be achieved by increasing sales to those customers accounting for only 10 per cent of company volume. A third way to achieve sales growth is to stimulate sales at particular times. These may be times of the day, week, month, or year. Whenever seasonal fluctuations in sales are encountered, overall sales growth usually is attained when sales are increased during slack periods.

To maintain or improve market share   Success in sales is generally relative to competition. Absolute increases in sales sometimes may obscure the fact that competitors are growing even more rapidly. Thus, it usually is necessary to maintain or improve market share in order to occupy a strong position in the market.

To create or improve brand recognition, acceptance, or insistence   Brand recognition generally precedes both acceptance and demand. And such recognition usually is improved through creative and constructive promotional efforts. In fact, many companies assign a very high priority to creating or improving brand awareness. As self-service and mass distribution through supermarkets became more and more widespread, the need to develop strong consumer demand stimulated the desire for higher and higher levels of brand recognition. The marketing of almost all consumer and many industrial products has been characterized by intensive promotional efforts to create and improve brand position.

To create a favorable climate for future sales   This type of promotional objective is commonly encountered in industrial marketing. It also is pertinent to certain aspects of consumer selling; for instance, the marketing of consumer durables. The promotional objective in such cases is not to create an immediate sales response. Rather, it is to precondition the prospective customer to react favorably to the seller's product when a need for it does arise in the future.

To inform and educate the market   A company's marketing program may be called on to perform a purely educational service. The end result of this effort should be to enhance the sales possibilities of the product; however, the immediate objective is definitely to transmit ideas or instructions to the marketplace. These ideas may relate to almost any topic of importance to the seller, and it usually is through them that nonmarketing objectives are carried out. Informing the public about the company's history, its position with respect to proposed legislation, its arguments in a pending labor negotiation, and the like are all appropriate subjects for transmittal to the public. Of closer concern to marketing might be such subjects as instructions for more efficient use or greater enjoyment in consumption (for example, recipes), helpful hints to improve the consumer's buying process (suggestions as to where and how to shop for certain goods and services), or even ways to save by consuming less (suggestions on energy conservation).

To create a competitive difference   Closely related to favorable brand recognition is the opportunity to create a competitive difference through promotion. Admittedly, the most effective competitive differences are established through product and package. However, the seller also can differentiate the image of a product. This may be the only avenue open to achieve a differential advantage, and the strategist must rely on promotion to accomplish the task.

To improve promotional efficiency   Unfortunately, relatively little is known about the effects of promotion. Because results are difficult to identify, there is reasonable suspicion that too much effort may be committed to the promotional function. For this reason, there usually is considerable interest in improving the efficiency of the promotion program. Since efficiency refers to the relationship between measured input and output, the first step in implementing such an objective is to set up controlled research projects designed to measure advertising effectiveness and ultimately to determine the optimum level of promotional effort.

General Promotional Issues and Problems

There are a number of general issues that must be considered in the development of a promotion strategy. These issues can be identified and resolved. The fact that many businesspeople seem to develop promotion programs on a helter-skelter basis does not mean that a systematic approach cannot be applied to promotional decision making. Considerable progress has been made in perfecting the planning process in promotion management. One of the earliest studies of the Marketing Science Institute (MSI) proposed an "adaptive planning and control sequence."[3]

The Promotion Decision Sequence

Michael Ray has presented a decision sequence for marketing communications.[4] It is

[3]P. J. Robinson and D. J. Luck, *Promotional Decision-Making: Practice and Theory* (New York: McGraw-Hill, 1964), pp. 3–4.

[4]M. L. Ray, "A Decision Sequence Analysis of Developments in Marketing Communications," *Journal of Marketing*, January 1973, pp. 29–38.

shown in Figure 14.4. The major elements in Ray's systematic approach are

1. Analyzing the situation
2. Setting objectives
3. Determining the communications budget
4. Determining the tentative promotion mix
5. Developing the details for each mix element
6. Implementing the decisions
7. Controlling the program

It should be noted that there is considerable similarity between the process shown in Figure 14.4 and the overall approach to market planning developed in Chapter 3. The merit of the system here is that it focuses on the special problems and issues that arise in promotion management. These problems and issues are described in the following pages. The discussion starts with the basic question: Is there an opportunity to promote at all? Subsequent issues and problems focus on fundamental decisions regarding receivers, media, and messages. The problem of how much to spend on promotion and how to allocate this sum to various promotional forms also are reviewed. Finally, the questions of how to approach the measurement of promotional effectiveness and how to organize for efficient promotion management are considered.

Is There a Promotion Opportunity?

Not all companies can make effective use of promotion, as we have noted. Whether the marketing program should rely heavily on promotion depends on the nature and extent of the promotion opportunity. Typically,

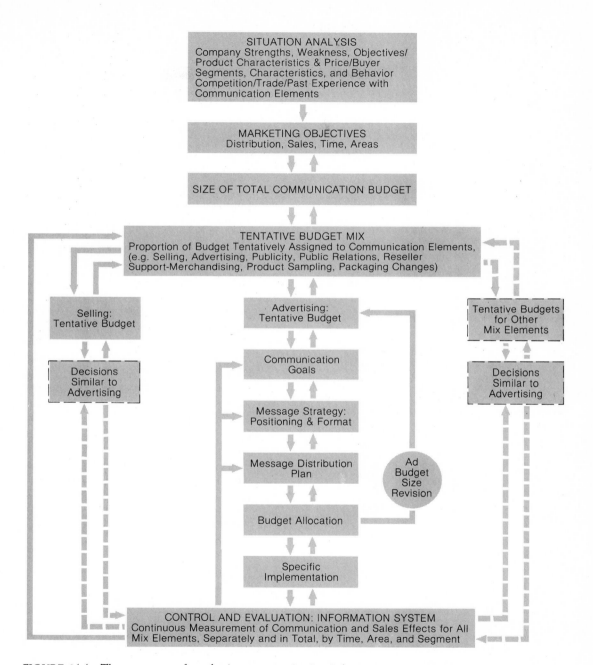

FIGURE 14.4   The sequence of marketing-communication information gathering and decision

Source: Reprinted from "A Decision Sequence Analysis of Developments in Marketing Communications" by M. L. Ray, *Journal of Marketing,* January 1973, p. 31, published by the American Marketing Association.

five key conditions indicate a favorable opportunity to promote. Although these conditions are concerned specifically with the opportunity to advertise, they also tend to create the opportunity to promote generally.

There should be a favorable trend in demand It always is easier to promote effectively when moving *with* the current of consumer demand. Although it is possible to slow down the rate of decline of a product or service for which demand is diminishing, it is unreasonable to hope that promotion alone can reverse such a trend altogether. On the other hand, it has been demonstrated that promotional effort can accelerate an increase in demand if the trend already is favorable. For example, most coffee companies are promoting the sale of their instant coffee rather than the old-style ground variety. The per capita consumption of soluble instant coffee has been increasing, whereas the consumption of the traditional product is on the decline.

There should be strong product differentiation Only if a product or service can be clearly differentiated from competitors' offerings will promotion really be effective. Although one of the objectives of promotion may be to make the best of minor differentiating characteristics, such promotion is bound to be less effective than that which capitalizes on major differences.

There should be some hidden qualities in the product Promotional opportunities are greater when hidden qualities of the product are more important to the consumer than external features that can be readily identified. In order to take advantage of hidden qualities, such as flavor in foods, purity in drugs, and cleaning power in detergents, consumers often rely on brand identification and promotional appeals when making purchase decisions.

Emotional buying motives should exist The opportunity to promote effectively, especially to motivate or convince consumers, increases when strong emotional buying motives are associated with the consumer buying process. Thus, a great deal of promotional effort is designed either to influence consumers' attitudes directly or to change the psychological climate within which purchase decisions are made.

Adequate funds should be available Before a company undertakes a promotional program, sufficient funds must be available. Of course, it is the manager's responsibility to determine how elaborate the program must be and how much it will cost. But unless there are adequate financial resources to develop a program of the scope required, a genuine promotional opportunity does not exist.

Whether this and the other four conditions of a good promotional opportunity exist can be determined by market research. A study of the marketing situation should suggest the nature and extent of the required promotional program and whether the firm can afford it.

To Whom Should We Promote?

This is a vital question in the development of a communications program. Strangely enough, a great deal of promotional effort is undertaken without a clear definition of the promotional target. Too often it is thought that a company's only available approach is mass communications. Nothing could be farther from the truth. The fact is that market segmentation *requires* that promotional messages be directed at the specific target for which the overall marketing program is being designed.

However, this does not mean that the question "To whom should we promote?" can be answered by identifying a single group of consumers. Many individuals affect the buying process, and the promotional program must be designed to reach all of them. In addition to customers and purchasers, purchase influencers also must be considered. For example, consumers usually rely heavily on the assistance of others in purchasing such products as home decoration items, landscaping services, central air conditioning, and medicines. Whether the purchase influencers are interior decorators, landscape architects, consulting engineers, or physicians, promotional effort must be directed to and through these individuals in order to deliver a convincing message to the ultimate users or purchasers. Thus, it is extremely important in resolving the promotional issues to identify accurately not only those who consume and buy the product but also those who influence its purchase.

Selecting the Message

What message should we communicate in order to achieve promotional objectives? The answer to this question may be the key to successful promotion. The heart of promotion is the transmission of ideas. Whether these ideas are received and perceived depends in large part on the skill used in developing the promotional appeal. The good salesperson realizes that it is not enough to know the product and be able to talk about it. Rather, as one author states it

in the subtitle of his book on salesmanship, selling involves "helping prospects buy."[5] The secret of doing this is to offer solutions to their problems. From this follows the importance of understanding consumers' needs. An effective promotional message is not one that describes the seller's product in great detail, but rather one that convinces the buyer that the product will satisfy his or her need. Therefore, choosing the right message is one of the major issues that must be resolved in developing a promotional strategy.

In most cases the promotional planner is not involved personally in the preparation of creative materials, but is responsible for defining the objectives of the promotional message. Creative specialists must be instructed concerning the kind and amount of information or persuasion that is necessary to improve consumer knowledge, alter attitudes, improve brand recognition, and motivate users, purchasers, and purchase influencers. *What* the creative content of promotion should accomplish is the responsibility of the promotion planner. *How* the creative content should accomplish it is the responsibility of copywriters, art directors, and sales promotion specialists.

How Much Should Be Spent on Promotion?

This is one of the most difficult problems in market planning. Promotional effort can involve huge sums of money. For example, a one-page, four-color ad in *Reader's Digest* magazine in 1977 cost $66,295, excluding production costs. A thirty-second television announcement on the CBS network in 1976

[5]C. A. Kirkpatrick, *Salesmanship: Helping Prospects Buy* (Cincinnati: Southwestern Publishing, 1971).

cost about $75,000 for the time alone. Many salespeople are relatively well paid; a good number earn annual incomes of $100,000 or more. The president of a large advertising agency is reported to be the highest paid woman in American business. In spite of these high figures, however, promotion is relatively inexpensive when compared with the other costs involved in manufacturing and marketing. Moreover, the apparently large sums spent for promotional purposes appear much more modest when the number of consumers reached is considered. For example, in 1977 the circulation of *Reader's Digest* was approximately 18.2 million. Accordingly, the cost per reader of a $65,000 advertisement was about $.004. Similarly, if a network television broadcast is seen in 20 million homes, the cost of reaching each household also will be less than a penny. Moreover, when related to the value of products or services sold, promotional expenditures are not exorbitant. Industrial advertisers spend, on the average, less than 1 per cent of sales on advertising and about 5 per cent on all promotion. In selling to the ultimate consumers, the cost of promotion per dollar of sales is larger—usually between 5 and 10 per cent of the final consumer selling price—although, of course, some companies are reported to spend much more.

In theory the determination of how much to spend on promotion should be relatively easy. We would use the marginality principle, selecting the level of spending that equates marginal gross profit and marginal promotion cost. That is, the last dollar spent on promotion produces exactly one dollar of incremental gross margin. In practice, however, this is very difficult to do. In the first place, it is very hard to measure the incremental effect of promotion on sales and profit. Second, it is not always true that the purpose of promotion is to increase income.

It might be, for example, to effect some kind of attitude change. We will look at these problems as they relate to advertising in more detail in Chapter 15.

How Should Promotion Funds Be Allocated?

A second problem that arises in determining how much should be spent on promotion involves the allocation of funds to the various elements of the promotional mix. The amounts to be spent on personal selling, advertising, and sales promotion must be decided. If the overall promotional budget is built up by the determination of the amounts that should be spent on each of these activities, then the allocation of the total among the parts is not difficult, even if some general promotional overhead is incurred. However, if the overall appropriation is determined without reference to the specific activities, the distribution of the total budget to the various parts of the mix is an important issue that must be resolved.

Conceptually it also should be possible to obtain an optimum allocation of the promotional budget by using marginal analysis. This might involve, for example, shifting dollars from personal selling to advertising until no further improvement in sales could be achieved. In other words, assuming the sales results of advertising, selling, and sales promotion could be measured directly, the market planner would allocate funds among these three ingredients in such a way as to equate the sales achieved by the marginal dollar spent on each of them.

Those of you familiar with economic theory will recognize this as a problem of optimum factor combination. The various combinations of advertising and personal selling that will produce a given sales response can be plotted. There would be one

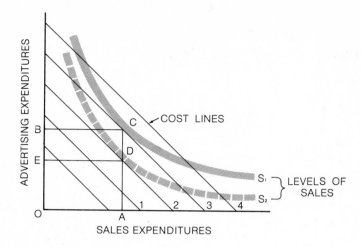

FIGURE 14.5   Allocation of the promotion budget to two factors

such curve for every level of sales. Cost lines showing the various quantities of the two factors that can be purchased with a given promotional outlay also can be plotted. If a certain total sales response is required, the cost line that is just tangent to the relevant factor-combination curve shows the amount of total promotional outlay required and the appropriate promotion mix. Or, viewed in terms of an overall budget constraint, the factor-combination curve that is just tangent to the expenditure line will indicate the allocation of that budget to the two factors and the total level of sales that can be expected. Figure 14.5 illustrates this approach.

Suppose a company wants to achieve a level of sales represented by the solid curve (S_1). This curve is tangent to the promotional budget line 3 at point C. At this point, OA dollars of sales expense and OB dollars of advertising expense would be used. On the other hand, if the company is limited in its available funds to budget line 2, a somewhat lower level of sales can be expected. This level is represented by the broken curve

(S_2). With such a budget, OA dollars of sales expense would still be used, but advertising outlays would be cut back to OE.

Again, it should be noted that the application of this theoretical approach is limited, since it is difficult and expensive to measure promotional effectiveness with the precision required. However, the approach does serve as a conceptual guide in a practical attempt to attain an optimum distribution of funds among the various promotional activities.

Measuring the Results of Promotion

There are three extremely difficult tasks that must be completed when we attempt to measure the results of promotion. First, standards or bench marks for measuring promotional effectiveness must be established. This means that the market planner must have an understanding of exactly what the promotion is intended to accomplish. For measurement purposes, the standards should be identified in specific quantitative terms. Second, actual promotional performance must be monitored. To do this, it usually is necessary to conduct experiments in which the effects of other variables are either excluded or controlled. For example, if the relative efficiency of two different promotional methods is being studied, variations in distribution strategy, pricing, or competitors' behavior should not be allowed to distort the measurements. Indigenous variables usually can be excluded fairly easily. However, the control of exogenous variables is very difficult. Moreover, devices for measuring results other than direct sales response are relatively crude. For instance, sensitive measurements of changes in customer attitudes or brand acceptance are difficult to obtain. The third step in measuring promotional efficiency is to compare the performance measures against the standards. In so doing, it is possible to determine the most effective method of promotion.

The effectiveness of promotion often is assessed at three stages. *Pretests* are conducted during the planning process to determine the most suitable of alternative promotional approaches. *Concurrent tests* are conducted while a promotional program actually is under way. *Posttests* are conducted at the conclusion of the plan to measure the achieved effect of the promotional program after it has been completed.

Organizing for Promotion

The way in which a company organizes for promotion depends first on the degree to which it wants to perform the promotional function internally or to assign this task to outside agencies.[6] Typically, the sales func-

tion is performed internally. Occasionally, as when manufacturer's agents are used, outside organizations are employed to perform personal selling. Advertising services may be performed internally or externally. In part because of a traditional method of agency compensation whereby agencies are paid by advertising media in the form of commissions, such outside organizations usually are retained when commissionable media are employed.[7]

Since direct-mail and point-of-purchase advertising are noncommissionable media, they often are handled internally. Sales promotion activities also usually are developed in house, although it is not uncommon for advertising agencies to be consulted in connection with sales promotion plans. When sales promotion is handled internally, a separate department may be created, or sales promotion may be the responsibility of the advertising manager.

The subject of marketing organization was introduced in Chapter 2. As was indicated, one of the oldest methods of organizing the marketing operation is along functional lines. If a sizable proportion of the advertising function is performed within a firm, an advertising department may be created. The advertising manager may report either to sales or to marketing management. A few advertising departments do most of the work of preparing advertisements, including layout, copy preparation, and even some mechanical procedures, such as the paste-up and printing of direct-mail material. A few also make media buys.

In consumer–packaged goods firms, the

[6]For a discussion of the ways in which the promotion function is organized and implemented, see S. Banks, "Trends Affecting the Implementation of Advertising and Promotion," *Journal of Marketing,* January 1973, pp. 19–28.

[7]Commissionable media include most of those in common use except local newspapers, local radio, direct mail, and point of purchase. Local media frequently establish differential rate structures—those for national advertisers (which are commissionable) and those for local advertisers (which are not commissionable). Recent years have seen a considerable departure from the traditional agency commission arrangement.

product or brand manager system has become very popular. In most cases advertising management is an important part of the product manager's job. In fact, it comprises almost the total responsibility of some brand managers. Where this situation prevails there may be no need for an advertising manager, especially when the brand manager works closely with a full-service advertising agency. On the other hand, some firms maintain an advertising department to supply creative services for the brand managers, to produce collateral material, and even to perform some media buying. There may also be a role for a corporate advertising director to manage this department, to develop corporate (as opposed to brand) advertising, to act as an expert consultant to the brand managers, and to assist in the shaping of overall promotion policies and strategies.

It is also well to realize that the implementation of a new promotional program may require changes in a company's organizational structure. This is most likely when dramatic departures in promotional activity are envisioned. If a company that has been relatively inactive in the promotional area adopts a new marketing strategy involving a heavy promotional commitment, it may be forced for the first time to consider better ways of organizing. For example, in many industrial firms the advertising function is supervised by the sales manager. As advertising and sales promotion become more and more important in the industrial field, however, advertising departments with their own managers tend to develop. In some cases, these managers report directly to the sales manager, while in other cases they have been given more autonomous responsibilities and report to a general marketing executive.

Of course, organizational problems also are involved if a company decides to change the division of promotional tasks between its own staff and outside agencies. An expanded promotional program may mean expanded organizational requirements for both the firm and its advertising agency, or it may imply a shift of responsibility from one to the other. In an experienced marketing company, it is not likely that the development of any one marketing strategy will result in much organizational strain. However, for a new or rapidly expanding company, it is probable that organizational stresses will be felt as market planning reaches the promotional stage. If this occurs, proper attention to future organization and staffing should be made in the proposed marketing plan.

Summary

Promotion in general refers to demand-creating or demand-stimulating activities. Specifically, the tools of promotion are personal selling, advertising, publicity, and sales promotion. Personal selling involves face-to-face communications between buyer and seller. Advertising is the nonpersonal presentation of a promotional message to a group of potential customers. Publicity is similar, but it is not paid for and its source is not identified. Sales promotion is a catchall term that includes all methods of stimulating demand not specifically identified as either personal selling or advertising.

The purposes of promotion are to communicate, convince, and compete. These purposes can be viewed in terms of the various aspects of consumer behavior that they are intended to affect. We found that there is hardly a point in the consumers' perceptive and decision processes that is not influenced, at least to some degree, by the promotional activities of marketing departments or companies.

Promotion is probably best understood as a communications flow from seller to potential customers. Several important elements of the communications flow bear directly on the promotion function. Among these are the source, the message, the medium, and the receiver. For promotion to be effective, a message must flow undistorted from a source to a receiver. In this context, promotion management involves the design and operation of an efficient communications system linking sources and receivers.

Of course, such a system must be designed so that it will attain general and specific company objectives. General objectives may stem from the company's overall goals or from broad marketing objectives. More particularly, promotion may be used to reach such goals as increased sales, improved market position, or strengthened customer awareness or acceptance of a product or brand.

In the development of the promotional plan a number of special issues or problems arise. As these issues and problems are resolved, the promotion strategy takes shape. The first issue that must be faced squarely is whether a particular marketing situation offers the opportunity to promote. Most marketing plans do include an important promotional ingredient; but some do not. Detailed guidelines exist to help the manager appraise the opportunity to stimulate market demand. Most of the other basic promotional issues relate specifically to the communications function of promotion. The manager must decide on a target audience, the message to be communicated, and the media to use.

Promotion is costly, and the manager usually does not have unlimited funds to spend on it. From this arises the necessity of allocating resources to the various elements in the promotion mix. Partly because of the considerable investment involved and partly because of the importance of promotion in the marketing program, the manager also needs to evaluate the effectiveness of the promotional plan. Promotion results can be measured in various ways. Unfortunately, no method is completely reliable, and considerable argument still exists as to the overall effectiveness of demand-creating activities in marketing.

A final issue in promotion involves the proper method of organizing the function. Much promotional activity is assigned to specialist firms, such as advertising agencies and sales promotion companies. Recently, in some companies the responsibility for developing promotion strategy has been placed in the hands of the product or brand manager.

Questions and Problems

1. Why does the author suggest that the development of promotion strategy pushes the planner to the "very frontiers of marketing knowledge"?

2. On the basis of your concept of consumer behavior, do you believe that promotion can create or stimulate demand? Explain your position.

3. Suppose you were asked to make suggestions on how sales promotion might be used to stimulate business for a local automobile agency. What kinds of things would you recommend? If the business had been a bank, would you have answered the same way? Explain any differences.

4. In early 1978 the Department of

Health, Education, and Welfare announced a $20 million campaign to discourage smoking. What do you think of the idea of using promotion to destroy demand? What problems do you think this campaign will face? What promotion mix would you recommend?

5. Many energy companies (oil companies, public utilities, and the like) have been subjected to considerable public hostility—principally because of the ever-increasing rates charged for their products and services. Assume you are the marketing director of an investor-owned (not municipally owned) electric utility. You have two objectives: (1) to convince people that the utility has not been charging exploitive rates, and (2) to persuade customers to conserve energy by using less electricity. What promotion tools would you use? How effective do you think they would be?

6. Why do you think a number of important supermarket chains have abandoned trading stamps in the past few years?

7. Consider a recent purchase that you have made. Identify all of the marketer-supplied information that was provided to you. Can you determine whether each item of information was intended to communicate, to convince, or to compete?

8. Suggest ways in which the concepts of specific, selective, and mass communications might be used by a department store in planning its promotion of summer furniture.

9. In what ways do the objectives of a promotion program relate to the problem of measuring its results? In your answer, give examples of specific objectives for which promotion might be used.

10. An executive of an advertising agency is in charge of several different advertisers' accounts. She is considering the promotion opportunity available to each of the accounts she handles. These include
    a. A medicated soap for dry skin
    b. A local ice-cream company
    c. A national computer software company
    d. A regional not-for-profit hospital insurance plan
    e. A national marketer of hydraulic brake fluid for automobiles and trucks
    f. A feeder airline

What is your opinion of the opportunity to promote each of these products or services?

11. Marketing managers often challenge their product managers and advertising agencies to come up with "the big idea." What they are looking for is a fresh message. Can you suggest any method by which a promotion executive might start to create a big idea?

12. A marketing consultant was nearly fired on the spot when he suggested to a company that it could decrease its selling expense by increasing its advertising outlays. Fortunately, he was able to explain what he meant. How would you go about explaining his statement?

15

Promotion Strategy:
Special Issues
in Advertising

It has been traditional in marketing textbooks to give separate consideration to the topics of advertising and selling in order to make the subject of promotion more manageable. Moreover, selling and advertising are different, and each is important enough to warrant individual consideration. The differences between them fall into two categories. There are task differences and organizational differences. The task of selling and the problems that arise in carrying it out primarily involve interpersonal relations. These relations may be between the salesperson and customers or between the salesperson and the sales manager. The tasks and problems of advertising also involve people, but the emphasis is not so much on interpersonal relations as it is on mass communications. The distinction is a fine one, but it lends support to another reason for separating the two topics. This is the fact that historically the selling and advertising functions have been separated organizationally.

In this chapter we address some of the special problems and issues that arise in the area of advertising. As mentioned above these issues tend not to be as personal as those of sales management. Of course, people are involved in advertising, and the management of them does create some interesting challenges. But the human-relations problems are not predominant. Rather, the advertising issues involve problems of mass communications, concerned principally with messages and media. We have already touched on some aspects of these issues in Chapter 14. We will now look at them in more detail.

Defining Advertising Goals

If advertising can be said to have a goal apart from its contribution to the overall marketing effort, it must be to communicate. Indirectly, of course, advertising does influence sales; and in an instance such as a mail-order business, it is a principal means of selling. But for the most part, advertising makes its contribution to sales indirectly by performing two powerful assists. It *conditions* and it *reinforces*. Advertising helps prepare the way for the salesperson by informing the prospective customer of the values of the company's products or services. It may even lead the customer up to the very point of conviction, so that there is little or no obstacle to closing the sale. Moreover, advertising reinforces the sales effort by bringing powerful reminders to bear after the sales presentation has been made. To a customer who already has purchased, such advertising combats incipient dissonance. To a prospect who has not yet decided to buy, such advertising keeps up the communications pressure. Of course, this reinforcement has a continuous effect and becomes, in turn, a conditioning for the next personal sales visit.

These effects of advertising on actual and potential customers have been stated in different terms by R. H. Colley and others.[1] Colley's perspective is built on the idea that potential customers must move through several stages of awareness before they are ready to buy.[2] The total population of potential customers can be distributed accord-

[1] Colley's model is found in R. H. Colley, *Defining Advertising Goals for Measured Advertising Results* (New York: Association of National Advertisers, 1961), pp. 56–61. We previously discussed the adoption process posed by E. M. Rogers. Lavidge and Steiner introduced a hierarchy of effects model at about the same time as Colley's work was done. See R. L. Lavidge and G. A. Steiner, "A Model for Predictive Measurements of Advertising Effects," *Journal of Marketing,* October 1961, p. 61.

[2] The hierarchy of effects model has been challenged on two counts: first, that a hierarchy exists at all; second, that the effects are exclusively in the direction described. Most advertising people, however, continue to accept the underlying concept. For a brief but well documented review of the controversy, see D. A. Aaker and J. G. Myers, *Advertising Management* (Englewood Cliffs, N.J.: Prentice-Hall, 1975), pp. 114–117.

ing to these stages. The goal of advertising is to change this distribution—to move potential customers toward the stages of conviction and actual use. The Colley classification of awareness levels is shown in Figure 15.1.

A combination of the conviction-reinforcement concepts of advertising with the idea of awareness levels is shown in Figure 15.2. Here we see the awareness scheme as a barometer of a particular prospect's interest through 16 periods. Let us assume that a company has not aggressively advertised its product and that the prospective buyer has not been exposed to the little advertising that has appeared. A salesperson calls in period 1. The customer's awareness level is very low and the prospect refuses even to see the salesperson. No contact is made, although the salesperson leaves some company literature. Awareness rises slightly but falls again after the literature is filed away. Let us assume that advertising begins in period 3 (solid line) and continues until the salesperson makes a second call in period 5. This time the prospective buyer knows something about the company and its products and sees the salesperson. Awareness rises even higher but no sale results. After the visit, the advertising continues, and on the next trip to the customer in period 10, a sale is consummated. Following this sale, we see two possibilities. One is that the advertising continues and holds the customer in the conviction stage until the salesperson's next visit, when a repeat sale occurs. The other is that the customer's experience with the product is not completely satisfying. Conviction wanes for a while, but the next series of advertisements dispels the dissonance and the awareness level recovers.

The broken line in Figure 15.2 suggests what the awareness level of this same customer might have been without advertising to condition and reinforce. In such a situation, each successive sales call raises the

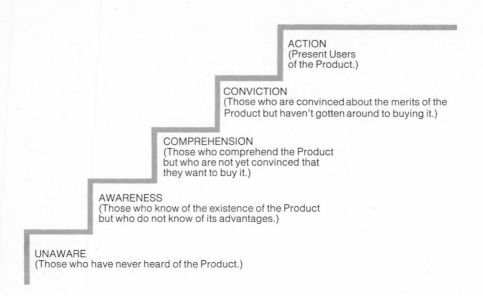

ACTION
(Present Users
of the Product.)

CONVICTION
(Those who are convinced about the merits of the
Product but haven't gotten around to buying it.)

COMPREHENSION
(Those who comprehend the Product
but who are not yet convinced that
they want to buy it.)

AWARENESS
(Those who know of the existence of the Product
but who do not know of its advantages.)

UNAWARE
(Those who have never heard of the Product.)

FIGURE 15.1   Awareness levels

Source: R. H. Colley, *Defining Advertising Goals for Measured Advertising Results* (New York: Association of National Advertisers, 1961), pp. 55–61.

level of awareness, but the four calls are not enough to bring the prospect to the point of action. We might expect this point to be reached eventually—perhaps in another eight or ten periods, if the present trend continues.

Although this example is purely hypothetical, it does suggest the effect that a consistent program of advertising can have on sales. It also points up the importance of having advertising goals coordinated with those of personal selling and, indeed, with those of the entire marketing program.

Determining the Advertising Budget

The high cost of promotion was mentioned in Chapter 14. Keeping the cost of advertis-

ing in line with the general marketing plan and obtaining maximum effectiveness for each dollar spent are extremely important considerations. Over the years, many methods of setting an advertising budget have been suggested. Each has advantages and limitations. All have been used by at least a few companies. However, only one—the task method—fits neatly into the systematic approach to promotional planning presented in this text. The task method, moreover, generally is recognized to be the most desirable. Before we can understand its advantages, however, we must look briefly at some of the other methods of determining an advertising budget.

The Marginal Approach

From a purely theoretical standpoint, the advertising appropriation should be set at

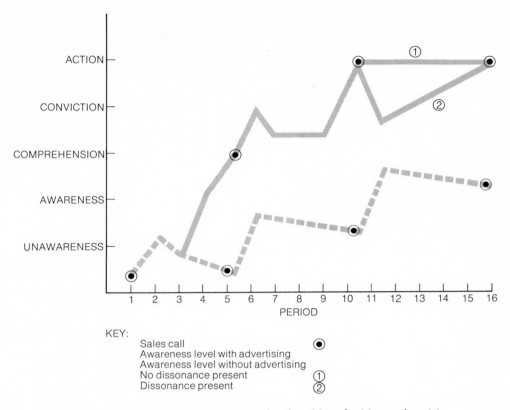

FIGURE 15.2   Changing a prospect's awareness level—with and without advertising

the level at which the last dollar spent exactly equals the incremental profit resulting from the effort. Figure 15.3 presents the application of the marginal approach to an advertising budget. In this particular example, we assume that marginal gross profit (selling price minus marginal manufacturing costs) is constant and that sales increases are associated with incremental advertising effort. Because of the increasing and then decreasing marginal productivity of advertising, marginal advertising cost is shown as a U-shaped curve. In the figure, advertising is

expanded until sales of Q units are obtained. At this sales level, marginal cost is equal to marginal gross profit, and profits are maximized. The total appropriation for promotion is determined by the area under the marginal advertising-cost curve.

The task of setting the advertising budget by the marginal approach is not nearly as simple as the preceding discussion might imply. Measurement of the effect of advertising on sales is extremely difficult, but some progress has been made and several econometric models of the advertising

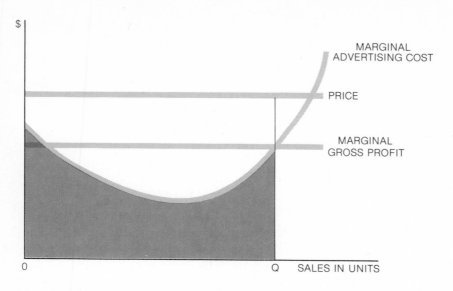

FIGURE 15.3   The marginal approach to setting the advertising budget

response function have been developed.[3] The difficulty is not simply that of trying to isolate the effect of a single determinant—although this is a serious measurement problem. In addition, there exists the fact that advertising results in any given period are affected by the carry-over effects of advertising done in previous periods. One of the first attempts to deal with this problem was the classic study by K. S. Palda, who attempted to measure the cumulative effect of advertising on the sales of a patent medicine.[4] The marketer of this product did not

[3]See V. R. Rao, "Alternative Econometric Models of Sales Advertising Relationships," *Journal of Marketing Research,* May 1972, pp. 177–181.

[4]K. S. Palda, *The Measurement of Cumulative Advertising Effect* (Englewood Cliffs, N.J.: Prentice-Hall, 1964), p. 80. A good discussion of advertising's delayed effects is also contained in J. Simon, *The Management of Advertising* (Englewood Cliffs, N.J.: Prentice-Hall, 1971), pp. 37–46. Recent treatments include D. A. Clarke, "Econometric Measurement of the Duration of Advertising Effect on Sales," *Journal of Marketing Research,* Novem-

employ most of the other elements of the marketing mix and spent approximately half of the product's sales revenue on advertising. Competitive action was minimal, moreover, since there were no close substitutes. By the use of a regression equation that incorporated the lagged effects of advertising, Palda was able to determine that each dollar of advertising generated only $.50 in additional sales in the short run, but produced $1.63 in sales in the long run. Clearly, this company was justified in its long-run policy of heavy advertising. It was also blessed with the option of making use of the marginal approach in setting its advertising budget. Not many firms are so fortunate. In fact most must resort to other methods.

ber 1976, pp. 354–357; and C. S. Craig, B. Sternthal, and C. Leavitt, "Advertising Wearout: An Experimental Analysis," *Journal of Marketing Research,* November 1976, pp. 365–372.

Arbitrary Approaches

Surprisingly, some marketing planners determine the amount to be spent on advertising by various arbitrary methods. There is no rationale for the amount spent other than that it is a sum that management is ready to approve. A statement such as "We never spend more than $100,000 a year on advertising" is typical of this approach. The approach ordinarily is used by management to limit the funds that can be directed into the promotional mix. In some instances, however, the arbitrary amount actually may exceed the sum that might be budgeted with some other approach.

A classic example of an arbitrary promotional appropriation was the decision of the famed Philadelphia merchant John Wanamaker to spend 100 per cent of gross receipts at the close of the first day of business in his new store on advertising for the next day.[5] The following sections detail several other arbitrary approaches.

Available-funds approach The commitment of available funds to promotion is an arbitrary and conservative appropriations approach. Sometimes it takes the form of committing dollars to all other manufacturing and marketing activities and then, if any money remains, spending the balance on advertising. This might be called the *total residual method.* Another form of the available-funds approach is the *cash residual method.* A firm in a weak cash position gener-

ally is not inclined to spend very much on advertising, although occasionally, as in the Wanamaker example above, a firm actually may spend all of its available dollars on promotion. There is no reason to assume that the available-funds approach produces the right budget, except by the purest coincidence. It might actually be wasteful, committing more dollars than needed. More likely, however, it generates too few dollars. It is generally assumed that a certain minimum level of spending is necessary to have any effect at all.[6] This is called the *threshold spending level* and it differs considerably from one marketing situation to the next. The threshold level is relatively high for consumer packaged goods, which are advertised in noise-laden communications systems. It is quite low for industrial products.

Competitive-parity approach One of the common criticisms of marketing is that many companies appear to match each other's advertising expenditures year after year on an ever-increasing scale. There is the implication that these firms, and the economy, would be better off if less were spent on advertising. Although such a conclusion might be valid, it would be next to impossible to persuade any firm to reduce its advertising effort unless all competitors agreed to do so. Making the reductions permanent would be even harder. The reasons for this reluctance to cut back on advertising outlays are rooted in the importance of maintaining market share. Many companies feel that in order to maintain market share they should spend at least as much on promotion as do their competitors. The effort to increase

---

[5]It was this same merchant who later was heard to say that he suspected half of the money spent on advertising was wasted. When asked why he didn't cut the ad budget in half, Wanamaker responded, "I can't because I don't know which half is productive and which half is wasteful." This bit of folklore appears to justify the larger arbitrary amount. Actually, it is a strong argument for the use of a marginal approach.

[6]See H. E. Krugman, "What Makes Advertising Effective," *Harvard Business Review,* March-April 1975, pp. 96–103.

share necessarily involves an even greater expenditure of funds. Since any increased promotional effort will probably be matched, it is more than likely that the budgets approved by each firm will be based on estimates of the amounts to be spent by other firms in the industry.[7]

Such a competitive parity approach might seem to imply that each competitor spends the same amount on promotion. This might be true in some cases. However, the approach also is applicable where different levels of promotional expenditure are involved. If, for example, GM increases its appropriation, it is quite probable that Ford will also increase its appropriation, either by a similar amount or by a similar proportion. In this way, market share should be stabilized even though the firms may spend different amounts on promotional activities.

Percentage-of-sales approach   The most traditional and also the easiest approach to setting the advertising budget is to designate a fixed percentage of sales. On the assumption that the money for advertising must be earned before it can be spent, this percentage frequently is computed on *last year's sales.* Thus, the method has the effect of accelerating advertising when sales are on the increase and of retracting it when sales are declining.

However, it is difficult to justify setting a promotional budget on the basis of sales in a previous period if the promotional effort is designed to affect future sales. Accordingly, many companies appropriate for advertising purposes by applying a fixed percentage to

forecasted sales. Using a percentage of forecasted sales is a fairly effective method of setting the promotional budget. It certainly is an improvement over the other arbitrary approaches mentioned to this point. However, it is based on the assumption that there is a direct relationship between advertising expenditures and sales. It assumes, for example, that if increased sales of 10 per cent are forecast, a 10 per cent increase in advertising also will be required. This may or may not be realistic, depending on such factors as the stage of the product in its life cycle, the level of the economy, competitors' marketing programs, and the overall strategy employed.

Fixed-sum-per-unit approach   This method is similar to the percentage-of-sales approach, except that a specific amount per unit is appropriated rather than a percentage of the dollar value of sales. The advertising appropriation may be based on units sold in a previous period or on a forecast of unit sales in a future period. The advantage of using a fixed sum per unit is that the appropriation for promotional purposes is not affected by changes in pricing strategy. If the appropriation, for example, were based on 10 per cent of an average selling price of $100, as could be the case in the percentage-of-sales approach, $10 would be spent for advertising. If the price were reduced to $90, the appropriation according to this method would be correspondingly lowered to $9 per unit. A fixed sum of $10 per unit, on the other hand, would leave the promotional budget unaffected. The fixed-sum method frequently is used in determining the advertising appropriations for industrial products and consumer durables, notably automobiles.

[7]For an interesting discussion of the high cost of the competition for market share, see W. E. Fruhan, Jr., "Pyrrhic Victories in the Fight for Market Share," *Harvard Business Review,* September-October 1972, pp. 100–107.

The Return-on-Investment Approach

The ROI approach in marketing has long been recognized as a theoretical ideal. It considers the advertising appropriations as an *investment* rather than as a current expense. Ideally, the amount to be appropriated for advertising should be based on the maximization of profits over a product's life cycle. The application of the technique demands that the planner forecast alternative revenues and costs for different levels of advertising. This method is comparable to a capital-budgeting decision. The promotion planner chooses between the alternative budgets by comparing the rate of return anticipated from each. The great difficulty of forecasting a product's life-cycle sales and the common disinclination to treat advertising outlays as investment expenditures, however, make the ROI method of little practical value in setting promotional budgets.

The Task-Method Approach

In view of the weaknesses and limitations in the other budget approaches, a comprehensive four-step budget procedure has been developed. The procedure emphasizes the tasks involved in constructing a promotional strategy. The four steps of this method are

1. *Conduct research* Make an analysis of the marketing situation to uncover the factual basis for the overall marketing and advertising approaches. Marketing opportunities and specific marketing targets for strategic development would be identified.
2. *Determine objectives* Set clear-cut short- and long-run advertising objectives.

3. *Identify the advertising tasks* Determine the message and media utilization required to achieve the advertising objectives.
4. *"Cost out" the advertising tasks* Estimate the cost of carrying out the tasks involved in the strategy. For example, the media schedule easily can be converted into an advertising budget by adding space or time costs to the cost of preparing the advertising materials.

Selecting Advertising Media

Decisions about the media to be used to transmit advertising messages are among the most important choices that an advertising manager must make. Not only do media decisions determine whom the messages will reach, but also the medium itself often influences the effect of advertising. In other words, the medium transmits the message, but it also adds or detracts something. For example, the strong impact of television advertising may result more from the power of that medium than from the actual message transmitted. Another reason why media decisions are so important is that media costs are the largest single item of expense in the advertising budget.

Media Classifications

Advertising methods vary tremendously from one medium to another. The greatest contrasts are found in comparisons of such obviously different media as newspapers and television. Similar but less dramatic differences, of both a functional and a mechanical nature, also are apparent among the other media, and sometimes they exist even within subgroups of a particular medium. For example, the mechanical preparations required for an advertisement in a supplement section of a Sunday newspaper are quite different from those required for a daily newspaper advertisement. Separate advertisements might have to be prepared for the *Reader's Digest* and for *Time* magazine because of the differences in page size. Let us look at some differences both within and among the major advertising media more carefully.

Newspapers Although newspapers are probably the oldest advertising medium, they are not nearly so standardized as we might suspect. There are daily newspapers, newspapers published exclusively on Saturday or Sunday, weekly newspapers, religious newspapers, foreign-language newspapers, and newspaper-distributed magazines, such as the Sunday supplements. Moreover, there is even a great deal of variation among daily newspapers. Some are published in the morning, and some in the evening. They range in size from the standard 15 inch by 23 inch to the smaller tabloid. In addition, daily newspapers can be local, regional, or national in circulation. Furthermore, some newspapers accept ads in color, while others are not equipped to handle them. We could expand this list of differences among daily newspapers, but it is sufficient to dramatize the variety that we encounter even within a single advertising medium.

Magazines There is even greater variety among magazines than among newspapers. These are classified first on the basis of general audience characteristics. The major categories are (a) consumer magazines, (b)

trade (business) papers, and (c) farm publications. Each of these major categories is then further subdivided into component groups.

Among the most important groups of consumer magazines are (1) mass-audience magazines, such as *Reader's Digest;* (2) special-audience magazines, such as *True Story, Playboy,* and *The New Yorker;* (3) shelter publications, such as *Good Housekeeping* and *Better Homes and Gardens;* and (4) special-interest magazines, such as *Popular Mechanics, Yachting,* and *Hot Rod.*

We can subdivide trade (business) papers into (1) general-audience publications, such as *Business Week* and *Fortune;* (2) vertical publications concerned with a particular industry, such as *Food Topics* and *Iron Age;* and (3) horizontal publications aimed at a given level of the trade channel, such as *Chain Store Age, Hardware Retailer,* and *Purchasing.*

Radio Although television programming has largely replaced network radio, local radio continues to be a very important advertising medium. It is less expensive than television and offers the advantage of being able to reach potential customers in their cars, at the beach, and other places where television has little or no impact.

Television Television ranks high among advertising media, but it is not as important as most consumers tend to believe. In terms of dollars spent, television still ranks behind newspapers. Like radio, television can be subdivided into *spot* (local) and network (national) broadcasting.

Direct mail Any type of mailing, whether a postcard or an elaborate brochure, is classified as direct-mail advertising. Direct mail is an extremely versatile form that can be used by all advertisers, large or small, and local, regional, or national.

Outdoor (billboard) advertising In spite of considerable public pressure to remove outdoor advertising from American highways, signs and billboards continue to be an important advertising medium. Much outdoor advertising is local in nature, but national coverage also can be obtained. Three types of outdoor advertisements are commonly used. The *thirty-sheet poster* is the standard form. The advertisement is printed on sheets of paper that are pasted on large wooden or metal frames. Such a display generally remains in good condition for at least thirty days. The advertiser can purchase different intensities of exposure, contracting for 25, 50, or 100 gross rating points—meaning 25, 50, or 100 per cent of the potential market. A 100 showing in Chicago would mean approximately three hundred posters; in Peoria, it would mean about forty. *Painted posters,* some of which are rotated every five or six weeks within a market by relocation of the entire display, are the second type of outdoor advertising. The third important version is the *electric spectacular,* such as seen in New York's Times Square. Stunning novel effects are obtained by the use of motion, sound, smoke, and other dramatic devices.

Transportation advertising Transportation advertising displays advertising material inside public transportation vehicles, attached to the outside of moving vehicles, or on the walls of subway stations, airport terminals, and the like. The interior transportation advertising frequently takes the form of *car cards.* Wrigley's chewing gum, for example, has been extensively advertised in this way.

The exterior or traveling displays appear on sides of buses, on the backs of taxicabs, and on panels attached to delivery vehicles.

Point-of-purchase advertising It is extremely difficult to distinguish between point-of-purchase advertising and sales promotion devices. However, since most advertisers closely coordinate point-of-purchase advertising with media promotion, the display material involved usually is considered part of the advertising program. Such point-of-purchase materials may include advertising attached to the package, window banners, simple or elaborate stages for displaying merchandise, "shelf talkers," merchandise tags, package stuffers, and information booklets.

Miscellaneous advertising media This classification is a catchall for all the other advertising media. These include motion-picture advertising, advertising specialties, house organs, *Yellow Pages* listings in the classified telephone directory, sky writing, and so on. This list covers most of the other familiar advertising media, but new methods of advertising constantly are being conceived and used experimentally. Others pass quickly away. The famous Burma-Shave signs are a good example.[8] In the days when lighter-than-air aircraft were common, advertising often was seen on the sides of blimps. A shoe store in a large metropolitan area once attracted a good deal of attention (and indignation from the city's street department) by painting large yellow footprints leading from

[8] For a popularized version of this bit of Americana, see W. K. Zinsser, "Good-Bye Burma-Shave," *Reader's Digest,* February 1965, pp. 203–206. The article ends with a typical jingle: "If you / don't know / whose signs / these are / you can't have / driven very far . . . Burma Shave."

TABLE 15.1   U.S. advertising volume according to media in 1950, 1960, 1970, and 1975
(Millions of dollars and per cent of total)

Medium	1950		1960		1970		1975	
Newspapers	2,076	36.3	3,703	31.0	5,745	29.3	8,450	29.8
Magazines								
Consumer	515	9.0	909	7.6	1,292	6.6	1,475	5.2
Business	251	4.4	609	5.1	740	3.8	920	3.3
Farm	21	.4	32	.3	n.a.	—	75	0.3
Television	121	3.0	1,590	13.3	3,596	18.3	5,325	18.8
Radio	605	10.6	692	5.8	1,308	6.7	2,020	7.1
Direct Mail	803	14.1	1,830	15.3	2,766	14.1	4,125	14.6
Outdoor	143	2.5	203	1.7	234	1.2	340	1.2
Miscellaneous*	1,125	19.7	2,364	19.8	3,919	20.0	5,590	19.7
	5,710	100.0	11,932	100.0	19,600	100.0	25,320	100.0

*Miscellaneous includes internal advertising-department expenditures, weekly newspapers, transportation advertising, point-of-purchase advertising, and all other categories not specified.

Source: 1950 and 1960 from *Printer's Ink;* 1970 and 1975 from *Advertising Age,* reprinted with permission from the 1970 and 1975 issues of *Advertising Age.* Copyright 1970, 1975 by Crain Communications.

a nearby intersection to the store entrance. You also may remember the familiar "sandwich man," carrying advertisements on panels hung over his shoulders. In one large city, the eight-pony hitch wagons of a brewery and of a local dairy still are fairly common sights. Obviously, these miscellaneous media are closely related to sales promotion and might properly be considered in that category as well.

A helpful summary of advertising media is found in Table 15.1. This table shows the dollars spent in the United States on the various media in selected years. The table also dramatizes the tremendous increases in advertising outlay since 1940. This outlay more than doubled between 1940 and 1950. From 1950 to 1964, volume increased by 145 per cent—faster than the rise in gross national product. The changing shape of the consumer-goods media mix also is indicated in the table. Radio (principally network), newspapers, magazines, and outdoor adver-

tising all increased in dollars expended but declined in relative importance, as television rose from insignificance in 1950 to become the second most important medium in 1975.

Selecting the Media Mix

Different advertising media require different types of messages. A message to be used in a radio commercial probably will be very different from one to be used on an outdoor poster. The medium, therefore, must be determined before an advertising message can be created.

In selecting the type of media to be used, a marketing approach should be followed. In exactly the same way that a planner develops a channel of distribution, so a media plan is conceived. It should not be hard to see why there is a great deal of similarity between the channel of distribution and the promotional channel. Both are subsystems involving components linked by specific flows. It is quite obvious, moreover, that the selection of media is not very different from the selection of resellers. The choice should be based on an understanding of how consumers, users, and purchase influencers receive information. A misconception somewhat like the shipping-platform approach must be avoided in selecting promotional media. Rather than asking, "In what magazines shall we advertise?" the promotion planner should ask, "With which advertising media (including magazines, newspapers, television, and so forth) do our ultimate users, purchasers, and purchase influencers come into contact?" For example, it is more important to know that ultimate users read *Time* magazine than for the advertiser to prefer some other publication because of its more sophisticated literary content. This is exactly the same way that a planner develops a channel system. The advertising planner works backward from the consumer in the selection of media, always matching the characteristics of users, purchasers, and purchase influencers with the audience characteristics of alternative media.

It is well to remember in connection with selecting media that dealer promotion often is required. Such dealer promotion falls into two categories. First, promotional effort may be aimed directly at resellers as a part of the general program to stimulate sales and to build a distribution system. This is called *advertising to the trade*. Promoting to the trade is designed to inform resellers about the manufacturer and the product line. It normally includes strong motivational appeals that relate directly to the reseller. Furthermore, promotion to the trade emphasizes such product service features as profit margin, merchandise turnover, and selling assistance provided by the manufacturer.

The second category of promotion that involves channel components is referred to as *advertising through the trade*. When the manufacturer advertises through the trade, the reseller becomes a type of promotion medium. A good example is the use of point-of-purchase advertising. The dealer displays banners, counter cards, shelf talkers, or special merchandise arrangements prepared by the manufacturer. Often, the dealer *readvertises* the manufacturer's product under the terms of a cooperative advertising agreement. To facilitate such an agreement, the manufacturer may prepare sample advertisements, radio commercials, videotapes, films, or transparencies for use by the reseller. It is interesting to note that this type of advertising serves two important purposes: First, it extends the manufacturer's advertising effort to ultimate users, purchasers, and purchase influencers; and, second, it develops dealer interest and goodwill.

Cost per reader Thus far we have been concerned with the qualitative aspects of media selection. Can quantitative evaluations be made? Indeed they can, and one criterion that has been used is the cost-per-reader criterion. An example of this was mentioned in Chapter 14 where the cost per reader of the *Reader's Digest* advertisement was about $.004. The more commonly used measure is *cost per thousand* (CPM). We compute the CPM as follows:

$$CPM = \frac{\text{page rate} \times 1,000}{\text{circulation}}$$

The cost per thousand for a four-color page in *Reader's Digest* in 1977 was $3.65. We calculate this by multiplying $66,295 (four-color-page cost) by 1,000, and dividing that

TABLE 15.2   Advertising cost per thousand for selected magazines

Magazine	Cost*	Circulation	CPM
Time	$53,195	4,522,776	$11.76
Newsweek	38,160	3,012,945	12.66
Sports Illustrated	34,010	2,310,897	14.72
Esquire	14,000	1,079,253	12.97
U.S. News & World Report	26,420	2,056,991	12.84
Psychology Today	17,595	1,108,822	15.86

*One-time cost for a full-page, four-color ad.
Source: Standard Rate and Data, *Consumer and Farm Magazines,* January 1977.

figure by 18.2 million (circulation). Because of the much lower price per unit of purchase, the per-reader cost for newspapers is the milline rate, or the line rate multiplied by 1 million and then divided by the circulation.

Presumably the marketing planner selects among available media vehicles those with the lowest cost per reader. Suppose qualitative analysis indicates that four magazines might be appropriate. The cost per thousand is calculated for each and the magazines ranked accordingly. Table 15.2 shows the cost of a single (one-time) insertion of a one-page, four-color advertisement in each of six general and news-oriented magazines. The total circulation and the cost per thousand are also given. On the basis of CPM figures, *Time* at $53,195.00 per page is the best buy with a CPM of $11.76. *Psychology Today* ranks sixth at $15.86, even though its page cost is about one third that of *Time*. Other things being equal, *Time* would be the first choice, followed by *Newsweek*.

But other things are seldom equal. Perhaps the advertiser can't afford $53,000. More important, suppose the campaign is intended for a special audience—say male college graduates, thirty-five years and older, with median income of $35,000.

Esquire might be a much better choice if its circulation is dominated by these kinds of readers. Or, suppose an ad is for a Head tennis racquet? The relatively high CPM for *Sports Illustrated* might not discourage the media planner in this instance, because of the magazine's superior editorial environment.

Probably the most damaging criticism of the cost-per-reader criterion is that it is an average and not a marginal value. Suppose that an ad manager, using the CPM data in Table 15.2, selects *Time*. Suppose also that the plan calls for three ads, not just one. Moreover, let's suppose that only a fourth of the readers actually are exposed to a given ad. We call this the *reach* of the vehicle. Now we can estimate the CPM for *new* readers for each ad.

	Cost	Reach	CPM
1st insertion	$53,195	1,130,694	$47.05
2d insertion	53,195	848,021	62.73
3d insertion	53,195	636,015	83.64

Making the same assumption about *Newsweek,* we can calculate the CPM for new readers as follows:

	Cost	Reach	CPM
1st insertion	$38,160	753,236	$50.66
2d insertion	38,160	564,927	67.55
3d insertion	38,160	423,696	90.06

On the basis of these numbers, the manager would place two insertions in *Time* and one in *Newsweek,* in this order: *Time, Newsweek, Time*—always selecting the magazine with the lowest incremental CPM. The improvement over three insertions in *Time* is noticeable.

	Total cost	Total reach	CPM
3 insertions in *Time*	$159,585	2,614,730	$61.03
2 insertions in *Time* and 1 in *Newsweek*	144,550	2,731,951	52.91

Of course, this analysis assumes that *Time* and *Newsweek* reach entirely separate audiences—which is not true. The duplicate coverage should be eliminated, but the process would unnecessarily complicate the example. Clearly, the selection of media on the basis of incremental cost is preferable to their selection on the basis of average cost.

The example also provides the occasion to discuss another dimension of media selection. This is the measure of *frequency,* or the number of times an average reader sees an ad in a given period of time. In the example, we assumed that the advertiser was only interested in *new* readers. The advertiser usually wants both reach and frequency. Using the same assumption that a fourth of a magazine's circulation sees a given ad, we could expect that running an ad twice in *Time* would produce a reach of 1,978,715. Actually 1,130,694 people would see the ad each time, but on the second insertion 282,673

(.25 times 1,130,694) would have seen it for the second time. With subsequent insertions, the amount of duplication increases and frequency occurs. After 6 insertions, a few readers (about 1,100) actually might have seen the ad 6 times, others 5 times, and so on. The average number of times would be 1.3, and this is the frequency of the 6-times schedule.

Media models Even before widespread use of computers, advertising media and their associations conducted elaborate studies of advertising. Such studies enabled planners to understand something of the effects of using specific media, either alone or in combination. But in spite of the amount of information available and to some extent because of the great difficulty of absorbing and using it, final decisions on the media mix remained largely subjective, reflecting the personal opinions and experiences of the strategist. More specific methods of determining the media mix gradually have been developed. With the advent of the computer and the invasion of marketing by operations research specialists, it became possible to combine information regarding markets and media (as well as subjective judgments) by the use of media models. *Media Models* are defined as decision models used in the design of the media mix. Young and Rubicam, Inc., a large advertising agency, is credited with the development and testing of the first media model.[9]

The first media models involved linear programming, and interest in using some aspect of the approach has continued. Let us look at how simple linear programming can

[9]See W. T. Moran, "Practical Media Decisions and the Computer," *Journal of Marketing,* July 1963, pp. 26–30.

provide insights into solving the media problem. Although there are limitations to such an approach, these can be controlled if we assume that

1. The measure of effectiveness will be total exposure.
2. Responses to media insertions are constant.
3. Costs of media insertions are constant.
4. There are no intermedia interaction effects.
5. The number of insertions is a continuous variable.[10]

The problem can be stated as

Maximize: Total advertising exposure =

$$\sum_{i=1}^{n} A_i x_i$$

subject to the following constraints:

$$\sum_{i=1}^{n} c_i x_i \leq B$$

$$x_i \leq u_i \quad \text{(for all } i = 1, 2, \ldots, n\text{)}$$

$$x_i \geq 0$$

where x_i = the number of insertions in the medium

A_i = the exposure value of an insertion in the medium

u_i = the maximum number of insertions possible in the medium

c_i = the cost per insertion in the medium

B = the available budget

[10]This list of assumptions and the model that follows appear in David B. Montgomery and Glen L. Urban, *Management Science in Marketing,* © 1969, pp. 143–144. Reprinted by permission of Prentice-Hall, Inc., Englewood Cliffs, New Jersey.

Consider the case of a company that is seeking to allocate a budget of $50,000 to two competing media during the next planning period so as to maximize the exposure of a selected advertisement. Magazine 1 has a readership of 4 million and is considered by management to be 80 per cent as effective as magazine 2, which has a readership of 3.3 million. The cost of a full page in magazine 1 is $16,000 per issue; in magazine 2, it is $11,000. During the planning period, four issues of magazine 1 and three issues of magazine 2 will be published. Given this information, we can state the problem as

Maximize: Exposure value[11] =
$$200x_1 + 300x_2$$

which is subject to the following constraints:

$$16,000x_1 + 11,000x_2 \leq 50,000$$

$$x_1 \leq 4$$

$$x_2 \leq 3$$

$$x_1, x_2 \geq 0$$

Now we can solve the problem graphically, as shown in Figure 15.4. We can see that the optimal schedule during the period in question is to utilize three full pages of magazine 2 and 1.06 pages of magazine 1.

Unfortunately, the linear-programming model produces some rather absurd results in actual practice. The principal reason is that it *is* linear; it assumes that repeat exposures have a constant marginal effect—a generalization we have already discredited.

[11]Exposure value calculated as readership relative effectiveness divided by cost per full page.

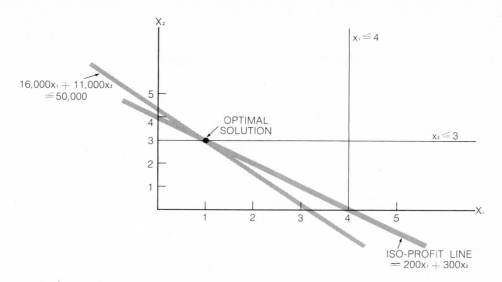

FIGURE 15.4   A graphic solution to a linear-programming media selection problem

Within five years of the first attempts to use mathematical programming, a number of improvements were made in the performance of media models. The best known of these is the MEDIAC model developed by Little and Lodish.[12] It searches among alternative schedules to find one that maximizes the objective function, subject to the given constraints. Unlike the linear-programming model just described, it does not produce a schedule; it only evaluates alternatives.

Other models have been developed by academics, ad agencies, and media-buying organizations. All make use of the extensive media information available—including cost data from *Standard Rate and Data* and audience information from Arbitron, W. R. Simmons, A. C. Nielsen, and Target Group

Index.[13] Some models attempt to determine the value of a schedule while others attempt to maximize reach and frequency. A model such as ADMOD entails very sophisticated measurements of advertising's impact on consumers' attitudes.[14] Most models are operated in a real-time computer mode, so that the planner can receive immediate feedback and continue to modify the media mix until the most satisfactory one has been identified.

Although media models have brought tremendous improvements, most media

[12]J. D. C. Little and L. M. Lodish, "A Media Planning Calculus," *Operations Research,* January-February 1969, pp. 1–35.

[13]These are four of the most widely used media audience research services. Arbitron and A. C. Nielsen provide audience and program ratings for electronic media, W. R. Simmons and Target Group Index provide print media data as well as information on product usage.

[14]D. A. Aaker, "ADMOD: An Advertising Model," *Journal of Marketing Research,* February 1975, pp. 37–45.

mixes still must be created by individual planners. Intelligently using the market information that is available and applying an understanding of promotional objectives, the planner must make decisions on the appropriate mix. Until science catches up, the artistry of media mixing will continue to shape the majority of advertising strategies, helpful though media models may be in the process.

Creating the Advertising Message

Information Requirements

Advertising messages are designed to change the awareness levels of specific audiences. These may be users, purchasers, or purchase influencers. Three specific kinds of audience information are almost mandatory for developing the advertising message. First, it is necessary to know how well informed these individuals are. Especially important is consumer knowledge of the company, its products, and its distribution arrangements. In addition, an appreciation of the extent of consumer knowledge about competitors, competitive products, and competitive distribution arrangements also assists in the development of an advertising message. Since the communications function of advertising is principally to disseminate accurate marketing information and to correct misapprehensions, knowing what consumers know (or do not know) is important in determining the kind of message that will be required.

Second, it is necessary to understand audience *attitudes* toward the company, its prod-

ucts, and its distribution channel. Attitudes, as we know, are subjective and often difficult to identify. But they are of vital significance, for in the consumer buying process all information relating to wants and satisfactions must pass through an attitude screening. Because of the competitive character of most advertising messages, it likewise is important to understand consumers' attitudes toward competitors, competitive products, and competitive distribution methods.

The third type of information that the planner needs is the extent to which consumers recognize, accept, or demand various competitive *brands*. Advertising effort can be directed toward improving brand recognition. Once recognition has been established, advertising can be directed toward the transmission of messages about strong selling features of the product or service, messages designed to build brand acceptance.

Creativity in Advertising

The task of preparing advertising messages, including illustrations and other forms of communication, usually is assigned to individuals trained in the field. Advertising agencies often perform this function. Occasionally some of the creative work is done in a company's own advertising department. For example, the animal feed divisions of Ralston Purina Company have long prepared most of the creative work in their advertisements. There are companies, however, that specialize in doing just creative work. Commercial art studios provide layout and illustration services; printing establishments provide assistance in copywriting; and radio and television stations often are equipped to produce commercials.

Regardless of who does the work, the task of translating advertising goals into effective advertising messages is a challenging and creative one. There are no fixed rules for creativity, although we know a great deal more about the creative process today than we did a few years ago. This knowledge is helping us to manage the creative function more intelligently. For example, it has taught us that creativity actually begins with good marketing information and that it is desirable to include art directors and copywriters in preliminary discussions of the market and marketing objectives. We also have been made aware of the fact that the creation of good advertising frequently involves a certain amount of trial and error, of experimentation and testing. Thus, long lead times often are required. Finally, it is important to recognize that advertising messages are a form of art and that the creative person in marketing cannot be expected to explain exactly the how and why of the work. Creative people generally are independent. "Rule book" managers find them the most exasperating individuals in business. But they are highly important to effective advertising; and their exceptional contributions usually are well rewarded.

Determining the Size and Timing of Advertising Messages

In planning an advertising program, two important decisions must be made that affect both its cost and its impact. These decisions concern the size of the advertisements that will be used and the strategic timing of their placement.

Size

Variations in size are most obvious in the case of published advertising. A wide range of sizes clearly is possible. Generally, the larger the advertisement, the more attention and readership it can produce. However, the rise in cost as the size of the advertisement increases usually is greater than the improvement in effectiveness. Accordingly, the most efficient size of an ad (cost in relationship to results) is seldom the largest size that can be obtained.

In electronic media (television and radio), the "size" of a commercial is measured by its length. Thirty seconds is now the accepted standard, although shorter (twenty-second and ten-second) spots are sold. Sixty-second commercials are still used quite frequently and even longer ones appear from time to time in specially sponsored programs.

Timing

Timing is of particular importance in relation to the rest of the marketing program, seasonal fluctuations, and the business cycle. The timing of advertising must be coordinated with the rest of the marketing program. Advertising should not start too early or too late. It generally is unwise to promote a new product before distribution has been obtained. Adherence to this principle sometimes complicates the implementation of a marketing program. A tobacco manufacturer introducing its first king-sized cigarette, for example, was forced to alter its schedule of introduction when a popular radio personality jumped the gun with an ad lib commercial. A drug manufacturer who encountered unexpected delays in manufacturing had to distribute the first lots of a new proprietary remedy by air freight in order not to lose the benefit of an already-scheduled advertising campaign.

We see an important exception to this general rule—that distribution should precede promotion—in the marketing of such specialty items as durable goods. A *teaser campaign* may be launched several weeks before the introduction of a new automobile, for example, in order to bring consumer and dealer interest to a peak at the time of the product's arrival on the market. The same type of promotional approach occasionally is used in industrial marketing. American Airlines used it to announce jet freight service many weeks before the company actually was ready to accept shipments.

Timing advertising with respect to seasonal fluctuations in demand is also an important consideration. Advertising seasonal items to consumers generally follows the above-stated principle that distribution should precede promotion. Thus, consumer advertising of summer sportswear normally does not begin until consumers are ready to shop for the season. However, trade advertising of summer sportswear should precede the consumer buying season by several months. For some products whose seasonal demand is the result of cultural rather than climatic influences, contraseasonal advertising might be used. The promotion of special flavors of ice cream originally was instituted in order to increase consumption in wintertime. Hotels, motels, and resorts frequently promote off-season attractions in order to increase business during slack periods. However, it usually is difficult to determine the effectiveness of contraseasonal promotion, because there is no easy way to measure the volume of business that might have been obtained without the additional promotional effort. Only in cases where sales response can be traced directly to a promotional campaign can the effectiveness of off-season promotion be estimated accurately.

Because advertising usually is more effective when business conditions are good or improving than when there is a recession or depression, many advertisers tend to cut back on their promotional efforts during a downturn in the business cycle. There are compelling reasons for such cutbacks. First, there is the common practice of relating promotional outlays to current sales. Low or declining sales mean low or declining advertising expenditures. Second, low profits and strained cash positions often dictate curtailment of the promotional budget. Third, advertising generally tends to be less effective in a recession than it is in prosperity. This is because the promotional elasticity of demand is known to fluctuate with changes in the level of business activity. Thus, the opportunity to advertise is definitely retarded during periods of economic slowdown. From a societal point of view, argument could be raised that contracyclical advertising would benefit the economy and therefore, indirectly, the advertiser. Although the experience of most companies has been that contracyclical promotion is not worthwhile, for certain products and services the promotional elasticity of demand might remain constant or even increase during a period of economic stress. Thus, increased promotion of such items as oleomargarine, public transportation, and similar substitutes for luxury products and services might be expected to be more effective when consumer incomes are down. For the bulk of products that have achieved success in the postwar era, however, contracyclical advertising is probably not advisable.

Measuring Advertising's Effectiveness

No issue in advertising strategy has caused more heated discussion than that of measuring the effectiveness of advertising. Confusion and disagreement characterize the issue, and, in spite of the attempts that have been made to resolve it, the effectiveness of advertising remains one of the most controversial topics in marketing.

Two Basic Concepts of What to Measure

Much of the disagreement about the feasibility of measuring advertising's effectiveness stems from differences of opinion as to what advertising is supposed to accomplish. Those who feel that advertising is essentially a *communications tool* want to measure its effectiveness in terms of the impact it has on consumers' attitudes and beliefs. They look to opinion research to supply the tools of measurement. In vivid contrast to this communications-effect school, are those who believe that the principal purpose of advertising is to *produce sales.* In their view, any measure other than sales avoids the basic question of advertising's effectiveness. The adherents of the sales-effect school turn to operations researchers for assistance in making measurements.

You should realize that there is no right or wrong to this division of opinion. Advertis-

ing is primarily a communications instrument, but it also is part of an overall marketing mix intended to produce profitable sales. To a degree, both elements are involved, and both can be measured—but not by the same methods. Unfortunately, the two viewpoints do not always correspond, especially in the short run. Thus, measurements of the effectiveness of advertising as a communications tool and as a sales tool may present ambiguous results. This is a dilemma that only a clear statement of advertising goals can resolve. If the purpose of a particular advertising campaign is to achieve a certain volume of sales, then that program's effectiveness should be measured in terms of sales results. If the goal is to achieve a change in consumer awareness, then it follows that the measurement of the advertising's effects should be made in terms of changing consumer attitudes.

The Timing of Advertising Measurements

In Chapter 14 we referred briefly to the use of *pretests, posttests,* and *concurrent tests* in measuring promotional effectiveness. These tests commonly are used in measuring advertising's effects. In addition, a continuous type of test—which we call *longitudinal measurement*—occasionally will be used.

Pretests Pretests are conducted before the advertising appears. These may be concept tests, in which the basic theme of the advertising is presented to consumers for their reactions. Or, completed print or broadcast advertisements may be tested prior to being committed to actual use. For example, a newly completed magazine ad may be inserted carefully in a current magazine. Consumers will be shown the magazine and later asked questions about the advertisements in it. Similarly, new television commercials often are shown to selected audiences in a theater setting to measure their impact prior to actual scheduling. The Schwerin Corporation conducts such tests with a stratified panel of television viewers. The company uses the viewers to measure changes in consumer opinion about a product before and after it is seen in a commercial. Another approach is actually to air rough television commercials (called *animatics*) and to obtain feedback (by interviews) that guides the final creative work.

Posttests   Posttests are conducted after the public has been exposed to the advertising. One important type of posttest determines whether people actually saw the advertising; another finds out if they remember anything about it. More specifically, *recognition tests* consist of showing a consumer a magazine or newspaper and asking the respondent to indicate which of the advertisements has been seen previously. *Recall tests* involve asking whether the consumer actually read the advertisement. This type of test, sometimes called an *impact study,* was originated by the Gallup and Robinson organization. It was first used with dummy magazines as a pretesting method; but it has since been used most extensively in postreadership studies. Many firms, such as Daniel Starch & Associates and Readex, Inc., also conduct aided-recall readership studies. Posttests of television are conducted by various methods, but the most widely used is the *day-after recall.* Telephone interviews are completed the day following the airing of a commercial. The proportion of persons determined to have watched a particular program and that

actually recalls having seen the commercial being tested is the measure of the ad's effectiveness. The Burke organization has conducted such tests for many years and has established historical bench marks for many product categories. A commercial generally is considered to be effective if it scores higher than its category norm.

Concurrent tests   Concurrent tests must be conducted while the consumer is being exposed to the advertising. A magazine or newspaper reader can be observed while reading or immediately after finishing. A radio listener or television viewer can be interviewed while a program is in progress. Outdoor advertising companies actually count the number of vehicles passing specific sign locations to estimate the number of potential viewers. Lengthy interviews simply cannot be conducted while the consumer is reading a magazine or viewing a favorite television program. In order to try to overcome this difficulty, mechanical devices, which record the stations to which sample sets are tuned, often are used in concurrent tests.

Longitudinal tests   Longitudinal tests are conducted over a period of time. One simple version is to repeat attitude studies at several intervals. Such tests often are called *bench mark studies.* The first study provides the bench mark against which subsequent changes in attitude can be compared. It is not uncommon for a company to conduct several bench mark studies while a major advertising campaign is in progress.

A more refined type of longitudinal test involves the use of a consumer panel that is studied over a considerable period of time. Measurements can be made of changes in brand awareness over time, and these changes can be directly related to actual exposure to advertising. Panel members keep extensive records of purchases and of associated activities, such as shopping and discussing consumer-buying issues. There are technical difficulties in conducting such longitudinal studies, but the possibilities of obtaining good ongoing information about the advertising's effectiveness make them a potentially useful method of advertising research.

Measuring the Communication Effects of Advertising

As we have said, the purpose of advertising according to the communications-effect school is to influence behavior. The ultimate goal of this influence may be to create a sale; but the impact of advertising is greatest on consumer awareness and the attitudes that precede a decision to buy. Such is the basic reasoning behind the attempt to measure the communications effects of advertising. The problem is that these effects often are difficult to measure. As a result, four different methods of making communications measurements have been devised. Within each of these methods, numerous specific measuring tools are used. Let us look at both the general methods and some of the specific tools for determining the nonsales impact of advertising.

Attitude and opinion studies   Attitude and opinion research delve into the mysteries of consumer behavior. We saw in Chapter 4 how psychological measurements are used to explore the existence and strength of consumer attitudes. Scaling techniques are the most commonly employed. Other methods

include intent to buy, brand preference, paired comparisons, ranking, and simulated buying studies. [15]

Memory tests   Attitude and opinion research methods are designed to discover latent views of consumers toward a product or advertising message. Memory tests, on the other hand, are intended to measure exactly how many people recall having been exposed to a commercial message and how much of that message they remember. We previously mentioned the recognition tests that are used to measure advertising readership. Recall tests, aided and unaided, also are intended to discover the residual impact of an advertising message.

In discussing consumer behavior, we looked at the volatile nature of memory. The tendency of humans to forget quickly much of what they learn and to forget all of certain things after a relatively short period of time limits the usefulness of memory tests in measuring advertising's effectiveness. However, since communications are intended to make a mental impression, it is particularly important that we make the attempt to measure what is retained in memory. Memory testing helps the advertiser learn how well the company is communicating ideas that retain their marketing impact for a reasonable length of time.

Psychophysical measurements   Suspicion of the unreliability of responses to opinion questions and even to the more refined attitude measuring devices has led to the use of some psychophysical tools. These are of rather limited importance, but they are

[15]Joel N. Axelrod, "Attitude Measures That Predict Purchase," *Journal of Advertising Research,* March 1968, p. 4.

interesting, and they do indicate the extent to which our concern about advertising's effectiveness has taken us.

The *tachistoscope* (sometimes called the *T-scope*) has been used by psychologists to measure reaction time and to study perception. It is a device that can control the length of time that an object (usually a projection on a screen) is exposed. In advertising, the tachistoscope is used to measure the length of time it takes a viewer to perceive the intended message of an illustration, a headline, or a piece of body copy. The technique likewise can be used to measure brand recognition and to evaluate alternative packages and logotypes.

The *psychogalvanometer* is a sensing device that measures the subject's reaction to a stimulus (such as an advertisement). It is much like a simple lie detector. Electrodes are attached to the arm and palm of the person being tested. When tension (or perhaps attention) causes the individual's palm to perspire, a difference in electrical resistance is detected between the two electrodes. The greater the tension impact of the stimulus, the more pronounced the measurement that the psychogalvanometer records.

These mechanical measuring devices are intriguing, but it is not certain how useful they really are. They are based on the assumption that physiological measurements are reflective of the psychological impact of an advertising message. In some instances, but certainly not in all, there may be a close relationship. It is possible, moreover, that the gadgetry involved interferes with the accuracy of the findings. And, as one might suspect, the psychophysical measuring methods are extremely expensive compared with the other techniques that are available.

Nonbuying response measurement As we have indicated, many marketing people in the communications-effect school do not expect advertising necessarily to result in a sale—at least not without considerable help from the rest of the marketing mix. But can't advertising trigger some measurable response short of an actual sale? In certain cases it can, especially if the advertisement is intended to create such a response. For example, it might be the purpose of an advertisement to get the reader to return a coupon asking for a catalog or some other type of promotional material. By carefully coding the response coupon, it is possible to measure the pulling power of a particular advertisement. Many industrial advertisers use this technique as the principal measurement of their advertising's effectiveness.

Measuring the Sales Effect of Advertising

Measuring the actual sales effect of advertising is not nearly so simple as we might assume. We cannot merely correlate advertising effort with sales and determine the extent to which sales vary. Unfortunately, many businesspeople do just this. Sometimes it leads them to extravagant expenditures on advertising—far more than its actual contribution justifies. More often, however, the people using this system are unable to detect any impact of advertising on sales, and they decide that their advertising "isn't doing any good." Accordingly, the advertising efforts are severely curtailed, and failing to see any immediate drop in sales the managers conclude that they made the right decision. The problem with this reasoning is that in reality we know that many variables affect sales, of which advertising is only one. Moreover, the cumulative, or lagged, effects may temporarily cover the real consequences of halting the advertising. Clearly, a better approach is needed.

There are three ways in which the sales effects of advertising can legitimately be measured. These are (1) direct measurement, (2) econometric analysis, and (3) controlled experimentation.

Direct measurement A substantial amount of selling is done exclusively by advertising, and thus the sales effects can be attributed almost exclusively to advertising. Magazines and other publishers have long used direct mail to solicit orders. Recently, major oil companies have launched extensive promotions of such products as luggage, radios, cookware, and so on through the mail. Offers are continuously made exclusively over television for phonograph records and household specialty items. It is possible to measure directly the sales effects of this kind of product advertising. Even if another mix variable (such as price) is at work, it can be controlled.[16]

Econometric analysis We have discussed the role of econometric analysis in establishing the response function as a step in the budgeting process. The same analysis is applicable here. We should remember that the measurement task is extremely difficult, principally because of the presence of other variables, some of which may not even be known. The method has further limitations as a measurement tool because it does not lend itself easily to the testing of qualitative decision inputs, such as message content and media mix. Notwithstanding these drawbacks, the method is important and has particular relevance to the measurement of the effects of the overall budget decision.

Controlled experimentation For a company that cannot measure directly the sales effects of advertising (and most cannot), the most reliable indirect method is the controlled experiment. This involves a special application of test marketing, the essence of which is to manipulate an advertising decision variable in a test area while controlling for other variables in another area.[17] All aspects of the advertising strategy can be tested in this way. Media, message, creative execution, and spending level all can be manipulated. Usually warehouse withdrawal or store-audit data are used to measure sales.

Helpful as this approach can be, it is not employed as often as we might suspect. It has limitations. It can be time consuming, requiring many months if lagged effects are to be picked up. It is costly—both to prepare advertising materials and to conduct the experiment. And, the approach enables competitors to learn almost as much as the advertiser. Nevertheless, controlled experiments are used by some large advertisers—at least to fine tune their programs if not to test them in the purest sense. Among the most sophisticated users of the method are duPont and Anheuser-Busch, both of which have used controlled experimentation to estimate the sales effects of their advertising programs.[18]

Summary

The major issues in advertising management involve the problems of mass communica-

[16]Simon, *Management of Advertising*, pp. 85–96.

[17]Ibid., pp. 13–26.
[18]R. L. Ackoff and J. R. Emshoff, "Advertising Research at Anheuser-Busch, Inc. (1963–1968)," *Sloan Management Review*, Winter 1975, pp. 1–15.

tions, principally those associated with messages and media. The proper solutions to these problems can be reached only if a statement of advertising goals has been made at the outset. For the most part, advertising contributes to the overall marketing program by conditioning and reinforcing. It helps prepare the way for the salesperson, and it continues to deliver the message afterwards. In both phases, the purpose of advertising is to improve customers' awareness levels by moving them from unawareness to action.

Exactly how much to spend on advertising is one of the most controversial issues in marketing. Almost no one is sure of the right amount to spend. Part of the difficulty is that a number of relatively unsound methods often are used for setting the advertising budget. Among these are the selection of an arbitrary amount, spending the amount that is available, matching a competitor's budget, or basing the budget on past or forecasted sales. Preferable methods are to base the budget on marginal analysis, on a targeted level of return on investment, or on the nature and scope of the tasks to be carried out.

Decisions about advertising media are among the most important and complex in marketing. Not only are there a number of general types of media, such as newspapers, magazines, television, and so on, but also there are literally hundreds of specific vehicles within each type. Thus, the number of possible media combinations is almost infinite. Fortunately, the task is simplified somewhat when customer orientation governs media selection. By starting with the customer, a company can narrow its options considerably. Media decisions, in other words, involve matching the socioeconomic characteristics of potential customers with media audiences. Here the computer is extremely helpful. Computer-based media models have been developed to identify the proper media to use and to allocate the advertising-space budget among them.

Creating the advertising message is also a very challenging task. To be effective, advertising must change the awareness levels of specific audiences. Thus, to prepare persuasive advertising messages (copy), the writer must begin with a knowledge of the customers' needs, attitudes, and buying behavior. The actual preparation of the message usually is assigned to special creative agencies, although a number of companies prefer to have their own people do this work.

All advertisements, of course, must be designed to appear in media according to a planned schedule. This schedule determines the size of the ad, the frequency of its use, and the exact timing of its appearance. The decisions on these issues are influenced both by the message and by the media to be employed. They also are affected by the amount of the advertising appropriation.

Closely related to the question of how much to spend on advertising is the issue of its effectiveness. Here two basic concepts of advertising's purpose come into conflict. One viewpoint is that advertising is a communications tool and that its effectiveness, therefore, should be measured in terms of its impact on customer knowledge and attitudes. The other viewpoint holds that advertising is a sales tool and should be held directly accountable for producing revenue. Different methods of measurement have been developed to support each concept. In both cases, tests can be conducted before, during, and after the appearance of the advertising. Communications effects can be measured by attitude and opinion studies, by memory tests, by psychophysical devices, and by nonbuying response measures. The sales effects of advertising seldom can be measured directly, except in the cases of catalog and direct-mail selling. Econometric studies of advertising outlays and sales volume are more useful in budget setting than in measuring ad effectiveness. It is possible to measure advertising's effect on sales by controlled experimentation.

Questions and Problems

1. Select six magazine advertisements for automobiles.

   a. Identify the apparent goals of each ad, using the Colley classification in Figure 15.1.
   b. Compare the promotional messages used. Explain the apparent reasons for using different creative approaches. Which message do you think is most effective? Why?

2. Two different departments in an advertising agency usually provide major inputs to a campaign. The media department selects the vehicles to be used and prepares the advertising schedule. The creative department prepares the layouts, illustrations, and copy. Sometimes the people engaged in these different tasks disagree about the relative importance of them. Is there any logical basis on which such a disagreement might be resolved, or is it simply a matter of personal opinion? Explain your answer.

3. Assume that you are in charge of advertising an instant tea. The product is intended to be used in making iced tea, but it also can be used in brewing hot tea. How would you distribute a $1.5 million budget for television advertising over the entire year? Explain.

4. A national marketer of soft drinks retained a management consultant to advise it on its advertising budgeting procedures. The consultant soon discovered that the firm set its budget at a given percentage of the previous year's sales. The consultant pointed out to the client that this resulted in several serious mistakes:

   a. Overall, the company was spending too little on advertising.
   b. Its advertising was badly distributed over the business cycle.
   c. The allocation of the budget to specific product lines was poor—too much being spent on mature products and too little on new ones.
   d. Because the company was only number four in its industry, it was not spending at a rate necessary to improve its market share.

   Based on these observations, what budgeting method(s) do you think the consultant recommended? Why?

5. Why is it that CPM (cost per thousand) is not by itself a satisfactory criterion for advertising-vehicle selection? Under what circumstances might an advertising manager select a vehicle with a relatively high CPM over one with a lower CPM?

6. How would the advertising manager of a company marketing a well-known soft drink use the marginal approach to set a budget? Be as specific as you can in outlining the methods that could be used to obtain the data.

7. What are some of the ways in which the two conflicting views of advertising's purpose might be reflected in various aspects of advertising management?

8. It is often assumed that the advertising of industrial products is different than the advertising of consumer packaged goods. Do you agree? What are the important points of difference? What similarities are there?

9. Advertisers of packaged consumer goods often rely on three measures of advertising impact: awareness, trial, and usage. Do you think there is a hierarchical relationship among these? Which would be most relevant for advertising a new product? A growth product? A mature product?

10. What is your opinion about the logic and ethics of advertising directly to children?

11. Suggest some reasons why it is important to know exactly how a product is distributed before trying to develop an advertising program.

12. Obtain a copy of a local or a campus newspaper. Select ten display advertisements. Interview approximately twenty people to find out whether they saw the ads and whether they remember the advertising messages. Use whatever techniques you want in your investigation. Write a brief report that includes a statement of your methodology and a summary of your findings. As a result of this study, what conclusions can you draw about the relative effectiveness of the ten ads?

16

Promotion Strategy: Special Issues in Personal Selling

In this chapter we will look at some of the special issues and problems involved in personal selling. We should recall that Chapter 14 presented an overview of all the promotional areas, including advertising, publicity, selling, and sales promotion. This integrated approach to promotion is mandatory in developing the marketing plan. Although the tasks of carrying out the various promotional components may well be assigned to different parts of the organization, they must be integrated in a common purpose by a single overall marketing strategy.

What kinds of decisions typically arise in the area of personal selling? Usually these are people decisions—decisions that involve the management of the sales force. We know that when human beings are the principal element in a business activity, the problems requiring decisions are extensive and complicated. A few of the most typical and important ones have been selected for discussion here. The purpose is not to explore

them extensively but to suggest the types of issues that arise in the area of personal selling and to indicate some of the ways that managers go about resolving them.[1]

What Kind of Sales Force?

Almost all marketing programs require some personal selling. Although there are a few

[1] Any number of excellent books are available on the subject of salesmanship and sales management. For example, in the area of selling, see F. A. Russell, F. H. Beach, and R. H. Buskirk, *Textbook of Salesmanship* (New York: McGraw-Hill, 1974); and J. W. Thompson, *Selling: A Managerial Behavioral Science Analysis* (New York: McGraw-Hill, 1973). In the area of sales management, you might inspect W. J. Stanton and R. H. Buskirk, *Management of the Sales Force* (Homewood, Ill.: Richard D. Irwin, 1974); R. S. Still and W. W. Cundiff, *Sales Management: Decisions, Policies and Cases* (Englewood Cliffs, N.J.: Prentice-Hall, 1976); and K. R. Davis and F. Webster, Jr., *Sales Force Management* (New York: Ronald Press, 1968).

firms that sell only through catalogs, magazine advertising, or direct mail, these are exceptions. Most companies use some type of personal promotion. The key question, therefore, is "What type?" Actually, this question involves two basic decisions. One relates to the structure of the selling effort and the other to its type per se.

Classification by Structure

The structure of the selling function corresponds closely to that of the channel of distribution. Accordingly, there are two major structural alternatives. These are

Direct selling   The company employs its own sales force, which calls directly on customers.

Indirect selling   The company uses the employees of owning or nonowning middlemen to solicit sales.

The difficult choice between direct and indirect selling is affected by a number of factors, and is illustrated by the dilemma faced by a moderate-sized company selling a line of fireplace fixtures and accessories. The arguments in favor of using manufacturers' representatives were

1. Good reps know the market and have established access to and rapport with important customers.
2. Representatives are paid a commission on sales (not a salary or expenses). The cost therefore is completely variable.
3. Fireplace products are seasonal, and the company would incur sales expense only as sales are made. A direct sales force would involve year-round expense.

On the other hand, using a company sales force had some advantages:

1. The company would not be competing for the rep's time.
2. A direct sales force is actually cheaper when selling to large customers. This is illustrated in Figure 16.1, which shows that if representatives are paid a 7 per cent commission, it is more profitable to service directly any account over $75,000 than to use an agent.
3. Company salespeople are easier to motivate and control.
4. In some market areas it is almost impossible to find a satisfactory representative.

Weighing the merits of each approach, the firm (principally because of its size and seasonal business) decided to continue to use indirect selling except for the private-label business it did with a large chain organization. This account, amounting to about 20 per cent of the company's entire sales volume, was serviced directly by the sales manager.

In addition to deciding on the structure of selling, a choice must be made between several distinctly different types of selling.

Classification by Type

Cold-canvass selling versus lead selling   The salesperson who calls on a one-shot basis with no knowledge as to whether the prospect has a need for the product is engaged in cold-canvass selling. Cold canvassing of a market was much more common a generation ago than it is today. Restrictive local ordinances, the mobility of householders, the high proportion of working women, and

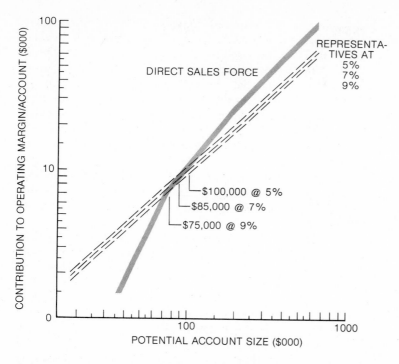

FIGURE 16.1   A comparison of profit contribution of direct and indirect selling methods

Source: Reprinted from "A Quantitative Method for Structuring a Profitable Sales Force" by J. W. Kokus, *Journal of Marketing,* July 1973, p. 14, published by the American Marketing Association.

the general disinclination of consumers to buy in this fashion have made it increasingly difficult to operate a cold-canvassing sales program. Even the Fuller Brush man and the Avon lady follow, for the most part, a planned route of calling on established customers and referred prospects.

The lead (pronounced "leed") salesperson calls only on prospects known or suspected to be interested in a company's product or service. Leads can be obtained in many ways. Lists of prime prospects can be purchased, or individuals responding to advertising offers can be called on. In addition, customers often suggest the names of prospects. One common method of prospecting is by the use of an *endless-chain system.* The salesperson attempts to obtain the names of at least two or three new prospects from each person called on. In this way, even if most of the names do not prove out, there usually is a backlog of prospects on whom to call.

Planned versus "canned" selling   The day of the unplanned, ad lib sale is past. All sales presentations are planned to some degree. The extreme in planning is the so-called canned sales talk. The salesperson using the approach presents it in the approved fashion, deviating only as permitted by a supervisor to adapt the presentation to special or peculiar circumstances. Careful observation of the selling of such items as debit life insurance, encyclopedias, and vacuum cleaners has shown that relatively unskilled persons can perform efficiently when using the canned sales approach. In contrast, experienced salespeople prefer to use a more flexible approach. But a sales plan will be used. It may be elaborate or simple, depending on the sales opportunity and the training and inclination of the salesperson. Sales engineers develop very elaborate customer strategies to guide them in their selling. The essence of any such strategy is to identify a sales objective and outline the manner in which the sales interview will be conducted to accomplish the goal.

Developmental versus competitive selling Developmental selling involves the cultivation of future sales opportunities instead of the solicitation of immediate business. In doing developmental selling, the salesperson works closely with prospective customers and with the selling company's research and development department. The goal is to create a good working relationship and to build up the customer's confidence. Eventually, through close cooperation, a product or service can be developed to meet the customer's particular need. In contrast, competitive selling implies the presentation of products in direct competition with substitutes that are readily available on the market. Much time and effort also may be required to close a sale under these conditions; however, the sales approach is notably different from that involved in developmental work. Competitive selling requires greater skill in the techniques of salesmanship. Generally, a more aggressive approach

is required. In one large chemical company, for example, entirely different individuals are used for the two types of selling. Developmental sales work is the responsibility of a special market development department, while the regular sales department is in charge of selling existing products to established customers. In fact, the developmental work is so closely related to technical R&D that it actually is not considered a sales assignment. But it really is a type of selling, since it is designed to establish a favorable climate for future sales.

Missionary versus order selling The missionary salesperson represents the manufacturer, calling on customers, resellers, and purchase influencers in order to stimulate demand and to assist resellers in developing their selling programs for the manufacturer's product. Ordinarily, a missionary salesperson does not accept orders. In contrast, the order salesperson concentrates on booking business. Similar in some respects to competitive selling, order selling involves making sales in the face of intense competition. However, the competitive salesperson often is technically trained and is found mostly in the industrial field. The order salesperson, on the other hand, is encountered in the marketing of resale items, especially packaged goods distributed through wholesale-retail trade channels. The order taker usually works for a wholesaler or jobber, although a vertically integrated manufacturer with an extensive product line may also employ the same type of person. Moreover, this type often works from a catalog or from a stock list, making only token efforts to promote special items. The principal objective is to obtain orders for as many items as possible and to increase the dollar value of the overall order.

Pretransaction selling versus posttransaction servicing   Pretransaction selling is similar in some respects to developmental selling. However, it need not necessarily involve the development of new products or services. It may simply involve a conditioning of the prospective customer. In any case, the objective of pretransaction selling is to evolve a long-standing relationship between the supplier and customer. Posttransaction servicing is a different type of selling effort. It is often assigned to individuals other than those who closed the sale. For instance, postsales servicing of electronic data-processing equipment usually is assigned to technicians. In contrast, the electric typewriter salesperson frequently is expected to make minor postsales adjustments on the machines. The objective of postsales servicing is to keep a customer satisfied and, as in pretransaction selling, conditioned for future sales. In spite of the emphasis on service, it is considered a type of selling effort.

Defining the Sales Task

Just what is a salesperson expected to do? The typical salesperson answers this question by saying, "Too much." The sales manager would agree that many demands are made on salespeople above and beyond the solicitation of business. The company looks on the salesperson as a manager of a territory or a group of customers. This difference in viewpoint often lies at the heart of the problems that arise in the sales area. The marketing view of the sales task recognizes the extreme importance of personal contact with customers and at the same time insists that this activity be planned, directed, and controlled in the same way that all other aspects of marketing are managed.

The sales task in an industrial-products company is outlined in Exhibit 16.1. This exhibit is a position description for a district sales representative. It is apparent from the description that this job entails many responsibilities besides selling. While companies differ in the specific nonselling demands they make, this position description illustrates the scope and character of many typical requirements. It goes without saying that the selling task in a completely different type of industry—consumer food products, for example—would be quite different.

Determining the Size of the Sales Force

Sometimes the size of a company's sales force staggers the imagination. National Biscuit Company has more than three thousand salespeople. How does a company decide whether it should have three thousand or two thousand or twenty in its sales force? This is an important issue in marketing to which there are two major approaches.

The Workload Approach

A company might determine the number of salespeople needed by estimating the extent of the selling task and dividing this task by the amount of it that a single person could handle.[2]

[2]The example in this section is based on a discussion in Walter J. Semlow, "How Many Salesmen Do You Need?" *Harvard Business Review,* May-June 1959, pp. 126–132. Copyright © 1959 by the President and Fellows of Harvard College; all rights reserved.

EXHIBIT 16.1 Position description

JOB TITLE: District Sales Representative

REPORTS TO: District Sales Manager

BASIC FUNCTION

Represent the Company with assigned accounts and execute sales policies and programs for the purpose of attaining and maintaining programmed levels of profit for the Company's products.

DUTIES AND RESPONSIBILITIES

1. Perform the functions of selling as assigned by the District Sales Manager. Maintain or increase volume and profit margins for sales. Directly and actively pursue solicitation of orders for the Company's products. Seek new customers or uses of the Company's products.
2. Promote the use of the Company's products to architects, engineers, contractors, owners, distributors, dealers, and other customers or potential customers.
3. Seek out and recommend distribution outlets for approval.
4. Train distributor's personnel on uses of the Company's products. Train and keep distributor's staff informed on the Company's policies, pricing procedures, and delivery schedules.
5. See that established price policies are maintained. After review with District Sales Manager, obtain approval of the Product Manager for exceptions to pricing policy.
6. Keep informed of marketing activities of competitors and report changes, trends, and new developments to the District Sales Manager. Also report new competitive products and uses of existing products to the District Sales Manager.
7. Keep informed of market conditions and pertinent information obtained by personal contacts and report them to the District Sales Manager.
8. Confirm in writing quotations to customers of all special prices for Company's products.
9. Record and transmit in writing with adequate lead time to the Customer Service Department complete information regarding orders. This includes the purchase order or contract, pricing, plans and specifications or bill of materials, delivery requirements, and other information pertinent to acceptance and handling of orders.
10. Where special conditions preclude selling through established outlets, bid on projects directly in the Company's name after approval of the District Sales Manager.
11. Handle inquiries in district office or see that they are handled by qualified persons in the distributor's organization.
12. Provide service after the sale to customer (status of order; transmittal of order, bill of material, or plans and specifications; shipping information; job visits, and so on).

Suppose, for example, that a well-known manufacturer of industrial machinery sells to two classes of customers: end users and dealers. In a selected market, there are 500 end users and 100 dealers. Management wants to determine the number of salespeople necessary to make 12 calls on each of the end users and 24 calls on each of the dealers during a single year.

As an aid to this determination we can use the following formula:

$$N = \frac{\sum\limits_{i=1}^{2} F_i C_i}{K}$$

where N = the number of salespeople
F = the call frequency required for a given customer class
C = the number of customers in a given class
K = the average number of calls a salesperson can make during the year

From past history it is known that the average salesperson can make approximately 600 sales calls during the year. Utilizing this figure in the above formula, management finds that

$$N = \frac{1}{600} [12(500) + 24(100)]$$

$$= \frac{1}{600} [6000 + 2400]$$

$$= 14$$

Thus, on the basis of the number of customers to be reached and the average number of calls made per person per year, the company

decides that it should assign a force of 14 people to this particular sales task.

The Marginal Approach

Most managers are faced with the problem of making adjustments in the size of an existing sales force. Although marginal analysis also enables a company to determine the optimum size of a total sales organization, a more practical application involves making day-to-day decisions about hiring and releasing personnel. A manager knows two basic facts about changing the size of an existing sales force. If an additional person is hired, total sales should increase, and so will total selling costs. If a salesperson is dismissed, sales will decline, and so will expenses. In general, another person should be hired if the gross margin on the additional sales volume rises more than selling cost increases—that is, if the extra person will contribute more in gross profit than in cost. In firing (or not replacing) people, the opposite reasoning applies. If the cost that is saved exceeds the gross profit that is sacrificed, the company is better off with a smaller sales force.

This approach is illustrated in Table 16.1. Suppose that a company is now employing 20 salespeople. Its total sales cost is $600,000. Its sales force produces $1,000,000 in gross profit contribution. A senior person has announced plans to retire. Four qualified applicants are seeking employment. The manager has several options.

The retiring salesperson would not be replaced. (Total sales force would then be 19.)

One applicant could be hired to replace the retired person. (Total sales force would remain at 20.)

TABLE 16.1   Marginal approach to changes in size of sales force

Number of salespeople	Profit contribution		Selling cost	
	Total	Marginal	Total	Marginal
19	$ 940,000		$570,000	
		60,000		30,000
20	1,000,000		600,000	
		50,000		30,000
21	1,050,000		630,000	
		30,000		30,000
22	1,080,000		660,000	
		20,000		30,000
23	1,100,000		690,000	

The size of the sales force can be expanded by hiring two or more applicants. (Sales force size would be at least 21.)

Table 16.1 indicates that hiring three persons is the most desirable course to follow. If the manager does not replace the retiring individual, gross profit will drop $60,000 while only $30,000 in cost will be saved. At least one person should be hired to replace the one who is leaving. Hiring two will increase total net profit by $20,000; hiring three will not change total net profit, but sales and market share will be larger. Hiring four is not practical, since the added profit contribution would be less than the cost of the fourth salesperson. It is clear from the table that 22 is the optimum sales force size, since the marginal profit contribution is equal to marginal selling cost at this size.

Allocating the Sales Force to Territories or Segments

Once the overall size of the sales force has been determined, it must be decided how this staff will be allocated.[3] The most common allocation problem is that of assigning salespersons to territories. The marginality principle is applied, the goal being to equate the marginal net profit earned in all territories. An example of this approach was presented in Chapter 8 to illustrate the application of marginal analysis.

The sales force can be allocated to customer segments. For example, a major fuse manufacturer assigns some salespeople to call on wholesalers and others to call on original-equipment manufacturers. Robert Buzzell suggests a deterministic approach to the assignment of sales personnel to each of two segments.[4] His example deals with an engineering-products firm that utilized two principal marketing channels for the distri-

[3]Of course, the size of the total sales force might be determined by calculating the optimum number for each territory or segment and adding these to obtain the overall figure. If this approach is followed, no allocation is required.

[4]Robert D. Buzzell, *Mathematical Models and Marketing Management* (Boston: Division of Research, Graduate School of Business Administration, Harvard University, 1964), pp. 136–156.

THE RELATIONSHIP OF SALES RESPONSE TO NUMBER OF SALESPERSONS
FOR A GIVEN LEVEL OF MARKET SATURATION

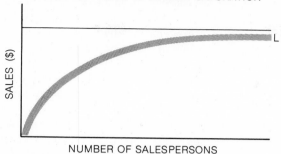

FIGURE 16.2   The relationship of sales response to number of salespersons for a given level of market saturation

bution of its products: direct sales to customers and sales through independent wholesale distributors.

In developing the model to allocate salespeople, it was first necessary to build into the model some relationship between sales effort (number of salespersons) and market response (sales volume). To determine this relationship the following assumptions were made:

1. The two methods of selling served separate markets.
2. In each market, there was an absolute maximum level of sales *(saturation level)* that could be attained by the firm.
3. The saturation level sales in each market was the same and equal to $12 million.
4. In each market, sales approached the saturation level exponentially.

Thus, for each market the sales response curve is given by the formula

$$S = L \left(1 - e^{-an}\right)$$

where S = the sales in dollars
L = the saturation level
a = a constant
n = the number of salespeople

The formula is depicted graphically in Figure 16.2.

Historically, the following sales information was available:

	Direct	Wholesale
Number of salespeople	40	2
Net sales (in dollars)	6 million	1.5 million

This information, together with the four assumptions, was used to establish two equations.[5] The first, for wholesale sales:

$$1,500 = 12,000 \left(1 - e^{-2\,a_w}\right)$$

[5]All figures in these equations are in thousands of dollars.

The second, for direct sales:

$$6,000 = 12,000 (1 - e^{-40\, a_d})$$

Solving these two equations we find that

$$a_w = .065$$
$$a_d = .0175$$

Additional accounting information showed that the fixed costs of selling the firm's product were $2 million and that gross margins per $1,000 sales were $377 for direct sales and $318 for wholesale sales. It also was assumed that the average compensation paid a salesperson was $12,000. On the basis of these additional figures, it was possible to develop a profit equation (in thousands of dollars).

Profit = (gross margin on direct sales × direct sales)
+ (gross margin on wholesale sales × wholesale sales)
− $12,000 (number of salespeople)
− fixed costs

$$= .377[\$12,000 (1 - e^{-.01725 n_d})]$$
$$+ .318[\$12,000 (1 - e^{-.065 n_w})]$$
$$- \$12,000(n_d + n_w) - \$2,000$$

It was assumed that the total number of salespeople would be kept at 42. And application of the differential calculus to the profit equation led to the conclusion that the most profitable assignment was 19 direct salespersons and 23 wholesale salespersons.

Sales Force Organization

We considered sales force organization briefly in Chapter 2 in connection with the marketing management system. The exis-

tence of a sales department indicates that a decision to organize on a functional basis has already been reached. This is the normal arrangement when the marketing program requires extensive personal contact with customers. Even if indirect selling methods are used, the outside selling arm must be supervised to carry out the sales responsibility effectively.

Line sales authority can be delegated on several bases. It can be divided according to product lines. Some salespeople and their respective managers may be responsible for one part of the company's line. Other groups will be in charge of other products. The method is used when a company's line is extremely broad, perhaps even involving some internal competition. Separate sales forces may be used in such cases, even if they call on the same accounts.

An almost inescapable way of organizing the sales force is along geographical lines. A salesperson can be thought of as a manager of a territory, responsible for developing business within it. Such an arrangement works fairly well in companies with short or homogeneous product lines and in cases where extreme market segmentation is not encountered. However, if a territory contains several different types of industries, it often is difficult for one individual to be familiar with the special needs of each. The St. Louis market, for example, has a high concentration of shoe-manufacturing firms and a number of important aerospace and electronics companies. It also boasts several large retailing organizations, a pair of major chemical companies, several other major corporation headquarters, and two major military establishments. A computer sales representative might be hampered in approaching these diverse types of firms with widely varying computer requirements.

This dilemma often leads to the assignment of salespeople on a customer or market basis. One group may deal with the electronics customers while another group handles the shoe manufacturers. Or the customers may be divided on the basis of size. Large and small customers tend to demand different services. A third basis for the assignment of salespeople can be the level or type of customer. In our computer example, different salespeople might call on manufacturing, wholesale, and retail accounts.

As in the case of company organization, it is common to find various combinations of these methods of sales organization. Any number of combinations is possible. An extremely large company might combine all four bases of sales organization: product, territory, customer, and size. For instance, a cash register representative might be assigned to a group calling on independent retail stores in a northeastern territory. The same company might have a bookkeeping-equipment sales force assigned to call on large banks and savings and loan institutions in the Midwest. Ordinarily such an extreme division of effort is not necessary, but it is commonplace to find a combination of at least two bases of sales organization: product and territory or territory and customer type.

Designing Territories

Most companies use some type of geographical basis in assigning the sales force. The wide geographical dispersion of customers and the great expense of reaching them from a single location make the geographical assignment an economical way of managing the personal-selling effort. In addition, it is much easier to render good competitive

service on a localized basis. A salesperson needs to be familiar with local problems and competitive conditions. This usually can be done best when the salesperson lives in the territory. Finally, morale is better if traveling is minimized.

There is almost always the question of which comes first, however, the design of the sales force or the design of the territories? The two are closely related. A sales force may be designed to serve specific territories, or the territorial structure may be adapted to the size and capabilities of the existing sales organization. Since we already looked at the first approach when we considered the size and allocation of the sales force, we will focus here on the second approach and some of its implications.

Fitting the Sales Territory to the Sales Force

If a company has a sales force of a certain size and ability, it may choose to develop its territories around these people. This is normally done when the sales force is limited in size or is particularly trained in certain products or markets. In such cases, a manager determines approximately how many territories the sales force can handle effectively. Then the total market is divided into this number of geographical areas. Alternatively, the optimum size of territory for a single salesperson is determined. The territories are then arranged in the order of their attractiveness to the firm, and people are assigned to the territories at the head of the list. The first alternative results in thin coverage of most territories; the second may leave a number of markets uncovered. There are risks and losses of potential sales in both alternatives, but there is little choice as long as the size of the sales force is limited. Assigning too large an area means that fewer calls will be made than desirable on some good customers and less frequent calls on all. On the other hand, by not covering some markets it is possible to develop others intensively. Obviously, a certain amount of volume is sacrificed, and the danger that competitors may establish a foothold in the uncovered markets is a serious threat.

Determining the Shape of Territories

There are two practical problems in designing territories. One is to determine the shape of the territory; the other is to establish its size. Of course, a territory is only part of an entire market, and the parts must fit together. Within this limitation, however, the territorial parts can be of almost any shape—even a jigsaw configuration is possible. Although rectangles are the easiest to construct, circular areas are the most economical to serve. As a practical matter, territories are constructed by combining smaller geographical or political units into larger ones. States are often used, but a more intricate territorial design may be based on county boundaries. The smaller the building blocks, the easier it is to obtain the desired configuration. Counties are particularly good building blocks because they are the smallest areas for which market data are available.

Figure 16.3 (parts A, B, and C) shows how an area might be divided in several geometric ways. In the *rectangular* shape (part A), the total market is divided into equal parts by vertical and horizontal lines. The result is extremely artificial and offers no obvious advantages except that the territories are of absolutely equal geographical size. The *circular* territory (part B) also has this advantage in addition to minimizing travel distances if customers are located evenly throughout the area and the salesperson is located in the center of the circle. (Since it is impossible to fill a surface completely by circles, hexagonal territories are shown in the figure.)

Part C of Figure 16.3 illustrates two special territorial configurations. The *cloverleaf* design represents the shape of a territory with a clustering of customers in five locations. The salesperson would be located at the center and make special trips to each of the four peripheral markets. The *wedge* design is part of a larger circular territory. The rectangle at the point of the wedge represents a major metropolitan market. Several individuals divide the market, each one taking a wedge-shaped territory. This may be the most equitable method of allocating such a market if the best customers are found in its center. No one salesperson gets all of the preferred accounts. Rather, each is located at the point of the wedge, concentrating calls in one part of the metropolitan area and making occasional trips to the periphery of the market.

Since customers usually are scattered unevenly throughout an area, territories with such neat rectangular, circular, cloverleaf, and wedge shapes rarely are possible. Political boundaries and topological phenomena also make it impractical for territories to conform to these ideal configurations. For example, customers tend to be concentrated in urban centers, which may be historically or accidentally situated. A major river or other impediment to travel may dictate a deviation from the ideal territorial shape. In practice, the design of territories only begins with the theoretical ideal and ends with rather massive compromises to fit each terri-

(A) RECTANGULAR

(B) HEXAGONAL (CIRCULAR)

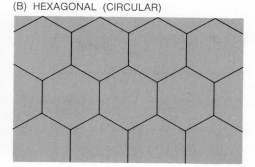

(C) CLOVERLEAF AND WEDGE

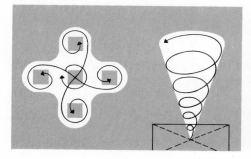

(D) TOPOGRAPHICAL

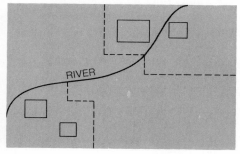

RIVER

FIGURE 16.3   Different shapes of sales territories

tory to the physical, political, and demographic characteristics that are peculiar to the given market. Figure 16.3, part D, illustrates such an arrangement.

Determining the Size of Territories

The size of a territory depends on several considerations. It is highly desirable that territories be about equal—both in terms of potential and in terms of difficulty of servicing. Although complete equality is never possible, approximate equality is a basic objective in territory design. Not only is it easier to compare sales performance when

territories are approximately equal, but also morale is better, and bickering or negotiating over territorial assignments is held to a minimum.[6]

A problem frequently arises, however, when a sales manager attempts to design territories that are equal both in potential and in workload. Since customers are not evenly distributed, we inevitably find pockets of high-potential concentration. For example, the New York City school system is

[6]A few companies consciously construct some inequality into territories in order to reward senior or productive salespeople. Ordinarily, however, this practice complicates other aspects of the sales management task.

second only to the armed forces in the number of people for whom it provides food service. This one customer might constitute an appropriate territory for a food products salesperson. Another individual might have the rest of the city of New York, while a third might be asked to cover the balance of the state. It would not be unreasonable, however, for the same company to assign one person to cover all of the states of Utah, Nevada, Idaho, and Wyoming, if this was the only way the potentials would be equalized. There is no ready solution to the problem. It is solved only by compromise. For example, an exceptionally large customer like the New York City school system often is handled by a corporate executive as a house account. Or the New York City quota may be a high percentage of potential in recognition of the ease of coverage. Still another solution might be to pay the person in the western states a more attractive salary.

Sales Compensation

The Importance of the Compensation Plan

The discussion of territorial inequality has led us to the subject of sales compensation. The territorial workload is only one factor that affects the payment of salespeople. In general, we find that sales compensation is related to the overall task of acquiring and maintaining an effective sales organization. To attract and hold good people, a compensation plan must meet the requirements of the employees. And to make such employees productive—that is, to make sure their efforts are profitable and are directed in accordance with the company's overall mar-

keting program—the compensation plan also must meet the requirements of the company. Balancing these two sets of requirements is not easy. Salespeople want to receive an adequate income on a regular basis and want to be rewarded for their contribution to the firm. From the standpoint of the firm, however, sales compensation is an expense that must be paid to retain able people, to stimulate them to be productive, and to provide the company with some control over the way the sales effort is directed.

Types of Compensation

Salary The straight salary provides a fixed sum at regular intervals. An expense allowance or reimbursement for expenses usually is provided. The straight salary plan is good from the salesperson's point of view. An income is assured, but there is no immediate reward for exceptional performance. From the company's point of view, the straight salary is a fixed sales cost. Such a cost is controlled, and as long as sales are satisfactory the burden is not serious. If sales slip, however, a fixed sales cost becomes a problem. Also, straight salary is not a good way to motivate people to extra effort. However, it does permit the sales manager to require the performance of nonselling activities, which people paid on a commission basis tend to avoid.

Commission The straight commission plan eliminates some of the deficiencies in the salary arrangement, but it raises problems of its own. Under a commission plan, the salesperson is paid a fixed or sliding rate of earnings based on sales volume or profit contribution. The commission is a reward for doing a job well. It also motivates a

TABLE 16.2   Trends in sales compensation

Type of plan	Per cent of companies using	
	Prior plan	Current plan
Straight salary	15	3
Straight commission	47	14
Combination	38	83

Source: D. A. Weeks, *Incentive Plans for Salesmen* (New York: National Industrial Conference Board, 1970), p. 3.

salesperson to exceed established standards of productivity. The company benefits from an incentive tool by which it can stimulate performance. Since the commission is calculated on the basis of current sales, it virtually pays for itself and has the great merit of being a completely variable cost.

Combination   A combination plan, as one would expect, involves both salary and incentive. The base salary usually is high enough to provide the financial security that the employee desires. It also is low enough so that its fixed-cost character does not seriously affect the firm in periods of declining sales. In addition to the base salary, an incentive is paid in the form of a commission—usually on sales greater than a set quota. Thus, the salesperson benefits from extra income for better-than-standard performance, and the firm benefits from a partly variable sales expense and some financial incentive to encourage and control marketing effort.

There is a trend toward such combination plans. The Conference Board has reported on a study of sales compensation plans now in effect compared with those used in years past. In a group of two hundred companies, 83 per cent reported that they currently were using a combination plan—up from 38 per

cent using such a plan during the period from 1955 to 1965.[7] The complete data on the use of the three types of plans are shown in Table 16.2.

Staffing the Sales Organization

The starting point in staffing the sales organization is an understanding of the sales tasks to be performed. Good position descriptions are the first step. The second step is the determination of those abilities and characteristics that best equip a person to fill the position requirements. Such specifications for filling the sales position become the criteria for evaluating job applicants. They also may be the basis for recruiting. The big question, however, is just what abilities and characteristics make a good salesperson. It is reasonably clear that some combination of intelligence, personality, and experience is desirable. Determining how to measure these elements and what weights to assign to them in selecting people is less clear. Various types of testing and rating devices have been designed for this purpose. Some correlation between performance and the scores on such devices has been found, but the relationship is far from absolute. Although testing and rating devices do provide management with one tool, formal testing and rating procedures cannot substitute for the manager's own judgment in determining the degree of fit between the applicant and the job to be filled.

Once applicants have been hired, they

[7] D. A. Weeks, *Incentive Plans for Salesmen* (New York: National Industrial Conference Board, 1970), p. 3.

usually must be trained. Training for sales is a vast and complicated subject. In brief, it involves not only an orientation to the company and its products, but also an attempt to fill the gaps between present ability and the needs of the new position. The position description is the basis for designing a training program that can accomplish these two goals. Such a program may be extremely lengthy and involved. A trainee may be given an orientation and then be sent to a district office for a number of months in order to gain practical experience. After this, there may be a stint at the home office to undergo several weeks of intensive training. Next may come an inside assignment for a number of months. While on the inside job, the trainee will be included in a pool waiting to fill a vacancy in the field. In this ideal procedure, the field selling organization is never short staffed, nor does it have to wait for a person to be trained to fill a vacancy. In most companies, however, sales training lags behind the need for new people, and there is a tendency to send individuals into the field before they are ready to operate effectively.

Directing the Sales Force

Implementing the Sales Plan

The issues involved in building a working sales organization have been reviewed in the preceding pages. In a sense, the resolution of these issues equips a company to implement its marketing plan. How well the sales organization carries out its assignment within that plan depends largely on how effectively its managers supervise and lead. We will now look at some of the aspects of directive leadership that are so important to

a successful selling program. These aspects are worthy of our attention, because it is clear that simply issuing instructions will not ensure adequate implementation of the marketing plan. Rather, implementation must be brought about through the process of directive leadership, which involves a number of different but functionally related activities. Each activity helps to make sure that the marketing program is carried out intelligently, enthusiastically, and effectively. We may think of these activities as the eight specific steps in the process of directive leadership.

The Process of Directive Leadership

Check organizational readiness Before attempting to issue instructions or to supervise the implementation of a marketing plan, the sales manager should check the organization's readiness to compete. Checking organizational readiness is much like the pre-flight check carried out by an aircraft commander prior to takeoff. It is doubtful that many marketing organizations actually have formal checking procedures, but certainly some type of informal evaluation is desirable. To a degree, the thoroughness of the evaluation will depend on the program to be initiated. A traditional marketing program may require only a routine check of organizational readiness. However, a program that involves a dramatic departure from the company's historical methods of selling demands a much more careful inspection.

Regardless of whether the inspection is routine or detailed, three different areas usually are involved. First, the manager confirms that the organization is *operational*. In effect, this means that personnel are thoroughly familiar with company methods and procedures and that they have had adequate training or experience in dealing with various selling situations. A second area that requires checking is the *capability* of the organization. It is not enough for people to know how to carry out a marketing program; they also must be capable of doing so. A sales force, for example, might be ready to undertake a routine seasonal promotion, but it might be completely unqualified to launch an entirely new line or to open up a new channel of distribution. In such a case, a thorough program of training and stimulation would be required before the new plan could be implemented. A final factor, one that is often difficult to check out, is *morale*. The mental readiness of an organization is as important as its physical and technical capabilities.

Issue instructions Instructions are communications regarding how a program should be carried out. They can be verbal or written. *Verbal instructions* have the advantage that they can be given quickly and with a great deal of emotional impact. However, verbal instructions may not be understood, and they easily can be forgotten. If verbal instructions are used, they should be backed up by written instructions.

Explain the strategic rationale In marketing, it often is desirable to explain the reason for a set of instructions. Generally, this means that at least two aspects of the strategic rationale should be made clear. First, the marketing target(s) should be carefully identified. In order to carry out a marketing plan effectively, the salesperson must know exactly which customer segment is being approached, so that prospecting and selling activities can be directed accordingly. A salesperson also should have some idea of the overall marketing strategy of which the selling effort is a part. This facilitates coordination with the rest of the organization.

Transmit bench marks of performance The salesperson should understand that field performance will be measured and controlled. Two types of measures are available. One is designed to measure the *effort* put forth, the other to measure *results*. The most frequently used bench marks of effort are the sales expense budget and the sales call plan. For example, a salesperson may be alloted $1,000 a month for travel and entertainment expense or may be instructed to limit such expenditures to a certain percentage of sales. The call plan is a statement of which customers will be visited and with what frequency.

While budgets of this type are used to measure effort, *quotas* generally are used as the bench marks of output. The quota sets forth the results that are expected. Quotas may be set for sales, for new customers obtained, for orders taken for particular merchandise, or indeed for almost any type of marketing activity. A performance quota also may be used to provide a psychological benefit. For example, a company may deliberately set a low quota in order to allow a person to surpass it easily. This often is done when financial incentives are tied to quota attainment. Occasionally, a company may set a deliberately high quota in order to impel extraordinary effort. However, the major role of quotas in the process of directive leadership is to provide a standard by which performance can be evaluated. Recently, salespeople themselves have participated in setting their quotas.[8]

Follow up on instructions Ultimately, the sales manager is responsible for perform-

[8]L. Winer, "The Effect of Product Sales Quotas on Sales Force Productivity," *Journal of Marketing Research*, May 1973, pp. 180–183; and T. R. Wotruba and M. L. Thurlow, "Sales Force Participation in Quota Setting and Sales Forecasting," *Journal of Marketing*, April 1976, pp. 11–16.

ance. It usually is desirable for the manager to check to see that instructions have been received and understood and that action has been initiated. This is especially important if instructions are transmitted impersonally, say, by routine mail. The difficulty here is that one of the common weaknesses of salespeople is the tendency to procrastinate in taking care of home-office mail. Days or even weeks may go by before the salesperson even reads a change of instructions.

Engage in consultative direction Once instructions have been issued and bench marks of performance have been transmitted, it theoretically would be possible to direct the organization simply by comparing results to the predetermined standards. Unfortunately, this type of direction seldom enables the manager to detect weaknesses in time to correct them or in time to discover the real reasons behind them. What is needed instead is a continuous program of supervision. We call such a program *consultative direction*. Its essence is communication. The salesperson is encouraged to discuss achievements and problems. This provides the manager with an opportunity to make suggestions for correcting or improving performance. Sometimes it may be necessary to repeat or amplify instructions issued earlier. And at times the manager can use the discussion to encourage and motivate the salesperson.

Provide tactical leadership Tactical leadership is provided when the sales manager works out special approaches for handling conditions not anticipated in the marketing program. Such tactical changes in approach should, of course, fit into the overall marketing strategy. For example, if a marketing plan calls for three personal contacts with a particular customer during a marketing campaign, a tactical change to increase or decrease this number of calls might be made as the result of consultative direction.

Provide inspirational leadership In the course of giving consultative direction, it may become clear to the manager that inspirational leadership is required to maintain or restore morale. Particularly in marketing programs that continue over a considerable period of time, it is quite common for the field organization to lose steam. Inspirational leadership is useful in rekindling enthusiasm, which many believe to be the single most important factor explaining sales success.[9]

Motivation and Discipline in the Sales Force

There are many occasions when the sales manager must use personal influence to achieve desired results. The reason is obvious. Instructions must be more than understood; they must be accepted and carried out intelligently and enthusiastically. In order for this to happen, personal influence often is required in the form of motivation or discipline. Motivation can be viewed as the use of positive incentives, while discipline involves the use of negative incentives.

Motivation: Using Positive Incentives

Financial rewards Financial rewards are important inducements in every line of

[9]See G. A. Churchill, Jr., N. M. Ford, and O. C. Walker, Jr., "Organizational Climate and Job Satisfaction in the Sales Force," *Journal of Marketing Research,* November 1976, pp. 322–332.

work. They are particularly useful in marketing, where effort cannot be as carefully controlled as it can in some other areas of business. For example, a salesperson cannot be forced to drive a few more miles or call on a few more customers each day. It is much more likely to be done, however, when the financial rewards for increasing effort are clear. But it cannot be assumed that financial incentives alone impel a salesperson.[10]

Opportunity for advancement Advancement in marketing is seldom routine. One cannot simply put in time and expect to qualify for a higher and more responsible position. It usually is advantageous, however, to have some type of promotion policy that motivates salespeople to do a good job.

Personal status Personal-status expectations can be quite specific. For example, giving a person a special title may affect performance. It generally is more effective to call a person a *sales representative* or an *account executive* than to use the more prosaic term *salesperson.* Similarly, most people relish holding manager status. For this reason, the typical marketing organization is replete with "managers." At least one company with which the writer is familiar has only managers in its organization. Salespeople are called *territory managers;* their immediate superiors are called *district managers* (in effect, they are regional managers); above these individuals are *general sales managers*—some of whom also enjoy the status of being vice presidents. The genuine value of such organizational nomenclature within the firm is doubtful, since everybody knows the relative importance of each manager; but it certainly enhances the status of territorial representatives with their customers to be called managers rather than salespeople.

Security In the past, sales positions have not been known for their security. In part this reflects the dynamic nature of marketing, and in part it reflects the kinds of people who are attracted to it. However, the advantages of job security in motivating personnel are obvious. People usually perform better when they are not fearful of being fired. The fact that more and more companies are abandoning straight commission methods of sales compensation in favor of the psychological advantage of some assurance of financial security shows that they are becoming increasingly sensitive to this fear. But security involves much more than guaranteed income. The secure person is also one who is well adjusted to the environment. A very effective way of generating higher productivity is to establish security in this sense.

Pleasant working conditions Good working conditions tend to improve productivity. Although this is not an especially critical problem in marketing, it has received some attention. For example, one of the most unpleasant aspects of sales employment has been the long hours of work required. Except in retailing, however, it has been found possible through proper scheduling and time control to cut back drastically the number of hours required for certain tasks. Throughout marketing, in fact, there is a general trend toward making the conditions of employment as attractive as possible. For example, most salespeople are accustomed to living well, to driving a relatively new automobile, and to dining and staying at better hotels and motels on the road. Unquestionably, a marketing manager could economize by cutting

---

[10]R. Y. Darmon, "Salesmen's Response to Financial Incentives," *Journal of Marketing Research,* November 1974, pp. 418–426.

back on these apparent extravagances. However, it is generally conceded that they are important factors influencing morale and, therefore, the efficiency of the selling organization.

A worthwhile job   One of the most effective motivational devices is to convince an employee that the job is important. In recent years, however, there have been numerous public attacks on selling. These attacks, whether on economic or ethical grounds, have raised serious doubts in the minds of many people as to the worthiness of selling careers. Even within the organization, selling positions are sometimes less respected than others. Currently, for example, scientific research is at the top of the status ladder; sales is often near the bottom. There *is* an opportunity to raise the status of selling. In companies where this has been done, morale in the sales department seldom is a problem.

Personal power   Aside from status expectations, many individuals enjoy a sense of personal authority. A very effective way of motivating some salespeople is to give them opportunities to increase their authority. It usually is possible to delegate far more authority than is realized. In the example cited above of the organization composed exclusively of managers, the sense of authority possessed by the firm's territorial representatives was considerable. Although the technique has certain disadvantages, it is clear that personal power, as well as personal status, was involved in motivating these individuals.

Self-determination   Most individuals also like to be independent. They resent being told what they should do and how they

should do it. It is possible to establish a considerable degree of self-determination in the selling organization. This is accomplished by delegating as much authority and responsibility as possible to lower levels in the organization. It also is facilitated by substituting marketing plans for marketing commands. If the individual actually participates in the development of the marketing plan, the work will be regarded, at least in part, as self-determined.

Discipline: Using Negative Incentives

Negative incentives are less commonly used today than they were a generation ago. However, it is impossible to operate an effective organization without discipline and therefore without some negative incentives. The essence of discipline is setting minimum standards of performance and establishing appropriate sanctions for a failure to achieve them.

There are two methods of discipline. The first method—the one used most widely in cases of minor infractions—is to *reprimand* the violator. The second method of discipline is to impose a *penalty*. The ultimate penalty for breaking an organizational rule is, of course, the termination of employment. Penalties may, on the other hand, involve withholding rewards for those who are being disciplined. Failure to grant a promotion would be among the most serious penalties imposed. Salespeople who fail to meet assigned quotas may not be invited to attend special meetings or conventions. Although the use of discipline in selling is the exception rather than the rule, it is wise to establish the managerial prerogative of using negative incentives when necessary. Some discipline is essential for good morale, and failure to enforce it can jeopardize an entire marketing operation. This fact is sometimes forgotten in training sales managers. It is one of the reasons why salespeople frequently do not make good managers. They are unwilling to establish minimum standards for their former associates and unable to enforce them. This unwillingness, of course, is a critical weakness in a manager who must be able not only to motivate but also to discipline, in order to direct the staff in the performance of its tasks.

All for One and One for All

We have looked rather deeply into a number of the special issues and problems involved in the areas of personal selling and advertising. The concepts presented and the methods suggested for solving the specific problems of sales and advertising management may have distracted the reader from an important point made in the opening section of Chapter 14. This point is that the firm does not have separate strategies of advertising, selling, and sales promotion. It has instead one promotional mix, and this mix is part of the overall marketing plan. All methods of demand creation and communications with customers exist for a single purpose—to reach the overall marketing objectives of the company.

The elements of the promotional mix, moreover, are not independent strategies that somehow are blended into an overall approach. Rather each one supports the others. We have seen how advertising conditions and reinforces. Of course, selling supports the advertising program. Sales promotion relates to both selling and advertising.

Taken together, selling, advertising, and promotion are the three musketeers of marketing. Their motto, too, should be "All for one and one for all!" This is what we mean when we refer to the integrated promotion mix.

Summary

It has been traditional in marketing to separate the functions of personal selling and advertising—both in theoretical discussions and in actual business practice. But there has been a recent trend to merge these topics, as we did generally in Chapter 14. Moreover, companies that have adopted the marketing concept always attempt to integrate the advertising and personal-selling components of promotion to some extent. Notwithstanding such developments, it still is convenient to consider advertising and personal selling separately. There are a number of special issues and problems that are peculiar to each. This chapter reviewed those that relate to personal selling.

The special issues and problems that arise in connection with personal selling are principally people oriented. In particular, they involve the management of the sales force. Most companies require the services of a considerable number of salespeople in the field. The organization of this sales force and its administration are the major decision areas in the management of personal selling.

The first specific decision that must be made involves the structure of the sales force. The basic choice is between employing a company's own group or using the services of another selling organization. We call the first method direct selling and the second method indirect selling. The kinds of sales efforts that a company can use also vary considerably. We have seen that there are important distinctions between cold-canvass selling and lead selling, and between planned and canned selling. Other differences were found between developmental and competitive selling, between missionary and order selling, and between pretransaction selling and posttransaction servicing.

Once the type of selling has been determined, it is necessary to decide how large a sales force should be used and how it should be assigned to cover the market. There are two basic approaches in determining the proper size of the sales force. In the workload approach, an attempt is made to measure how much work is to be done, and this is then divided by the amount that can be handled by a single salesperson. The marginal approach attempts to match the cost of hiring an additional salesperson with the gross profit contribution that the additional salesperson will make.

Salespeople usually are assigned to specific territories. Sometimes, the size of the sales force is influenced by the area that has to be covered. In other cases, the territorial coverage is fitted to the given size and abilities of an already-established sales force. Territories can have different shapes, each reflecting a different method of coverage. In practice, however, territorial design options often are limited by such considerations as the density of customers and the topography. Usually a compromise between the ideal and the practical is necessary.

Decisions involving the administration of the sales force are closely related to those involving its organization and structure. Administration, of course, requires a definition of the sales task to be performed. Producing a position description of the sales job is a first step. From the description it is possible to determine the staffing requirements. Personnel can then be recruited, selected, hired, and trained. Having an appropriate compensation plan is also an important part of sales administration. Basic types are the straight salary plan, the straight commission plan, and the combination plan.

After the major decisions on the nature of the personal selling program have been made, directing the sales force toward those actions that will achieve sales objectives becomes the critical management function. A number of important elements are involved. When the sales manager knows that the organization is ready to take to the field, instructions must be issued and explained. The manager must follow up to see that instructions are being carried out and must exercise leadership, as necessary, to make sure that the sales program is successful. Most salespeople need to be motivated, and a few must be disciplined from time to time.

Having looked at the special issues and problems of advertising in Chapter 15 and at those of personal selling in this chapter, it is important for us to return to the concept of the promotional mix. The firm does not really have separate strategies for personal selling and advertising. Rather it has a single, integrated promotional mix, and this mix is part of an overall marketing plan.

Questions and Problems

1. Briefly explain which type of sales force you feel would be used by each of the following companies:
   a. A management-consulting company
   b. An office equipment manufacturer

    c. A breakfast cereal company

    d. An importer of Japanese photographic equipment

    e. A farm equipment manufacturer

2. Cite at least three examples of marketing situations in which posttransaction servicing may be more important than pretransaction selling.

3. The Olympia Sporting Goods Company sells a broad line of professional and scholastic athletic equipment and supplies. Sales are made directly to professional teams, sporting-goods wholesalers, and large dealers. Smaller sporting-goods stores are serviced by the wholesalers' salespeople. In the Midwest, there are 50 professional and semiprofessional teams, 24 sporting-goods wholesalers, and 150 large dealers. There are also 10 large universities that want to buy directly from the company. The company's marketing plan requires that each wholesaler be called on twice a month and each dealer and university at least four times a year. A salesperson in this line can make an average of 500 calls a year. Using the workload approach, calculate the number of salespeople Olympia needs in the midwestern territory.

4. Referring to question 3, how would your answer differ if the sales force also was expected to make at least two calls a year on each of 300 other small sporting-goods stores in the region?

5. The marketing director of a large architectural firm wants to know how much should be spent in trying to develop a promising client—a rapidly growing department store chain. The manager believes that this potential client would generate fees of $50,000 a year for at least a five-year period. The architectural firm earns a profit margin of 15 per cent on its fees. Its before-tax return on investment is 20 per cent. How much can this firm afford to spend in trying to acquire this client? What suggestions do you have about the way the money should be spent?

6. Explain the rationale of the hexagonal (circular), cloverleaf, and wedge territorial shapes.

7. Research has shown that salespeople are notoriously poor at gathering and transmitting marketing information. Why do you think this is so? What do you think might be done about it?

8. There has been a recent trend toward having salespeople participate in the setting of their own quotas. What do you think might be the reasons for doing this? Do you see any problems in this method?

9. Most companies use some type of combination plan for compensating salespeople. Explain why this is so, using arguments from both the management's and the salesperson's point of view.

10. How might an understanding of communications theory be applied in the direction of the sales force?

11. What relationship does motivating the sales force have to the efficiency of marketing? To the social criticisms of marketing?

12. A sales manager once said, "I never discipline my salespeople. I don't believe that a good manager needs to use negative incentives." Comment on this statement.

17

Pricing Strategy: A General Approach

We are now ready to consider the challenging task of formulating a pricing strategy. As we have seen, it would have been extremely difficult to discuss the problems and issues of price setting without first developing the other elements of the marketing mix. Many aspects of pricing depend on decisions made at each of the previous stages of marketing planning.

Pricing is probably the most complex and difficult of the strategy-making tasks. In approaching it, we will look first at the basic role of pricing in marketing planning. We will see that the complexity and importance of pricing require a systematic approach, involving the setting of objectives and the development of a pricing structure to achieve them. These topics are the concern of this chapter. A number of critical problems and issues must be resolved before a complete pricing strategy materializes. We will look at each of these, as well as at some

of the methods of analysis and decision making used in solving them, in Chapter 18.

Defining the Role of Price

What Is Price?

Superficially, price is easy to define. A *price* is the amount we pay for a good or service. When a shopper asks, "What is its price?" a reply that appears to answer the question completely might be, "Its price is ten dollars." However, the real meaning of the term *price* is not nearly so simple. There are several reasons.

In the first place, buyer and seller have quite different views of the meaning of price. Second, owing to the proliferation of products and services, the geographical dis-person of consumers, the segmentation of most markets, and an almost infinite array of different conditions surrounding market transactions, it is virtually impossible to specify a single prevailing price for any one product or service. A third factor complicating the meaning of price is the conflict that may arise within a firm, within its channel system, or between a firm and its environment in connection with pricing. Finally, price is only one of several competitive weapons that can be used by the seller. The problem of setting the right price is made more difficult by the need to coordinate competitive pricing with indirect and non-price competitive strategies. Let us consider these conditions in greater detail.

Price from the buyer's point of view   A marketing (consumer-oriented) approach to pricing requires that the market planner understand the meaning of a price to ultimate consumers and resellers. To the ultimate consumer, the price paid for a product or service represents a sacrifice of purchasing power. Money spent on one product is not available for something else. Although the affluence of the average American consumer has been rising, almost everyone finds it necessary to choose among alternative ways of spending. Even the big spender is bound by this limitation and purchases in ways that will yield the greatest satisfaction. A four year old standing before a candy counter, clutching a nickel tightly, offers a good example of the meaning of price as a buyer sacrifice. Eventually, the child may select a lollipop or Tootsie Roll or may even turn reluctantly away because a favorite chocolate bar has risen in price to 20 cents. Most consumers face the same hard decisions all their lives. Moreover, the dealer who buys goods for resale, views price in

about the same way. Prices paid by resellers are sacrifices too.

Price from the seller's point of view   From the seller's point of view (either the manufacturer's or the reseller's), price can mean something quite different from what it means to the buyer. The seller knows that price is a source of revenue and a prime determinant of profit. The price a seller sets for a product is the *revenue expectation from a sale.* Closely related to this conception of price is the notion of price as a platform on which to assemble the costs of manufacturing and marketing. Especially when a cost-plus pricing method is used, the seller tends to view price as an *accumulation of costs.* Such a view is most commonly held by financial executives and manufacturing-oriented personnel. In contrast, the marketing manager's conception of price is related to the entire marketing program. Optimistically, the marketing person thinks of price as a *product feature.* A relatively high price may be viewed as evidence of quality; a price that is low relative to prices charged by other sellers may be viewed as a differential advantage. The marketing manager always bears in mind that price is a part of the marketing mix and seldom focuses on price alone. Price is important, but it has real meaning only in terms of its relationship to the entire marketing program.

An Example of Pricing Complexity

The complexity and ambiguity of the term *price* can be further dramatized by asking and answering such questions as "What is the price of a new car?"; "What is the price of an insurance policy?"; "What is the price of a box of tea?" You will immediately recognize that it is impossible to respond to such questions categorically and without major qualifying assumptions. Consider, for example, the price of a Chevrolet. In 1977 it was possible for a consumer to purchase an eight-cylinder, four-door sedan Impala in St. Louis, for approximately $5,223. The price of the car would vary considerably, however, depending on the extras or accessories ordered. On the assumption that the customer wanted a stripped-down model devoid of all extras except a radio, heater, and air conditioner, the price quoted above was a typical cash price for a Chevrolet of this description. In contrast, another motorist might have paid as much as $8,000 for a Caprice hardtop with such accessories as T-top, cruise control, FM radio, power brakes, and power steering. In this example, the differences in product explain the differences in price. However, consider the hypothetical case of two almost identical Chevrolet automobiles sold in the same market. Mr. Jones purchases a four-door Impala sedan with radio and heater for family use. He trades in a four-year-old automobile, for which he is allowed $1,500. He purchases his new car in August, toward the end of the model year. Although he pays cash for the difference between the asking price and the value of his trade-in, he borrows this sum from a local bank for a three-year period at 6 per cent interest. The price that Mr. Jones eventually agrees to pay for his automobile is $4,303 and his old car. Nine months previously, the local police chief purchased a four-door Impala for $3,700. He traded in a two-year-old police car that had been driven 210,000 miles, for which the Chevrolet dealer allowed $500. The price was quoted by a competitive sealed bid and awarded to the lowest bidder. It was a cash transaction, involving local vehicle registration funds that had been previously collected.

Basic Price

It is clear from the above example that many variables affect the actual price a buyer pays. It would be impossible for a marketing manager to anticipate all of these different variables. Instead, a general approach to pricing that will be flexible enough to permit the minor changes required to adjust the final-user price to prevailing market conditions is needed. A useful approach is found in the concept of basic price.[1] A *basic price* is a reference price. It is a price from which actual prices can be determined by adding extras and deducting discounts. *Actual prices* deviate from the basic price for two important reasons. The first reason is that product-line pricing requires pricing differentials associated with the different products in a multiple line. The second reason is that actual prices reflect differentials from the basic price because of market structure, geographical location, competitive conditions, and the terms of individual transactions. We can see that a company's pricing strategy can be divided into three elements on the basis of the following factors:

1. The determination of basic price
2. The determination of the relationship among the prices of the various items in the line
3. The selection of a discount pricing structure to adapt specific product prices to actual market conditions

Conflicting Forces in Pricing

By now we should be quite accustomed to contending with conflicting elements in pre-

[1] J. Dean, *Managerial Economics* (Englewood Cliffs, N.J.: Prentice-Hall, 1951), p. 398. This is a classic discussion of pricing and is recommended reading for all serious students.

paring market strategy. Although conflict is encountered in product development, channel system design, and the creation of a promotional mix, disagreements about pricing are more heated than those in any other area of marketing planning. Pricing conflicts arise at three system levels. They arise within the firm itself, within the channel system, and between the firm and its environment—especially with competitors and the government.

Conflict within the firm Within the firm, three types of conflict regarding prices are important. First, in many firms there is considerable disagreement about the basic function of pricing. In some situations it is assumed that the function of pricing is to generate sales volume; in others it is assumed that the function of pricing is to produce profits. While it might seem that these objectives should not be in conflict, they are, as a matter of fact, usually quite incompatible—at least in the short run. Forces within the firm interested in such considerations as rate of return, pay-back, and cash flow ordinarily support high prices. In contrast, sales personnel interested in increasing volume and improving market share are equally strong in supporting low prices. They argue for the long-run economies of scale that low prices make possible, while at the same time the proponents of high prices emphasize the high costs associated with diminishing returns in marketing.

A second conflict that may arise within the firm relates to the proper starting point in setting prices. Financial and technical personnel are inclined to begin with the product and its costs of manufacture and distribution. Customer-oriented marketing planners want to begin at the other end of the channel, with the price the customer is willing and able to pay, and work backward to

determine the amount that the firm can spend on production and distribution.

A third aspect of internal conflict regarding prices is found in large decentralized establishments in which one department sells to another department in the same firm. This problem is even more complicated when sales are made both internally and externally. What price should one operating department charge another? Several types of solutions have been worked out. One department may sell to another at the market price. A second approach is to transfer products from one department in a company to another at the direct-cost figure; that is, no overhead or departmental profit is charged. A third method is simply to charge the other department an arbitrary price somewhere between direct cost and market price. The adversary roles of seller and buyer are likely to arise internally. Unfortunately, the conflict is not as easily resolved because within a firm some final agreement must be reached, whereas on the open market no such necessity exists.

Conflict within the channel Similar conflicts about price often arise among components of the channel system. For reasons already mentioned, the most obvious conflicts arise between purchaser and seller— whether a direct-selling manufacturer or a reseller. The reseller, as buyer, may disagree with the manufacturer's policy. The issue is not unlike the intracompany pricing conflict, because a well-structured channel system is similar to the vertically integrated organization. Thus, channel components tend to react to buying prices in much the same way as company-owned departments.

Another notable price conflict within distribution channels relates to resale price maintenance. This issue was mentioned in connection with working with channel components. Many resellers voluntarily comply with the manufacturers' suggested resale prices. Others, however, for reasons quite sound in their particular situations, do not. We will look more closely at resale price maintenance in Chapter 18 when we consider some of the special issues and problems of pricing.

Conflict with the environment   A company's pricing strategy may be at variance with numerous elements in the environment. Conflicts are seen most clearly in relationships with competitors and public policy. The most critical conflicts with competitors arise in oligopolistic markets because of the extent to which one company's price affects its competitors' sales. Under more competitive conditions with minimal product differentiation, pricing conflict is a key factor explaining competitive behavior. Even the monopolist is not entirely free from competitive pressure—either from remote substitutes or, more important, from potential competitors.

The reason that company pricing strategy is often at odds with public policy are equally obvious. Pricing strategy must be developed within the framework of existing laws and enforcement practices; but these factors may lead to pricing decisions that are contrary to the company's marketing objectives. Conflict with public policy is generally a matter of degree. It is possible to identify some prices that are clearly legal and others that are definitely illegal. In between is a vast gray area of prices that may or may not be legal, depending on the decisions of administrative commissions and courts. Even a legal pricing move may be in conflict with public policy. For example, the efforts of steel firms and automobile manufacturers to increase prices always face extremely hostile reactions from Washington.

Price Is a Powerful Marketing Instrument

The power of price to produce results in the marketplace is not equaled by any other element in the marketing mix. For this reason it is a dangerous and explosive marketing force. It must be used with caution. The damage done by improper pricing may completely destroy the effectiveness of the rest of a well-conceived marketing program. It may doom a good product to failure. Some pricing decisions, notably low pricing strategies, usually are irreversible; they must be used correctly from the outset. As a marketing weapon, pricing is the big gun. It should be triggered exclusively by those thoroughly familiar with its possibilities and dangers. But unlike most big weapons, pricing cannot be used only when the danger of its misuse is at a minimum. Every marketing plan involves a pricing decision. Therefore, all marketing planners should be equipped to make correct pricing decisions.

Price Is a Competitive Weapon

Price is an important competitive weapon, and it must be understood in these terms. Three basic considerations relate pricing to a company's competitive position. First, a company should have some policies concerning pricing. The most important is the policy defining the kind of pricing approach to be used. Regardless of whether a company is selling high-, medium-, or low-priced merchandise, it always has to decide whether its specific prices will be *above, equal to,* or *below* its competition. This is a basic policy question that affects the entire market planning process. Ordinarily, it is not possible for a company to occupy extreme positions at the same time. That is, it cannot offer some products priced above and others priced below competition.

A second important competitive consideration is the relationship of pricing to other elements in the marketing mix. Price does not stand alone as a device for achieving a competitive advantage. In fact, indirect and nonprice competitive techniques often are more desirable, because they are difficult for competitors to match. An overall competitive approach, including price and nonprice elements, should be utilized.

A third consideration in competitive pricing is the relationship between pricing and the product life cycle. There are notable differences in the kinds of pricing that should be used in different stages. Within a particular stage, such as the introductory stage, there also are clear-cut alternatives that must be considered. Since the product's life span is directly related to the product's competitive distinctiveness, pricing at any point in the cycle should reflect prevailing competitive conditions. We will discuss the practical aspects of this concept in Chapter 18.

Pricing Objectives

Sources of Pricing Objectives

As in the other areas of marketing planning, pricing strategy begins with the determination of objectives. These objectives may arise from within the marketing organization or from other parts of the firm. Let us look first at some of the nonmarketing sources of pricing objectives.

The nonmarketing sources often are extremely influential because the consequences of pricing pervade the entire company. In profit-directed firms almost all decisions are studied in the light of their impact on pricing. A request by the manufacturing manager to buy new equipment, a chief engineer's recommendation that more draftsmen be hired and trained, and a treasurer's suggestion that a quarterly dividend to stockholders be increased may involve considerations of pricing. It is not uncommon, therefore, for pricing objectives to originate outside the marketing department.

Unfortunately, there is no assurance that the pricing requirements of a decision on a capital expenditure, on a personnel change, or on a stockholders' dividend will be consistent with each other or with objectives that relate directly to marketing. This is why it is especially important that corporate pricing objectives be considered carefully to make sure that they meet the tests of consistency and realism.

Of course, pricing objectives also arise strictly within the marketing area. Product development opportunities always are closely tied to pricing considerations. In the design of a distribution system, pricing (especially margins to resellers) is an important influence on the type of channel used. The design of a promotional strategy also requires the careful study of pricing. In other words, the process of developing the rest of the marketing mix actually may create pricing objectives.

Typical Pricing Objectives

Most business managers approach pricing with a fair understanding of its objectives. Because of the complexity of pricing decisions and their importance to company profits, marketing planners in virtually all large companies and in many smaller firms have been quite conscientious about delineating pricing policies and about directing pricing decisions toward particular objectives.[2] A selection of some typical pricing objectives is presented in the following paragraphs.

Growth in sales   When used wisely, a strategic price can move merchandise faster than almost any other marketing tool. If corporate growth plans call for increased sales of particular products, to particular customers, or at particular times, pricing objectives may be established to accomplish these goals. Normally, the objective is not phrased in terms of charging a particular price. Rather, this is left to the tactician's discretion.

It should not be assumed, however, that a price designed to increase sales must of necessity be a *low* price. The objective is to determine the *right* price to stimulate the desired sales increase. Of course, price by itself seldom is expected to generate sales increases. Price and nonprice objectives should be coordinated to produce the desired result.

Maintaining or improving market share   Sales increases per se do not necessarily result in an improved market position, since competitors may enjoy even greater sales increases. Paradoxically, a company's competitive position actually might be improved at the same time that an overall sales decline is experienced. This is why few companies operating under the marketing concept use sales volume objectives as their sole guide to pricing strategy. Market share, or sales in relation to competition, is a far more meaningful bench mark of survival and

success. Accordingly, many firms establish as pricing objectives the maintenance or improvement of market position. A&P for example, gained from its inception a reputation for low prices in food retailing. Its objective was to establish a niche in the market and progressively increase its share of that market. This objective of improving market position was a principal factor guiding A&P's pricing for many years.[3]

Managing cash flow   Pricing decisions are extremely important to the financial manager. Before World War II, marketing plans did not as a rule make major claims on a company's cash reserves. However, the rapid expansion of new-product research and decentralized distribution networks and the explosion of aggressive selling have made it necessary to commit large sums of money to marketing. Since there are many other demands within a firm for the same funds, it is understandable that a principal pricing objective is to return as much cash as possible within a given period of time. Firms in the chemical, electronics, and pharmaceutical industries, for example, typically incur heavy product development costs. Consumer–packaged goods marketers incur heavy introduction costs—notably advertising. The relatively high introductory prices charged by these companies often reflect the desire to recover these sunk costs as early as possible in the product's life cycle.

Achieving a predetermined profit   Pricing for profit would appear to be the most logical of

[2]For a very worthwhile classic treatment of pricing objectives, see A. H. Kaplan, J. D. Dirlam, and R. S. Lanzillotti, *Pricing in Big Business* (Washington, D.C.: Brookings Institution, 1958).

[3]This same low price strategy proved in later years to be inappropriate for A&P due largely to the changed competitive situation. For an analysis of the company's WEO disaster, see R. Hartley, *Marketing Mistakes* (Columbus: Grid, 1976), pp. 97–108.

all pricing objectives. In practice the typical approach has been *cost-plus.* We must understand, however, that cost plus a reasonable profit is not an objective; it is a pricing technique. Pricing to attain predetermined profits involves the establishment of specific profit goals—either as a percentage of sales, or preferably as a rate of return on investment (ROI) or assets managed (ROAM). Decisions based on return are becoming common in marketing. Research, development, and promotional expenditures often are justified on the basis of an anticipated rate of return. For example, GM is assumed to price its products in order to realize a 15 to 20 per cent rate of return on invested capital.[4] Some companies may have target returns that are somewhat lower; others run considerably higher. A pricing objective based on an anticipated rate of return for new products usually is different from that for mature products. As one would expect, the anticipated return from a product innovation would be considerably higher than that from a mature product. Not only would research and development costs be higher, but the risks associated with the project would be correspondingly greater.

Stabilizing prices and margins In oligopolistic industries, the stabilization of price levels or of operating margins may be more critical than the maintenance of a certain level of short-run profits. This objective easily might be reworded in terms of pricing in relation to competition. For example, in the marketing of most basic metals, it is the accepted practice of the majority of firms to follow the price leader. Although

public attention is drawn more frequently toward price increases, downward adjustments of prices are not unknown. Both types of adjustments are generally the result of increasing or decreasing cost pressures throughout an industry. Thus, the practice of price leadership and followership has developed as an acceptable means of avoiding the inherent hazards of unilateral pricing adjustments without the danger of violating antitrust laws. The role of price leader is generally that of maintaining stable prices in an industry in which erratic and irresponsible pricing moves would result in undesirable changes in market share and profits.

A Systematic Marketing Approach to Pricing

There is probably no area of marketing planning in which it is more important to follow a systematic approach than in pricing. A price is objective and quantitative; it demands a precise and logical method of determination—one that begins at the proper place. As we have indicated, the most widely used pricing method begins with costs. Since prices should cover costs, we find it difficult to argue with the thesis that an intelligent approach to pricing is to accumulate costs and add a profit. This cost-plus-a-reasonable-profit explanation of pricing generally is understandable and acceptable to legislators, Justice Department attorneys, and ultimate customers. The marketing manager knows, however, that the cost-plus doctrine of pricing is self-defeating. Pricing strategy must be based on

[4]Kaplan, Dirlam, and Lanzillotti, *Pricing in Big Business,* pp. 131–135.

the consumer, just as product, distribution, and promotion strategies are. To start at any point other than the market in the determination of pricing is to start at the wrong place.

The following steps present a marketing approach to pricing. Costs are not ignored, but they are relegated to their proper place in the pricing process. The ultimate goal of that process is to set a price that is compatible with the rest of the marketing mix and that will enable the firm to achieve its objectives. This is not an easy task, but the approach that offers the most hope of meeting these requirements is the one that starts in the market and works back to the manufacturer's pricing plan. We call this *market-minus pricing.*

Step 1. Identify the Potential Customer

The ultimate purchasers are the ones who pay the final price for a product or service. They are, therefore, the focal point in pricing strategy. How these people respond to price determines to a large extent whether a marketing program succeeds or fails. It is extremely shortsighted to select a pricing strategy without first identifying those people whom the pricing plan is supposed to affect. Of course, the identification of such market components is not a new step in market planning. The users, purchasers, and purchase influencers who are important in pricing are exactly the same individuals whose needs and attitudes were explored in the development of the rest of the marketing mix. The novelty of identifying these individuals for pricing purposes lies not in the task of doing it but rather in the role they play. This role will become more obvious as succeeding steps are unfolded.

Step 2. Estimate Demand

Prices are seldom set for each user.[5] Rather, users are grouped together into market segments. These may be regional, economic, demographic, or psychographic segments whose members are reasonably similar. For each market segment it is necessary to determine the relationship of alternative prices to potential demand. The discovery of these relationships may require a deep penetration by the market planner into the nature of the demand for the product and the factors that influence it.

This demand analysis should have been part of the research activity that preceded the first step in planning. Empirical studies of demand should have produced demand schedules for each market segment. This should permit the planner to judge fairly accurately the range of prices that might be charged and the price elasticity of demand within that range. If the company has had no experience with a particular market segment or lacks the opportunity to engage in statistical analysis or controlled experimentation, the planner is forced to reach decisions at this stage on the basis of subjective assessments of the market.

Step 3. Determine Competitors' Prices

The importance of pricing in relation to competition makes it mandatory for the market planner to know exactly what competitors are charging. One might think that this information would be readily available. However, in practice, competitive pricing information is usually closely guarded. Nor-

---

[5]Custom manufacturing, such as machine tool making and portrait painting, is an important exception to this generalization.

mally, it is not difficult to obtain information about competitors' *list prices*. But it often is a real challenge to discover a competitor's actual pricing structure. Discount sheets on which a manufacturer prints the current pricing structure are generally distributed with great care. Ordinarily, only salespeople, representatives, and key dealers receive this information. Often discounts are printed in the form of code numerals, so that it is difficult for an outsider to interpret the sheet correctly.

There are several ways in which these obstacles to obtaining competitive pricing information can be overcome. Most sellers establish excellent rapport with a few *key customers*. These customers, for their part, find it useful to provide selected manufacturers with information about prices quoted by competitors. One difficulty encountered in this connection is the temptation of some of the customers to play suppliers against each other by reporting lower (sometimes fictitious) prices from one in order to lure another into offering even greater discounts.

It is also possible to obtain information on competitors' pricing strategies by *comparative shopping*. This type of shopping involves the observation of prices actually charged by competitors. Many types of retailers engage in comparative shopping. Often, it is done by a buyer, although full-time comparative shoppers are on the payroll of some retail establishments.

within which the company chooses to compete and the price elasticity that exists. The wider the range and the greater the cross-elasticity of demand, the greater the number of pricing alternatives that must be considered. If the range is narrow and cross-elasticity low, there should be only two or three distinct pricing alternatives.

A convenient way of considering these alternatives is to set up a *pricing work sheet.* Such a work sheet is shown in Table 17.1. Each column represents an alternative basic price or price reference point. The quantity that is expected to be sold at each price (line 2) is estimated from the preceding demand analysis and from judgments regarding the probable reactions of competitors.

It should be stressed that, although it may never be applied to any particular product or selling situation, the basic price in the table is a realistic market price. It is not an arbitrary reference point, rather it resembles an ideal price. If a company sold a single product to only one customer and if the selling conditions never varied (for instance, if the customer always purchased on the same payment terms), then the basic price might closely conform to the price that actually would be charged. But such pricing circumstances are most unlikely. The basic price is, therefore, only a starting point in the determination of what is going to be a more complicated pricing structure.

Step 4. Identify Alternative Basic Prices

After pinpointing the market, estimating demand, and discovering competitors' prices, it usually is possible to identify basic pricing alternatives. The number of alternatives will depend on the range of prices

Step 5. Calculate Manufacturer's Net Price

On the assumption that most manufacturers use some type of middleman, it is necessary to calculate the amount of the basic price that will be returned to the manufacturer

TABLE 17.1   Work sheet for alternative pricing strategies

Line	Alternative basic prices				
1. Basic price	$300.00	$250.00	$200.00	$150.00	$100.00
2. Expected volume in units	25,000	40,000	60,000	75,000	100,000
3. Channel discounts*	123.24	101.88	81.50	61.13	40.75
4. Manufacturer's net price	177.76	148.12	118.50	88.87	59.25
5. Fixed cost per unit	120.00	75.00	50.00	40.00	30.00
Depreciation	40.00	25.00	16.67	13.33	10.00
Rent and interest	20.00	12.50	8.33	6.67	5.00
General administrative	60.00	37.50	25.00	20.00	15.00
6. Variable cost per unit	40.00	40.00	40.00	40.00	40.00
Direct material	20.00	20.00	20.00	20.00	20.00
Direct labor	20.00	20.00	20.00	20.00	20.00
7. Total cost per unit	160.00	115.00	90.00	80.00	70.00
8. Total revenue (2 × 4)	4,444,000	5,924,800	7,110,000	6,665,250	5,925,000
9. Total costs (2 × 7)	4,000,000	4,600,000	5,400,000	6,000,000	7,000,000
10. Total profit (loss) (8 − 9)	444,000	1,324,800	1,710,000	665,250	(1,075,000)

*In this example, list less 30-10-5, 1/10 net 90.

and the amount that will be retained by the channel member(s). Only if the manufacturer sells direct to the final buyer will the basic price and the manufacturer's net price be the same. The various kinds of discounts that are offered to resellers are discussed in Chapter 18; and it will suffice here to point out that in Table 17.1 the manufacturer's net is calculated by deducting a chain discount of 30-10-5, 1/10 net 90. In the case of a basic price of $300.00, the channel discounts amount to $123.24, so that the manufacturer's net price is $177.76. If the company expects to make a profit, all costs (including overhead) must be less than this amount.

Step 6. Estimate Costs

Fixed costs are those expenses that do not vary in total with changes in sales. In Table. 17.1, fixed costs (line 5) are depreciation, rent and interest, and other general adminis-

trative expenses. Although these costs do not vary in total, they do decline per unit as sales are expanded. Thus, since total fixed costs are assumed to be $3 million, fixed costs per unit range from a high of $120 (for sales of 25,000 units at $300 each) to a low of $30 (for sales of 100,000 units at $100 each). Variable costs, on the other hand, are those that do vary in total with output. They are, therefore, constant per unit. In Table 17.1, variable costs (line 6) are $40 per unit.[6]

Step 7. Calculate Expected Profit

Total expected profits for each of the alternative prices are shown on line 10 of Table

[6]Usually there also are *semivariable costs,* such as the expenses of maintaining equipment, that tend to rise somewhat (although not directly) with increases in output. For purposes of simplifying the analysis in Table 17.1, it has been assumed that all costs are either fixed or directly variable. The analysis would not be changed significantly by including semivariable expenses.

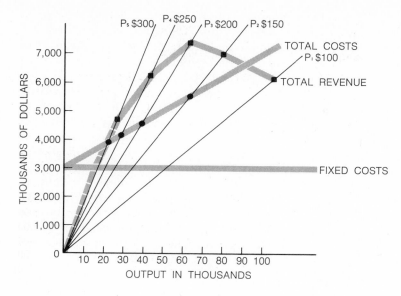

FIGURE 17.1   The break-even approach to pricing

17.1. These are obtained by multiplying total cost per unit (line 7) by expected volume (line 2) and subtracting this amount from the total revenue anticipated by the manufacturer (line 8).[7] It is obvious from the table that a basic price of $200 is the most profitable. All other prices except $100 also would produce profits, but not as great a return as a $200 basic price.

It is interesting to look at the data in Table 17.1 in graphic form. The most convenient way of doing this is to use a break-even analysis such as that seen in Figure 17.1. The break-even chart shows the relationship between total costs and total revenue at alternative pricing levels. Fixed costs are constant at $3 million. Variable costs rise from zero at zero output to a total of $4 million at an

[7]The same result could, of course, be obtained by subtracting unit costs from the manufacturer's net price and multiplying the remainder by the expected volume.

output of 100,000 units. Total costs are shown as the sum of fixed and variable costs. Price lines are shown for each of the alternative basic prices. These lines represent the total revenue that would be obtained at various outputs at each of the alternative basic prices. The higher the price the final user is charged, the greater the total revenue received by the manufacturer. The more output that is sold at any price, the greater the level of total revenue. In traditional break-even analysis, attention is focused on the intersection of total revenue and total cost. The various break-even points are noted in Figure 17.1 by black circles at the intersections of the total-cost line with the various price lines. Only for P_1 (basic price of $100) is the revenue line below the total-cost line. Losses would thus be incurred at all levels of output at this price. Profits are enjoyed at all outputs to the right of the break-even point. As you would expect, the higher the price, the lower the break-even point.

Although it is always useful to be able to identify the break-even point, this point is not of particular importance in selecting the most profitable price. Emphasis on break-even analysis can be misleading. The assumption that an infinite quantity of goods can be sold at each of the alternative prices is not consistent with the pricing information in Table 17.1. True, more can be sold at lower prices than at higher prices, but at every price there is an absolute number of units that can be sold. These values, of course, would lie along the demand curve and are shown in Table 17.1 by the volumes that appear on line 2. There is, accordingly, only one significant point on each of the respective price lines in Figure 17.1. This is the total revenue that would be derived from selling the expected volume at that price. These points are shown by black squares on the total-revenue line in the figure. A smooth curve drawn through the expected-revenue squares represents a portion of the total-revenue curve. This curve is extended in Figure 17.1 to the origin by the use of a broken line. When total revenue is plotted as a curve, rather than as the straight line used in break-even analysis, it is relatively easy to determine the most profitable output and price. Theoretically, the market planner should select that output at which there is the widest spread between total costs and total revenue.[8] In Figure 17.1, this is seen to be 60,000 units, exactly the same output that is shown to be most profitable in Table 17.1.

It is also interesting to note that there are *two* break-even points—one at an output of

---

[8]These concepts can also be expressed in marginal terms, as was illustrated in Chapter 8.

approximately 18,000 units and another at 85,000 units. These break-even points are important because they indicate the range of profitable operations. Any output between 18,000 and 85,000 units is profitable. A wide range of profitable operations is particularly helpful for a company that finds it difficult to forecast sales or one that is plagued with drastic fluctuations in sales as a result of conditions beyond its control. A decline in demand or an increase in total costs would narrow this range of profitable output, as well as to lower profits at every level. An increase in demand or a reduction in total costs would both widen the range of profitable operations and increase profits at every output within the range.

Step 8. Repeat the Analysis for Each Major Segment

If the analysis of the marketing situation were to reveal the existence of more than one major market segment, it might be necessary to develop separate pricing strategies for each segment. It is not uncommon for markets that are homogeneous in all other respects to be segmented on a price basis. Segmentation does not necessarily mean that the manufacturer must attempt to serve all segments, but it is important to recognize the existence of other market groups in making a final decision on the marketing approach. For example, the price-volume relationships presented in Table 17.1 may have applied to only one of three possible market segments. These segments are shown in Figure 17.2 as demand curves D_1, D_2, and D_3. D_1 is the market segment analyzed in Table 17.1. D_2 is an extremely elastic demand, representing a segment of the market willing to pay only

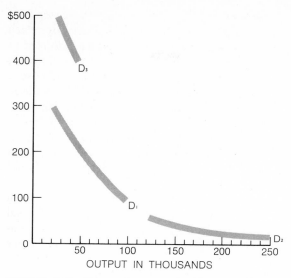

FIGURE 17.2 Demand curves for three market segments

the lowest possible price for the product. D_3 is the prestige market. It is a small segment, but it represents a demand of extreme inelasticity. In considering these other market segments, it becomes obvious that the product developed for D_1 will not be appropriate for either D_2 or D_3. As we recall from Table 17.1, any price for that product below $40 would be less than variable costs. Thus, if the firm expects to develop the market, a different product and probably an entirely different marketing mix will be required. A different product, and probably different channel and promotion strategies, also might be necessary to reach market segment D_3. Buyers in market D_3 would be expected to demand better performance and higher quality than those in D_1. Since any price on D_3 would be profitable, it clearly would be possible to build in the necessary product improvements in order to cater to this segment.

Setting Basic Price Under Uncertainty

In the preceding discussion of setting basic price, we saw that it was necessary for the marketing planner to estimate the volume that would be sold at each of several alternative basic prices. This is no easy task. A great deal of uncertainty surrounds the attempt to forecast sales volume at particular prices. The planner, forced to make a decision, selects that volume which appears most likely, even though not absolutely sure of the accuracy of the projection.

An approach for this problem involves the use of decision theory, which was described in Chapter 8.[9] The technique allows the marketing executive to establish a range

[9]See also W. R. Darden, "An Operational Approach to Product Pricing," *Journal of Marketing,* April 1968, pp. 29–32.

TABLE 17.2   Schedules of estimated demand

Price per unit	Units demanded		
	Q_p	Q_m	Q_o
$ 50	13,000	15,000	17,000
60	11,000	13,000	15,000
70	9,000	11,000	13,000
80	7,000	9,000	11,000
90	5,000	7,000	9,000
100	3,000	5,000	7,000

from which to select an acceptable price. An example of the application of this technique to a pricing problem follows.

Suppose that for any price under consideration by the decisionmaker three estimates of resulting demand can be made. They can be termed optimistic demand Q_o, most likely demand Q_m, and pessimistic demand Q_p.

Table 17.2 gives Q_o, Q_m, and Q_p estimates for six prices under consideration. Each of the columns of Table 17.2 can be thought of as representing a demand curve. These curves are presented in Figure 17.3, together with their associated total-revenue curves. If it is assumed that there is a fixed cost of $300,000 associated with producing the product and a variable cost of $33.33 per unit, then a total-cost curve also can be depicted.

From the figure it can be seen that at price P_1 ($85) a quantity of 6,000 units will be our pessimistic demand. This can be interpreted as the upper limit of the price range at which zero profits will be generated. Similarly, at P_2 ($60) a quantity of 11,000 units will be demanded, and this can be interpreted as the lower limit of the price range at which zero profits will be generated.

After establishing the feasible range with-

in which to select a price, the next step is to calculate the payoff for each price for each condition of demand. These are inserted in the payoff table (see Table 17.3). We must now impose some criterion and choose a price that best meets this criterion. Assume that the criterion is to maximize expected profits. Assigning weights (subjective probabilities) to each estimate of demand (.2 to Q_p, .6 to Q_m, and .2 to Q_o), we can calculate the expected profit for each pricing alternative. These values are shown in the last column of Table 17.3. The pricing strategy of $80 has the highest expected profit, so this is the basic price that would be selected in this example.

Summary

What is a price? We have seen that this question is far more difficult to answer than most people might think. In part, this is due to the complicated and many-faceted nature of pricing issues. For example, there are the differences in the meaning of price when viewed from the customer's standpoint and from the seller's perspective. The customer views a price as a sacrifice; the seller sees it as an indicator of expected revenue. Moreover, the seller often is in conflict over pricing with the government, with channel members, and with the environment at large.

Some of the confusion about pricing can be lessened when we view pricing strategy as being made up of a basic price, or reference price, and a pricing structure. There is less difference among prices when they are compared at the basic level. Thus, the variations in the level of most quoted prices can be

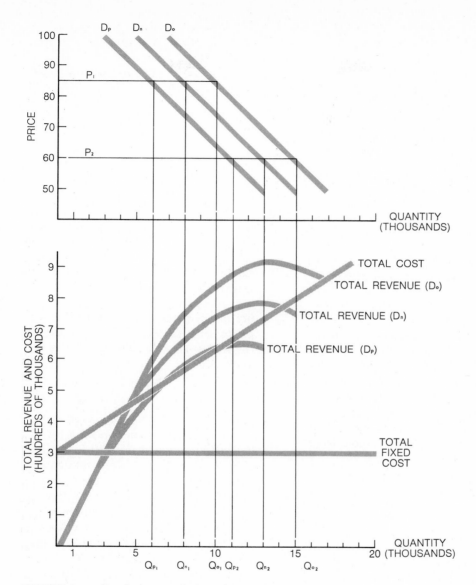

FIGURE 17.3   Break-even analysis under uncertainty

explained by specific aspects of the pricing structure.

The development of pricing strategy begins, of course, with the identification of

pricing objectives. Among these may be company growth, increased market share, control over cash flow and profit, and the stabilization of prices and margins. Such

407

TABLE 17.3   Payoff matrix for alternative prices (Profit payoffs in thousands of dollars)

Price strategy	Q_p (p = .2)	Q_m (p = .6)	Q_o (p = .2)	Expected profit
$ 50	(83.3)*	(50.0)*	(16.6)*	(50.0)*
60	(6.6)*	46.7	100.1	46.7
70	30.0	103.4	176.7	103.4
80	26.7	120.0	213.4	120.0
90	(16.7)*	96.7	210.0	96.7
100	(100.0)*	33.4	166.7	33.4

*Loss.

objectives usually can be attained when a pricing plan is formulated systematically.

The systematic approach commences, as should any marketing-oriented aspect of strategy, with a study of the consumer. Obviously competition is not ignored, and generally several alternative basic prices are identified, so that a choice must be made. Usually, this is accomplished by comparing the revenues, costs, and profits associated with the various alternatives and making a selection that seems to achieve the company's pricing objectives. The approach can be modified to reflect the degree of uncertainty faced. And, of course, basic prices may have to be set for various products in a company's total line of offerings or for customers in different segments of the market.

Questions and Problems

1. Describe the manner in which price can be used as a competitive weapon by
   a. A department store
   b. An encyclopedia salesperson
   c. A hamburger stand
   d. An electrical-apparatus manufacturer

2. Select a product, such as a gallon can of latex paint, a package of noodles, a toothbrush, or a 19-inch color television set. Shop for this product in at least three different stores. Find out if only one price is charged for this product in any given store and if different prices are charged in two or more of the stores. How can any differences be explained?

3. What is the difference between cost-plus and market-minus pricing?

4. A company that manufactures room air conditioners has experienced a lot of disagreement on what its pricing policy should be. Finally, in desperation, the president created a pricing committee composed of the marketing director, the director of manufacturing, the sales manager, and the controller. What do you think of the idea of using a pricing committee? Who should be appointed chairperson? As regards pricing decisions generally, what positions do you think each of the committee members might be expected to take?

5. The statement is made in the chapter that price is potentially a dangerous and explosive marketing force. Why do you think this is so?

6. Generally a company charges a high price when it wishes to recover cash quickly—as in the introduction of a new product that incurred heavy development costs. Can you think of circumstances in which a fast pay-back might be achieved better by a low price?

7. Reexamine the alternative pricing prices in Table 17.1 using the following estimates of demand:

Price	Expected volume
$300.00	25,000
250.00	50,000
200.00	75,000
150.00	90,000
100.00	100,000

Assume that costs remain the same as in Table 17.1, with the following exceptions:
   Variable material costs are $22.50.
   Variable labor costs are $27.50.
   General administrative costs are $1.25 million in total.
   Depreciation is also $1.25 million in total.

8. The Schmelly Chemical Company introduced its now obsolete Polyusterplus in January 1971. At the time of its introduction, this product was the only one of its particular kind. The manufacturing process was patented, and the trade name Polyusterplus was registered. The chemical basis of the plastic, however, was not difficult to discover, and Schmelly executives believed that other firms would be able to duplicate the product within eighteen months.
   a. List and explain briefly the pricing objectives that might be relevant for this company.
   b. What pricing alternatives were probably considered for Polyusterplus at the time of its introduction? Explain these alternatives and indicate the one that you ordinarily would recommend for a new industrial chemical facing this type of situation.

9. What is meant by basic price?

10. Isn't the consequence of every pricing decision uncertain? If so, what is so special about the concept of pricing under conditions of uncertainty?

18

Pricing Strategy: Issues and Problems

The systematic approach to pricing outlined in Chapter 17 may make the pricing process appear simpler than it actually is. In reality, pricing is extremely complicated. Each of the steps involved in the development of a market-oriented pricing strategy presents the market planner with intricate issues and problems requiring sophisticated techniques for their analysis and solution. We will now look at the major issues and problems that arise in developing a pricing strategy and at some of the methods for their resolution.

Pricing the Product Line

What is the pricing procedure if a manufacturer has a line of products? Such a line ordinarily would be required to meet the diverse needs of the various users. For ex-

ample, the line that a manufacturer of power lawn mowers offers includes six major products, some in a number of models:

5 staggered-wheel rotaries, priced from $90.00 to $129.95

6 in-line deck rotaries, priced from $99.50 to $139.95

4 heavy-duty rotaries, priced from $139.95 to $225.00

1 ride mower, priced at $589.95

1 commercial-institutional mower, priced at $449.50

1 edge trimmer, priced at $87.50

In marketing a line of products for a particular market segment, pricing differentials must be established for each of the items in the line. It is important to stress that these are differentials from the basic price.

The amount of the differential depends, in part, on differences in volume expectation, costs, and performance. Dramatic differences in the performance and costs of riding and self-propelled mowers compared to other mowers in the line result in their prices being near the upper extreme. Prices of conventional power mowers, on the other hand, fall somewhere below the basic price. The line also might include a promotional item that would be sold at less than average total costs in order to attract potential customers. Dealers would be encouraged to trade up customers to better-performing and higher-priced merchandise.

Of course, the theoretical goal in setting product-line prices is to improve the marketability and profitability of the entire line. In order to be competitive, to satisfy diverse user requirements, and to meet the demands of resellers, however, it often is necessary to make compromises. For example, a traditional pricing method used in department stores is known as *price lining*. The merchant selects a set of pricing differentials that are applied to all items sold. The price line selected for a dress shop might be as follows:

$14.95
 17.95
 22.95
 27.95
 35.00
 50.00

When retailers and their wholesalers practice price lining, it is necessary for manufacturers to set their prices accordingly. In order to market profitably at these levels, the manufacturer must carefully control the design features and manufacturing costs. Price lining is an excellent example of the backward push of the market on the manufacturer's prices. Although price lining is less formally followed in other areas of marketing, the pressure of consumers and the trade dictates to a large degree the pricing alternatives open to any manufacturer. This market pressure reaffirms why a cost-plus approach to pricing is not desirable. Rather, the manufacturer must use the market-minus pricing approach, in which the margins of resellers and the manufacturer's own profit expectations are deducted from the final price in order to determine the amount to commit to the costs of manufacturing a product.

The Discount Structure

The group of discounts established to adjust for variations in product offerings, customer requirements, and competition constitutes the pricing structure.[1] Although discounts (and extras) can be designed to fit almost any pricing situation, there are a number of typical situations for which traditional forms of discounts have been developed.

Trade (Functional) Discounts

Over the years, marketers have granted discounts on the basis of a customer's position in the channel system. The various trade status positions that are recognized by

---

[1] It should be pointed out that the pricing structure can include extras as well as discounts. An *extra* is a charge added to a basic price to compensate the seller for the cost of unusual buyer requirements. For example, if a steel customer requires that steel sheets be trimmed to a certain size, or if a department store requires that its supplier package a product in some special way, the price probably would be raised.

discounts are retail (dealer), jobber, whole-saler (distributor), and manufacturer. A discount granted to a system component for performing status functions in the marketing channel is called a *trade discount,* or occasionally a *functional discount.* Trade discounts generally conform to historical patterns and reflect the typical cost and profit configurations of the customer. The important point to remember in connection with trade discounts is that they are awarded on the basis of the trade position exclusively. Every retailer in a channel system qualifies for the same trade discount. No wholesaler, regardless of size, can obtain it. Such discounts might seem at first to be highly discriminatory. However, since wholesalers, at least theoretically, are not in direct competition with retailers, any difference in discount on the basis of trade status should have no restraining effect on competition.

Quantity Discounts

It is quite common for a seller to accept a lower unit price for items sold in large quantities than for items sold in small lots. There are two types of quantity discounts: cumulative and noncumulative. The *cumulative discount* is based on the total amount of business done by a seller with a particular customer over a period of time. It is calculated according to either anticipated volume or past experience. The *noncumulative discount* is based only on the quantity included in a particular order.

There are important legal requirements to be satisfied when quantity discounts are used. The legal status of the cumulative discount is seriously in doubt, because it is extremely difficult to defend on the basis of cost savings. Shorn of this defense, the

cumulative discount in most cases is apt to violate the Robinson-Patman Act. The noncumulative discount, on the other hand, usually is legal provided that the difference in discount can be justified by differences in costs incurred. The Federal Trade Commission also has ruled that no quantity discount schedules can be discriminatory, even though the differences in discount reflect actual cost savings. For example, if only one or two firms qualify for the largest quantity discount, the commission might rule, as it has in the past, that the effect on competition of granting the lower price to only one or two customers would be unfair.

Promotional Allowances

Promotional discounts also take two forms—permanent and special. In working with resellers in the trade channel, it is common to set up *permanent* schedules of allowances for performing promotional activities. For example, a cooperative advertising program may be established in order to encourage resellers to advertise the manufacturer's products. The *special* promotional allowance, in contrast, is a short-term allowance that usually is related to a particular promotional campaign. For example, in order to build up retail stocks in advance of a large-scale consumer promotion, a manufacturer may offer a special promotional incentive to resellers. This may be a direct discount or it may be in the form of free goods.

Promotional allowances also are regulated by specific provisions in the Robinson-Patman Act. They must be offered to all customers, they must be proportional to the amount of business done with each customer, and they must be used by the customer solely for promotional purposes. It is the intent of the law to prohibit promotional allowances from becoming convenient disguises for discriminatory pricing offers.

Locational Discounts

One of the thorniest problems in pricing arises in connection with the location of customers. It should be clear that the cost of moving a finished product from the manufacturer's location to the customer's location is a marketing cost. It is a cost that, like other costs incurred by the seller, must be covered if the transaction is to be profitable. The difficulty arises when considering the most appropriate way in which to cover such transportation costs. It might seem that the fairest and easiest method would be to add the cost of transportation to the manufacturer's selling price in order to determine the delivered cost to the customer. This is, in fact, a common method and is referred to as *F.O.B. pricing.*[2] Although simple to understand and easy to quote, F.O.B. pricing is quite difficult to administer, especially for a firm with a broad line and a wide geographical dispersion of customers. Under an F.O.B. pricing system, customers ordinarily expect the manufacturer to ship the merchandise by the most economical method. This means that the manufacturer must maintain a sizable traffic and transportation department to route shipments and to determine the freight charges to be billed to the customer. F.O.B. pricing, moreover, usually places certain sellers at a pricing disadvantage in comparison with competitors located closer

[2]The initials FOB stand for *free on board* and mean that the legal title to the goods passes to the customer when the merchandise is accepted by the carrier and that the customer is liable for all transportation costs incurred.

to the customer's place of business. In order to avoid the costly and thankless tasks of determining freight charges for each and every sale and in order to meet competitors' prices, manufacturers have developed various discount arrangements based on customer location.

Uniform delivered pricing Technically, a uniform delivered pricing system involves no discount on the basis of location. The same delivered price is charged to each customer. The uniform system is used frequently in the sale of products for which transportation costs are low relative to the value of the goods. It also is used if there is an advantage in advertising a single price throughout the country. This is true of products that are sold at so-called customary prices, such as magazines, men's shirts, and electric shavers. Uniform delivered pricing occasionally is called *postage stamp pricing,* because the customer's price, in effect, includes a fixed average cost of transportation. It is obvious, however, that uniform delivered pricing does involve differentials in price according to customer location. If the manufacturer's price is considered to be the *mill-net*—that is, the price charged the customer minus the actual cost of transportation—it is clear that a distant customer pays a lower price than does one located close to the shipping point. Nevertheless, in most cases where uniform delivered pricing is used, the transportation costs are so small that the differential is insignificant.

Zone pricing If transportation costs are large in relation to the value of the goods but the seller wishes to retain the advantages of uniform delivered pricing, a zone pricing system is adopted. Zone pricing is similar to uniform delivered pricing, except that delivered prices differ from one zone to the next. A familiar example is the practice of some appliance sellers of charging "slightly higher prices west of the Rockies." Industrial firms frequently use multiple zones, perhaps as many as there are territorial sales districts.

Pricing differentials in zone pricing arise in two ways. They are illustrated in Figure 18.1. In this exhibit, a manufacturer located at point A uses a pricing structure that involves uniform delivered pricing in each of three zones, shown by the concentric circles around point A. Pricing differentials can be seen by inspecting the effect of this pricing system on three different customers—one at location B, another at location C, and a third at location D. Customers B and C pay the same delivered price, because they are in the same zone. Customer C, however, actually pays a lower price (mill net) than does customer B. Customer D pays a higher price than either B or C, even though located only a few miles away.[3] Such zone prices, as we shall see, sometimes can avoid the legal problems connected with another method of providing location discounts—basing-point pricing.

Basing-point pricing   Basing-point pricing has more historical than immediate importance in marketing.[4] Under this method of pricing, a firm would designate selected locations as basing points from which transportation charges to customers were determined. It did not matter under this system whether goods actually came from the basing

point; transport costs still were calculated as if the basing point had been the place from which they were shipped. Most companies in an industry used the same basing points. Therefore, the price of a product to any customer would be about the same for all competitors, regardless of location. Many companies that once used basing-point pricing systems have shifted to zone or F.O.B. pricing. In large part, these shifts have been the result of rising doubts concerning the legal status of basing-point pricing. The abandonment of this system also was stimulated by the proliferation of competition that attended its use and by the shifting geographical patterns of industrial activity.[5] It should not be assumed, however, that basing-point pricing is unimportant in today's market. A well-known example is the pricing of motor vehicles, in which F.O.B. Detroit is still the common pricing method.

Unsystematic freight equalization   Unsystematic freight equalization[6] is the practice of meeting competitors' delivered prices in order to maintain market share. In other words, sellers offer locational discounts to particular customers through the absorption of freight costs. Freight absorption has been a very common practice in the highly competitive sectors of the steel industry since the abandonment of the multiple basing-

---

[3]Actually, this type of zone arrangement would not be allowed. Zone boundaries must not be set in such a way as to create unfair pricing differences.

[4]In spite of its obsolescence as a pricing method, basing-point pricing should be understood by the marketing student. Not only is it important historically, but it also is important because it demonstrates the actual and potential discriminations that are inherent in almost any type of geographical pricing system.

[5]This point is well illustrated by U.S. Steel Corp., which abandoned the multiple basing-point selling system in 1948. A study by the Maryland State Planning Commission revealed that the effect of changing from basing-point to F.O.B. mill pricing on the company's Sparrow's Point, Maryland, mill resulted in a net gain of 1.4 million tons of steel business for the Sparrow's Point mill. See Maryland State Planning Commission, *Survey of the Impact of F.O.B. Mill Pricing on Maryland Manufacturers,* Publication No. 61 (Baltimore: Maryland State Planning Commission, 1949), p. 60.

[6]A *systematic system* of freight equalization would be so similar to a multiple basing-point pricing system in which all shipping points were treated as basing points that it need not be discussed separately.

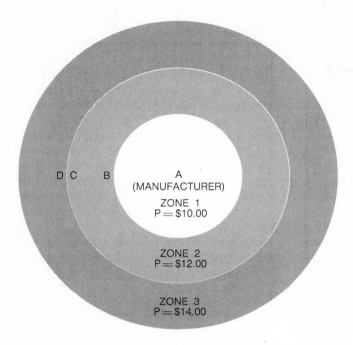

FIGURE 18.1   An example of zone pricing

point pricing system. This is because it is mandatory for a firm with heavy fixed costs and extensive capacity to maintain volume and share of market. When used aggressively or in a predatory fashion, freight equalization is considered an unfair pricing practice. However, when used independently and in order to meet competition, an unsystematic method of freight equalization is permissible. It is feasible in the long run only when the incremental profit from the added business more than offsets the cost of freight absorption.

Terms of Payment

Arrangements for payment can be of almost any type; however, they usually are classi-

fied as either cash or time payment discounts. In order to induce prompt payment, sellers may offer a cash discount. The *cash discount* provides a specific percentage reduction for prompt payment of the invoice, and it stipulates the period of time within which payment must be made. The most commonly quoted cash discount is 2/10, net 30. This means that the customer may deduct 2 per cent from the value of the invoice if paid within 10 days of the invoice date, and the full invoice amount is due in 30 days. Many variations of this type of discount are offered, the differences reflecting traditional methods in particular lines of trade. For example, in sales of seasonal merchandise, it is common to date invoices so that payment is not required until the start of the buyer's selling season.

Methods of Quoting Prices

Before concluding the discussion of pricing structure, it is necessary to describe how decisions regarding basic price and discounts are translated into actual selling prices. The technique most commonly used by manufacturers is to establish a so-called list price for each item. This list price may be identical to the basic price or it may represent some modification thereof. For example, the basic price might be adjusted downward slightly to establish a list price below that of major competitors. The list price also provides a convenient way of stating prices. List prices can be advertised or printed in expensive catalogs without any loss in the flexibility that is needed for quoting actual prices. It is much easier and quicker to change the discount structure than to change the list prices mentioned in catalogs or advertisements. Moreover, different discount sheets can be distributed to different customer groups without raising unnecessary questions or undue concern over possible discrimination.

In quoting an actual price to a particular customer, the seller always begins with the list price. From this is deducted, in succession, each of the discounts for which the customer qualifies. Trade discounts typically are quoted in the form of a *chain*. Quantity, promotional, and cash discounts usually are deducted after the trade discount has been determined. Actual transportation charges are added to the list price minus all the buyer discounts. For example, suppose that a manufacturer sells 100 wrench sets to a warehouse distributor. This distributor would be the first link in a distribution system that might also include a jobber and a dealer. Assuming that the list price (which is also the manufacturer's suggested retail price) is $200, the manufacturer might offer a chain discount of 20-15-10-10-5, 2/10 net 30. This discount means that the distributor would deduct in succession each of these percentages from a constantly reducing base. (Note that the discounts are not simply added up to obtain a total discount.)

In our example, the amount that the distributor would pay for the 100 wrench sets is $11,505.70 or $115.06 each. The computation is shown in Table 18.1. Each discount in the chain is deducted separately, and the succeeding discount is computed on the basis of a new net value. The cash discount is offered only on the final net and no discounts are allowed on transportation and insurance costs. The distributor, in turn, would price the wrench set to a jobber at $200 list less a chain discount of 20-15, 2/10 net 30. The jobber, in turn, would charge the dealer $200 less 20, 2/10 net 30. The retailer would be encouraged to charge the ultimate buyer the manufacturer's suggested list price of $200.

Pricing and the Product Life Cycle

The decision on pricing is closely tied to the position of the product in its life cycle. Early in its history, a product possesses its greatest degree of differentiation. If its distinctiveness is considerable, pricing above the market may be feasible and desirable. In the growth stages and in the early period of maturity, competitive parity of prices is far more common. In the declining stages, when the product's uniqueness has deteriorated substantially, pricing below competition may be the only effective way of slowing down the decline in sales.

TABLE 18.1 Computation of a distributor's price by use of a chain discount, 20-15-10-10-5, 2/10 net 30

List price $200 (F.O.B. St. Louis)	Per unit	Total
List	$200.00	
less 20%	40.00	
leaves a net of	160.00	
less 15%	24.00	
leaves a net of	136.00	
less 10%	13.60	
leaves a net of	122.40	
less 10%	12.24	
leaves a net of	110.16	
less 5%	5.51	
leaves a net of	104.65 × 100	$10,465.00
less 2% cash discount		209.30
		10,255.70
Plus insurance and transportation from St. Louis, Missouri		1,250.00
		$11,505.70

The Introductory Stage

As we have indicated, the appropriate pricing strategy for a new product depends on its *degree* of distinctiveness and the *duration* of the period that this distinctiveness is expected to last. Products of little or no distinctiveness must be priced close to the prices of substitute products. Of course, the logic of introducing a new product or service without truly differentiating characteristics should always be challenged on general principles. Now we also should question the soundness of introducing an undifferentiated product on pricing grounds. Without distinguishing characteristics, the only possibility a product has for success lies in selling it at a price lower than competitors'. This type of pricing strategy is extremely tenuous

and never offers as good an opportunity for profit as the pricing of a product that does have considerable distinctiveness. The duration of the distinctiveness is also of critical importance, because, if the market strategist can anticipate a period of three to five years during which the unique character of the product is unlikely to be challenged by potential competitors, the pricing decision can be approached from the standpoint of maximizing profits.

Pricing a product of lasting distinctiveness is quite comparable to pricing in a monopoly situation. A monopoly pricing model is shown in Figure 18.2. Using this model, the seller of a product of lasting distinctiveness equates marginal cost and marginal revenue to determine the price that should be charged and the quantity that should be sold.[7] Profits are maximized at this price and output. Note in Figure 18.2 that profit maximization is determined by *marginal cost,* not average total cost (ATC). The reason for this was explored in Chapter 8. The ATC curve is shown only because it is useful in calculating total profits at the most profitable price and output. (ATC is total cost divided by quantity.) Total profits are shown in the model by the shaded rectangle. Of course, price *P* is a first approximation to the appropriate price. For reasons other than maximizing profits, the seller may decide to price at a somewhat lower level. These reasons usually arise from an awareness of the public environment. Public opinion, union tactics, or federal antitrust activities, for example, may lead the seller to price somewhat below *P.* The cost of such a pricing concession can

[7]You should recognize that this marginal criterion is the same as maximizing the spread between total revenue and total cost. This relationship was explained in Chapter 8.

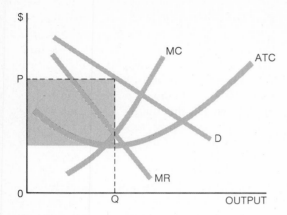

FIGURE 18.2   Pricing in the introductory stage (a product of lasting distinctiveness)

be measured directly by the reduction in total profits.

Intriguing as monopoly pricing strategy may be, a market planner seldom can anticipate three or more years of lasting distinctiveness. Accordingly, the planner usually must price in the introductory period on the assumption that the distinctiveness of the product will decline rapidly as a result of competitors entering the market. The appropriate pricing strategy for the introduction of a product of perishable distinctiveness is either a skimming or a penetration price. Both are strategic prices. The *skimming price* is higher than the monopoly price, and the *penetration price* is certainly lower. Neither is a profits-maximizing price. In fact, skimming and penetration prices are charged in order to achieve pricing objectives other than maximization of profits.

The decision of whether to skim or to penetrate is based principally on the elasticity of demand for the new product. If the demand is inelastic, a skimming price is used. If the demand is elastic, a penetration price is in order. Both prices, of course,

should be considered in relation to costs. However, pricing in the introductory period need not be closely related to immediate costs. It is the long-run strategy of profit attainment over the entire product life cycle that is significant. It is important that the pricing strategist never attempt a compromise by pricing somewhere between the two levels. An in-between price has the awkward result of being encumbered with the disadvantages of both while possessing the advantages of neither.

These general concepts are shown in Figure 18.3. The demand curve D_1 represents a new product with an inelastic demand. Clearly, a skimming price such as P_1 would be in order for this product. Quantity Q_1 would be sold. D_2 represents a new product with an elastic demand. The price for this product should be a penetration price, such as P_2. At P_2, a quantity Q_2 would be sold. P_3, a compromise price, might be considered for either product. It is clear, however, that P_3 is much too low for D_1 and much too high for D_2. At P_3, Q_3 would be sold on either demand curve. Total revenues in either case would be much less than would be achieved by the appropriate pricing strategy.

The Growth Stage

Pricing in the growth stage of the life cycle involves pricing in direct relationship to competition. In the growth stage, it is expected that potential competitors will have made their way into the market. Pricing to maintain market share and pricing in relation to the rest of the market mix usually are involved. The exact pricing conditions that prevail in the growth stage depend principally on the number of potential competitors—that is, whether oligopolistic

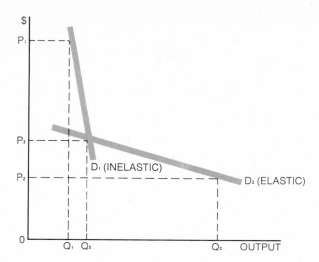

FIGURE 18.3   Pricing in the introductory stage (a product of perishable distinctiveness)

or monopolistic competition exists.

It is in the growth and early-maturity stages of a product's life cycle that oligopolistic market conditions are most likely to develop. An *oligopoly* is a market in which a limited number of firms account for a large proportion of total industry sales. The dependence of a seller's pricing strategy on the pricing practices of oligopolistic competitors is well illustrated by the famous kinked demand curve. In contrast to the demand curve presented in Chapter 7, the *kinked demand curve* of an oligopolist has two distinct segments, each with a different slope. This is shown in Figure 18.4. On the realistic assumption that the pricing structures of the competitors have become more or less stable, we may use the manufacturer's list price (P_1) as a reference point in describing this kinked demand curve. If the seller contemplates a price increase (say, to P_2), there is the reasonable expectation that less will be sold. Just how many fewer units will depend on the overall demand elasticity for the product and the behavior of competition. In Figure 18.4 a broken line *DD* has been extended through P_1 at point *A* representing the slope of the industry demand curve.[8] We will call this line *(DD)* the *industry reference curve.* If other sellers matched the manufacturer's price increase, sales would fall to Q_2 as indicated by the industry reference curve. In practice, however, it is not likely that competing firms would raise prices in the absence of price leadership, collusion, or industry-wide cost pressures. If competing firms do not raise prices, or raise them to less than P_2, sales will decrease more sharply than would be expected if all firms matched the price rise—perhaps a decrease to Q_3. The effect on the manufacturer would be a

[8]This is not the industry demand curve, which would be far to the right of the curve depicted. It has, however, the same slope.

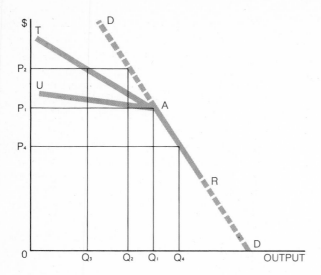

FIGURE 18.4   Pricing in the growth stage (oligopoly pricing)

decline in market share resulting from the new price, which is high in relation to competition. Since failure to match a price increase is the competitors' most probable reaction, it is assumed that the actual schedule of sales that the oligopolist would experience would be along a line AT. For a truly differentiated oligopolist, this curve might not depart very much from the upper segment of the industry reference curve. For an undifferentiated oligopolist, however, any price differential in favor of competitors would mean drastic losses in market share. This is shown in Figure 18.4 by the line AU.

Considering next the effect of lowering price (say, to P_4), the oligopolist must assume that competitors would exactly match any price reduction. This assumption is based on the realistic conclusion that competitors could not afford to lose market share by being undercut, nor would they be willing to risk the dangers of a price war by

pricing even lower. Since all firms would be selling at identical but lower prices, the sales that the manufacturer might expect would fall along a line approximating the position of the industry reference curve. The lower length of this kinked demand curve is shown by line AR.

The kinked demand curve demonstrates the importance of the interaction of competitors. No seller can price unilaterally. Pricing strategy can be developed only after careful consideration of competitors' pricing tactics and their expected reactions to any price changes initiated. Second, the kinked demand curve suggests why price stability frequently is encountered in American markets. In all probability, the demand segment AR is quite inelastic. This means that a price reduction would result in decreases in total revenue for each competitor. Since the demand segment AT (and definitely the demand segment AU) must be considered

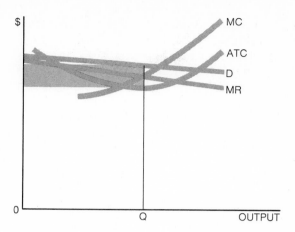

FIGURE 18.5 Pricing in maturity (monopolistic competition)

elastic, a price increase under these conditions also would decrease total revenue. Thus, since total revenue would be expected to decline with *any* price change, the desire to stabilize price is easy to understand.

The Maturity Stage

The mature stage of a product's life cycle develops when the rate of sales growth begins to decline rapidly. The product in this stage is usually one of waning distinctiveness. Depending on the number of competitors, either undifferentiated oligopoly or monopolistic competition prevails. The latter condition, a fairly common occurrence in mature pricing situations, involves a large number of competitors. That is, the monopolistic competitor faces critical competition from many close substitutes. Such a seller attempts to maximize profits by equating marginal cost and marginal revenue as shown in Figure 18.5. However, because of the high price elasticity of demand and the con-

stant pressure on market share that results from easy entry into the market, there is very little margin of profit, which is shown in the figure by the shaded area. The seller cannot afford to price very much above the market. Normally, any substantial deviation from the prices of competitors results either in a substantial loss of market share (at too high a price) or in the threat of an undesirable price war (at too low a price). The best examples of monopolistic competition in marketing are found in the area of retail trade, especially in gasoline and fast-foods marketing.

Pricing in maturity frequently is plagued by the entrance of vigorous price cutters. Notable among these are late comers into the field and large distributors marketing private-brand merchandise. The seller of a product in its mature stage is thus faced with a constant squeeze between lowered margins and rising costs.

The Decline Stage

Products are seldom abandoned the moment they turn into the decline stage. As long as they are sold, they must be priced. A product in the decline stage possesses either zero or inferior distinctiveness. Accordingly, the marketer of such a product often prices below the market. This may be the point in the product's life cycle when it is used as a loss leader. An unprofitable declining product should be sold only as long as it is needed to fill out a product line or until a new product is ready to replace it. The pricing of products with little or no distinctiveness in the declining stage is quite comparable to the pricing of products under conditions of pure competition. The firm probably can sell adequate volumes at the going market price.

If product distinctiveness is inferior, however, the price has to be lower than market in order to retain any customers at all.

Psychological Pricing

A market planner must consider not only the fairly tangible relationship between pricing and the product life cycle but the less tangible issue of psychological pricing as well. A *psychological price* is one that is supposed to produce sales responses as a result of emotional reactions rather than as a result of economic considerations. Psychological pricing is used most often on the retail level, although it is not unknown in industrial marketing. Four types of price adjustments are commonly made on the basis of their psychological effects.

Odd Pricing

Odd pricing refers to the practice of setting resale prices that end in odd numbers. There is no doubt that odd prices are commonly found in retailing, but whether it is true that consumers react more favorably to odd prices than to even ones has not been established. Odd pricing is probably the least important of the psychological pricing practices, and it often is used in conjunction with markdowns and discounts designed to produce additional psychological effects.

Customary Prices

Customary prices are those that consumers expect to pay. For years, $.05 was the estab-lished or customary price for a carbonated beverage or a cup of coffee. Today, a cup of coffee or a bottle of pop carries a customary price of $.25 or higher. Customary prices also are encountered in the marketing of soft goods, services, and even some industrial products. Such prices are psychological in the sense that they are established by consumer attitudes and by sellers' unwillingness to violate the norms.

Prestige Pricing

Prestige pricing involves setting high prices for certain products because of their unique or unusual character. The assumption is that more units of a prestige item can be sold at a higher price than at a lower price. New products, especially those that are somewhat bizarre, often command relatively high prices and would not be purchased by some customers at lower prices. Although many factors influence the price of a new product, prestige pricing is clearly an important consideration. For example, when the Polaroid camera was first introduced, it represented a remarkable innovation in amateur photography. Certainly the demand for this item was extremely inelastic; the company could have picked almost any price that it wanted to. It is possible that the public might not have expected an inexpensive camera to perform so remarkably, and for this reason fewer units might have been sold at a price under $100 than were actually sold at a price almost twice that amount. Similarly, when the first home laundry equipment was introduced in the 1930s, market research indicated a greater demand for the product at high than at low prices. Obviously, there is a limit to which this psychological advantage can be pushed, but within the relevant range of

(A) PRESTIGE PRICING

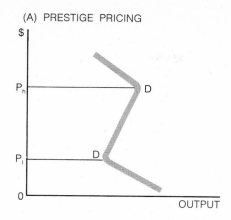

(B) PSYCHOLOGICAL DISCOUNTING

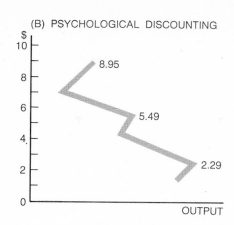

FIGURE 18.6   Psychological pricing

pricing alternatives there may be a definite advantage in prestige pricing.

Part A of Figure 18.6 shows the demand curve for a prestige product. The segment of the curve labeled *DD* represents the area within which the psychological advantage of prestige pricing is obtained. At prices higher than P_h, sales ordinarily would be expected to decline. This is shown by the upward extension of the demand curve. Similarly, prices lower than P_1 might reasonably be expected to increase sales volume again. Given a choice of where to price in such a demand situation without regard to cost, the seller should always price at P_h or higher.

Psychological Discounting

Psychological discounting is the practice of using certain prices that give the illusion of markdowns from higher prices. For example, a buyer might expect a price of $8.95 to have been reduced from $10.00. A $2.29 price might be associated with an original $3.00 value. The assumption follows that a merchant can sell more at a price that gives

the illusion of being a discount than at a somewhat lower price. This is illustrated in part B of Figure 18.6.

Closely related to psychological discounting is the prevalent practice of using fictitious comparative-pricing promotion. Better Business Bureaus and the FTC have diligently attacked the practice. A typical example would be that of a merchant displaying merchandise in a store window with a sign that reads "Was $25.00. Now $12.95." Neither the BBB or the FTC objects to legitimate markdowns, but in many instances the original price was never actually charged. In fact, the discount price is sometimes higher than normal retail value.

Psychological prices, except prestige prices, ordinarily are set at the retail level. They are not, accordingly, of extreme importance to the manufacturer in developing a market mix. However, in view of the fact that the reseller's price has substantial bearing on the manufacturer's volume and profits, it is important for the market planner to anticipate the opportunity or the need for psychological pricing. Where this exists, part of the challenge of working with resellers is to urge

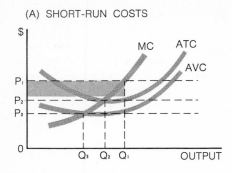

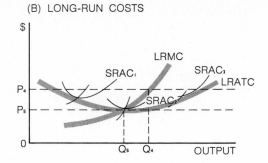

FIGURE 18.7   The relation of price to typical cost curves

them to adopt the appropriate psychological pricing tactics.

Pricing in Relation to Cost

Almost everyone agrees that prices should cover costs. However, it would be quite wrong to insist that every product should be priced to cover its own individual costs. Also, since there are many ways of measuring cost, there must be many ways of viewing the problem of pricing in relation to costs. The issue can be clarified by considering some of the relationships between price and several of the key cost concepts.[9] These curves are reproduced in Figure 18.7. Part A shows the typical short-run cost curves, and part B the behavior of long-run costs.

Pricing and Short-Run Cost

Three types of cost are important in short-run pricing situations. These are *marginal cost, average total cost,* and *average variable cost.*

[9]The various cost functions are explained in some detail in Chapter 22.

In the short run, profits can be maximized if a price (P_1) is set equal to marginal cost. At this price, quantity Q_1 would be manufactured and sold. It can be readily seen that profits are maximized at output Q_1, because any further increase in sales would result in incremental costs in excess of price. Any sales quantity less than Q_1 would be less profitable, because profits could be improved if output were increased. In fact, as long as price exceeds marginal costs, profits can be improved by increases in output. The profits yielded by this pricing strategy are shown in the shaded rectangle of Figure 18.7, part A. The profit can be computed by determining the difference between price and average total cost at Q_1 and multiplying this value by the quantity sold. Such a profit exists because the seller possesses a unique cost structure. This uniqueness, however, is likely to deteriorate as equally efficient competitors become more active. In the face of competition, the seller is forced to lower price, constantly equating marginal costs and price to determine the most profitable output. Under these conditions, but still in the short run, two particular prices are of special importance. The lowest price that the seller can charge and still recover all costs is P_2. This is the low point on the average-total-cost curve and is indicated by the intersection of marginal cost and average total cost. Q_2 would be sold at this price. This is a significant price, because any price lower than P_2 fails to cover average total cost and accordingly results in a loss on the sale of the product. However, sales could be made at prices *below* average total cost. It is as important to *minimize losses* as it is to maximize profits in the short run. But we must ask how far below average total cost a company should price. The answer to this question is P_3. This is the lowest point on the average-variable-cost curve. All prices higher than P_3 contribute something to fixed costs, even though losses are incurred. A price lower than P_3 would involve out-of-pocket expenses in excess of revenue. For this reason, price always should be equal to or greater than average variable costs. At P_3, quantity Q_3 would be manufactured and sold.[10]

Pricing and Long-Run Cost

Part B of Figure 18.7 illustrates the relationship between price and long-run cost. In the long run, a company has the opportunity to adjust its capacity, and for this reason all costs are variable. As in the short run, a price should be set that maximizes profits. Losses in the long run are indications either of a declining market opportunity or of unnecessarily high costs. The solution to a loss problem, therefore, is found in a shift in company strategy. Profits are maximized in the long run by equating long-run marginal cost and price. In the exhibit, this occurs at

P_4. (Q_4 would be sold.) Even in the long run, competitive pressures can develop. In the face of such competition, long-run prices decline. The lowest price that should be charged in the long run is P_5. At Q_5, price is equal to long-run marginal cost and long-run average total cost. It is also equal to short-run average cost and short-run marginal cost. This is the classic condition of equilibrium, toward which economists assume that market conditions tend.

The Experience Curve

A different approach to pricing in relation to cost has been taken by a number of successful firms. The approach utilizes the experience cost curve. An example is shown in Figure 18.8. Unit cost declines with cumulative volume over time, hence the phrase *experience curve.* Through time, the firm develops versions of the product with lower costs and discovers more efficient methods of manufacturing. The classical explanations of declining unit cost also apply, but the forces causing increasing costs are assumed to be offset by the benefits of experience.

How does a firm price in relation to the experience curve? It is impractical to attempt to apply the classical profits-maximizing criteria. Instead, the concept fits best with strategic pricing over the life cycle. Using Figure 18.8, suppose the Minex Company (a fictitious electronics firm) introduces a digital watch in period 1. Its initial price, P_1, is a skimming price, high enough to recover much of the research and development cost already committed. Unit costs are high in period 1, but Minex is familiar with integrated-circuit technology and anticipates the experience cost curve depicted. Thus, the experience cost curve is a planning tool—it is a forecast of what costs are

[10]For competitive reasons, in the absence of legal restraints a marketer can charge any price desired, whether or not it covers the average variable cost. Such a price might be necessary in order to meet the price of a competitor with a lower average-variable-cost curve. In other circumstances prices of this sort tend to be leader or bait prices.

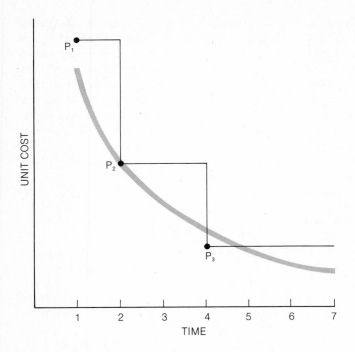

FIGURE 18.8   Pricing in relation to a hypothetical experience
curve

expected to be with cumulative volume.[11]
Clearly, prices can be lowered over time if
sufficient volume can be generated; Minex
accordingly develops a long-run (seven-
period) marketing plan involving price and
nonprice strategies intended to produce the
needed volume. According to this plan, P_1
would prevail in period 1 (introduction). In
period 2, price would be lowered drastically
to P_2—presumably a break-even price at that
point. This reduction, plus planned promotional efforts, should expand volume substantially. P_2 prevails through period 4 when
another drastic cut is made—this time to P_3,
momentarily unprofitable. But volume is
expected to surge again and P_3 will produce

[11]This is not a distortion of the use of cost functions.
In fact, the classical long-run average-cost curve (Figure
18.7, part B) is sometimes called a *planning curve*.

profits through period 7, where our example
ends.

Some electronics firms selling hand-held
calculators and digital watches are thought to
use strategies of this kind, although price
reductions on these items have taken place
more frequently and have been less dramatic. But the end result has been the same.

Pricing in Relation to Promotion

Although pricing decisions must fit into the
overall approach and harmonize with the
entire marketing mix, it is especially important for pricing strategy to be coordinated
with promotion. We recall that the purposes
of promotion are threefold: to communi-

cate, to convince, and to compete. Price is, first of all, a competitive weapon. However, communicating with consumers and convincing them to buy also are related to pricing. Consumers must be aware of prices in order to be influenced by them. Information about pricing is an important message that can be transmitted to potential purchasers. In advertising for instance, the subject of pricing is of such importance that the phrase *price copy* has been coined to designate message content devoted to pricing information. Food retailers, discount stores, furniture and appliance merchandisers, and department stores make extensive use of promotional media to announce pricing decisions.

A second place where the pricing effects of promotion are felt is in the area of demand creation. Promotion increases sales by altering one or more of the basic determinants of demand. In economic terms, the effect of promotional effort is to shift the demand curve upward and to the right. Efficient promotion should enable the manufacturer to sell more merchandise at the same or even higher prices. Higher prices often are possible as a result of effective promotion, because the differentiated features of the product make customers willing to pay more for it. In addition to shifting the demand curve, effective promotional effort can alter its slope and thereby change the price elasticity values all along it. Normally, promotional efforts result in a less-elastic demand, that is, promotion tends to reinforce the differentiating features and to intensify consumer insistence. In some cases, however, especially in the development of entirely new markets, promotion may be directed toward increasing the price elasticity of demand. If there are potential long-run economies of scale, it may be desirable to use a penetrating price to open up a large

market. This cannot be done, of course, until consumers are ready to respond to low prices—that is, when the demand has become sufficiently elastic. Promotional effort can make a demand more elastic by improving a product's substitutability for established products. Since the position of the demand curve and the price elasticity at each point are important factors in pricing, we should consider the probable effect of the promotional strategy on these factors. When the general marketing plan was set forth, a tentative pricing approach was included. The appropriateness of the promotional program in relationship to this tentative pricing approach should also be carefully studied.

Leader and Bait Pricing

Ordinarily pricing below cost is not desirable. However, aggressive marketers, especially at the retail level, frequently charge prices below cost for promotional purposes. A *loss leader* is a dramatically low price that is offered on one item in order to attract customers. It is hoped that the profits on the sale of regularly priced products will more than offset the losses incurred on the loss leader. When using a loss leader the advertised items are actually sold at this price. In contrast, some merchants use bait pricing. A *bait price* is intended to hook a customer who is then switched to another, more expensive item. It is never intended that sales will be made at the lower-than-cost bait price. Bait pricing is distinctly unethical, and some states have passed laws prohibiting this practice.[12] Sales below cost, whether leader or

[12]So-called unfair trade practice acts prohibit sales below cost. These laws have generally been difficult to enforce because of the administrative impossibility of defining the term *costs*. The FTC has declared bait and switch to be an unfair competitive practice.

bait, can only be justified from a marketing point of view when they permit the marketer to improve total profits.

Pricing to Close a Sale

Pricing does not have to be below cost to be a potent factor in convincing the consumer to buy the advertiser's product. A particularly attractive but still above-cost price may be just what is needed to persuade the consumer. In fact, the tactical use of pricing information is often crucial in speeding consumer conviction. Two commonly used methods of obtaining this conviction or of closing sales involve pricing. A salesperson or an advertisement may emphasize an impending event relating to price. For example, the headline of a newspaper advertisement might read "Memorial Day Special—25% Off On All Picnic Supplies—Two Days Only—Sale Ends May 29." Or a salesperson may suggest to a prospect that there is reason to believe that a price increase is about to be announced and that, if the buyer wishes to take advantage of the current price, the purchase should be made immediately.

Managing Price Changes

There are situations in which prices should be changed; and there may be long periods when they will remain constant. Generally speaking, there should be a reason for any price change. Prices, correctly conceived, are determined by working back from the market. Thus, major market changes such as shifts in consumer preferences or the intrusion of a new competitor may alter demand seriously enough to warrant a reconsideration of basic price. Changed market conditions of this kind are likely to occur over a product's life cycle. Since different pricing strategies are called for in each of the four stages of the life cycle, major price changes, therefore, would be made whenever it is well established that the product has moved from one life-cycle stage to the next.

The timing of price changes can be very important. While price reductions often are timed to coincide with a general promotional event, there probably is never a really good time to raise prices. However, certain times are better than others. In periods of economic prosperity, buyers usually expect prices to rise. It is also easier to effect a price increase when other vendors are doing the same. In the absence of a general rise in the price level, price increases probably can best be instituted when tied to major changes in the marketing mix. The introduction of a new product or a dramatic change in distribution may make it possible to put a higher price into effect without serious consequences. Frequently, the forces that require a pricing change also create the need to alter some of the other marketing elements. Thus, a total marketing solution to a problem is demanded rather than a pricing solution to a part of the problem. This requires more work but generally leads to sound pricing decisions.

Price Discrimination

To discriminate in pricing means to charge different markups over marginal cost to different customers. The Robinson-Patman

Act specifically prohibits price discriminations that tend to lessen competition. This means, in effect, that it is illegal to discriminate in price between customers when these customers are in competition with each other. However, many customers are not in competition with each other because they operate either at different levels of the channel or in different market areas. For this reason, different prices might legally be charged to these noncompeting customers by the use of trade or geographical discounts.[13]

Even though charging different prices to different customers might be legal, it is not desirable unless it also is profitable. Discrimination in pricing is most likely to be profitable when a firm sells to two or more market segments and when three specific conditions exist. First, the customers should be separated—either geographically or by trade status. Second, these customers' demands should be of different magnitudes and price elasticities. Third, remarketing by one customer to another should be impossible. When these conditions prevail, a firm maximizes its profits by first determining its most profitable rate of overall operation. This is done by equating marginal cost and overall marginal revenue, as is shown in Figure 18.9, where the two markets, D_1 and D_2, conform to the three conditions mentioned above. For these two markets, MR_1 and MR_2 are added horizontally to obtain the aggregate marginal revenue (AMR). AMR is equal to

marginal cost at the quantity Q, the output that should be produced. The seller must then apportion this output between the two markets in such a way as to maximize revenue. This is accomplished by equating the marginal revenue obtained in each market, as shown in the illustration by a horizontal broken line drawn to the vertical axis from the intersection of MC and AMR. The intersection of this line and the respective marginal-revenue curves indicates the quantities to be sold in each market and, accordingly, the correct allocation of Q. The prices to be charged in each market are found on their respective demand curves.

Resale Price Maintenance

Whether to attempt to control resale prices is another difficult question for a manufacturer to answer. For many years, such companies as GE, Sunbeam, and Columbia Records attempted to enforce fair-trade contracts as part of their continuing marketing programs. Pharmaceutical companies, sporting-goods manufacturers, and proprietary-drug manufacturers also have been leaders in resale price maintenance. The reasons for price maintenance differ somewhat from one industry to another, but there are four basic considerations that have caused manufacturers to control resellers' prices. The first and foremost reason has been the desire to maintain control over pricing throughout the channel system. Although in some instances this may be the result of a desire to fix prices, the more typical reason has been the desire to prevent destructive price cutting in the channel. Price cutting at the retail level tends to work

---

[13]If, however, trade customers (not consumers) of these noncompeting customers are in competition, the discrimination may be illegal. For example, assume that a manufacturer (M) sells to two noncompeting wholesalers (W_1 and W_2). If these wholesalers in turn sell to retailers (R_1, R_2, and R_3) who are in competition with each other, a lower price charged to W_1 would be discriminatory if W_1's retail customer R_1 were able to compete unfairly with retail customers of W_2.

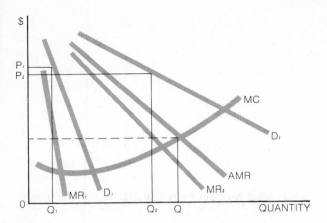

FIGURE 18.9   Price discrimination in two markets

its way back up the channel. Retailers who cut prices to meet competition ask for special pricing concessions from wholesalers and manufacturers. On the theory that the best way to stop this seepage of price cutting is to prevent it from starting at all, manufacturers have adopted resale price maintenance.

Another reason for attempting to maintain resale prices is the desire of the manufacturer to advertise its own user prices. The tendency of retailers either to price above the manufacturer's suggested list price or to discount below it makes it extremely difficult for the manufacturer to promote these user prices. In marketing such products as small electric appliances or phonograph records, it is highly desirable to establish prices to appear in consumer advertising.

A third closely related reason for maintaining resale prices is the need to protect dealers from predatory price cutting by competitors. Historically, retail druggists were among the strongest proponents of so-called fair-trade legislation, because independent drugstores were among the first victims of

cut-rate merchandising. They demanded and obtained the support of their suppliers in restraining predatory price cutting by discount drugstores.

A final reason for maintaining resale prices is to uphold the integrity of the marketing mix. If a price is worked out in relation to the rest of the marketing program, it is highly desirable that this price be maintained. A product that becomes a pricing football may plunge immediately into the mature stage of the life cycle and is probably doomed to an early end. Even if such a drastic development fails to materialize, it is frustrating and disappointing to find that forces beyond the manufacturer's control dictate important parts of the marketing mix. Thus, in order to retain the authority to develop an integrated marketing program, it may be necessary to enforce resale price maintenance.

Although these reasons for maintaining resale prices are strong, there are other equally valid reasons why most manufacturers move slowly to implement such a decision. First of all, it deprives the manufacturer of considerable merchandising flexibility. It may be desirable under some circumstances to encourage certain dealers to sell at lower prices than others. Or, as in the case of large discount operations, it may be virtually impossible to stop them. If a manufacturer wants to develop business through discount channels, a willingness to tolerate strategic price cutting by customers is necessary. A second reason for not setting resale prices is that such a strategy inevitably invites competition, either from other manufacturers or in the form of private-label merchandise. Paradoxically, some manufacturers maintain prices on their own products and at the same time manufacture almost identical items for sale by distributors under private brands. Sooner or later, consumers detect the source of private-label merchandise, and the resale price strategy becomes a liability rather than an asset.

Probably the strongest reason for not attempting to maintain resale prices, however, is the difficulty of enforcing them. For many years, enforcement was possible by utilizing the state fair-trade laws and the federal enabling legislation to write price maintenance contracts with resellers. A fair-trade law permitted a manufacturer of branded merchandise to establish minimum resale prices. Under the nonsigners clause, all retailers in a given state were bound by the contract signed by the manufacturer with any one retailer in that state. A federal law, the McGuire Act of 1952, permitted price maintenance of goods sold in interstate commerce provided that a state law existed in the market served. Under such fair-trade legislation, it was the responsibility of the manufacturer to enforce the fair-trade contracts.

However, the courts made it increasingly difficult for manufacturers wishing to en-force fair trade contracts. A number of state supreme courts invalidated their laws. Some state legislatures actually repealed them. In 1975, the McGuire Act (and its forerunner, the Miller-Tydings Act) were repealed by Congress. Fair trade was effectively ended.[14] Notwithstanding, resale price maintenance continues to be practiced in vertical marketing systems wherever the need and legal opportunity exist.

Organizing for Pricing

It is extremely important that there be some organizational provision for pricing. Pricing is an essential function and should be assigned to specific individuals within an organization. Historically, however, this seldom has been done. In some cases, the strategic importance of pricing has not been recognized, and the pricing function has been transformed into a clerical operation. At the other extreme, the pricing task has been so jealously guarded by top management that no authority to consider or set prices has been delegated to marketing management. In between these two extremes lies a wide range of other organizational possibilities. Ideally, as part of the marketing mix, pricing is the responsibility of the marketing manager. Pricing decisions affect all levels and all departments in a firm. The marketing manager, for this reason, often is involved in discussions with manufacturing, finance, engineering, and accounting executives. If these interdepartmental influences on price

[14]M. L. Bell and D. Hays, "Fair Trade, 1931–1975: An Obituary," *Proceedings of the Southern Marketing Association*, October 26–29, 1977, pp. 25–28.

are particularly strong, a coordinating organizational group may be formed. This may be a permanent pricing committee or an ad hoc group meeting as required to formulate pricing decisions.

Summary

The discount structure is developed to fit the basic price to the particular marketing methods used by a firm. Discounts are offered to customers to reflect their trade status, the quantities that they purchase, or specific promotional objectives that a seller may wish to attain. In addition, discounts (or extras) may be charged because of special aspects of an order, a customer's location, and the like. Terms of sale also may affect the discount structure, as when a customer is offered a discount for payment within a specified period of time. Methods of quoting prices generally reflect the basic price as well as the discount structure.

Pricing plays a particularly significant role in a company's strategy at different stages of the product life cycle. The economic models of monopoly, monopolistic competition, and oligopoly can be adapted to the special conditions of pricing in the introductory, growth, maturity, and decline stages of the life cycle. An interesting aspect of pricing at all stages is the use of psychological pricing to convey favorable attitudes toward the prices charged.

Prices, of course, produce revenues for the seller. Whether these prices also produce profits depends on the relationship of price to cost. The relationship differs in the short run and in the long run, since different costs are relevant for decision making in the two time scales. Pricing in relation to the experience cost curve is practiced by some successful companies. Cost relationships are also important for sales at or below cost. Leader pricing, for example, involves charging low prices intended to attract customers. Price discrimination involves charging different prices to customers based on differences in the marginal costs of serving them.

A final aspect of pricing concerns resale price maintenance to encourage resellers to maintain the manufacturer's suggested prices. So-called fair-trade laws, which prevented a customer from pricing below an agreed resale price, were used for many years.

Questions and Problems

1. Select an item that has worked its way through its life cycle. Interview a retailer and find out the prices charged for this product in each of its stages. (Note: The retailer may not be familiar with the life-cycle concept. Ask only for a history of the price of the product from the time it was first introduced.)

2. A product has a list price of $189.50. The discount structure calls for the following jobber price: list less 25-10-5-5, 2/10 net 30. What price does the jobber pay?

3. Why is the cumulative quantity discount usually considered to be discriminatory?

4. Visit an automobile showroom, a boat dealer, a furniture store, an appliance

store, or some similar establishment that sells a line of products at different prices. Select one manufacturer's line and identify its various pricing points. Then determine the retailer's overall assortment, identifying the various pricing levels for which various manufacturers' products have been selected. What conclusions do you draw from these observations.

5. One might assume that an objective in pricing a new product would be to discourage competitors from entering the market. In fact, this is a common argument used to support penetration pricing. However, a few companies appear purposely to encourage the entry of competitors into a market by setting a high introductory price. What is the logic of this type of pricing approach? Find examples of companies that have apparently priced in this manner.

6. The Schmelly Chemical Corporation introduced Polyusterplus in 1971. Sales for the six years following its introduction were as follows:

In thousands of pounds

	1971	1972	1973	1974	1975	1976
1st qtr.	50	225	675	1,375	1,825	1,875
2d qtr.	75	300	800	1,550	1,850	1,850
3d qtr.	100	400	1,000	1,650	1,875	1,800
4th qtr.	150	525	1,200	1,750	1,900	1,700

Three critical pricing situations arose over the six-year period. Answer the following questions posed about these pricing situations:

a. About July 1972, Schmelly learned from an equipment supplier that the Gigantic Chemical Company hoped to introduce its version of Polyusterplus within three to six months. What pricing decision should Schmelly have made at this point?

b. By July 1974, four major plastics manufacturers were producing almost identical products, although each carried its own trade name. Prices charged by these companies were almost identical, although Schmelly's Polyusterplus was priced slightly higher than the other three. Explain the pricing dilemma faced by Schmelly under these circumstances.

c. After July 1973, sales increases were almost imperceptible. Starting in January 1976, sales actually declined. How should Polyusterplus have been priced in this kind of situation?

7. Visit a shopping district. Find several examples of each type of psychological price.

8. In 1973, the Schmelly Chemical Company began exporting Polyusterplus to Western Europe. Until French and German chemical producers became active in this field about 1975, Schmelly found it possible to charge a considerably higher price in Europe than in the United States. Why do you think that this was possible? Explain, with an appropriate diagram, how the company would have maximized profits by following the theory of imperfect price discrimination.

9. How might the technique of pricing

under conditions of uncertainty be applied to the problem of oligopolistic pricing?

10. It is generally believed that Texas Instruments has utilized the concept of the experience curve in establishing a pricing strategy on its hand-held calculators. Research this situation to see if you can find information that relates TI's pricing practices to the cost structure in the electronics industry.

19

The Integrated Marketing Plan

As the preceding chapters have shown, the marketing activities of a firm are diversified and complex. They are influenced not only by almost every facet of an enterprise but also by conditions external to it. A company's overall objectives as well as the minute details to the marketing mix must be considered. At times it might be difficult to relate the many and diverse elements of the mix and to coordinate them with corporate objectives. But in spite of the complexity and the diversity, in spite of the many internal and external influences, it is absolutely imperative that the marketing manager develop a thoroughly integrated marketing program. A firm should not have a collection of marketing plans—that is, a selling plan, a product development plan, a distribution plan, an adveritising plan, and a pricing plan. Any firm that expects to operate effectively under the marketing management concept must

compete with a single comprehensive marketing program.

Unfortunately, it has been necessary for us to take up the development of this program in a somewhat artificial fashion. The market planner does not, in actuality, move rigidly from product to channel to promotion and finally to pricing. Rather, since the objective is to create an integrated and coordinated overall marketing program, all of the elements involved must be considered simultaneously. However, it is extremely difficult to describe such a comprehensive planning assignment without using a procedure that breaks the assignment into separate components. Often, this traditional method of treating marketing planning leaves the impression that the marketing manager is concerned with developing separate plans or policies in each of the four strategy areas. To dispel such an illusion, this chapter presents a summary of the entire planning process. It is in fact a review of Chapters 8 through 18.

This chapter utilizes a model of the planning process. Since we have looked at all of the aspects of that process except the integration of the final plan, it should not be surprising that much of the material in this chapter is familiar. Obviously the model resembles those presented in the earlier chapters. Accordingly, the model begins with the prerequisites of marketing planning: mission, objectives, policies, and organization. It presupposes the use of the management tools that are necessary to analyze the marketing situation and to make decisions. And finally, it considers in detail the development of strategy in each of the four areas of the marketing mix—products, channels, promotion, and pricing. Thus the model in this final chapter performs two useful functions: first, it provides a review of the strategy-making topics; and second, it integrates these topics into a single comprehensive view of the marketing plan.

The complete planning process in marketing management is illustrated in Figures 19.1 through 19.4. These figures conform to generally accepted flow chart design. As such, they are largely self-explanatory. The activities enclosed in rectangles constitute the steps actually involved in the planning process, and the activities enclosed in diamonds represent the testing or checking procedures required to determine which step should be taken next. Although our overall model is not extremely complex as flow models go, it is convenient to break it into four separate parts or fields. We will discuss each field briefly, taking special note of those aspects of it that contribute to the development of the overall plan. Field One is composed of the basic planning activities involved in creating two or more alternative grand strategies. Field Two includes the planning activi-

ties necessary to create a marketing mix for one of these grand strategies. Field Three involves a summary and review of the developing plan. And Field Four encompasses the soliciting of management approval and the preparation of the tactical plan.

Field One: Preliminary Planning Activities

The preliminary planning activities are shown in Figure 19.1. This segment of the flow chart is patterned after Figure 3.2, although only the first phase of the general planning-process model is included here. Each of the preliminary steps in the model was discussed in Chapter 3, and there is no reason to repeat them now. It is necessary only to point out that the preliminary planning process stops at the point where a suitable grand strategy, or general overall plan, has been selected for development in detail.

Field Two: Developing the Marketing Mix

The second part of the overall planning process is shown in Figure 19.2. As we know, the marketing mix is the combination of marketing instruments used to reach marketing targets. In Chapters 9 through 18, we were provided with detailed discussions of each of the mix elements: product, channel, promotion, and price. It is now necessary to show how the decisions reached in planning these mix elements are blended together into a complete marketing program. A sys-

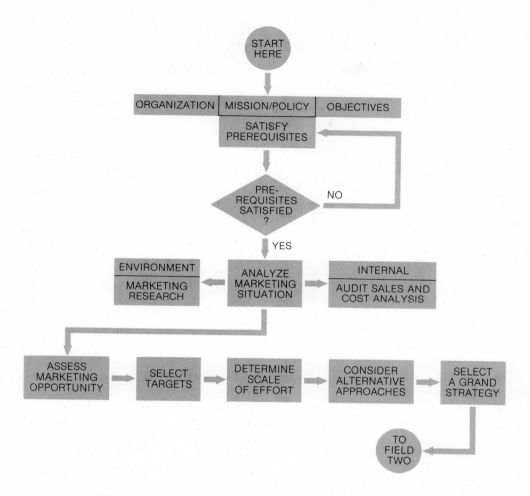

FIGURE 19.1   The marketing planning process: Field One: Preliminary activities

tematic, sequential approach to this task is followed. We begin, as in Chapter 9, with the development of product strategy.

Product Strategy

Figure 19.2 indicates that there are five parallel steps to be taken in developing each of the four strategy elements of the market-

ing mix. The pattern is established in the development of product strategy. The first step requires the planner to determine the specific product objectives that must be satisfied. In the second step, the various issues and problems that face the manager in connection with product planning must be identified. Next, these issues and problems must be resolved. Finally, the product strategy that has been developed must be reviewed

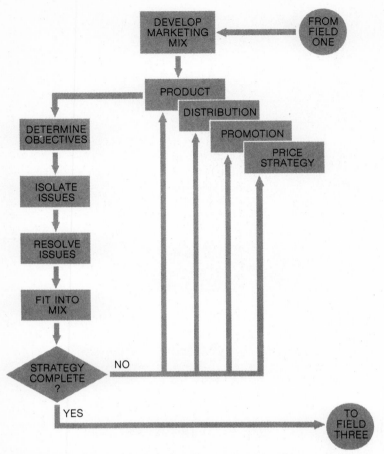

FIGURE 19.2   The marketing planning process: Field Two: Developing the marketing mix

and, if necessary, modified to make sure that it fits into the rest of the marketing mix.

Satisfy the prerequisites for product strategy The development of product strategy requires the prior completion of the first seven steps in operational planning. These were shown in Figure 19.1. Product planning cannot commence until these steps have been completed, because they provide the objectives, policies, organization, marketing intelligence, and general direction that the manager needs before making decisions about product offerings.

Determine product subobjectives In Chapter 9 we looked at a number of typical product objectives and considered why the setting of these objectives is important to marketing management. It is at this point that the manager becomes particularly conscious of the relationship among product objectives, broad marketing objectives, and corporate objectives. Needless to say, this hierarchy of objectives must harmonize in order to be used by the planner as a basis for developing product strategy.

Isolate product issues and problems The special issues and problems involved in marketing new and mature products were identified in Chapters 10 and 11. Not all of these issues and problems arise in connection with each marketing plan, of course. If the grand strategy requires the introduction of a new product, the issues and problems described in Chapter 10 come into play. If the overall approach involves the marketing of an existing line, some of the issues and problems associated with mature products may have to be resolved. In either case, the identification of the relevant issues and problems is a major step in this stage of the planning process. For example, the planner may isolate any or all of the following:

What products to sell
What new product(s), if any, to add
How broad a product line to offer
What product(s), if any, to drop
When product additions and/or deletions should be made
How the product(s) should be packaged
How the product(s) should be identified
The kinds of postsales servicing required
The amount to spend on product, package, and identification
The firm's organization to implement product strategy effectively

Resolve product issues and problems Each of the relevant issues and problems identified in the preceding step must be resolved. The

solutions reached at this stage give form to the evolving product strategy. These solutions are found by turning to the market. The planner determines the consumers' use specifications and adapts the product offerings to them. In the same fashion, all product problems and issues are approached from the standpoint of customer orientation, not production orientation. Thus, the raw material of decisions about product offerings is good marketing intelligence—intelligence that has been gathered in the preliminary step of analyzing the marketing situation. This intelligence will help to resolve product strategy issues by making it possible to complete these steps:

Identify ultimate user(s)

Determine use (satisfaction) specifications

Determine resale specifications of resellers

Match use specifications and resale specifications with design, performance, and cost specifications of product

Determine product identification requirements

Match product identification requirements with brand name and trademark

Fit immediate product decisions into a long-run product-line program involving future products, products to be deleted, and timing of product-line changes

Estimate the cost of this product strategy and prepare a preliminary budget

Test new or improved product(s) by engineering, manufacturing, and marketing criteria

Evaluate the product strategy Since product strategy is the first of the four mix elements to be developed, it is unlikely that the problem of fitting it into the overall marketing plan will arise. However, the process of product planning is lengthy, and often compromises are made to meet the requirements of consumers, resellers, and nonmarketing interests within a firm. It is quite possible that the product strategy finally developed may drift in some respects away from the general plan that was first envisioned.

The product strategy must be evaluated as it relates to the overall marketing mix. Specifically, the planner must consider the effects of product decisions on channel, promotion, and pricing. For example, if the overall plan did not anticipate the need for a new distribution system but the product strategy that has been developed makes such a channel decision necessary, it may be wise to reconsider the overall approach that has been selected, Generally, however, such a major reconsideration would not be necessary. Rather product decisions simply raise certain warning signals that must be heeded carefully as the planner moves through the rest of the planning process. For example, if the product that has been designed requires extensive postsales servicing, this particular requirement will be important in determining the type and location of retail outlets.

Modify product strategy to fit the mix The final step in the development of product strategy is the alteration or adaptation of that strategy to fit it into the general plan of marketing action. On rare occasions this may involve starting all over again. However, in most cases, going back to the drawing board is not necessary. It is much more likely that the evaluation of product strategy will reveal that it deviates from the general plan only in certain minor respects. Modest changes, for example, in the size or color of a package, can easily be made. Major changes, like

those in the degree of engineering precision or the quality of raw materials utilized, may be more difficult.

Channel Strategy

The approach used in developing channel strategy is the same as that followed in formulating product strategy. Let us look at these steps as applied to the design of a distribution plan.

Identify channel subobjectives Chapters 12 and 13 were concerned with trade channel and physical-distribution strategies. You recall that channel objectives exist and must be taken into account in the marketing plan. It goes without saying that these objectives must be hierarchical, consistent, and realistic if a sound channel strategy is to be developed.

Isolate channel issues and problems As a particular plan is being developed, channel problems and issues must be isolated so that solutions can be found. For example, most of the following questions will probably have to be dealt with:

Should we sell direct?

What type(s) of system components should we use?

How many components of each type should we use?

Should we use multiple channels?
    1. Complementary (noncompetitive)
    2. Competitive

What special assistance or control activities will be necessary to maintain an effective channel system?

How much should we spend on channel development and control?

How should our firm be organized to make the most effective use of the channel system?

Resolve channel issues and problems The customer is the place to begin the search for solutions to channel issues and problems. The type and dimension of the channel are best determined by working backward through the system. The shipping-platform approach, as we know, leads to incorrect channel decisions. Rather, these decisions should be made by balancing the level of service required by customers with the cost of providing it. We use the following steps in the systematic marketing approach to resolve channel issues:

Identify ultimate users and purchasers (if different)

Determine buying specifications of these users and purchasers

Match buying specifications with location and performance specifications of resellers

Determine number of retailers in each market required to serve purchasers. Adjust by manufacturer's distribution objectives and by retailers' needs for exclusive distribution

Determine buying specifications of retailers

Match retailers' buying specifications with location and performance specifications of wholesalers

Determine the number of wholesalers required to serve the number of retailers. Adjust to meet wholesalers' needs for exclusive distribution

Determine buying specifications of wholesalers

Determine facilitating and other channel function specifications

Match these other channel function specifications with location and performance specifications of other channel components

Determine the special problems of training, motivation, and control expected to arise within the channel system

Estimate the cost of this channel strategy and prepare a preliminary budget

Test the channel by marketing criteria

Institute the organizational changes required to implement the channel strategy

Evaluate the channel strategy If channel strategy is designed to achieve coordinated marketing objectives, it should not conflict with the overall plan. However, in a few cases conflict does occur, for reasons that are not too difficult to understand. Decisions that seem most appropriate in light of the many influences affecting the channel may result in the development of a plan that does not conform to the general marketing program. A channel plan designed in this fashion is not necessarily wrong. It may be a good plan when considered only in terms of distribution problems. However, the plan must be more than a good distribution plan; as we know, it also must fit into the overall marketing approach. It is imperative, therefore, to evaluate the channel strategy in light of its contribution to an integrated marketing program.

In every case, it is important to evaluate the proposed channel plan according to the channel subobjectives that have been set out. For instance, a subobjective might be to achieve some predetermined method or level of distribution. A manufacturer of an industrial hand cleanser identified a channel subobjective of achieving distribution in grocery stores. Another firm with products already in about one fourth of the potential outlets decided in its plan to attempt to increase its level of distribution to 50 per cent. In each case, the planner needed to evaluate the channel strategy in terms of the specific subobjectives that had been set.

The third step in fitting channel strategy into the overall plan is to examine the consequences, if any, of the decisions reached for the rest of the marketing mix. Some of these consequences, especially those that relate to product decisions, were mentioned previously. Channel decisions also have considerable importance for promotion, as we saw in our discussion of the problems of assisting and supervising the activities of channel components. A consideration of the overall plan should suggest ways in which channel strategy can be coordinated with plans for direct selling, advertising (especially cooperative advertising), and sales promotion. For example, it is possible that the need for missionary or detail-type sales personnel might not be recognized until consideration has been given to the relationship between channel decisions and promotional strategy. Or channel decisions might indicate the need for market push or market pull tactics.

Channel decisions also have an important bearing on pricing. This fact is grasped when we realize that channel costs, especially the margins of resellers, come off the top of the final consumer price. The marketing approach to pricing requires that the final consumer price be set without initial regard to either manufacturing or distributional costs. Nevertheless, channel decisions have an important effect on the profit that remains to the manufacturer after subtracting reseller margins and manufacturing expenses. It is not uncommon for profit stresses to begin to emerge at this point in planning. Perhaps a

firm may have to move somewhat higher in the range of acceptable market prices than had previously been contemplated. Alternatively some compromise in product design or channel structure may be required.

Modify channel strategy to fit the mix The whole purpose of the evaluation of the channel decisions is to permit the planner to make necessary changes in channel strategy before proceeding to the consideration of promotion. It is easy to change some elements in the channel strategy, but rather hard to change others. Alterations in the types of resellers to be used, for example, would be very difficult to make without disrupting the overall plan. Since this kind of change tends to distort the entire channel structure, both above and below the point at which the change is made, it is not advisable to attempt major adjustments in the vertical arrangements of the channel. If such adjustments appear to be mandatory in order to fit the channel into the overall plan, it would be better to scrap the entire marketing plan and begin again.

The horizontal arrangements of the channel system can be more easily adjusted. A shift to more or less extensive distribution probably can be effected without a great deal of stress. The most flexible aspect of channel strategy consists of the activities involved in working with channel components. The scope of these activities easily can be increased, changed, or decreased, depending on the need to fit the channel program into the rest of the marketing plan.

Promotion Strategy

The planner is now in a position to tackle the problem of creating the promotional mix. If the systematic approach has been followed, the general kind of promotion program already is known. But the details still must be worked out, and this, of course, involves the same basic steps as were used in designing product and channel strategies.

Determine promotion subobjectives Demand creation is an important part of marketing, and good communications are vital to its success. Thus, it is not unusual to find promotion objectives among the most compelling that the planner must consider. In Chapter 14 we looked at some typical promotion objectives. For the most part, these objectives involve either selling products or communicating ideas—and the two are often related. In addition, there may be corporate or overall marketing objectives that require some particular type of promotional activity. All of these objectives of promotion must be identified before the marketing planner can proceed to design a program.

Isolate promotion issues and problems There are a number of important and difficult issues and problems that arise in developing promotional plans. We looked at these in Chapters 15 and 16. Since selling and advertising are the basic communications tools of marketing, most of the issues and problems center on the creation of compelling messages and the selection of appropriate communications vehicles. Of course, managing the cost of promotion is also an important issue, as is the difficult task of measuring its performance. All of these are among the promotion issues listed below.

The promotion opportunity
The promotion target
The methods and/or media to use
The promotional message or appeal to use
The timing of promotion
The amount to spend on promotion in total

The allocation of the total among the various elements in the promotional mix?
The effectiveness of the promotion, and the ways in which it can be improved
The organization of the firm in order to make the most effective use of promotion

Resolve promotion issues and problems A pattern of looking to the market to resolve the issues and problems that arise in marketing planning has been set. This pattern holds for the design of promotion strategy. The answers to the questions that face the promotion planner are found in information about customers, purchasers, and purchase influencers. We cannot expect to find the solution to the promotion issues by gazing fondly at the product. Rather, we must look to its ultimate users and direct our communications through the media to which these users are exposed. The following steps may seem elaborate and complicated; but they are a foolproof approach to resolving promotion issues and developing a sound promotional program:

Identify ultimate users, purchasers, and purchase influencers by determining
1. Their *knowledge* of the company, its products, and competitive companies and their products
2. Their *attitudes* toward the company, its products, and competitive companies and products
3. Their *recognition* of company brands and of competitors' brands

Determine *how* users, purchasers, and purchase influencers are motivated

Determine the kind and amount of assistance, information, or persuasion that will alter knowledge, attitudes, recognition, and motivation of users, purchasers, and purchase influencers

Identify the sources of information or personal influence from which users, purchasers, and purchase influencers obtain their information and attitudes

Develop a promotional message—a compelling story of potential satisfactions

Determine the magnitude and frequency of exposure necessary to transmit the selected promotional message

Select a promotional mix, defining the exact contribution and cost of each element (sales, advertising, publicity, and sales promotion)

Prepare a coordinated promotional schedule

Estimate the total cost of the promotion strategy, and prepare a preliminary budget

Establish standards of promotional effectiveness, and pretest proposed promotion

Institute the organizational changes required to implement promotion strategy

Evaluate the promotion strategy   Having formulated a promotion strategy, the market planner is on the home stretch in the development of the total marketing mix. Promotion strategy involves several elements and usually a number of different individuals as well. It requires a considerable amount of specialized creative talent that is difficult to direct and control. Moreover, designers of promotional material often are overimpressed with the importance of their function. All of these factors tend to push promotion strategy away from the overall plan that has been selected. They often encourage the creation of more ambitious promotional programs than are actually required. They frequently misdirect the promotional effort into areas not directly related to corporate marketing objectives. The best way to make sure that the promotion strategy fits into the overall plan, therefore, is to evaluate it carefully before proceeding with the final step in the development of the marketing mix.

The designer of promotion strategy should evaluate the plan in terms of the opportunity the company hopes to seize. If the opportunity is to create a competitive advantage or to carve out a market niche, heavy emphasis normally will be placed on the promotional content of the marketing program. The planner must, therefore, carefully scrutinize the promotional plan to make sure that it is working toward that opportunity. Unfortunately, many promotional programs go astray at this point. Is the promotional effort aimed at the precise market segment that the company hopes to reach? Have the sales methods and advertising media been well selected to reach this particular target? Is the promotional message designed to appeal to exactly the same market for which product strategy and distribution strategy have been developed? These are important questions, and they must be answered affirmatively. If, for some reason, the promotional plan has veered from the original marketing target, it should be brought back on course before being incorporated into the overall plan.

In the development of product and channel strategies, an attempt was made to anticipate the effects of these strategies on the promotional program and to make any necessary adjustments. In evaluating the promotional plan, the reverse procedure is used. The promotional plan is adapted to fit the product-channel strategy. For instance, the planner must ask, "Does the promotion plan make effective use of product features—such as packaging, performance specifications, and the like?"; "Does the promotional program include the required dealer promotion?"; "Has advertising (for example) to and through the trade been considered in the promotional plan?'' This type of evaluation ensures the thorough integration of the various elements of the marketing mix.

Modify promotion strategy to fit the mix If the preceding evaluation process has revealed certain aspects of the promotional plan in which marketing objectives or the rest of the market mix have been ignored or distorted, changes in the promotional approach must be made. Fortunately, there is considerable flexibility in the promotional area—more than in either product or channel strategy. Dramatic changes in the overall promotional plan can be achieved simply by changing the media mix. For example, a regional food manufacturer dropped all television advertising and replaced it with four-color ads in regional magazines and local saturation advertising in newspapers, on radio, and on outdoor posters. Not only was the cost of the program dramatically reduced, but important local and regional differences in demand were exploited.

Pricing Strategy

The planner is now three fourths of the way through the development of the marketing mix; but some of the hardest decisions have yet to be made. These involve pricing. Of course, the planner has anticipated the pricing problem and is ready to attack it in light of the general approach already chosen and by means of the same step-by-step procedure used in developing the rest of the marketing mix.

Determine pricing subobjectives Because prices produce revenue and hoped-for prof-

it, pricing recommendations can arise from almost anywhere within a firm. The government may want a price rolled back, a labor union may want a price increase that will finance a wage demand; dealers may want price relief or price protection. In order for these various demands, as well as the requirments of the marketing program itself to be met, specific pricing objectives must be set. We looked at some typical pricing objectives in Chapter 17. The planner has now reached the point where something must be done about achieving them.

Isolate pricing issues and problems More issues and problems arise in pricing than in any other area of marketing planning. And they pose tough questions, often defying easy solution. Compromises are frequently necessary—as when, for example, conflicting demands are felt from inside and outside the company. Although we discussed the various pricing issues and problems in Chapters 17 and 18, it is well to review them here.

What should be the basic price?
What discounts should we allow for the following:

1. Trade status
2. Quantity
3. Promotion
4. Location
5. Terms of payment

How should we price in relation to competition?
Should we use psychological prices?
What is the proper relationship between cost and price, especially for sales below cost?
How should we price in relation to promotion strategy?
When and how often should we change prices?
Should we discriminate in pricing?

Should we attempt to maintain resale prices? How should our company be organized for the most effective use of pricing strategy?

Not all of these questions arise in every planning situation, but basic price always must be set and discounts always must be determined.

Resolve pricing issues and problems We have seen that costs are not the place to start in resolving pricing problems. Instead, a market-minus approach has been suggested. Chapter 17 demonstrated the importance of understanding the consumer in developing the right pricing strategy. In the following steps, we see once more that overall marketing, rather than cost considerations alone, dominate the pricing process:

Identify ultimate users, purchasers, and purchase influencers

For each market segment, determine the relationship of price to demand

Determine prices *actually* charged by competitors

Determine discount requirements of product, channel, and promotion strategies

Deduct margins and discounts of channel components and channel transfer costs (if any) to determine manufacturer's net sales price. Multiply by expected volume(s) to obtain alternative total-revenue possibilities

Estimate total fixed and variable costs of alternative sales volume

Deduct total costs from total revenue to obtain alternative profits

Repeat all of the above steps for each segment

If necessary, adjust the prices of individual products to improve the marketability of the entire line

Adjust final-user price to conform to the most appropriate psychological price

Determine the likelihood of reseller price cutting and its effect on pricing objectives. If necessary, institute a program of resale price maintenance

Pretest the pricing strategy

Institue any organizational changes required to implement the pricing strategy

The answers to pricing questions are not easy to find. Good demand analysis, accurate forecasting, and the use of research to test alternative prices are the basic tools for resolving pricing issues. Newer techniques, such as Bayesian analysis, also contribute to the solution of pricing problems. But in the last analysis the marketing planner makes the decision. How well the pricing issues are resolved probably determines more than anything else the success of the entire marketing program. If the consumer feels the price is right, the plan may work—provided everything else also is well conceived. But if the price is not right, it is doubtful that correct decisions in the rest of the planning sequence will compensate for a serious pricing mistake. Thus we see again the folly of relying on costs to guide the manager to correct pricing decisions.

Evaluate the pricing strategy The marketing strategist has now completed what might be called a rough draft of the entire marketing mix. It is still rough in the sense that the preliminary decisions reached in the pricing area may not be consistent with the overall plan. Stresses and strains are apt to develop as the plan reaches its final stages. After resolving the pricing issues, therefore, the planner must review the pricing strategy carefully to make sure that it fits into the overall marketing plan.

Unfortunately, pricing decisions are quite

likely to stray off course. In part, this is attributable to the fact that often several departments and a number of different individuals in the firm play a role in formulating the pricing plan. Pricing objectives, for example, may reflect financial as well as marketing goals. Undue concern over costs or the adherence to cost-plus pricing doctrines by nonmarketing personnel may so completely warp the pricing decision that it becomes incompatible with the rest of the marketing mix. In some companies, pricing is not even the responsibility of the marketing manager. In such a case, it becomes all the more imperative that the marketing strategist carefully review the implications for the marketing program of the pricing decisions reached by others. Such pricing conflicts seldom are easy to resolve, but a marketing manager who is held responsible for the total consequences of a marketing program should not implement that program unless all of its elements are combined harmoniously.

Pricing subobjectives, like objectives of the rest of the marketing mix, represent demands on the marketing function. Whatever these objectives may be, whether to control cash flow or to stabilize competitive conditions, the pricing plan must demonstrably contribute to them. Pricing is not an end in itself. Rather, it is a means for achieving other results. Although traditional methods of pricing have tended to hide its functional character, the market-minus approach that we have used in this book places emphasis on the task that price is supposed to perform. For example, pricing has a particularly important task to perform when a firm is attempting to create a differential advantage or to carve out a market niche. If these objectives require the introduction of a new product, penetration pricing may be used to establish a marketing beachhead. A

penetration price, however, ordinarily will not permit a firm to maintain its market position. It is a common error in market planning to assume that a pricing differential will establish a permanent competitive difference. Once competitors have had an opportunity to adjust their strategies, any advantage gained by a penetration price quickly disappears. What is needed instead is a continuing program of total marketing action. That is, price, working with product, channel, and promotion strategies, can establish and maintain a competitive difference; but price cannot do it alone.

It is when price strategy is reviewed in terms of the overall plan that the greatest stresses are likely to be encountered. The first test is whether the pricing strategy closely resembles the original pricing intention. Any deviation from the price approach incorporated in the overall plan should be carefully questioned. A number of factors might cause such a deviation. Failure in the early stages to understand the nature of market segments or a lack of knowledge about competitors' prices might lead to a preliminary pricing guideline that later proves to be unworkable. On the other hand, if nonmarketing pressures have caused the market planner to pursue a pricing strategy not anticipated in the general plan, a fundamental flaw in the marketing approach is almost inevitable. This type of flaw must be corrected, either by changing the general plan or by correcting the pricing strategy.

Even though the pricing strategy may fit the general plan, it may be in conflict with some other part or parts of the marketing mix. The basic price and pricing structure, therefore, should be reviewed carefully in terms of previous decisions on product, channel, and promotion strategies. Some typical stresses in these strategy areas have already been mentioned. For example, a decision to skim, to penetrate, or to use prestige pricing may drastically affect product design. Pricing decisions also may affect channel and promotion activities. Thus, a decision to price for two different market segments may require the development of different channels of distribution and certainly will require different promotional strategies. The only acceptable course at this point is to review carefully the effect of each of the pricing decisions on the rest of the marketing mix. This is frequently a time-consuming and laborious process; however, it is more than justified if fundamental inconsistencies in the marketing mix are detected.

Modify pricing strategy to fit the mix   The pricing task and the entire assignment of developing the integrated marketing mix are now almost complete. The planner need only make necessary alterations in the tentative pricing strategy to bring it into line with the overall plan and with the other elements of the marketing mix. Frequently these final alterations are difficult to make. A marketing mix is not like a jigsaw puzzle—all of the pieces do not fit neatly together. If we could visualize the puzzle pieces floating on the agitated surface of a pan of water, we might better appreciate the task of bringing together the various mix elements. The best that the market planner can hope to do is to get the elements reasonably in line. Changing market conditions and dynamic reactions from competitors make any tighter integration of the marketing mix impossible. But the market planner must have the right pieces of the puzzle. They must belong in the same program. None should be left out, and each should be present in its correct proportion. Any final adjustments should be made now. These may be adjustments of previous decisions in the product, channel,

or promotional areas. On the other hand, they may involve a revision of the pricing strategy itself. The adjustment process is completed when the planner is reasonably satisfied that an integrated marketing plan has been produced that will achieve the objectives set forth. In some respects, planning never ceases. There are always new ways to improve a plan. In the last analysis, however, results are achieved from doing—not from planning. At the earliest possible moment in the planning process, therefore, the planner should complete the marketing program and move on to its implementation.

Field Three: Summary and Review of the Plan

We have constructed a complete marketing strategy based on decisions in the areas of product development, channel arrangements, promotional methods, and pricing. By using a systematic approach, we have tried to build this strategy as a coordinated marketing program, in which all the parts fit together. It is now time to see whether this is actually the case. We do so by subjecting the completed marketing strategy to a final review. Such a review involves three important steps: (1) summarization of the complete plan; (2) review and if necessary revision; and (3) preparation of a final written plan. The steps in this procedure are shown in Figure 19.3.

Summarize the Plan

At this stage, the planner actually has at hand four subplans, or strategies, for product,

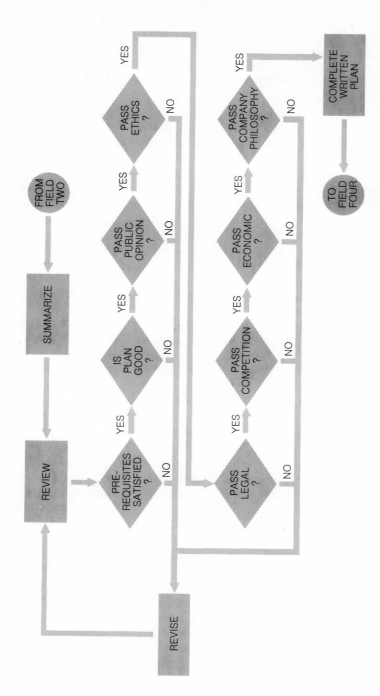

FIGURE 19.3   The marketing planning process: Field Three: Summary and review

channel, promotion, and price. The implications of these strategies on each other and on the company's overall approach have been considered. But the subplans must now be pulled together into one complete marketing plan.

Although the final written document is not produced until the plan has been thoroughly reviewed and possibly revised, it is necessary to begin to assemble the various subplans into a single working manuscript. Introductory materials need to be prepared. Relevant marketing data should be summarized and appropriate exhibits produced. The purpose, scope, and overall approach should be spelled out. The various substrategies should be outlined and placed together in a single rough draft of the integrated plan. When the elements of the plan have been pulled together in this way, the marketing manager is ready to review it carefully prior to final revision and write-up.

Review the Integrated Plan

Have the planning prerequisites been satisfied? The final plan should be reviewed in terms of company objectives—corporate goals in general and marketing objectives in particular. Moreover, the marketing program as an operating plan should be reviewed in terms of the company's policies. It goes without saying that a total marketing plan should also rest on sound marketing intelligence. The need for a factual basis for marketing strategy should never be neglected.

It is imperative that a total marketing plan be opportunity oriented and target directed. The marketing opportunities must be as clear at the end of the planning process as they were at the beginning. The same applies to target direction. Marketing effort

unless it is aimed at specific marketing targets is very likely to be misdirected. The importance of selecting specific marketing targets was emphasized in each of the strategy areas. Obviously, the same targets should apply to each part of the mix as apply to the overall plan. If any deviation from this single target direction occurs in the planning process, it usually can be detected in a final review.

As for the capabilities prerequisite, the total expected cost of a proposed marketing program seldom can be known until the planning process has been completed. It is imperative, however, that this expected cost fall within the budget restrictions. One of the most critical final reviewing steps therefore is an inspection of the financial commitment that the company will be asked to make. This commitment must be reasonable if there is any hope that the plan will be approved.

The last step in reviewing the complete marketing plan involves comparing it to the grand strategy that management intends to pursue. This overall strategy was outlined in the preliminary planning stage. When the planner has completed the marketing mix, it is possible to ask, "Is this the type of plan that we set out to create?" Strange as it may seem, the planning process sometimes results in programs that bear only modest resemblance to the grand strategy that originally was intended. Obviously, such a plan cannot be approved. There is no recourse except to retrace the planning steps to discover where procedures were not followed correctly. Once the errors are corrected, the plan can be cycled once more through the review procedure.

Is the plan a good plan? A proposed marketing plan may fall within the boundaries set by company policy, it may be aimed at reaching established goals and objectives, and it may involve an appropriate scale of effort. Nevertheless, it still may fall short of being a *good* marketing plan. From the marketing manager's point of view, a good plan should meet certain other specific requirements. Although the perfect plan has probably never been devised, any proposed program should be carefully considered in terms of each of these requirements:

It has been kept confidential.
It is appropriate to the company.
It is feasible.
It is comprehensible.
It is flexible.
It includes a schedule.
It includes a budget.
It is in writing.
It provides for implementation.

Reviewing the plan in light of environmental factors As the strategy is developed, the marketing manager is concerned for the most part with the firm and its customers. This preoccupation does not mean, however, that the planner can be oblivious to external forces affecting the company's marketing activities. Any suspected conflict with these forces should be studied carefully. Of course a marketing program cannot be all things to all people. However, it should not raise more serious environmental problems than it is intended to solve. Frequently, for example, minor changes in strategy may make a marketing plan more environmentally acceptable from either a public-opinion or an ethical point of view. On the other hand, if a marketing program involves clear-cut violations of the legal environment, it may require more drastic alterations. If a marketing strategy treads the narrow line between legality and illegality, the risks it will run must be carefully assessed. Ultimately, any marketing program involves some risk of clashing with public policy, but a careful review of the plan in the light of the contemporary environment should indicate the probable degree of risk to anticipate.

Generally speaking, the economic environment also must be favorable for an ambitious marketing program to succeed. Although it would be impossible to wait for the perfect moment at which to launch a marketing program, a final review of the economic environment can avoid a costly marketing failure if it reveals that it is desirable to postpone the program to a time when economic conditions will be more favorable.

A review of the marketing plan also involves an assessment of competitive conditions. The typical marketing plan is intended to be competitive—it is intended to prolong a product's competitive life expectancy. Unfortunately, however, the opposite result frequently occurs. A marketing program can completely disrupt competitive conditions by evoking massive retaliation from strong competitors who seek to doom the program to failure. Because of this retaliation, the planner is forced to make tactical changes, such as modifications in product design, early recourse to penetration pricing, and purely competitive promotion. Such changes bring many products to an early end. However, a careful review of the marketing program in advance usually will provide some clues as to whether intensive competitive reaction can be expected. The appropriate course of action depends on the competitive role the company elects to assume. Modest changes in the marketing approach may make it possible to avoid drastic competitive retaliation. On the other hand, if such reactions are considered unavoidable, alterations must be made in the marketing plan to make it as difficult as possible for competitors to upset its success.

The Final Written Plan

Having carefully reviewed the integrated marketing program in terms of planning prerequisites, the characteristics of a good plan, and environmental factors, the planner must prepare a final written document. Actually, much of the document will have been completed well in advance of this stage. Its final preparation, therefore, is largely a matter of assembling the material to be included and writing the summary portions. There are many ways in which a final written document can be organized.[1] A typical one might be set up as Exhibit 19.1.

Field Four: Finalizing the Plan

The integrated marketing plan has been reviewed, and a written document has been prepared. But the plan still must be put into final form before it can be put into action. The major steps involved in this process are shown in Figure 19.4.

The Upstream Presentation: Soliciting Top Management's Approval

It should be emphasized that for a marketing plan to be accepted by top management it

[1]For some excellent examples of the way various companies organize their marketing plans, see D. Hopkins, *The Short-Term Marketing Plan* (New York: The Conference Board, 1976).

must deserve approval. The top managements of most companies today are market oriented. They are familiar with the marketing management concept and with the rigorous standards it demands. Thus, a marketing plan cannot be poorly conceived or carelessly presented if it is to win top management's approval.

Very often, in fact, a marketing plan must be sold to top management. Occasionally, when production or financial viewpoints dominate a firm, top management is hostile to marketing. In other cases, management takes the position that it should challenge any proposal involving the commitment of company resources. In such situations, at least four selling principles should be utilized in an effort to convince top management to approve the plan. First, the marketing group must be ready to *demonstrate* that the plan is a good plan—that it is, in fact, the best that they can propose. One way of making this clear is to use the checklist of the characteristics of a good plan. Second, the presentation of a marketing plan always is improved by the use of good *visual aids*. The complete written plan should never simply be read to top management. The executive summary, highlights of the plan, and its expected results can be far more dramatically presented by the use of flip charts, slides, advertising layouts, and the like. A third important factor in selling a marketing plan is that it should be presented in a *polished performance*. The marketing group should rehearse the presentation of the plan as often as is necessary to achieve the desired effect. Finally, the marketing group should present its plan with *enthusiasm*. The zeal of the marketing group should be based on a thorough understanding of the underlying marketing situation and a conviction that the best and most appropriate plan has been conceived.

EXHIBIT 19.1 A.B.C. Manufacturing Company: 1979 marketing plan

PART I *Executive Summary*

The executive summary of the marketing plan is provided for the use of top-management personnel. It enables the manager to understand at a glance the scope and character of the proposed plan. The ideal executive summary should be short—between 500 and 1,000 words in length. It should be well organized and should indicate clearly the significant features of the program, including departures from previous marketing programs.

PART II *Background of the Plan*

The background of the marketing plan should include a report of changing environmental conditions, a summary of company objectives underlying the proposed program, and, if necessary, a brief description of the planning organization and procedures used.

PART III *Analysis of the Marketing Situation*

A complete picture of the current marketing situation usually is presented. The factual basis for the marketing plan should be summarized and its significance to the company's marketing program pointed out. Specifically, highlights of the marketing audit, of marketing-research studies, and of the sales forecast are included in this section.

PART IV *Summary of Objectives and Identification of Marketing Targets*

This section should indicate the objectives of the marketing plan and the specific targets that have been selected. There should be absolutely no question as to the intent of the proposed plan.

PART V *The Scope of the Marketing Program*

One of the principal considerations that must be weighed carefully in reviewing a proposal for marketing action is the scale of effort that will be required. The scope of the plan should clearly fall within the range that top management considers appropriate. Especially helpful at this stage is a comparison of the magnitude of the proposed program with others followed in the past.

PART VI *Alternative Approaches and the Grand Strategy of the Current Plan*

Management always is concerned that alternative courses of action have been carefully considered, since there usually are several different ways of developing marketing strategy to achieve a given set of objectives. Each of the alternative overall marketing approaches that was considered can be briefly described here. The reasons for rejecting all but the proposed approach should be noted. Finally, the proposed approach that is the core of the marketing plan also should be briefly described. (Amplification of this plan will be found in the following parts of the written plan.)

PART VII *The Detailed Marketing Mix*

In this section the details of the plan are revealed. Ordinarily, it is possible to separate the discussion of marketing strategy into its component parts. The objectives of each part, the issues to be faced, and the methods by which these issues are to be resolved should be presented. The integrating features of the marketing strategy should be emphasized throughout. Finally, the overall scope and nature of the marketing strategy should be set forth in a summary of the marketing mix.

PART VIII *Providing for Implementation and Control*

In order to facilitate implementation and to provide for adequate control of the marketing program, the plan should include three elements. These are

1. A comprehensive schedule
2. Detailed sales and cost budgets
3. Standards of expected performance

The schedule provides a time control to ensure that the program is initiated and completed according to plan. Sales and cost budgets provide basic criteria by which the success or failure of the plan will be judged. Standards of expected performance, whether in the form of quotas or productivity standards, will permit the evaluation of particular parts of the marketing program. In the last analysis, top management is interested in results—not in plans. They are interested in adequate controls to assure that deviations from expected results will be quickly and accurately detected. To design a marketing plan without such controls is like equipping an aircraft without navigation instruments. In some respects, the control features of the marketing plan are the most important from top management's point of view.

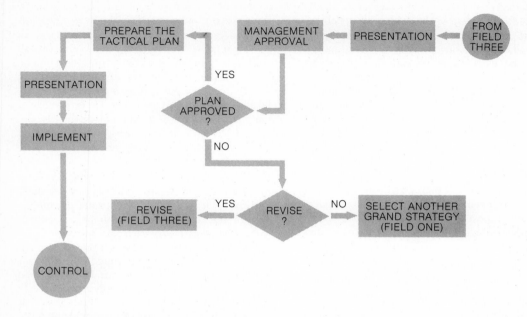

FIGURE 19.4 The marketing planning process: Field Four: Finalization

After presenting the plan, the marketing group should not allow it to be left in limbo without the authorization to begin implementation. It should not be permitted to gather dust on the executive bookshelf while management directs its attention to other matters. The marketing group should ask for an approval and obtain either authorization to proceed or specific instructions regarding how the proposed plan should be changed. Planning executives, especially staff managers, sometimes are reluctant to press top management for a decision on a proposed program. However, this pressure sometimes is necessary, for the marketing manager too is interested in more than just planning. Results can be obtained only by putting the plan into action. Since action commences with top management's approval, getting this approval is the prime objective of the presentation.

The Tactical (Short-Term) Marketing Plan

Approval of the long-range plan is the signal to finalize the development of the short-term, or tactical, plan. The long-range plan is not directly implementable. Rather, as we saw in Chapter 3, specific action plans need to be developed in each area of the marketing mix. The specific elements in the tactical plan are

1. A statement of the specific actions to be taken

2. An identification of the specific individuals responsible for each action

3. A schedule of when each action is to be initiated and completed

4. A comprehensive budget that specifies the expected cost of each action

5. A statement of the anticipated outcome of each action

The tactical marketing plan also should be a written document. It becomes the blueprint by which day-to-day marketing activities are carried out. Since it is in written form, it becomes a means for communicating instructions to those who will carry out the program. It also becomes a control instrument, because actual performance can be compared to the outcomes specified in the plan.

The Downstream Presentation

Figure 19.4 shows a second presentation as well. This is a presentation of the tactical plan. Whereas the first presentation was to top management to obtain approval of the overall approach, the second presentation (and sometimes there may be several) is made to those who will carry out the programs. We can call the first presentation *upstream* and the second presentation *downstream.*

The downstream presentation can be very important to the ultimate success of the program, for on it may depend the willingness and ability of the line organization to carry out the short-term action plan. For example, a product manager typically makes a formal presentation of the marketing plan to the sales organization. This presentation is not simply to let these people know what they will be doing and what other marketing activities will be taking place. It is also to stimulate and motivate the sales organization. A product manager often competes for the time of the sales force. Salespeople tend to sell the products they like personally or which they are able to sell easily. Part of the product manager's job is to convince the salespeople that time and attention should be devoted to the manager's brand. The

downstream presentation is one way of doing this.

On to Implementation and Control

The implementation of a marketing plan is the responsibility of line marketing management. Implementation is initiated by the process of direction. It is sustained through the activities of leadership. It is restrained and guided by control processes. These latter processes take us beyond the planning process. But, in a larger sense, we have merely completed a circle, since one of the purposes of control is to tell us when and how to begin planning again.

The implementation and control processes may indicate that a revision in strategy is needed. Minor tactical changes can be made at any time. Even substantial modifications might be made if the nature of the grand strategy is not disturbed. If the plan is a good one, it should allow for modifications. Flexibility, as we have seen, is a characteristic of a good marketing plan.

Ultimately, however, even a good marketing plan wears out. The environment changes. Contending with competitive reactions becomes more and more difficult. Customers become bored or disenchanted. Perhaps, a saturation level is reached. Most likely, it is an instance of the product's life cycle having run its course. Recycle efforts probably have been attempted and have kept the program going at least temporarily. But eventually the point is reached when further revision of the marketing plan is impractical.

Where does the marketing manager go from this point? "Back to the beginning" is the obvious and correct answer. The planner goes back to Field One, and a completely new cycle of marketing planning is set in motion. And so the process of marketing management goes on.

Summary

This chapter has itself summarized the marketing planning process. A summary of a summary is superfluous. We have now been introduced to a wide range of marketing concepts and to the ways in which these concepts become the basis for marketing planning and problem solving. We set out in Chapter 1 to portray marketing as a perspective on business—a view that bridges the gap between consumer needs and the traditional business functions of making and distributing goods. In the rapidly changing environment of business, such a perspective on marketing should serve the manager well— both in performing the job and in providing satisfactions to consumers. This, after all, is what marketing planning is all about.

Questions and Problems

1. At one time a large chemical company was reported to have a critical-path model for the introduction of new products that included over five hundred different marketing activities. What does this tell you about the complex nature of the marketing mix?

2. The planning model presented in this chapter suggests that the mix elements should be attacked in a specified order: product, distribution, promotion, and price. Explain the rationale of this sequence. Under what circumstances do you think a different order might be justified?

3. Explain how the subobjectives of each element of the marketing mix are developed.

4. What is meant by an *issue* in the planning-process model?

5. Throughout the model presented in this chapter, the resolution of the various issues involves a study of the ultimate user or buyer. Does this mean that the marketing planner must interrupt the planning process to do marketing research?

6. Why is the fit of each element of the mix stressed in the planning-process model?

7. Why is it important to keep a marketing plan confidential?

8. A marketing executive once said, "Until it is written down, it's not a plan." What was meant by this statement?

9. Which is more important: to develop a sound plan or to monitor and modify a somewhat less than perfect program?

10. Select a product or service designed to serve a market with which you are familiar. Assume that a company serving this market has asked you to develop an integrated marketing plan. Using the model presented in this chapter, develop a marketing strategy and its marketing mix for the firm.

Four

Marketing Information

20

The Marketing Information System

We have looked at the way in which the marketing company develops strategies to deliver customer satisfactions. A key step in the process of developing strategies is to make use of marketing intelligence to assess the problems and opportunities that exist in the marketplace. Ultimately, the evaluation and control of a program also depend on marketing intelligence, which makes it possible to compare actual results with the objectives of the strategy. *Intelligence* in these contexts refers to marketing information that has been screened, classified, and organized for management to use in developing its plans. Raw marketing data can come to the manager in a disorganized, confusing clutter of relevant and irrelevant facts; or it can come in an orderly, meaningful manner as the output of a marketing information system. In this chapter, we will look at the general framework of the marketing information system and its relationship to planning and control. In the next chapter we will

look at the role of marketing research, probably the most important part of the system for a consumer-oriented company. Chapter 22 explores the critical topic of marketing cost and profitability analysis—a process that feeds invaluable data into the marketing information system.

Using Marketing Information for Planning and Control

A model showing the relationship between the flow of information and the processes of planning and controlling is shown in Figure 20.1. Two flows are indicated. The first is the flow of information involved in the development of marketing plans and their implementation. The second is the flow of feedback information necessary to evaluate performance and to exercise control. In the

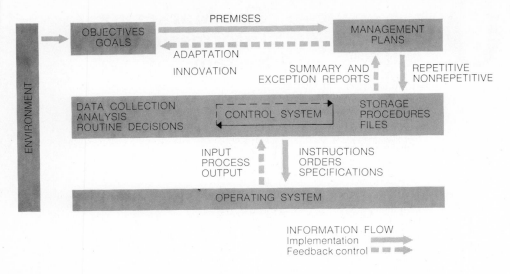

FIGURE 20.1   Information flows in a planning and control system

Source: Adapted from *The Theory and Management of Systems* by R. A. Johnson, F. C.Kast, and J. C. Rosenzweig. Copyright © 1973 McGraw-Hill Book Co., Inc. Used with permission of McGraw-Hill Book Company.

model, marketing information flows from the environment to the firm. This information is used in the specification of goals and objectives, which in turn become the premises on which management plans are based. These management plans in turn become part of the information system. Along with other types of data not specified in the diagram, they constitute the basis of implementing instructions and, ultimately, of operational control. Feedback of results originates in the operating system and flows back to the control system. Performance is compared to plan, routine adjustments are made, and summary and exception reports are issued. From the evaluation of performance in relation to plan may arise modifications to tactics or strategies or even an adjustment in the firm's objectives.

Very little modification would have to be made in this model to convert it into an adaptive control system. All that would be required is to include data inputs describing the performance of a normative operating system. Given adequate information about the operation being controlled, the system itself could issue necessary instructions to bring performance into line with the expected norm. This type of adaptive control process has been successfully used in automated manufacturing systems, such as chemical processing. In marketing, discussions of adaptive control systems are still at the theoretical level. However, the kind of system shown in Figure 20.1 is being used for marketing control purposes. In fact, control has become so vital in many firms that there is a tendency to think of information flows almost exclusively in terms of control data. The importance of marketing control cannot be overemphasized, and we will return to this topic later in the chapter. But we recognize that control is only one element of an overall marketing information system. The other is its contribution to the design of long- and short-run marketing plans.

The Development of Marketing Information Systems

What Is a Marketing Information System?

The marketing information system has stemmed from two developments: First, there has been the emergence of the general systems approach to marketing; second, there has been increasing disenchantment with traditional approaches to marketing research. The principal reason for this disenchantment is that marketing research has been very narrowly circumscribed. It has failed to provide all of the information required by managers for planning and problem solving. The coincidence of these two developments resulted in the application of a systems approach to the management of information. According to L. Adler, "The role of a systems approach is to help evolve a *marketing intelligence* system tailored to the needs of each marketer. Such a system would serve as the ever-alert nerve center of the marketing operation."[1] From this concept of its role, a definition of the marketing information system has evolved.

A structured, interacting complex of persons, machines, and procedures designed to generate an orderly flow of pertinent information, collected from both intra- and extra-firm sources, for

use as the basis for decision-making in specified responsibility areas of marketing management.[2]

This definition is widely accepted in the field of marketing. It gives proper recognition to the fact that the system is composed of people, computers, and information flows. It stresses that the ultimate purpose of the system is to assist managers in making marketing decisions.

Figure 20.2 illustrates how an elementary marketing information system operates. The information system, presumably computer based, is located in the center of the diagram. The system is activated by the management decision structure—possibly a product manager preparing to develop an annual marketing plan. This activation takes the form of an interrogation of the information system—that is, the product manager asks for data needed to make a planning choice.[3] The information that is needed may already exist in the information system's data bank. If this is the case, the product manager receives an immediate response. However, the information may not be in the system, in which case research is necessary. An inquiry is directed at the market environment and a response is received. Ultimately, the response is transmitted to the product manager who initiated the request for information. Figure 20.2 also contains the feedback flow required for an elementary control system, but we will temporarily postpone a discussion of this aspect of the information

---

[1] L. Alder, "Systems Approach to Marketing," *Harvard Business Review,* May-June 1967, p. 110.

[2] S. V. Smith, R. H. Brien, and J. E. Stafford, "Marketing Information Systems: An Introductory Overview," in *Readings in Marketing Information Systems* (Boston: Houghton Mifflin, 1968), p. 7.

[3] Of course, the information system can anticipate the information needs of the decision structure and routinely communicate selected key facts that can be used in the development of marketing programs. Not surprisingly, the same data also are used for control purposes.

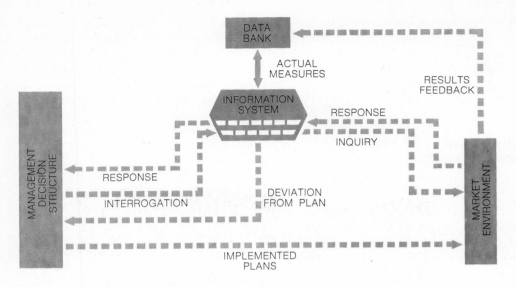

FIGURE 20.2   A marketing information system

Source: Reprinted from "The Marketing Executive and Management Information Systems" by A. E. Amstutz in R. M. Haas (ed.), *Science, Technology, and Marketing,* 1966, p. 85, published by the American Marketing Association.

system while we look at the kinds of data required for planning and decision making.

Information Requirements

What kinds of information are pertinent for making marketing decisions? The answer really depends on the specific decisions to be made and the decision tools that will be applied.[4] However, we can generalize about four types of information that are sought by most marketing managers.

1. *Information about customers and markets* These nonroutine data, which are re-

---

[4]This point is well illustrated in the description of an information system developed for use at General Mills. See L. D. Gibson et al., "An Evolutionary Approach to Marketing Information Systems," *Journal of Marketing,* April 1973, pp. 2–6.

quired to help management solve particular problems, are obtained by marketing research. Chapter 21 deals with this topic.

2. *Information about past and expected sales* Through routine analyses of past sales and forecasts of future sales, the manager obtains information useful in evaluating the effectiveness of current programs and in planning future strategies. The use of sales analysis for control purposes is explored later in this chapter.

3. *Cost information* Expense data related to the products and programs for which the manager is responsible are obtained through techniques of marketing cost analysis and marketing profitability accounting. We will look at this subject in Chapter 22.

4. *Information about the environment* Every-

thing outside the company constitutes its environment. This means that the information system should possess data about the channel system, the industry system, and the macromarketing system of which the marketing company is a component part.[5] Specifically, the information system generates and stores information about the economic, competitive, and public-policy environments. Selected environmental forces are reviewed in Chapter 23.

The Current Status of Marketing Information Systems

The development of marketing information systems is still in its infancy. A study by Cox and Good revealed that

very few companies have developed advanced systems, and not all of these are in operation. Some might even best be classified as subsystems, since they related to only a portion of the marketing decisions made.

Some companies, perhaps 15, are actively upgrading their systems to a high level. Of course, about half seem to be progressing well; the others have been much less successful. Many other companies are contemplating plans to develop sophisticated systems.[6]

More recent discussions reveal that the progress in integrating the computer into a meaningful information system has been painfully slow.[7] The slowness is attributed to two facts: (1) Decision-making problems in business are much more difficult than originally perceived, and (2) the computer does not necessarily fit all of the information needs of the manager.

Notwithstanding the relatively slow pace at which marketing information systems are being developed, there is little question that they will become increasingly important. More information is available today than ever before, and managers are learning how better to use these data in making increasingly complex marketing decisions. The information system will become more and more important as each year goes by. At present, it provides us with an excellent example of the application of the systems approach to marketing. It demonstrates clearly that the component parts of the organization must be meaningfully linked by a formal communications flow. The management of the organization as a whole unquestionably is facilitated by the proper direction of the information flows within it. So far as marketing planning is concerned, having the right information about customers, competitors, and other environmental influences is essential.

Marketing Control Systems

The ultimate of an information system is automated control. At present, most firms

---

[5]W. R. King and D. I. Cleland, "Environmental Information Systems for Strategic Marketing Planning," *Journal of Marketing*, October 1974, pp. 35–40.

[6]Donald F. Cox and Robert E. Good, "How to Build a Marketing Information System," *Harvard Business Review*, May-June 1967, p. 148. Copyright © 1967 by the President and Fellows of Harvard College; all rights reserved.

[7]M. McNiven and B. D. Hilton, "Reassessing Marketing Information Systems," *Journal of Advertising Research*, January 1970, p. 3; and L. Winer, "Putting the Computer to Work in Marketing Management," *Business Horizons*, December 1974, pp. 71–79.

are not even close to this ideal, which must be approached gradually through the design of more and more sophisticated information systems. The development process might begin with an elementary information system, such as that shown in Figure 20.2, in which internal and environmental data are used by the management decision structure in the formulation of marketing plans. Results feedback also is shown entering the information system, and this is the beginning of an elementary control process. We should now look more closely at the control mechanism in order to understand the implications of a comprehensive and, eventually, a completely automated marketing control system.

The Nature and Importance of Marketing Control

Although the concept of control goes beyond the transmission of information, data feedback is a most important aspect of a control system. Performance data enable a manager to evaluate how well various components are achieving system goals. With this knowledge, the manager is in a position to take corrective action. We can illustrate the use of control information by the simple model shown in Figure 20.3. As we see from the model, control feedback leads either to the modification of the existing plan or to the alteration of objectives. In either case, the impact on planning is clear—revised plans eventually must be developed, and control data become a vital input for the marketing planner.

To exercise control means far more than to exercise authority. As a marketing function, *control* includes all those activities that are necessary to exert a guiding and restraining influence over the operations of a marketing organization as it attempts to achieve its objectives.[8] The concept of control has become quite commonplace in recent years. Almost every American is familiar with the words, "This is Houston Control," which are broadcast during American manned flights into space. As a matter of fact, the analogy of missile control is useful in describing the nature and importance of marketing control. The rocket with its payload (the space capsule) is launched into a predetermined orbit at a planned velocity. Malfunction in the system, changes in atmospheric conditions, an unexpected shift in the target site, or an error in human judgment might occur at any time. Control is necessary to detect such threats to the flight plan and to indicate the changes required to get the missile back on target. A space vehicle is an extremely complicated technical device, and there are literally hundreds of strategic points at which control must be exercised. The rapid and simultaneous control of a large number of variables is facilitated by the use of a *control system,* or an interconnected group of tracking, measuring, and computing components. The system receives information (data feedback) at periodic intervals or at strategic checkpoints. Flight data then are compared to the predetermined flight plan. If deviation from the plan is indicated, a corrective action is initiated.

From the example just cited, it is apparent that the control process involves three basic steps: (1) setting standards of performance at strategic points, (2) checking and reporting on performance, and (3) taking corrective action. These three activities are common to

---

[8]Probably the most comprehensive treatment of control is found in R. Anthony, *Planning and Control Systems: A Framework for Analysis* (Boston: Division of Research, Graduate School of Business, Harvard University, 1965).

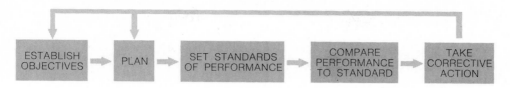

FIGURE 20.3   The elements of a marketing control system

every type of control system. They are inherent in the process of exercising a guiding and restraining influence. The system may be simple or complex; it may be manual or automated; it may involve qualitative or quantitative information. But in every instance, setting standards, checking performance, and taking corrective action are involved.

Control in Marketing

Marketing control is the regulating device of a marketing program. Like missile control, it detects each threat to the program's progress and indicates necessary adjustments. A marketing program is launched into a market environment that is much like outer space. Atmospheric conditions, the rotation of the entire solar system, shifts in target location, malfunction of the space vehicle, and human error, all have counterparts in the implementation of a marketing plan. Much as space exploration requires thorough and systematic control, so does marketing. The variables of the marketplace necessitate such control. The marketing manager establishes policies and makes plans, determines budgets and procedures, and employs and trains an operating organization. But long before the ultimate goal of a successful marketing operation is achieved, almost all of the marketing phenomena on which the program

was established change. Control is necessary to identify the changes in these factors, to assess the impact of these factors on the program, and to indicate any needed adjustments in strategy.

The marketing manager is well aware of the changing environment and expects to make decisions to adjust the program as the need arises. But in practice it is seldom easy to determine when these decisions must be made or when a marketing program is off target. Marketing management, like a space flight, is a complex of interrelated activities. It is extremely difficult for the marketing manager to be on top of all of these activities. In accordance with good management practice, the manager should not have to be intimately involved with them but must be ready to make decisions in any area when required. To complicate the situation, most issues arise far down the organizational ladder. They frequently spring up at distant geographical locations. A good control system is designed to uncover problems in remote parts of the marketing organization. It also is supposed to detect such situations quickly, for generally a firm that is able to adjust quickly succeeds most conclusively.

The Marketing Controller

We have seen that controlling is an important part of marketing management and that the marketing information system inputs data for evaluating performance. A question arises: Who does the controlling? The first and most obvious answer is that the manager, the person who is also the planner, must control. Indeed, the planner must control in order to make sure that the plan produces the desired results. The purpose of planning is not simply to produce a plan; it is to get things done. It is performance that produces results—not a plan. Thus the idea of a planner-controller emerges—a planner who is also the controller. In this controlling capacity, the planner analyzes feedback, determines that the effort called for in the plan is carried out, compares actual with expected results, analyzes variances, and sets in motion actions to modify the program or even to substitute a different strategy for one that is not working.

A few years ago, S. R. Goodman suggested that a position be established in the marketing department that would have the responsibility for performing the control function.[9] He even suggested calling the person filling this assignment a *marketing controller.* Among the duties of the marketing controller would be

Maintain records of adherence to profit plans.
Closely control media expense.
Prepare brand manager's budgets.
Advise on optimum timing for strategies.
Measure the efficiency of promotions.
Analyze media production costs.
Evaluate customer and geographic profitability.
Present sales-oriented financial reports.
Assist direct accounts to optimize purchasing and inventory policies.
Educate the marketing area to financial implications of decisions.[10]

[9]S. R. Goodman, *Techniques of Profitability Analysis* (New York: Wiley-Interscience, 1970).
[10]Ibid., pp. 17–18.

Goodman's research indicated the presence of an impasse between finance and marketing and the need to bring these two functions closer together. There has not been widespread acceptance of the marketing controller concept, although the author has discovered a dozen or more large companies that make use of it. Instead, the merging of finance and marketing is taking place in the types of demands being made on marketing managers and the academic training they are receiving. Understanding financial concepts and knowing how to use various techniques of financial analysis have become important talents for the marketing manager to have.[11] We will look in more detail at one aspect of this in Chapter 22.

Toward an Automated Planning and Control System.

We noted at the beginning of this section that we are still a long way from the ideal of an automated control system. Nevertheless, the systems approach is a step in the right direction. And we can move even closer to our ideal through the use of simulation models like those shown in Figure 20.4. Historical data are the basis for the construction of such simulation models. Proposed plans, based on hypothetical conditions, are tested in the model; and simulated results are returned to the decision unit as a foundation for making final plans. In this type of process, the simulation models can be con-

[11]For two excellent treatments of the financial control aspects of marketing management, see M. Schiff, "Finance and Financial Analysis in Marketing," in V. P. Buell, ed., *Handbook of Modern Marketing* (New York: McGraw-Hill, 1970) pp. 15-3–15-21; and V. H. Kirpalani and S. S. Shapiro, "Financial Dimensions of Marketing Management," *Journal of Marketing,* July 1973, pp. 40–47.

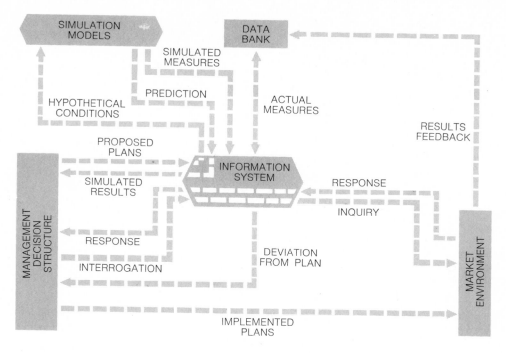

FIGURE 20.4   An advanced marketing control system

Source: Adapted from *The Theory and Management of Systems* by R. A. Johnson, F. C. Kast, and J. C. Rosenzweig. Copyright © 1973 McGraw-Hill Book Co., Inc. Used with permission of McGraw-Hill Book Company.

stantly improved and updated by current data.

Conversion of this system into a completely automated control system requires only the substitution of a control model for the simulation model. Performance data are fed directly to the control model as well as to the information system. Routine deviations from plan can be noted and corrective instructions issued. If deviations from plan are beyond the ranges of those that can be controlled by the automatic system, warning signals can be directed to the decision structure.

At this point in the development of management information systems, companies have experimented with the use of such simulation models only for planning purposes. Whether completely automated control systems will be feasible in marketing is yet to be determined.

The Marketing Audit

The financial audit is one of the established instruments of financial control. Periodically, usually on an annual basis, a careful study is made of a company's financial performance. The accuracy of financial reports is verified. These audited statements become the basis for assessing the financial strengths and weaknesses of a company, and in turn lead to the development of financial strategies.

The idea of a marketing audit—a systematic and thorough examination of a company's marketing position—has existed for many years; but, like the concept of marketing controllership to which it is closely related, it has not been widely adopted. It is, however, an important aspect of marketing management and logically can be considered an element in a total marketing information system.

With few exceptions the concept of the marketing audit has been a neglected topic in the literature of marketing—at least compared with such topics as marketing research and applications of management science. Even its origin is difficult to trace. The first formal discussion of the topic appeared in 1959, when the American Management Association published a booklet that carried the subtitle "Marketing Audits in Theory and Practice."[12] It became a landmark in marketing literature, and most of the subsequent works on the subject refer to this AMA study.

For reasons that are somewhat hard to identify, the marketing audit has not taken hold, in spite of the fact that interest in it continues.[13] As we shall see, marketing au-

diting is a difficult procedure in that it requires a great deal of time, effort, and money. Neither internal nor external marketing auditing staffs exist in significant numbers, as do such staffs in the area of financial auditing. Most companies apparently do not feel the need for a marketing audit until a serious breakdown occurs. Unfortunately, in a crisis there usually is not enough time to conduct a thorough marketing audit. It also is probable that the marketing audits that are conducted are not well publicized, since the methods used and the results obtained are considered confidential. Marketing consulting firms do not publish the results of their work. It is reasonable to believe that more work of an auditing type is being done in marketing than might be apparent from an inspection of contemporary marketing literature. On balance, it appears that marketing auditing is of sufficient interest and importance to merit increased attention. Potentially it can be extremely valuable to a company seeking to improve its marketing planning and performance.

What Is a Marketing Audit?

A *marketing audit* is a systematic and thorough examination of a company's marketing position. In much the same manner that a company's financial condition is highly complex and ever changing, so its marketing activity is immensely complicated and dynamic. Almost the same reasons that prompt a firm to review its financial position and have its reports and procedures audited make it desirable for the company to have its marketing position examined.

In some respects, a marketing audit probes deeper into the essence of a compa-

---

[12]*Analyzing and Improving Marketing Performance, Report No. 32* (New York: American Management Association, 1959).

[13]Besides the treatment of the marketing audit in the first edition of this text, other authors have devoted some attention to it. See G. Fisk, *Marketing Systems: An Introductory Analysis* (New York: Harper & Row, 1967); P. Kotler, *Marketing Management* (Englewood Cliffs, N.J.: Prentice-Hall, 1976); and D. T. Kollat, R. D. Blackwell, and J. F. Robeson, *Strategic Marketing* (New York: Holt, Rinehart and Winston, 1972).

ny's operation than does a financial audit. Although it is concerned principally with appraising marketing performance, it also focuses on the most fundamental facets of a company's marketing effort—its philosophy, objectives, policies, and organization. Stated in another way, the marketing audit explores the conceptual basis of a firm's marketing activities. Professor Shuchman clearly defines the marketing audit as

a systematic, critical, and impartial review and appraisal of the total marketing operation: of the basic objectives and policies of the operation and the assumptions which underlie them as well as of the methods, procedures, personnel, and organization employed to implement the policies and achieve the objectives.[14]

Types of Marketing Audits

Although marketing audits can be conducted in a number of ways, three general bases suffice for our purposes. First, there is the *degree* of thoroughness or complexity involved in the audit. On this basis, we can distinguish between partial and complete audits. A *partial audit* involves something short of an exhaustive investigation of all aspects of the activity under study. A *complete audit* involves a comprehensive examination, including internal and external primary research.

Second, there is the *number* of marketing elements or activities that are being studied. From this viewpoint Richard Crisp distinguishes between *horizontal* and *vertical* audits.

The horizontal audit examines all of the elements that go into the marketing whole, with particular emphasis upon the relative importance of these elements and the "mix" between them. It is often referred to as a "marketing mix" audit. The vertical audit singles out certain functional elements of the marketing operation and subjects them to thorough, searching study and evaluation.[15]

Philip Kotler suggests a third basis of distinguishing marketing audits. He describes the *activity-level audit,* suggesting that audits can be conducted along various strata of the marketing organization.[16] At the top there is the system- or corporate-level audit. There also can be audits along a divisional level, such as a product-line division, and finally audits can be conducted at an even lower level, for example, in one segment of the distribution system.

An audit of a company's advertising program or of its sales organization would be a *vertical* audit. An investigation encompassing both advertising and selling as well as other related activities, including product management and marketing research, would be *horizontal*. Both vertical and horizontal audits can be conducted at one or more levels. Figure 20.5 shows the relationship between vertical, horizontal, and activity-level audits. The vertical audits involve specific functions, labeled A, B, and C. They ordinarily are conducted at all levels of the firm. Horizontal audits encompass two or more of these functions. These are indicated by the platforms in the diagram. Since two platforms are shown in Figure 20.5, we differen-

---

[14]A. Shuchman, "The Marketing Audit: Its Nature, Purposes, and Problems," in *Analyzing and Improving Marketing Performance, Report No. 32* (New York: American Management Association, 1959), p. 13.

[15]Richard D. Crisp, "Auditing the Functional Elements of a Marketing Operation," in *Analyzing and Improving Marketing Performance, Report No. 32* (New York: American Management Association, 1959), pp. 16–17.

[16]Kotler, *Marketing Management,* pp. 596–602.

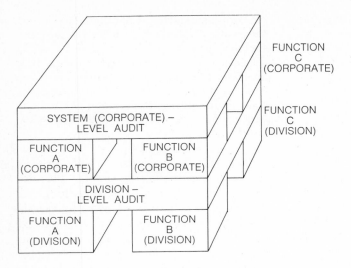

FIGURE 20.6   Types of marketing audits

tiate between them on the basis of activity level. In this example, there is a system or corporate-level audit and a division-level audit. Obviously there also can be purely vertical audits at the divisional level. A study of a single function at the divisional level could be called a *division-level vertical marketing audit.*

The matrix in Figure 20.6 illustrates all three types of marketing audits. Three activity levels are shown—system (corporate), group, and division. These correspond to the three levels of planning most frequently encountered. Vertical and horizontal audits are represented, as are audits that are either complete or partial. Within this particular arrangement, twelve different types of audits might be conducted. Clearly, however, it is the type of audit shown by the shaded area in Figure 20.6 that identifies the concept of the marketing audit presented in this chapter. This concept is the system-level, complete horizontal (integrated) marketing audit.

The Focal Points of a Marketing Audit

Actually, no aspect of a firm's marketing operation is beyond the scope of the system-level, complete horizontal audit. For convenience, however, we shall focus on three particularly important points in marketing auditing. These are the company's assets, its performance, and its competitive effectiveness.

Marketing assets   A marketing program involves the commitment of assets to the achievement of marketing objectives. In a marketing audit, the following questions regarding assets are explored: What are the company's assets? Are these assets modern or obsolete? Are other or improved assets needed to meet future marketing opportunities? Some of the more typical marketing assets evaluated in a marketing audit include the marketing department organization, the trade channel structure, product lines, com-

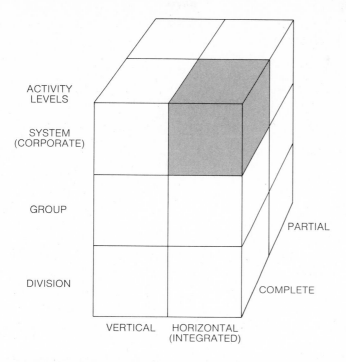

ACTIVITY
LEVELS

SYSTEM
(CORPORATE)

GROUP

DIVISION

PARTIAL

COMPLETE

VERTICAL   HORIZONTAL
(INTEGRATED)

FIGURE 20.5   Horizontal and vertical marketing audits at two
levels

pany image and reputation, and marketing skill and philosophy.

Some of these assets are intangible and can be evaluated only indirectly and only in a highly subjective manner. Nevertheless, all of these are elements with which a company builds its marketing program, and their assessment as well as an evaluation of performance in using them constitute one of the most important aspects of the marketing audit.

Performance evaluation   The key to evaluating marketing performance is found in comparing actual results against expected standards or norms. The measurement of actual results, for example sales, and the subsequent comparison against the forecast

are continuous analytical activities. They are part of the overall analysis of the marketing situation and go beyond the occasional marketing audit.

Competitive effectiveness   It is important constantly to be aware that the marketing program is a competitive business weapon. Its purpose is to create a differential advantage and thereby carve out a well-defined market niche. For this reason, the competitive aspects of a company's marketing effort must be scrutinized. In the course of a marketing audit, questions such as the following are raised: Who are the competitors? What are their market objectives? How do they market their products? Why? What are the specific competitive strengths and weaknesses in the company's marketing effort? What apparent directions are competitors taking? Why?

Techniques of Marketing Auditing

In our definition of the marketing audit, the first word was "systematic." A *systematic* investigation requires that the audit be conducted according to a step-by-step procedure. Experience has shown that is is desirable to move from the general to the specific and from the upper to the lower level of the activity being studied. In the course of this process, certain procedures have proven to be successful.

1. The audit usually is conducted by means of a detailed questionnaire exploring all areas of importance. An example of the type and depth of question raised in a marketing audit is shown in Exhibit 20.1. Of course, the questions posed in a marketing audit are tailored to a particular company. However, the questions shown are typical of those used in exploring the distribution phase of a company's marketing activities.

2. The marketing audit is a careful and comprehensive study. Accordingly, each topic in the audit is examined thoroughly before the next is considered. The marketing auditor is accustomed to working with written documents, such as statements of policy, job descriptions, organization charts, plans, market research studies, and the like. Material pertinent to each part of the marketing audit is collected and compiled prior to discussions of the area involved. Insofar as it is practical, discussions are limited to the topic under consideration. Preliminary findings are prepared for each stage or step.

3. It is desirable in marketing auditing to obtain a diversity of viewpoints. The composite picture is required for a thorough understanding. Group sessions in which a number of executives participate or individual discussions with key personnel usually are undertaken.

4. Since the support and participation of top management are important in successful market auditing, the general practice is to begin with the highest echelons of the company and work down to the tactical marketing positions.

5. For the most part, the preliminary discussions of each topic are concerned with historical and descriptive aspects. Only after the historical development and present condition of a particular activity have been thoroughly explored is an effort made to extend the discussion to future plans.

6. Marketing auditing is a lengthy process and frequently tends to consume more time than is necessary. To expedite the procedure, an audit schedule is desirable, and every effort is made to keep the analysis on time.

7. The final report of a market audit is a written document covering the entire scope of the investigation. Because of the breadth of a marketing audit, it is usual for the report to be divided into several parts, these divisions depending on the nature of the analysis and the findings. The audit report represents the best judgment of the analyst regarding the company's capability to engage in effective marketing action. For the most part, this judgment is based on the weighing of evidence obtained in the

---

EXHIBIT 20.1   Selected marketing-audit questions

Questions to be answered about the firm's distribution strategy

A.   Sales organization

1.   Please describe the channel or channels of distribution used to reach ultimate users of the products sold by your firm. For each major channel, please indicate:
    a.   The number of resellers (that is, retailers, wholesalers, direct-mail establishments, and so on) by type
    b.   The location of resellers by type
    c.   The number and location of your representatives

2.   Describe the methods you have used in building your trade channels.

3.   Describe in detail the sales management organization, including line and staff activities utilized by your firm.

4.   Please describe the relations with resellers of your products.
    a.   Outline the job responsibilities of your resellers.
    b.   How are resellers selected?
    c.   How are resellers indoctrinated?
    d.   What methods of reseller supervision and control are used?

    e.   What techniques are used to stimulate resellers?
    f.   What functional (trade) discounts are allowed to resellers?

5.   What types of sales organizations are used by your important competitors? Indicate especially how their distribution channels may differ from yours. Any observations as to reasons for such differences will be very helpful.

B.   Physical distribution

1.   Please describe the physical-distribution arrangements by which your firm's products move to the consumer.

2.   How are warehousing points selected?

3.   What procedure is used for the selection of particular warehouse firms?

4.   What are the advantages and disadvantages of the present system of physical distribution?

5.   How do major competitors arrange for the physical distribution of their products? Please explain any significant differences in approach.

---

course of the investigation. Documentary evidence as well as the opinions of the auditor are included. The marketing auditor, whether a company executive or an outside consultant, should be completely objective. This objectivity should ensure an unbiased report and reflect the best marketing judgment that can be brought to bear on the study of the company's marketing activities. Such a report generally concludes with recommendations for changes in such areas as goals and objectives, organiza-

tion, policies, planning and control procedures, and the development of marketing strategy.

Problems in Conducting a Marketing Audit

Since the evaluation of a company's marketing efforts is of such importance, why then is marketing auditing often neglected? The answer to this question lies in a number of problems connected with carrying out an audit.

Expense Considerable expense is involved in carrying out a thorough audit of a company's marketing activities, especially when an outside auditor is retained. Even internal auditing may be quite costly in terms of the time of the executives involved.

Time A marketing audit requires the time of top management as well as of marketing personnel. Often this time is given with reluctance. However, general managers should not only see that time is made available, but they also should realize that audits have to be conducted periodically and according to a definite timetable.

Selection of auditors Finding an appropriate auditor can pose a problem. There is no one best way to select marketing auditors. What the controller should look for in making such a choice is objectivity and a knowledge of the activity being investigated. Shuchman commented on this problem as follows:

As implied by the definition of the audit, such people (i.e. auditors) must be not only critical and impartial but also knowledgeable and creative. They must not be so involved with or "married" to existing policies and procedures that they cannot really be critical and objective in their assessments. In addition, they must possess the experience, know-how, and creative imagination needed to recognize problems and opportunities that are just beginning to appear on the horizon of the company's marketing situation and to define feasible courses of action for solving the problems and exploiting the opportunities.[17]

A. R. Oxenfeldt suggests several sources of auditing services that can be either internal or external.[18] *Internal* sources of auditing include

Persons from "above in the organization and in charge of the activity being studied"

Persons engaged in other (though related) activities on the same functional level as the activity being appraised

A task force composed of individuals within the company of varied training and background

Persons responsible for the activity being appraised (self-appraisal)

In a few companies there are formalized internal consulting departments that provide the staff for internal auditing. Corporate marketing-planning groups sometimes assist in internal auditing, as well.

External sources of marketing appraisal include

Marketing consultants
Management services departments of public accounting firms
Marketing-research firms capable of providing audit services

Marketing Audits in the Future

For the reasons presented in the preceding section, relatively few companies have availed themselves of the benefits of marketing audits. The time and expense involved

---

[17]Shuchman, "The Marketing Audit," p. 18.

[18]A. R. Oxenfeldt first presented a classification of sources of auditing in "The Marketing Audit as a Total Evaluation Program," in *Analyzing and Improving Marketing Performance, Report No. 32* (New York: American Management Association, 1959), pp. 35–36. The same material is found in his text, *Executive Action in Marketing* (Belmont, Calif.: Wadsworth, 1966), pp. 756–757.

militate against the widespread use of this analytical tool. Few consulting firms specialize in performing the service. However, the marketing audit is of considerable importance to scientific marketing management. It may once have been appropriate only for the largest and wealthiest companies, but now the marketing audit can be utilized by almost any firm. All that is required is careful adherence to the basic intent and fundamental procedures of market auditing. The internal audit, audits conducted by advertising agencies for their clients, and audits performed by management consultants will become of increasing importance in the future.

Controlling Sales

The analysis of sales is of great importance in checking marketing performance. Together with measurements of potential, actual sales data enable the manager to answer the question, "Have we sold all that we could?" Sales data used for this purpose take many forms. For example, orders, bookings, shipments, backlog (cumulative unfilled orders), receipts, and billings are common methods of reporting sales. Sales may be recorded in dollar values or in units. Generally speaking, when multiple products are involved, the sales dollar is the most convenient form of recording sales information.[19] In view of the many forms in which sales information is obtained and the diversity of uses to which it can be put, it should not be surprising that

there also are many different methods of analysis.

The most common methods of analyzing sales are by time period, product, territory, customer or customer group, and company organizational unit. In many cases, combination analyses are made. For example, product sales also may be analyzed according to customer. Territorial sales may be analyzed by customer, by product, or by salesperson. If a computer is available to process the data, there is virtually no limit to the number and type of analyses that can be made. A good example of the diversity of the types and sources of sales data is shown in Exhibit 20.2. This exhibit is a composite drawn from the experience of many firms. Any one company would be unlikely to use more than two or three of the various types of sales information.

Here is an example of how a marketing manager should analyze the sales data for a particular firm (see Table 20.1). The data in this case are hypothetical, although the situation is based on the sales control procedures used by a major home-furnishings company.[20] The example is particularly realistic because it dramatizes how aggregate sales data may cover up serious problems in particular sectors of the marketing operation. In our example, Fyne Furniture Company's marketing manager, B. J. Sanders, has no indication initially that anything is wrong. A routine quarterly review of sales reveals that the entire marketing program appears to be running smoothly. However,

---

[19]In isolated cases, other aggregative measures are used. A refinery measures sales in barrels; a steel company uses tons of product. This is not a very useful method for a diversified company, however.

[20]In constructing this example, the author has adapted material that originally appeared in an article by S. J. Robinson, "Trouble Spots in Sales: How We Localize and Cure Them," *Sales Management, The Marketing Magazine,* 15 December 1949, pp. 44–50. Adapted by permission from *Sales and Marketing Management* magazine, copyright © 1949.

EXHIBIT 20.2   Types and sources of sales information

Document	Source information provided	Document	Source information provided
1. Order forms and invoices*	Customer name, number, and location Product(s) or service(s) sold Volume and dollar amount of the transaction Salesperson (or agent) responsible for the sale End use of product sold Location of customer facility where product is to be shipped Location of customer facility where product is to be used Customer's industry, class of trade, and/or channel of distribution Terms of sale and applicable discount Freight paid and/or to be collected Shipment point for the order Transportation used in shipment		Sales by company (in dollars and/or units by product or service by location of customer facility) Customer's industry, class of trade, and/or trade channel Estimated total annual usage of each product or service sold by the company Estimated annual purchases from the company of each such product or service Location (in terms of company sales territory)
		6. Financial records	Sales revenue (by products, geographical markets, customers, class of trade, unit of sales organization, and so on) Direct sales expenses (similarly classified) Overhead sales costs (similarly classified) Profits (similarly classified)
2. Cash register receipts	Type (cash or credit) and dollar amount of transaction by department and by sales person		
3. Salespeople's call reports	Customers and prospects called on (company and individual seen; planned or unplanned calls) Products discussed Orders obtained Customers' product needs and usage Other significant information about customers Distribution of salespersons time among customer calls, travel, and office work Sales related activities: meetings, conventions, and so on	7. Credit memos	Returns and allowances
		8. Warranty cards	Indirect measures of dealer sales Customer service
		9. Summary reports from distributors and dealers	Sales by product, geographic area, class of customer, and so on
		10. Store audits	Unit and dollar volume and market share of consumer purchases of the company's brands in selected retail outlets
4. Salespeople's expense accounts	Expenses by day by item (hotel, meals, travel, and so on)	11. Consumer diaries (as a rule they cover only packaged foods and personal-care items)	Unit volume of purchases by package size of company's brand (and competing brands) made by selected families Details about prices, special deals, and types of outlets in which the purchases were made
5. Individual customer (and prospect) records	Name and location and customer number Number of calls by company salespeople (or agents)		

*The source of most information about company sales is the order form and invoice, but various other documents, records, and reports also serve as raw material for sales reports, as the tabulation indicates. Of course a single company is likely to draw on only two or three of these sources of sales information.

Source: National Industrial Conference Board, *Sales Analysis* (New York: National Industrial Conference Board, 1965), p. 68.

TABLE 20.1   Fyne Furniture Company sales microanalysis

Sales analysis activity	Focus	Sales data				Comment
		Sales ($000)	Goal ($000)	Over or under ($000)	Per cent over or under	
1. Sanders conducts a quarterly sales review, comparing actual with goal for the overall marketing program	Total company	5,060	5,000	60	1.2	No apparent problem
2. Microanalysis by reviewing sales in eight regions	Mideast	995	1,000	−5	−.5	Mideast region off by $5,000, which is 0.5% of goal
	Great Lakes	1,050	1,000	50	5.0	
	Northeast	301	300	1	.3	
	Plains	403	400	3	.8	
	Southeast	1,047	1,050	−2	−.2	
	Southwest	510	500	10	2.0	
	Rocky Mountains	96	100	−2	−2.0	
	Far Northwest	757	750	5	.7	
3. Microanalysis by reviewing sales in the Mideast region at four districts	Baltimore	270	250	20	8.0	All of the Mideast region's problem is in the Philadelphia district
	Pittsburgh	315	300	15	5.0	
	Philadelphia	140	200	−60	−30.0	
	Richmond	270	250	20	8.0	
4. Microanalysis by reviewing sales in Philadelphia at three focal points:						
a. Customer	Katz Brothers	15	15	—	—	The problem in Philadelphia is centered in two large customers— one of which bought nothing during the quarter
	Williams & Foote	0	40	−40	−100.0	
	Maurice Bentley	10	40	−30	−75.0	
	Furniture Fair	25	15	10	66.7	
	All other	90	90	—	—	
b. Salesperson	Johnson	10	60	−50	−83.0	Johnson and Avery are the focal points of the problem, with Johnson alone accounting for $50,000 loss in sales
	Avery	25	50	−25	−50.0	
	Blomberg	45	45	—	—	
	Fenton	60	45	15	33.3	
c. Product line	Heritage	30	40	−10	−25.0	Sales loss is concentrated in the Colonial group—a highly competitive line of Early American reproductions; Avente, a modern line, showed unexpected strength
	Colonial	20	70	−50	−71.4	
	Grenada	40	60	−20	−33.3	
	Avente	50	30	20	66.7	

Sanders knows that a thorough sales analysis involves the inspection of performance at several points and accordingly checks sales in relation to quota beginning with the first of eight marketing regions. It is immediately apparent that the aggregate sales picture is misleading. The Mideast region is 0.5 per cent off its goal. Although the deficiency is modest, it is a danger signal that calls for further analysis. The next step, accordingly, is to continue the microanalysis by inspecting sales performance in the Mideast. This analysis reveals that sales are off drastically in Philadelphia. In order to discover the exact trouble spot, a more detailed analysis of sales in the Philadelphia district is made.

There are three focal points in the company's marketing operation—the customer, the salesperson, and the product (or product line). Any one or combination of the three might lie at the root of the problem. The analysis of district sales by major customers indicates that almost all of the problem is centered at two customers (Williams & Foote and Maurice Bentley). An analysis of sales performance by salespersons reveals that two senior salespeople (Johnson and Avery) who carry the load of the district, are 83 and 50 per cent below quota. As might be expected, their major accounts are the same ones that are far behind their assigned quotas of sales. The product analysis further reveals that the Colonial line accounts for most of the district's sales problem.

Thus, the Philadelphia district's sales problem centers on two salespeople and their inability to keep two major customers going and to produce orders for the most important group in the line. It appears, therefore, that the problem in Philadelphia is unique in character and probably has no serious implications for the entire marketing program. However, remedial steps should be taken to correct the localized situation. These might include

1. A thorough analysis of the company's relationships with its major customers in the district, with the particular purpose of discovering why sales in the leading outlets have been so far below expectations.
2. A review of the two salesperson's work habits, especially their handling of major accounts and their methods of presenting the Colonial line. In this example, the district sales manager was able to redirect the salespersons' activities. Together they worked out a change in selling tactics that resulted in the recovery of most of the lost Colonial business with the key accounts.

Sanders, continuing with the microanalysis, would next look into the Great Lakes region. The $50,000 over goal reflects a special order from Sears. Then, in turn, Sanders would continue to inspect each district, further analyzing those districts that show a difference (plus or minus) from anticipated sales.

Summary

Before the marketing manager can begin to develop a strategy, marketing intelligence must be used to assess the situation in which to plan and make decisions. This intelligence comes through a marketing information system. The need for such a system to gather, process, store, and report information has arisen because of the information explosion that has taken place in recent years. Among the most potent forces behind this information explosion is, of course, the computer.

The systems approach is one such method applied to the management of marketing information. The result has been the development of a formal marketing information system designed to generate an orderly flow of pertinent data from within and without the company. One of the principal functions of a marketing information system is to provide the mechanism for marketing control. The systems approach has three key elements: (1) setting standards of performance at strategic points in the operation, (2) comparing the actual performance with the standard, and (3) taking corrective action. The combination of the systems approach to control with an advanced marketing information system is a major step toward the ultimate in marketing management—the completely automated control system.

The marketing audit is a systematic and thorough examination of a company's marketing position. There are several types of marketing audits, and combinations of the types are possible. Audits can be partial or complete in their coverage of a marketing operation. A horizontal audit embraces all marketing activities at a particular level of a company. A system-level audit encompasses the entire firm; group and divisional audits involve the investigation of part of a firm. These are called activity-level audits. A vertical audit would involve a study of a single function at all levels of the firm.

The marketing audit focuses on several important aspects of a company's marketing operation. These include its marketing assets, its marketing performance, and its competitive effectiveness. In the exploration of these areas, several techniques of auditing are utilized. Interviewing, observation, and data analysis usually are involved.

A number of problems arise in connection with conducting a marketing audit. Not the least of these is its expense. Also, it is almost inevitably a lengthy process. Selecting the proper people to do the auditing is another difficult problem. And a final issue involves the lack of cooperation that sometimes arises when a company or department is being investigated.

Notwithstanding the slow pace at which marketing auditing has been adopted, there is currently more interest in it than there was a few years ago. As more people become familiar with marketing auditing, it should be more widely used. It is, after all, a powerful tool for the marketing planner.

Analyzing past sales is a critical aspect of controlling the marketing operation. The key to effective sales control is having a system that permits the rapid pinpointing of trouble spots. Data must be presented in such a way as to isolate particular problems quickly. Most sales analysis systems report sales by product classification, territory, customer, and salesperson. By combining these data and comparing them with forecasts or with measures of potential, it usually is possible to evaluate sales performance quickly and objectively.

Questions and Problems

1. A manager of marketing information remarked after a particularly frustrating day of work that "managing information is harder than managing people." What reasons might this person have had for making such a remark?

2. Even if marketing information reaches the decisionmaker, it is often seriously

distorted. Why is this so? Approach your answer

  (a) From the standpoint of communications theory (Chapter 14)

  (b) From the standpoint of the practical problems involved in transmitting marketing information

3. What is the relationship between marketing information and the functions of planning and control?

4. Some companies have decentralized their marketing information services. Others use centralized information departments. What reasons might explain these different approaches to fitting the marketing information system into existing organizational structures?

5. What is marketing control, and how is it exercised in marketing? Who should be the marketing controller?

6. Some persons maintain that it is impossible to exercise control in marketing. Why do they say this? Do you agree?

7. List as many of the activities in a department store as you can that you think might be subjected to some degree of control. Be specific as to the kinds of controls that might be used.

8. If you were a manager in charge of a group of franchised fast-food establishments, what would be the critical points in your operation at which you would collect and study control information?

9. Marketing audits have not taken hold in business. Why do you think this is so?

10. Financial audits are concerned with the past; marketing audits are future ori-ented. What does this difference mean in the kind of activities involved in the two types of audits?

11. The accounting profession and state regulatory groups have established the requirements for the CPA (certified public accountant), who is said to be qualified to conduct financial audits. What do you think would be some of the requirements that should be established if the position of CMA (certified marketing auditor) were to be developed?

12. The owner-manager of three music stores is concerned because the stores' sales have declined modestly in spite of a population growth of almost 25 per cent in the surrounding area in the past five years. The stores handle a complete line of organs and pianos, a top line of stereophonic equipment, and a wide assortment of classical records and tapes. In addition they provide piano and organ lessons to pupils. The main store is located in the central shopping district of a large city. Two branch stores have been opened in important regional shopping centers—one to the east and the other to the north of the city. (The areas to the south and west are either industrial or low-income residential in character.) The branch stores are located in highly populated, middle- to upper-class suburban areas. The owner has asked you to outline a marketing audit and to explain what the benefits of conducting a marketing audit for the firm would be. In responding to this request, identify the areas (topics) to which you would devote particular attention.

21

Marketing Research

The major method of fact finding undertaken in most companies to supply their marketing information systems with nonroutine data is known as *marketing research*. Informal and, by today's standards, crude attempts to analyze the market date back to the early 1900s. Only in recent years, however, has the role of research as it relates to management been clearly recognized. The earlier conception of marketing research is expressed in the definition adopted by the Definitions Committee of the American Marketing Association in 1948: "The gathering, recording, and analyzing of all facts about problems relating to the transfer and sale of goods and services from producer to consumer."[1] Although the word "problems" is

used in the AMA's definition, it clearly is subordinate to the mechanics of recording, analyzing, and interpreting data.

A 1969 report of the Conference Board on current organization and practices in marketing research indicates a strong trend toward its use as a tool in problem solving.

Underlying most alterations of one kind or another in companies' marketing research operations is a single aim—that of enabling the department to contribute more directly and effectively to the solution of company problems. Typical is the firm in which marketing research is said to be moving "away from simple surveys to action-oriented, decision-oriented, problem-solving research."[2]

It is difficult to determine just how widespread the use of marketing research actually is. For an arm of industry that is concerned with facts, there is a surprising lack of information about the extent of its use. It is clear,

[1] R. S. Alexander (Chairman, Committee on Definitions, American Marketing Association), "Report of the Definitions Committee," *Journal of Marketing*, October 1948, p. 210. This definition was not changed in the 1960 revision of the glossary of marketing terms. See R. S. Alexander (Chairman, Committee on Definitions, American Marketing Association), *Marketing Definitions: A Glossary of Marketing Terms* (Chicago: American Marketing Association, 1960), pp. 16–17.

[2] L. W. Forman and E. L. Bailey, *The Role and Organization of Marketing Research* (New York: National Industrial Conference Board, 1969), p. 23.

however, that more and more companies are turning to marketing fact finding.

Reflecting this change in orientation, the following definition of marketing research is offered: Marketing research is the gathering of nonroutine marketing information undertaken to help management solve marketing problems. It is important to understand that marketing research is not the same as the complete marketing information system. Marketing research is one of several activities that provide data for the information system. Marketing-research data are nonroutine. They are collected for a particular purpose, to help solve a special problem. This is in contrast to the processing of routine data that flow from sales and cost analyses.

What Needs Researching in Marketing?

An easy and truthful answer to this question is "Everything." There is no aspect of marketing to which research cannot be applied. Every concept presented in this text and every element involved in the marketing management process can be subjected to a great deal of careful research.

The most obvious point to begin the search for marketing facts is with the ultimate consumer. Customer orientation demands a great deal of careful marketing research. Many important questions relating to the consumer can be raised.

Who is the customer?
What does the consumer want in the way of satisfactions?
Where does the buyer choose to purchase?
When are purchases made?

What are the motives for buying? For not buying?
How does the shopper go about seeking satisfactions in the market?
How is the product used? Or not used? Or misused?
What are the postpurchase reactions to using the product?

The Conference Board's study of marketing-research activities in 237 manufacturing and nonmanufacturing companies indicated that American businesses "are relying more heavily on marketing research than ever before." It also found that a "great many are also attempting to link these efforts even more closely . . . to planning and decision making."[3] Accordingly, a great deal of marketing research is directed toward rather specialized areas of management. These activities are broken down into five major areas of marketing research.

Research on markets—market trends, market share, market potentials, market characteristics, competition, other market intelligence.

Research on products—new-product research, product features, brand image, concept tests, product tests, market tests.

Research on sales—sales analysis, sales forecasting, quota-setting, sales territory design, sales performance measurement, trade channels, distribution costs, inventories.

Research on advertising and promotion—promotion concepts, copy research, media research, merchandising, packaging, advertising, effectiveness measurement.

Research on corporate growth and development—economic and technological forecasting, cor-

[3]Forman and Bailey, *Role and Organization of Marketing Research,* p. 1.

porate planning inputs, corporate image, profitability measurement, merger and acquisition studies, facilities location.[4]

Procedures and Techniques in Marketing Research

It is important for a marketing manager to be familiar with the basic procedures and techniques in marketing research.[5] It is true that many businesspeople will never have occasion to engage personally in marketing research. However, it is quite likely that they will be faced with a need either to supervise an internal marketing-research activity or to work with an outside marketing-research firm. The manager who understands the research function is in a position to judge the proposals made by research specialists and to evaluate their findings and recommendations.

There is no single set of steps in a market research procedure that is accepted by all. Indeed, each marketing-research problem requires, to some degree, its own peculiar procedure. However, there is general agreement that four major activities should be performed in a thorough marketing-research project. These are (1) making a preliminary investigation, (2) creating the research de-

[4]Ibid., p. 5.

[5]Many textbooks on marketing research are available. For example, see H. W. Boyd *Marketing Research* (Homewood, Ill.: Richard D. Irwin, 1977); K. P. Uhl and B. Schoner, *Marketing Research: Information Systems and Decision Making* (New York: Wiley, 1975); D. J. Luck, H. G. Wales, and D. A. Taylor, *Marketing Research* (Englewood Cliffs, N.J.: Prentice-Hall, 1974); G. A. Churchill, *Marketing Research: Methodological Foundations* (Hinsdale, Ill.: Dryden Press, 1976); and D. Tull and D. I. Hawkins, *Marketing Research* (New York: Macmillan, 1976).

sign, (3) conducting the investigation, and (4) processing the data.

Making a Preliminary Investigation

The preliminary investigation has two phases. The first involves the determination of the purpose and scope of the research. The second involves an informal investigation of the marketing environment.

Determining the purpose and scope of the research Many years ago, Richard Crisp proposed what he called the "Iceberg Principle," holding that the basic problem in marketing is seldom the problem that appears on the surface. It is therefore necessary to explore beneath the surface to ascertain the nature and size of the problem. This is a vital first step and must be done correctly. Every subsequent phase of the project is directed at solving the basic problem. For the research to be worthwhile—indeed, for it not to be a waste of resources—the problem must be stated clearly and correctly. The failure to do so is the most serious research mistake. The author once heard a lecturer on operations research discuss the errors in problem solving. These were

A third-degree error Interpreting the facts improperly

A second-degree error Gathering the wrong facts for interpretation

A first-degree error Selecting the wrong problem

It is easier to stress the importance of finding the right problem than it is to suggest how this should be done. Two types of situations generally give rise to issues that can be resolved by engaging in marketing research. The first arises in connection with planning. Whenever a manager must choose between alternative courses of action, facts must be obtained about the market in order to select the strategy that is best suited to the company's marketing objectives. The second type of situation in which a manager must look for a basic problem is in connection with marketing control. As we have seen, part of the planning process involves setting standards of performance. When actual performance fails to measure up to the standard, there may be a need to engage in marketing research to discover the reasons for the failure.

Remember, the purpose of research is not to solve the problem. This is the manager's responsibility; research only can provide the information necessary to solve it. Therefore, the second step in determining the purpose and scope of the survey is to translate the problem into its informational elements. We do this by posing two questions regarding the problem. First, what information do we need to solve the problem? In planning, this means that the manager must set forth a description of the kinds of data needed in order to decide between alternative courses of marketing effort. In analyzing past performance, it means that the analyst sets forth the facts needed to explain a deviation from standard and, it is hoped, to point to the changes required to bring performance into line. Some of this information should already be on hand. This leads to the second question: Of the needed information, what is already available? The answer to this question eliminates from the list of required facts those that are already at hand. Those that remain to be collected constitute the purpose and scope of the survey.

The informal investigation The second important phase of the preliminary investigation is called the *informal investigation*. The informal investigation is an unstructured search of the marketing environment. It enables the research designer to become familiar with the problem setting.

The informal investigation goes beyond merely getting acquainted with the problem and its marketing setting, however. The final result of the preliminary investigation is the creation of a set of research hypotheses. In marketing research, a *hypothesis* is a tentative solution to a problem. For example, if a marketing manager is trying to solve a problem that involves an important loss of market share in a particular area of the country, an informal investigation might reveal several possible reasons for the decline in market position.

In searching for possible explanations, the researcher examines company records to uncover new sources of information or to discover relationships in old data bearing on the current problem. Interviews with company executives and operating personnel usually are conducted. The statistical sampling of opinions is not nearly so important as is a thorough search for all important ideas bearing on the problem. Interviews also are conducted with various persons outside the company whose opinions might be expected to have some bearing on the problem. As in the case of internal interviews, sampling is not critical, since no valid statistical findings are expected. The preliminary search always is limited to obtaining an insight into the problem and into possible solutions for it.

Often, the interviewer is not certain as to the insights being sought and is anxious to obtain as many different ideas as possible. Having exhausted the sources available, the research designer analyzes the obtained results and restates them in the form of research hypotheses. In the market share problem mentioned above, the informal findings might be distilled as follows:

1. The decline in market share is the result of increased advertising by competitors.
2. The decline in market share is the result of the introduction of a new product by a major competitor.
3. The decline in market share is the result of stock-outs at the retail level.

Creating a Research Design

The design of a marketing-research project is the plan for testing the hypotheses—a plan for collecting and processing information. *Design* means more than is involved in simply using good market research procedure. Every research project should be conceived individually to produce the specific information needed to solve a particular problem. For this reason, no two market research projects are ever exactly alike. The word *design* also suggests the application of the systems concept. Marketing research involves the flow of information through system components. Five steps are involved in creating a research design.

Choosing the approach Three alternative approaches are possible in creating a research design. They are not mutually exclusive, but in most cases the design of a research plan is limited to the use of one of the three.

The first approach is the *experimental approach*. This approach utilizes the research hypotheses generated in the informal investigation to impose a structure on the subsequent stages of the research. The structure permits the systematic testing of the hypotheses using appropriate statistical methodology.

In a market experiment, information relating to the basic problem is obtained through the use of a small-scale simulated program designed to test a specific research hypothesis. Suppose, for example, that we wish to test the hypothesis that differences in regional tastes are important in explaining differences in the consumption of a particular soft drink, say Dr. Pepper. The first step would be to establish the null or negative hypothesis that for a given time period the average fluid ounces purchased in each city was the same. Next, a sample of the families with similar socioeconomic characteristics in each city would be selected, and a survey would be taken to determine the number of ounces purchased by each family. Once this was done, an analysis of variance technique would be used to test the hypothesis. If statistically significant differences in purchases of Dr. Pepper were noted, the null hypothesis would be rejected, and it could be concluded that geographical location does influence the amount of this soft drink purchased by families with the same characteristics. Of course, other hypotheses about soft drink purchasing also could have been tested using a slightly different method. For example, the effect of television advertising on the purchase of Dr. Pepper might have been studied by inspecting purchases in two or more cities in the same general area of the country (such as the Southwest) but in which different levels of television advertising had been used.

Some success also has been achieved in experimental marketing research by introducing the use of *control areas*. A control area is matched in all important respects with an experimental market area. For example, it is matched in population size, income levels, educational levels, and the like. There is no manipulation of any variable in the control situation. Applying this technique to the example above, suppose Dr. Pepper is considering the use of an entirely different medium of advertising, such as outdoor posters. In the control area, no use would be made of the outdoor posters. However, different levels of outdoor advertising might be used in two or more other markets similar to the control area. Again, a null hypothesis would be formulated, stating that the purchases of Dr. Pepper would be the same in each area, including the control area. Purchase data would be gathered as before and appropriate statistical analyses made. In this way, the exact effect of outdoor advertising on Dr. Pepper sales could be measured. Of course, the accuracy of the findings would depend on the ability of the research designer to control all elements except the variable being measured.

The experimental approach has had wide acceptance in marketing research; however, its application appears to be best suited to narrow areas of problem solving. In solving marketing problems in which many variables are involved, the experimental approach becomes extremely difficult to apply.

The second approach is called the *observation method*. Using this approach, the researcher schedules a series of occasions to watch some aspect of a marketing situation and to record what is observed. For example, a buyer of television, radio, and stereo equipment needs to know whether to merchandise primarily to men, to women, or to both. The store's research director might suggest a project to observe the shoppers in the department for a period of several weeks. The method is simple and relatively inexpensive. A good deal can be learned about any marketing situation simply by observing it carefully. But the method has severe limitations. It tells us nothing about the *reasons* for the observed behavior. Moreover, an observation may actually be misleading. For example, in the television department example we might observe that

women make up 60 per cent of the shoppers in the department. In fact, however, men play the dominant role in electronics purchasing. They simply do not shop as extensively as do women, and therefore they are less likely to be found in the department. A different research method would be needed to uncover this phenomenon.

The third method that can be used in designing a marketing-research plan is the *survey approach*. In the survey approach, marketing information is collected by interviewing. In contrast to the experimental method, in which the data are factually related to the problem, the survey approach necessarily involves more subjectivity and intuition on the part of the researcher.

Watching a customer make a purchase of a new television reveals next to nothing about motives; simply asking the customer "Why?" is not much better. Drawing conclusions from either observations of behavior or from the opinions offered by respondents in interviews is fraught with dangers of interviewer and respondent bias. These dangers, however, can be minimized by the use of tested marketing-survey techniques. The survey method is flexible. It can be adapted to almost any type of research problem. For this reason, and because of the difficulties in creating marketing experiments and in relying on observation, the survey approach is used extensively in marketing research.

Determining the types of data needed There are three types of data: facts, opinions, and motivational information. The types of data required are identified in part by the nature of the problem to be solved. For instance, if the problem relates to production and inventory scheduling, the *facts* that are needed relate to market and sales potential. On the other hand, if the problem revolves around the choice between two new products, the *opinions* of potential customers will be important considerations. Finally, if a problem involves the choice of an appropriate selling appeal, buyers' *motivations* probably will be most important. Facts are quantitative or descriptive information that can be verified. Opinions are ideas relating to a problem that are expressed by people involved in the solution. Motivations are basic reasons, recognized or unrecognized, that explain behavior.

Locating the sources of data   There are two general sources of market information: secondary sources and primary sources. *Secondary-source information* has been previously published and can be either internal or external. Company records and previously prepared marketing-research reports are typical of *internal* secondary source material. *External* secondary source data are widely available. It is not possible in this chapter to list these sources in detail. Bibliographies of marketing-research information are available.[6] Ferber, Blankertz, and Hollander mention seven sources of secondary market information.[7]

1. Public libraries.
2. Universities—library facilities and bureaus of business and economic research.
3. Government agencies—especially departments of commerce, agriculture and labor.
4. Professional and trade associations.
5. Commercial publishers—especially trade publications.
6. Research and nonprofit organizations.
7. Conferences and personal contact.

There are tremendous advantages in using data from secondary sources. In the first place, the expense of gathering information from secondary sources is a fraction of the cost of collecting primary data. Secondary sources usually can be searched with considerable dispatch and the results analyzed promptly. Recently developed computer search services have accelerated the pace at which secondary sources can be studied. The time required to plan and execute a primary marketing-research project is always greater. In the writer's experience, it usually takes from four to ten times as long to collect primary information as it does to gather secondary-source data.

The inherent limitations of using secondary-source data are that (1) the information is frequently outdated, and (2) seldom are secondary data collected for precisely the same reasons that the information is sought to solve a current marketing problem. In spite of these limitations, the advantages of secondary research are so great that it is a common procedure not to proceed with the collection of primary data until a thorough search of secondary sources has been made. There is nothing more discouraging or wasteful than the collection of marketing information that already is available from secondary sources.

Primary marketing information is obtained directly from its source. It involves data that are not available in published form or in

[6]See, for example, S. H. Britt and I. A. Shapiro, "Where to Find Marketing Facts," *Harvard Business Review,* September-October 1964, p. 44; E. Gunther and F. A. Goldstein, *Current Sources of Marketing Information,* Bibliograph Series No. 6 (Chicago: American Marketing Association, 1960); and H. G. Wales and R. Ferber, *A Basic Bibliography on Market Research* (Chicago: American Marketing Association, 1956).

[7]Robert Ferber, Donald F. Blankertz, and Sidney Hollander, Jr., *Marketing Research* (New York: Ronald Press, 1964), pp. 357–360.

company records. The sources of primary marketing information, however, cannot be as easily identified as can the sources of secondary market data. Actually, the identification of possible sources is a logical step beyond the determination of the purpose and scope of the survey. In step one, having identified the information required to help management solve a problem, it usually is possible to identify the person or persons possessing the information desired. In some cases, the information can be obtained from one of several sources. In other situations, the information can be obtained only by contacting several different sources. For example, a manufacturer of vitamins for children discovered that it was necessary to obtain information from the users (children), purchasers (parents), sellers (for the most part druggists), and purchase influencers (pediatricians). Similarly, a manufacturer of feed for dairy cattle found it desirable to seek market information from farmers, feed dealers, and dairy specialists. Obviously, it is expensive to collect marketing information from multiple sources, and it often is time consuming. These two disadvantages are offset by the fact that the information so obtained is tailored to the specific problem at hand. Ultimately, the question as to which source of market information to use depends on (1) where the information is located, and (2) the value of the information in relation to the time and cost required to gather it.

Choosing a method of collecting data   As we have learned, there are various methods of collecting data. Experimentation seldom is easy in marketing because of the great difficulty of controlling the host of other variables in a test situation. As noted earlier, the method most frequently used in marketing,

especially for collecting primary information, is the survey method.

The *survey method* makes use of the technique of asking questions and recording answers. Questionnaires may be distributed by mail and responses returned in the same way, or they can be administered during a telephone inquiry or a personal interview. Although mail surveys can be helpful, they cannot be relied on to produce very accurate results, particularly when lengthy or complicated questions are asked. In addition, the response rate from a mail questionnaire usually is quite low; and nonresponse tends to bias the information that is obtained. A more convenient and faster way of gathering market information is to conduct a telephone survey. A telephone inquiry is limited in several important respects, such as the difficulty of reaching the correct respondent, the problem of completing the interview if the respondent decides to hang up, and the inability to eliminate the bias introduced by not interviewing individuals with unlisted numbers and nontelephone subscribers. In recent years, however, because of the very large proportion of households with phones, the effect of this last limitation is considered to be relatively trivial. And, in spite of all its limitations, the telephone survey is frequently used.

The principal technique used in the survey method in marketing research is *personal interviewing.* It is the most effective and most flexible way of soliciting primary information. The specific questions to be asked and the manner of inquiry can be tailored exactly to the information source. For example, very different interviewing techniques are used when interviewing business executives, homemakers, and children. Years of experience in collecting primary market information by the survey method have enabled market research specialists to develop a great deal of knowledge about questionnaire construction and use.

Marketing researchers also are fully aware of the deficiencies and limitations of personal interviewing. Eliciting market facts from respondents, especially ultimate consumers, is difficult. For several reasons consumers often provide misleading information. A common explanation is that respondents do not understand all questions and are unwilling to admit their confusion. In some situations, consumers volunteer false information. Consistently, consumer respondents in market research surveys overstate their incomes, understate their ages, and fail to admit to attitudes that run counter to those generally accepted. A third reason for failing to provide accurate answers to survey questions is that the consumers actually do not possess the information. In some cases, respondents simply refuse to answer; in others, and this is often hard to detect, consumers give false responses rather than admit a lack of knowledge. This often is encountered when research is in the area of consumer behavior. It is seldom wise to accept a consumer's own explanation of motivation. Consumers are, generally speaking, the least reliable source of direct information on the subject of their own behavior.

Questions can be asked in different ways. Respondents may be interviewed singly or in groups. *A focused group interview* is a research technique in which a trained interviewer, often a psychologist, leads a group discussion of topics related to the research problem. The method often generates answers that might be difficult to produce in a set of single interviews. The members of the group react to each other's comments and feed on one another's ideas to produce much more depth than is possible when persons are interviewed separately. The group interview is an economical method of interviewing several individuals in depth and at the same time obtaining the benefits of group thinking on a marketing question.

When interviews are conducted with single respondents, one or a combination of three different techniques can be used. The simplest and most obvious technique is known as *direct interviewing,* in which relatively clear-cut questions that call for objective facts or obvious attitudes are asked.

The second method of asking questions in a personal survey is by *depth interviewing.* When using a depth technique, the interviewer attempts to probe behind the immediate and obvious answer to a question. The use of depth interviewing requires skill and experience. The results must be interpreted with care. When used correctly, the depth interview produces extremely useful market research information at relatively low cost. One reason for the low cost is that only a small number of depth interviews generally are required. The tabulations of findings are almost impossible to construct, however, and they are very difficult to verify by statistical methods.

A third technique of personal interviewing is used when it is difficult to obtain direct or indirect responses through depth interviewing. According to a psychologically proven premise, it is possible by impersonalizing questions to obtain information that a respondent would not, or could not, otherwise provide. This method involves the use of the *projective technique,* an even more oblique method than the depth interview. The intent of the projective technique is to give respondents an opportunity to answer questions without the embarrassment or confusion created by direct involvement. There are various methods of applying the projective technique. Familiar psychological tests, such as word association and sentence completion, are used. A particularly interesting approach is the psychodrama, in which the respondent is asked to provide information about an artificial marketing situation. Probably the best known example of the psychodrama is the classic Nescafé test. In this experiment, conducted by Mason Haire in one of the first projective market surveys, two statistically identical samples of respondents were given grocery shopping lists. These lists were identical in all respects except for the item of coffee. One list called for Nescafé instant coffee; the other specified regular Maxwell House coffee. Respondents were given one or the other of the lists and asked to describe the type of person using it. Since the only difference between the two lists was the difference in the coffee specified, distinctions drawn by respondents between the types of consumers had to be attributable to the coffee consumption factor. Instant coffee was in its infancy at the time of this study. It was somewhat surprising to discover that respondents viewed the person who used instant coffee as being a sort of second-class housekeeper who was too lazy or too indifferent to go to the trouble of preparing regular coffee. This negative prejudice toward instant coffee was assumed to be a projected attitude of the respondents. A shift was made in the promotion of instant coffee to emphasize the positive benefits that might be found in using the product.

Preparing a sample plan   In survey work in marketing it seldom is necessary to conduct a complete census. To do so is time consuming and expensive. For this reason most marketing surveys make use of samples. A *sample* is a group of elements (persons, stores, financial reports) chosen from among a population or universe. It is up to the researcher to determine how the sample will be chosen.

The *sampling unit* is the basic element in the sample. In general, the units correspond to the individual respondents in a survey. The selection of the sampling unit is reached directly from the earlier decision about the source of the primary information.

The selection of the precise sampling units to be investigated requires a master list, or a framework, from which they may be selected. The sampling frame is the population or statistical universe from which the sample units will be selected. For example, the frame for a survey of attitudes of credit customers of a department store would be the company's list of customers having charge accounts.

Although there are many kinds of sample designs, all of them can be classified as either probability samples or nonprobability samples. In a *probability sample,* each unit has a known chance of being selected for inclusion in the sample. Its simplest version is the *simple random sample,* in which each unit in the sample frame has exactly the same chance of selection.

In cases where the expense of undertaking a simple random sample outweighs the value of the information obtained and where more homogeneous sample groups are desired, alternative methods of selecting a probability sample may be employed. These methods include stratified sampling and area probability sampling.

In a *stratified sample,* the sampling frame is divided into two or more groups, and each group is sampled separately. A sampling frame consisting of people may be stratified on the basis of such factors as age, income, educational level, and occupation. Such

490

stratified sampling is economical, because it permits fitting the sample size to each group. Different sampling rates can be used for different segments, depending on the population of the segment and the necessary accuracy of the data. For example, if upper-income respondents are especially important in a particular study of a suburban market area, all upper-income households could be sampled, whereas a much lower sampling rate (perhaps one out of five) might be used to survey middle-income households.

Area probability sampling is used most frequently to identify the individuals or households of a sampling frame when no satisfactory list with this information can be obtained. According to this method, geographic areas are selected from a map by a random process, and the households in the selected areas are included in the sample.

What is the overall advantage to be gained from using probability sampling techniques? The answer lies with the theory of probability. According to probability theory, the amount of sampling error included in the research results can be estimated. By the very nature of sampling, we know that the results obtained from samples are *estimated values*. The difference between an estimate derived from a sample and the true value obtained from a survey of the entire frame is called the *sampling error*. Even though the true value of a population is not known, probability theory allows us to measure the probable sampling error. We can then determine the size of the sample needed given the degree of accuracy desired.

In a *nonprobability sample* the sampling units are selected arbitrarily. To return to our department store example, instead of using a random process to select a sample of charge customers, an arbitrary and more convenient method simply would be to take the first fifty or sixty names on the list. As was previously mentioned, the advantage of a probability sample is that the errors due to sampling can be measured and the results of the project evaluated with statistical methods. However, the errors due to sampling in nonprobability samples cannot be measured, and therefore the precision of the final results is open to doubt. As a matter of fact, in many so-called probability surveys the sampling units that are eventually utilized probably do not constitute a purely random sample. In such cases, nonprobability samples may be just as accurate, and they certainly are less costly.

Conducting the Investigation

The implementation of a research plan seldom is easy. Often a research program requires extra effort from already busy personnel in the company. In other cases, outsiders must be recruited, hired, and trained. In either situation, carrying out a marketing-research plan is difficult and requires very close supervision and control. To the extent that the research design has been well conceived, supervision and control are restricted to making sure that the research activities called for in the plan are carried out according to schedule and in the manner prescribed. In particular, care must continuously be exercised to minimize the effect of bias.

Various types of errors, or survey bias, tend to arise in collecting primary information. *Bias* is defined as any difference due to causes other than sampling variation between the value determined in the survey and the true value. In contrast to sampling error, very little is known on the subject of survey bias and the measurement of nonsampling errors appears to be impossible. Ferber, Blankertz, and Hollander summarize the importance of supervision and control as related to the problem of minimizing nonsampling errors as follows:

Included in non-sampling errors are all the innumerable influences that tend to distort, or bias, estimates obtained from samples. Arbitrary selection of sample members, prejudicial wording of questions, preconceived interviewer attitudes, faulty editing, and many other factors can produce sample values that will not average out to the true population values, no matter how large the sample. Unlike sampling error, bias is largely invariant, regardless of sample size.

Because it is so difficult to control nonsampling errors, and virtually impossible to measure them, initial emphasis in sample design is on assuring a minimum precision of estimates, with additional precautions taken to control the various possible sources of non-sampling errors. Accordingly, an effort is made to train the inverviewers properly; to avoid disclosing to the respondents (and often to the interviewers) the hypotheses being tested; to ask questions in a way that will not prejudice people's answers; to select the samples so that particular parts of the frame are not accidentally omitted (such as a dwelling unit at the rear of the house); and to obtain some idea of the extent to which the opinions of non-respondents in the sample differ from those of the respondents. These are all highly subjective procedures, but are nevertheless indispensable for the proper conduct of a survey.[8]

Processing the Data

Processing the data obtained in a market survey involves transforming the information obtained into a report that can be used by management. Four steps are involved: (1)

[8]Ferber, Blankertz, and Hollander, *Marketing Research*, p. 200.

editing, (2) tabulating, (3) interpreting, and (4) presenting the data. Obviously, great care must be exercised to make sure that the plan for tabulating the data actually fits the kinds of information obtained. Also, it is never wise to limit data analysis to the techniques anticipated in the survey design. Information obtained in a survey may suggest other methods of analysis. A good plan for the analysis and interpretation of the data is of immense assistance in bringing a project to a successful conclusion, but it should never limit the kinds of interpretations that eventually are made or restrict the content of the final report.

Imagination, intuition, and creative insight are valuable assets in analyzing marketing data. The usefulness of a marketing report often depends on the ingenuity demonstrated in the analysis and presentation of the findings. There is some danger at this stage of the research that analytical bias may influence the conclusions drawn. Because of the well-established fact that "one sees what one wants to see," it sometimes is possible for two individuals to interpret the same marketing data quite differently. Interpretation is governed by insight and judgment. Where different interpretations of research findings are encountered, the reason usually can be traced to confusion as to the purpose and scope of the survey.

When purpose and scope are understood, only conceptual divergences can explain differences in data interpretations. Here good marketing concepts enable a manager to make a sound interpretation of marketing-research findings.

The final report of a primary marketing survey should ordinarily be written. Since vast amounts of data often are involved, the written report is the only appropriate method of presenting these findings. The written report also has the advantage of being permanent, permitting management to study the findings carefully and to refer to them in the future. Unfortunately, many marketing-research projects are never translated into management action—sometimes because the research conclusions do not directly contribute to the solution of the problem, sometimes because the report is too technical and difficult to understand, and sometimes because the report writer has not offered specific suggestions as to how the report should be translated into management strategy.

There are legitimate differences of opinion as to whether a research manager should push for the adoption of specific recommendations. Clearly, it is not the research manager's responsibility to make the management decision. However, many executives are neither marketing nor research minded. If they are ever to use marketing research to help solve problems, they often must be persuaded that the fact-finding approach is worthwhile. If the margin of difference between the acceptance or the neglect of a marketing-research project lies in the willingness of the research team to sell its findings, this effort should surely be made.

Organizing the Marketing-Research Function

On the assumption that the research function is handled internally, the preceding discussion of marketing research indicates that the following kinds of tasks are ordinarily performed:

1. Research design, including sample design

2. Information gathering, including experimentation, observation, and interviewing

3. Supervision and control of information gathering

4. Data processing

5. Information analysis

6. Report preparation and presentation

All of these activities, with the possible exception of information gathering, might logically be assigned to a single department—possibly even to one individual. In larger firms, each of these tasks might be assigned to a separate individual. A model of a hypothetical research department is shown in Figure 21.1. In this exhibit, as is often the case, a large information-gathering section is not employed. When needed, outside field research services can be retained for this purpose.

When we consider the organization of the marketing-research activity in a large company, several important questions arise. Among these is, "Should marketing research be centralized or decentralized?" Closely related is another question: "To whom or to what department should marketing research report?" A third issue that arises as marketing research becomes more important in a company's operation is, "What should be the organizational and functional relationship between market research and technical (engineering) research?" No quick answers are available.

Some years ago, the Conference Board proposed three criteria that should be considered when positioning a marketing-research department within a company organization. These still apply today.

1. The marketing research department should be free from the influence of those whom its work affects.

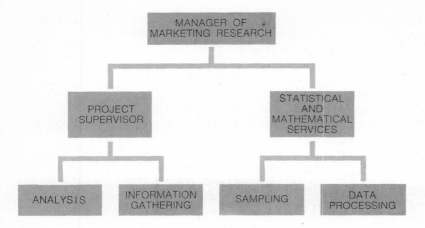

FIGURE 21.1 The organization of a marketing research department (hypothetical)

2. The location of the marketing research department should be conducive to maximum efficiency.
3. Marketing research should have the wholehearted support of the executives to whom it reports.[9]

There is apparently a tendency to keep marketing research at a fairly centralized point in the organization. Table 21.1 indicates that 43 per cent of 147 companies surveyed use only a corporate marketing-research staff, and another 29 per cent use both corporate and divisional or group departments. Only slightly more than one in four firms rely exclusively on decentralized marketing research.

In general, when marketing research is departmentalized—either along functional or along product lines—the work tends not to be free from the influence of the department to which it is assigned. For example, when marketing research is placed in the sales department, it seldom is encouraged (or even permitted) to initiate studies directly relating to the performance of the sales organization. More likely, the research department is assigned to routine activities, such as sales territory analysis, quota assignments, and the like.

The criteria above suggest also that marketing research should report directly to the chief marketing executive, and according to the Conference Board study about two out of three marketing research heads do so.[10] The marketing manager should be in the best position to offer "wholehearted support" to the process of market fact finding. Other executives, such as presidents, executive vice presidents, controllers, and technical-research directors, seldom have enough time or interest to devote to marketing research.

We can answer the third question in the

[9]National Industrial Conference Board, *Studies in Business Policy,* No. 72 (New York: National Industrial Conference Board, 1955), p. 7.

[10]Forman and Bailey, *Role and Organization of Marketing Research,* p. 17.

TABLE 21.2   Location of the Marketing Research Function

Location of marketing-research function(s)	Total	Divisionalized companies reporting			Nonmanu-facturing
		Manufacturing			
		Total	Consumer products	Industrial products	
Corporate level only	43%	41%	51%	38%	64%
Division-group level only	28	30	35	28	7
Both levels	29	29	14	34	29
	100%	100%	100%	100%	100%

Note: Data based on responses of 147 divisionalized companies: 37 consumer-products manufacturers, 96 industrial-products manufacturers, and 14 nonmanufacturing firms. Not all companies with marketing research at both headquarters and divisions maintain the function in every one of their divisions.

Source: L. W. Forman and E. L. Bailey, *The Role and Organization of Marketing Research* (New York: National Industrial Conference Board, 1969), p. 9.

implementation of the marketing-management concept. No greater need for coordination exists than that between marketing and technical research. As we saw in Chapter 10, coordination is especially critical in connection with new-product development. It is not wise to place these activities in the same organizational niche; however, it is imperative that the activities of the two departments be closely correlated. One organizational device for achieving this coordination is the creation of a special department. In some companies this is a *development department;* in other firms it is a *new-product development department;* and in still others it is called a *new-venture department.*

The Value of Marketing Research

It is important to point out that it is not always necessary to conduct research before attempting to solve a problem in marketing management. The manager may already know enough to make a good decision. In a few instances, there may be no choice among alternatives and hence no decision to make. But in most business situations, the manager must make a choice among two or more courses of action. This is where fact finding to help make the choice enters in.

But even if a manager would like more information in order to make a decision, it is not always wise to conduct the necessary research. One reason is that it may take too much time. Another compelling reason is that the cost of the research may exceed its contribution. In principle, it is easy to understand how such a cost test might be applied. If the cost of conducting the research is less than its contribution to the improvement of the decision, the research should be carried out. If its cost is greater, it should not be conducted. We have seen in Chapter 8 how this principle can be applied in the attempt to eliminate uncertainty and to estimate the value of perfect information.

Summary

Marketing research is the gathering of information to help management solve marketing problems. As a function in marketing, research is over half a century old; but it only recently has become a full-fledged partner in marketing management. This is due to the fact that the orientation in marketing research has changed from merely making surveys to finding solutions to operating problems. Researchable problems are found in all areas of marketing: in selecting market segments, in directing sales effort, in developing new products, in designing promotion, and in pricing.

There are four major elements involved in undertaking marketing research. The first element is a preliminary investigation. This initial study permits the researcher to determine the purpose and scope of the research as well as to identify tentative hypotheses.

Creating a research design to test the hypotheses is the most important and most complicated aspect of marketing research. It commences with the selection of the approach to be taken. The three most commonly used are controlled experiments, observation, and surveys. Any given project may use one or more of the three. It also is necessary to determine the types of data that will be needed to solve the marketing problem and to locate sources where this information can be obtained. Sources generally are classified as either secondary or primary. Secondary data are made up of previously collected information and are obtained from historical records, publications, government documents, and the like. Primary data are gathered by observation, experimentation, and surveys. The survey method is the most frequently used in marketing. Data are gathered by personal interview, telephone, and mail. The development of survey techniques, including depth and group interviewing and projective questioning, has progressed rapidly.

Another critical aspect of most marketing-research projects is the selection of the sample. This is important because few marketing studies involve surveys of an entire population. Developing a sampling plan involves choosing the sampling unit, selecting a suitable sample frame, and drawing the sample. Once the frame has been identified, either a probability or a nonprobability sample can be drawn. A probability sample involves the selection of respondents in such a way that every unit in the frame has a known chance of being selected. A nonprobability sample is drawn on a judgmental basis; the respondents are selected because they are considered to be representative of the frame from which they are drawn.

The final aspect of the research design is the decision as to how the data will be summarized and reported. It is becoming more and more common in large marketing-research projects to make use of a computer for the processing and tabulation of the research results.

If the research has been well designed, its implementation should not be difficult. Some problems usually arise, however, and careful supervision and control of the data collection activities are important. It is particularly critical to guard against various kinds of survey bias that can creep into a project.

The marketing-research function is organized in different ways. In some firms, it is concentrated in a centralized department; in others, it is decentralized. Certain firms utilize both corporate and divisional marketing-research departments. Regardless of whether the department is centralized, however, its function is to help line managers solve marketing problems. To accomplish this, it should be located reasonably close to where these decisions are made, it should be free from undue influence by those who will use the results, and it must have the wholehearted support of marketing management. Probably the greatest organizational difficulty that remains is to find ways to achieve more and better coordination between marketing and technical research.

Marketing research can contribute to the solution of most marketing problems, but sometimes the cost does not warrant the effort. In general, research should be undertaken if the expected value of the research exceeds its cost.

Questions and Problems

1. Marketing research is sometimes referred to as a *problem-solving tool*. Explain what this means.

2. It often is argued that only such fields as physics, chemistry, and mathematics are really scientific and that marketing research, in common with all behavioral research, cannot be scientific. How would you respond to someone who states this opinion?

3. Do you think that a distinction can be made between *pure* and *applied* research in marketing?

4. Select a local or campus enterprise with which you are familiar. Identify a marketing problem that it faces. (You may need to interview the manager of the establishment.) Translate this marketing problem into its informational elements. Conduct a small-scale informal investigation. On the basis of this preliminary investigation, answer the following questions:
    a. What tentative hypotheses can you develop?
    b. What types of research design do you believe would be necessary to test these hypotheses?

5. A small manufacturer of highly specialized medical laboratory equipment and a manufacturer of a proprietary (nonprescription) cold remedy need information to assist in planning new-product introductions. What would be the advantages and drawbacks of using primary versus secondary marketing information for each firm?

6. A market research expert once said that using mail questionnaires is like counting the mail that arrives at the White House. What do you think this person meant, and what is its implication to the many companies that continue to use mail surveys?

7. A random system for interviewing people by telephone has been developed. It is called *random digit dialing.* A table of random numbers is used to identify the specific telephone numbers to be called. What advantages and disadvantages do you see in this method of selecting a sample?

8. What problems, if any, do you see in the following questions that might be included in a questionnaire directed at ultimate consumers:
    a. What is your spouse's favorite television program?
    b. How many cups of coffee did you serve in your house last year?

c. How much money do you have in a savings account?

d. Should members of the Communist party be allowed to run for public office?

e. Do you think that electric utility rates are too high?

9. You are the advertising manager of a company that manufactures professional athletic equipment—everything from knee pads to wrestling mats. Your firm employs fifty field salespeople who make periodic calls on sporting-goods dealers, large schools and colleges, and professional athletic organizations. You also place full-page advertisements in a trade publication for the sporting-goods industry, *Scholastic Coach*. The president of your company has questioned the use of this publication and has asked you to find out how effective it is in increasing consumer awareness of your products and in stimulating sales. How would you go about this task?

10. In 1976 Chevrolet introduced its subcompact automobile, the Monza. Suppose you had been a marketing-research analyst working for another car manufacturer. What kinds of primary and secondary marketing research would you have conducted to evaluate the success of this new-product introduction?

11. A large church organization is concerned about the apparent decline in interest in religion and wants to study the reasons for it. Why might a projective technique be suitable for this project? Suggest a way that a projective technique might be used to research this rather sensitive question.

12. A rather commonly accepted practice is to allocate about 5 per cent of an overall marketing budget to marketing research. Thus, a company with a total marketing budget of $1 million, would spend about $50,000 on research. What is good and what is bad about this practice?

22

Marketing Cost and Profitability Analysis

Another important component of the marketing information system is data about marketing cost and profit. The purpose of marketing is not simply to sell things; it is to provide customer satisfaction and to do so profitably. Only when the manager understands how to control both income and costs is the ability to plan and control marketing profits attained.

The Theory of Marketing-Cost Behavior

Economic theories concerning cost explain much that is important to marketing. In economic theory, the study of forces determining supply rests principally on decisions made regarding the quantity of goods offered in the marketplace. This schedule of supply is dictated by the costs of manufacturing and marketing. In applying economic concepts of cost to the latter, we should not be too disturbed by the difficulties involved. The limitation lies not with the concepts but with the problem of producing empirical data to which to apply the cost concepts. We shall tackle that problem in a later discussion of specific methods and the control of marketing costs. At this point our emphasis is on those economic forces that affect marketing costs.

Cost Distinctions According to Time Period

The significance of costs to management varies according to the time period under consideration. This may be seen clearly when time periods are classified in terms of increasing duration. First, although modest attention is paid to it in economic theory, is the *market period,* sometimes called the *short, short run.* The market period quite frequently is significant in real marketing situations. It is a period of time in which a manager must make decisions regarding price and sales effort for a fixed stock of goods. In the market period, there is not enough time to increase inventory by manufacture or purchase. The only options open to the seller are to sell, to hold, or to destroy.

The *short run,* in contrast, is a period of time in which a manager can change inventory through procurement or through manufacturing with existing facilities. There is not time in the short run, however, to increase capacity or to expand operations by acquiring additional capital assets. In marketing terms, for example, the short run is a period in which a firm can attempt to increase sales by intensifying its effort with the existing sales force, but there would not be enough time to hire and train additional salespeople.

The *long run* is a period of sufficient duration to permit a firm to increase (or decrease) capacity. In general, it is any period of time longer than the short run. Long-run considerations are important in market planning because many market plans involve changes in company capacity. Expanding facilities, acquiring subsidiaries, and introducing new products are examples of long-run decisions. Although it may be difficult in actual practice to distinguish between short-run and long-run situations, the distinction is important in clarifying economic theories of cost.

Determinants of Short-Run Costs

Once a marketing program has been launched almost anything can influence its cost.[1] As we shall see, it is very difficult to anticipate all the costs that will be involved in a marketing program. The experienced executive is aware of this fact, and considerable attention is paid in marketing management to the budgeting of marketing expenditures and the control of marketing costs. Proper budgeting or planning of costs starts with an understanding of those factors that determine cost behavior.

In the short run there are four major determinants of cost: (1) technology and factor combination, (2) efficiency of productive factors, (3) price of factors, and (4) rate of plant use.

Technology and factor combination   The first major determinant of a firm's costs are found in the types of inputs that it has at its disposal and the manner in which they can be combined within the framework of existing facilities. Ordinarily, a manufacturing or distribution system is designed to operate according to a set technology, so that the kinds of inputs—capital, labor, or raw materials—and the proportions in which they are combined are restricted by the type and size of the system. In contrast, most marketing situations permit some degree of flexibility in factor combination. For instance, in the allocation of effort to a promotional program, it usually is possible to vary the proportion devoted to advertising with that devoted to personal selling. In general, the development of an appropriate marketing mix involves the selection of the correct factor combination within a given marketing technology.

In summary, technology limits the number of different factor combinations that are

---

[1]Unless otherwise stated, the term *cost* is used in the sense of unit or average cost.

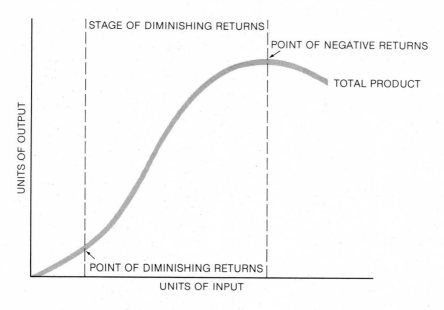

FIGURE 22.1   A productivity curve

possible, and the factor combination selected directly determines cost. This is true especially if the prices of the various factors are not the same. Economic logic suggests that equal amounts of total output might be attained by a number of different factor combinations. Clearly, some of these combinations require fewer factors than do others. Accordingly, output per unit is greatest when the number of required factor units is lowest. Unit costs of production are correspondingly lower.

Efficiency of productive factors   An important economic principle that is basic to almost all marketing effort is the law of diminishing marginal productivity. Frequently referred to as the *law of diminishing returns,* it states that in most business situations the successive application of units of effort to a given objective (all other influences remain-

ing unchanged) results in varying levels of incremental productivity. This can be seen in Figure 22.1.[2] As successive units of the input variable are applied (with all other input factors held constant), total output rises rapidly, at first at an increasing rate. But the rate of increase in total output quickly reaches a maximum and subsequently declines. The point at which a total product *begins to increase at a decreasing rate* is known as the *point of diminishing returns.* Following this, and generally for a considerable range of output, total product continues to increase, although at continually decreasing rates. Ultimately, a point is reached at which maximum total product is achieved. Any further application of input units in such a situation results in a decline of total output. This is the *point of negative returns.*

[2]This curve is the same as the response function presented previously in this text on several occasions.

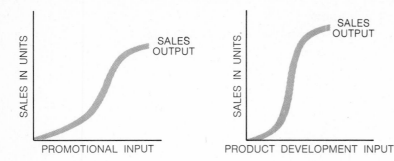

FIGURE 22.2   Marketing productivity curves

This phenomenon of diminishing returns is commonplace in marketing. Largely because of the resistances of market saturation and competition, additional inputs of marketing tend to manifest diminishing marginal productivity—often rather early. Two hypothetical total-product curves for marketing are presented in Figure 22.2. The marketing inputs are promotion and product development. Although the two curves have different shapes, both conform generally to the model shown in Figure 22.1.

Price of factors   In economic analysis, it often is assumed that factor prices do not change. In actual practice, however, an important determinant of cost is the price that must be paid for an input factor. The practice of granting quantity discounts suggests that factor prices might be expected to decline modestly as additional input is acquired. On the other hand, if there is a limited supply of a particular input factor, increased demand for this factor might be expected to raise its price. In the analysis of costs it is important to know a great deal about factor prices and any changes that may take place. For example, in marketing, a change in sales compensation or an increase

in advertising media rates alters the shape of the marketing cost curves.

Rate of plant use   As a cost determinant, rate of plant utilization refers to the fact that as a firm increases or decreases output, its unit costs vary according to the level of capacity at which it operates.[3] In part, these cost changes are explained by the determinants already discussed. In addition, one more aspect of plant utilization affects the level of average costs. In the short run, certain costs are said to be *fixed*—that is, they are constant in total without regard to the level of output. Fixed costs decline per unit as output is increased. This decline is an important factor that influences the level of costs and is directly associated with the rate of plant utilization. Many marketing operations have relatively high fixed costs. These may be the costs of maintaining an expensive store or an automated warehouse. They also may include the costs of maintaining a corporate-planning or research staff, or a salaried sales force.

[3]The term *plant* refers to any fixed resource, the cost of which is constant irrespective of the extent of its use. It does not refer exclusively to a manufacturing facility.

Determinants of Long-Run Costs

The long run, as we know, is a period of sufficient duration to permit management to alter capacity. Conceptually, the long run is viewed as a succession of short-run periods. But the businessperson, although aware of the importance of long-run planning, always operates and incurs costs in the present. It is important, however, to understand the relationship between the current cost position and those alternatives that are available through capacity adjustments. In evaluating these long-run adjustments, there are two major determinants of cost that we should consider: technology and returns to scale.

Technology   Just as technology is an important factor affecting short-run costs, it is of comparable significance in the long run, except that in the longer period usually more than one alternative technology is open for management's consideration. The size of a business and the scope of its marketing opportunity frequently determine which of the alternative technologies will be most appropriate. The use of electronic data-processing equipment is a good example. Until recently, a small firm seldom found it advantageous to purchase its own computer. A moderate-sized operation might make efficient use of a modest installation. A large company with multiple product lines probably would find that its sales and distribution cost analyses justify a large facility. Ordinarily, the cost per unit of output of the larger facility is lower than that of the smaller. However, the larger equipment must be used at or near its optimum in order for this generalization to hold true.

Returns to scale   Closely related to technology is the economic phenomenon known as *returns to scale,* which refers to the behavior of costs in the long run as the capacity of a firm is changed. Typically, although not exclusively, long-run costs are assumed to decline as the size of the business increases, to reach a low point (called *optimum*), and subsequently to rise. The principal determinant of the decreasing phase of long-run average costs is the utilization of larger and more efficient technologies. Eventually, however, the advantages of expansion are offset by diseconomies of size. These diseconomies are the result of the lack of coordination and control often encountered in larger companies. The duplication of effort, red tape, and breakdowns in communications explain increases in long-run average costs.

A related, but not identical, concept of cost is the so-called experience cost curve.[4] Instead of relating unit costs to volume representing utilization of different sizes of plant, the experience curve relates unit costs to cumulative volume—that is, total output over time. This cumulative volume brings experience, and the experience enables the company to reduce its average costs. An experience curve is shown in Figure 22.3. The marketing significance of this concept is that it leads the firm that adopts it to aggressive programs to achieve high market share, often by the use of a penetration pricing strategy.

The Behavior of Costs

A useful method of dramatizing cost behavior is found in the cost curve used in eco-

[4]*Perspectives on Experience* (Boston: The Boston Consulting Group, 1972), pp. 12–27. The concept was discussed earlier in connection with pricing.

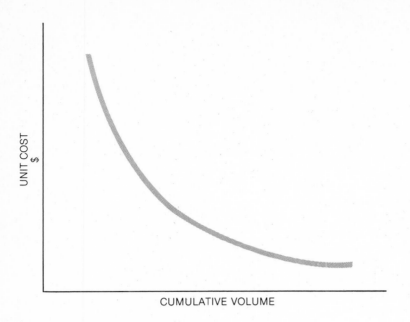

FIGURE 22.3   The experience cost curve (hypothetical)

nomic analysis. Figure 22.4 portrays a set of short-run cost curves, while Figure 22.5 presents a set of long-run cost curves. In Figure 22.4, the average-fixed-cost curve (AFC) is shown to be a succession of constantly declining values as total fixed costs are spread over greater and greater output. Marginal cost (MC), the increase in total cost resulting from a unit increase in output, falls briefly during the stage of increasing marginal productivity and subsequently rises throughout the stage of diminishing returns. The average total cost (ATC) curve is dipper shaped. The decreasing phase of this curve is attributable to the decline in average fixed costs and in marginal costs. Ultimately, however, the benefits of spreading fixed costs are offset by decreasing marginal productivity; thus, the average-total-cost curve reaches its low point and subsequently rises.

To illustrate long-run costs, Figure 22.5 has four parts. Part A depicts the long-run average-cost curve assuming no returns to scale—that is, constant long-run average costs. This implies that the technology of a larger plant is no more efficient than the technology of a smaller plant. The curve in part B represents a long-run average-cost curve based on the assumption of constantly increasing returns to scale. Part B supposes that each successively larger plant permits the firm to operate at lower average total costs of production and sales. Part C represents the opposite situation, that of increasing long-run costs. Here, the assumption is that any increase in size is associated with an increase in average costs. Finally, part D illustrates the saucer shape of the long-run average-cost curve that generally is assumed to prevail. The reasons for this saucer shape

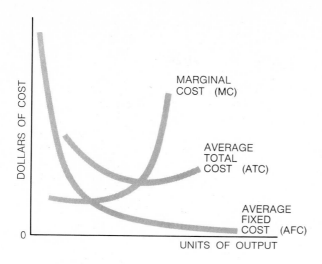

FIGURE 22.4   The behavior of short-run average costs

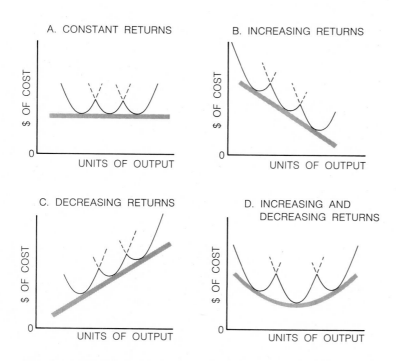

FIGURE 22.5   The behavior of long-run average costs

are the diseconomies of scale that at some point offset the advantages of larger size.

In each of the sections of Figure 22.5 several selected short-run cost curves have been inserted. This technique is used to emphasize the fact that the long run is always considered a set of short-run periods. Nevertheless, long-run cost concepts are vital to business planning. In fact, the saucer-shaped curve in part D is often called a *planning curve.*

Analyzing Marketing Costs

Analyzing marketing costs in the context of traditional accounting procedures presents some serious problems. Almost all marketing costs are incurred in support of several products, customers, territories, or salespeople. They are, for the most part, common costs. Economists and accountants have recognized this fact for many years, noting that business costs seldom are assembled according to marketing divisions.[5] For example, a marketing manager is hired to plan, direct, and control a company's marketing activities. The manager's salary is incurred on behalf of the marketing of all company products. In order to obtain a useful estimate of the cost and ultimately of the profitability of a particular product, it is necessary to distribute or allocate the manager's salary to the various products. Techniques for making such allocations have been developed as part of the branch of marketing in-

formation known as *marketing cost accounting.*

Another serious aspect of the overhead nature of marketing cost is the fact that it often is difficult to differentiate between marketing and nonmarketing costs. For instance, the president of a company typically spends time working on marketing problems and time working on nonmarketing problems. What is the marketing cost? This distinction, moreover, is not restricted to the allocation of top-executive time. It also may be difficult to determine whether product-related expenditures are marketing or nonmarketing costs. For example, should product design and development be considered an engineering or a marketing cost? Should costs of maintaining finished-goods inventory be charged to manufacturing or to sales?

The issue raised here, of course, may be academic (although it seldom is considered such by the individual departmental managers involved). Indeed, the marketing concept suggests that the arbitrary distinction between marketing and production is artificial. In almost any firm, management may gain new insight by abandoning the endless arguments as to the costlines of each. Certainly, the overall objective of a firm is to achieve profits—whether through manufacturing efficiency or marketing excellence. This can be achieved only when both functions are performed in accordance with a unified company plan. Even if accounting records make it possible, the assignment of cost or profit to either manufacturing or marketing is pointless so long as the two functions must be integrated in order to make any profit at all. Rather than distribute costs between marketing and nonmarketing, management should concentrate on their allocation among alternative decisions—such as products, customers, and territories. It is in connection with this type of analysis that

---

[5]For example, see the classic by J. M. Clark, *Economics of Overhead Costs* (Chicago: University of Chicago Press, 1923); and J. B. Heckert, *The Analysis and Control of Distribution Costs* (New York: Ronald Press, 1940).

the overhead aspect of marketing cost is most critical.

Traditional Techniques of Marketing Cost Analysis

Some of the limitations to the study of marketing costs, which we have just discussed, are being overcome.[6] Marketing managers have continued to ask for good cost information, and now the development of electronic data-processing systems has made it possible to undertake analyses by computer that formerly required more time and effort than the results could justify. In fact, two separate approaches to marketing cost analysis have been developed. One is based on the use of traditional accounting data and involves the assignment of expenses to marketing functions, often using computers to handle the data processing involved. In contrast to this traditional approach, the second method of marketing cost analysis involves the use of entirely new accounting concepts and reporting systems. We call it *direct cost, variable cost,* or *profitability* accounting. In this chapter, we will use the third term, since the basic purpose of cost analysis is to determine the relative profitability of alternative courses of action.

Marketing costs can be analyzed at three

---

[6]A number of books have been written on the subject of analyzing marketing costs. In addition to those mentioned in other footnotes, see: R. D. Crisp, *How to Reduce Distribution Costs* (New York: Funk and Wagnalls, 1948); J. W. Culliton, *The Management of Marketing Costs* (Boston: Graduate School of Business Administration, Harvard University, 1948); D. R. Longman and M. Schiff, *Practical Distribution Cost Analysis* (Homewood, Ill.: Richard D. Irwin, 1955); C. H. Sevin, *Marketing Productivity Analysis* (New York: McGraw-Hill, 1965); and L. G. Rayburn, *Financial Tools for Marketing Administration* (New York: American Management Association, 1975).

different levels, each falling within the traditional framework but each representing a different degree of analytical sophistication. The most basic type of cost analysis involves the use of the profit and loss statement prepared for other accounting purposes. The second type of analysis centers on the costs of particular marketing functions. In the third and most complex method, costs are studied according to the purposes for which they are incurred.

The analysis of natural expenses The simplest type of cost analysis utilizes the company's profit and loss statement. This operating statement is a summary of *natural expenses*—that is, expenses classified according to the nature of the cost, not the reason for which it was incurred. A typical analysis of operating (natural) expenses for a hypothetical firm is shown in Table 22.1. As this table demonstrates, two types of comparisons usually are made. First, current expenses can be compared with those of a previous period. Second, actual expenditures can be compared with those budgeted for the period. Of these, the historical comparisons of cost are the easiest to make, but they usually are the least reliable for planning purposes. Changing market conditions, major alterations in marketing programs, and fluctuations in the value of the dollar make year-to-year comparisons somewhat misleading.

The analysis of marketing costs in terms of natural-expense comparisons is quite commonplace. Its advantages are that it is simple and inexpensive. The operating statement is understood by most managers. However, the technique is not sufficiently analytical to provide clear-cut guides to improved performance. Its principal drawback is that it collects costs according to the nature of the expense rather than the purpose for which

TABLE 22.1   Analysis of operating (natural) expenses

Item	Current year Dollars	Current year Per cent	Budget Dollars	Budget Per cent	Variance (dollars)	Previous year Dollars	Previous year Per cent
Gross sales	5,000,000	100.5	4,800,000	100.4	−200,000	4,500,000	100.4
Less: Returns and allowances	25,000	0.5	20,000	.4	−5,000	20,000	.4
Net sales	4,975,000	100.0	4,780,000	100.0	−195,000	4,480,000	100.0
Cost of goods sold							
Beginning inventory	200,000	4.0	200,000	4.2	—	180,000	4.0
Cost of goods purchased	2,500,000	50.3	2,400,000	50.2	−100,000	2,250,000	50.2
Total merchandise handled	2,700,000	54.3	2,600,000	54.4	−100,000	2,430,000	54.2
Ending inventory	250,000	5.1	200,000	4.2	−50,000	200,000	4.0
Cost of goods sold	2,450,000	49.2	2,400,000	50.2	−50,000	2,230,000	49.8
Gross profit	2,525,000	50.8	2,380,000	49.8	−145,000	2,250,000	50.2
Direct marketing expenses							
Sales salaries	750,000	15.1	700,000	14.7	−50,000	680,000	15.2
Sales expenses	500,000	10.1	450,000	9.4	−50,000	430,000	9.6
Advertising	250,000	5.0	200,000	4.2	−50,000	190,000	4.2
Warehousing and shipping	360,000	7.2	350,000	7.3	−10,000	330,000	7.4
Payroll taxes and insurance	35,000	.7	30,000	.6	−5,000	30,000	.7
Regional and district office expense	150,000	3.0	150,000	3.1	—	140,000	3.1
Total direct marketing expense	2,045,000	41.1	1,880,000	39.3	−165,000	1,800,000	40.2
General administrative expense							
Executive salaries	150,000	3.0	150,000	3.1	—	140,000	3.1
Clerical expense	100,000	2.0	100,000	2.1	—	95,000	2.1
Payroll taxes and insurance	2,500	.1	2,500	.1	—	2,500	.1
Office expenses	60,000	1.2	55,000	1.2	−5,000	54,000	1.2
Depreciation	12,000	.2	12,500	.3	+500	12,500	.3
Credit and collection	35,000	.7	25,000	.5	−10,000	20,000	.4
Other expenses	50,000	1.0	55,000	1.1	+5,000	51,000	1.1
Total general administrative expense	409,500	8.2	400,000	8.4	−9,500	375,000	8.3
Total expenses	2,454,500	49.3	2,280,000	47.7	−174,500	2,175,000	48.5
Net profit	70,500	1.5	100,000	2.1	−29,500	75,000	1.7

the cost was incurred. For example, the function of a firm is not to pay salaries but to produce sales. The purpose of a firm is not to minimize costs but to generate profits. Profits are attained through programs of marketing action, and unless costs are analyzed either along functional lines or in terms of specific marketing programs, no real assessments of strategy are possible.

Functional cost analysis The second type of traditional cost analysis is functional. The

purpose of functional analysis is to control internal operations by classifying and studying expenses according to the functions for which they are incurred. Costs can thereby be directly related to specific areas of marketing performance. Although there are a number of ways that functional costs can be determined, the method most frequently suggested is as follows:

1. Natural expenses are reclassified according to the functions of the organiza-

tion for which they are incurred. There is little agreement, however, as to what the correct functional classifications are. Examples include selling, advertising, credit, warehousing, and delivery. Many different sets of functions have been developed for costing purposes, but the important point to remember is that a given function should represent a group of relatively homogeneous activities.

2. A service unit (a unit of measuring functional output) is then selected for each function. For example, the service unit of assembling and checking orders by a wholesaler is the completed order. If some orders contain many more items than do others, however, the invoice line is a better measure of the assembly and checking function. On the other hand, if the merchandise handled varies considerably in size or weight, as in hardware wholesaling, the volume unit, rather than the order or invoice line, might be used.

3. The final step is to determine the unit cost for each function by dividing the total cost of that function by the number of service units produced. Thus, if the total cost of assembling and checking orders in a given period was $1,000, and 5,000 orders were processed in the same period, the unit cost of assembling and checking orders would be $.20.

This type of functional cost analysis is a useful device for the internal control of marketing operations. It is helpful in preparing expense budgets and in comparing actual costs with budgeted values. Functional cost analysis also can be used in setting cost standards for each function.

Marketing cost analysis by manner of application When we speak of cost analysis by manner of application, we refer to the basic purpose of the study.[7] For example, a marketing manager may want to know the relative profitability of various products. On the other hand, interest may focus on the difference in cost between using one type of distribution method and another. These particular applications of cost study become the *objects* of the analysis. Many other objects could be mentioned, such as departments, territories, customers, order sizes, and the like.

The procedure of marketing cost analysis by manner of application is as follows:

1. With respect to the type of analysis desired, subdivide the marketing tasks into homogeneous functions capable of being related to specific items of cost. For example, C. H. Sevin suggests that the following functions be used in the allocation of costs to commodities (products):[8]
   a. Storage
   b. Investment
   c. Handling
   d. Delivery
   e. Order routine
   f. Promotion
   g. Reimbursement

[7] The phrase *cost analysis by manner of application* was introduced to the writer by Professor R. F. Breyer, who, to the best of the writer's knowledge, has taught the only comprehensive university course in marketing control. Professor Breyer's study of channel costs is a classic in marketing literature. See R. F. Breyer, *Quantitative Systematic Analysis and Control* (Philadelphia: R. F. Breyer, 1949). In a recent article, Beik and Byzby use the phrase *analysis by market segment* to refer to the same type of study. See L. L. Beik and S. L. Byzby, "Profitability Analysis by Market Segment," *Journal of Marketing,* July 1973, pp. 48–53. The use of the term *segment,* however, is apt to be misleading if it is thought to refer to market segments as described in Chapter 6.

[8] C. H. Sevin, *Distribution Cost Analysis* (Washington, D.C.: U.S. Department of Commerce, 1946), pp. 19–20.

2. Reclassify natural expenses according to the functions selected in step 1. Almost without exception, all so-called natural expenses are incurred directly for particular functions. If allocations of natural expenses must be made to various functions, this usually can be accomplished by judgment or by the use of simple time and duty studies.

3. Functional costs incurred directly for the object of analysis (customer, product, territory, and the like) are assigned immediately. For example, if salespersons are paid a straight commission, this cost of selling can be charged directly to products. Similarly, if a sales manager's time is devoted exclusively to one territory, all salary and expenses can be applied directly to that territory.

4. Costs of marketing functions that are wholly inapplicable to the object of analysis are excluded. For example, if the object of the analysis is to determine the relative profitability of products, credit and collection expense would not be assigned because products have no bearing on customers' payment performance.

5. Appropriate service units are identified for each function. (This step is comparable to step 2 in functional cost analysis.)

6. Calculate the unit cost for each function by dividing its cost by the number of service units produced. (Step 3 in functional cost analysis.)

7. Ascertain the number of functional service units required by the object of analysis. For example, in the allocation of physical-handling expense to a particular commodity, it is necessary to ascertain the number of standard handling units accounted for by this product.

8. The cost of each function in relation to the object of analysis is obtained by multiplying the number of service units required (step 7) by the unit functional cost (step 6).

9. Total marketing cost is obtained by adding the direct cost (step 3) and the allocated functional cost (step 8).

This method of marketing costing enables the manager to determine the actual cost of marketing particular commodities, of selling to individual customers, of servicing specific territories, and the like. The cost information can then be studied in other ways. For example, the costs of handling specific commodities, serving particular customers, or maintaining a certain sales territory can be compared to the costs of other products, customers, or territories. Comparisons to past performance also can be made. Finally, actual distribution costs can be compared to predetermined cost standards.

An Example of Marketing Cost Analysis

The Ajax Wholesale Hardware Company sells two separate lines of merchandise to the retail hardware trade. Both lines are sold by the same sales force, and some of the hardware customers carry both lines while others buy only one. Salespeople are paid on a straight commission basis, the rate being 3 per cent of net sales. The company delivers both lines of products directly to customers. No advertising is done, but merchandising aids such as display cards, posters, and so forth are furnished to hardware dealers. Gross profit taken by the company has always been the same (15 per cent) on both product groups, on the theory that any differences in the cost of distribution must be negligible and that competitive forces have never dictated any reason for lowering or raising markups.

During 1977, however, the marketing manager of the Ajax Hardware Company noted a decline in sales of Product A. Also,

TABLE 22.2   Ajax Wholesale Hardware Company Profit and Loss Statement (1976)

	Total Firm	Product A	Product B
Net sales	$2,500,000	$1,500,000	$1,000,000
Cost of goods sold	2,125,000	1,275,000	850,000
Gross profit	375,000	225,000	150,000
Expenses			
Sales commissions	75,000		
Sales expenses	7,000		
Salaries	25,000		
Promotional expense	10,000		
Warehouse and delivery	215,000		
Credits and collections	25,000		
Total expenses	$ 357,000		
Net profit	$ 18,000		

the president of the firm was concerned because the net profit of the business the previous year had not been satisfactory. The profit and loss statement for the Ajax Wholesale Hardware Company is shown in Table 22.2. In this statement, sales of the two product categories are presented separately, but marketing costs are reported only for the overall operation.

In the hope of obtaining information on which to base possible changes in marketing strategy, the marketing manager decided to attempt a reasonably accurate calculation of the costs of marketing each of the two product groups. The method of cost analysis outlined above was followed.

Step 1.   For the commodity (product) analysis the manager selected the marketing functions shown in Table 22.3.

Step 2.   Marketing expenses as shown on the profit and loss statement (Table 22.2) were reclassified according to function. This is illustrated in column 1 of Table 22.3, part A.

Step 3.   Costs incurred directly for com-

modities were assigned. These included salespeople's commissions and promotional materials.

Step 4.   Since all functional costs were to be allocated to commodities, none were excluded from the analysis.[9]

Step 5.   Appropriate service units were selected for each function. They are shown in Table 22.4, part B.

Step 6.   Unit functional costs, excluding those costs assigned directly to products, were calculated (see Table 22.4, part A).

Step 7.   The number of functional service units required for each product was ascertained. These are shown in Table 22.4, part A.

Step 8.   The total cost of performing each function for Product A and Product B was calculated by multiplying the number of service units by the unit costs. This is shown in Table 22.3, part A.

[9]The decision to allocate "reimbursement" to commodities is questionable, but is done in order to fully absorb (allocate) all costs. A reconciliation with the overall P&L statement is thereby facilitated.

TABLE 22.3   Ajax Wholesale Hardware Company profit and loss by products

(A) Functional analysis and marketing costs

Function	Total Cost	Service units			Unit Cost	Allocation to products	
		Total	A	B		A	B
Maintenance							
Investment	10,000	400,000	160,000	240,000	$0.025	4,000	6,000
Storage	50,000	300,000	100,000	200,000	0.167	16,667	33,333
Movement							
Physical handling	70,000	120,000	55,000	65,000	0.583	32,065	37,935
Order processing	65,000	200,000	80,000	120,000	0.325	26,000	39,000
Delivery	20,000	120,000	55,000	65,000	0.167	9,185	10,815
Promotion							
Salespeople commissions	75,000	Direct			—	45,000	30,000
Salespeople expenses	7,000	2,500,000	1,500,000	1,000,000	0.0028	4,200	2,800
Management salaries	25,000	2,500,000	1,500,000	1,000,000	0.01	15,000	10,000
Promotion materials	10,000	Direct			—	5,000	5,000
Reimbursement							
Clerical	13,000	2,500,000	1,500,000	1,000,000	0.0052	7,800	5,200
Financial	12,000	250,000	140,000	110,000	0.048	6,720	5,280
Total marketing costs	357,000					171,637	185,363

(B) Recapitulation: Profit and loss by products

			A	B
Net sales	2,500,000		1,500,000	1,000,000
Cost of goods sold	2,125,000		1,275,000	850,000
Gross profit	375,000		225,000	150,000
Expenses	357,000		171,637	185,363
Net profit (loss)	18,000		53,363	(35,363)

Step 9.   The total marketing cost of Product A and Product B was determined by adding the direct and functional costs. The total marketing costs of the two products are shown at the bottom of the last two columns of Table 22.3, part A.

The profitability of each product is found in the recapitulation in part B of Table 22.3. It indicates, contrary to management's prior opinion, that Product A in spite of its declining sales accounted for all of the company's profit. Product B, on the other hand, had been marketed at a loss. Clearly, some type of management action was called for. Whether the action should relate to methods of marketing Product B or to its pricing

TABLE 22.4   Ajax Wholesale Hardware Company allocation data

(A) Data for allocation of functional costs

	Total	Product A	Product B
Average value of inventory	$400,000	$160,000	$240,000
Number of standard handling units	120,000	55,000	65,000
Average amount outstanding	250,000	140,000	110,000
Floor space occupied (sq. ft.)	300,000	100,000	200,000
Number of invoice lines	200,000	80,000	120,000
Promotional materials (direct)	10,000	5,000	5,000

(B) Bases of allocation*

Functional cost groups	Bases of allocation
Maintenance	
A. Investment	Average inventory value
B. Storage	Floor space occupied
Movement	
A. Physical handling	No. of standard handling units
B. Order routine	No. of invoice lines
C. Delivery	No. of standard handling units
Promotion	
A. Salespeople's commissions	Direct—3% of sales
B. Sales expenses	Dollar value of sales
C. Management salaries	Dollar value of sales
D. Dealer helps, etc.	Direct to product group
Reimbursement	
A. Clerical	Dollar value of sales
B. Financial & collection	Average amount outstanding

*For a comprehensive list of allocation bases see M. Schiff, "Finance and Financial Analysis in Marketing," in V. Buell, ed., *Handbook of Modern Marketing* (New York: McGraw-Hill, 1970), pp. 15-8–15-9.

became a matter of executive concern. Eventually, a strategy involving a price increase and tighter cost control was adopted.

Profitability Accounting for Marketing

Up to this point, we have been considering the traditional methods of marketing cost analysis. A more sophisticated method has received attention in recent years.[10] *Profitability accounting* is a total accounting system that reports only those revenues and costs that are directly related to a particular prod-

[10] A number of managerial accounting texts discuss variable costing. For a relatively simple treatment, see H. Bierman, Jr., and A. R. Drebin, *Managerial Accounting* (New York: Macmillan, 1968), pp. 130–143. For a discussion of the application of profitability accounting to marketing, see S. Simon, *Managing Marketing Profitability* (New York: American Management Association, 1969); and F. M. Mossman, P. Fisher, and W. J. E. Crissy, "New Approaches to Analyzing Marketing Profitability," *Journal of Marketing,* April 1974, pp. 43–48.

uct, territory, or other object of profit control. No overhead or even indirect costs are assigned. Thus, it is a partial cost system as opposed to the traditional full-absorption systems of accounting, which assign all costs, direct and indirect, to the various functions.

The starting point of profitability accounting is a reclassification of expenses in such a way as to permit their identification as direct or fixed with respect to particular profit centers in the business. A *direct cost* is a variable cost—one that varies with the volume or activity. A *fixed cost* is one that does not vary with volume or activity. Implicit in these definitions is the idea that a variable cost is incurred because activity has taken place and that this cost would not have been incurred if the activity had been eliminated.[11] If a decisionmaker is really interested in controlling costs, fixed costs should not be assigned to profit centers. Variable costs of selling and standard manufacturing costs are assigned, however, as are certain other costs incurred specifically for the profit center involved.

These latter costs are called programmed or specific costs. They may be of a nonvariable or a semivariable character. They are not necessarily directly variable; but they are escapable. Examples of such programmed marketing costs might include sales promotion and advertising costs that are planned for particular products or territories. In addition, a particular department or profit center may have some other types of programmed costs that properly are charged against it in profitability accounting. The

expense of maintaining a departmental marketing-research staff would be an example.

Table 22.5 compares a profitability accounting earnings statement with a profit and loss report prepared in the traditional manner. Two notable differences can be seen. First, the profitability statement is a partial statement. It emphasizes a product's contribution—not net profits. Second, the classification of expenses and the order in which they appear in the statement are different. The reason for these differences should be clear. The traditional statement jumbles costs between marketing and manufacturing so that the resulting profit figure cannot be used solely for marketing planning or control purposes. The profitability-accounting statement isolates those costs that are the specific responsibility of the marketing decisionmaker. Manufacturing overhead and general administrative expense are not charged against the marketing department.

The discussion of marketing profitability accounting can be clarified with an example of its use by a hardware manufacturing company. Handy Hardware makes three lines of products. Its small household appliance line is composed of fans, small space heaters, kitchen toasters, and waffle irons. This line is sold through hardware wholesalers, department stores, and discount houses. Handy also manufactures a line of power lawn mowers, which it sells to large, direct-buying mass merchandisers and to hardware wholesalers. The third line is industrial shelving, which is sold to industrial distributors, large direct buyers, and the government. All lines are sold by salaried company salespeople.

At the end of 1976, the director of marketing received a year-end profit and loss statement for the company as a whole. With

[11]Sometimes the terms *escapable* and *inescapable* are used. An escapable cost is one that would be avoided if an activity were not undertaken; an inescapable cost would continue in any event. Escapable costs, then, tend to resemble marginal costs; as, of course, do variable costs.

TABLE 22.5   Comparison of traditional and profitability-accounting earnings statements

Traditional accounting		Profitability accounting	
Net sales	$29,733	Gross sales	$29,964
Cost of goods sold		Variable costs	19,072
Direct materials	13,100		
Direct labor	2,057		
Manufacturing overhead	4,217		
	19,374		
Gross profit	10,359	Profit contribution	10,892
Selling expenses			
Salaries	3,091		
Advertising and promotion	1,104	Specific product expenses	
Shipping	970	Discounts and allowances	231
Other	1,202	Advertising and promotion	2,068
	6,367		2,299
General and administrative expenses	2,000	Product earnings	8,593
Earnings before taxes	1,992		
Provision for taxes	956		
Net profit after provision for taxes	1,036		

some dismay, it was noted that not only had Handy failed to achieve its target sales volume of $37 million, but net earnings for the year actually were below the 1975 level. Return on investment was below the goal set by top management. The director of marketing believed that a thorough analysis of marketing costs should be made. The company's accountant was asked to prepare a profit and loss statement by major product lines. Because of the detailed analysis required, it took about sixty days to complete this report; and it was not until March 15 that the new statement of earnings was available. This statement is shown in Table 22.6. The controller sent a memorandum with the analysis, indicating that a meeting should be called to discuss the immediate dropping of industrial shelving. "We're losing money on this (industrial) line even before it leaves the factory" was the memo's opening sentence.

The director of marketing was not so sure about this, believing that the report as shown in Table 22.6 did not accurately reflect the actual profit picture. This marketing executive was familiar with profitability accounting and asked the accountant to revise the product-group profit and loss statement to show variable and specific costs and the profit contribution of each product group. Although this involved another time-consuming examination of accounting documents, the report was prepared. The new statement, shown in Table 22.7, revealed some interesting things. First, the shelving line actually made a contribution to factory and general overhead in 1976. Unless a new line could be found to take its place, the immediate removal of industrial shelving would lower Handy's profits even more. Nevertheless, the shelving line was not contributing nearly so much as the other two

TABLE 22.6   Example of traditional profit and loss statement by product group

Handy Hardware Company
Statement of Profit and Loss by Product Group
Year Ending 12/31/76
($000)

	Total company	Housewares	Lawn mowers	Industrial shelving
Net sales	29,733	20,051	5,005	4,677
Cost of goods sold				
Direct materials	13,100	7,765	1,986	3,349
Direct labor	2,057	1,352	305	400
Manufacturing overhead	4,217	2,786	453	978
	19,374	11,903	2,744	4,727
Gross profit	10,359	8,148	2,261	(50)
Percentage	34.8			
Selling expenses				
Salaries	3,091	2,211	377	503
Advertising and promotion	1,104	785	264	55
Shipping	970	655	165	150
Other	1,202	905	232	65
	6,367	4,556	1,038	773
General and administrative expenses	2,000	1,350	340	310
Earnings before taxes	1,992	2,242	883	(1,133)
Provision for taxes	956			
Net earnings after provision for taxes	1,036			

lines. Its overall profit contribution was only 9.8 per cent, compared to over 40 per cent for the houseware and lawnmower lines. The production department maintained that its costs were not out of line, however. Raw materials were purchased competitively, and the cutting, stamping, and painting operations were routine and well controlled. The director of marketing believed that the problem was in the pricing of the line. Before making a decision to raise shelving prices generally, another report was prepared that showed the sales of shelving by type of customer. Three major types of accounts were served: large, direct-buying industrial users; industrial distributors; and government departments and agencies. Table 22.8 shows the breakdown of sales and the profit contribution for each shelving customer group. At last the culprit emerged! Direct sales of shelving to the government actually cost Handy Hardware Company $208,000 in 1976. On further investigation, the reason became all too clear. Prices quoted in bids on government contracts were low—too low, in fact, even to cover the direct cost of manufacture. Most government orders, it was discovered, were for 8-foot-high shelving, which required 20 per cent more steel than the standard 6-foot-high units on which the firm's standard costs were based.

TABLE 22.7   Example of profitability-accounting statement of earnings by product group

Handy Hardware Company
Statement of Earnings by Product Group
Year Ending 12/31/76
($000)

	Total company	Housewares	Lawn mowers	Industrial shelving
Gross sales	29,964	20,238	5,016	4,710
Variable costs	19,072	11,933	2,893	4,246
Profit contribution	10,892	8,305	2,123	464
Specific product expenses				
Discounts and allowances	231	187	11	33
Advertising and promotion	2,068	693	1,120	255
	2,299	880	1,131	288
Product earnings	8,593	7,425	992	176
General expenses	6,601			
Earnings before taxes	1,992			

As a result of this study Handy's director of marketing immediately initiated a policy of pricing on government orders to yield a profit contribution of no less than 25 per cent. The sales force objected at first, maintaining that it could not get any business at the higher prices. As it turned out, however, Handy was able to compete favorably on some of the patented items in its line and was even able to obtain orders for its standard line of shelving because of its history of quality and prompt delivery.

TABLE 22.8   Example of profitability-accounting statement of earnings by customer group

Handy Hardware Company
Statement of Earnings for Industrial Shelving by Customer Group
Year Ending 12/31/76
($000)

	All customers	Industrial (direct)	Industrial distributors	Government
Gross sales	$4,710	$471	$1,413	$2,826
Variable costs	4,246	353	989	2,904
Profit contribution	464	118	424	(78)
Specific product expenses				
Discounts and allowances	33	8	20	5
Advertising and promotion	255	30	100	125
	288	38	120	130
Product earnings	176	80	304	(208)

The executive committee of Handy Hardware was so impressed with the improved information provided by the profitability-accounting reports that it instructed the accountant to convert the entire accounting system to this basis. In the following year, the director of marketing received periodic reports on the profit contribution of the various product lines. As a result, midyear corrections were instituted during 1978 that enabled the firm to reach its target levels of sales and return on investment.

The Control of Marketing Costs

We have seen how profitability accounting can be used to report those costs for which marketing managers are responsible. It is relatively easy to see how the same type of cost concepts used to analyze the Handy Hardware Company's past performance can be used to establish standards for the future.

Following the successful use of profitability accounting to isolate the problems in the line of industrial shelving sold to the government, the director of marketing decided to use the same cost concepts as a basis for controlling marketing costs in 1978. A detailed forecast of sales for the first six months of 1978 was made. Next, the accounting department established standard costs of direct material and labor at the expected rate of operations. These permitted an estimate of the profit contribution for each product group. Product managers were required to submit detailed marketing plans for 1978, including budgets for advertising and sales promotion. The director of marketing discussed the promotional plans with each of the product managers. Agreement was

reached with the general sales manager on the limits to which special deals and allowances would be made. With these commitments it was possible for a complete budget of anticipated product earnings to be prepared. By comparing the quarterly reports of actual performance with this budget, the director of marketing was able to work out with the product managers changes in promotion and pricing strategy that resulted in further improvements in the company's profits by the end of the year.

The overall control illustrated in the Handy Hardware Company case may be as close as managers can come to the control of marketing costs. This is particularly true when the activities over which they must exercise control, such as advertising and pricing, do not lend themselves to the setting of precise standards.

However, there are aspects of marketing that can be routinized and for which fairly rigid cost standards can be set. In setting standards for routinized or repetitive operations, such as telephone selling, clerical work, and warehousing, the following steps are involved:

1. *Establish the most efficient work procedures* These procedures are not ideal but represent realistic job performance.
2. *Compute the standard input required* This input may be computed for any or all of the various factors, such as labor, materials, power, and so forth.
3. *"Cost out" the standard input to determine the cost of performing the most efficient procedure* Since the costs of the various kinds of inputs are known or readily obtainable, it is relatively easy to determine the total number of dollars required to perform a given task.
4. *Compute the standard output* It is neces-

sary to measure the number of output units created when the required job procedure is followed.

5. *Compute the standard cost per unit of output* By dividing the total cost of a given procedure by standard output, it is possible to compute the standard cost per unit. These steps are the same as those generally followed in the establishment of standards for manufacturing costs. No attempt has been made to allocate a portion of general overhead or administrative costs to a particular task, although this is sometimes done by companies using absorption-accounting procedures.

6. *Compare actual to standard* At the end of each accounting period actual costs of performing a routine function are reported. In addition, records must be maintained to ascertain the amount of output. Total cost of performing the function is divided by the output to determine actual unit cost. This actual is then compared to the standard.

7. *Analyze variances* The differences, if any, between actual and standard must be studied. This is called *variance analysis*. A favorable variance means that a particular function was performed more efficiently than was anticipated in the preparation of the standard. An unfavorable variance implies a decline in productivity. Since only direct functional costs were included in the standard and only direct costs actually charged against it, any difference between actual and standard is attributable to unexpected changes in the prices of materials or labor or to the productivity of the function. Variance due to changes in material prices or wage rates can be easily discovered and removed. The remaining

variance, either positive or negative, is the result of performance.

If an allocation of overhead was made in the computation of the standard, an additional step in variance analysis is involved. Since overhead is fixed in total, it varies per output unit according to the rate of operation. A standard rate of operation must be determined before a standard overhead can be determined. If a standard-overhead factor is added to a standard cost, variance analysis also involves an inspection of variation in the rate of operations, which requires computation of what the standard cost would have been at the level of operations actually achieved. Any variance from this standard is then studied for productivity changes that may have occurred.

Summary

Marketing cost data constitute an essential element in the marketing information system. Unfortunately, cost study is the least advanced area of data analysis in marketing. However, there is a body of theory regarding marketing cost behavior as well as a number of techniques for the analysis and control of actual costs.

The theory of marketing cost behavior rests largely on concepts developed in economics. Economic reasoning suggests that we can best understand marketing costs by looking at the various time spans involved. The market period is a time span in which the marketer has a fixed supply of goods to sell. The short run is a time period in which the manager can increase the stock of goods but cannot increase capacity. In the long run, the marketing manager has complete flexibility as to the range of decisions that can be made. Economic theory assists the manager in making all decisions involving cost by identifying the various determinants that affect the behavior of costs in each of these time periods.

Techniques of marketing cost analysis have been available to the marketing manager for many years, although they have been infrequently used until recently. These techniques have involved three different approaches. One approach has been to inspect marketing expenses by the use of conventional accounting reports. Another has been to assign marketing expenses to the various functions performed and then to analyze total and unit functional costs. The third approach involves allocating functional costs to various objects of the marketing effort—products, customers, territories, and so on. This method has been called marketing cost analysis by manner of application.

More recently, developments in managerial accounting have made it possible to report and analyze marketing costs in a new way. This method of analysis, which we call marketing profitability accounting, assigns only direct costs to a marketing profit center. These costs may be variable or fixed, but they are strictly escapable. That is, if the particular marketing activity, such as a product or a territory, were abandoned, its cost would disappear. By the same token, any profit produced by this activity can be attributed directly to it. Reporting costs and profits in this way permits managers to make intelligent decisions about those activities for which they are responsible.

Our discussion of marketing cost information closed with a treatment of cost control. We found that the techniques of profitability accounting are directly applicable to budgeting and control. Variance analysis between budgeted and actual costs can be made. Even if profitability accounting is not used in a company, the costs of performing routine marketing activities can be controlled by the use of cost standards. This method, too, involves variance analysis of differences between standard cost and actual cost. Reasons for the variance can be isolated and corrective action taken.

Questions and Problems

1. Distinguish among long-run, short-run, and market periods. Why is this distinction useful in analyzing marketing costs?

2. Retailing and wholesaling have both been affected by important technological changes in the past twenty-five years. Identify at least two important changes for each and indicate the effect you think each has had on marketing costs.

3. Why is it that a firm always should operate in the stage of diminishing returns? Can you cite any exceptions to this general principle?

4. Marketing establishments seem to be getting bigger and bigger. Draw a sketch of what you think the long-run cost curve of a large department store might be. Explain your diagram.

5. Over the years it has been believed that most marketing costs are indirect or overhead costs. Do you think this may be less true today? Why or why not?

6. How can the marketing department be

a profit center if it does not control manufacturing costs and general overhead?

7. What are the differences between traditional profit and loss statements and profitability-accounting report forms?

8. Obtain a copy of a marketing company's annual report. What does its earnings statement tell you about the company's marketing costs?

9. If you were going to establish a cost control system for a routine marketing activity, what steps would you take? What problems do you think you would encounter, and how would you handle each?

10. The chapter presented a method for analyzing marketing cost variances. How would you go about analyzing profit variances (the difference between planned and actual profits)?

Five

**Extending
the Marketing
Concept**

23

Environmental Impacts on Marketing

We have completed an inspection of the micromarketing system. We have discovered how it is organized, how it operates, how it responds to the consumer, and how it processes information for planning and control. We have been exposed to a wide range of marketing concepts, and we have mastered a number of analytical and problem-solving techniques. We have covered a great deal of ground; but as the lyrics of the song popularized by Peggy Lee ask, "Is that all there is?"

By no means is that all there is to marketing. We have explored only a system within an arbitrarily drawn boundary. What if we extend that boundary? What if we plunge beyond the frontier of marketing management within the business firm and embrace marketing's environment in our thought?

We discovered in Chapter 2 that a marketing system is composed of a set of related components. A system boundary encloses these components, and everything outside of this boundary is called the *environment*. As we learned, most marketing systems are subject to the influence of external factors, such as economic conditions, technological developments, cultural impacts, public opinion, and political pressures. This chapter will be concerned with three of the most critical environmental impacts on marketing. They are (1) the public environment, (2) the legal environment, and (3) the competitive environment.

The Public Environment

American society constitutes the public environment of marketing. Its basic element is the influences that people as citizens (rather than as consumers) have on marketing. These influences are many and varied, reflecting the dynamic and complex forces that influence society itself.

Public influence on marketing is manifested in several ways. People's attitudes, opinions, and prejudices are important *informal* influences on marketing behavior. Eventually, some informal public attitudes are formalized into administrative *rulings* and *laws*. The influence of the public on marketing can be expressed individually or collectively. *Individual* public influence is encountered when a single person, usually someone in an important position, makes a strong pronouncement on some issue related to marketing. Estes Kefauver, Philip Hart, and William Proxmire waged running battles with big business during their careers in the U.S. Senate. Outside of politics, the popular author Vance Packard and consumer protector Ralph Nader are important individual influences within the public environment of marketing. *Collective* public influence arises whenever group action is taken. Group action, whether by a strong labor organization, such as the AFL-CIO, or a local parent-teacher association, is a vital factor in American society and of tremendous importance to marketing. The public presence influences marketing in two important ways.

1. Through public opinions and attitudes, currently articulated in the new consumerism
2. Through public policy as directed by federal, state, and local governments

The New Consumerism

In 1962, for the first time in more than a quarter of a century, an American president took note of public opinion toward marketing in a special message to the Congress.

Much like Franklin Roosevelt's famous "Four Freedoms," John F. Kennedy's proposal outlined a "strengthening of programs for protection of consumer interest" based on four fundamental consumer rights. The importance that he apparently placed on consumerism is reflected in the following excerpt from his special message to Congress:

Marketing is increasingly impersonal. Consumer choice is influenced by mass advertising utilizing highly developed arts of persuasion. The consumer typically cannot know whether drug preparations meet minimum standards of safety, quality, and efficacy. He usually does not know how much he pays for consumer credit; whether one prepared food has more nutritional value than others; whether the performance of a product will in fact meet his needs; or whether the "large economy size" really is a bargain.

Nearly all the programs offered by this administration—e.g., the expansion of world trade, the improvement of medical care, the reduction of passenger taxes, the strengthening of mass transit, the development of conservation and recreation areas and low-cost power—are of direct or inherent importance to consumers. Additional legislative and administrative action is required, however, if the Federal Government is to meet its responsibility to consumers in the exercise of their rights. These rights include:

1. The right to safety—to be protected against the marketing of goods which are hazardous to health or life.
2. The right to be informed—to be protected against fraudulent, deceitful, or grossly misleading information, advertising, labeling, or other practices, and to be given the facts he needs to make an informed choice.
3. The right to choose—to be assured, wherever possible, access to a variety of products and services at competitive prices; and in those industries in which competition is not workable and government regulation is

substituted, an assurance of satisfactory quality and service at fair prices.

4. The right to be heard—to be assured that consumer interest will receive full and sympathetic consideration in the formulation of government policy, and fair and expeditious treatment in its administrative tribunals.[1]

Following this summary of the dilemma of the consumer in the face of contemporary marketing practices, the president proposed the extension of public policy in three areas: (1) strengthening of existing programs, (2) improvement of governmental organization, and (3) passing new legislation. Although President Kennedy and those who followed him in office did not succeed wholly in implementing these goals, they are indicative of the trend of federal interest in marketing. This trend will continue in the future.

Thus, in the early 1960s the new consumerism appeared. Is consumerism really new? No, because public influencers have been speaking on behalf of consumers for over seventy years. Extremely bitter criticisms of marketing practices were raised in the 1920s. The first consumer protection laws were passed in the early years of this century, and a slow but certain course of public policy emerged. Thus, a good case can be made that the new consumerism is not unique in marketing history but is actually the form in which consumer interest is now being expressed. We will look briefly at some of the older expressions of consumerism before

discussing the ways that it affects marketing today.

The Consumer Movement

We can demonstrate historically that the consumer protection movement has been tied to the rising importance of the individual as a consumer, starting when mass production began to dominate American industry.[2] As soon as productive and distributive capacity ran ahead of effective demand, competition for customer purchasing power became intense. At the same time, a vast array of new and complicated products made buying difficult and confusing. General buyer frustration appeared in the form of a fairly well defined protest during the late 1920s. This protest became known as the *consumer movement*.

So-called guinea pig books appeared. A consumer club launched by one of the early writers developed into a nonprofit testing agency we know as Consumers Research, Inc. Probably the most famous of the consumer movement books was *100,000,000 Guinea Pigs* by Kallet and Schlink, which remained on the best-seller list for two years.[3] It made millions of American consumers wary of the products they purchased. Beware the rosy apple—it may be covered with an arsenic insecticide; avoid the unknown hamburger or hot dog—poisonous preservatives or impure products may be in

[1]Kennedy, J. F. *Message from the President of the United States Relative to Consumers' Protection and Interest Program,* Document 364, House of Representatives, 87th Congress, 2nd Session, 15 March 1962 (Washington, D.C.: U.S. Government Printing Office, 1962), p. 2.

[2]We must go back to textbooks and articles published over thirty years ago. For example, see R. S. Alexander et al., *Marketing* (Boston: Ginn, 1940), pp. 661–883. Most libraries are more likely to have a classic article by K. Dameron, "The Consumer Movement," *Harvard Business Review,* Spring 1939, pp. 271–289.

[3]A. Kallet and F. J. Schlink, *100,000,000 Guinea Pigs* (New York: Vanguard Press, 1932).

it. According to one source, the 1936 amendments to the Federal Food and Drug Act resulted directly from Franklin Roosevelt's interest in *100,000,000 Guinea Pigs.*

The president and the American people had far more serious problems confronting them in the 1930s than those of consumer protection. The Great Depression overshadowed the consumer movement. Having something to eat understandably was more important than having the purest of products to consume. Consequently, in the 1930s the movement appeared to pass out of sight, and the wartime years that followed gave little incentive to its resurrection. World War II employment opportunities improved the economic lot of most consumers, but the conversion from a peacetime to a wartime economy forced the withdrawal of many consumer products from the market. A complaining consumer was a complaining American. Patriotism prevailed in the marketplace.

Nor did the consumer movement revive immediately after World War II. Pent-up demands for consumer products, veterans accustomed to the primitive consumption standards of military service, and a torrent of exciting new products combined to make consumers tolerant of marketing's performance. Moreover, many consumers in the 1950s had been raised during the lean years of the depression. The relative abundance of goods and an insatiable demand for them made these consumers uncritical of abuses that existed in the marketing process.

Marketing actually had not changed. New faces, new products, and some new tactics for distribution and selling had appeared. But the underlying potential for consumer abuse remained. Some observers suggest that it had increased dangerously. A new wave of social criticism began to build.

Vance Packard's, *Hidden Persuaders,* Rachel Carson's *Silent Spring,* and Jessica Mitford's *American Way of Death* focused attention at least temporarily on the damage caused by modern marketing on consumers and society as a whole. Public critics increased in number and eloquence. The 1960s was a decade of new criticism. Public opinion as well as public policy reflected the rise of the protection movement now known as the *new consumerism.*

Consumerist Issues

The consumerists' bill of complaints focuses on four major areas: high prices, product quality and safety, false and misleading advertising, and environmental pollution. None of these stands out as of compelling importance, and each has received its share of attention at one time or another. The author's studies for the Better Business Bureau indicate that the principal concern of most consumers relates to the persistent *escalation of prices* of consumer goods and services. On unaided-recall questions, the issue of high prices is the only criticism to emerge with frequency.

Once consumers have vented their irritation over high prices, a number of other issues materialize. *Deteriorating product quality* is a common complaint. "They just don't make _____ like they used to" reflects disappointment in shoddy goods and expensive repair services. Product safety is also a widespread concern, because in almost four out of five households persons are hurt, disabled, or killed in product-related incidents (excluding automobile accidents) each year. The extensive publicity given to the dangers in food additives and to durable-goods recalls, and the hazards of such products as hair sprays, insecticides, and over-the-counter drugs serves to focus a general concern of consumers regarding the quality and safety of the products they use.

Another important area of consumer complaint has to do with the *truthfulness of advertising.* In an MSI study, nearly half of the respondents reported that they found most television advertising to be seriously misleading.[4] The reaction to print advertising is less strong—only about one fourth of the survey respondents are critical. According to S. A. Greyser, who has studied this topic for many years, there has been "an erosion of the public's traditional tolerance of puffery in advertising in recent years."[5] This tougher appraisal has led both to criticism and to new methods of advertising that are more informational in their copy approach. Comparative advertising, in which a company actually contrasts its product's features with those of a competitor's, is a good example.

A fourth area of consumer complaint, which has been sparked by very articulate consumer activist groups, is *environmental pollution.* Industrial pollution of soil, water, and atmosphere is the principal target; but the impact of marketing also is criticized. The discharge of fluorocarbons from aerosol containers, the emission of toxic exhaust fumes from automobiles, the littering of streets and parks with wrappers and nonreturnable bottles and cans, and the scarring of the landscape by highway billboards are examples of consumer complaints against marketing pollution. Voluntary self-regulation and public enforcement have merged to restrain these particular types of pollution,

at least to a degree. But there will be continuing criticism, because the problems have not been solved completely, and the general challenge of improving and preserving the environment remains.

Why Has Marketing Served Consumers Poorly?

Since the purpose of marketing is to provide customer satisfactions, why has the system done so poorly? In response, it should be recognized that not everyone agrees that the complaints voiced in the new consumerism accurately reflect how well marketing has performed. For example, marketing people ask if it is really right for consumers to blame them for high prices. They argue that high levels of government spending and other monetary and fiscal factors have been the principal culprits in creating inflation. It is also maintained in the defense of marketing that the majority of American consumers seem pleased with the goods and services provided. Social critics and articulate complainers, so they say, overstate the case for the new consumerism.

Although the criticisms may be exaggerated and distorted, a basis for complaint does exist. One possible reason marketing may have failed to perform adequately is that marketing executives have construed too narrowly the meaning of customer orientation. It is not solely mechanical—matching products and services to customer needs. It is also philosophical, involving a genuine concern for the consumers' welfare.[6] The proper response to the challenge of the new

---

[4]S. A. Greyser, *Americans' Attitudes Toward Consumerism* (Cambridge: Marketing Science Institute, 1977), p. 4.

[5]Ibid.

[6]M. Bell and C. W. Emory, "The Faltering Marketing Concept," *Journal of Marketing,* October 1971, pp. 37–42.

consumerism is to accept that there is room for improvement in marketing's economic and social performance and to agree that something can be done—in short, to become genuinely concerned. This is part of the challenge of marketing management. It is imperative to do the job; it is highly desirable to do it efficiently. Part of the manager's responsibility is to identify areas in which the company's products and services fail to measure up to consumer expectations and to initiate programs to provide the kinds of satisfactions that consumers demand.

Business' Response to Consumerism

A number of companies have responded effectively to the new consumerism. Others seem to do so as a last resort. *Business Week* described the stages that a business seems to go through in arriving at a decision to take action in response to consumer pressure.[7] These steps are

1. Deny everything
2. Blame wrongdoing on the small, marginal companies
3. Discredit the critics
4. Hire a public-relations person
5. Defang the legislation
6. Launch a fact-finding committee
7. Actually do something

[7]Concept reprinted from "Business Responds to Consumerism," 6 September 1969, *Business Week*, p. 100, © 1969 McGraw-Hill, Inc., 1221 Avenue of the Americas, New York, N.Y. 10020. All rights reserved. For two more contemporary assessments of business response to consumerism, see N. Kangun and others, "Consumerism and Marketing Management," *Journal of Marketing*, April 1975, pp. 3–10; and S. A. Greyser and S. L. Diamond, "Business Is Adapting to Consumerism," *Harvard Business Review*, September-October 1974, pp. 38–60.

Among the companies that have successfully attempted to do something is Whirlpool Corporation. Other companies have similar programs, but the Whirlpool approach indicates that a sincere but relatively modest program of response to consumerism actually pays off, not only in fewer consumer complaints but in profits as well. The Whirlpool program includes

A 24-hour "cool line," free-of-charge, enabling customers to telephone from anywhere in the country to gripe, ask about service, get product and usage information, or request such things as spare owner manuals. The two-year-old service has fielded some 11,000 calls so far this year, and averages 125 per day.

A letter in housewife's language in place of warranty certificates, telling customers what they can expect.

"Reputation" ads, for which Whirlpool has been spending about 20% of its advertising budget. A notable one ran last October in *Life* and *Look*. "If you have a gripe," it ran, "let the manufacturer know." The ad offered a preaddressed letter which the reader simply scribbled on and mailed, "Dear Mr. Upton," it began— and the rest was blank. "We got about 2,700 responses to that," says Stephen Upton, Whirlpool's consumer services vice-president, "and they're still coming in."

A buy-guide that is attached to appliances, showing major product characteristics and features: motor size, operating time, water temperature and pressure, water consumption, weight. The head of a consumer testing organization points out that the guide tells the housewife everything but how well the washing machine will wash clothes.

Whirlpool was also the first company in the industry to pay for all in-warranty service calls. "Back in the early 1960's," says Upton, "the discount store was taking a larger and larger percentage of sales. But because they were working on a smaller profit margin, many did not lay aside an amount for the in-warranty labor for which they were responsible."

So Whirlpool took the warranty service out of the dealers' hands. "The service agent just writes out a regular bill to us, sends it in at his regular out-of-warranty rates so that he makes a profit, and we pay it," Upton explains. "It also gives us a complete record of all in-warranty claims anywhere in the country so we can see immediately what components are failing."[8]

The starting point of a company program to respond to consumerism is effective communications. The Whirlpool cool line is one example. Or a firm might have a consumer *ombudsman*—an executive charged with the responsibility of representing the consumer and carrying complaints directly to top management. More typically a firm will try to build some type of communications system with its consumers, usually involving component members of its channel of distribution. A series of studies of consumer communications systems in the automobile, tire, gasoline, cereal, meat, and sporting-arms industries showed that, although groundwork for consumer communications has been provided, more must be done to make these systems effective and efficient.[9]

A few firms have established top level units in the organization to deal with consumerist issues.[10] In exceptionally large companies the responsibility may be decentralized. This is the way it is handled at GM. Each division—Chevrolet, Pontiac, Oldsmobile, Buick, Cadillac, and GMC—has a customer relations department. Each of these divisions, in turn, assigns local customer relations responsibilities to the various zone offices. By the use of this elaborate vertical system, the company reaches down to the market and responds quickly to consumer complaints.

Public Policy

Public policy involves the legal framework constructed to govern and protect society and its institutions.[11] Institutionally viewed, public policy is a reflection not only of contemporary needs but also of the past. For example, antitrust laws enacted over half a century ago still provide the basis of public policy. Judicial review and administrative enforcement keep older legislation meaningful.

The U.S. Constitution created three branches of government: legislative, judicial, and executive. The general responsibilities of each branch are well known. It is also important to recognize that, in performing their respective tasks of lawmaking, interpretation, and administration, these

---

[8]"Appliance Maker Comes Clean," p. 100. Reprinted from the 6 September 1969 *Business Week.* Copyright © 1969 by McGraw-Hill, Inc., 1221 Avenue of the Americas, New York, N.Y. 10020. All rights reserved.

[9]D. Cohen, ed., *Communications Systems Between Management and the Consumer in Selected Industries* (New York: Hofstra University, 1969).

[10]See E. P. McGuire, *The Consumer Affairs Department: Organization and Function* (New York: The Conference Board, 1973).

[11]The relationship between marketing and public policy has been of interest to a number of marketing scholars. At the forefront of these was E. T. Grether, whose interest dates back to the 1930s. For Professor Grether's most recent essay dealing with market structure and public policy, see E. T. Grether, "Marketing and Public Policy: A Contemporary View," *Journal of Marketing,* July 1974, pp. 2–7. Another useful article on the same general topic is P. N. Bloom and N. Dholakia, "Marketer Behavior and Public Policy," *Journal of Marketing,* October 1973, pp. 63–67.

branches perform other functions that affect public policy as well.

The *legislative branch,* of course, is primarily responsible for creating and passing legislation. Except for constitutional prohibitions, there is virtually no limit to the directions in which Congress can act. The wide range of marketing-related legislation that has been enacted since the turn of the century shows the many activities that are regulated by law. We will inspect some of these statutes later in the chapter.

Important as the law-making function of the legislative branch is, it is not its only activity. It also has broad *investigative* powers. The congressional investigation has become a part of twentieth-century America. Television coverage of inquiries conducted by the House Internal Security Committee, the House Labor Committee, and the Senate Subcommittee on Antitrust and Monopoly brought the investigative powers of the legislative branch to the public awareness.

The principal function of the *judicial branch* is to review and interpret the law. The basic interpretation is constitutional. However, laws are also carefully studied in the context of the evolving legal framework. The legislature is not permitted indiscriminately and erratically to change its position on the legality or illegality of specific practices. Precedent is an important factor in evaluating particular laws. There are hierarchies of judicial review, with the Supreme Court of the United States at the apex of the system. In recent years this high tribunal has exerted great influence on public policy. Most of its important decisions relate to social issues, such as integration and civil rights. But American business practice has not been exempt, and a number of important Supreme Court decisions have substantially altered the legal framework of American marketing.

The *executive branch* is responsible for the administration of constitutional government and the enforcement of law. As chief executive, the president defines public policy by deciding to enforce or not to enforce certain programs, to investigate or not to investigate specific practices; to support or not to support programs financially; and to encourage or not to encourage the Congress to enact particular legislation. With the centralization of power in the federal government, the role of the president has become extremely important.

The White House does not act alone. For example, several hundred federal agencies and departments are directly involved in consumer affairs. At the executive level these are focused in a number of major departments and agencies, including the Federal Trade Commission and the Departments of Justice, Commerce, and Health, Education, and Welfare. All of these executive agencies and departments were created by legislation. They act within and enforce the laws affecting marketing. It is important, therefore, to inspect the laws that directly bear on the practice of marketing management.

The Legal Framework of Marketing

The antecedent of the legal framework of marketing was the *common law,* which governed commercial activities prior to the development of modern business law. In general, the common law supported the free-enterprise system, as well as the institutions and behavior to maintain it. Although the common law was based on a tremendous body of judicial precedent, it failed to provide a clear or comprehensive set of legal guidelines. Specific activities, which were injurious to competitors or to the public, seldom were restrained under the common law. In fact, under the common law free enterprise seemed to be self-defeating. The result of competition seemed to be the decline of competition. Unless the free-enterprise system could be regulated to remove the effects of its own undoing, it was doubtful that economic freedom and political freedom could remain compatible. M. C. Howard well summarizes the deficiencies of the common law in the following excerpt:

But the common law itself was not a clear-cut body of doctrine. Generally speaking, agreements and restraint of trade such as price fixing, pooling arrangements, cornering the market, division of markets along territorial or commodity lines, or restriction of sales had been treated simply as being unenforceable in the courts. Such practices as sales below cost, exclusive dealing, and tying arrangements have usually been deemed by the common law courts to constitute legitimate market behavior even when employed to eliminate a competitor. And relief of third parties through damage suits had generally been obtainable only if the methods of the restraint were considered criminal or highly unorthodox. As for business combinations, the businessmen had little reason to fear prosecution for conspiracy unless violence or fraud were involved. Finally, the common law had provided only the framework to permit private redress from private wrongs. Such a legal framework thus required private initiative and could hardly have been expected to constitute more than an implied statement of public policy.[12]

Because of the deficiencies in the common law and the scandals resulting from the

[12]M. C. Howard, *Legal Aspects of Marketing* (New York: McGraw-Hill, 1964), pp. 4–5. Used with permission of McGraw-Hill Book Company.

combinations and trusts of the late nineteenth century, the first of the so-called antitrust laws were passed. Today the *antitrust laws* are the foundation of the legal framework of marketing. They are intended to preserve competition—the competition that regulates and preserves free enterprise. Each of these laws, important amendments to them, and selected judicial interpretations of them are described below.

The Sherman Antitrust Act (1890)

This law has two major provisions.

1. It is illegal, either openly or conspiratorily, for persons to enter into agreements with each other to restrain or restrict interstate trade.

2. It is illegal for any person to monopolize or to attempt to monopolize any portion of interstate commerce.

The Sherman Act was passed over a decade before the development of modern marketing. It remains, however, the basic regulatory force in the legal environment. A violation of the act is the most serious charge that can be brought against an American business. As a result of the general tightening of the interpretation of the words *monopolize* and *attempt to monopolize,* it has become extremely difficult for businesses to achieve the size and power of corporations that existed seventy-five years ago. Most states have similar antitrust laws governing intrastate commerce.

In spite of its importance in American legal history, it was many years before the Sherman Act had significant impact. Some perplexing court decisions as well as the somewhat vague terminology of the Sherman Act resulted in the failure of the Justice Department to initiate a large number of antitrust suits or to win those that were started. It required a series of supplementary laws, as well as the passage of time, to make the law effective.

The Federal Trade Commission Act (1914)

The Federal Trade Commission Act was passed in 1914 to establish an administrative body that would have the responsibility of studying and rendering reliable judgment on antitrust matters. It was hoped, therefore, that the FTC would stop up the loophole in the antitrust laws created by the "rule of reason."[13] The commission was given broad powers to investigate and render judgments on Section 5, which provided that "unfair methods of competition in commerce, and unfair or deceptive acts or practices in commerce, are hereby declared unlawful." Regarding those acts that the commission judged to be "unfair methods of competition," it was empowered to issue cease and desist orders. Until 1938, however, the commission had no power to enforce its orders. In that year, the Wheeler-Lea Amendment to the Federal Trade Commission Act made it mandatory for defendants either to comply to FTC orders or to appeal to the federal courts within sixty days. The amendment also established schedules of fines for violations of commission orders that were upheld

by the courts. Today, the Federal Trade Commission is the most powerful regulatory agency in the legal environment of marketing.

Section 5 of the act has been broadly interpreted to include not only restraints of trade that tend to monopolize but also those practices that injure competitors or the public. For example, the commission has issued complaints and/or cease and desist orders concerning the following:

False advertising of a drug preparation as a cure for rheumatism, arthritis, insomnia, constipation, and blindness

False advertising of vitamin or mineral preparations for tiredness, poor appetite, or weakened resistance, without disclosing that most persons who experience such symptoms will not derive benefit from the use of such preparations

False advertising of a test purporting to show the superiority of a certain toothpaste in preventing tooth decay

Misrepresentation of computer-programming courses through false claims of employment and earnings

Deceptive pricing of clothing, electrical appliances, tires, housewares, auto seat covers, and other merchandise

Misrepresentation of the country of origin and fictitious pricing of perfume

Deceptive use of the terms *guaranteed* and *free*

False claims that a preparation will cure a common cold or shorten its duration

Use of deceptive television demonstrations for gasoline, nasal spray, antifreeze, soups, and toothpaste

Claims that certain dangerous sedatives are harmless and safe to take

---

[13]The "rule of reason" rendered by the Court—see especially *Standard Oil of New Jersey et al.* v. *United States;* 221 U.S. 1 (1911)—adopted the principle that each instance of restraint should be considered on its own merits to determine whether it was "reasonable" (legal) or "unreasonable" (illegal).

Use of misleading statements to designate the caloric content or weight-reducing properties of bread

Preticketing and other fictitious pricing of merchandise

In addition to its regulatory activities, the commission encourages voluntary compliance with the law and endeavors to assist business in improving its own trade practices. When it appears that industry compliance is probable, the commission may organize a trade practice conference at which commission members and industry representatives meet and discuss guidelines for industry behavior. *Trade practice rules* that evolve from these conferences are advisory in nature and do not constitute an extension of specific regulations governing business.

Since 1962, the commission has had the authority to issue trade practice rules that summarize the commission's experience and judgments concerning the statutes it administers. For example, the commission has issued proposed trade practice rules involving mandatory inclusion in advertising of nutritional ingredients of food products and therapeutic characteristics of over-the-counter drugs. The FTC also conducts investigations into industry practices. These eventually may lead to trade practice rules and regulations or to the issuance of reports to assist consumers.

In the 1970s, the FTC assumed a much more aggressive posture than it had in the past. Instead of merely responding to complaints from injured citizens and consumers, it began to initiate actions to regulate and alter the pattern of competitive activity. Not only has its power been extended by Congress, but its commissioners and staff members have taken strong positions on such issues as advertising to children, substantia-

tion of advertising claims, and the use of corrective advertising by advertisers whose claims have been found to be untruthful or misleading. The FTC is not, of course, alone in assuming this protective stance. Other regulatory agencies have followed the same path. The Food and Drug Administration, the Federal Communications Commission, and the Environmental Protection Agency —to name a few—have become very active in taking the initiative to curb or control various aspects of business behavior.

The FTC is specifically responsible for administering the Federal Trade Commission Act; the Clayton Act; the Webb-Pomerene Export Act; the Flammable Fabrics Act; the Wool, Fur, and Textile Fiber Products Labeling Acts, and numerous others.

The Clayton Antitrust Act (1914)

In order to clarify the Sherman Antitrust Act and to prohibit specific monopolistic practices, Congress passed the Clayton Act in 1914. Among the most important provisions of this act are the following:

1. Section 2 prohibits price discrimination. (This section was subsequently extended and clarified by the Robinson-Patman Act of 1936.)
2. Section 3 prohibits tying agreements. This provision makes it illegal to require customers not to handle competitors' products.
3. Section 7 prohibits the acquisition of the capital stock of a competitor where the effect of the acquisition is to restrain trade. (This section was strengthened in 1950 by the Celler-Kefauver Act, which prohibits the acquisition of assets as well as the capital stock of a competitor.)

4. Section 8 prohibits interlocking direc-
    torates of large companies that are in
    competition with each other.

The Robinson-Patman Act (1936)

In spite of its clarification of the Sherman
Act and the provision (in the Federal Trade
Commission Act) for a commission for its
enforcement, the Clayton Act, too, was
subject only to sporadic and limited enforcement. Moreover, not until the growth of
large corporate chains in the late 1920s was
concern voiced over the threat to competition posed by big retailers. As a result of the
growing strength of large retail organizations, the price discrimination provisions in
Section 2(a) of the Clayton Act were revised
and expanded in 1936. Specifically, Congress
was concerned with the following kinds of
activities: giving and receiving discriminatory prices; asking and demanding fictitious
brokerage allowances; and asking, receiving,
and misusing promotional allowances. In
order not to prohibit genuine price concessions based on economies in manufacturing
and marketing, Congress clearly set forth
the conditions under which pricing differences, brokerage allowances, and promotional allowances could be offered.

Section 2(a) prohibits price discrimination—that is, charging a different price for
goods of like grade and quality to one customer than is charged to another where
the effect of the difference may be to lessen competition substantially. The section
provides, however, that the prohibition does
not prevent differentials due to differences
in the cost of manufacturing and marketing.
Nor does it prohibit the normal changes in
price that must be made due to changing
conditions in the market.

Section 2(b) provides a defense against
charges of price discrimination in those instances where a seller can demonstrate that a
lower price was quoted "in good faith" to
match a competitor's offer.

Section 2(c) prohibits dummy brokerage allowances, a subterfuge alleged to have been
practiced by large chain organizations. A
dummy brokerage firm (wholly owned by
the chain but performing nothing but a
paper-passing function) would be paid a
trade discount—thus giving the chain a pref-
erentially lower price.

Section 2(e) further requires that promotional allowances must be offered on a proportional basis to all customers, not just to a
preferred few large accounts.

Section 2(f) states that a buyer is culpable if a
discriminatory price has been knowingly in-
duced or received.

This digest of the provisions of the
Robinson-Patman Act only hints at the tremendous significance of the law. It is the
most direct of all the federal laws affecting
marketing management. It has eliminated
the most flagrant types of unfair pricing, but
it also has severely hampered the use of
pricing as a competitive strategy. On balance, it is a necessary law that the conscientious seller must understand and obey.

Many Federal Trade Commission orders
and court decisions have clarified and modified the Robinson-Patman Act. Two are of
particular note. In the Morton Salt case, the
Court ruled that a lower price to one customer may be discriminatory even if this
customer is not in direct competition with
one that receives a higher price.[14] It could
be discriminatory if the customers of these
two buyers are in competition with each

[14]*FTC* v. *Morton Salt Co.*, 334 U.S. 37 (1948).

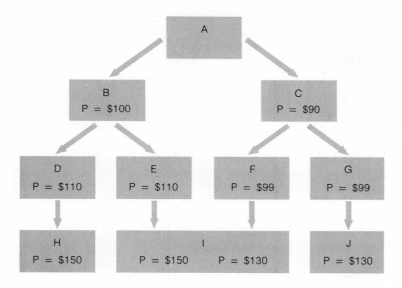

FIGURE 23.1   An example of illegal and legal price discrimination

other (see Figure 23.1). A is a manufacturer selling to two wholesalers, B and C, who are not direct competitors, each having its own separate set of customers. The $10 difference in price is not discriminatory. However, according to the Morton decision, if B and C have customers who are competitors, in this example E and F, the $90 price to C is discriminatory. It would give F an unfair advantage over E, because F can sell at less than can its competitor.

The Borden case dealt with private-label products.[15] In a complicated but typical process of appeals to higher courts, decisions on some issues, and remanding to lower courts for others, it was established that private labeling alone does not create a different product. There must be a physical difference to justify a lower price. We again can use Figure 23.1 to illustrate this point. If the

[15]*Borden Co.* v. *FTC,* 339 F. 2d 953 (7th Cir. 1964), revised 383 U.S. 637 (1966).

product sold to C is physically different than that sold to B, there is no discrimination any place in the system. If, however, the product is physically identical, even though labeled differently, the price difference would be illegal if there are no cost savings and if competition is judged to be adversely affected.

Other Important Federal Legislation

So far we have reviewed the major federal laws affecting marketing. There are many others, but we will not describe them in detail. Table 23.1 gives a summary list. However, two additional areas of federal laws affecting pricing and promotion are of particular importance. The first now has only historical significance but was so much a part of marketing over the past forty years that it deserves our brief attention.

TABLE 23.1   A summary of important federal laws affecting marketing

Act	Year passed	Major provisions
Sherman Act	1890	Prohibits contracts, combinations, and conspiracies in restraint of trade as well as monopolizing or attempts to monopolize
Pure Food and Drug Act	1906	Forbids adulterations and misbranding of foods and drugs sold in interstate commerce; amended in 1938 and 1962
Meat Inspection Act	1907	Provides for inspection of slaughtering, packing, and canning plants that ship products in interstate commerce; amended in 1967 to require states to match federal meat inspection standards
Clayton Act	1914	Prohibits price discrimination and selected practices in acquiring control of competing establishments
Federal Trade Commission Act	1914	Established the FTC, and declares unlawful all unfair methods of competition
Webb-Pomerene Act	1918	Exempts firms engaged in foreign trade from the provisions of the Sherman Act
Capper-Volstead Act	1922	Exempts farm marketing cooperatives from the provisions of the Sherman Act
Agricultural Marketing Agreements Act	1929	First attempt to establish orderly marketing of agricultural commodities; created the Federal Farm Board and encourages the development of farm marketing cooperatives
Perishable Agricultural Commodities Act	1930	Designed to prevent unfair and fraudulent practices in the marketing of perishable agricultural commodities
National Industrial Recovery Act	1933	Although subsequently declared unconstitutional, set the stage for subsequent public policy; act regulated work hours, credit terms, sales below cost, and methods of unfair competition
Robinson-Patman Act	1936	An amendment to Section 2 of the Clayton Act; prohibits price discrimination, dummy brokerage discounts, discriminatory promotional allowances, and buyer acceptance of discriminatory prices
Wheeler-Lea Act	1937	An amendment to the Federal Trade Commission Act, which tightened the commission's enforcement machinery and gives

TABLE 23.1   A summary of important federal laws affecting marketing (*cont.*)

Act	Year passed	Major provisions
		the FTC jurisdiction over advertising of food, drugs, cosmetics, and therapeutic devices
Federal Food, Drugs, and Cosmetic Act	1938	Extends the FTC's authority over packaging, misbranding, and labeling to include food, drugs, cosmetics, and therapeutic devices
Wool Products Labeling Act	1939	Requires that the labels on wool products indicate the percentages of wool, reprocessed wool, and reused wool
Lanham Trademark Act	1946	Provides for the registry of trademarks, collective marks, and certification marks
Celler-Kefauver Antimerger Act	1950	An amendment to the Clayton Act; prohibits the acquisition of assets (as opposed to capital stock) of a competitor if the effect of a merger would tend to lessen competition
Fur Products Labeling Act	1951	Prohibits false advertising and misleading labeling of fur products
Flammable Fabrics Act	1953	Prohibits manufacture and sale of apparel that is dangerously flammable; extended by amendment in 1968 to cover household furnishings, fabrics, and materials
Poultry Products Inspection Act	1957	Empowers the Department of Agriculture to inspect poultry sold in interstate commerce; amended in 1968 to encourage states to upgrade their poultry inspection practices
Automobile Information Disclosure Act	1958	Designed to prevent deceptive pricing practices in the sale of automobiles; requires that dealers affix to new automobiles the manufacturer's suggested retail price of the automobile and factory-installed accessories
Textile Fiber Products Identification Act	1958	Regulates the labeling of textile products by requiring the identification of the different textile fibers by percentage content, the name of the manufacturer or distributor; and the country of origin (if imported); also synthetic fibers must be identified by generic names assigned by the FTC
Hazardous Substances Labeling Act	1960	Requires that the proper labels be attached

TABLE 23.1   A summary of important federal laws affecting marketing (*cont.*)

Act	Year passed	Major provisions
		to toxic, corrosive, irritating, or flammable goods that tend to enter into ordinary household use; labels must be specific as to the nature and extent of the danger involved
Fair Packaging and Labeling Act	1966	Through mandatory and discretionary provisions assures accurate labeling and informative packaging of most household products
National Traffic and Motor Vehicle Safety Act	1966	Directs the Secretary of Transportation to issue safety standards for new and used motor vehicles
Consumer Credit Protection Act	1968	Requires disclosure of credit terms and annual rates of interest of finance charges on loans and installment purchases
Consumer Protection Act	1970	Provides protection by amending the Federal Trade Commission Act to enable the FTC to take corrective action against deceptive practices merely "affecting" interstate commerce; permits the attorney general to bring actions and following this or FTC action, for consumers to file individual or class suits for damages
Fair Credit Reporting Act	1970	Requires that a consumer's credit report contain only accurate, relevant, and recent information, and that it must be handled confidentially
Consumer Product Safety Act	1972	Created the Consumer Product Safety Commission with power to set safety standards or otherwise to regulate the marketing of unsafe products
Warranty-FTC Improvement Act	1975	Establishes minimum disclosure standards for written consumer-product warranties; identifies minimum content standards; and allows FTC to prescribe rules governing the use of product warranties
Consumer Goods Pricing Act	1975	Repealed both federal resale price maintenance enabling laws—the Miller-Tydings Act of 1937 and the McGuire-Keogh Act of 1952

The Miller-Tydings Resale Price Maintenance Act (1937), the McGuire-Keogh Fair-Trade Act (1952), and the Consumers Goods Pricing Act (1975)   The Miller-Tydings Act, an amendment to the Sherman Antitrust Act, exempted vertical price-fixing contracts from the antitrust laws wherever such contracts were legal in the respective states. Between the years of 1931 and 1937, state fair-trade laws were passed in forty-five states. These laws were effective in restraining price cutting because of the *nonsigners clause* which stated that if a manufacturer succeeded in signing a resale price maintenance contract with even one retailer in a state, all other retailers were bound by the same contractual agreement. In 1951, the Supreme Court ruled the Miller-Tydings Act did not apply to the nonsigner provisions of the various fair-trade laws. In the following year, Congress passed the McGuire Act, an amendment to Section 5 of the Federal Trade Commission Act, specifically to restore the nonsigners provision to the federal fair-trade legislation. The constitutionality of the McGuire-Keogh Act subsequently was upheld in the courts, but efforts to pass a federal fair-trade law were defeated permanently in 1963. The Miller-Tydings Act and the McGuire-Keogh Act were repealed by the Consumer Goods Pricing Act of 1975. Resale price maintenance by then was out of vogue and unenforceable. It passed quietly out of existence.[16]

The Lanham Trademark Act (1946)   The Lanham Act summarizes the evolving federal law relating to trademarks and sets forth the procedure required for registration and protection. The law provides for primary registration in the Principal Register or secondary registration in the Supplemental Register. Registry of a trademark in the Principal Register is held to be prima facie evidence of exclusive ownership.[17] Registration in the Supplemental Register is for information purposes only. Under the Lanham Act, four types of trademarks may be registered.

1. Trademarks, which are distinctive designs identifying a product, that may be imprinted on the product, on its package, or on the manufacturer's literature
2. Service marks, identifying the services of one person
3. Certification marks, identifying an independent agency that certifies to the quality or performance of another party
4. Collective marks, used by cooperative groups or other associations

The Legal Aspects of Consumerism

To this point we have considered laws designed primarily either to regulate or benefit business. What about consumer protection?

---

[16]For two articles recapitulating the stormy history of fair trade, see M. L. Bell and D. Hays, "Fair Trade, 1931–1975: An Obituary," *Proceedings of the Southern Marketing Association, 1977,* pp. 25–28; and J. C. Johnson and L. E. Boone, "Farewell to Fair Trade," *MSU Business Topics,* Spring 1976, pp. 22–30.

[17]Although registration of a trademark is prima facie evidence of ownership, the trademark generally must be used to be protected. Moreover, prior use of a trademark usually is grounds for challenging the registration of any particular trademark. Ordinarily, if a firm uses a trademark for a period of five years without being contested, its legal right to permanent registration is acknowledged. Care must be taken in usage to avoid having the trademark ruled generic by the courts. Such a fate befell aspirin, celluloid, cellophane, lanolin, and escalator. The successful use of a trade name can lead to even more serious problems. In 1976 the FTC issued a complaint against the Borden Company requiring it to license the use by others of its trade name Real Lemon on the grounds that Borden's exclusive right to the name constituted a restraint of trade in the market for reconstituted lemon juice. The issue has not been finally resolved.

Over the years, a number of laws specifically intended to benefit consumers directly have been passed. While antitrust legislation appears most directly to protect competitive businesses, there are consumer benefits as well, including lower prices. More specifically, however, federal laws have been passed that concern consumers directly.

One of the earliest consumer-oriented laws was the Pure Food and Drug Act (1906), which subsequently was amended to cover cosmetics and therapeutic devices (1938) and to tighten federal inspection and regulation of drug marketing (1962). A Federal Meat Inspection Act was passed in 1907. A Poultry Products Inspection Act was enacted in 1957, and amendments to both the meat and poultry laws were passed in 1967 and in 1968. Over the years, a number of federal laws have been passed governing the labeling and advertising of products. These include the Wool Products Labeling Act (1939), the Fur Products Labeling Act (1951), the Automobile Information Disclosure Act (1958), the Textile Fiber Products Identification Act (1958), and the Hazardous Substances Labeling Act (1960). A Fair Packaging and Labeling Act, frequently called the *truth in packaging law*, was passed in 1966. Two years later a *truth in lending* bill, the Consumer Credit Protection Act of 1968, was enacted. Two national commissions were established in the mid-1960s; one was the President's Commission on Food Marketing, and the second was the National Commission on Product Safety. The latter was established to study the scope and adequacy of measures to protect consumers from unreasonable risk of injuries caused by hazardous household products. The National Traffic and Motor Vehicle Safety Act of 1966 established temporary federal safety standards for new automobiles. Modifications of these standards are issued by the Department of Transportation from time to time. Federal regulation of cigarette marketing was initiated by the Federal Cigarette Labeling and Advertising Act of 1965, which required that cigarette packages carry the warning, "Caution: Cigarette smoking may be hazardous to your health." By subsequent legislation, Congress instructed the FCC to tighten the printed warning and to ban all advertising of cigarettes from television and radio by January 2, 1971.

The year 1972 brought the passage of the Consumer Product Safety Act. This law created the Consumer Product Safety Commission, an independent federal regulatory agency that has the responsibility for establishing mandatory product safety standards to reduce the unreasonable risk of injury to consumers. It also has the authority to ban hazardous products. The only product categories that are exempt from the jurisdiction of the commission are items regulated by other government agencies or departments.[18]

It is apparent from this list of federal laws affecting marketing that the tempo of consumer protection legislation increased markedly in the 1960s. And, it is reasonable to expect that Congress will continue to devote considerable attention to the area of consumer protection.

The Competitive Environment

Paradoxically, competition is at once an opportunity and a barrier in marketing. It is the

[18]W. Jensen, Jr., E. M. Kazze, and D. N. Stern, "The Consumer Product Safety Act: A Special Case in Consumerism," *Journal of Marketing*, October 1973, pp. 68–71.

struggle among firms for shares of the market that creates competition. Marketing success usually depends on the skill with which a company succeeds in creating and maintaining a competitive advantage. Marketing failures are often the result of competitors' superior accomplishments. Competition, on the one hand, appears intense.

On the other hand, the fostering of monopoly is one of a number of complaints about marketing. Changes in competitive behavior have resulted in a shift in emphasis from price to nonprice competition. This new competition is notably different from the kind of competition presumed to exist in the models of classical economic theory.

One of the purposes of this chapter is to resolve this apparent disagreement concerning the nature of the competitive environment of marketing. In large part, the disagreement stems from differences in points of view. Hopefully, these differing perspectives can be blended into a single meaningful concept of competition.

Two Views of Competition

The economic view of competition In economics, competition is a condition of rivalry. Depending on the market circumstances, this rivalry is either perfect or imperfect. *Perfect competition* is said to exist when no single seller or buyer is large enough to exercise an appreciable influence over the market. The following conditions create perfect competition:

1. A large number of buyers and sellers
2. Homogeneous (undifferentiated) products
3. Freedom of market entry and exit
4. Accurate knowledge on the part of buyers and sellers

5. Rational decisions to buy or sell

These requirements of perfect competition may seem very unrealistic; and most economists agree that perfect competition seldom is encountered. Nevertheless, the concept of perfect competition is helpful for understanding some aspects of marketing. Bach suggests that it roughly approximates behavior in a number of important marketing situations. He says, "Most of agriculture, broad areas of retailing, wholesaling, and service establishments and important sectors of manufacturing where a moderate scale of plant is big enough for efficient production, come reasonably close to the pure competition model." [19]

Imperfect competition exists in any market where one or more of the conditions of perfect competition are absent. The two most commonly encountered departures from perfect competition are

1. A limited number of buyers and sellers
2. Differentiated products

The term *imperfect* does not imply that such competition is less desirable. In fact in the modern American economy where so much attention is paid to the development of new and differentiated products, the best competitors are to be found engaged in competition of a decidedly imperfect type.

Various kinds of competitive situations may be encountered in the American economy, as indicated by the model of the various types of market structures in Table 23.2. In this table, two principal determinants of the condition of competition are shown: the number of sellers and the degree of product differentiation. Although the terminology

[19]L. Bach, *Economics* (Englewood Cliffs, N.J.: Prentice-Hall, 1963), p. 371.

TABLE 23.2 Economic concepts of competition

Number of sellers	Extent of Differentiation	
	Undifferentiated products	Differentiated products
One seller	Monopoly	
Few sellers	Undifferentiated oligopoly	Differentiated oligopoly
Many sellers	Perfect competition	Monopolistic competition

used is borrowed from economic theory, most of these terms frequently are encountered in marketing and should be recognized as a part of our marketing concept of competition.

Inspection of Table 23.2 shows us that under perfect competition there is no product differentiation. We might ask, "What marketing opportunities exist for such a firm?" Virtually none, because if a firm succeeds in differentiating its product or service it moves into the category of imperfect competition. The only opportunity for the perfect competitor is the chance to operate more efficiently. However, with perfect knowledge this advantage would quickly disappear, and all firms would operate at the lowest possible costs. In fact, this is the equilibrium toward which perfect competition is presumed to tend.

Contrary to popular opinion, monopolists do not always sell differentiated products. The condition of monopoly may result from the absence of other sellers or from exclusive control of an economic resource, such as a raw material or a mode of transport. A monopolist always faces the possibility of potential competition, either from new entrants into the market or from remote substitutes. For obvious reasons, monopolies are carefully regulated by public policy.

In today's economy we frequently encounter *oligopoly,* in which a limited number

of sellers compete. An oligopolist can sell either a differentiated or an undifferentiated product. The *differentiated oligopolist* is in the most enviable position. Some latitude exists in pricing and there are opportunities to compete on a nonprice basis as well. GM is a good example. The *undifferentiated oligopolist,* a steel company for instance, usually is caught on one of two horns of a difficult competitive dilemma: Either the company can run the serious risk of a price war by lowering prices or it can run afoul of the law by attempting to maintain price stability. Undifferentiated oligopolists, like perfect competitors, search constantly for ways to compete in terms of product difference—usually with little success.

As a guide to enterprise competitive behavior, the economist's theory of the firm leaves untouched many of the subtleties and practicalities of real-life competition. These aspects must be added to create a total viewpoint toward competition that is meaningful and helpful in marketing management.

The business view of competition The business person views competition as a struggle among firms for shares of the market. The attainment of market share, its defense, or its increase are major objectives in marketing planning. On occasion, share competition among firms becomes so fierce or so unbalanced that either government or the competitors themselves act to control it.

Cooperative efforts among businesses to control or limit competition sometimes are attempted. Most horizontal agreements of this type are illegal, although some cooperative endeavors (as in agriculture) actually are encouraged under the law. Competition, rather than cooperation, is generally preferred by most marketing managers. This is because the ability to act independently and to take advantage of competitive opportunities is sacrificed when one firm agrees to act jointly with others. Moreover, there is usually a maverick that refuses to go along with the rest of the group, and this split in group solidarity often spells the breakdown of a collusive effort.

Competition and Marketing

The occasion to compete is a basic marketing opportunity. Almost every marketing effort has as its direct or indirect goal the creation of a differential advantage. Peculiarly, some persons engaged in marketing fail to recognize how important a clear-cut competitive philosophy can be. Two divergent schools of thought exist. There always has been a fraternity of executives who feel that it is better to live and let live and, if necessary, to meet secretly with competitors in order to avoid open conflict with them. A second group of executives spurns this philosophy and believes that the only ethical and economic course is to meet head-on in vigorous competition. Members of this second group revel in the prospect of competition, and well they should because success is often directly related to the determination to compete aggressively.

Some managers trained in nonmarketing sectors of business tend to shy away from competition because of their lack of familiarity with it. The president of a small manufacturing company once remarked about his firm's marketing effort that "competing was the last thing that we learned to do well in this company." By this he meant that products were designed from an engineering point of view, priced on a cost-plus basis, and promoted without regard to the opportunities to carve out a sizable market share. Years of steady but only modest growth brought the realization that something was lacking in the company's marketing effort —it had no competitive vigor.

A Marketing Approach to Competition

The proper marketing approach to competition involves a two-step procedure. The first step requires the choice among several competitive philosophies. The second is the selection of an appropriate competitive technique.

Competitive philosophies Of the three possible philosophical approaches to competition, the first is the *aggressive philosophy*. This attitude toward competition is taken by those who believe that the ultimate success of a marketing program depends more on the intensity and skill with which it is promoted than on the merits of the program itself. It is well established that numerous good products have not succeeded in the market while many mediocre products have achieved amazing success. The margin of difference usually has been the agressiveness with which the respective products have been marketed.

A second competitive philosophy is *conservative*. A competitor acting under this philosophy does nothing to upset the apple cart. A constant but moderate competitive pressure is exerted in order to maintain market share. But the firm does not compete vigorously enough to cut deeply into competitors' sales. Adoption of the conservative competitive philosophy results in modest and slow-paced product introductions. It also is possible for this type of competitive philosophy to prevail in a period of market growth. As long as the total market expands, an individual competitor need not extend selling efforts in order to grow. On some occasions, a firm may aggressively promote a new product but subsequently lapse into a conservative approach. The introductory momentum carries it forward. However, even the neutral competitor tolerates no substantial decrease in market share. In order to maintain satisfactory sales and earnings, a firm will react firmly and with adequate strength against the threats of competitors.

A third philosophical approach to competition is *passive*. The passive competitor is content to engage only in the amount of competition required to survive. The passive competitor relies on industry growth to increase sales. Reacting slowly to competitive intrusions, the passive competitor hesitates to engage in defensive activities even when market share and sales decline. It is forced to retreat to ever smaller segments of the market until a point is reached where it must withdraw completely.

Competitive techniques   The second step in developing a competitive approach is the selection of a competitive technique. There are three methods of competing in marketing, and these can be used separately or in combination. They are (1) price competition, (2) indirect price competition, and (3) nonprice competition. *Price competition* involves the struggle for market share by the strategic use of price. Increased sales as a result of price reductions are based on two economic facts. First, overall consumer demand may respond to lower prices. All firms enjoy greater sales. Increased sales as a result of price competition also are based on the fact that each seller, in some respects, provides a differentiated product, which possesses its own unique demand. Increases in sales in this case are achieved as a result of customers' shifting from one company to another because of price differentials between firms. It is this second aspect of pricing that makes it an especially effective competitive weapon. It might be assumed that all an injured competitor need do is match an antagonist's price reduction in order to recover the lost sales volume. While this frequently occurs, often it is not possible. Differences in cost structure, company policy, and distributors' margins can make it unprofitable or impossible to meet a competitor's lower price. Thus, a firm with a cost advantage or some special market flexibility is in a position to increase market share by the use of direct price competition.

Indirect price competition refers to a competitive situation in which a seller offers customers a benefit that does not take the form of an outright price concession but has much the same economic effect. For instance, if a seller offers to price goods on a delivered basis (for example, F.O.B. customer's warehouse) the transportation savings to the buyer result in a lower net delivered cost of the goods. A buyer is very likely to order from a vendor offering such an indirect price benefit. Similar types of selling benefits include advertising allowances, dealer training programs, free merchandising services, and the like. Obviously, such benefits can be offered by several competing firms. However, in some cases a seller may not be in a position to offer comparable indirect price benefits, and the firm that is able to do so achieves a corresponding competitive advantage. For example, a company with a broad line of frozen-food products can afford to deliver directly to large customers by combining orders for several products into a single truckload. A one-product company could not do this.

Nonprice competition includes all efforts to increase market share other than by price changes and indirect price concessions. The definition is broad and involves hundreds of specific methods of increasing company sales. These methods include merchandising, advertising, personal selling, and sales promotion. Even a casual observation of American marketing highlights the fact that nonprice techniques are used extensively. The wide extent of product, service and enterprise differentiation suggests that all sellers eagerly search for means and methods of competing on the basis of differentiated offerings. Even a superficial investigation of the market reveals that ultimate consumers and industrial customers alike are bombarded incessantly with hard-hitting and persuasive selling campaigns. Estimates of the dollars spent each year on advertising and personal selling suggest that these may add up to as much as 10 per cent of the gross national product. The conclusion appears irrefutable: Marketing is dominated by nonprice competition.

Marketing and Nonprice Competition

We have seen that marketing is dominated by nonprice competition. It is important to understand why this is so. The explanation of nonprice competition in the American market is not simply that many sellers prefer to compete this way. The reasons for it lie, rather, in some basic marketing factors explaining business and consumer behavior.

Foundations of nonprice competition   Probably the most important factor influencing the use of nonprice competitive techniques by marketing firms is the *nature of the ultimate consumer.* Differences in consumer tastes and needs are pronounced. The wide range of requirements and tastes among consumers ordinarily can best be satisfied only by differentiated products. The constant desire of consumers for new and different products or services gives rise to the efforts of sellers to provide these satisfactions. It also is commonly accepted in marketing circles that consumers tend to buy on the basis of emotional considerations. Most nonprice competitive efforts are closely tuned to this type of buying. Finally, the modern American consumer enjoys unprecedented levels of income. The affluence of the typical American consumer permits acting on many considerations other than purely economic ones.

The *nature of the marketing system* also explains the importance of nonprice competition. The goals of most marketing firms are closely tied to survival and growth. Maintenance and increase in market share are common measures of success. Product, service, or enterprise differentiation provides the means by which growth is achieved. The competing firm also is encouraged to engage in nonprice competition by its desire to avoid the hazards of direct, and even of indirect, price competition. Because a high degree of substitutability among competing products exists, price reductions on the part of one firm usually are quickly matched by competitors. The result is almost inevitably a decline in revenue and little change in market share for each firm. The dangers of runaway price wars are well known.

An environment, as we have seen, is composed of cultural and material elements. The highly refined selling techniques that are necessary to successful nonprice competition, but absolutely unimportant in price competition, are vital elements in the marketing environment. The existence of an elaborate system of mass media provides the channels through which nonprice competitive efforts are directed. An advanced understanding of human behavior has led to the development of refined skills in persuasion and sales supervision.

The legal and ethical environments in which marketing takes place tolerate and occasionally encourage nonprice competition. The illegal status of discriminatory pricing and the prohibition of cutthroat pricing has turned some sellers to nonprice competitive methods. New legislation and recent administrative rulings have made it increasingly difficult to administer some aspects of nonprice competition, such as cooperative advertising, contests, and other special promotions. The fact remains, however, that the law recognizes and allows nonprice competition. The ethical climate in which marketing takes place is more hostile. Some consumers are irritated, others are amused, a few are misled, and a good many are benefited by these nonprice efforts. Most consumers accept the fact that sellers compete vigorously on nonprice terms for their loyalty.

Thus the marketing establishment, coming into contact with its marketing environments, is driven naturally toward nonprice competition. This is not to say that price is unimportant in the marketing effort; it merely substantiates the conclusion that competition in the American economy is essentially of a nonprice nature.

The economic and social effects of nonprice competition   It is important for the marketing manager to be aware of the economic and social consequences of competitive activities. The economic consequences are objective and less controversial than are the social ones. However, some disagreement on economic consequences exists. The principal argument hinges on whether aggregate demand is influenced by nonprice competitive activities. The question is not merely academic. An increasing standard of living requires constantly expanding production and consumption levels. Economists generally concede that in the absence of innovation an economy tends toward stagnation rather than growth. This stabilization of the economy, it usually is assumed, also occurs at levels of economic activity when some factors (notably labor) are not fully employed. Taking a positive position, a marketing economist might contend that marketing opportunities give rise to both innovative possibilities and full resource utilization. By stimulating consumer wants and directing a constant flow of new and improved products to satisfy these wants, it is believed that growth pressures are injected into the system. The result is not only increased output but increased real income with which consumers can satisfy their wants.

There are other economic consequences of nonprice competition as well. A narrow viewpoint suggests that prices in general are higher when nonprice competition is used. If prices are administered, criticisms of output restriction also are encountered. Some economists believe too that nonprice competition results in meaningless waste. Evidence cited includes the duplications of modestly differentiated products and the accelerated obsolesence of products replaced by new but only slightly differentiated versions.

Ethical criticisms of nonprice competition also are raised. Reductions in product quality and the superficial differentiation of features give rise to arguments that consumers are not benefited by nonprice competitive efforts. It is suggested also that nonprice competition tends to misinform an already poorly informed public. Information in nonprice competitive programs frequently is biased and sometimes is misleading. Falsification occurs. The commercialization and degradation of entertainment and educational media are condemned. The materialistic basis of modern American life and its corresponding de-emphasis of higher values frequently is attributed to the efforts of sellers to dramatize unreal and emotional product benefits. To the marketing manager, such criticisms often are difficult to understand. The important point, however, is that they constitute part of the public environment, and they are largely directed at the nonprice competitor.

Nonprice competition does benefit the individual firm. Maintenance of market share and increases in share at the expense of competitors are everyday occurrences. Increases in sales and company growth are the inevitable results of successful nonprice competition. But it has a corresponding impact on costs. Increased sales through nonprice competition usually are dearly won. Whether nonprice competition is profitable is the important issue. Nonprice competition is profitable only when the margins produced by the effort more than offset the marketing costs incurred. It is this important relationship among incremental marketing effort, additional marketing costs, and resulting profit that is the key to profitable marketing management.

Restraints on nonprice competiton   Restraints on nonprice competitive activities that have resulted from economic and social criticism are important. Some of these take the form of legislative, judicial, or administrative rulings as to what methods of nonprice competi-

tition can be used. Voluntary restraints are occasionally imposed. Some companies have policies that govern the types of nonprice competition in which they engage. Advertising media reserve the right to refuse untruthful or distasteful advertising copy. Better Business Bureaus require members to conform to strict rules governing the use of advertising. Nonmembers are encouraged to comply as well, and local bureaus often maintain records of consumer complaints about particular firms. Self-regulation of advertising at both the national and local levels is attempted by advertising review boards composed of industry and public members who investigate and attempt to resolve complaints about advertising before the matter becomes an issue in court. In the last analysis, a firm operating under the marketing concept finds itself conscientiously attempting to govern its methods of nonprice competition in order to increase the probability of long-run customer satisfaction. Ultimately, its survival depends on the same kind of relation with the rest of its environment. Responding to external and internal pressures, a firm must adapt its methods of nonprice competition to conform to the existing legal and ethical codes.

Summary

A new age in marketing—an age of public and consumer concern—may well be dawning. On the other hand, the development of the new consumerism in the 1960s may be only another stage in the long cycle of history. Public concern over business, particularly marketing, has appeared and reappeared with almost predictable regularity, and whether the present excitement represents a basic shift or a temporary interest is not yet clear.

In this chapter we have looked at the public, legal, and competitive environments of marketing. A most significant development in the public environment of marketing has been the emergence of the new consumerism. Actually consumerism is not new. The so-called consumer movement can be traced to the early years of the twentieth century. The decade of the 1960s saw only an era of new criticism. New opinion leaders arose, and a new bill of consumer complaints was drawn up.

Business responded defensively at first, but then turned to more positive programs. Government responded with new legislation and administrative changes. Most important, there was an awakening of marketing's social responsibility, which goes beyond the marketing concept to the acceptance of the ideas that marketing is not an end in itself and that it is not the exclusive province of business management. It must provide goods and services for consumers, but it also must serve society. It must have a genuine concern for the consumers' welfare.

Public policy reflects opinion, perhaps not very promptly and possibly not always accurately; but it is the formal expression of the will of society. It is manifested in law, judicial decisions, and administrative action. Thus each of the three major branches of government plays an important part in the development of public policy.

The legal framework of marketing is complex. Although there are laws that affect marketing at every level of government, the U.S. Code is the most important, since it governs the marketing of goods in interstate commerce. There are a number of basic federal laws that provide the legal foundation of marketing practice. The Sherman Act, the Clayton Act, the Federal Trade Commission Act, and the Robinson-Patman Act are the most important. There are also other selected laws, particularly those involving the protection of consumers, that have a direct bearing on the way in which marketing is carried out.

Marketing takes place in a competitive environment; but this environment is viewed quite differently by economists and businesspeople. The economist sees perfect competition as the normative condition prevailing among many firms selling more or less identical products. Any deviation from this condition is considered imperfect; and the economist sees a great deal of imperfection in competition. The businessperson, on the other hand, sees competition as a rivalry among firms for market share. This is the competition that characterizes contemporary American marketing.

A company's marketing approach to competiton involves two elements. There is the philosophy and there is the technique. A competitive philosophy can be aggressive, conservative, or passive. The major techniques of competition in marketing are price, indirect price, and nonprice competition. Of these, nonprice competition is the most prevalent. It has both economic and social consequences that can lead to complaints about marketing practice. Restraints against the potential abuses of nonprice competition have been introduced through public policy and by the voluntary actions of competitors themselves.

Questions and Problems

1. Investigate the status of the consumerist movement in your state. What public interest groups are functioning?

What public agencies exist for the purpose of protecting consumers? What position does the political leadership take on consumerist issues?

2. Several issues in consumerism were mentioned in this chapter. Have any new issues arisen since this book was published? What are they? What are their implications to marketing management?

3. The chapter mentions four consumer rights that John F. Kennedy proclaimed. Name at least two others that you think might be appropriate. How would you suggest that these rights be guaranteed to consumers.

4. It is widely recognized that some consumers take advantage of the marketing companies that sell them goods and services—for example, unreasonable claims for service long after the warranty period has expired, excessive exercise of the privilege of returning goods, shoplifting, and slow or non-payment for goods purchased on credit. Do you think there ought to be a marketers' bill of rights to protect them against unscrupulous or dishonest consumers?

5. Assume you are the president of a consumer-products company that has been the object of a good deal of consumer complaint. What organizational plans might you consider to help remedy the situation?

6. Why is the Sherman Antitrust Act of such fundamental importance to marketing?

7. At a sales training session, a number of questions were asked by the trainees about what they could and could not do

in the way of competing. Specifically, they wanted to know

a. If they could lower a price to one customer and not to another
b. If they could offer a cumulative quantity discount
c. If they could work up a special advertising allowance for an important customer
d. If they had to have proof of a competitor's lower price before matching it

How would you answer each of these questions?

8. You are the president of a food-products company, and you want to acquire a chain of retail food outlets. Your personal lawyer has told you that the law only prohibits horizontal mergers and that this vertical acquisition would be perfectly legal. Would you seek another legal opinion? Why or why not?

9. You are the marketing director of an electronics company that sells such products as television sets, high-fidelity equipment, and the like through a nationwide organization of retail stores. Exclusive agency contracts have been used with each local outlet, and you have long required your agents to carry only your line. One of your important outlets in Los Angeles, however, recently has taken on a competing line of portable television sets. What should you do about it? How will the legal framework of marketing affect your decision?

10. Since much competitive activity is intended to influence the prospective buyer to purchase a particular brand, isn't this kind of competition contrary to the idea of customer orientation? In

fact, aren't competition and customer orientation basically incompatible?

11. Suppose that you were in charge of introducing a new frozen dessert. (Frozen dessert is similar to ice cream except that it is made with vegetable fat instead of cream.) Recognizing that the success of this product probably will depend on the skill with which it is differentiated, list all of the ways this could be done. Select those methods of differentiation that you would recommend using and briefly explain the reasons for your choices.

12. Identify at least one major American company that follows one of the following competitive philosophies:
a. The aggressive philosophy
b. The conservative philosophy
c. The passive philosophy
What was your basis for judgment? To what factors might you attribute the differences in the competitive approach taken by these firms?

24

Frontiers of Marketing Management

Marketing, as we learned in Chapter 1, can be looked at from a macroviewpoint. In part, the purpose of this chapter is to escape the traditional boundaries of the micromarketing system and explore the broader applications of marketing concepts. In doing this, we will cross several of the frontiers of marketing management.

In part, the purpose of this chapter also is to fill in some holes in our coverage of traditional marketing management. These holes are not massive gaps; they are areas of marketing management that purposely have not been stressed. The focus in this book has been on the marketing of consumer goods. Reference to the marketing of services and to the marketing of industrial products has been made, but these areas of marketing management have not been considered separately. Two considerations led to this approach. First, all readers of this book are consumers, already familiar with the market-

ing of consumer goods as seen through the buyer's eyes. This frame of reference has made it possible to discuss marketing in ways that generally are recognized by most people. This is a tremendous advantage to any writer, and the author freely has taken advantage of it. The second reason for focusing almost exclusively on consumer-goods marketing is that the marketing of services and industrial goods is not substantially different. True there are differences, and we touch on some of these in this chapter. But the essential character of marketing is the same. In the interest of simplicity and relevance to your frame of reference, therefore, this book has not yet probed either of these important areas of marketing. A second purpose of this chapter, then, is to devote some attention to them.

Beyond the frontier of traditional marketing management lie three other relatively unexplored areas. The first of these is the area of international and multinational marketing. We will look at this vast expanse of marketing opportunity in a section called "Beyond the Twelve-Mile Limit." Past a second frontier lies the field of not-for-profit marketing. As we discovered in Chapter 1, the profit motive traditionally has been closely tied to the marketing concept. There are many who believe that this relationship is not mandatory and that marketing concepts and practices can be applied in the not-for-profit sector. We will look at this application of marketing in a section called "Beyond Profits."

At the outer limits of marketing, we discover an area that opens the mind to its almost unlimited applications. The view of marketing as a social process is concerned with the most fundamental reason for the existence of any social institution—marketing included—which is the fulfillment in the best possible manner of all people's needs and wants. The section that deals with this frontier of marketing carries the name generally associated with this broad view of marketing's purpose and role—"Societal Marketing."

Beyond the Marketing of Consumer Goods

As we noted above, there are two important areas of marketing management that have not been stressed in this book. They are the marketing of consumer services and the marketing of industrial goods and services. These do not represent fields where massive differences in marketing methods are encountered. But the distinctions are important enough to require some discussion before we complete the subject of marketing.

The Marketing of Consumer Services

A *service* is an act performed by one person or organization on behalf of another. In marketing, a *service establishment* is a business that has as its purpose the satisfaction of customer wants by performing acts for which a customer is willing to pay a price. Historically, the term *service* was used to describe a number of so-called free benefits that sellers provided their customers. These free services included such things as alterations to garments, delivery, and credit. Whether these services actually were free is debatable, since the cost of performing these acts had to be covered in the prices charged for the goods that the merchants sold. In view of this, these services could more properly be considered extensions of the merchant's product offering—a concept consistent with the definition of *product* presented in Chapter 9.

There always have been opportunities to market services.[1] Today's hotels and resorts find their forerunners in the inns and taverns patronized by travelers hundreds of years ago. The blacksmiths of the eighteenth century are the auto mechanics of the twentieth.

[1]One of the first efforts to describe the marketing of consumer services is found in a monograph by D. D. Parker, *The Marketing of Consumer Services* (Seattle: University of Washington Bureau of Business Research, 1960) For more current discussions, see G. L. Shastack, "Breaking Free from Product Marketing," *Journal of Marketing,* April 1977, pp. 73–80; and W. E. Sasser, "Match Supply and Demand in Service Industries," *Harvard Business Review,* November 1976, pp. 133–140. A very interesting treatment of service marketing in Great Britain is found in R. Lewis, *The New Service Society* (London: Longman, 1973). An approach to the marketing of health services (a hot topic at present) is found in G. Zaltman and I. Vertinsky, "Health Service Marketing: A Suggested Model," *Journal of Marketing,* July 1971, pp. 19–27. And, an excellent summary of service marketing, including a comprehensive bibliography, is found in Englier et al., *Marketing Consumer Services: New Insights* (Cambridge: Marketing Science Institute, 1977).

The supersonic jet is not really so different from the graceful clipper ship of a hundred years ago. Technology has changed the form but not the function of the service establishment.

Services are not completely divorced from products, just as products cannot be separated from the services that are offered in connection with their sale. Restaurants prepare and serve food. Dry cleaners return garments on hangers and in sanitary bags. But the service dominates the offering and the product simply augments it. There almost always is a product-service mix; and in the case of service marketing, it is the service elements that dominate.

A good case can be made that the marketing of goods is actually the marketing of a service. What does the customer want—a thing or a satisfaction? A famous writer on the art of selling once said, "Sell the 'sizzle' and not the steak." In the final analysis, the delivery of a satisfaction is the rendering of a service. As the marketer focuses on this aspect of the task, the differences between goods marketing and services marketing fade rapidly.[2] However, this distinction is not clearly understood by all, and there are some specific aspects of service marketing that deserve our attention.

Extent of service marketing   Table 24.1 presents a summary of service establishments and their receipts in 1972 as reported by the U.S. Department of Commerce. In 1972 there were 1.4 million service establishments, and this does not include service-delivering institutions such as hospitals,

schools, banks, transportation companies, and the like. Calculation of the aggregate amount of service marketing is just about impossible, but the data in Table 24.1 suggest that the overall sum must be very large indeed.

Unique aspects of service marketing   While we have been stressing the similarities between goods marketing and services marketing, it is true that there are some interesting points of dissimilarity. These differences are that (1) services are intangible, (2) services suffer from lack of uniformity in quality, and (3) services are perishable.

It is readily apparent that a service is not a tangible commodity. An act is not a thing although, as noted above, it may be accompanied by a physical product. Because a service is intangible, it cannot be inspected prior to use; it cannot be packaged; it cannot be transported or stored. All that is done to physical things in marketing is irrelevent to the marketing of services.

Since a product is intangible, its ownership is hard to establish. It cannot, in the conventional sense, be resold. However, a *claim* on a service may be established. Tickets to a Broadway show or to an Islander hockey game provide good examples. Such claims can be transferred to another, and there are resellers of service claims—both merchant and agent middlemen.

Services, or acts, generally must be performed by one person for another. Since each person's need is somewhat unique and each server is likely to develop a special way of rendering a service, it is not strange that there is little uniformity in services offered. Consider hair styling, for example. Each customer has a set of physical characteristics and need perceptions to which the stylist brings a personal set of skills and attitudes. The quality of service that eventually is

---

[2]One student struggled valiantly to demonstrate the differences, only to conclude that goods marketing and service marketing are very similar. E. M. Johnson, *Are Goods and Services Different? An Exercise in Marketing Theory,* unpublished DBA dissertation (St. Louis, Mo.: Washington University, 1969).

TABLE 24.1   Service establishments in the United States, 1972

	Number of establishments	Receipts in millions of dollars
Hotels, motels, and so on	79.7	10,638
Personal services	506.4	14,361
Business services	320.7	36,355
Auto repair and service	169.0	12,081
Other repair service	149.0	5,941
Motion pictures	21.5	4,804
Other amusement	124.3	8,635
All services	1,370.6	92,815

Source: U.S. Census of Selected Service Industries, 1972.

rendered depends on how well the server is able to adapt to the needs of the customer. In contrast to the relatively objective satisfaction that a tangible product may be expected to deliver, the degree to which a service lives up to a customer's expectations is very hard to determine. This fact also contributes to the general belief that the quality of service delivery is variable and often poor. The problem is particularly vexing to companies engaged in the marketing of consumer services. If the quality of service sags for even a short period of time, this tends to drive customers away permanently. Notice how many service establishments encourage their patrons to report on the quality of service—obviously in an effort to quickly identify a potential problem.

The third characteristic of a service is that it is extremely perishable. Some commodities also are perishable—fruits and vegetables and fashion goods, for example. But consider how perishable is a service. An unfilled seat in an airplane, an unoccupied hospital bed, an unsold thirty seconds of television commercial time—these potential services can never be rendered again once the single opportunity has passed. The service cannot be stored until another time

when the demand is greater. A service is perishable in the extreme. This places a severe burden on the service marketer to forecast accurately and then to use as much creativity as possible to overcome the problem. Consider how some airlines have solved part of the underload problem. A leisure fare is offered that does not guarantee a reserved seat. If a leisure fare–ticketed traveler arrives at the gate and discovers that other customers have taken all of the available space, the airline stands ready to refund the price of the ticket and to transport the traveler on the next flight at no cost. What is the advantage to the airline if it has to carry the passenger free? Actually not much. But, because some travelers make duplicate reservations and because a goodly number fail to show up at the gate, there usually is room for the leisure traveler. And the leisure fare, although less than the regular fare, is almost all profit. Unfortunately, not all service marketers can juggle demand in this way, and the perishability of service is one of the more serious problems they face.

The service marketing mix   The distinctive character of services gives rise to some differences in the service marketing mix. The intangibility of services seems to deny the idea of a product offering, but we can dispel this illusion by remembering that a service is a *product* in the broadest meaning of the term. The services to be offered must be determined in exactly the same way that a product offering is identified. One must be customer oriented and respond to consumer's needs and wants in deciding what services to provide.

The channel issues tend not to be very important in service marketing.[3] Most services are sold directly to the buyer, although, as we noted earlier, it is possible to resell a claim on a service. There is some franchising of service establishments. Fast-food organizations and motel chains are the best examples, although the recent trend has been to abandon franchising in favor of outright ownership—primarily to ensure control over the quality of service rendered. There are also franchised real estate offices, car rental agencies, dental and optometry services, dry-cleaning establishments, and so on. These franchised networks have many of the characteristics of conventional trade channels, except that the flows that bind the components seldom include the movement of physical product.

Services can be promoted, although there are industries in which members have discouraged the practice. The medical and legal professions have spurned promotion as unethical. Recent court action has held that the self-imposed prohibitions against advertising by lawyers are in violation of the antitrust laws. At least a few lawyers have begun to advertise as a result of these judicial opinions. In other areas of service marketing the use of promotion is extensive. Airlines, ho-

tels, movie companies, and professional sports teams engage in very aggressive promotion. They utilize all of the promotional tools, including advertising, personal selling, and sales promotion.

The pricing of services is somewhat unique. In a field such as fast-food retailing, the one-price system prevails. Each customer pays the same price. But there are notable exceptions. Prices charged by physicians and attorneys often are tailored to a customer's ability to pay as well as to the value of the service rendered. Price discrimination is widely practiced. A convention guest at a hotel pays a lower rate than does a walk-in customer. Also, the prices of services can be negotiated. An architect may negotiate a fee with a client, just as a typist may work out a price with a college student for the typing of a thesis. And, we have noted how the airlines adapt their prices to meet the peculiar nature of the demand for air transportation.

You may feel that the author has been stretching to come up with differences in the marketing mix for services. As mentioned previously, there are more similarities than there are differences. Customers want satisfactions, not things per se. Goods marketers and service marketers must respond to these wants. It is not surprising that the marketing mixes are similar. While there are differences, they are not substantial; and an understanding of goods marketing can be effectively applied to the marketing of consumer services.

The Marketing of Industrial Goods and Services

Industrial goods are those goods that are sold for business use or for resale. Numerous examples of the marketing of industrial products have been mentioned throughout

[3]For a commentary on service channels, see J. H. Donnelly, Jr., "Intermediaries in Channels of Distribution for Services," *Journal of Marketing,* January 1976, pp. 55–57.

this book.[4] The subject of industrial buyer behavior was discussed, and a classification of industrial goods was presented. These treatments seem to imply that the marketing of industrial goods and services does not differ significantly from the marketing of consumer goods. In the most fundamental sense this is true; and it explains both the integration of industrial marketing examples and the author's decision not to attempt a separate discussion of the subject up to this point in the book.

Although there are no fundamental differences between the marketing of consumer products and industrial products, there do exist several distinguishing characteristics of industrial marketing that deserve comment and that take us beyond the boundary of consumer-goods marketing. Several of these distinguishing features have been mentioned earlier in the book—for example, buyer behavior and the classification of goods. It is worthwhile, however, to look again at these and at other distinguishing factors of industrial marketing.

The unique characteristics of industrial products Industrial goods and services do appear to be different from consumer goods and services, in at least some respects, even though the basic nature of their marketing is similar. In the first place, many industrial goods are highly complex, technical products. Even a commodity-type product, such as steel sheet or copper tubing, is the result of highly sophisticated metallurgical and process research. Many industrial products are extremely expensive or are purchased in

such large quantities that very large sums of money are involved. Industrial products tend to have much longer life cycles than do consumer products. Each stage of the cycle is protracted. Introductions are slower paced; growth is achieved over a longer period of time; and mature industrial products flourish for years before going into decline. Even in the decline stage, the industrial product tends to survive far longer than does its consumer counterpart. Relatively few industrial products are perishable, although some, such as chemicals, do lose their purity or potency over time. Some industrial products are toxic, or flammable, or dangerous in some other way and they require extremely careful handling in transit and storage. Each of these characteristics explains, in part, the kinds of marketing activities that are necessary; but they are not nearly so critical in this respect as are the differences that we can note in the nature of industrial markets.

The unique aspects of industrial markets In Chapter 5 we looked at the nature of the business buying process. We will not repeat that discussion here except to recall that the rational, problem-solving approach dominates industrial buying behavior. There is almost no place in business buying for emotional, impulsive purchasing. We noted also that industrial buying is characterized by formal buying procedures, multiple purchase influences, and inventory-level concerns. While each of these can be found in some aspects of consumer buying, there is no question that they arise frequently in the buying of industrial goods and services.

The demand for most industrial products is said to be *derived*—that is, it stems from the existence of a demand for something else. The demand for a machine tool exists because there is a demand for the item that

[4]Texts on industrial marketing include E. R. Corey, *Industrial Marketing: Cases and Concepts*, 2nd ed. (Englewood Cliffs, N.J.: Prentice-Hall, 1976); P. W. Haas, *Industrial Marketing Management* (New York: Petrocelli-Charter, 1976); and R. M. Hill, R. S. Alexander, and J. S. Cross, *Industrial Marketing*, 4th ed. (Homewood, Ill.: Richard D. Irwin, 1975).

the tool can make. There is a demand for oil rig replacement parts because there is a demand for petroleum. At first glance, this might seem to be helpful; but in fact it is a mixed blessing. True, the industrial marketer is not faced with the necessity of creating demand. On the other hand, the demand tends to be highly cyclical. This is because relatively modest changes in final demand can impact drastically on the derived demand. Suppose that an industrial company sells injection-molding machines for the plastics industry. Its biggest customer regularly buys about $150,000 of equipment each year for expansion and replacement of old equipment. In 1975, however, affected by a 15 per cent decline in its business due to a shortage of raw materials, this customer decided not only to refrain from increasing its capacity but also to not replace some older equipment. Instead of buying $150,000 of new molding equipment, it purchased only $50,000 worth. What was a 15 per cent decline for the customer resulted in a 66.7 per cent decrease for the industrial firm. Of course, if the customer's business had increased by 15 per cent, the equipment manufacturer's sales would have been disproportionately higher. This derived relationship results in very drastic swings in the sales of industrial products—swings that make both forecasting and marketing planning very difficult.

Industrial markets are segmented differently than are consumer markets.[5] The concept of segmentation prevails, but the bases differ. Geographic segmentation occurs, but the similarity ends there. The demographics of industrial marketing do not relate to age, income, education, and the like; rather, they refer to the nature of the industrial customer's business. Three major distinctions can be drawn: functional, product, and channel. In *functional* segmentation, the industrial marketer distinguishes among segments on the basis of the nature of the customer's business. A customer that incorporates the seller's product in some manufactured item is called an *original equipment manufacturer* (OEM). Another major function is resale, as when a distributor buys an industrial product and then resells it to industrial customers or to other resellers, such as jobbers and dealers. Industrial marketers often segment according to the kinds of *products* that their customers make. For example, the Donaldson Company sells air filters and purifiers to the automotive market, the farm equipment market, and the construction equipment market. A third method of industrial market segmentation is by *channel of distribution*. Here the principal difference is between direct sale and the use of middlemen. Large direct-buying accounts must be dealt with differently than are smaller customers who are frequently serviced by distributors. It is evident that these three bases of segmentation overlap, just as demographic and psychographic segmentation overlap. Nevertheless, it should be clear that the bases used to segment industrial markets are different than those used to segment the markets for consumer goods.

The industrial-goods marketing mix The concept of the marketing mix is applied in industrial marketing. Marketing programs embracing product, distribution, promotion, and pricing decisions are commonplace. However, the character of the industrial marketing mix is likely to be quite different from that of the consumer-product marketing mix.

We have noted some of the unique features of the industrial market and of indus-

[5]E. R. Corey, ''Key Options in Market Selection and Product Planning,'' *Harvard Business Review,* September-October 1975, pp. 110–128.

trial products, both of which affect the kinds of product strategies used by industrial marketers. Industrial products are often complex and technical. They are so because these kinds of products are necessary to meet the rigid specifications established by industrial buyers. There is much more customizing of industrial products than there is of consumer products. This results in very broad product lines that reflect thousands of relatively minor variations.

New-product development is important in industrial marketing, but it tends to be more technically directed than market-directed. True, industrial product managers work closely with key customers in the development of new products to meet those customers' needs, but a substantial proportion of the ideas for new products are generated within the seller's R&D and engineering departments.

Industrial products often require extensive service. This is especially true of capital goods, such as machine tools, printing presses, and computers. The industrial product is almost always an augmented product, including technical consultation, maintenance and repair service, and in some cases purchase financing.

Industrial-marketing channels are somewhat unique. Many industrial sales are made direct to the user, as to OEM accounts; whereas, this occurs with relative infrequency in consumer marketing. Regretfully, the shipping-platform philosophy appears to dominate industrial channel selection. The author knows of at least half a dozen industrial marketing companies that sell through distributors and do not know what happens to their products once they have been shipped from the factory. Partly to overcome this problem, some industrial firms have integrated forward and have acquired their own distributors. Others have used franchising or other contractual arrangements to establish some vertical control over their channel of distribution.

In promotion, industrial marketers make extensive use of personal selling and comparatively little use of mass communications. This may be the single most obvious difference between the consumer-product marketing mix and the industrial marketing mix. Most industrial selling strategies are aimed at *pushing* a product down the channel to the ultimate user. Most consumer-goods marketing involves direct appeals through advertising to the user with the hope that consumer demand will *pull* a product through the system. This is not to say, however, that industrial firms do not advertise. Many do; but the use of mass communications is limited and the amounts of money spent on it are considerably less than in consumer-goods marketing.

Industrial pricing is extremely complex, due largely to the many variations in customer status and product line that are involved. In the extreme, a price is established for each transaction. Always it is subject to negotiation, even if the seller wants to establish some uniformity in the pricing approach. Demand for industrial products (except highly standardized items, such as lumber) tends to be inelastic in the short run, although substitutability of one firm's product (for example, an electric motor) for that of another company often is possible. Thus, the seller does not always have the upper hand. Reliance on a limited number of large customers (whether user or reseller) gives the buyer a great deal of bargaining power.

These differences in product, distribution, promotion, and pricing approaches for the industrial marketer are important because they lead to rather different overall strategies than one encounters in consumer-goods marketing. But the planning process by which the industrial strategy is developed and the concepts on which the industrial program are based are not fundamentally different. So, while the discussion of industrial marketing takes us beyond the frontier of consumer-goods marketing, we have not wandered very far beyond the management concepts with which we are familiar.

Beyond the Twelve-Mile Limit

The twelve-mile coastal limit symbolizes the beginning of the high seas and the frontier of domestic commerce. Beyond that line lies a market of stupendous potential—a market that lures many American firms to seek business in other lands and those abroad to find markets in the United States. More and more companies are taking advantage of the opportunity to achieve growth through the development of international business, and a discussion of marketing would be incomplete without some treatment of the international aspects of marketing management.[6]

International and Multinational Marketing

International marketing refers to the carrying out of marketing across national boundaries.

[6]Here are four useful texts on international marketing: P. R. Cateora, *International Marketing* (Homewood, Ill.: Richard D. Irwin, 1975); J. Fayerweather, *International Marketing* (Englewood Cliffs, N.J.: Prentice-Hall, 1970; G. E. Miracle and G. Albaum, *International Marketing Management* (Homewood, Ill.: Richard D. Irwin, 1970); and H. B. Thorelli, *International Marketing Strategy* (Harmondsworth, England: Penguin, 1973).

The sale of a Japanese automobile in the United States is international marketing. The sale of American wheat to the Soviet Union is international marketing. The sale of Belgian textiles in a Canadian department store is international marketing. In each case, a marketer in one country seeks out and serves customers in another.

Multinational marketing is an extension of international marketing. The multinational marketer actually establishes an operations base—whether manufacturing or distribution—in several countries and manages this complex system to achieve overall corporate goals.

The distinction between international and multinational marketing is one of degree and does not drastically affect the kind of marketing that takes place. Multinational marketing seems to suggest a greater commitment and a substantially larger investment. It implies that companies or facilities operated in other countries might be managed by nationals of that country or would, at least, be very solidly tuned to specific needs of its consumers. International marketing, on the other hand, usually is directed from abroad and may be less sensitive to the individualities of the countries in which the company is attempting to sell. However, this need not be the case; and good marketing practice requires that the international marketer, as well as the multinational marketer, be customer oriented and thoroughly familiar with the environment in which the marketing effort is to be made.

International Marketing: Is It Different?

Is marketing beyond the twelve-mile limit different from the marketing that takes place at home?[7] In a very general way we must admit that it is not. Marketing is marketing, without regard to the latitude and longitude of where it takes place. The marketing concept is applicable. The systems concept can be utilized to identify the components engaged in international marketing. The processes of planning, decision making, and control are virtually identical. Marketing information plays a critical role. And the concept of the marketing mix can be applied.

But there are differences, and these exist largely in the environmental impacts on marketing abroad. While it is impossible to deal with the many factors that affect international marketing, a brief discussion of several primary issues should serve to illustrate the importance of fitting the overseas marketing effort to the market. It is not that there exists a separate set of environmental impactors for international marketing, because the external influences impacting on foreign marketing are much the same as those affecting domestic marketing. Culture, the economic climate, and political-legal considerations are as important in defining foreign marketing opportunities as they are in establishing domestic markets. It is simply that these dimensions take on different values

and create distinctly different climates in which marketing must take place.

Cultural Differences

Culture creates a vastly different climate for marketing in different parts of the world. As a term, *culture* describes the totality of a society's pattern of beliefs and behaviors. Extreme cultural differences are displayed throughout the world, and these differences explain in large part the kinds of marketing opportunities that exist. Certainly the drastic contrasts that can be drawn between oriental and occidental consumers can best be understood in terms of culture and only secondarily in terms of individual psychical and physical differences. Differences in behavior among various Western nations, for instance France and the United Kingdom, also can be explained adequately by cultural distinctions. Consider, for example, life styles in Paris and in Tokyo; then compare Paris and London, and London and Los Angeles. These are cities of roughly the same size and climate, but how different are the behaviors of the people living there!

The Economic Environment

Many different types of economic systems have appeared throughout history. Archeologists and anthropologists have discovered evidence of fairly advanced economic systems that existed in civilizations long since extinct. Even the economic history of the Western world reveals a considerable number of different economic systems. Each culture tends to develop its own economic system. However, many of these differ only in detail, and when considered in broad outline fall into four major categories: (1)

[7]This question has been around for quite a while. Bartels contended that marketing has universal validity. See R. Bartels, ''Are Domestic and International Marketing Dissimilar?'' *Journal of Marketing,* July 1968, pp. 56–61. Buzzell suggested at about the same time that while a standardized approach is possible, there are not genuine rules of thumb that can be applied. See R. D. Buzzell, ''Can You Standardize Multinational Marketing?'' *Harvard Business Review,* November-December 1968, pp. 102–113. More recent treatments include S. H. Britt, ''Standardizing Marketing for the International Market,'' *Columbia Journal of World Business,* Winter 1974, pp. 39–45; and R. E. Sorenson and U. E. Wiechmann, ''How Multi-nationals View Marketing Standardization,'' *Harvard Business Review,* May-June 1975, pp. 42–56.

the primitive or underdeveloped system; (2) the collective or cooperative system; (3) the authoritarian or command system; and (4) the free-enterprise, capitalist, price, or market system. Since the economic systems prevailing in all countries can be classified into one of these general types, we will examine the general systems rather than the economic environments in specific foreign lands.

Primitive systems   Although great strides have been made in raising the standard of living in the so-called underdeveloped countries, the fact is that a large portion of economic life (about two thirds of the world population) is still in an extremely primitive stage. In a primitive system emphasis is placed on survival. Paramount in importance is the production of food to maintain the population at even a subsistence level. Without adequate mechanization and soil fertilization, this often proves to be difficult, as indicated by the conditions that prevail in much of Africa, Asia, and South America. Because of the emphasis on agriculture, virtually no capital surpluses are created and no savings for the future purchase of nonagricultural products is possible. There is little specialization. For these reasons little or no exchange takes place, and marketing as we know it does not exist. As more efficient methods of farming are discovered or imported and as outside capital flows into the primitive system, increases in agricultural productivity follow and eventually both capital and food surpluses are created. This usually is a time-consuming process, and progress in improving the standard of living is painfully slow. One reason why the peoples of primitive systems turn so readily to the authoritarian economic system is its promise of quick results.

Collective systems   Theoretically, one solution to the problems of the primitive economic system is found through collective action. If the efforts and resources, although limited, of the members of a society can be pooled into a larger effort, it is possible (at least in theory) to achieve some of the advantages of specialization and the division of labor. It also is feasible to acquire and fully utilize certain types of labor-saving equipment.

In spite of its improvement over the primitive type, the cooperative system is characterized by an extreme scarcity of resources relative to wants. For this reason, the output of the system generally is distributed by common consent on the basis of need rather than on the basis of ability to purchase or to produce. Under such a distribution system, it is theoretically possible to set aside some of the output of the system for capital accumulation (investment). It is hoped that such forced savings will raise the relatively low rate of productivity. Because of this arbitrary method of distribution according to need, there is no market or exchange process in the collective system. The result is that the consumer has no way to voice a reaction to the goods that are provided. There is no feedback from a marketplace to provide guidance as to what goods and services are needed and desired. Dissatisfaction with this method of allocation and discontent with job assignments (which are equally arbitrary) explain why most cooperative systems have expired quickly or have been transformed into another type of economic system.

Command systems   Superficially, a command system might not appear to differ much from either the collective or the free-enterprise arrangements. In principal it differs drastically, and its social effects are quite dissimilar. All economic decisions regarding the allocation of resources and the distribution of products rest with the government, usually a strong central authority. Rather than permit a loose sense of general purpose to guide the allocation process, the authoritarian system involves both long-run and short-run master plans for economic survival and growth. The intention of the economic leadership usually is to build up the industrial sector of the economy as quickly as possible. This involves an arbitrary and disproportionate diversion of resources to the creation of capital goods. In order to distribute the little that remains for personal consumption, systems of rationing and price control are imposed. Whereas very little attention is placed on methods of promotion, display, and sale, a great deal of attention is devoted to the efficient physical handling of goods. In order to encourage the output of capital goods, a premium is placed on high productivity in these areas. Still, production standards or quotas alone have not been entirely satisfactory, and ingenious incentives are used to stimulate production. Among these are status symbols and monetary rewards.

The effect of the authoritarian system is a tendency toward a low standard of consumer life but extremely high levels of national output. Therefore, successful authoritarian systems have been able to rise rapidly in economic and military strength—somewhat to the surprise and dismay of capitalistic economies, in which recent growth rates have been far less dramatic.

Market systems   The market system, identified alternatively as a *capitalist, price* or *free-enterprise* system, often is characterized by an apparent lack of overall planning. This is not to say, however, that there is no planning or that the central government takes no interest in the operation of the free-enterprise system. On the contrary, the government acts as a strong partner as well as a guardian and watchdog of the economic process.

In common with other types of systems, the market system is characterized by a scarcity of resources relative to wants. However, it places emphasis on several principles of economic behavior that other systems either cannot afford or choose not to permit. The first of these is the institution of private property. In a free-enterprise system, the owners of resources and capital goods are protected in the exercise of their rights to direct the economic disposition of their wealth. In the free-enterprise system, profit incentives are recognized and accepted. In addition, it is critical to the operation of the system that freedom of choice and action belong to the institutions and individuals within the system. Thus, the consumer is free to select or reject any product or service. By the same token, almost any business is free to enter into and withdraw from the marketplace.

The free-enterprise system also is based on the assumption that businesses must compete with each other for market acceptance. While heavy reliance is placed on price as a force tending to allocate resources and as a mechanism for establishing economic balance between supply and demand, methods of nonprice competition also are encouraged. Nonprice competition not only tends to encourage higher levels of consumption but is the only sensible approach in a situation where price competition would become purely destructive. In the market system, a premium is placed on growth rather than on mere survival. The exercise of ingenuity and creativity in the development of new and profitable marketing ventures leads to new investment and the creation of capital goods. The emphasis on profit making (subject to social constraints) leads to extreme pressure for financial efficiency through cost control. At the same time, profits also are made through improved selling efficiency. To this end emphasis is placed upon marketing—on the customer and the satisfaction of wants.

To some degree at least, a number of countries besides the United States operate under the market system. These include the Western European democracies, the British Commonwealth nations, and certain countries in the Middle East, South America, and Asia. These are the places where American marketing operates best and also the places that host most of the world's multinational businesses. While marketing effort is directed at and through some command governments, the general application of marketing management is toward customers in the countries where some form of market system operates.

Critical Decision Areas in International Marketing

The marketing decision process knows no national frontiers. In a very real way, the decision variables that guide domestic marketing are those that forge international marketing strategies.[8] Yet, international marketing is different—even if only with respect to the methods used to reach and serve foreign customers. It is reasonable, therefore, to inspect briefly critical decision areas in international marketing management.

[8] Y. Wind, S. P. Douglas, and H. V. Perlmutter, "Guidelines for Developing International Marketing Strategies," *Journal of Marketing*, April 1973, pp. 14–23.

Assessing the international marketing opportunity Opportunities in international markets often are quite different than those in the United States. Cultural differences and differences in the stage of economic development compel the development of different marketing approaches. We recognize here an obvious example of segmentation, because it is readily apparent that consumers in one cultural-economic setting (for example, an emerging country in equatorial Africa) have dramatically different needs and express different behaviors than do consumers in a completely developed environment (say, Norway).

Apart from the obvious segmentation that exists in international marketing, the opportunity analysis process is similar to that which is employed in domestic marketing. The fundamental opportunity always is to provide customer satisfactions, so the principal effort is to locate areas of unfulfilled customer need.

The big problem is not whether opportunities exist in international marketing but whether any given firm should choose to devote its resources to the development of these opportunities. A decision to commit capital and managerial effort to international marketing is an issue in corporate strategy. It must represent a viable means of achieving a company's long-range business objectives. For a company to decide that it should commit itself to international marketing, it must assess the expected return from that investment and compare it with other business alternatives. In recent years, the apparent motive for expanding into international business has been the desire to maintain the rates of growth enjoyed in the 1950s and 1960s. At some point, the expected return from international marketing will appear to be greater than the expected return from continued emphasis on domestic operations. David Leighton suggests that the decision to enter international markets should be made when the expected rate of· return on the investment in that effort exceeds the expected rate of return on other strategic alternatives. The steps involved in the determination of the expected return on international marketing are identical to those employed in the assessment of domestic markets.

In general, the process of predicting profitability of an international venture usually should follow a rough sequence of steps:

1. Estimates are made of the existing markets in the foreign country for the product or products being considered.
2. Forecasts are made for these markets for some period into the future, usually five or ten years.
3. Estimates are made of reasonable market-share targets for the company, based on an analysis of present and anticipated competition.
4. *Pro forma* profit-and-loss statements are developed for each year of the planning period.
5. Cash requirements and cash flows are estimated for the planning period, not only for physical facilities but also for working capital in the form of accounts receivable, inventories, etc.
6. A suitable discount rate may be applied to the cash flows to take account of the fact that a dollar of income some years hence is worth less than a dollar today. The resultant rate of return should be compared to the company's cost of capital and alternative uses of funds, and those projects showing a rate of return above the cost of capital should be chosen.[9]

[9]D. S. Leighton, "Deciding When to Enter International Markets," in V. P. Buell, ed., *Handbook of Modern Marketing* (New York: McGraw-Hill, 1970), p. 20-4.

The selection process might be further refined by applying decision theory and structuring the choice by the use of a payoff matrix. This refinement enables the decisionmaker to incorporate such uncertainties as the future state of the world economy, political developments, and the threat of international competition. Thus, we see that the process of deciding to enter international marketing and of selecting particular countries in which to operate is not substantially different from the process used in selecting among alternative strategies in domestic marketing management.

We should note two major exceptions to the similarity. First, it is much more difficult to obtain reliable market information about foreign markets than it is to obtain comparable data concerning conditions in the United States. The inability in some cases to gather any data at all and the incompatibility of various data bases make estimates of foreign market potential extremely unreliable. Second, due to the great uncertainty that pervades the foreign market environment, the discount rate chosen to determine the present value of the investment probably should be somewhat higher than the rate used in determining the present value of domestic strategies. Uncertainty creates risk, and the greater the uncertainty, the higher the discount rate should be. The effect of these two exceptions is that conservative estimates are obtained on the worth of the international marketing opportunity. Some reasonably good prospects are passed up. But, obviously, not every international venture fails to pass this harsh test—assuming it is made. There is today a considerable number of extremely large international and multinational corporations; and there is an even larger number of smaller firms engaged in international business. This means that the international marketing opportunity is substantial and that a careful analysis of strategic alternatives by any company may very well lead to a decision to engage in international marketing.

The international marketing system Any company engaged in international marketing, or one that is thinking about it, must consider the way in which it will fit into the international marketing system. The basic decision appears to be whether to export goods manufactured at home or to produce (or otherwise acquire) goods abroad. Many factors affect this fundamental decision, including the desire to reduce costs for a competitive advantage, to avoid heavy import duties on finished goods, or to conform in other ways to the political-economic environment that prevails abroad. Of course these are not the only considerations involved. The decision to manufacture products offshore also is based on a number of nonmarketing factors that we need not develop here.

Once the basic question of where manufacture will take place has been answered, the problem of establishing a channel system that will serve the international market effectively arises. Figure 24.1 illustrates the system alternatives that exist for a company manufacturing at home and exporting to a foreign market. Exporting presents two alternatives—indirect or direct. *Indirect exporting* is established by the use of one of two types of exporter. The *export merchant* purchases goods from the manufacturer, assembles these with products of other companies, and then presents this assortment to buyers located in foreign countries—both direct customers and resellers. Once a domestic manufacturer has delivered the product to the export merchant, total responsibility for

subsequent marketing lies in the hands of the new owner of the goods, and the original manufacturer has next to no control over what happens to them. Another method of indirect exporting involves the use of an export agent. An *export agent* is similar to a manufacturer's representative, in that this middleman does not take title and often does not take physical possession of the goods. The export agent travels abroad calling on potential customers and attempts to sell the manufacturer's products. Once sold, these goods may be delivered from distribution points located abroad or they may be shipped directly from their manufacturing locations at home. A third method of indirect exporting involves the use of a cooperative organization that undertakes exporting responsibility for several different manufacturers. The *export association,* in common with other cooperatives, enjoys some tax exemptions and is used most frequently by companies engaged in the marketing of primary products, especially agricultural goods.

Direct exporting involves either the use of a company's internal sales organization to reach its foreign customers or the use of foreign-based merchant or agent middlemen. A company that elects to perform the exporting function itself may create a department for this purpose, or it may establish a network of overseas sales branches that is supervised by the company's regular sales management organization. A company that has grown beyond the use of indirect exporting but has not yet achieved the penetration in foreign markets that might justify the establishment of branch offices abroad often will use the export department as a means of focusing attention on its international program without going so far as establishing its own sales branches abroad. The export manager may select from a number of alternative

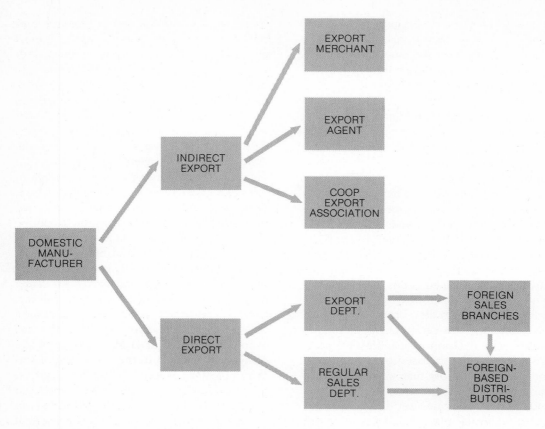

FIGURE 24.1   Alternative methods of foreign-market entry

channel choices, including either domestic- or foreign-based merchant or agent middlemen. It could, of course, establish a network of foreign branches. These, in turn, may either sell direct to foreign users or make use of resellers. If sales branches are used without the services of an export department to supervise their activities, there usually will be an export sales manager within the domestic sales department to supervise them.

A final option of direct marketing involves the use of a company's sales force to visit foreign markets and to establish working relationships with resellers. Quite frequently this task is assumed by a senior marketing executive or by one of the other officers of the firm.

The methods of establishing manufacturing bases abroad are of less interest to us, but they are important in understanding the structure of the international marketing system. There are four basic approaches. Under a *licensing* agreement, a foreign manufacturer is offered the right to use a process, a patent, or a brand name, paying a fee or royalty for the privilege. This foreign company then assumes the sole responsibility for the making and marketing of the product. It is a relatively inexpensive and easy way to get involved in foreign marketing, but its returns are limited to the licensing fee or royalty, which is entirely dependent on the success of the licensee in establishing a strong market position.

A second approach is to *contract* with a foreign manufacturer to produce goods abroad that are then sold by the exporting company's sales organization. Somewhat more risk is involved in contract manufacturing than in licensing, but the potential profit is correspondingly greater. The system's principal advantage is that it eliminates the necessity of a substantial capital investment in foreign manufacturing facilities. It has the disadvantage that the exporter has limited control over production scheduling and quality of manufacture.

A third method of establishing foreign-based production is the *joint venture*. This is a relatively popular method of foreign market entry, and in some countries it is a mandatory approach if public policy requires that a substantial proportion of ownership be retained by nationals.

Ultimately, if the political environment permits, a firm committed to international marketing considers the wisdom of having its own *foreign manufacturing operations*. From a marketing point of view, foreign-based manufacture has some distinct advantages. First, it permits the production of goods at lower unit costs. Second, there may be a psychological advantage in producing locally. The products may be more acceptable to foreign consumers, and the company may enjoy more congenial relations with the governments of the countries in which it operates. Of course there are correspond-

ing risks. The political environment may change; and, as has happened in many parts of the world, the facilities may be expropriated, requiring massive write-offs of the investment. But this risk has not deterred a great number of companies from establishing substantial foreign operations. As satellite communications and supersonic transportation have diminished the obstacles to global communication, the feasibility of multinational business has increased significantly. The available evidence today suggests that international marketing in some form will be of increasing importance in the future.

The international marketing mix   It goes without saying that marketing strategies must be fitted to marketing targets. International consumers, like all segment members, tend to be more like each other than they are like the market as a whole. Product, promotion, distribution, and pricing must be positioned to satisfy the conditions in each market in which an international marketing effort is made. There exists no basis on which to draw significant differences in the conceptual approach to the development of international versus domestic marketing. However, the strategies themselves are likely to be quite different. This is, as we have said, because the customers whom these programs are intended to serve are different.

True, there are some companies that have been remarkably successful with undifferentiated international marketing programs. The domestic programs seem to have suited well the needs of most potential customers throughout the world. These firms have made only minor variations in their domestic marketing approaches to adapt them to foreign marketing conditions. Probably the best example is Coca-Cola, whose international marketing operation represents an extension of its domestic program. In contrast, other food-products marketing companies have found it extremely difficult to take their American products and sell them in exactly the same form and in the same packages in foreign markets. The same can be said of consumer durables and of industrial goods. In most cases, it is necessary to work backward from the market to determine the specifications of the product offering. All too frequently, unfortunately, domestic marketers have discovered this fundamental truth only after encountering considerable resistance to their efforts to sell their products abroad. For example, most European car manufacturers had little success in penetrating the American market. The exceptions were luxury and sports car manufacturers, and Volkswagen, which carved out an entirely new market niche for itself in the United States.

We have commented on distribution methods in our discussion of the international marketing system. If we apply the same logic to the development of an international marketing channel as we should to the development of a domestic system, we find that it is imperative to adapt the channel to local preferences and practices.[10] Export marketers have been notoriously guilty of following the shipping-platform approach. They do this partly because of an unfamiliarity with the foreign marketing system, and also because they have forgotten that channels, like products, must be built backward from the marketplace. The author is familiar with one industrial-products company that, in its enthusiasm to obtain foreign sales, created three distinctly different channel

[10]D. R. McIntyre, "Your Overseas Distributor Action Plan," *Journal of Marketing*, April 1977, pp. 88–90.

arrangements. Considerable duplication of effort and unnecessary price competition developed among the three channels. Although multiple (and even competing) channels sometimes are desirable, in this case it appeared to create confusion abroad and it reduced profits at home. The problem was solved only after an export manager was appointed and assumed sole responsibility for the company's international marketing. The competing channels were eliminated quickly, and price stability was restored.

Promotion and communication programs can be similarly tailored to the foreign market. Foreign consumers have different media viewing habits and they shop in different ways. By American standards, some foreign advertising is very unsophisticated; but a number of American firms have discovered that an attempt to use creative materials that had been developed for the American market has not been successful in other countries. Good foreign advertisements tend to be more product than personality oriented. They are less subtle and appeal less to emotional buying motives. But this does not mean that these ads are less effective; they are simply different because they are keyed to a different audience.

Price, as we know, is a powerful marketing tool. Because many foreign consumers are not as affluent as Americans, it usually is wise to price exported goods at somewhat lower levels than the prices at which they sell at home. Moreover these may not be the same products. Frills may be removed; packages may be simplified. The somewhat lower standard of living in most parts of the world means that consumers there must attempt to satisfy somewhat different needs than do American consumers; they also have considerably less income with which to do it. The importance, then, of pricing strategically to stimulate consumption in the face of these basic economic obstacles should be readily apparent.

These differences in the mix elements imply the necessity of separate marketing programs for international operations. This is, as we noted at the beginning of this section, the key lesson of market segmentation. Therefore, it should come as no surprise to discover that many companies use foreign nationals to help develop their marketing programs and utilize foreign-based advertising agencies to create their communications strategies. One distinct advantage of the multinational corporation is its ability to build its marketing operation around its foreign manufacturing base. The company at the greatest disadvantage in this regard is the domestic concern using indirect exporting as a means of reaching the foreign market. The lesson would seem clear: If a firm is seriously interested in capitalizing on the international opportunity, it must move as quickly as possible to a customer-oriented structure and strategy.

Beyond Profits

For many years, marketing was considered the sole property of profit-making organizations. Unquestionably this was the result of the great influence that economics has had on the theory and practice of marketing as well as the basic nature of the free-enterprise economic system within which marketing flourishes.

The conviction that marketing and profit making are inseparable was first challenged by those interested in *comparative marketing*

—that is, the comparison of marketing in different economic environments. These observers discovered that marketing also exists in other economic systems. Marketing, although not as it has been presented in this book, can take place in a cooperative system, such as Sweden, and in an authoritarian system, such as the Soviet Union. Products are produced and distributed; there is some advertising; and prices are set. True, these elements of the marketing mix are determined not so much through customer orientation as through administrative edict; but the final effect is similar. A second development that has caused marketing people to challenge the dominant role of profit making is the response to consumerism. There is a direct conflict between satisfying customers and maximizing profits. Companies committed to customers have had to sacrifice profits, at least in the short run. Some have done this under extreme pressure; others have done it as a result of rethinking the purpose and function of the modern business. This reevaluation of the purpose of business has led, in turn, to challenges to the traditional role of profits in management. Peter Drucker summarized the advanced view succinctly. He says, "Profitability is not the purpose of but a limiting factor on business enterprise."[11] Profits are necessary to ensure long-run survival; but they are not the proper measure of a firm's success in satisfying customers. Partly due to this decline in the conviction of the inseparability of profits and marketing and partly due to the rapidly increasing number of not-for-profit organizations, interest has been directed by some scholars toward the application of marketing in the not-for-profit

[11]P. Drucker, *Management* (New York: Harper & Row, 1974), p. 60.

sector.[12] It is the purpose of this section to review this new frontier of marketing management.

The Logic of Not-for-Profit Marketing

When we recall that the purpose of marketing is to provide customer satisfactions, it is no great jump to the recognition that satisfactions can be delivered in many ways. These may be delivered by profit-making marketing organizations. They may, on the other hand, be provided by government or by charitable organizations. Does marketing occur when a not-for-profit organization attempts to satisfy a human need? In part, it must; for this is marketing's fundamental purpose.

The most compelling argument for considering the activities of not-for-profit organizations as marketing is found in the view of marketing as an *exchange process*.[13] Market transactions involve exchanges between buyer and seller. But not all exchanges take place in the conventional marketplace. Whenever one person transfers an object or commitment to another and accepts in compensation some sacrifice from the other party, an exchange takes place. A candidate for public office promises to support a particular piece of legislation in return for a constituent's vote. An exchange has occurred. A fire department offers emergency protection, and in exchange citizens pay taxes and cooperate with fire and accident prevention programs sponsored by the department. It should be clear that exchanges are not limited to the marketplace. But the question remains. Can marketing techniques be used

to affect or improve the efficiency of nonmarket exchanges? Yes, they can. There is a customer, or client, whose need must be identified and satisfied. There is a product or service. Information regarding the availability of that product or service must be communicated to its potential users. There is a sacrifice, if not a price, involved. When these elements of the marketing process are encountered in transactions of any kind, we must accept that marketing is taking place.

Organizations Engaged in Not-for-Profit Marketing

A businessperson once remarked, "In my career, I've worked for two not-for-profit organizations. One tried to make a profit but couldn't. The other didn't try; it was a not-for-profit organization." Our interest here is only in the second type—the organization that does not have profit as one of its goals.

Not-for-profit organizations can be classified either according to the type of product or service rendered or by the nature of their ownership. This is illustrated in Table 24.2. For example, the federal government provides many services and even a few products. The table shows examples of services and products offered by all levels of government, as well as by cooperatives and privately supported institutions. One has simply to inspect the budget of any governmental unit to discover the nature and magnitude of its involvement in the marketing of goods and services. *Cooperatives* are associations of producers or consumers who band together for their mutual benefit. If a profit (*residual,* as they call it) is earned on a cooperative's activities, it is returned to its members and patrons. In the United States, there are thousands of not-for-profit organizations offering

---

[12]P. Kotler, *Marketing for Nonprofit Organizations* (Englewood Cliffs, N.J.: Prentice-Hall, 1975).

[13]R. P. Bagozzi, "Marketing as Exchange," *Journal of Marketing,* October 1975, pp. 32–39.

TABLE 24.2   A classification of not-for-profit organizations

| Ownership | Type of service rendered | | | | |
	Health	Education	Welfare	Other	Products
Government					
Federal	Veterans hospital	Naval Academy	Job training	National parks	Postage stamps
State	Mental institution	State university	Employment service	Penitentiary	License plates
Local	City hospital	Community college	Drug clinic	Sports arena	Refuse bags
Cooperative	Blue Cross	Elementary school	Child care	Savings bank	Agricultural chemicals
Private	Hospital	College	Shelter	Travel club	Used clothing

services of many kinds. Private institutions arise to answer an unfilled need for a service of some type. If the need is compelling and the purchasing power of its potential users is strong, a regular profit-making venture would respond to meet it. On the other hand, if the need is not supported by adequate purchasing power and if it is not adequately met by government, a not-for-profit organization may emerge in an attempt to satisfy it. Hospitals, schools, welfare agencies, recreational associations, and publishing and broadcasting entities—all of a not-for-profit character—may arise.

The private not-for-profit organization enjoys several advantages. Contributions to its support generally are legitimate deductions from the donor's income for tax purposes. It also enjoys special rates on selected government services, such as the postal service. Finally a not-for-profit organization frequently is exempt from local property taxes, so long as its facility is used directly in the delivery of a public service.

The Concept of the Public

The not-for-profit organization can be viewed in a systems context. In this respect, it is not very different from the profit-making organization. It can be viewed as an organism existing within an environment. We sometimes refer to these environmental impactors on a not-for-profit organization as its *publics*. Figure 24.2 illustrates a not-for-profit organization, the United Fund, and its major publics. The United Fund's purpose is to solicit contributions for the support of various social services, such as community health, recreation, and welfare. It has several publics. *Input publics* are those that contribute moneys to the support of the fund. They are roughly comparable to the suppliers of raw materials in a conventional marketing system. These input publics can be individual donors, companies, or foundations. *Agent publics* are those organizations through which services actually are rendered and that the United Fund supports financially. The *consumer publics* are those who are the beneficiaries of these services. We call them *clients.*

We can draw a boundary between this system and the environment (the broken line in Figure 24.2), thereby distinguishing its internal publics from those that belong in the environment. *Environmental publics* of this system include the government, which regulates its financial activities through tax auditing; the public press, which through reporting the fund's work affects not only the financial support that flows to the fund but the extent to which the public is aware of

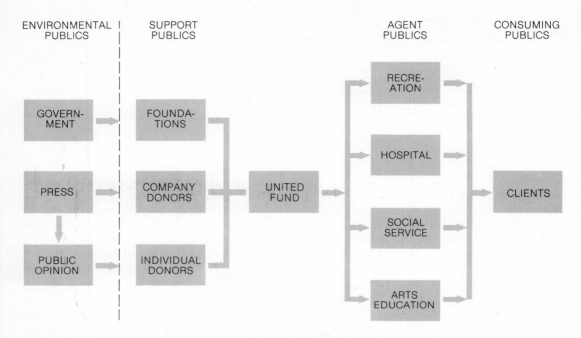

FIGURE 24.2   A not-for-profit system and its various publics

the work that it does; and the public itself, which both supports the fund and receives the benefit of its social services. About the only difference between this system and the regular marketing system is found in the terminology we used. Customers or consumers are called *clients;* the *agent publics* constitute the organization's channel of distribution; the *donor publics* are its resources.

Applying Marketing Concepts to Not-for-Profit Marketing

In looking at not-for-profit marketing, we are impressed first with the general similarity in approach to profit-making marketing. Indeed, more similarities are found than differences; but, as we shall see, these differ-ences are noteworthy. The fact that there are remarkable similarities means that the framework of concepts and techniques presented in this book generally are applicable in not-for-profit marketing.

Similarities of for-profit and not-for-profit marketing   Concepts and techniques of marketing planning can be applied. The most serious difficulties arise in the area of setting objectives. Profit objectives are not relevant. Conventional sales goals and share-of-market goals are similarly inappropriate. The objective of a not-for-profit organization is to maximize outgo, not income. This means that objectives must be defined in terms of the numbers of clients served or the units of service rendered. For example, how many outpatients did Mercy Hospital treat in 1977? Or, how many hot Christmas dinners did the Salvation Army serve in Chicago in the same year? Of course, the quality of the service must be maintained, and sheer volume of output is not the best sole criterion for judging performance. Outpatients must be given prompt and good attention. The Salvation Army's turkey dinner must be nutritious, tasty, and served with dignity.

Once goals have been set, strategies can be formulated. A strategy is always a statement of how an organization intends to achieve an objective. A not-for-profit organization has financial, production, and marketing strategies. The financial strategy governs the manner in which the various services are funded. Production strategy relates to the manner in which the service is created and rendered. The marketing strategy identifies clients' needs and directs the organization's resources to their satisfaction.

The not-for-profit organization often faces a segmented market. The demands for services from not-for-profit organizations are as heterogeneous as are the demands faced by profit-seeking companies. Segments can be defined on geographic, demographic, and psychographic bases. Different segments have different needs and intensities of desire. A large hospital, for instance, may have a portion of its facilities set aside for those who want luxurious accommodations. These patients are charged substantially higher fees than normal, and the income from this segment is used to offset in part the losses incurred in other areas of the hospital. And we can mention other examples of segmentation. The Boy Scout and Girl Scout organizations have different programs for young people of different ages. Universities provide schools or programs to meet the demands for different kinds of learning. Indeed, it might seem that when the criterion of ability to pay is removed, the segmentation possibilities in the demand for client services are almost infinite.

Because the markets that not-for-profit organizations seek to serve are segmented, the concept of targeting or positioning becomes relevant. The organization must select the segments that it intends to serve and then develop programs to meet the needs of its selected client groups. If we assume that the segments respond differently to the efforts of organizations to satisfy their wants (and they must if true segments exist), the challenge to the planner in the not-for-profit organization is to design a program that best meets the segment clients' needs.

As already mentioned, the marketing strategy of the not-for-profit organization includes a marketing mix. This mix embraces everything except the conventional aspects of pricing. A product-service offering must be identified. There should be no difference between the product-service mix of a not-for-profit organization and its profit-making counterpart, if the objective of each is to provide customer satisfaction. It may be compromised to some degree by what the organization can afford to provide, given its financial limitations. But it cannot compromise too far or for too long. Free dental care, if it is painful, will not be sought; inept instruction in public classrooms will not be endured; housing or parks that are noisy, dirty, or unsafe will be shunned.

Not-for-profit organizations, especially those that provide services, often deal directly with their clients. Others, however, such as the funding agency illustrated in Figure 24.2, utilize agent publics to create and distribute services. To this extent channel decisions are involved. If they are not, it is not because of the not-for-profit complexion of the organization, but because it is dealing in direct service marketing rather than goods marketing.

Promotion plays an important role in not-for-profit marketing. The demands for many social welfare services are latent and must be cultivated. Many potential clients may not be aware of a service; others may be misinformed or too embarrassed to inquire about it. Certain services suffer from cultural taboos, such as suicide prevention services, drug abuse clinics, and family-planning offices. Such agencies sometimes find it difficult to generate interest and cooperation. On the other hand, criticism often is leveled at not-for-profit organizations that do promote their work extensively. It is assumed that too much is taken from donors' contributions to pay for this communications program. In some cases the criticism is warranted, because a relatively high percentage of the funds raised is expended to pay for the promotional campaign. Many organizations, however, utilize voluntary workers and agencies and keep the promotional cost to a fraction of the total amount raised.

Pricing plays a unique role in the not-for-profit marketing mix. It consitutes one of the important differences in the marketing approach of these organizations. We will look at the unusual role of price in the next section.

Differences in for-profit and not-for-profit marketing Pricing obviously is not very important in the not-for-profit marketing mix. It plays a distinctly secondary role because it is not a principal consideration in the exchange process. Indeed, there may be no price at all, since the organization may offer its services without charge to its clients. Even if a token price is charged, it is more symbolic than real. It may add dignity to the exchange or simply reflect a client's ability to pay.

Although price certainly is not a strategic element in the client-serving part of an organization, the reverse may very well be true in its relations with its donor publics. The price, again, reflects ability to pay, and there is no specific relationship to the worth of the other side of the exchange process. Why does an individual contribute to the support of a local welfare organization? In most cases, it is a result of a sense of public obligation and concern. There is some satisfaction in being part of the solution to a social problem. Does more satisfaction result from a large donation than a small one? Probably, but it is doubtful that the relationship is linear. A $10 contribution to the Heart Fund from an office secretary may yield far more satisfaction than a manager's $100 gift. So, again, we can see the general, if not the specific, applicability of the concept of price to the not-for-profit marketing mix.

The smaller role of price is closely related to other important differences. The not-for-profit organization cannot use sales income as a measure of its performance. It may measure its donor contributions or the sum of all moneys received (including government grants and such prices as clients are asked to pay). This aggregate flow of funds does correspond to the sales income of a profit-making business. It represents the limit to which a nonprofit organization can finance the services that it provides. This income measure, however, could prove misleading if the organization's goals were set in terms of its maximization. The function of the organization might become that of fund raising rather than of client serving. And this would be fatal to the long-term viability of a not-for-profit organization.

If neither profits nor sales income is an adequate measure of the performance of a not-for-profit organization, what can we use to evaluate its efficiency? This is a tough question. There are no clear-cut measures of the output of a social service. As we noted previously, some measure of effort expended or the number of clients served would be helpful, but these are relatively crude—especially if the quality of service is difficult to monitor and maintain. Again, indirectly, the willingness of donors to contribute funds could be used as a guage of performance.

Societal Marketing

Although marketing managers always have operated within an environment of public opinion, it was not until the decade of the 1960s that they realized its overriding importance. Pressure from public influencers and a rising swell of consumer discontent forced marketing practitioners and academicians to reappraise marketing's social responsibility —indeed to begin to think in even broader terms of using marketing to achieve societal goals. Thus emerged a new frontier: societal marketing.[14]

Lazer discussed marketing's changing social relationships as follows:

Marketing is not an end in itself. It is not the exclusive province of business management. Marketing must serve not only business but also the goals of society. It must act in concert with broad public interest. For marketing does not end with the buy-sell transaction—its responsibilities extend well beyond making profits. Marketing shares in the problems and goals of society and its contributions extend well beyond the formal boundaries of the firm.[15]

If marketing is not an end in itself, it must be a means to some other end. This is true of marketing as a business activity of which the goal is commercial success, usually measured by profits. But, as Lazer points out, marketing is also a means to achieve societal goals. Marketing in the macro sense is more than an economic system; it is a social process by which want-satisfying goods and services are made available to consumers. Thus marketing can be a means to either business or social ends. But can it satisfy both goals at the same time? Is there not an inherent or at least a potential conflict between the two kinds of goals? Adam Smith tangled with this very question when first theorizing about the free-enterprise system. He accepted that the underlying purpose of business is to perform a social service by channeling useful goods and services to consumers. He reasoned that an "invisible hand" of long-run self-interest and competition would ensure a meeting of business and social goals. Thus, the same means could satisfy both goals. In some ways, the system has worked remarkably well; but the complaints of consumers indicate that businesspeople have not succeeded in resolving this conflict as well as the architects of free enterprise hoped that they would.

How will marketing meet this changing

[14]The list of noteworthy contributions to the literature of societal marketing is growing rapidly. Among these, several can be mentioned. S. J. Levy and G. Zaltman, *Marketing, Society, and Conflict* (Englewood Cliffs, N.J.: Prentice-Hall, 1975); W. Lazer and E. J. Kelley, eds., *Social Marketing: Perspectives and Viewpoints* (Homewood, Ill.: Richard D. Irwin, 1973); P. Kotler and S. J. Levy, "Broadening the Concept of Marketing," *Journal of Marketing,* January 1969, pp. 10–15; B. Enis, "Deepening the Concept of Marketing," *Journal of Marketing,* October 1973, pp. 57–62; and J. Arndt, "The Proper Scope and Content of Marketing," *Journal of Marketing* (forthcoming).

[15]Reprinted from W. Lazer, "Marketing's Changing Social Relationships," *Journal of Marketing,* January 1969, p. 3, published by the American Marketing Association.

societal responsibility? The first step must involve the adoption of the marketing concept in its most basic meaning. The purpose of marketing is to provide customer satisfactions. Consumer orientation in any lesser meaning is obsolete. Simply to know the customer will not be enough. Marketing must be genuinely concerned for the consumer's well-being.[16] In the short run, at least, this could mean a reduction in profits. In the long run, it may mean that profits cease to be the overriding consideration affecting business decisions. Lazer suggests that marketing companies may well have to look "beyond the realm of profit"

One of the next marketing frontiers may well be related to markets that extend beyond mere profit considerations to intrinsic values—to markets based on social concern, markets of the mind, and markets concerned with the development of people to the fullest extent of their capabilities. This may be considered a macro frontier of marketing, one geared to interpersonal and social development, to social concern.[17]

No one claims that it is exclusively marketing's responsibility to solve social problems. Consumers have their parts to play. It is a challenge faced by all sectors of society—consumers, businesses, and government. We do not suggest that profit as a reward for venture and investment will disappear. We claim only that businesspeople will look beyond profit to the longer-run responsibilities that all segments of modern society face.

[16]M. L. Bell and C. W. Emory, "The Faltering Marketing Concept," *Journal of Marketing,* October 1971, pp. 37–42.

[17]Reprinted from W. Lazer, "Marketing's Changing Social Relationships," *Journal of Marketing,* January 1969, p. 4, published by the American Marketing Association.

There are some immediate and important ways in which marketing can contribute. Looking beyond profits and beyond the expectation of immediate societal acceptance, marketing establishments can help work toward solutions to contemporary social problems. Many companies have done so. For example, a number of firms are involved in programs of urban renewal, environmental protection and renewal, training and jobs for the hard-core unemployed, and low-cost distribution to feed and clothe the poor. The effort to date is minuscule compared to the need, and some social critics are convinced that these are only token or showcase experiments. Time will tell. But it is clear that, as it seeks to meet its evolving social responsibilities, business will become more and more involved in projects of this kind.

Summary

We have completed our exploration of marketing management. The opportunity is now presented to look beyond the frontiers of the micromarketing system and inspect some of the broader aspects of marketing.

We have looked beyond the marketing of consumer goods to the marketing of services and the marketing of industrial products. A service is an act performed by one party on behalf of another, and many such acts are needed by consumers. This has given rise to a substantial service industry, which annually renders billions of dollars worth of service to American consumers.

There are some unique aspects of services; although in general we must recognize that the marketing of services is not unlike the marketing of goods. Services are noteworthy because they are intangible, because they suffer from variations in quality, and because they are perishable. These features, in turn, give rise to some interesting differences in the marketing mix, although in total these differences are not substantial.

The marketing of industrial goods and services also differs in some modest respects from the marketing of consumer goods. The mix elements are identical, but the blending is different. Product lines are longer and products are more complex and technical. Channels tend to be short. Promotion relies heavily on personal selling. Pricing is complex and often tailored to each customer.

Beyond the twelve-mile limit lies the world market. In a very broad sense, there are not very significant differences between domestic and international marketing. Such differences as are found are explained largely in terms of the different environments in which international marketing takes place. Cultural differences and differences in the type of economic systems are the dominant factors. The principal decision area in international marketing is whether to engage in it in the first place. This strategy should be pursued if the expected rate of return on a proposed international venture is greater than the expected rate of return on all other investment alternatives faced by a company.

A company, having decided to enter the international marketing arena, must then determine how it will fit into the international marketing system. It can employ indirect or direct exporting, and it can choose among four different methods of obtaining products overseas. With its organizational arrangements determined, an international marketing program must be developed. Here the differences between domestic and international marketing fade, except for the fact that the specifics of the marketing mix must

be tailored to a company's international consumers, who may be quite unlike those served at home.

The next frontier discussed was the not-for-profit field. For many years, it was thought that marketing had no role to play unless profits were the goal of the organization. This view has changed, and today marketing concepts and techniques are being applied in not-for-profit organizations. Of these there are several types, including governmental, cooperative, and private agencies. They offer a wide range of services and sometimes provide goods. There are many similarities in profit and not-for-profit marketing, and there are some notable differences—the most important of which is the unique role that pricing plays in not-for-profit marketing. In many cases, there is no price; in others, it is merely symbolic.

The final frontier of marketing that was discussed in this chapter is marketing's social responsibility—referred to here as societal marketing. This application of marketing means that its attentions must be directed to the solution of broad social problems and the achievement of broad social goals. Marketing is not an end; it is a means. It can be a means to more than business goals. Ultimately, marketing's goal must be to help provide a richer and more meaningful life for all.

Questions and Problems

1. Several frontiers of marketing management have been discussed in this chapter. Can you think of others? What are they? What are the special marketing considerations involved in each?

2. You are a marketing manager working for a telephone company and have received an announcement of a forthcoming seminar on marketing planning. Your superior doubts that the principles and techniques of marketing goods can be applied in the marketing of communications services. What do you think?

3. There is no doubt that the industrial buyer and the industrial buying process differ in some important respects from consumer buying circumstances. Does this mean, however, that the marketing of industrial goods is essentially different from the marketing of consumer goods and services? Explain.

4. Most industrial companies make relatively little use of advertising, except in trade magazines. From time to time, however, a major industrial firm will place commercials on television and insert impressive ads in consumer publications. Do you think the firm is really trying to sell its products? If not, why does it engage in this kind of advertising?

5. Many American manufacturers are very anxious to develop markets overseas, but at the same time others are violently opposed to the importation of goods from other countries. How do you explain this difference in viewpoints?

6. What is the difference between international marketing and multinational marketing?

7. If you were asked to go to a foreign country and investigate the possibilities of marketing your company's products there, what would be the focus of your investigation? Establish some priority, or order of importance, to your list of things to study.

8. Is it possible for a marketing company headquartered in a free-enterprise nation to market effectively in an authoritarian economic environment? What adjustments would have to be made?

9. If profit is an inherent element in the marketing concept, how can marketing be applied in a not-for-profit organization?

10. You have been hired by an automobile club in your city to be its first director of marketing. The club is a not-for-profit organization that provides a number of services for its members, who pay an annual membership fee of $30. The club participates in a national auto insurance program that produces some revenue. It also generates income from its auto diagnostic facility and its travel agency. Nevertheless, recently the club has been going further and further into the red. The organization has been losing members quite steadily, and the principal complaint seems to be the lack of value for the relatively high membership fee. Outline a marketing program that you might pursue to improve this situation.

11. What is societal marketing? What relationship, if any, does it hold to marketing management?

12. Do you agree that the ultimate goal of marketing is to provide a richer and more meaningful life to all? If so, what are the ways in which marketing companies can respond to this challenge? Do you see it interfering in any way with the traditional approaches to marketing management?

Index

ABCDEFGHIJ-H-8210/79